The Counselor's Handbook

Intext Series in Guidance and Counseling

Series Editor: PHILIP A. PERRONE

LIST OF CONTRIBUTORS

Gene M. Abroms
Dugald S. Arbuckle
Edward S. Bordin
Angelo V. Boy
Arnold H. Chin
John J. Cody
Harold F. Cottingham
Constantine A. Dallis
Gail F. Farwell
Alan R. Feirstein
Jesse D. Geller
Eugene T. Gendlin
Douglas R. Gross
Tim Gust
Norman C. Gysbers
Ray E. Hosford
Chris D. Kehas
Paul T. King

Barbara A. Kirk
DeWayne J. Kurpius
James L. Lee
David L. Livers
David Donald Malcolm
Richard Mowsesian
Cecil H. Patterson
Anthony C. Riccio
Edward C. Roeber
Michael Helge Ronnestad
Marshall P. Sanborn
Randolph S. Thrush
David V. Tiedeman
Leona E. Tyler
Gary R. Walz
Carl A. Whitaker
Patricia L. Wolleat
Janet P. Wollersheim

The Counselor's Handbook

EDITED BY

Gail F. Farwell
University of Wisconsin—Madison

Neal R. Gamsky
Illinois State University

Philippa Mathieu-Coughlan
Wesleyan University

INTEXT EDUCATIONAL PUBLISHERS
NEW YORK AND LONDON

Library of Congress Cataloging in Publication Data
Farwell, Gail F.
    The counselor's handbook.
    (The Intext series in guidance and counseling)
    Bibliography: p.
    1. Counseling.   I. Gamsky, Neal R., ed.
II. Mathieu-Coughlan, Philippa L., ed.   III. Title.
BF637.C6F33   361.3'2   73-18384
ISBN 0-7002-2451-3

Intext Educational Publishers
257 Park Avenue South
New York, New York 10010

Text design by Paula Wiener

Contents

Preface

We are aware that the responsibility of editing a handbook for any discipline should not be undertaken lightly.

In the first place, the discipline must not only evince a need for such a compendium, but its concerns must have become focused and its methodology and practice must have achieved a certain maturity and refinement before the taking stock and evaluation that are implied by the compilation of a handbook can be justified. Above all, while the editors may be correct in their assessment that the effort is warranted and willing to expend that effort, they cannot hope to succeed without the energy, talents, and full-hearted support of the contributors whose work they solicit.

Our combined academic and professional experience suggested that counseling and counselor education had reached that stage of professional development where a professional reference work might be of value to the profession as a report of achievement, past and present, and of unsolved problems; a forecast of needed development; and perhaps as a stimulus not only to development but also to a more well-rounded and professional approach to both problem and practice. If this were in fact true and our colleagues agreeable, then such a work could hope to be of use both to counselors in service and those in training.

It has been our good fortune that so many of our colleagues were sympathetic to our aims in preparing this handbook. Their essays deal with professional education, community service agencies, schools, counseling centers, public facilities, and private practice. They discuss supervision, research, administration, consultation, and clinical practice.

Since we hope this handbook will be useful to both student and practitioner, we have tried to make it as easy as possible for the reader to locate specific content. At the beginning of a chapter, we present a brief overview of each topic and a description of the scope of the contributor's presentation. At the end of the chapter, we offer a discussion of issues, a bibliographic listing of related articles in selected journals, and suggestions for further reading.

Thanks have to be extended to so many people in connection with the development of this publication that no attempt will be made to list them here. Each essayist is thanked for his or her contribution to the book, as well as his or her patience with the editors in the development and fruition of the total enterprise.

Finally, inasmuch as a prime function of professional associations is the professionalization of their membership through professional training and continuing education, the royalties from this book will be distributed equally to The American Personnel and Guidance Association and The American Psychological Association.

The Counselor's Handbook

CHAPTER 1

Introduction

Gail F. Farwell

University of Wisconsin—Madison

A controversy of long standing focuses on the degree and scope of preparation that should be required of those who want to become *helping persons*—particularly, in this discussion, the type of helping persons that we call *counselors*. The argument includes, for example, the debate between supporters of "rap centers," who advocate the use of lay persons who have "lived" (whatever that means), and those who want helping persons to have undergone extensive psychoanalysis. This book is concerned with the preparation of *professionals*. In the bias of this writer, professionalism implies knowledge, experience, skill, and evaluation.

Several points come to mind. Who should become a counselor? What experiences are requisite for entry into the field? What is the scope of the learning contract developed for the counselor-candidate? Are there identifiable criteria that can be translated into competencies that ought to be demonstrated by counselor-candidates? What procedures in counselor education would facilitate the growth of candidates toward professionalism? Can we differentiate stages of professionalism, so that some consensus might be reached about minimum expectancies, and then envisage continuing growth experiences that would bring the practitioner to a more mature level of operation? What demands for expertise and competency are made by different users of counselors?

As the reader can see, there are many questions to be answered. Candidates preparing to become professional counselors ask themselves similar questions. For example: Why do I consider counseling as a profession for me? What do I need to know? Why? What experiences am I going to acquire in a counselor-preparation program? Why do I need to know such-and-such (whatever it might be)? Why does the faculty insist that I study this particular subject? Why supervision? Why research?

Many applicants inquire about becoming counselor-candidates with very little in their minds except a vague idea of becoming a counselor. Their other

1

thoughts on professional development in the field are ambiguous, and sometimes they know nothing about it at all.

Hiring personnel are often confused about the competencies and preparation of counselors. When such a situation exists, the counselor's expertise is often misused. This results in dissatisfaction with the services provided, leading to disgruntlement with the goals attained, and in the long-run public attitudes become negative or dubious about the viability and relevance of counseling. At the same time, when a person has prepared himself professionally and then finds his expertise misused and misunderstood, he may become discouraged, recalcitrant, or blasé, thus presenting an image that negates any positive input in the counseling setting.

Counselor-educators also have many questions and should engage in constant investigation of ideas and procedures relevant to the professionalizing of counselor-candidates.

As a counselor-educator, I view the preparation process as one that never ends. The continual need for assimilation (integration-reintegration) action in light of changing environmental conditions, new developments, and the human condition makes renewal a constant demand upon the counselor.

Thus, this book has several purposes.

One is to acquaint counselor-candidates with the thoughts of many persons about the multidimensional possibilities that exist in both preparation and practice. In regard to these, the counselor-candidate must make decisions and find ways to cope. In our view, decision making and coping should be predicated on considered judgment, which by definition implies knowledge and competency.

Another purpose of this book is the edification of persons who have hiring responsibilities in other fields. If the principal of a school or the director of a social agency is to hire and effectively utilize professional staff, he should have a realistic base from which to operate. This implies that he must know what competencies to expect of a counselor and how these can be integrated into the strategies employed by his institution for attaining its stated goals. It would be helpful for an employer to know what kind of preparation his employees have had.

This book is also directed to persons involved in the preparation of counselors. The various chapters should stimulate those in counselor education to renewed vigor in reviewing their own programs and being concerned about personal and program development and renewal.

Such a book could have been written by one person or by co-authors. However, we, the editor-collators and contributors, sought original essays from many persons, some well known through previous writing and research, and others who are just developing a professional reputation. We followed this route because we wanted both "seasoned" thinking and the insights that newcomers to our field can bring to bear on the concepts, issues, problems, procedures, and research involved in the preparation of counselors. Persons of various orientations and from many different settings were invited to contribute to this book; geographical factors were also taken into consideration.

A POSITION

It is a basic premise, in the development of the materials that follow, that counseling is a professional activity. Some observers equate counseling with friendship, rapping, casual conversation, advice, and other "talk" factors. An element common to each of these is communication; however, one must ask, "Communication for what?" In other words, it is desirable and necessary to specify goals, to formulate assumptions about human beings and their development as biological organisms responding to the influence of environmental inputs as nurturance elements of life-style. We maintain that the essence of humanness or selfhood is at the forefront of the helping person's concern. Counselors are helping persons. We must ask, however, *in what way* they are helpers and *to what end.*

At least part of the reason for the professional preparation of counselors lies in the premise that they should be knowledgeable about the human condition and the numerous environmental influences that are salient in the development, growth, and modification of human behavior. Strategies of intervention are employed. Professional preparation implies that the candidate will become knowledgeable about these intervention strategies. The counselor should not just be doing, but should be informed about what he is doing.

It is just as important for the counselor-preparation program to specify its goals as it is for the counselor to have an understanding of what he is trying to accomplish when working with a counselee.

An employer has the right to expect that his employees know what they are about and how they propose to get there. He has the right to hold them accountable for their professional behavior, which implies that he expects them to define objectives and goals and to utilize evaluation strategies.

THE COUNSELOR-CANDIDATE

There are many reasons why a person decides to enter a helping profession, too many to mention them all here. In one case, for instance, an individual has been afforded a viable model of counseling from a setting in which he has been involved. In another, a person has been involved in a counseling relationship as a counselee, views what happened positively, and tells himself he would like to become the same kind of a helper. Still another entered a counseling relationship and found it unsatisfactory, yet sees purpose in counseling intervention and wants to make a contribution to the field. Another individual has a bachelor's degree in a social-science discipline (sociology, psychology, education, anthropology, philosophy, etc.) and hopes to apply his training in a related field that will provide him with a marketable competency. Or a person seeking help for himself may gravitate toward a professional area that allows him to focus on his own needs. Or a particular significant "other" may encourage someone to go in the direction of counseling because he sees in him potential for meaningfully implementing the functions of a counselor. Finally, a person may see a fertile field of research opening up to him should he acquire the necessary qualifications.

Inescapably, candidates bring their own experiences to the preparation program. How have they integrated these experiences? Where has this integration taken them regarding talents, limitation, attitudes, values, knowledge, competencies, and needs? Candidates apply to counselor-education/psychology programs immediately after college graduation, or as late as in their fifties and sixties. They come from almost every undergraduate major, although the majority have a social-science discipline as a base. Some have had no work experience; others have had thirty-plus years of gainful employment. Some come from "majority" groups; others from "minority" groups; there are foreign students—individuals from countries other than the United States.

Considering the range of diversity among applicants, every preparing program focuses on the critical question of the criteria utilized in identifying candidates for admission. When that has been established, comes the next question: What vehicle do we develop to meet what ends? What kind of learning experiences, what range of opportunities are needed, and what form should the degree contract take?

Some candidates come to a preparation program with the assumption that they already have the tools and only need the license. Other candidates, fully aware of their lack of experience and preparation, seek specific assistance in identifying a sequence of experiences that will qualify them both for a degree and for employment upon completion of the program. Not infrequently, a candidate is quite far along in his preparation in a related helping field, changes his mind, and decides to transfer to counselor education, using as much of his current base as possible. The areas most frequently contributing this type of candidate are communication arts, social work, clinical psychology, and education.

Because of the vast range of undergraduate, graduate, and work-experience credentials offered to a preparing program, it seems probable that the learning *contract* is the soundest approach to program planning. This approach permits the basic principles of guidance and counseling to be applied, with the candidate himself taking into account the route he has followed to date and the path needed to qualify him for acquiring credentials and securing employment.

One of the purposes of this book is to assist counselor candidates to gain a perspective on the "what" and "why" of the experiences offered in the preparation program—also, on some of the many viewpoints, issues, and ethical questions confronted in counseling and counselor preparation.

THE PROGRAM

Preparation programs in counselor education take on many forms and shapes. This is as it should be; the structure of institutions and the composition of faculties dictate that there be recognition of differences and variation in design. Moreover, the setting of the institution dictates the possibilities available for laboratory, practicum,[1] and internship experiences. Nonetheless, this does not militate against the preparation of some acceptable broad-gauged guidelines establishing parameters for the structure of learning experiences in counselor education.

Counseling involves human beings and a professional helper surely should be knowledgeable about the human condition and human development. Counseling involves learning about self-in-situation; therefore, it is critically important to have knowledge about motivation theories, learning strategies, the development of values, and the attitudes and influence of culture and society. Counseling involves intervention strategies; thus, tools and procedures of intervention must be understood, and must be practiced until competency is acquired. Listening and communication are at the heart and core of counseling. Because counselors become involved both directly and indirectly with their counselees, one can argue the need for skills in interviewing, in group procedures, in consultation, and in environmental change. Institutional parameters are frequently a reality for the practicing counselor; thus, one can ask what differences in awareness and sensitivity, if any, are required of school counselors or of employment and rehabilitation counselors. Evaluation skills are a legitimate expectancy.

Establishment of curriculum and methodology is the unique responsibility of each institution and its faculty. On the other hand, it is legitimate to expect that the goals of the program be explicated, and that strategies for reaching these goals be clearly outlined and serve as the substance of the counselor-preparation program.

In the last decade, both the American Personnel and Guidance Association,

---

[1]For the purposes of this and other essays in this volume, the word *practicum* refers to a *counseling* practicum.

through several of its divisions, and the American Psychological Association, primarily through the Division of Counseling Psychology (Division 17), have spent untold man-hours in studying counseling and counselor preparation. As a result, several guideline statements and standards have been presented, which serve as spring-boards for establishing preparation programs. Professionalism of counseling and counselor-preparation demands that the profession continue to search for answers to critical questions about goals, intervention strategies, theories, evaluation, and societal impact, and, perhaps most important of all, about man himself and how the human essence can be maximized in constructive ways.

The guides for standards, licensure, certification, and degrees are not sacrosanct and unchangeable. One of the characteristics of a profession is the obligation to continually evaluate, upgrade, and discipline itself so as to maintain quality in its procedures and its outcomes. It is essential for counselor-educators, counselors, and counselor-candidates to constantly investigate, evaluate, and modify programs, adopting new findings into the mainstream of counseling.

In the past few years, two words have been utilized repeatedly as points of emphasis—*relevant* and *significant.* In my judgment, these must be understood in several ways. Take the concept of *relevancy.* What is done in the name of counselor education must be relevant to the purveyor as well as to the recipient. Generally, standards, precedents, and guidelines, established by associations, boards, and preparing institutions, condition the relevancy of the input and experiences demanded by the purveyor. Are these so sacrosanct that modification is not in order? No, *but* bringing about change can be difficult, it can pose threats, and it inevitably results in stirring up those who would defend the status quo. An easy out is to operate from the current base; experience says that what we are doing has achieved satisfactory results so far, so keep on with the same learning paradigm. This is the ostrich's "head in the sand" approach—an immediate denial of the change that goes on all around us. The *real message* of history is man's dissatisfaction with the status quo and his desire to "get on with it"—to reach out, to explore, to discover, to seek. Surely the results of such searching should be incorporated with the best of the past. In such ways, programs can keep on top of things; they can be relevant and significant.

The student perceives relevancy and significance much more personally. He is concerned and anxious about the appropriateness of his learning in self-application and in contributing to the applications he must make when working with counselees in his laboratory, practicum, and internship settings. Learning is relevant for him when he achieves some immediate feedback on the pluses of his applications and when the negatives are used in constructive ways for improvement. A good preparation program needs constant feedback from candidates for a continuing effort in maintaining an up-to-date sequence of learning experiences. For a candidate, relevancy and significance are a very existential phenomenon; his current needs are that immediacy prevails. He comes with a need for competency; he is being evaluated; he is expected to provide help to other persons; he is in a setting (for his practice) that has a strong sense of responsibility to the clientele it serves; and the recipients of his help have their own notions of whether this helper (the candidate) is relevant to their concepts and needs.

All of this seems to indicate the desirability of (1) appropriate knowledge for making professional judgments, (2) salient experience in respect to the "current scene," and (3) competency in putting these together so that meaningful application with counselees is the resultant. A preparation program should facilitate these ends.

THE CONSUMER

The products of a preparation program, the counselor-candidates, most frequently end up in some form of institutional employment. This is not to say that some persons do not work for themselves, but the numbers going in this direction are few. The work locale will usually be in educational institutions, social agencies, employment agencies, rehabilitation units, business and industry, and hospitals. In recent years there has been some inclination to use counselors for such operations as rap centers, hot lines, crisis centers, and outreach, although it is often argued that it is better to use persons indigenous to the population being serviced, regardless of their competencies in intervention strategies or their foundational bases for making sense out of the behaviors being presented. Such workers should be viewed as paraprofessionals.

Many consumers have distorted views of the goals, procedures, and foundations possessed by counselors. When this is the case, the counselor may be misused because erroneous specifications are developed for his position. In other instances, unrealistic expectations for accomplishment may be utilized for accountability procedures. If expectancies are unreasonable, the consumer may dislocate responsibility and blame the inadequacy of the program on the candidate, when, in fact, the fault lies in the criteria.

Part of the purpose of the material in this book is to enable people in many different fields and areas to grapple with the content, procedures, and functions of helping persons who focus on the personal life-style of subjects. Focus on the personal life-style involves the bringing together of the subject's experience, whether it falls in the realm of content knowledge, attitudes, values, feelings, or mores.

If I, as a consumer, have a viable perception of a counselor-candidate's preparation and competencies, I am in a much better position to work out, with the candidate, an appropriate role-description for my agency. I am in a better position to incorporate his skills and knowledge into the institutional team. It is possible to better utilize his competency in meeting the needs of the institution and the clientele it serves.

Employers, like everyone else, operate from an experiential base, and if their experiences are not of sufficient breadth to encompass a reasonable range of behaviors, erroneous interpretations result and generalizations are applied that do not fit the individual candidate, or that result in job specifications that serve to encapsulate the candidate in a restrictive operation that does not utilize his talents, initiative, and creativeness.

Adequate preparation of counselors is a relatively new phenomenon, although persons with the title "counselor" have been employed for many decades. A criterion frequently employed in the past was whether an individual happened to get along well with others. Let us use the school as an example. Any employee of a school who is worth his salt gets along well with children and adolescents. It is immaterial whether he is a teacher, a principal, a counselor, or a bus driver—the worker must get along with kids. Does this mean that anyone who gets along well with kids should instruct in the field of chemistry? No, because not everyone is knowledgeable about valences, chemical formulae, the union of elements, and so forth. Counseling is much more than just relating to others: a salesman relates, a bartender relates, a foreman relates, a mechanic relates. Would you call such persons counselors? Of course not!! Good *professional counseling* relies on a positive relationship with others, but it also requires a counselor who can employ theoretical knowledge, situational sensitivity, and intervention strategies toward the end of reaching positive behaviors with the clientele being served. These positive behaviors must be identified realistically and at levels appropriate to the developmental stages of the persons being assisted. The subject matter for counselors is the personal makeup and integration of experience that continually modifies the life-style and behavior of the individual. The subject matter for the chemistry teacher is influencing the behavior of a learner through examining the chemical medium.

When an employer has an adequate understanding of the strengths a well-prepared counselor can provide, and of the limitations that are also present, then, we can assume, the counselor-candidate will be involved in developing a role compatible with his experience, his competency, and the needs of the institution and the persons subject to the institution's intervention.

It is as essential for an employer to know how to properly utilize the knowledge, skills, and talents of a counselor as it is critical for the counselor to have these commodities. Both parties should possess an understanding of the application and useability of these commodities in reaching meaningful goals.

WHAT FOLLOWS?

On subsequent pages the reader will find materials written by many different essayists. Topics were selected by the editors, and contributions were then elicited. An effort was made to obtain a range of viewpoints. In each chapter grouping, the editors have sought to do several things:

1. An introductory statement is offered.
2. Research materials pertaining to the topic are presented.
3. A selected annotated bibliography of these research materials and other supportive documents has been included.

The stimulation provided by these materials should result in informational input and the development of a perspective that gives direction, raises questions, and encourages counselor-candidates and practitioners, counselor-educators, and consumers to operationalize the *professionalism* sought through the development of this resource.

CHAPTER 2

Distinctions and Commonalities between Counseling and Psychotherapy

Some readers will look at the title of this chapter and decide that once again the poor dead horse is being beaten; others will eagerly turn the pages, hopeful that the provocative controversy has at last been resolved. The more relevant matter, however, is that differences do exist among the tacit assumptions made by practitioners, educators, and administrators about counseling and psychotherapy. Just exactly how these two fields are supposed to differ is not always clear. For example, in the most popular long-standing view, counseling refers to the treatment of simpler, less serious problems, tending to concentrate on problems of an educational, vocational, or behavioral nature, which can be resolved in a matter of a few sessions—the settings for this are usually schools and agencies. Psychotherapy, on the other hand, is considered, in the same view, to be the domain of practitioners who deal exclusively with serious emotional problems, which often require hospitalization and are resolved only through extended, long-term sessions, usually conducted by professionals in private practice, in hospitals, or in intensive-treatment units. The tendency is to see the "counselor" as less well prepared and the "therapist" as a professional with extensive, multidimensional expertise.

At first glance this view might seem reasonable, for surely it is one way of classifying different types of problems and different modes of treatment. But for anyone who has worked in the mental health field, this is not the way "things really are." Titles, in this context, like diagnostic categories, create more problems than they cure. The person who ostensibly has a career-choice problem may well turn out to be a borderline schizophrenic who needs intensive treatment but can only be in treatment for a short period of time. In other words, counselee problems are seldom so precisely divided, and schools and hospitals are not characteristically sources of such homogeneously simple and serious behavior populations.

What really happens is that practitioners deal with all kinds of experiences, behaviors, and problems, and thus should be prepared to deal with them. They may provide the treatment or they may refer the individual, but in some way they have to intervene and contend with the person and the behaviors presented.

The main practical damage done by the popular view cited above is that it confuses reality and miseducates, and thereby perpetuates itself in a curious way. The fact that it is a "popular" view is very important, because in many cases it becomes the only available guideline for the layman seeking help; and, more often than not, unable to accurately classify his behavior(s) he chooses a counselor or therapist on the basis of whether his troubles are more or less complex, whether he needs medication or not, whether he "wants" long-term treatment. The second aspect affected by this view is within the different disciplines, where the lack of growth-producing self-assessment, and the prevalence of external reinforcement in the form of client self-selection, perpetuates the sense among counselors that they deal with the less serious behaviors and experiences, and among therapists that they are the high priests for the truly emotionally disturbed. As a result, there very often is a lack of flexibility of treatment programs among practitioners and the consequent imposition on the counselee by the practitioner of his "special form of treatment" or of premature and sometimes ill-suited referrals.

There is an overwhelming need for well-qualified, responsible professional personnel to help individuals of all ages and socioeducational-economic groupings with the widest spectrum of personal experiences and concerns. This demand indicates that, as a way of efficiently treating the large numbers of people seeking help, there is value in encouraging the development of specialists who are especially well equipped to deal with specific behavior areas (e.g., sex, marriage, drugs, interpersonal relationships). But the need for specialization in no way contradicts the more basic need for professionals who are competent to treat a broad range of behaviors regardless of what they call themselves.

The three authors in this chapter present very individualistic positions with regard to the similarities and differences between counseling and psychotherapy. These essays give new vitality to a by-now classic debate. Patterson reviews in some detail the various criteria for differentiation, and critiques each before proceeding to a consideration of the similarities. He presents implicit evidence for a hierarchy of functions.

Sanborn argues a distinctive thesis convincingly and offers six postulates in support of his contentions. His use of a detailed case example does much to clarify his exposition and adds greatly to the reader's understanding of the basic issues.

Tyler persues the ramifications of the major arguments and looks for some mediation. A critical evaluation is made of the substantiveness of each view, of the operational differences, and of the implications for education at the graduate level.

Distinctions and Commonalities between Counseling and Psychotherapy

Cecil H. Patterson

University of Illinois

In commenting on my chapter (Patterson, 1967) in his review of Arbuckle's *Counseling and Psychotherapy: An Overview,* Abeles (1968) refers to my discussion of the "old saw" about the difference between counseling and psychotherapy. Abeles apparently "knows" that there is a significant difference, but like many others who claim to possess this supernatural knowledge, he does not let us in on what this difference is. He does not even attempt to define a difference, but simply implies, from his lofty position of knowledge, that anyone who does not see the difference is just too stupid to be let in on the secret. It appears from his later comments that psychotherapy is equated with psychoanalysis, and counseling is something less.

The concern over whether counseling and psychotherapy are different may be an "old saw," but it is such precisely because no one has been able to differentiate between them in any way that commands respect or agreement, although it cannot be said that many valiant attempts have not been made. I have briefly reviewed some of these attempts elsewhere (Patterson, 1959, 1963, 1966a, 1966b, 1967), as have Stefflre and Grant (1972). Whether it is an "old saw" or not, it appears that the controversy deserves extended attention, particularly in view of current concerns and developments in counselor preparation and counselor role and functions, and of recent research illuminating the nature of the conditions for facilitative interpersonal relationships.

DEFINITIONS OF COUNSELING AND PSYCHOTHERAPY

Many writers, perhaps beginning with Rogers (1942), make no attempt to distinguish counseling from psychotherapy. Others, such as Brammer and Shostrom (1968), Stefflre and Grant (1972), and Tyler (1961), attempt to differentiate them. Some of those who make this attempt, perhaps not able to

13

convince themselves of a difference, end up by deciding to use the terms interchangeably (e.g., Brammer & Shostrom, 1968, p. 8).

In an attempt to differentiate between counseling and psychotherapy, we will review a number of definitions to determine whether there is any agreement on differential meaning or use of the terms.

Differentiation in Terms of Severity of Client Disturbance. Many differential definitions revolve around the seriousness of the disturbance manifested by the client. A 1950 conference on the training of counselors (Bordin, 1951), while unable to agree on a clear distinction, felt that "counseling is concerned with the essentially normal individual [p. 9]." The Committee on Definition of the Division of Counseling Psychology of the American Psychological Association (1956) took essentially the same position, and saw the counseling psychologist as helping essentially normal people "toward overcoming obstacles to their personal growth, wherever these may be encountered, and toward achieving optimum development of their personal resources [p. 283]," while psychotherapy deals with the more extreme problems presented by "individuals who are in need of emergency treatment [p. 283]," "whose emotional growth has been severely distorted or stunted [p. 283]," or who represent "psychological disasters [p. 283]."

Hahn and MacLean (1955) accept the concept of severity when they state that part of the unique pattern of the counseling psychologist is "his concern with clients in the 'normal' range [p. 11]." He leaves the "deviates [p. 12]" to the therapists.

There are several difficulties with this distinction between "normal" and severely disturbed ("neurotic" or "psychotic") individuals. Those who propose this distinction recognize that no sharp line can be drawn to distinguish between the two categories of clients. Even the distinction between psychosis and lack of psychosis is not highly reliable, and depends on the individual making the judgment. Second, this position implies that a client being "treated" by a psychotherapist no longer needs the special skills or help of the therapist once he reaches "normality" (assuming that this could be reliably determined), but should then be transferred to a counselor if he still desires further help. The psychotherapist at some point would presumably say to a patient something like the following: "You are now no longer abnormal, so I am going to transfer you to a counselor to help you solve your remaining problems." Some of those who make this distinction go on to note that counseling cannot be limited to the normal person, but applies also to the abnormal or severely maladjusted person. Here, however, the qualification is added that counseling deals with "the normalities even of abnormal persons, with locating and developing personal and social resources and adaptive tendencies so that the individual can be assisted in making more effective use of them [Super, 1955]."

Differentiation in Terms of Problems. This indicates another proposed distinction. Rather than, or perhaps in addition to, the severity of the disturbance, it is the nature of the problem that defines whether what is done is counseling or psychotherapy. In this distinction, counseling deals with reality-oriented problems, problems of an environmental or situational nature, rather than intrapersonal problems or internal personality conflicts. Counseling deals with *decisions* related to educational, vocational, or other choices; psychotherapy is concerned with attitudes, feelings, and emotions within the self. Counseling deals with *cognitive* problems, psychotherapy with *affective* problems.

This distinction also breaks down, however, when one examines it closely. Reality problems are not all cognitive in nature; the paranoid person has situational or environmental problems. And interpersonal problems, while in one sense reality problems, are also personality problems.

Distinctions Involving Goals. The whole matter of the goals of counseling or psychotherapy is in a state of confusion (Mahrer, 1967), and it is only natural that this confusion should be reflected in attempts to distinguish between counseling and psychotherapy in terms of goals. The Committee on Definition, referred to above, speaks of counseling as helping individuals to overcome obstacles to personal growth. Tyler (1958), however, states that it is *not* the job of the counselor "to remove physical and mental handicaps or to get rid of limitations [p. 8]." Counseling, according to Tyler, does not attempt to "repair damage done to [the client] in the past, to stimulate inadequate [*sic*] development of some stunted aspect of his personality [p. 18]," but is a process of "helping a person attain a clear sense of personal identity, along with the acceptance of limitations [p. 8]." This latter sounds like the goal of existential psychotherapists. Many psychotherapists include the removal, reduction, or elimination of blocks as goals of psychotherapy (Mahrer, 1967, p. 263).

Psychotherapy, according to Tyler (1961, p. 12), is directed toward "personality change of some sort." Counseling, she states, refers "to a helping process the aim of which is not to change the person, but to enable him to utilize the sources he now has for coping with life." Related to this distinction is the attempt to define psychotherapy as remedial in nature and counseling as preventive. Hahn and MacLean (1955, pp. 31–32), and Bordin (1951), among many others, make this distinction.

This distinction is no more clear-cut than the others we have considered. It hardly seems possible to separate personality change, even reorganization of the basic personality structure (whatever that is), from changes represented in greater utilization of the capacities of the individual. Personality could no more change without the potential being present than could a utilization of resources be achieved without their being latently there. Tyler rejects a distinction in terms of superficiality versus depth, noting that "the way a person sees his work, his religious beliefs, or his relationships to his wife and children are as deep and fundamental a part of him as are his anxieties over sexual or aggressive motivation [Tyler, 1961, p. 13]."[1] Changes in perceptions, attitudes, beliefs, values, feelings, and emotions all occur as a result of counseling. Who would say that these are not basic personality changes?

Tyler also appears to be inconsistent when she describes "minimum change therapy." She defines this as counseling, since it is concerned with "*exploration of resources*" rather than "personality weaknesses [Tyler, 1961, p. 213]." Yet she calls it therapy. (In the 3rd edition of her book there is no reference to minimum change therapy.)

Differentiation in Terms of Methods or Techniques. If one reviews the literature on techniques proposed or used, on the one hand, by those calling themselves counselors or professing to engage in counseling, and, on the other, by those calling themselves psychotherapists or engaging in psychotherapy, there appears to be no technique or method used exclusively by one and not by the other. A possible exception might be the use of drugs by those calling themselves psychotherapists. The use of drugs can hardly be called psychotherapy, however. There are some who claim that certain techniques, such as interpretation, probing and uncovering, are more frequently used by psychotherapists. No quantitative evidence is presented, however, and certainly these techniques are widely used by those engaging in what is called counseling.

On the other hand, the similarities in methods and techniques are widely recognized. Everyone, except extremists who talk about "computer counseling," seems to agree that counseling and psychotherapy are both personal relationships involving personal interaction, mainly verbal but also on a nonverbal level, and characterized by attentive listening, empathic understanding, a nonpossessive warmth, respect, and acceptance, and a genuine, real, honest relationship. Attempts to specify further characteristics differentiating counseling and psychotherapy have not been successful. Counseling is said to involve more cognitive techniques of problem-solving, to be more rational in its methods and approach. But one need only consider Ellis's rational psychotherapy to dismiss this argument (Ellis, 1962).

Again, as with the other attempted distinctions, the differences exist more in the mind of the person who wants differences to exist than in any objective reality. Thus Stefflre and Grant (1972, p. 21) write: "In distinguishing counseling from psychotherapy on the basis of difference of methods, we should run counter to the advice of Patterson (1959, p. 10) who sees no difference between

---

[1]In her third edition, Tyler (1969) makes no clear differentiation between counseling and psychotherapy. She talks about *choice* counselors and *change* counselors, indicating that the latter are often called therapists (p. 174).

them." They fail to offer any reasons for their "should." Incidently, Stefflre and Grant (1972, p. 16) present what they claim is a quotation from me, regarding the characteristics of a counseling-psychotherapy continuum, which I am unable to find in the reference cited.

The attempt to separate remediation from prevention is likewise futile. Clearly, what is remedial at one point in time may be preventive when considered at another point. Moreover, counselors do not refuse to deal with current problems or difficulties in which clients find themselves. And certainly psychotherapists are concerned with the prevention of more serious or future disturbances. As Blocher (1965, p.799) notes, "Much of what is attempted in the name of counseling has been as remediative and adjustive as anything attempted in the name of psychotherapy [p. 799]."

SIGNIFICANT DIFFERENCES HAVE NOT BEEN ESTABLISHED

It should be apparent that efforts to make a distinction between counseling and psychotherapy have not been successful. Even terms like *client* and *patient,* *counselor* and *therapist,* and others supposedly differentiating between the processes and goals of the two fields, have been used in descriptions of both counseling and psychotherapy. Authors of chapters on counseling and psychotherapy in the *Annual Review of Psychology* have struggled for years to find some reasonable criteria to separate the literature covered in their respective areas. None have been found. Articles with *counseling* in the titles have been reviewed in chapters titled *Psychotherapy,* and vice versa. The only general agreement has been to include studies reporting work in a medical setting, or reported in medical or psychiatric journals, in reviews of psychotherapy, while studies conducted in a nonmedical setting and reported in other journals are reviewed in chapters on counseling. Even this distinction is not always adhered to.

In practice, *professionally trained* counselors and psychotherapists do not attempt to make distinctions about whether they are engaging in counseling or psychotherapy. They do not attempt to make fine evaluations about whether a client is abnormal in a pathological sense or is facing temporary or situational problems. They do not attempt to distinguish between efforts to change basic personality structure and efforts to resolve current problems or dissatisfactions. They do not concern themselves with whether they are engaged in bringing a client with "pathology" up to a "normal" level where they will then terminate, or whether they will only accept a client who is "normal" and work towards helping him increase the use of his potentials. All counselors or psychotherapists, within the broad limits of the accessibility of the client to a counseling or psychotherapeutic approach, take the client where he is and continue with him as far as he can or will go. There is no concern about regulating the depth, intensity, or length of the relationship to keep it at a "counseling" level or at a psychotherapy level. Tyler (1960) in her discussion of minimum-change therapy, which is supposedly a limited, short-term therapy, does not set a limit. She points out that "the experience of having someone really care about him is such an indispensable part of what counseling means for a client that we must be especially careful never to jeopardize it [p. 475]." Setting a time-limit, she suggests, may make the client feel he is only worth ten hours, or twenty hours. Likewise, other aspects of the relationship cannot be limited. A counselor cannot limit a relationship with a client and still be his real self, genuine and spontaneous. A counselor cannot commit himself only partially to a counseling relationship. You cannot go swimming without getting wet all over. Tyler (1960) notes that:

We can best control the duration of counseling contacts [and I would say depth, intensity, goals and outcome, also] by adopting consistently an attitude of respect for what each individual client now is and lending him support and understanding while he comes to terms with this unique self of his. Whether it takes him two hours or two hundred, if he succeeds, the effort will have been very worthwhile. [p. 479]

All this applies, of course, to the professionally trained (not necessarily doctorally trained) counselor. The source of much of the confusion, for those like Stefflre and Grant, is the number of untrained persons calling themselves counselors. Such persons are not psychotherapists—neither are they counselors—and what they do is neither counseling nor psychotherapy.

In view of this failure to reach any generally accepted or compelling distinctions, it would appear to be a tenable conclusion that there are no essential differences between counseling and psychotherapy. But the amazing thing is that the existence of a difference is only more stoutly, if irrationally, claimed. There *must* be a difference, it is declared—if only it could be discovered! The irrationality of some goes even further. Hahn (1953), summarizing agreements, notes that counseling and psychotherapy cannot be distinguished clearly, that counselors practice what psychotherapists consider to be psychotherapy and psychotherapists practice what counselors consider to be counseling, but nonetheless asserts that there is agreement that they are different. Stefflre and Grant (1972, p. 15) state openly that "a distinction *must* be made. If it is not present in nature, it must be invented." Their reasoning is that since what many who have the title "counselor" are doing is not psychotherapy, there must be something called "counseling" to *define* what they are doing. This conclusion is quite unreasonable. It might more logically be concluded that such persons are not in fact counselors. It may be that the resistance against recognizing that there is no essential difference between counseling and psychotherapy is rooted in the dawning recognition that what many, if not most, counselors do, though it may be called counseling, is not really counseling, and is indeed a far cry from it. Counseling is made to mean whatever anyone wants it to mean. Thus, counseling is (it *must* be) whatever persons called counselors do.

Others have attempted to resolve the problem by asserting that counseling and psychotherapy are on a continuum. They do not specify what the continuum is. Moreover, they place counseling on one end of the continuum and psychotherapy on the other, and then point at it, saying: "See, there is obviously a difference between the two ends of the continuum." No one so far, to my knowledge, at least, has appealed to statistics to bolster this claim, in the form of stating that there is a difference of six standard deviations between the ends of a normal continuum, clearly a significant difference!

Goldman (1964) has used an analogy to support the continuum argument. Put in logical form, his argument is as follows: (1) counseling equals light; (2) psychotherapy equals darkness; (3) light is clearly different from darkness; (4) therefore counseling is different from psychotherapy. Stated in this form, the fallacious logic is clearly apparent, but it is an argument accepted by many. The difference is assumed, and then "proven."

BASIC SIMILARITIES OF COUNSELING AND PSYCHOTHERAPY

Counseling and psychotherapy may indeed be placed on a continuum—But only on a continuum of helping activities, not an arbitrary and unnamed continuum with the two ends designated as counseling and psychotherapy, with no identification or description of the underlying variable or variables. The kind of "reasoning" that does not identify or describe variables is simply a way of expressing or illustrating a conclusion already reached and has no relationship to the relevance or validity of the conclusion.

The continuum on which counseling and psychotherapy may be placed is shown in Figure 1.

The major variable underlying this continuum of helping relationships is affect, or its opposite, cognition. It is not suggested, however, that affect is completely lacking at the cognitive end; or that cognition is completely lacking at the affect end. It is a matter of more or less, since all relationships involve both affective and cognitive elements. A slightly different way of putting it is to say that in teaching, for example, the relationship is the *medium,* whereas in counseling or psychotherapy it is the *substance* or *essence.*

Other related variables, which appear to underlie the continuum, are the personal nature of the relationship and the generality or specificity of the goals

Information giving	Teaching	Behavior modification	Behavior "therapy"	Counseling psychotherapy
Cognitive	←		→	Affective
Impersonal	←		→	Personal
Specificity	←		→	Generality

Figure 1. A Continuum of Psychological Helping Relationships

of the relationship. Counseling or psychotherapy is highly personal, and its goals are broader or more general than teaching or behavior modification. A fourth variable that may be related to the continuum is the presence or absence of appropriate responses in the repertoire of the recipient in the relationship. At one end of the continuum the appropriate responses are not present; the purpose of teaching and skill training is to develop appropriate responses, and that of behavior modification is to eliminate inappropriate responses and substitute new, appropriate responses. In counseling or psychotherapy, appropriate responses are in the response repertoire of the client but are inhibited or blocked for some reason. While this variable appears to be related to the continuum, it is probably, to some extent at least, independent of it.

It is impossible not to conclude, after a review of the discussions of the differences between counseling and psychotherapy, that they are fundamentally the same in terms of the essential elements. Both consist of a relationship in which an individual seeks help from a person skilled in providing a helping relationship. The help needed, or problem, is of a general nature, rather than information or solution of a specific problem. The problem involves affect, or feeling, and is not mainly a cognitive problem resolvable on a purely objective or rational basis. Since an effective counseling or psychotherapy relationship consists of the core facilitative conditions (Carkhuff & Berenson, 1967) of empathic understanding, respect or nonpossessive warmth, and genuineness, both counseling and psychotherapy should be restricted to relationships in which these (and perhaps certain other related conditions) are sufficient for positive results. These conditions are also necessary, to some degree, for all effective helping relationships, but are not sufficient in all cases, as, for example, where information is lacking.

When other conditions are necessary, the relationship is not counseling or psychotherapy, but a different kind of helping relationship. The incidental inclusion of other elements in a relationship that essentially consists of the core facilitative conditions, however, may not justify calling the process something other than counseling or psychotherapy. A case in point is the use of tests and occupational information in vocational counseling. If the relationship is a counseling relationship, then the focus is not upon information-giving, but upon the affective aspects of the client's acceptance and use of the information in the process of developing a (vocational) self-concept. On the other hand, if the relationship is one of providing information without regard to its emotional or personal effects on the client, either because there is little such effect or because the counselor ignores it, then the process is not counseling but information-giving, or possibly teaching.

The difficulty inherent in attempts to differentiate counseling from psychotherapy is that when such differentiation appears to be achieved, the resulting relationship called counseling is essentially teaching. These attempts emphasize the cognitive nature of counseling—problem-solving, decision-making or choice, testing and information-giving. The nature of the relationship, in terms of the core conditions, is minimized or neglected. Such a concept of counseling is little different from teaching—in fact, it is individual teaching. The "counseling" depicted in the film *Challenge of Change: The Case for Counseling* (NET Film Service, Indiana University, Bloomington, Ind.) is of this type. It is interesting that what the counselor does in the so-called counseling interview in this film bears no relation to the instruction in counseling he receives earlier in the film. In the instruction the emphasis is on understanding the feelings and attitudes of the client from the internal frame of reference, while in the interview the approach is purely external, with information-giving, encouragement, and suggestion.

It should be apparent that the differences between counseling and psychotherapy are not related to essentials. The basic nature of the relationship, the major methods or techniques, the general goals, are all essentially the same. If the function is performed in a medical setting, or presumably under medical supervision, it is called psychotherapy and its practitioners are referred to as psychotherapists. If it is performed in a nonmedical setting, it is called counseling and its practitioners are referred to as counselors.

It is of course true that there are broad differences between medical and nonmedical settings in regard to the nature of clients and problems treated. There are also differences in the duration of the process, in terms of number of interviews. But the overlap is great, and the variation within each setting is great. To use a statistical analogy, the range of differences within settings, on variables such as type of client, degree of severity, methods, goals, and so forth, is so much greater than the differences between settings, that discrimination or differentiation is not significant.

IMPLICATIONS FOR PREPARATION

If there are no significant differences between counseling and psychotherapy, there should be no basic differences in programs of preparation for counselors and psychotherapists. If we compare programs preparing professional counselors (not "guidance workers") with programs preparing psychologists to engage in psychotherapy, we find essential commonality in those aspects of the programs related to theory and practice. Most programs in both cases are probably inadequate, to be sure, but they are similar.

If counselors are really counselors, and not information-givers, teachers, or dispensers of M & M's and other mechanical reinforcements, they must be prepared to deal with and relate to a wide variety of people in close interpersonal relationships. This requires intensive preparation and training in the provision of the core conditions of facilitative interpersonal relationships, as developed by Truax and Carkhuff (1967), Carkhuff and Berenson (1967), and Carkhuff (1969), all of whom are referred to above.

The work of these writers has shown that an intensive program of 100 hours of didactic and experiential preparation can lead to the development, in persons without a college degree or any specific background in psychology, of the ability to offer a relationship characterized by levels of these core conditions approximating those of professional counselors or therapists. If this is the case, then it would follow that counseling and psychotherapy are not a profession, since one of the marks of a profession is that it requires unique knowledge and skills that are not possessed by those without professional training, which is usually offered at the graduate level.

If counseling and psychotherapy are to be considered professions, they must consist of more than this. Providing a therapeutic relationship is not a unique function, and is not a monopoly of psychiatrists, social workers, psychologists, and counselors.

A professional is distinguished from others, in part, by being skilled in providing higher levels of therapeutic relationship. But if this can be achieved without professional training, it is merely a technical achievement. What is it, then, that makes, or can make, counselors and psychotherapists professionals?

A characteristic of a professional is his autonomy. He is able to function independently, without supervision. He is able to determine when it is appropriate to use his specific skills and when something else is required. He is able to use and apply his specific skills with a wide variety of clients in a wide variety of situations requiring judgment and adaptation. Thus, the professional counselor can determine when and with whom to function as a counselor, when to discontinue, and when to refer. The technician must have his clients selected for him, and must be constantly supervised or monitored to determine the appropriateness of counseling, when a referral is indicated, and when counseling can be concluded.

The professional counselor thus must be prepared to take responsibility for his clients, or the clients of the technicians he is supervising. He must be able to recognize the needs of clients for other assistance or services in addition to the counseling relationship, and must be prepared to offer these in combination with counseling (e.g., testing and occupational information) or to make appropriate referrals (e.g., tutoring or remedial reading). Counselors may vary in the extent to which they themselves provide specific services or use referral sources, depending upon their specific preparation and interests. Some counselors may offer services that are not specifically counseling, but are in the teaching or information-giving range of the continuum of helping relationships. But every professional counselor must be able to determine the kind or kinds of helping relationship needed by the client, both before and during the counseling relationship, and to see that the client's needs are adequately met.

Preparation for such a level of professional functioning requires general undergraduate education in the behavioral sciences, and more specific graduate preparation in psychology and the related areas included in the recommendations of professional organizations (APGA, 1964; APA, 1962; ACES, 1967).

As a major emphasis, all programs should concentrate on developing the ability of students to offer the core conditions of a helping relationship. These core conditions are basic to all helping relationships, and are necessary for effective counseling or psychotherapy with all clients with all kinds of problems in all settings.

However, since counselors tend to specialize in working in a particular setting with certain kinds of clients with certain kinds of problems, some differences in programs of preparation are desirable. These differences are in general of two kinds.

The first relates to the kinds of clients with whom the counselor is expected to spend most of his time. If the counselor is to achieve the necessary degree of empathic understanding of his clients, he must have some general background and preparation to help him relate to and understand them. Thus the counselor or psychotherapist who is to work in a mental hospital or with severely disturbed clients must have considerable preparation in abnormal psychology. The counselor who is to work with adolescents must have preparation in adolescent psychology, while the counselor who is going to work with younger children needs preparation in child development. The counselor who is to work with physically disabled clients in rehabilitation counseling needs preparation that includes work in the nature of physical disabilities and the psychology or social psychology of disability. And the counselor who is to work with other kinds of clients, such as members of one or another minority, racial, or socioeconomic group, should also have preparation for understanding them.

All of this special preparation, however, is based upon and in addition to general preparation in human behavior, and in personality and development. Moreover, overspecialization must be avoided, both because counselors work with a variety of clients, and because a counselor may someday wish to change the setting in which he works, and thus the kinds of clients he sees. The elementary-school counselor must work with, and to some extent counsel, teachers and parents. And he may wish to leave elementary-school counseling for another setting, either within or outside the school system.

Related to differences in clients are differences in problem areas. Such areas include education, vocation, marriage, and aging or retirement. Counselors expecting to work with adolescents or young adults, particularly in a school setting, should be prepared to deal with educational and vocational problems, and should be prepared in both the theory (vocational development) and technical aspects (tests and measurements, occupational information) necessary to understand and work with clients having problems in these areas.

The second area of difference in the preparation of counselors is the providing of background in the setting in which they are to work. Counselors who are to work in an educational setting receive some special preparation for this, as do rehabilitation counselors for the setting in which they are to work. Such preparation, again, should not be too specific or rigid, making it difficult or impossible for a counselor to move from one setting to another. It would appear to be too restrictive to insist that preparation for counseling in a school must include qualification for a teaching certificate and teaching experience.

In any case, it should be recognized that a major part of the preparation of counselors is the same for all settings. Segregation of counseling students in terms of the settings in which they are to work, with entirely separate curriculums, in separate departments or schools, is undesirable.

CONCLUSION

The issue of whether counseling and psychotherapy are significantly different has been complicated recently by the extension of the use of the word *counseling*. While *psychotherapy* has continued to have a relatively constant meaning, *counseling* is used by many as words were used by Humpty Dumpty in Lewis Carroll's *Through the Looking-Glass:* "When *I* use a word, it means just what I choose it to mean." *Counseling* now means anything that anyone who is called a counselor does—or can be induced to do. It covers all services to the individual—a variety of activities beyond the private, interpersonal relationship, which has always been considered the essense of counseling. It includes all helping activities, all methods of attempting to influence and change the behavior of others.

Thus it is difficult to object when the word is used by those with no professional preparation or training: beauty counselors, travel counselors, loan counselors. I recently heard of a rug counselor, though I have never seen a rug that needed counseling.

We are now in a state of confusion. As Alice said to Humpty Dumpty: "The question is, whether you *can* make words mean so many different things." It is necessary to restrict, or delimit, the meaning of the word *counseling* so that it has a clear, denotative meaning. And when this is done, we reach a definition that does not differ in any essential repsect from a definition of *psychotherapy*.

It may be that we ought to abandon the term *counseling* for *psychotherapy*, but we must recognize the practical difficulties attached to this. For example, the practice of psychotherapy is restricted by law in many places to medical doctors. Also, the term has some undesirable connotations.

It certainly would be useful to retain the term *counseling*. However, the fact that it is not legally restricted, and is now used by persons with no preparation or qualifications to engage in a (professional) counseling relationship, constitutes a problem. We need some way to distinguish professional counselors from others who use the title or have it as a job-title without adequate preparation. I have suggested the use of the term *psychological counselor* for this purpose (Patterson, 1968).

The fact that no significant or important differences command general agreement and acceptance, despite all the efforts to differentiate counseling and psychotherapy, is strong evidence that there are no significant differences. The null hypothesis of no difference has not been disaproved.

REFERENCES

Abeles, N. Review of D. S. Arbuckle (Ed.), Counseling and psychotherapy: An overview. *Personnel and Guidance Journal,* 1968, **46**, 702–704.

Albert, G. If counseling *is* psychotherapy—what then? *Personnel and Guidance Journal,* 1966, **45**, 125–129.

American Personnel and Guidance Association. The counselor: Professional preparation and role —a statement of policy. *Personnel and Guidance Journal,* 1964, **42**, 536–541.

American Psychological Association, Division of Counseling Psychology, Committee on Definition. Counseling psychology as a specialty. *American Psychologist,* 1956, **11**, 282–285.

American Psychological Association, Division of Counseling Psychology. The scope and standards of preparation in psychology for school counselors. *American Psychologist,* 1962, **17**, 149–152.

Association for Counselor Education and Supervision. Standards for the preparation of secondary school counselors-1967. *Personnel and Guidance Journal,* 1967, **46**, 96–106.

Blocher, D. H. Issues in counseling: Elusive and illusional. *Personnel and Guidance Journal,* 1965, **43**, 796–800.

Bordin, E. S. (Ed.) *Training of Psychological Counselors.* Ann Arbor: University of Michigan Press, 1951.

Brammer, L. M., & Shostrom, E. L. *Therapeutic psychology.* (2nd ed.) Englewood Cliffs, N.J.: Prentice-Hall, 1968.

Carkhuff, R. R. *Helping and human relations.* Vols. 1 and 2. New York: Holt, Rinehart & Winston, 1969.

Carkhuff, R. R., & Berenson, B. G. *Beyond counseling and therapy.* New York: Holt, Rinehart & Winston, 1967.

Ellis, A. *Reason and emotion in psychotherapy.* New York: Lyle Stuart, 1962.

Goldman, L. Comment: Another log. *American Psychologist,* 1964, **19**, 418–419.

Hahn, M. E. Conceptual trends in counseling. *Personnel and Guidance Journal,* 1953, **31**, 231–235.

Hahn, M. E., & MacLean, M. S. *Counseling psychology.* (2nd ed.) New York: McGraw-Hill, 1955.

Mahrer, A. R. (Ed.) *The goals of psychotherapy.* New York: Appleton-Century-Crofts, 1967.

Patterson, C. H. *Counseling and psychotherapy: Theory and practice.* New York: Harper & Row, 1959.

Patterson, C. H. Comment: Counseling and/or psychotherapy. *American Psychologist,* 1963, **18**, 667–669.

Patterson, C. H. Counseling. *Annual Review of Psychology,* 1966, **17**, 79–110. (a)

Patterson, C. H. *Theories of counseling and psychotherapy.* (2nd ed.) New York: Harper & Row, 1973. (b)

Patterson, C. H. Psychotherapy in the school. In D. S. Arbuckle (Ed.), *Counseling and psychotherapy: An overview.* New York: McGraw-Hill, 1967.

Patterson, C. H. Rehabilitation counseling: A profession or a trade? *Personnel and Guidance Journal,* 1968, **46**, 567–571.

Rogers, C. R. *Counseling and psychotherapy.* Boston: Houghton Mifflin, 1942.

Rogers, C. R. (Ed.) *The therapeutic relationship and its impact.* Madison: University of Wisconsin Press, 1967.

Stefflre, B., & Grant, W. H. (Eds.) *Theories of counseling.* (2nd ed.) New York: McGraw-Hill, 1972.

Super, D. E. Transition from vocational guidance to counseling psychology. *Journal of Counseling Psychology,* 1955, **2**, 3–9.

Truax, C. B., & Carkhuff, R. R. *Toward effective counseling and psychotherapy.* Chicago: Aldine, 1967.

Tyler, Leona E. Theoretical principles underlying the counseling process. *Journal of Counseling Psychology,* 1958, **5**, 3–8.

Tyler, Leona E. Minimum change therapy. *Personnel and Guidance Journal,* 1960, **38**, 475–479.

Tyler, Leona E. *The work of the counselor.* (2nd ed.) New York: Appleton-Century-Crofts, 1961.

Tyler, Leona E. *The work of the counselor.* (3rd ed.) New York: Appleton-Century-Crofts, 1969.

School Counseling: Emphatically *Not* a Therapy Service

Marshall P. Sanborn

University of Wisconsin—Madison

There has been a considerable amount of discussion in our profession about whether counseling differs in any important way from psychotherapy. In fact, so many arguments have already been presented on this issue that it may well be superfluous to present another. At least insofar as the general question is concerned, the potentialities for a novel position seem to be fairly well exhausted. No matter what point of view one takes, it has already been taken before. Furthermore, it appears that whoever has asserted himself (or herself) on the issue thus far has been met with at least one formidable rebuttal. Although I cannot see that anyone yet has had the last word, I nevertheless believe that to pursue the general question further is possibly to beat a dead horse—or else a live mule. Whoever does so risks the indignity of receiving either no response at all—or else one bigger than he bargained for.

Some people argue that the difference between counseling and psychotherapy is mainly a matter of depth or intensity. Blocher (1965, p. 798) has aptly summarized this position:

Writers such as Perry (1955) and Brammer and Shostrom (1960) have characterized human personality in terms of a sort of onionskin analogy, with the counselor busy peeling away the outer layers . . . while the therapist penetrates to the inner and apparently more pungent layers of the onion core. Presumably, every counselor should stop at whatever point his eyes begin to water.

Most people who take this position also argue, either implicitly or explicitly, that psychotherapy, being the deeper and more complex task, calls for a higher level of training and competence than does counseling (e.g., Patterson, 1959; Stefflre, 1965). It follows, of course, that in many circles the psychotherapist is accorded more prestige than the counselor. Were it not for this fact, I suspect, we would have more counselors than we do, and fewer psychotherapists.

27

Quite a few professionals and a large segment of the lay public view counseling as mainly a developmental activity and psychotherapy as mainly a remedial one. They see counselors as dealing with "normal" individuals, primarily at conscious, rational levels, with decision-making tasks; whereas psychotherapists work primarily with "abnormal" persons, usually in search of unconscious, irrational factors, which must be identified and corrected. Lewis (1970) provides a definition of counseling representative of this point of view, and Wolberg (1967) offers one for psychotherapy. Among those who differentiate in this manner, psychotherapy again is usually regarded as the more complex process.

Some writers emphasize a third differentiating factor. That is the degree of impact upon the client. In general they see psychotherapy as an activity which, if successful, may lead to major or basic personality restructuring. Counseling would call for nothing of such magnitude. Thus, whatever client changes occur during successful psychotherapy may be somewhat more difficult to achieve, and perhaps more dramatic to observe, than would be expected of the changes in a counselee who has had a successful counseling experience. Probably most people who emphasize either of the aforementioned differentiations would also recognize this one. Factors such as intensity, depth, identification of unconscious forces and needs, and remediation all seem to go hand in hand with the concept of dramatic personality restructuring.

Most writers who argue that counseling and psychotherapy are different seem to believe that the difference is mainly a matter of degree. They apparently conceptualize counseling and psychotherapy as two ends of the same continuum. Looking at it this way, it is easy to tell the difference at the extremes, but the problem of where to draw the line in the middle is not so simple. At what level, or what degree of intensity, does counseling stop and psychotherapy begin? What is the boundary between the "normal" and the "abnormal"? Should the counselor ever attempt to deal with motives or needs the counselee has not been aware of before, or should he refer to a psychotherapist whenever these enter the picture?

Leona Tyler (1961) attempted to relieve this problem by introducing a middle ground, which she called "minimum-change therapy." Those who find her position attractive differentiate three ways instead of two. *Counseling* is a developmental activity focused on plans, choice, and decisions, usually of an educational or vocational nature. *Minimum-change therapy* is an activity like counseling, but the focus is on personal and social problems the client is encountering. It is a rational process, for the most part, which can be done by "counselors who are not psychotherapists (p. 232)" (school-counselors, for instance), so long as they are careful to stay within the limits of minimum-change goals. Tyler defines minimum change as a change in direction, chosen from among alternatives that have been identified during the interviews. She does not specify any maximum to compare with "minimum," and this may be difficult to do in any exact way. She does suggest, however, that minimum-change therapy ought not take an inordinate amount of time; and we may safely presume, I think, that any turn executed by the client would be somewhat less than 90 degrees—more a matter of getting back on a favorable course than of setting an entirely new destination. *Psychotherapy*, then, is a process reserved for use with those who are classified as "neurotic" or something worse.

It would appear that type of problem, degree of depth, intensity, impact on the client, and complexity of problem are all relevant distinctions for Tyler, as they are for others who differentiate between counseling and psychotherapy. Another distinction she alludes to—and a very practical one, I think—is the setting in which the activity is carried on. In settings such as schools, she asserts, where counseling is expected but where sanctions do not extend to psychotherapy, we should not be using much time in psychotherapeutic pursuits.

Through nearly all the arguments for differentiating between counseling and psychotherapy (with the exception, perhaps, of a distinction based on setting), there seems to be the implication that all qualified psychotherapists possess the skills and understanding necessary to do counseling, but not all qualified counselors can do psychotherapy. A good psychotherapist is a good counselor and *then* some. One writer who takes exception to this implication is Lewis (1970). He argues that counseling is a different process rather than merely a limited case of psychotherapy, and that competence in either activity does not necessarily insure competence in the other. I agree. The skills and understanding required and the general strategies employed in school counseling should differ qualitatively, not quantitatively, from those demanded in psychotherapy.

There are some persons, of course, who subscribe to none of the positions discussed above. Writers such as Rogers (1951) and Arbuckle (1961) have taken the position that no meaningful distinction can be made between counseling and psychotherapy. To them, counseling *is* therapy; and although they make frequent use of both terms, they apparently do so mainly in the interest of smooth sentence structure, and not for the purpose of differentiating one activity from the other.

Perhaps they would argue that no matter what we call ourselves—counselors or psychotherapists—our ideal goals, and the directions we take to attain goals, are not very different. Both counselors and psychotherapists hope to assist individuals toward enhanced self-concepts; better capacities for meeting and coping with new problems, experiences, and challenges in their lives; improved capabilities for making choices and decisions and otherwise exercising independent control over their own experiences and outcomes; more meaningful and harmonious relationships with others; and so forth and so on.

It may well be that the closer we come to attaining these ideal goals, the fewer differences we will be able to detect between counseling and psychotherapy. In the long run they may be one and the same. But we are far, in either profession, from attaining ideal goals in any general way; and within the limits of what we can realistically expect to accomplish, I think it is safe to assert that both the purposes and the processes of good school counseling are—and ought to be—different from those currently employed in psychotherapy.

Not long ago I was present at a conference where a psychotherapist was reporting on a research project involving comparisons of "successful" and "unsuccessful" psychotherapeutic cases. When I asked him what the criterion of success was, he looked at me for a long moment and then said, "We defined successful cases as those who were able to operate in society after therapy, without being returned to the institution." That, I thought, may suffice for psychotherapists, but it certainly would not do for school-counselors. We start at different points; we work on different tasks; and hopefully we end with different outcomes.

THE CASE FOR DIFFERENTIATION IN SCHOOLS

There are perhaps two basic reasons why school-counselors should emphasize that their work is counseling and not psychotherapy. The first is to talk accurately among ourselves, and the second is to talk accurately to teachers, administrators, students, parents, and taxpayers about what we ought to be accomplishing in schools, why, how we do our work, with whom, and how counseling fits into the larger picture of education. To facilitate accurate description among all concerned, it helps to use words that are most likely to convey accurate meanings. The words *psychotherapy* and *therapy* are likely to be misleading. Both denotatively and connotatively they are inappropriate for educational counseling and guidance programs, since they tend to promote the idea that the services and activities involved are crisis-intervention procedures predicated on trouble. The school-counseling program ought to be a developmental program predicated on sound general objectives for the personal, social, educational, and vocational growth of all youngsters.

School-counselors who fancy themselves psychotherapists are unlikely to devote much energy and ingenuity to the task of programming meaningful counseling and guidance activities for the general school population. Their priorities usually lie with the many interesting crisis cases that come to light. Psychotherapeutic problems do occur among schoolchildren, of course, since virtually the entire population goes through the schools. But at best the school-counselor will experience good success with only a few of these cases, marginal success with some, and no success at all with most children in the school who need psychotherapy, which the school has neither resources nor sanctions to provide. For the vast majority of the pupils, such a counselor will have no impact at all, his attention being elsewhere. Over the years he is likely to establish a reputation as a person to whom children go—or are sent—only when in trouble, and who doesn't get very dramatic results among those with whom he works. Anyone who questions this need only go into the schools to find that it has happened, and is happening.

Another negative consequence of viewing school counseling as psychotherapy is that the public may come to believe it is providing needed psychological services, which, in fact, it is not. School-counselors need adequate community mental-health resources to which they can refer psychotherapeutic cases beyond the scope of the school-counseling program. In many communities such resources do not exist at all, and sometimes where they do exist they serve only those who can afford to pay the high costs of self-sustaining psychotherapeutic agencies.

I will remember my own years as a school-counselor in a small town in western Colorado. As might be expected in any community, we had a few youngsters each year who, together with their families, needed psychotherapeutic help. The nearest useful resource was the University of Colorado Diagnostic Center in Denver—200 mountain miles away. We could send children there for diagnostic evaluation, and they would be returned with case information and suggestions for follow-through. These suggestions made good sense in terms of the needs of the individuals in question, but almost no sense at all in terms of the capacities of the school, family, and community to carry them out. By committing inordinate amounts of time and resources to a minuscule proportion of the school population we could "make do." This we did as best we could. In some instances costs were very high in terms of neglected needs of other pupils in the school. They were high also, I suspect, in terms of delayed public awareness of mental health needs in the community, which were not being appropriately met.

Teachers, administrators, and counselors who operate schools day in and day out are certain to encounter instances where they realize that a child or a family needs psychotherapeutic help, just as they are certain to identify some children who need medical or dental attention. These children should be referred to appropriate resources outside the school so that school people can, as quickly as possible, get back to their responsibilities of designing and carrying out educational and developmental activities aimed at all pupils.

SOME POSTULATES

Further on in this essay I will outline for the reader a few features of school counseling that are essential to a good program and are obviously not crisis-intervention procedures. Hopefully such a discussion will show how school counseling differs from psychotherapy. Before doing this, however, it seems important to clarify things a little—or else to confuse them once and for all —by listing several postulates, which, I have come to believe, are true and are important to consider in differentiating between counseling and psychotherapy.

It should be obvious that *I view psychotherapy as primarily a corrective, remedial process and counseling as primarily a developmental one.* This is not to say that nothing developmental goes on in psychotherapy, or that nothing remedial goes on in counseling. But the *primary* characteristics of the two activities, both in purpose and in process, differ in this respect. Psychotherapists operate primarily on a crisis-intervention model. They enter the life of the individual at some point where things have gone awry, or at a point where it is thought that whatever is awry can best be corrected through use of a psychotherapist. Until such a point is reached, the psychotherapist has virtually no formal impact upon the individual.

The school-counselor, on the other hand, has the responsibility of initiating an orderly program of experiences, which may lead to positive personal, social, educational, and vocational growth of individuals. He will encounter crises from time to time, but he intervenes whether there is a crisis or not. Crises are relevant to the counselor's work, as are any factors that enhance or impede progress toward developmental goals, but crises are kept in proper perspective in the total pattern of counselor activities, and are not the predominant factors underwriting daily routines and functions. The predominant factor is a coherent program (curriculum, if you will) based on goals and objectives the counselor can serve in the interest of fulfilling the mission of the school.

The psychotherapist's role is essentially reactive; whereas the school-counselor's role ought to be essentially proactive. Unlike the psychotherapist, the school-counselor does not "hang out a shingle" and then wait for troubled individuals to walk through his door. He should go after individuals and groups with a series of activities designed to help them learn to think about themselves, their environment, and the important issues and choice-points in their lives. He should attempt to assist other school people in providing a simplified environment wherein learning steps can be ordered and implemented. Individual interviews with pupils should usually be carried on with a suitable background of self-exploration experiences prior to the interview— experiences which the counselor has planned and instigated and which prepare both counselor and counselee to use short-term one-to-one contacts efficiently.

The counselor's responsibility is not only to assist individual students to change and improve their relationships with self, society, and the school, but also to improve the way the school relates to individual students. Because of his position and function in the school, the counselor is able to secure an overview of student-school relationships and needs. With this information at hand he has a responsibility to try to assist teachers and administrators to improve the school's ability to respond appropriately to the characteristics and needs of individuals and groups. When evaluation of school counseling is done, it should include not only consideration of student growth and change, but also consideration of the impact the counselor has had on school practice.

Personal, social, educational, and vocational problems and issues are often inextricably interrelated. It makes no sense to try to categorize school-counselors as dealing with educational and vocational questions but not with personal-social ones. Whether such a separation can be made or not depends entirely upon the degree of personal investment a counselee has in his educational and vocational concerns. This varies from counselee to counselee, but no school-counselor can expect to do his work very long without encountering a fair number of students who have intense personal values, feelings, and motives connected with their educational and vocational goals and problems. I know of no reasonable way to sort out the educational-vocational from the personal, so as to deal only with one and not with the other in a counseling relationship. For many students, school is life. It is where virtually all significant associations outside the family are formed and sustained. For many individuals a career is life. It is their principal means of self-expression. This is very likely true even for those who write books and give lectures to the effect that it is not.

It is not reliable to attempt to distinguish between counseling and psychotherapy on the basis of depth, intensity, level of rationality, degree of impact upon the client, or degree of nonnormalcy of the client. Counseling can involve any degree of depth or intensity. It often must necessarily involve examination of thoughts, attitudes, values, feelings, motives, hopes, fears, and objectives hitherto unrecognized by the counselee. A good counseling program is complex, as we shall discuss below, and often calls for a wider variety of skills and activities, more systematic long-range planning, and sometimes a more complicated approach to integration and dissemination of information than does psychotherapy. Often also, it requires skillful solicitation and coordination of efforts of other persons in the counselee's life, and highly concerted efforts to effect environmental changes in circumstances where strong resistance to appropriate change is present.

Changes sought and attained by the counselee may be "minimum" or they may be very significant, with a profound effect on the counselee's future. Good counseling does not differ from psychotherapy in this respect.

Nor is "normalcy" of clientele a suitable criterion. All kinds of individuals attend schools. The current trend toward deinstitutionalization of "nonnormal" persons probably means that an even wider range of personalities will be found in schools in the future. School-counselors must program for and deal with all these individuals, whether "normal" or not, and whether they are engaged in psychotherapy or not. Thus the school-counselor must expect to provide useful experiences to a much broader range of individuals than the psychotherapist is likely to encounter.

As an aside, which perhaps is not much aside, I feel compelled to add here that it is foolish to believe that "normalcy" is a condition we can afford to ignore in school counseling. It is just as foolish to believe that nonnormalcy is a condition that requires remediation.

Counseling differs from psychotherapy in terms of its intended purposes, and in terms of the total pattern of processes upon which counseling is predicated and which counseling facilitates. I have already suggested that the primary purposes of school counseling are developmental and not remedial, and that the counselor should primarily be a proactive agent in the students' life and not merely a reactive one. For the most part, counseling interviews with individual students should be predicated on prior work the counselor has done to prepare youngsters for counseling. He does not depend primarily on long series of interviews with students as his means of assisting them, but rather on shorter-term interviewing contacts, which fit a pattern of pre- and post-interview activities. This pattern is further explained below.

CLARIFYING THE SCHOOL-COUNSELOR'S ROLE

As I have stressed, an adequate school-counseling program differs from an adequate psychotherapeutic service in several important respects. Perhaps the most encompassing way to say it is that school counseling ought to be viewed as a program rather than as a service. The program should consist of several interrelated activities, which are designed and coordinated to achieve the goals school-counselors serve.

The essence of a good school-counseling program is a sound communication system whereby information and points of view from various persons in the student's life—teachers, parents, administrators, the counselor, the student—can be freely given, received, and put to use so as to enhance the student's awareness and understanding of himself and to improve the ability of others to respond and plan appropriately for the student. Although there may be a number of ways to classify school-counselor activities, I have chosen to classify them as follows:

THE APPRAISAL FUNCTION

The counselor studies the individual student. He assembles relevant information from several sources regarding each student. He provides meaningful information about the student to the student himself, to parents, and to members of the school staff. He assists them in interpretation of such information, and he solicits their cooperation in constructive planning and action based on appraisal data.

But a good appraisal program is more than merely a means of securing information. *It is a program whereby the counselor can help students learn how to think about themselves while others learn how to think about them more effectively.* A well-ordered appraisal program will serve both these purposes. It will lead both students and others step-by-step through processes designed to stimulate their thinking on specified topics, to improve their ability to assign meaning to information from other sources on those topics, and to identify situations where additional information is needed.

The appraisal program, like any other aspect of the school program, should be ordered so as to begin at simplified levels and proceed through more complex ones as students develop and mature. Everything else the counselor does will usually depend, for its quality, on the quality of the appraisal program.

Essential Steps. The appraisal program involves five essential steps, none of which can be bypassed or omitted without sacrificing quality. These steps are:

1. Activities designed to generate and secure ideas and information concerning the individual student from various sources—student behavior, performance, and point of view; information from parents, faculty, and others.
2. Collecting, assembling, ordering, digesting, integrating the above.
3. Interpretation, assigning meaning to appraisal data.
4. Feedback of information and interpretations to those who generated it, resulting in both validation and modification of points of view.
5. Follow-through activities. The various functionaries in the student's school life modify plans and actions on the basis of steps 1–4 above.

In order to implement these steps adequately, the counselor must promote a free-flowing, open system of communication. He does not usually collect information *about* the student without intending to communicate such information appropriately *to* the student. The practice of obtaining IQ's on all the students and then keeping such information secret from the students, for example, cannot be justified as a counselor activity. The school may have some reason for doing it, but the counselor does not.

The responsibility to provide useful feedback to those who need it poses special issues for school-counselors, which go beyond those common in more clinical settings. Even though it is not systematically sought in the appraisal program, highly private and confidential information will come to the counselor from time to time. It is a consistently recurring problem to know how to tell the difference between information that should be devulged and information that should not. The school-counselor, in most states, does not have privileged communication. He cannot withhold, willy-nilly, any information that comes his way. Even if he could, he can hardly expect to have much of an impact if he does not communicate accurately and effectively with the teachers, administrators, and parents who control the life and experience of a minor child. He is almost totally dependent on these persons for accomplishment of the developmental goals of school counseling.

Sound implementation of a feedback system is critical to the success of school counseling, and is by no means a simple task. To my way of thinking it requires skill in making practical and ethical judgments far beyond that required of most psychotherapists.

Expected Outcomes. An adequate appraisal program should result in better student self-knowledge and development of abilities to think on topics regarding the self. It should yield concrete examples of the individual's own ideas and thoughts on a variety of topics thought to be important considerations in personal, social, educational, and vocational development. It should also enable teachers and other school personnel to increase their knowledge of the characteristics and needs of individual students and groups of students. And it should lead to better awareness of a variety of viewpoints regarding students, and of the reasons why differing viewpoints exist. It should lead to a better balance of personal attention on all students, and not merely on those who are troubled, or who trouble us. Finally, we might expect to see ideas generated and action taken toward specific goals based on individual student characteristics.

Appraisal activities are not brought into play at the time the student encounters a problem or gets into trouble. They are brought into play when he enters school and are sustained throughout his attendance in the school. They systematically keep us in touch with the student—trouble or no trouble—and they stimulate his thinking along lines we believe to be important during the process of growing toward independent adulthood. Such a program requires a set of skills, interests, and activities different from what we might expect of the psychotherapist.

THE COUNSELING FUNCTION

Of all the definitions of counseling which I have seen, I like this one best:

Counseling is many things. It is a technique of informing and assessing. It is a vehicle designed to modify behavior. It is an experience in communication. Most of all, I think, it is a mutual search for meaning in one's life, with the growth of love as an essential concomitant and consequence of the search. To me, all the rest is fairly trivial or downright senseless without the search for meaning. Indeed, that search is really what living is, and counseling is just a special intensification of the quest.[1]

This definition, which was formulated by R.W. Strowig, carries all the connotations I associate with the best potentialities of school counseling. In it, the focus is on positive growth and development, and on the relationship of counseling to daily life. In schools, counseling should be just that—an intensified, personal activity focused on discovery of the self.

School counseling, for the most part, is predicated on prior activities and experiences the student has been exposed to for the purpose of achieving self-discovery goals. Oftentimes counseling is initiated by the counselor, but as the student is given proper background experiences, he should come to know counseling as a means of communicating questions, examining issues, solving problems, making choices, laying plans for his own life. It is likely that as this occurs more counseling interviews will be student-initiated. Impetus for seeking counseling, or for a particular focus in a counseling interview, is likely to come from a combination of factors prior to the interview—some of which are introduced into the life of the students by the counselor.

Perhaps an example will help to illustrate how classroom, social, personal, and appraisal factors combine to lead an adolescent counselee to focus with his counselor on a personal question important to his current life and future choices.

A Case in Point. Let us consider a ninth-grade boy whom I will call Mark.[2] Mark participated in the Research and Guidance Laboratory for Superior

[1]This quotation appears on a plaque at the University of Wisconsin, Department of Counseling and Guidance, whereon the names of recipients of the Strowig Memorial Award are recorded.
[2]Excerpts of this same case have appeared in print elsewhere. Teachers' comments and the student essay below, together with other case material not presented here, are to be found in Bruce Amble and Richard Bradley, *Pupils as Persons* (New York and London: Chandler, 1973).

Students, University of Wisconsin (Rothney & Sanborn, 1966) throughout his four years of high school. I was his counselor during the first three years, and J. W. M. Rothney was his counselor during his senior year. All our activities with Mark, including counseling interviews, were scheduled by us. The example involves a counseling session that was part of a coherent program initiated by the counselors in grade 9 and sustained throughout high school. Mark participated in a variety of appraisal, counseling, and counseling-related activities. We concentrate here only on those that are relevant to the fourth of a series of eight scheduled counseling interviews carried on with Mark while he was in high school. This was the last interview held during the sophomore year.

TEACHER COMMENTS

Mark's ninth-grade teachers were asked to submit their observations and comments about the boy. They were free to focus on anything they felt would reveal their own points of view about Mark on the basis of having had him in class. The only requirements were that they be as brief as possible, and that they let the counselor know what they felt were important characteristics Mark showed during grade 9. Also, they were not to say anything *about* the student that they were unwilling to have said or interpreted *to* the student:

TEACHERS' COMMENTS

BIOLOGY: Mark is one of the hardest workers that I have ever encountered. He is very meticulous in his work and tries hard to improve his "weak" points. Sometimes I feel that his concern for little insignificant points may be hampering his overall progress.

ENGLISH: Mark is especially adept in oral expression and his ideas and opinions are valued by his classmates. He isn't afraid to argue any matter about which he feels strongly, nor does he hesitate to question decisions, corrections, even authority if he feels it necessary, but he never loses his consideration for others in the process. He is quick to grasp ideas and concepts and to analyze situations in literature. He is a thinker and an excellent writer, although his writing is a bit careless from the standpoint of mechanics.

GEOMETRY: Could be very good but he is spread too thin. Does not possess the keen analytical mind needed in math. If he would concentrate in this one area it could easily be developed. The intelligence is there.

PHYSICAL
EDUCATION: Mark at times can be a follower rather than a leader. Has to learn to lose along with winning.

SOCIAL
STUDIES: Tries hard, and succeeds. Has a good sense of humor too.

Without belaboring the above comments, we can see both consistency and inconsistency among them. We see also that some teachers, if they could, would have Mark learn to behave differently in ways they feel would be better for his own welfare. We can surmise that the reactions of the teachers to Mark, and perhaps even their plans for providing him with learning experiences, may at times be based on the points of view expressed above. Any teacher worth his salt will try to help a student learn what he believes the student should learn, whether it is an academic matter or a personal one. The counselor probably should provide these teachers with additional information with which they might better decide whether, and how, to assist Mark in personal developments they are concerned about.

THE STUDENT'S VIEWPOINT

During each of his high school years Mark was asked to write a personal essay. Our purpose was to stimulate his thinking about himself in relation to others, and to encourage him to move gradually from thinking about the impact of others and his environment on *himself* to expressing his own hopes and objectives that might have an impact on *others*. The unedited essay below was written by Mark during his ninth-grade year. It reveals his own viewpoint on issues that seem closely related to those covered by the teacher comments. He helps us to understand why his teachers say what they say.

FRESHMAN ESSAY

You will be given this hour to write an essay about yourself entitled, "The Dominant Forces That Have Directed My Life." Perhaps it would help if you keep the following questions in mind while you write.

1. In what ways have certain persons influenced my life most?
2. What other factors have caused me to be the person I am?
3. How will the above two factors aid or hinder me in attaining what I hope to become?

I think that the forces and factors which have most profoundly influenced me are the unfortunate events of my family life, Mr. Jack Haley and Mr. John Hartwick, the time and general environment in which I was brought up, and the fact that I was handicapped as a result of a birth defect.

In discussing the effects of several unfortunate events upon my life I think that one thing that I have gained as a result of them is a personality that is able to withstand severe pain and strain. My life up to the time of my mother's death was largely uneventful except that in this time a surgical operation, orthodontic treatment, and speech therapy helped me to begin to overcome my birth defect—a cleft pallet. At the time of my mother's death I think that I gained a great deal of faith in God. The remarriage of my father several years following the death of my mother I think of as a transition period in which I learned all about the great happiness of marriage. This marked a period of "relative happiness" which ended just recently with the divorce of my father and stepmother. I then lapsed into a period of depression. The only really good thing to come out of the whole situation was that I am presently stronger, more flexible, and better equipped to adjust to unfavorable and unhappy situations. As a result of this I think that I have learned how to accept disappointments in stride.

My understanding of the responsibilities of leadership and the workings of a democracy has been furthered greatly by the Student Council advisor, Mr. John Hartwick and principal, Mr. Jack Haley of Smith Jr. High. I have learned many object lessons from these two men. From Mr. Hartwick I have learned how to be subordinate, that there are times when nothing is said, and the necessity of co-operation and good rapport between all parties involved in an issue in order for anything to be accomplished. I believe that Mr. Haley has taught me the meaning of patriotism and the meaning of the phrase "Never give up." Together, in summary I would like to say that, these men have shown me how to respect authority.

Obviously my family background would tend to have a profound effect on my thinking and my set of morals and values. My thinking, by virtue of my background has given me a tendency to dislike labor unions and favor management, support the Republican Party, to hold conservative views, and to be outspoken—to stand up when the situation demands it—at times.

My birth defect, already having been discussed in a previous paragraph, is the last major factor which has greatly influenced my life. It has been a handicap to be sure, but in another respect it has given me something to work for. It has given me something to prove—that I can lead a normal life and that I can excel in anything I desire regardless of the defect. It has further helped in understanding the problems and goals of others.

During his tenth-grade year, Mark met with me for two scheduled counseling interviews. He utilized the time talking about his own personal characteristics and motives so as to shed more light on topics mentioned in case material of the previous year. The counseling interviews were predicated on another personal essay (not included here) and on something that happened in Mark's English class shortly before he was to be interviewed. Mark brought the personal essay with him to the interview, handed it to the counselor, and said:

MARK:	My writing hasn't improved much over the year, has it?
COUNSELOR:	You mean the appearance of it?
MARK:	Appearance of it, anyway. [*pause*] My handwriting—I think, I—I don't know—. I started out—and I started one way, and I got to thinking—I think somewhere in the middle of the paper, or in the middle of the theme, I switched points of view almost entirely.
COUNSELOR:	Is that right? From what to what?
MARK:	I don't know—exactly why I switched, but I—. Well, about in the middle of the paper I had the feeling I was talking about something entirely different than when I started out.
COUNSELOR:	Different than what you began to say.
MARK:	My idea was to—ah, originally—to, ah, try and take a character trait that I thought that I had and try and trace back why or how this had developed and why I felt this way now.
COUNSELOR:	Uh huh.
MARK:	I don't know how well I answered, you know, that type of question.
COUNSELOR:	You get the feeling that you might have got sidetracked somewhere along the way—
MARK:	Uh huh.
COUNSELOR:	—that to try to understand this—
MARK:	I really don't quite understand where or how I did it, but I felt like I was talking about something—you know—the unity that I tried to start out with was all lost by the end of it.
COUNSELOR:	It just broke down in the middle.
MARK:	Uh huh. [*pause*]
COUNSELOR:	Well, what did you have in mind? Could you tell me what you had in mind?

At this point in the interview Mark tried to state more clearly the personality characteristic he was wondering about. It was a characteristic he said "some people would call 'compulsion,' or 'power-drive' or 'competitiveness.'" He had difficulty stating exactly what he meant by these terms, but he apparently had been thinking about them as possibly descriptive of himself before he began to write the autobiography.

My response to him was to suggest that perhaps this was the case. We shall pick up the interview again there.

During the remainder of this 50-minute interview, we discussed Mark's motives. The excerpts that follow are examples of interview material that bear on appraisal data already shown.

COUNSELING INTERVIEW³

COUNSELOR:	You had this on your mind before you went in there to write.
MARK:	Yeah.
COUNSELOR:	So—so you just thought maybe you'd—
MARK:	So, so—that, that was one of the things I, I got sidetracked on. I just don't know whether I wrote everything down. I was just sort of thinking about it and trying to—you know —write as fast as I could to keep up with the line of thought, and—
COUNSELOR:	Trying to organize your own thoughts about this.
MARK:	Uh huh.
COUNSELOR:	And still do the assignment—as far as writing it out was concerned.
MARK:	Yeah.
COUNSELOR:	I gather that—. Go ahead.
MARK:	Oh no, that's alright.
COUNSELOR:	Well, I was just going to say, I gather that—that this—that on this particular topic you still find that you aren't really —you haven't really organized it well enough to say what you think about it.
MARK:	Well, I hadn't really observed myself—well, if you want to put it that way, "observed myself." I don't know if that's what I want to say. But I hadn't really, uh, noticed— observed how, I exactly, how I feel about this.
COUNSELOR:	Um Hum. It's kinda hard to stand back somewhere and take a look at yourself as maybe somebody else would.
MARK:	Um Hm. That's, that's what I tried to do. I don't know if I succeeded in doing it or not. [*pause*] But would you say that I, I would have a, this power hunger—this type of thing? I'm—and if I do have it, it is something I should try to avoid, or try to control or limit?
COUNSELOR:	I gather that somebody said this to you. Somebody implied it.
MARK:	We were discussing this the other day, or not, not that, but we were discussing, ah Tennyson's *Idylls of the King*.
COUNSELOR:	Yes.
MARK:	And—I've forgotten. [*pause*] You know, he always writes in these allegories—

³Excerpts from this interview also appear in J. W. M. Rothney, *Adaptive Counseling in Schools* (Englewood Cliffs, N.J.: Prentice-Hall, 1972).

COUNSELOR: Yes. Um Hm.

MARK: —in this allegoric fashion, and everything comes out—you know, and you can, you try to apply it to, you know, situations that you come across in your, ah, your daily life. This type of thing. And we discussed this other person who, whose name was not given, but who said in the discussion of ah "power hunger," and, ah, put it this way—material symbols, of popularity or something like that—. It was in connection—. Now I remember—with the Holy Grail and how some of the knights of the Round Table had this compulsion to see it, and others did, it didn't make any difference whether they did or they didn't.

COUNSELOR: Um Hm. Some of them had a real hunger for this and others could get along tolerably well without it.

MARK: Um Hm. They, they didn't think it was important. Because all it really was was a symbol—of the, you know of strength of their faith.

COUNSELOR: Yes. For those who needed a symbol, it had meaning.

MARK: And some—just knowing, just having the faith to start out with—that was enough, but for other people, they needed it.

COUNSELOR: Some people could live with—that is, some people could accept the idea and just believe in it, and others had to keep searching for it—to try to prove it—to try to figure out some concrete proof to whatever this idea was.

MARK: Um Hm. And well—and anyway, that's how we got into it. And someone—joke—I don't know if he meant it jokingly or not—I hope he didn't. I don't know. But—ah—he said—he—they—he pointed at me; and I just laughed at the time, but I've been thinking about it. I don't know, what do you think about it, about that? Do you think that—

COUNSELOR: You laughed at the time, but you're not sure it was funny.

MARK: No. I'm not sure. Well, ah, ah, ah, what do you do when someone—you know? You've gotta respond somehow, and didn't know what to say.

COUNSELOR: You couldn't bust him in the nose.

MARK: [*laughs*] No. So I didn't know what to do.

COUNSELOR: But you sort of hoped he wasn't completely in earnest.

MARK: He, he was, he—no I don't—I didn't know if he was or if he wasn't.

COUNSELOR: But you sorta suspect he was, I gather, or you wouldn't have been so concerned about it since.

MARK: I don't know. I don't, I really don't. He, he could have been —I don't know. But I just don't want to let, or give people the idea that I, that I want this type of thing for, purely for the sake of having it.

COUNSELOR: That is—you may recognize that you've done some things that might lead somebody to conclude this—

MARK: Um Hm.

COUNSELOR: —*but not*

MARK: Well, I would hope—

COUNSELOR: for that sake alone—

MARK: I would hope that this was not my motive.

COUNSELOR: It's a better purpose that you have in mind than just—just to have just to have power.

MARK: The point is—well, I was trying to examine my motive in doing some of the things that I do. I don't know why I do them.

*   *   *

MARK: I think when I was about twelve or thirteen—I don't think you could have found a—a shyer person around because I really think I was shy at that time.

COUNSELOR: Um Hm.

MARK: And for some reason—I have no idea why I did it—I got —I, I, was, I was put up as a candidate for student council in the eighth grade.

COUNSELOR: Even if, if you were shy, somebody nominated you.

MARK: Yeah. So I—somehow I, I got—I was elected—by one vote.

COUNSELOR: Um Hm.

MARK: And from there, uh, I, ah, next year I was elected president of the class. It was really surprising.

COUNSELOR: And it felt good, didn't it?

MARK: Um Hm. Um Hm. And it's sort of—oh, they say—a taste of power, and ah, ah you want more of this type of thing.

COUNSELOR: Was it power? Was it power that you liked about it?

MARK: I don't know. I don't think it was really—I don't know what it was. I don't think it was really—I hope that it wasn't the power, and I can't decide whether it was or it wasn't.

COUNSELOR: Whatever it was, it was something you liked, though, because you have continued to do that type of thing since.

MARK: Um Hm.

COUNSELOR: Now if you could just figure out what it was.

MARK: Yeah—whether—yeah. [*pause*]

COUNSELOR: You said you were really shy before.

MARK:	No. Well, in this—then the second point was that even, ah, after last year, I think I was still—though everybody didn't think of me as being shy at all, but uh, I really still was shy.
COUNSELOR:	Other people might—
MARK:	But I, I—I, I—in other words, I could be—project myself outward at times, but at other times, I'd be a real introvert —you know, keep to myself and I don't think it has been until almost halfway through this year that I've started to change this too—and get rid of the shyness altogether.
COUNSELOR:	There have been times in the past when although maybe others didn't know it, you knew that you were feeling a little uncomfortable or maybe not as secure as you look.
MARK:	Um Hm.
COUNSELOR:	But now you're beginning to feel more secure underneath the surface, though. You know that this shyness thing is something you're really overcoming. It's not just a big front you're putting on.
MARK:	Um Hm. No. I think that's to a large extent what it was last year.
COUNSELOR:	A big front.
MARK:	Yeah. Well, yeah and that's what it was.
COUNSELOR:	But now you feel a little more comfortable in this role of being kind of a leader and somebody the other kids vote for, and look to.
MARK:	Um Hm.
COUNSELOR:	I imagine that felt pretty good, didn't it? If you were—you know—if you sort of felt that you weren't worth much, and shy, and staying away from others, not being aggressive— and suddenly they come along and vote you into a leadership position. That must have felt good.
MARK:	Um Hm. I think—uh—I think that sort of changed my sense of values. I think—uh—up until about halfway through the first semester I was very intellectually—well, not really intellectually—but I, I placed, I, my, my entire emphasis on you know, schoolwork and schoolwork and more schoolwork. And going down from there I tried to—well—broaden my base, if you want to call it that.
COUNSELOR:	Yeah. You sort of buried yourself in schoolwork—
MARK:	Um Hm.
COUNSELOR:	—and you realized that that's not all there is to life—just the intellectual side.
MARK:	Um Hm.

COUNSELOR: There's a feeling side too.

MARK: No—well, I—I ob—observed several seniors that I fel—I felt were—well, they were, they were thought of as sort of snobs because they were intellectual, and I didn't want, I didn't want this to happen to me.

COUNSELOR: You didn't want to be that kind of a narrow intellectual-ist—

MARK: Um Hm.

COUNSELOR: —because there's more—uh—there are some really impor-tant things that aren't necessarily intellectual things.

MARK: Yeah. [*pause*]

COUNSELOR: So then you set out to broaden yourself a little bit—

MARK: Um Hm.

COUNSELOR: Not only in your own eyes, but in other people's eyes too.

MARK: Hmmm. [*long pause*]

MARK: See—I, I just— [*pause*]

MARK: I, I'm so absent-minded too. Every once in a while—hmm, and you, did—that ever happen to you? When, when all of a sudden you think of something, and all of a sudden there it is, and there it isn't.

COUNSELOR: It was there, and then it's gone. I suppose sometimes when it's kind of tough to verbalize it, you know, it's elusive. [*pause*]

MARK: Well what was that—I guess, ah—well—I don't know—is there anything that you think we ought to discuss? I'm afraid I've been—you know, just more or less—

COUNSELOR: No. This is your time. And, and really, the question you ask is your responsibility to answer. I can't—I can't answer it. [*pause*]

MARK: Oh, I—now I remember what it was. It's something—I think I mentioned that in—uh—in the paper there someplace [*points to the essay*]—all those—oh, I think I had a desire to be liked. [*pause*] I resp—well, not, not even—I don't really want to be respected. I just want to be accepted, rather than being respected.

COUNSELOR: Yeah. This has been a big thing for you.

MARK: Um Hm.

MARK: Oh I still would—I, I still don't think I mainly place what some people would say too much stress on ah—other people the way other people take something that I say—that rather than just saying what I think you know, right out. There's some—there, there's a couple of people that I know that are very outspoken and if, if they, you know, if they, if they decide that they don't like someone they just say—they just say—well they just let them know about it—whereas—I don't know—I seem to have the attitude that I don't want to offend anybody, or—in other words, I want to make everybody—the politician-type attitude that you want, to make everybody happy and you don't want to make anybody mad at you.

COUNSELOR: You don't want to alienate anybody.

MARK: Right. Um Hm.

COUNSELOR: And this is partly because you don't want to hurt them and partly because you don't want to hurt yourself.

MARK: Um Hm. Because I ah—I don't, I don't know how far back this goes, but it gets to this idea. I think it all goes back to the fact that ah when I was smaller I used to play with the neighbor boy all the time. And as it happened he went to a parochial school and I went to a public school, and so I didn't have very many friends to start out with in school.

COUNSELOR: You lost the one good one you had

MARK: Well he—he, he

COUNSELOR: because he went one way and you went another.

MARK: Well, he moved away, and so then he, we couldn't even play together after school. And so then I gradually developed friends—I, well, well acquaintances—I, I don't really know that I have what you'd call a really good friend.

COUNSELOR: Even now you're not sure you do.

MARK: Well, I don't know. We, that's something else we talked about in English the other day. Uh—we all agreed that really in your lifetime you could not get more than one or two true friends—in the truest sense of the word.

COUNSELOR: If you think about it as a really deep relationship, then there aren't going to be many of them. You just can't spread yourself that thin.

MARK: No.

COUNSELOR: Yes. [*pause*] But you're wondering—. I gather—when you went back to—to when you were quite small, and you said you had one good friend, and then he moved away, that it wasn't so easy to form a new friendship.

MARK: Right.

COUNSELOR: This is something that you didn't do easily.

MARK: Right. I found, I found it difficult. I think—I—I don't know why, why, why it was that way, but I guess that's just the way it was.

COUNSELOR: You mentioned the fact that you had a speech defect and a birth defect.

MARK: Um Hm. Well, I don't know. That's another thing. Ah, I don't know if that's the reason. But one rationalization that occurred was that maybe even though I had this birth defect that I could still be normal in that type of thing.

COUNSELOR: You mean, insofar as what you're doing now.

MARK: Yeah, prove, prove that prove, proving to myself that I can do anything that anybody else can do, and that I am indeed normal.

*   *   *

MARK: I was in debate. I, I didn't think I was going to like that too much, but surprisingly enough I really had a pretty good time doing it.

COUNSELOR: You felt fairly successful at it.

MARK: Well, I, I think we won more than we lost, if that's a measure of success, but—uh—I think—uh really if, if, if you're going out for debate you have to be going out for the experience rather than for the wins and losses.

*   *   *

COUNSELOR: I—uh—read your paper—I talked to you last year, and I've thought about all the things that have happened to you. That you haven't had all the good breaks in the world. You've had some—you've had some bad ones. It occurred to me that perhaps many of the things that you seem to have chosen to do reflect a—a determination to overcome what you see as your own handicaps—your own disadvantages— that you're willing to work on these things—to really give it the old "college try" instead of shying away from them or making excuses for them. That sort of occurred to me.

MARK: Yeah. I think that, that, that's probably part of it. I, but I don't know—it's just, it's not that, ah con, I consciously say, "Well, I, I have these handicaps, now let's go out and do this."

COUNSELOR: This isn't—

MARK: No. I just, I just, no, I just get the idea, well, today it would be nice to try this.

COUNSELOR: So you've never thought of this as—

MARK: And so I go out and try it.

COUNSELOR: It could be more basic—

MARK: More basic than that.

COUNSELOR: —than just an outlined program that you have. It could be something that's really—uh—satisfying needs that you have.

*   *   *

COUNSELOR: Well, our time is up. You brought up an interesting topic, and I can see that it would be one that really concerns you; and—ah—I don't know—I guess if I sat and thought about it awhile I might have suspected that you'd have this question to answer for yourself sooner or later—

MARK: Um Hm.

COUNSELOR: You know, "Why am I really doing these things? Do I just want to prove something, or am I after power, or is my motive, ah, higher than that?" Ah, just from what I know I would have—I guess I would have suspected that you had a lot of determination, for one thing, to overcome those aspects of yourself that you thought needed improvement. And you've done some good hard work on them. I guess when you described this first time you were elected in the eighth grade—how this was kind of a major turning point—maybe you discovered how meaningful it could be to have other people, you know, care about you too, and give you some encouragement to go on—that this is a real important thing. And I suppose it is for all of us. What other people think does count, and should, because we're social animals. And then another question I guess you have to work out is —is you seem to have thought about—is—you know—ah— "At what length should I go to make sure that I don't offend other people? How honest should I be at the risk of hurting other people, or alienating them from me?" You've done some real thinking about this. I think more than most people your age. And you've tried to trace this back to some early things and some real basic qualities that you might have. Ah, probably you're on the right track as far as working these things out. I'd encourage you to talk more about it if you ah, if you want to pursue this and don't feel like you can do it on your own . . ."

*   *   *

I have tried to give the reader a sample of this school-counseling interview large enough to demonstrate several important features which, I believe, should characterize school counseling:

1. It qualifies according to a definition of counseling (Strowig) properly focused for school-counseling work.
2. It exemplifies relevance of the counseling interview to prior and current appraisal activities, and to the current life of the student in school.
3. It shows how the student can utilize the counselor to discuss a topic that is important at the time, even though the interview was counselor-initiated.
4. It illustrates a counseling interview on a personal topic that falls well within normal limits of adolescent concerns during the process of self-identification and maturation.
5. It provides information we may utilize to better understand teachers' viewpoints about Mark.

Mark's school behavior, both in academic and in extracurricular choices and accomplishments, was related to the personal issue he was examining in this interview. It could also be shown that his choice and pursuit of post–high school education and career were related in critical ways to the personal motives and characteristics discussed in the interview, but we shall not belabor that point here. Suffice it to say that the characteristic he is wondering about plays a major role in his being the person he is. Were he to change this, I would call it a major change. Mark is a young man beginning to establish his own life-style and to set his own life-goals. At this point even a small change in direction could lead, in the long run, to a major difference in his experience.

THE COORDINATING FUNCTION

On the basis of appraisal and counseling experiences with the students, a school-counselor, to attain counseling goals, often must secure and sustain the cooperation of other persons. Return to the comments, for example, given us by Mark's biology and physical education teachers. Would information from the essay and the interview help them to understand Mark better? Are they in a position to help or hinder him in his struggle to determine his own motives and needs, and to change or improve himself? If so, the counselor has a responsibility to assist in forming a team that will work for Mark and not, unwittingly, against him.

Coordination of follow-through activities is a routine part of the school-counselor's job. On the basis of personal knowledge of the student, and commitment to all aspects of his development, the counselor acts to bring coherence to the efforts of all concerned with his development. Put briefly, the counselor assists all functionaries, including the student, to know the student as well as possible—and then to act as if we know him. I believe that most school-counseling interviews should lead to change and improvement in the way the school responds to the student. This cannot be expected to happen unless there is systematic follow-through by the counselor after counseling.

THE EVALUATION FUNCTION

Counselors must show what they have accomplished. Unlike some psychotherapists, they cannot do it in terms of closures. Everybody leaves school sooner or later. Every case is eventually closed. What we need to know, when the case is closed, is how the individual is better for having had counseling? We cannot measure success in terms of a return to "normalcy" of our clientele. Most of them have been "normal" all along. So what do we measure? How do we tell whether we have succeeded or not in the large responsibility for schoolchildren-in-general? I will leave the reader, I think, with these questions. They are somewhat more complicated than the questions faced by psychotherapists at evaluation time. They require some careful thought about how one can help young people learn to thrive in a free society, and to help sustain a society in which freedom is a continuing possibility for themselves, for others, and for those who are to come, in which "normalcy" for the next generation is a condition better than it has been for this one. If this cannot be taught and learned, then I think school counseling makes little sense. It is what school counseling is all about.

REFERENCES

Amble, B., and Bradley, R. *Pupils as persons.* New York and London: Chandler, 1973.

Arbuckle, D. S. *Counseling: An introduction.* Boston: Allyn & Bacon, 1961.

Blocher, D. H. Issues in counseling: Elusive and illusional. *Personnel and Guidance Journal,* 1965, **43**, 796–800.

Brammer, L., & Shostrom, E. *Therapeutic psychology: Fundamentals of counseling and psychotherapy.* Englewood Cliffs, N.J.: Prentice-Hall, 1960.

Lewis, E. C. *The psychology of counseling.* New York: Holt, Rinehart and Winston, 1970.

Patterson, C. H. *Counseling and psychotherapy.* New York: Harper & Row, 1959.

Perry, W. G. On the relation of psychotherapy and counseling. *Annals of the New York Academy of Sciences,* 1955, **63**, 396–407.

Rogers, C. R. *Client-centered therapy.* Boston: Houghton Mifflin, 1951.

Rothney, J. W. M. *Adaptive counseling in schools.* Englewood Cliffs, N.J.: Prentice-Hall, 1972.

Rothney, J. W. M., and Sanborn, M. P. Wisconsin's research through service program for superior students. *Personnel and Guidance Journal,* 1966, **44**, 694–699.

Stefflre, B. S. Function and present status of counseling theory. In B. S. Stefflre (Ed.), *Theories of counseling.* New York: McGraw-Hill, 1965.

Tyler, Leona E. *The work of the counselor.* New York: Appleton-Century-Crofts, 1961.

Wolberg, L. R. *The technique of psychotherapy.* (2nd ed.) New York: Grune & Stratton, 1967.

Commonalities and Distinctions between Counseling and Psychotherapy

Leona E. Tyler

University of Oregon

ACADEMIC AND TRADITIONAL ARGUMENTS

When we try to differentiate between counseling and psychotherapy, we find ourselves paying more attention to the connotations the words carry than to their actual denotative significance. *Counseling* is the broader and older of the two terms. The word is a part of our common speech; the function is a part of basic human experience. Kings have had counselors to help them make important decisions. Counselors-at-law, camp counselors, and investment counselors all have as good a right to the counselor title as do the psychologists and educators who have preempted it. *Psychotherapy,* in contrast, is a comparatively new word in the English language, and carries strong connotations of illness, treatment, and cure. It brings to mind images of a man in a white coat or of a patient on a couch recounting his dreams to a wise psychoanalyst. We assume that psychotherapy will be sought only by persons who are anxious, troubled, or maladjusted, persons with "problems."

During the 1940s, 1950s, and 1960s, distinctions between counseling and psychotherapy became more and more blurred. Some practitioners applauded this convergence and helped it along; others opposed it but without much success. The lines they have tried to draw are most commonly based on quantitative rather than qualitative distinctions. Most frequently attention has been focused on the ambiguous variable, DEPTH; psychotherapy is said to be deeper, in some sense, than counseling. Those who advocate this kind of distinction consider that talk about early memories is "deeper" than talk about the day's events, talk about sexual attitudes "deeper" than talk about vocational plans, and talk about dreams "deeper" than talk about relationships with friends and family. It would be difficult to produce evidence, however,

53

that this scaling of depth corresponds to anything meaningful in the psychology of personality.

Two other kinds of distinction that are sometimes made correspond in some ways to this distinction based on depth. One has to do with the closeness of the relationship between the helping person and the person being helped. Counseling relationships are considered to be more superficial and less enduring than psychotherapeutic relationships. The other is based on the seriousness of the problems presented. An essentially normal person experiencing some difficulty at home, at school, or on the job is considered a candidate for counseling; the person diagnosed as neurotic, psychotic, or psychopathic is presumed to need therapy. Like the depth distinction, these too are difficult to justify on rational grounds, and as special varieties and techniques of counseling and psychotherapy have multiplied, there is more and more overlap between the two domains.

Another rather different basis for distinguishing counseling from psychotherapy has to do with the qualifications required for the practitioners and the nature of the agencies providing the service. Counseling has been considered to be a legitimate activity for people with various kinds of special training— or no special training at all. Clinics dispensed therapy; schools provided counseling. Until quite recently, most of the counseling that went on in schools was the responsibility of teachers released from classroom duties for a part of the day to enable them to engage in this activity. They did not consider themselves therapists. Many of them realized that they were not adequately equipped for the counseling task and found their way into courses and programs designed to fill the gaps in their preparation. But the fact that untrained persons could function after a fashion as counselors contributed to the impression that counseling is a superficial sort of helping activity. Similar things happened in other settings as well—employment offices, rehabilitation agencies, correctional institutions. The development of professional standards for counselors of many special varieties made great progress during the decade of the sixties, so that the concept of counseling as an activity carried on by well-meaning but untrained amateurs has now become less tenable, but the meaning people attach to the term is still influenced by this history.

In clinics, hospitals, and other medically oriented agencies, the term *psychotherapy* is generally used as a label for any sort of psychological treatment provided, regardless of its nature. In contrast to the agencies in which counselors have carried on their work, these clinics attempted from the beginning to establish and maintain high standards for therapists. The direction of change, as time has passed, has been to liberalize these standards somewhat rather than to raise them.

The result of these two opposite movements has been to decrease the professional differences between counselors and psychotherapists. It is still true, however, that the amount of time required to prepare a person to become a recognized psychotherapist tends to be longer than the time required to prepare for what are designated as counseling positions. For psychotherapy, a doctor's degree of some kind has been the standard;for counseling, a master's degree; often, it is true, a two-year graduate program, rather than a minimum of one year of advanced study, is the norm. For many years, psychiatrists insisted that only medically trained persons could really provide psychotherapy, although they were willing that various kinds of paramedical workers should carry on counseling. The rapid rise of clinical and counseling psychology after World War II led to a widespread challenging of this restriction, and, as a result, the right of psychologists with proper qualifications to practice as psychotherapists has been written into the laws of many states. A doctoral degree, Ph.D. or Ed.D., is usually specified in such legislation as a minimum essential for psychotherapeutic practice. In legislation governing the certification of school-counselors, rehabilitation-counselors, employment-counselors, and the like, the doctor's degree is seldom if ever specified.

We can sum up the various distinctions between counseling and psychotherapy in the one word *prestige*. This is an elusive quality, difficult to define in any precise way. But, especially for persons in professional lines of work, it operates as a powerful motivational force. Because psychotherapy has been automatically ranked higher than counseling on the prestige scale used by professional workers in schools and social agencies, there has been a tendency for the kinds of counseling that could be classified as therapy to increase in comparison with nontherapy kinds of activity. The more professional counselors became, or the more special training they obtained, the more they were likely to slant their work in this direction.

This tendency has had some unfortunate consequences. While it has made therapeutic counseling available to increasing numbers of people in various kinds of trouble—problem children, anxious employees, underachieving students, for example—it has led to neglect or avoidance of some of the kinds of interpersonal activity that constitute major contributions counseling can make to human development. By reemphasizing the idea that *counseling* is a broader term than *psychotherapy,* that it covers other kinds of helping activity, some of them very important to the welfare of society whether they are prestigious or not, counselors and the educators who prepare them for their work can right this balance. There is a large area of overlap between counseling and psychotherapy, but the overlap is not complete.

PRACTICAL DIFFERENTIATION

What counseling consists of in addition to psychotherapy can best be explained under two principal headings, to some extent related to one another. First, counseling is for *everybody,* not just for the maladjusted, the people with "problems." Historically, as was mentioned in the preceding section, it has been the leaders of society, not its misfits, who were most likely to have access to "professional" counseling. In ancient times, for example, important people from the farthest corners of the Greek world used to climb the long road to the Temple of Apollo at Delphi to seek counseling from the oracle. The oracles have long since fallen silent, but I know of no evidence that our modern world no longer needs social arrangements that will permit individuals to talk over their thoughts, decisions, and plans with a wise and interested outsider at critical turning points in their lives.

The second kind of distinction that can be made between counseling and psychotherapy is that counseling is concerned, in a major way, with people's *choices, decisions,* and *plans* for their lives, as well as with the changes in personality or behavior toward which psychotherapy is directed. One of the principal roots out of which the present-day counseling professions grew was vocational guidance, and this is still considered to be a counseling task. In the drift of the profession toward therapy, the responsibility of helping people to make good vocational choices, and suitable plans for the education or training through which occupational objectives are attained, has sometimes been slighted or deemphasized, but it can never be sloughed off completely. The occupational world is very complex—far more complex now than it was a half-century ago when vocational guidance was initiated. Not only boys and girls preparing to enter the working world, but adults at all stages of life, may need help in finding places within it that suit them well. The skills required to analyze the characteristics of individuals and of occupations are different from the skills required for psychotherapy. Sensitivity to what a client wants from life, and to what kinds of work would bring him most satisfaction, has something in common with the therapist's sensitivity to general feelings about people, self, and situation, but the two are not identical. Vocational counseling is not psychotherapy.

Besides the choice of an occupation, many other kinds of choices face the individual in our complex, mobile, changing society. Some of these involve other persons and one's relationships with them. In the college situation, for example, the question of whether or not to join a sorority, while it may appear trivial to a psychologist oriented toward depth therapy, is worth a counselor's serious consideration because of its implications for the direction the student's life will take during the critical college years. Other kinds of choices are in the realm of values and beliefs. The individual encounters people, books, and films representing markedly different ways of life. Sorting out what he believes and developing a code he is content to live by may be facilitated by counseling directed toward choice-making rather than toward personality change.

The two bases upon which counseling has been distinguished from psycho-therapy—that it is a service for the well-adjusted as well as for persons with problems, and that it focuses on the making of wise choices as well as the facilitation of changes in persons and their situations—do not differentiate sharply between the two functions, and no hard-and-fast line can be drawn between counseling and psychotherapy in practice. The difference is a matter of differing emphases rather than complete separation of roles. What a professional worker must avoid doing, if he wishes to be of service to the many kinds of persons who seek him out, is to define his role by *exclusion*. A high-school counselor does this when he states proudly that he no longer helps tenth-graders plan their programs but spends all his time in "therapy" with underachievers. A college counselor does this when he has no time for "routine" cases, meaning students who seek help in choosing a major and making career plans, and turns such cases over to inexperienced trainees. This kind of prestige-oriented exclusion keeps counseling from making the full contribution to human welfare it is capable of making. To a counselor who understands the full complexity of human life, *no* question is trivial. *No* case is routine.

IMPLICATIONS FOR TRAINING

The movement to define all counseling as psychotherapy has had one very beneficial effect upon training programs for counselors. It has focused attention on the *relationship* the counselor establishes with the client he is serving, and the qualities counselors must develop if they are to generate productive relationships. It was Freud who first emphasized that for psychoanalysis to succeed in its therapeutic endeavor with a patient there must be a powerful *transference*. Psychoanalysts have explored in great detail the nature of the emotional link that develops between patient and therapist. However, it was Carl Rogers (1957) who clarified the nature of this relationship in a way that showed its relevance to all sorts of counseling efforts. In recent years, Truax and Carkhuff (1967) have undergirded this set of concepts with a considerable body of research.

The three common elements in the interpersonal situation provided by good counselors and therapists are, to use the Truax and Carkhuff terms, *accurate empathy, nonpossessive warmth,* and *genuineness.* The first objective of a training program for practicing counselors at any level from counselor-aides to doctoral candidates thus becomes to develop these characteristics to the maximum degree in each of the trainees. Because individuals differ in their potentialities for this particular kind of development, it is advisable to select prospective trainees on the basis of this "aptitude" to the extent that such selection is possible. But it is becoming evident that even persons who at the outset manifest only moderate levels of aptitude can greatly increase their sensitivity and skill as they participate in educational programs designed to facilitate such increases.

Detailed arrangements vary, of course, from one training program to another. What is recognized in all of them, however, is that the crucial part of the program, so far as this objective is concerned, is practicum experience, and the crucial instructors are the practicum supervisors. Tape recordings, of both the audio and the video varieties, have been very valuable aids. They make it possible for the student to evaluate how successful he has been in providing the kind of counseling relationship a particular client needed. Freed from the task of constantly evaluating the performance of the trainees for whom he is responsible, the supervisor can make himself available as a source of support and ideas. Productive relationships between supervisors and trainees are built on the same essential qualities as those on which counselor-counselee relationships rest.

Professionally we have not yet faced up to all the implications of the assumption we are now making that certain personal qualities are more fundamental than anything else to success in counseling. How can we keep the competitive, stressful aspects of work for graduate degrees from interfering with the development of these essential counseling attitudes? What shall we do with the student who shows a great deal of interpersonal skill but does only mediocre course work? What about the opposite—the brilliant student who has no difficulty in obtaining a doctor's degree in clinical or counseling psychology, even though he is deficient in the basic interpersonal skills? Fortunately, the correlation between scholastic ability and the quality of heart and mind in which we are interested is not negative, so that it is quite possible for a person to be high on both scales. But, unfortunately, such positive correlation as there is does not seem to be very large. The result is that in today's world, which presents an almost unlimited demand for workers skilled in human service, some persons who might help meet this need cannot obtain the proper professional credentials. Setting up new positions for counselor-aides and similar paraprofessional workers will help to some extent, but eventually we may need to overhaul our whole system of basing credentials primarily on academic degrees if we are to follow through with the implications of what our study of therapeutic relationships has taught us.

So much for the implications for training of the commonality between counseling and psychotherapy. If we accept the conclusion that the overlap is not complete and analyze the differences in the way we did in the preceding section, several implications for the training of counselors become apparent. The first of these is that to help clients make good choices and wise plans, a counselor must be able to provide dependable *information* about the alternatives they consider. The training counselors undergo should prepare them to do this.

Obviously this does not mean that the well-trained counselor should be a walking encyclopedia of information about jobs, schools and colleges, social agencies, government programs, and the conditions of life at all stages in all parts of the world. Even if it were possible to package such detailed and diverse material into courses and to require all prospective counselors to take them, the knowledge would be at least partly obsolete before they began to apply it in counseling practice. What his training can provide the counselor with is, first, an understanding of the *kinds* of information that are relevant to particular kinds of decisions, and of *sources* of such information that can be considered sound and dependable.

Because of the responsibility counselors in many situations carry to help people make good vocational decisions, courses designed to give trainees an understanding of the occupational structure and its changing trends have usually been a part of the counseling curriculum. The trainee becomes familiar with books and pamphlets containing facts his clients will need to take into consideration, so that he knows where to look for them when occasion arises —facts about educational requirements, salaries, working conditions, prospects for advancement, and many other aspects of jobs and careers.

The other principal kind of information a client needs if he is to make good decisions is information about *himself*—his abilities, his interests, his needs and expectations from life. While much of this self-understanding can be generated through interviews, standardized tests can also play a prominent role in increasing it. Thus courses on testing have usually been included in training programs for counselors. Here, as in the occupational domain, a general background is more useful than a plethora of detailed factual information. What tests can and cannot accomplish, how to distinguish between good and poor tests, how to translate scores into usable information about individual strengths, weaknesses, and directions of development—these constitute the framework of knowledge a counselor should get as part of his training program.

It is because of the manysidedness of the informational component of counseling that specialization tends to develop within the counseling profession. School-counselors deal with kinds of choices and plans that are different from those dealt with by rehabilitation-counselors. Counselors in employment offices deal with people who are thinking in a different way about their futures than the students who come to a college counselor for assistance in choosing a major. Those who counsel the disadvantaged or the hard-core unemployed are specialized in still different directions.

The necessity for specialization can be taken care of partly by the differentiation of training programs, but it has other implications as well. It is very common for counselors trained for one special kind of practice to shift to another during the course of their professional careers. New fields of specialization develop; existing ones change their character. Hundreds of counselors, for example, moved into positions with the Job Corps and other antipoverty agencies in the 1960s. They needed quickly to become specialists in assisting disadvantaged individuals. If counseling is to make its maximum contribution to social progress, the training its practitioners get should not make them unfit to adapt to unpredicted shifts in social goals and social climate. Thus it seems that the general parts of the training should continue to receive more emphasis than the specialized parts. Furthermore, facilities for continuing education, such as short courses, institutes and workshops, and professional publications, should be made continuously available. In a very real sense, a counselor's education is never completed.

There is one other way in which the difference between counseling and psychotherapy has implications for training. The focus on the choices and decisions normal people must make in the real world leads to a concern with social groups and institutions as well as individual thoughts and feelings, the environment as well as the person. Thus, while a counselor must have a thorough grounding in psychology, he also can use knowledge of the other social sciences to good advantage—sociology, anthropology, economics. It is true that many psychotherapists are also now emphasizing this environmental aspect of their work, and consequently this difference in orientation is probably narrower now than it was in the days when most therapists tended to be Freudians oriented toward intrapersonal conflicts and difficulties. The point is that basic knowledge of the concepts and principles of the relevant social sciences must find a place in training programs for counselors.

What implications do any of the differences have for the level of training practitioners should be expected to attain? As mentioned in the first section, psychotherapists have typically held doctor's degrees, counselors master's degrees. I see no justification for this distinction. The counselor's work is fully as complex and requires fully as much preparation as the therapist's. There is a problem here, however. I know of no good evidence that the advanced levels of educational attainment, in either professional specialty, contribute very much to the trainee's *skill* as a practitioner. He acquires more abstract knowledge and more research skills in his work for a doctor's degree but, aside from internship experience, does not typically increase his skill in helping people. Therefore, I should be more inclined to advocate better training and more professional opportunities for psychotherapists who hold only master's degrees than to require that all counselors obtain doctor's degrees. And if we could get away from the overriding prestige considerations that so strongly motivate people now, we should be able to design advanced programs beyond the master's degree that would increase professional competence far more efffiectively than the traditional Ph.D. program does.

One way of summing up much of what I consider to be of greatest importance is to state that the counselor is an artist who works with human possibilities. Like other artists, he needs both richness of vision and skill in the use of materials. He must be creative. The first essential is that he be able to see possibilities, to think of possible directions development may take in the case of any individual with whom he is working—old or young, rich or poor, bright or retarded. Whatever stimulates creativity of this special sort is part of his preparation for counseling, whether or not it has been included in his formal training program. But in designing training programs we should provide for experiences that stimulate this kind of creativity, and we should make sure that it is not dampened or destroyed by the training process.

REFERENCES

Rogers, C. R. The necessary and sufficient conditions of therapeutic personality change. *Journal of Consulting Psychology,* 1957, **21**, 95–103.

Truax, C. B., and Carkhuff, R. R. *Toward effective counseling and psychotherapy.* Chicago: Aldine, 1967.

Issues

1. Since there are degrees of severity of problems, and since referrals are not always available (nor more competent), what should constitute the realm of the counseling professional and what factors ought to be included in his evaluation of severity and need for referral?
2. What is the value of discussing the possible differences between counseling and psychotherapy? Do any benefits accrue as a consequence for either or both of these professions?
3. Is prestige or function the more crucial variable in the perpetuation of the classic question of difference?
4. What would be the soundest and most helpful position to take on this debate for a department just initiating both a master's and a Ph.D. program? Would counselor education, counseling psychology, school psychology, and clinical psychology, among the various disciplines, agree on a position?

Annotated Readings

Anderson, W. P. The clinical-counseling dilemma. *Journal of Counseling Psychology,* 1965, **12** (1), 97–100.

There is an increased need to distinguish the fields of counseling and clinical psychology. Granting that in certain instances counseling psychology lacks adequate theoretical formulation, it is a mistake to assume that clinical psychotherapy is necessarily more universal in its application or of higher positive value as treatment.

Much of the current confusion stems from the practice of lumping clinical and consulting psychology together when, actually, they do not constitute one major area. Instead, there should be division and training for two types of applied psychology: one involving abnormal diagnosis, psychotherapy, and abnormal personality structure; the other handling selection of personnel, occupational and educational information and measurement, evaluation, normal personality, and various techniques improving the client's decision-making abilities. A training program that attempts to encompass both areas is liable to produce less-skilled personnel than would separate and specialized programs. In fact, to the extent that the background of the psychologist can influence problems developed by the client, training in clinical psychology would be a hindrance to the performance of counseling functions.

Differentiations of psychotherapy and counseling can help to alleviate the confusion of the roles of clinical and counseling psychology. Greater subspecialty definition, coupled with the psychologist's heightened awareness of his own realm of competence, can insure a method of treatment best suited to the client's problem.

Brammer, L. M. The counselor is a psychologist. *Personnel and Guidance Journal,* 1968, 47 (1), 4–9.

School-counselors are anxious about their status and identity as professional workers. They are criticized by other helping professions for their superficiality, and they are being dispossessed of their basic helping functions by school psychologists and social workers. Solutions proposed are abandonment of the guidance model for counselors, and adoption of the counseling-psychologist model geared to a two-year master's degree level. Counselors are being called upon increasingly to function as psychological specialists in behavior change and their training has become firmly based in the psychological aspects of behavioral science. Statements by the American School Counselors Association and a growing number of counselor-educators emphasize the psychological base of counseling practice.

Suggestions for Further Reading

Dörken, H. Utilization of psychologists in positions of responsibility in public mental health programs: A national survey. *American Psychologist,* 1970, **25**, 953–958.

Mandato, V. The training of school psychologists and implications for a professional school of psychology. *American Psychologist,* 1971, **26**, 1039.

Resnick, H., & Gelso, C. J. Differential perceptions of counseling role: A reexamination. *Journal of Counseling Psychology,* 1971, **18**, 549–553.

Thelen, M. H., & Ewing, D. R. Roles, functions, and training in clinical psychology: A survey of academic clinicians. *American Psychologist,* 1970, **25**, 550–554.

Warman, R. E. Differential perceptions of counseling role. *Journal of Counseling Psychology,* 1960, **7**, 269–274.

Warman, R. E. The counseling role of college and university centers. *Journal of Counseling Psychology,* 1961, **8**, 231–238.

CHAPTER 3

Preparation Practices in Different Disciplines

Is it indeed true that different clinical disciplines have different goals, values, and approaches to preparation? The best answer is probably yes and no. It is interesting to see how surprised people of one discipline are when they hear members of another discipline express enthusiasm for some value or method espoused by the first group. The expectation of difference seems more characteristic than any expectation of similarity. One is tempted to wonder whether communication gaps, differences of opinion, and professional rivalry might not be more the accouterments of the professions than essential elements of them. This is not to imply that all the clinical fields are in total accord, but rather that there are probably fewer differences and more similarities among experienced practitioners, whatever the discipline or group with which they are affiliated. While emphases may vary, it is not reasonable to assume, for example, that a medical model is less relationship-oriented than a nonmedical model, or vice versa.

The contributors to this chapter shed considerable light on the relative positions of four different programs in relation to issues of function and preparation. Abroms and Whitaker candidly discuss, in historical perspective, the weaknesses, nominal strengths, and on-going changes in psychiatric residency programs. The stereotype of the medically educated therapist is examined and some new insights are presented. The priorities of contemporary programs indicate a shift from established patterns toward an interdisciplinary collaboration. Explicit changes in program and role are thoroughly explored.

Bordin postulates an ideal relationship between learning and experience, recommending the sequence and content of courses best suited to prepare the counseling psychologist. He also comments on ways in which vital preparation time is too often wasted. The differences between goals for short-term programs (master's) and long-term programs (Ph.D.) are enumerated in accordance with professional function and expectations.

Kehas begins his coverage of the development of the school-counselor with the ominous prediction that perhaps there really is not any established function for the school-counselor. His focus is on the master's programs, with a great deal of emphasis placed on the design of the practicum experience. He asserts that professional organizations should concern themselves with the future of school counseling and the relationship of the school-counselor to the total process of education in the schools.

The applied psychologist working in a counseling center must be a combination scientist-professional, say King and Wollersheim. Without careful monitoring and continued evaluation of curriculum and of the changing needs of these centers, programs may tend to overemphasize research at the expense of clinical service, or vice versa. The appropriateness and value of experiential and didactic learning approaches are set forth in an authoritative and logical argument. The need for flexibility in programs is described, and is anchored to the rapidly changing functions and expectations with which the applied psychologist is confronted.

Malcolm considers the specific needs of the counselor if he or she is to function at the most qualified level in the schools—both elementary and secondary. The blend of didactic and clinical instruction provided over a carefully structured two-year program is presented. A variety of role models is described and reviewed.

New Approaches to Residency Training in Psychiatry

Carl A. Whitaker and Gene M. Abroms

University of Wisconsin—Madison

Until very recently, psychiatric residencies in this country could be divided roughly into three types. First, there were the programs located at large state hospitals, which usually did not constitute training at all. With virtually no supervision, residents were put in charge of hordes of broken-down men and women, with little means of helping them and no guidance in distinguishing who was responsive to treatment, why they might be so, and what methods were applicable. Whatever the avowed treatment philosophy of such institutions, the main lessons that trainees learned were the extent of human devaluation and the numbing pain of therapeutic impotence. The graduates of such programs are often recognized by their cynicism, their technical incompetence, and their discomfort in talking intimately with patients. An indiscriminate reliance on somatic treatments flags these underlying attributes.

Second, there were programs that aspired to teach some form of psychoanalytic theory and practice as applied primarily to individual patients. By far the most prestigious, this group included most of the residencies based at the better academic departments of psychiatry and at small private hospitals. This group also included so-called eclectic programs, which in fact taught an eclectic language while remaining essentially Freudian in practice. Starting from a humanistic commitment to foster understanding of patients in their historic and dynamic particularities, such programs sometimes ended up betraying their original purpose by encouraging closed-system thinking. Trainees were taught to make patients fit preformed theory. They were taught to provide psychotic patients with ever more penetrating intellectual insights, but rarely with the kind of emotional or physical encounter from which self-control and social mastery could be learned. Furthermore, in a major distortion of Freud's original notions, trainees were often taught to regard their patients as purely psychological beings to the neglect of their social contexts. Some of these psychiatrists saw nothing wrong, for example, in subjecting a psychotic

67

depressive patient to a lengthy analysis of questionable benefit while avoiding other interventions. Particularly, in bondage to the individual-psychology orientation of psychoanalytic theory, trainees were taught to neglect the patient's family and significant others, sometimes even casting them in the role of villains, thereby further imprisoning the patient in his precious singleness.

Finally, there were training institutions that retained a fundamental commitment to teaching the medical-disease concept of psychiatric disturbance. Rather than too little structure and supervision, such programs suffered from an excess of it, often of a rigid, authoritarian stripe. This medical approach, amply discussed in the literature, assumes that a disease process, either physiological or psychological, is taking place inside the patient independently of the functioning of other persons in the environment, including the psychiatrist. Rather than as a disturbance manifested in all the patient's interpersonal relationships and capable of exacerbating the therapist's anxieties and conflicts, thereby serving to bind both patient and therapist together in a common human undertaking, the patient's disturbance was perceived primarily as an occasion for the therapist to do something to or for him—that is, to straighten him out. With the task so conceived, the therapist could maintain a medically correct stance, aloof and superior and possessed of expert knowledge to be doled out in the customary manner to the underdeveloped. Therapists trained in this mode are known by their stiff formality and their omnipotent, one-up attitude towards patients. Even when Freudian, neo-Freudian, or existential theories are adduced to underpin the medical therapist's activities, he typically uses them as weaponry to further widen the gulf between the patient and himself, to foster secrecy about his person—in short, to obliterate any sense of his belonging to a common human family with his patient.

These portraits, although perhaps overdrawn and tending to caricature, do underline a rather widely held impression; namely, that the "products" of psychiatric training in the past commonly portrayed qualities of would-be omniscience and technical incompetence. As we discuss below, the structure of the various training programs tended to reinforce these attributes even though the psychiatrists who administered them were often competent, humane therapists. And yet it would be unfair to deny that these programs also had their offsetting good points. The programs that taught trainees to overvalue the individual relationship and the psychological word were yet most effective in fostering sensitivity to the depths of meaning of a patient's sufferings. Those that neglected psychological and interpersonal skills were at least hearty enough to instill respect for the person as a biological organism. Those that favored medical superiority and the disease model were straightforward in teaching the proper use of suggestive authority and structure in the treatment enterprise. But each of these approaches taken alone could not help but convince its trainees of the universal applicability of what were surely partial explanations and limited practices. This widespread provincialism, of psychiatrists taking a particular theory and practice born of a very restrictive clinical experience—for example, with outpatient hysterics or with chronic schizophrenic inpatients—and making them serve to explain and treat all mental illness, is surely one of the most characteristic and depressing features of psychiatric training in the first half of this century.

ECLECTICISM AND EXISTENTIALISM

The new approach to training, as we see it emerging, seeks to transcend such provincialism by a radical commitment to eclectic and existential values. Both these terms are of course encrusted with a residue of old meanings and require redefinition. Eclectic training in the past was more concerned with an ideological position than with real differences in practice. The line was drawn at Freud's biological instinctualism. The ideological eclectic maintained that the wellsprings of human behavior were to be found not only in the biological drives but in the prevailing cultural values and patterns of interpersonal relationships. Yet most "eclectic" therapists were still trained to do basically and quite exclusively a form of psychoanalytic practice with only some of the formal rules relaxed and the terminology altered. The new eclectism has less to do with a terminological, theoretical difference than with a felt necessity to master a very broad range of treatment techniques: not only the classic forms of individual and group psychotherapy, applicable after all only to the least sick members of society, but the increasingly refined applications of psychoactive drugs, behavioral-modification approaches, nonverbal communication, suggestion techniques, psychodrama and role playing, couple and family therapy, multiple-impact crisis intervention, and community social action— none of which is so bound to an excessively verbal, upper-class ethos. All the many pieces of such a program can be effectively organized by fitting them within the framework of a general systems model, as both Abroms (1969) and Duhl (1971) have suggested.

In sum, one of the new trends in residency training is to provide trainees with courses and practical experiences in the use of a very broad range of treatment modalities. No longer can a graduate feel comfortable in doing only individual analytic therapy and perhaps prescribing a few psychoactive drugs. In addition, he should certainly be able to sit down with families and to intervene effectively in whole social milieus. He should be able to direct patients to self-help educational activities and to utilize the disinhibiting effect of nonverbal, physical encounter. Finally, he should be able to appreciate the opportunities for research provided by all these activities and hopefully to do some himself. To accomplish these goals, a training program must have a community of faculty members who, in a spirit of mutual tolerance of differences, can teach the various skills and exemplify the values that such eclecticism implies.

But how does a training program foster a commitment to existential values? Clearly, no matter how technically proficient and broadly experienced, a psychiatrist may remain so aloof and grandiose that the potentialities of the therapy situation are never even remotely approached. Thus, even for practical reasons, a residency must cultivate basic existential qualities in its trainees; strength instead of grandioseness, humility instead of impotence, alliance instead of omnipotence, warmth instead of distance. In the past, existentially minded psychiatrists exhorted their residents to love and respect their patients as beings-in-the-world. Sometimes they were even able to demonstrate these qualities. But these exhortations and examples, however admirable, were rarely sufficient to develop the resident into an existential man.

The new existential psychiatry recognizes that a residency experience, not to mention the prior medical school experience, may have structural properties that inhibit human concern no matter how overtly it is valued. Conversely, there are ways of organizing the format of training that foster existential qualities—provided, of course, that the faculty can provide living examples and the resident is open to growth. In the following paragraphs we discuss a few of the structural arrangements that have altered the existential tone of our residency program at the University of Wisconsin.

SUPERVISION

The manner in which therapy supervision has been provided until now has tended to reinforce the trainee's emotional distance and intellectual elevation. Furthermore, it has perpetuated a destructive lie—namely, that the trainee does not need help in learning his craft. Typically, the resident meets privately with his supervisor (how often is the patient even told about it?), at which time he presents the "verbatim" notes or tapes of his interviews, suitably edited so as not to offend the supervisor's sensibilities. The supervisor then comments on the patient's dynamics and the therapeutic process, with particular attention to the trainee's interpretive technique. Although the avowed purpose of such supervision is to teach psychotherapy skills, what is primarily being learned is how to comment better on another person's productions. The supervisor comments on the trainee's report and then the trainee goes back and comments on his patient's remarks. The longer supervision continues, the more the comments of supervisor and trainee sound alike. While such an arrangement may be appropriate for learning how to examine biological excreta, it is less than optimal for learning to develop meaningful human relationships, therapeutic or otherwise.

If supervision really has the purpose of developing the ability to do therapy, then therapy must be practiced during the supervisory session, just as the piano must be played during a piano lesson. We know that such skills are best learned by first watching someone who knows how (the supervisor) and then trying it oneself with the supervisor watching and providing feedback. In practice, this means that psychotherapy supervision becomes co-therapy; the resident and his supervisor sit down together with a patient or family, the supervisor perhaps taking the lead early in treatment but the resident gradually becoming an equal and then earning the right to take the lead himself. During these sessions the supervisor and resident can talk about each other's techniques and counter-transferences as well as the patient's techniques and transferences—in front of the patient himself. Both the authors regard this so much as the ideal mode of supervision that they are reluctant to do it any other way.

Of course such a format requires a greater exposure of the supervisor's and resident's persons than is customary, and this may be initially uncomfortable for both. But the advantages become increasingly obvious with experience. The supervisor-resident collaboration is not only acknowledged but witnessed by the patient. That collaboration stands as the model for the resident-patient relationship. When it goes well, the patient as well as the resident and supervisor learn that each can show himself—both his good and his bad work—and be approved or contested and still not be disqualified as a person. It is difficult for anyone to remain grandiose or aloof in such a situation. But to be truly helpful it does require that the supervisor possess therapy and relationship skills that the resident does not yet have, and that the resident possess some that the patient is so far lacking. This is only fair. The old mode of supervision may only be a method of legislating the authority of supervisor and resident without either having to earn it in human terms.

CASE PRESENTATIONS

Residents are frequently asked to present their cases to colleagues and teachers for the purposes of deepening their intellectual understanding of patient's difficulties and formulating rational treatment plans. But the usual format for these presentations is more suggestive of a ritual celebration of medical superiority than a quest for learning. For the patient is "summed up" without being present to amend or accept the account. He is sometimes brought on briefly, sandwiched between the presentation and the formulation, to show his psychic lesions. But for both the preliminary hearing and the later sentencing, he is denied due process. His absence encourages the residents and other staff members to think and talk about him as if he were a pathological specimen. One is struck by the pejorative language, the condescending tone, the concentration on personality deficiencies, and the unchecked implications about hidden unsavory motivations that sometimes characterize these presentations. It is little wonder that the staff begins to feel that the "truth" about the patient is terrible and must be held in exclusive confidence. This may, however, be in part an artifact of the exclusive setting of the discussion.

Recently, we have undertaken to have the patient present when his history is discussed. In addition to the patient, nurses, nursing aides, members of the patient's family, and other patients are routinely invited. As we have gradually and sometimes painfully moved in this direction, we have noted that the trainee learns to think and talk about his patient's difficulties in a language that all can use as corrective feedback. The language inevitably becomes more descriptively exact; inferred patterns of behavior become more closely grounded in what is observable. By being allowed to take issue with the presentation, the patient and his partners can engage the staff in a meaningful dialogue. Instead of unilateral license to make pronouncements, the staff finds itself caught up in a dialectical exercise. Most importantly, the views of experienced staff members are immediately shared with patients to the enhancement of their self-knowledge. To talk about patients without patients being there certainly enhances the doctor's sense of importance, but it wastes information that could be used by the patients, who presumably need it most.

TEAM MEMBERSHIP

Even when case supervision is optimally arranged, the resident still spends the greatest part of his time in solo practice. No one is in a position to comment on his work. He is on his own. Many residency programs have been structured so that he is for most of the time a law unto himself. When he is on the inpatient service he writes orders and makes decisions that are to be carried out by the nursing staff without quibble. In many outpatient departments there simply are no other professional helpers. With so much power and so little experience, the infantile dream of grandiosity comes true.

Perhaps the greatest single contribution of the community-milieu movement in psychiatry will turn out to be the creation of an intellectual climate in which this kind of isolated and lonely individual burden is no longer thinkable. In a situation in which there are too many patients, too few doctors, but a largely untapped pool of mental-health workers (nurses, social workers, etc.), the greatest need will be for psychiatrists and psychologists who can work through and potentiate their less-trained, or at least less-credentialed, colleagues by providing consultative help, by delegating therapy responsibilities, by encouraging participation in formulating and carrying out programs—in short, by functioning as members of interdisciplinary teams.

This not only makes sense as a better delivery system of mental-health care than the solo-performer model, but from a training viewpoint it may save the soul of that erstwhile virtuoso soloist. For in the team setting, he has to learn to collaborate—to take account of other's wishes and talents and to receive their feedback in working together. The trainee is no longer imprisoned in the grandiose, omnipotent position. It may even help lower the extreme suicide rate amongst psychiatrists.

As in many residencies now, we require our trainees to spend periods of several months on team-oriented milieu-therapy services, either impatient, day-care, or crisis units. The trainee must here learn to negotiate the team-leader function in a spirit of mutual collaboration. Nurses, aides, social workers, occupational therapists, and patients are expected to give him feedback on how he exercises leadership: how authoritarian, unilateral, defensive, disqualifying of others, or how facilitating, mutually respectful, open to others, and so on. We think it highly desirable that the trainee join his co-professionals in an ongoing sensitivity-group or encounter-group experience as part of this milieu experience. Here the exchange of verbal and physical feedback between the various members can be monitored by an experienced trainer or communication analyst.

SUMMARY AND CONCLUSIONS

We have discussed some of the newer trends in residency training, which hopefully will contribute to a broader eclecticism and a deeper existential outlook on the part of psychiatrists of the future. The eclectic part of the picture is more easily realized in that it only requires instruction and experience in using a broad range of treatment techniques. Having a large armamentarium, the budding therapist should no longer be as prone as he was in the past to the perseverative reliance on a single approach that actually has a limited sphere of applicability. Without the need to support such delusionally monistic approaches, the old tendency to make premature and forced ideological commitments should similarly be discouraged, to the greater benefit of our patients. Training can instead address itself to improving the trainee's artistic talents, his interpersonal skills, and his scientific knowledge—all in a nonpartisan spirit.

The greatest enemy of human authenticity in conducting psychiatric treatment is, in our opinion, the grandiose, omnipotent fantasies and attitudes that most physicians bring to their missionary life among the sick. We have discussed several training practices that tend to reinforce rather than soften these trends and have recommended new formats to combat them. We have suggested that supervision, case presentations, and clinical assignments all be structured to maximize collaboration with patients and the other mental-health professionals and to open the trainee up to constructive feedback by these colleagues. We suspect that such a frontal assault on the old shibboleths of confidentiality and privacy, which served to protect the therapist's delusions, will have implications for the critical role of personal therapy in the future training of psychotherapists; it may no longer be so necessary as it is at present. But this is a subject that deserves future consideration. Finally, although changes in training procedures may be necessary conditions for fostering basic existential attitudes, they can by no means be sufficient ones. There are personal qualities involving both trainees and trainers at issue here that may transcend educational methods. Faced with such mystery, a training program must pursue ever more diligently the ideal of collecting a community of scholars who are dedicated as much to gaining wisdom as to possessing knowledge.

REFERENCES

Abroms, G. M. The new eclecticism. *Archives of General Psychiatry.* 1969, **20**, 514–523.
Duhl, F. J. A personal history of politics and programs in psychiatric training. In G. M. Abroms & N. S. Greenfield (Eds.), *The new hospital psychiatry.* New York: Academic Press, 1971.

Reflections on Preparation for Psychological Counseling

Edward S. Bordin

University of Michigan

Anyone who sets out to discuss the professional and personal preparation of counselors must first make clear what versions of this highly varied and ambiguously defined set of persons he is including within his purview. Unlike the term *psychotherapy,* which is associated with human troubles marked by extremity, chronicity, or both, *counseling* is associated with almost any human condition that invites intervention by another. All the dilemmas of life, whether momentous or trivial, become occasions for turning to another person for help of some sort. The young couple begins to wonder whether their marriage, initiated with seemingly deep attachments, can survive the increasingly frequent and ever more bitter quarrels. A college sophomore, still lacking that feeling of inner conviction and commitment for which he longs, approaches the time when he must "declare a major." These are significant dilemmas when measured against any scale of values. But advice, counsel, and aid are also sought about such more limited questions as how to apply for admission to a given college, where financial aid can be obtained to tide one over a temporarily disabling illness, and even where to shop for a specific cold cream.

For the purpose of defining the counseling functions with which I am concerned in this essay, it is useful to distinguish between the personal and instrumental aspects of human enterprises. *Instrumental* is used here in a broad sense to refer not only to how something is done but to the concepts and principles that underlie it—in short, the whole range of knowledge, from acquaintance with specific, concrete details, requisite crafts, and mechanical skills, to the ability to apply the complex ideas of a particular discipline. This is a sphere of operation occupied by coaches, teachers, and other technical advisers. They inform the person about technical requirements, guide his practice for needed skills, stimulate his curiosity and imagination, and extend his cognitions. *Personal* refers to the complex organization of motives which every individual superimposes upon his native drives, and which play such an important part in the kinds of enterprises he selects to engage in, the satisfactions he obtains, the strains he can endure, and his susceptibility to unnecessary strains. In short, we speak here of human personality, its development, its continuity and change.

Though the personal-instrumental distinction may be useful, it will not provide us with neat dichotomies. The ideal teacher is concerned not only with impersonalized mastery but with aiding his student to integrate knowledge or skill into his individual functioning. The effective teacher arranges learning experiences related to the student's motivations and relevant to the life he leads. To the extent that each student brings a different set of motivations and experiences, his education must be individualized in order to further it. Thus, we have a continuum: at one end, coaches, technical advisers, and others who concentrate on the instrumental; in the center, the educator, who gives balanced attention to the instrumental and personal; and at the other end, the counselor, whose primary concern is the personal. And, of course, the coach who pays no attention to the personal is a poor coach indeed, just as the counselor is prone to form grossly inaccurate perceptions and consequently to offer ineffective counseling, if his view of the person is uninformed by any acquaintance with the instrumental aspects of the person's life.

Another influence on the counselor's functions is the setting in which he works. The mainstream of counseling has from the beginning been located within educational systems, particularly secondary schools and colleges, and has been concerned with contributing to individual development during the formative years. This means that the counselor gives attention to the developmental tasks of early and late adolescence; the clarification of identity, particularly as it is expressed through occupation; the achievement of a maturely independent relationship with parents; the stabilization of habits of work and effort; and the ripening of sexual expression and the expression of intimacy. This is a time of discovery for the adolescent. He reaches out into the world of ideas, of people, and of social customs and institutions. In doing so, he becomes familiar with his own capacities and attitudes, tests out his talents or skills, and learns how much effort he can sustain. Correspondingly, the counselor must be conversant with the psychological demands made by various kinds of activities, and with the technical methods devised to help an individual assess his capacity to meet these demands. There are times when the counselor is called on to supplement the activities of the teacher in aiding the student in his exploration of his environment. This is often true with regard to occupational information. Frequently, there are socially backward youngsters who need special attention in exploring and mastering the customs of dress and other social skills that are part of the youth culture.

Inner-city schools, out-of-school youth in the black ghettos, school and community programs in rural poverty areas, all present new and formidable challenges to the counselor. He must free himself from a white, middle-class view of the sources of motivation, and of the development and expression of intellectual ingenuity, so that he can aid teachers to adapt their methods to the needs of these disadvantaged youngsters and be of direct aid to these young people in their search for self-realization in an alien world.

In growing numbers, counselors work in medical settings with patients temporarily or permanently disabled by inherited or prenatal disabilities, or as an aftermath of accident or illness. Individuals with early disabilities must learn during their formative years to adapt to these limitations. Those whose disabilities arise later through accident or disease must come to terms with this sudden change in their status; they must learn how to use the resources they have not lost to adapt to the losses of certain of their functions. Disability may not only require adaptations in carrying out specific activities, but frequently calls for changes of occupation or modification of roles in the family.

Rehabilitation counselors need to have special familiarity with the physical as well as the psychological demands of various kinds of activities and of their interaction. They need to be specially versed in methods of assessing this interaction. But, more than these specific technologies, they must be steeped in the role of the body, and of body image in personality development and in psychic functioning, so that they can understand and play a part in helping the individual to adapt to the experience of physical and psychological disability. They cannot concentrate their attention on the adolescent years; they must be fully aware of the social and psychological processes of the later years, marked by marriage, parenthood, and middle-career stages, and of the period of matured children and the beginnings of physical decline. They will need this fuller understanding of the life cycle to be able to gauge the impact of a particular illness and disability at a specific point in the cycle.

Counselors have always been concerned about influencing the individual's environment. Student personnel work received a good deal of its impetus and much of its intellectual nutriment from counselors. Because of their knowledge of individual development and its viscissitudes, counselors have been useful consultants to teachers in dealing with everyday problems in the classroom. They have also been useful in the design and administration of curricula and in many other aspects of the educational community. As counselors have moved into social settings outside the schools, they have become part of the larger movements of community psychology and social psychiatry. When one confronts the problems of the inner city or of poverty-ridden rural areas, it becomes imperative to develop methods to aid individuals to band together so as to exert influence over their environment, and to help these individuals create the conditions they need in order to expand their capacities and establish identities which reflect their special characteristics in a viable manner. To play a part in this kind of process, the counselor will need to be well versed in the principles and patterns of organization. He will need to have knowledge of group processes and sensitivities to group interpersonal relations. He will need to be skilled in methods of assessing group atmospheres, group resistances, and group resources.

This, then, is the context in which I propose to discuss the preparation of counselors. It should be apparent that their functions are centered around human behavior and development, which means that psychology is their foundation discipline. The range and complexity of the tasks subsumed and the size of the job to be done will naturally raise questions regarding levels of preparation, breadth or depth, emphasis on theory versus practice, and personal or professional emphasis. I do not propose to recapitualate the many foundation publications, which outline educational and professional preparation for counseling (e.g., APA, 1952a, 1952b; Bordin, 1951; Thompson & Super, 1964; Wrenn, 1962). Instead I will devote myself to defining the convictions about principles and procedures that I have acquired during twenty-five or more years of counseling, administration, supervising, and teaching.

LEVEL OF PREPARATION

The stereotype of counseling as little more than the kind of aid one might expect from a parental figure, which is not confined to laymen but has counterparts among clinicians, leads to underestimates of the amount of professional preparation needed. The fact that a counselor can be expected to serve a useful function at some stage of almost every person's life combines with the blending of teaching and counseling roles to push toward a minimizing of formal training. Despite the counteracting influence of a tendency toward more complete training (i.e., the summer and two-year-long institutes of the NDEA period), there remains a tendency to convert teachers into counselors by administrative fiat plus a course in psychological measurements. Our increasing understanding of the complexities of psychological growth and of human behavior pull us in the other direction—that of insisting on thorough grounding in psychology and related behavioral sciences.

Even after discounting stereotypes, we must find patterns of practice suitable for counselors whose level of preparation is short of the extended doctoral program prescribed for counseling psychologists. Though I am encouraged by the results of training experiments, such as those by Rioch (1963) or Truax and Carkhuff (1967), I do not find in them a carte blanche for the use of laymen or briefly trained counselors without regard to setting or particular goal. I have little doubt that there are features of counseling or therapeutic ways of relating that can be transmitted in brief, intensive training programs, and that counselors or therapists with only this limited experience behind them will be rated no differently than formally trained experienced therapists. But if my review of the influence of setting on the functions of the counselor and the demands on him has any merit, it suggests that the individual with more limited training must be pointed toward the particular setting in which he is to operate, with the understanding that his preparation does not necessarily transfer to other settings.

In considering how important extended academic and clinical preparation is for practice, we must take into account differences in effectiveness of doctoral programs. There is no doubt in my mind that many clinical and counseling-psychology programs, including a great many of those that survive certifying review, have not represented serious efforts to prepare students for practice. Too often they have retained too much of the earlier theoretical and experimental tradition, unchallenged and uninfluenced by the need to gear theory and research to naturalistic events, which, after all, is the goal of all science that has not descended to the state of scientism. If doctoral preparation for practice is to represent more than a barrier of rituals erected to protect a professional guild, courses and teachers must be geared to interact with accumulating field experience and practical sophistication. This means that direct observation and clinical experience must be introduced early and graded in complexity and responsibility. Opportunities to observe children and adults in schools, work settings, and clinics should be followed by clinical responsibilities for diagnostic tests and interviews and appropriately graded counseling or therapeutic responsibilities. Courses in general psychological theory and research need not offer immediate answers to practical problems, but they should be required to stand the test of being consistent with phenomena of behavior observed in their natural setting. Obviously, a doctoral program draws a particular kind of person, one who is willing to distance himself from the urgency of an immediate human problem, who has an appetite for abstraction and intellectual play. Elsewhere I have spoken of the diverse motivations of curiosity, compassion, and doubt to be found among psychologists, and the need for programs flexible enough to arouse and implement various combinations of these motives (Bordin, 1951). More importantly, I have suggested that too much doubting can undermine the effectiveness of a clinician (though he still needs a modicum of doubting), and that too much compassion may deflect the research worker from his task (though some empathy is needed to formulate significant problems).

Returning to the usefulness of more limited preparation for counseling, general theories of learning as well as common sense suggest that the way to get maximum effect in performance of a given task is to concentrate practice on that task. It is only when we seek maximum transferability that we pay attention to high-level abstractions of concept and principle. At a minimum, the limited training of counselors should include opportunities for them to observe, and to engage in some amount of reading and discussion about, the stages of personal development represented by their clientele and some of the specific facts and methods that are relevant to their work. The danger to be avoided is that of highly intellectualized discussion of poorly understood concepts. The proper antidote lies in direct observation of others and of themselves in counseling or kindred personal relationships. The counselor with limited training must be aided to separate those aspects of counseling relationships that invite more responsibility than he is prepared to accept from those that will make him a helpful person, even with his more limited experience. For example, the set to understand how another is experiencing the world and how to respond genuinely to him, seems certain to be helpful. On the other hand, insisting on unconditional positive regard, important though this be, may create just that threat to the counselor which will make it difficult for him to respond to his client in a genuine manner. In my view, the counselor accepts great responsibilities whenever he tries to establish a relationship marked by unlimited confiding, and whenever he tries to induce his client to communicate in a passive, free-flowing state that is not directed toward active problem-solving. Such conditions, I believe, have the potential for releasing and highlighting primitive and immature elements. Bringing them into direct experience can be an important growth experience for certain persons at the proper times and with an experienced helper. But an inexperienced, blundering counselor may only bring his client face to face with immaturities neither of them are prepared to face. Often our interest in an intimate counseling relationship, combined with our conceptions of being client-centered, psychoanalytic, or some other kind of psychodynamically oriented helper, translates into just such invitations to confide and to free-associate. I should add that another feature of genuineness in counseling is the willingness to inform a client regarding relevant facts or experiences he has acquired. In working with adolescents, a major task of the counselor is to aid the student to acquire information, skills, and conceptual tools, which will enable him to gain the ability to express his emotions and act on his motivations in a positive and constructive fashion. Too often our current awareness of the importance of emotions and motivations as determiners of action has led us to overlook the importance of knowledge and thought.

LEARNING VERSUS EXPERIENCING

Every generation produces its own version of the old dilemma of whether to emphasize discipline or spontaneity in education. Having passed through a period of renewed emphasis upon "basics," which must be part of the background of all (because it helps us compete with the Russians), we are now experiencing a counteracting emphasis on immediacy ("relevance") and the freedom of the individual to fashion his own curriculum. To one side's insistence that tool concepts must be acquired for meaningful response and that teachers are more than T group leaders, the other side responds that teaching is more than filling students full of bits of information as though they were empty vessels, and that meaningful learning requires the absence of external pressures such as grades, required courses, and the like. As is evident from the above, both sides of the controversy too frequently reduce their opponents to straw men, thereby obscuring what are surely enduring educational dilemmas.

It seems to me that we must continue to seek for ways to introduce sophistication, enrichment, and artistry into spontaneity, thereby modifying without destroying it. A Michelangelo or a Picasso tells us that discipline *and* spontaneity can be profitably combined. Naturally, we must beware of pedantry masquerading as a concern with an awareness of the rich range of intellectual thought reflected in a particular strand of ideas or as a concern with the development of sophisticated methods of observation and analysis to serve for the uncovering and verification of new knowledge. Conversely, we must not mistake encouragement of antiintellectualism, or tolerance of immature or shallow reactions, for the fostering and release of spontaneity. Spontaneity without selectivity loses the name of creativity, being more accurately designated as narcissism. Kris (1952), among others, has emphasized the interplay of discipline and spontaneity involved in artistic creation. While the inventor or creative artist must draw on primitively based inner forces, he must also be able to select the "bits of gold" from the associative flow and to enrich and fashion them into a truly creative product. Each moment of creation, of "truth," is accompanied by hours of disciplined effort in the fashioning of meaningful products. Parents and teachers share the problem of how to introduce external restraints and guided experiences so as to facilitate their transfer into self-discipline and self-initiating processes. Surely an important ingredient is the student's trust that his teacher shares his ultimate goals of self-expression.

Within the context of counselor education, this means that the student needs to have evidence that the experiences offered to him grow out of an acceptance of his professional goal. Where there is trust of the faculty's dedication to this goal, there can be tolerance of misperceived or even true discrepancies between any experiences and the goal. This is not to say that there will not be any grumbling during periods of frustration and great effort with courses that are required "because they offer good background," but this will not become a signal for alienation and rejection. The student must have evidence that the faculty carries on a continuing, thoughtful review of the role of course offerings. One of the surest ways of giving him this evidence, and one that is useful in its own right, is to invite students to play an active part in such reviews. This kind of cooperative review is especially necessary for the so-called basic courses, such as those in sensory processes and perception, physiological psychology, and learning. Social organization and social psychology are areas of content sufficiently close to the counselor as not to need as much of this kind of justification. But students should realize that a global approach to the individual should contain an awareness of more minute psychic processes. The analytic, sometimes artificial, views of the processes of registering experience and of modifying responses in successive experiences need not stultify. On the contrary, teachers with imagination, enthusiasm, and the desire to stimulate others can open the prospective counselor's eyes to new possibilities in observation and conceptualization, possibilities that he will be motivated to explore, hopefully, into new frontiers.

In courses dealing with counseling or psychological assessment, with personality development and psychopathology, the question is not the relevance of the particular area, but rather the dispersion of effort between direct experience and examination of research and theory. It seems axiomatic that before sophisticated efforts toward establishing and validating principles of counseling or psychotherapy can be appreciated, the student must have built up some familiarity with the range of phenomena encountered. This suggests that a continual, spiraling cycle of direct observation succeeded by theoretical and research analysis is best. The initial period of observation should be the longest possible without getting the student deeply immersed in clinical responsibilities. This limitation is not only dictated by the ethical consideration of protecting clients from untrained counselors, but by the danger of building up closed-mindedness in response to the premature experience of the threat created by the initial impact of professional responsibility. Field observations, particularly those calling for participant observations, films and tape recordings of various human-relations situations, especially counseling and psychotherapeutic situations, and participation in diagnostic testing and interviewing, should seem to be part of the first cycle of observations preparing for initial survey and discussions of personality development and psychopathology, counseling, and psychological assessment. As the student begins to take on further professional responsibilities, he is ready for more searching examinations of theory and research, hopefully moving toward greater independence of effort.

A source of continuing ambivalence in the counselor's preparation is the role of experience as a recipient of counseling. Applications of behavior therapy aside, the emphasis on the relationship aspects of counseling has led to almost uniform agreement that personal conflicts are likely to interfere with the counselor's effectiveness and that when they do, personal therapy is indicated. But there are those who believe that personal conflicts are sufficiently widespread and likely to interfere as to make it profitable to require personal therapy of all counselors or therapists. The ludicrous prospect of our limited counseling and psychotherapeutic resources being expended on counselors and therapists in training, rather than on clients, gives support to those who on other grounds advocate the use of interpersonal sensitivity-group experiences as an alternative. One difficulty with this latter kind of program is the difficulty in deciding whether to apply a teaching or a therapeutic ethic to it. Formal teaching, even where grading is minimized, retains certain authoritarian elements. The teacher must at least decide whether the student has progressed to the point where he can be admitted to a more advanced experience. He usually plays a part in deciding whether the student has qualified for a degree. His recommendations are solicited almost routinely in the awarding of fellowships or other prizes. By contrast, a major ethic of counseling and psychotherapy is that of respecting the client's confidences. Associated with this is the expectation that the counselor will not pass judgment on his client. Are *T* groups to be viewed as teaching or counseling? For the most part they are conducted as voluntary groups, which seems to remove them from one set of the restraints of the teaching situation. But what if the leader is also a faculty member, active in the formal teaching program and on the various committees that oversee it? To complicate things further, the *T* group has broken out of the pattern set by Lewin and his co-workers, which concentrated on the dynamics of group formation and how individual sensitivities and skills contribute to the effectiveness of group action. These groups have branched into "personal development," marathon meetings for personal release and true contact and dialogue, and so forth, which brings them into contiguity with psychotherapy. I am sure that the old-style *T* group can contribute without complications to the preparation of the counselor. The new style can also contribute, but students and faculty will have to come to clear understandings about the resulting role confusions.

ASSESSMENT AND DIAGNOSIS

Psychologists are confused and battered by cross-currents when thinking about assessment and diagnosis. From one side come the voices of the debunkers, underlining how far short of perfect accuracy is the forecasting provided by psychological tests. A subset of debunkers shout about the shortcomings of permitting clinical judgment to add to objectively derived and statistically processed data. From another side, counselors are assured that diagnosis is irrelevant or even detrimental to their task. Our review of the functions of counselors, I believe, has made clear that counselors will be working with individuals who are in the process of assessing or reassessing themselves. If we have resources, imperfect though they may be, useful for such activities, it seems evident that we are obliged to make them available to our clients. This means the full range of assessment skills that psychologists have to offer. Too frequently in the past, training in assessment has concentrated attention on pencil and paper devices and on their statistical evaluation. Knowledge of statistical evaluation is certainly necessary to a realistic, practical application of assessment methods. But it should not replace a thorough consideration of why particular sets of observations are useful in understanding an individual and for forecasting his responses. Further, the counselor should be taught the skills required for field observations. This is one of the main virtues of clinical tests of intelligence and personality. In these free-acting situations, he can learn that method of disciplined observation which registers phenomena in painstaking detail and separates observation from inference. Most importantly, he must learn to respond to actions in their individual rather than their social context. When he hears an utterance, he not only registers its manifest socially defined message but also its particular style—for example, whether it is pedantic or excessively colloquial—as well as the facial expression, gestures, and body position that accompany it.

Counselors are not only concerned with helping their clients to arrive at realistic assessments of themselves; they must make diagnostic judgments regarding their clients. Too often the need for diagnosis has been justified on bureaucratic or evaluative grounds. The fact is that any responsible counselor cannot escape having to make decisions about offering his services. At a minimum, the demand for service being what it is, he must decide which potential clients will profit from his help and which will not and therefore should be referred elsewhere; which ones ought to be seen immediately and which ones should be asked to wait. Those of us who believe that counseling methods are multidimensional, and must be adapted to the needs of the particular client, are obliged to seek the kind of understanding that will enable us to adapt ourselves to the needs of each client. Too great an emphasis on diagnosis as an ongoing process concurrent with counseling and psychotherapy, it seems to me, has served to obscure the special character of diagnostic interviewing. Here I refer to more than the direct observation of a person in action; I refer to a process of eliciting an anamnesis. Too many counselors rely on biographical questionnaires. Others conduct a diagnostic interview as if it were an orally administered questionnaire. A good diagnostic interview requires a combination of sophistication, sensitivity, and tact, seasoned with hard-headed directness.[1] The interviewer must be able to make clear the relevance of his questions to the client's reasons for consulting him, and to time his interventions to fit into the flow of the client's communications. Thus,

[1]Sullivan's discussion (1954) of the psychiatric interview is a good example.

questions about parents come at a time when the client is speaking of issues that naturally bring them to mind, even though he may not yet have spoken to them. Thus, the order of questions is dictated by the client rather than by the author of a questionnaire, and many questions are not asked at all because the client provides spontaneous answers. In addition, the flow of communication and observation stimulates half-formed understanding, which gives rise to questions that no standardized set could have included. The skill to conduct such an interview, it should be evident, must be founded on considerable sophistication regarding human personality and must be built up gradually through directed experiences.

SUPERVISION

Counseling is a set of activities that cannot be learned from books alone. It requires practice accompanied by effective supervision. Effective supervision, of course, requires that the supervisor be an experienced clinician, and that he and the student be willing to spend at least two hours a week in an intensive examination of the student's work with clients. This will be in addition to the time the student may spend in reviewing and cogitating over his interview and the time the supervisor may spend in reviewing records or listening to tape recordings of interviews. Effective supervision helps the student translate his book learning into a meaningful relationship. It should also help him take a critical look at the concepts and recommended procedures stimulated by the feedback of his own experience. Finally, and most importantly, it should sensitize him to the impact of his own attitudes, his fears, his tender spots, his rigidities, upon his working relationship with his clients. Eckstein and Wallerstein (1958) have called attention to the likelihood (they treat it as a certainty) that the student's working relationship with his supervisor will mirror his relationship with his client. They expect, and illustrate with instances, that the student, in seeking the supervisor's help, will play out exactly the resistances that he finds most troublesome in his own clients. Despite this emphasis, they do not propose that supervision become a form of personal therapy for the counselor in training, but simply a means for sensitizing him to his personal needs and impact, with expectation that he will then take them into account, so that they do not limit his counseling effectiveness, or, failing that, either get personal therapy or limit his counseling practice.

Though concern with the counselor's characteristic patterns of feeling and acting as a source of his difficulties in mastering counseling is paramount, the supervisor should not lose sight of inexperience as an initial source of difficulty. Much attention should be given to helping the student bring about a fuller integration between his intellectual mastery of basic concepts and procedures and his translation of these into action. He must be aided to rediscover such process concepts as transference, resistance, insight, and self-discovery, and such personality concepts as projection or identity formation, in his living experience with his clients. As both a didactic teacher and a supervisor, I have always been chastened and enlightened by the expression of dawning comprehension accompanied by the exclamation, "So that is what is meant by _____!" when I have tested whether the student was aware of the concept being illustrated by his own clinical experience. Because our working concepts and procedures are still in such a crude state, supervision can serve the very important purpose, for supervisor and student alike, of providing a continuing confrontation of the closeness of fit between theory and direct observation. The supervisory relationship ought to be an important spawning ground for significant clinical research. Altucher (1967) has given us some good discussions of how to maintain a balance of concern between the intellectual and the emotional issues in clinical supervision.

REFERENCES

Altucher, N. Constructive use of the supervisory relationship. *Journal of Counseling Psychology,* 1967, **14**, 165–170.

American Psychological Association, Division of Counseling and Guidance, Committee on Counselor Training. The practicum training of counseling psychologists. *American Psychologist,* 1952, 7, 182–188. (a)

American Psychological Association, Division of Counseling and Guidance, Committee on Counselor Training. Recommended standards for training psychologists at the doctoral level. *American Psychologist,* 1952, 7, 175–181. (b)

Bordin, E. S. (Ed.) *Training of psychological counselors.* Ann Arbor: University of Michigan, 1951.

Bordin, E. S. Curiosity, compassion, and doubt: The dilemma of the psychologist. *American Psychologist,* 1966, **21**, 116–121.

Ekstein, R., & Wallerstein, R. S. *The teaching and learning of psychotherapy.* New York: Basic Books, 1958.

Kris, E. *Psychoanalytic explorations in art.* New York: International Universities Press, 1952.

Rioch, M. J., Elkes, C., Flint, A. A., Udansky, B. S., Newman, R. G., & Silber, E. National Institute of Mental Health pilot study in training mental health counselors. *American Journal of Orthopsychiatry,* 1963, **33**, 678–689.

Sullivan, H. S. *The psychiatric interview.* New York: Norton, 1954.

Thompson, A. S., & Super, D. E. (Eds.) *The professional preparation of counseling psychologists: Report of the 1964 Greyston conference.* New York: Teachers College Press, 1964.

Truax, C. B., & Carkhuff, R. R. *Toward effective counseling and psychotherapy: Training and practice.* Chicago: Aldine, 1967.

Wrenn, C. G. *The counselor in a changing world.* Washington, D.C.: American Personnel and Guidance Association, 1962.

Counseling

Chris D. Kehas

Manchester, New Hampshire, Public Schools

PRESENT STATUS

The present status of counseling-in-education—that is, counseling as a process of schooling—can be described quite succinctly. Counseling is not an established function of schooling, and consequently there is wide disagreement regarding its role. Reactions to this fact take different forms. There is inordinately more concern on the part of interested professional organizations (such as the American School Counselor Association), schools of education, universities, *and* practitioners with *role establishment* and support than with functions. It is almost a case of asserting that we will clarify our functions *after* we establish our place and get it supported. Further, there appears to be far more concern with the duties of the office than with the cultivation of "skills" necessary to effective performance in the office, or with evaluation of performance—regardless of duties—and these are vastly different concerns. For example, more resources are spent in developing opportunities for "personal counseling" than in investigating the skills whereby change is facilitated in any counseling encounter; that is, with examining the personal aspects of so-called educational and vocational counseling. The activities engaged in by counselors are rarely related by either practitioners or professors into a substantive and conceptual pattern, but remain somewhat isolated activities linked by intention rather than process.

At present the training of counselors for schools is preparation for a somewhat tenuously established position—one that exists until budget cuts force priorities, thus revealing the underlying assumptive structure and the fragility of the entire enterprise. School-counselors are being trained for a function that has yet to be deemed essential to and integrated into the processes of schooling, and to be sanctioned by many school administrators and their communities. Contemporary counseling in schools may well be described as a practice in need of definition, purpose, and perspective.

THE FUNCTION OF COUNSELING IN SCHOOLING

Though the framework of the counseling function has been elaborated elsewhere (see Kehas, 1968, 1970), a word about my view on the subject may be in order. Recognizing that schooling is now primarily and almost exclusively concerned with instruction, I have argued that it ought to be deliberately and systematically concerned with the development of students as persons, that provision ought to be made within the processes of schooling for a student to examine his own experience and the self he is creating. Guidance would have the unique function of providing opportunity and assistance for a student to *develop intelligence about his self.* Such a posture would foster the development of coherence in the school's varied activities and involvements—indeed, decisions—pertaining to the personal dimensions of a student's life, such as college or work, peer relations, and so on ad infinitum. Teaching and guidance in this view would become complementary functions.

Acceptance of this position would require no less than a redefinition of what is basic to schooling. One consequence of acceptance is that a distinction becomes necessary between counselors working *in education* and counselors working *as educators.* Unlike school psychologists, school social workers, speech and hearing specialists, and other guidance specialists, the school-counselor has desired a continuing involvement with *each* student, a relationship heretofore enjoyed only by the teacher, who until recently has been quite unwilling to share it. A further consequence is that the relationship of the student with the counselor becomes more of an *intraview* than an interview. The personal dimensions of a student's life—his phenomenological life space —become a legitimate concern when the student desires it, not just when something is amiss with his academic learning: that is, there should be systematic and continuous concern with the development of intelligence about self. Let me hasten to add that there is as yet little public (or even professional) sanction nationally for this new posture, and perhaps appropriately so at this stage of development of the behavioral sciences. But it is a possible position, which has merit and deserves consideration.

The larger question, "Should counseling develop into a basic function of schooling?" and its corollary, "Can it?" remain just that at the moment— questions. Yet since training does go on, we shall turn to a consideration of the training of counselors for schools.

TRAINING PRACTICES

What is known about the training practices of counselors for educational environments, especially as regards the experiential components? There are two main sources in the literature, the triennial issue of the *Review of Educational Research* and the *Annual Review of Psychology*. We find that both the amount and quality of the research are seen as being somewhat limited. The findings will be reviewed briefly.

Stoughton (1957) found that much of the literature consisted of status studies and descriptive reports, concluding that there is much to be done in the development of adequate programs.

Hill and Green (1960) found the research disappointingly limited in scope and intensity. They also found that status studies predominate and that there was no basic longitudinal research on the selection, education, and subsequent effectiveness of school-counselors; they wondered if the shortage of counselors would prompt better research and more publication. Three years later, however, Stripling and Lister (1963) reported no significant increase in publications or research. Stripling and Lister also found that most work investigating the status of preparatory programs was conducted through questionnaire surveys; they reported that few counselor-education programs included any systematic evaluation of behavior changes in candidates. In 1966, Cash and Munger judged the methodology as being more sophisticated and meaningful, and attributed that situation to the fact that more resident counseling students had been available than in previous years. The NDEA Institutes, which accounted for large numbers of full-time counseling students, also made subjects more available for research purposes. However, Cash and Munger also reported "little basic or empirical research regarding supervision of practicum, school internship, or the supervisor role." [p. 258]

Most recently, Whiteley (1969), noting that Hill and Green some ten years earlier had not found any "major" longitudinal study of selection, training, and evaluation, concluded that their finding remains true today. Whiteley lamented the current stage of professional development in counseling, suggesting that it is one reason for the lack of good evaluation.

The two most recent reviews in the *Annual Review* yield very little with regard to research on training practices. Brayfield (1963) dealt with training only in passing. Patterson (1966) cited the preparation of counselors at the subdoctoral level as a major concern. He discussed the controversy regarding the nature of supervision of the student in the practicum, the newly developing use of videotape, changes in attitudes occurring as a result of instruction, and selection procedures.

It is not difficult to conclude that reported research on the training of school-counselors has been and remains quite minimal. In fairness it must be added that we do know informally, though perhaps not systematically, that the staffs of some counselor-education programs are dealing with these very problems most intensively and in a continuing fashion.

We may speculate a moment on why this is the situation. One contributing factor is that training is generally conceived of and acted on as a realm of application of what is known rather than as a realm of inquiry—i.e. of developing the known. Though somewhat artificial, this distinction prevails no less in other fields of practitioner preparation, such as medicine, law, social work, and teaching, than it does in counseling. A second contributing factor is that those involved in practicum preparation programs are not typically disposed to research. They become involved with research primarily through their advising of degree candidates, and in this regard often see their mission as one of facilitating completion of degree requirements rather than encouraging important inquiry. Third, and perhaps most important, there is a general apathy regarding educational research, which is not known for either its power or its influence on practice—that is, schooling is not a research-based practice.

Such speculation may or may not be helpful in understanding the current state. Since so little is known, we turn our attention to the heart of the preparation program, the practicum. We approach the practicum primarily from the viewpoint of our own experiences.

THE PRACTICUM

There is considerable evidence that the practicum is the most valued aspect of counselor preparation (e.g., Arnold & Hummel, 1958; Baker, 1959; Munger, Brown, & Needham, 1964). Paradoxically, it is not yet a requirement for licensing and certification in many states. The supervised practice experience, to be maximally effective, must take place in the setting of intended practice. For the school-counselor trainee, the practicum ought to be arranged in a school—especially so if he has not had any actual teaching experience. If he has been a teacher, the practicum should not be arranged or even allowed in his own school, for he will not have the freedom necessary to begin a new role. The schools—or, in general, the work sites—are essential for the complete training of a counselor; a university cannot go it alone any more than a medical school would attempt medical training without a teaching-hospital affiliation. The cooperation and collaboration of school and university is essential to the preparation of educational practitioners. Such relationships, however, have been developed only for the teacher, and only "practice teaching" is an acknowledged responsibility of schools. The situation is not yet as well established in the training of school-counselors and other guidance specialists.

There are some problems peculiar to making arrangements for "practice counseling," which may contribute to the current state. Though my suggestions are in a sense deceptively simple, we will discuss the process of making arrangements in order to highlight the necessary yet often "disturbing" components.

Arrangements are made with a school to secure the commitment of one of its staff members, who is designated as host counselor. The host counselor is interviewed to assess his promise as a supervisor and as a model for the trainee. Though oftentimes a principal—or a director of guidance or head counselor —offers to serve in that capacity, it is rarely a good arrangement. They are simply too busy with administrative demands to be able to give continuous and programmatic attention to the progress of the trainee. The host counselor must orient the trainee to the policies, procedures, and practices of the host school. The trainee should serve a minimum of two days a week in the school, and the host counselor must see to it that the trainee is kept unencumbered by "full-time job" expectations.

One of the first problems the host counselor faces is making it possible for his trainee to gain access to counselees. This is not as simple as practice teaching, where one works with classroom groups with increasing degrees of responsibility until finally taking over. It is a difficult and sensitive procedure to arrange for students to be assigned to a trainee, although these problems are lessened somewhat if the student is told that he will have more opportunity to see this counselor trainee than his regular counselor, whose time is quite limited because of his large "caseload." The trainee should receive students from all members of the staff, and he should have an opportunity to see "all kinds and types of kids." Especially should he be protected from the situation where the regular counselors turn over only their "hard-to-reach," "I've done all I can with him; let's see what you can do," students. Our expectations are that the counselor-trainee, to the extent possible and appropriate, will be given the opportunity to counsel with individual students. In the beginning he should not be seeing more than five or six different students each day; there should be variety and diversity in the age, sex, maturity, and concerns of the students he counsels; he should see one or two students over a period of time, on a continuing basis; and privacy during the interviews should be insured. Though *counseling with individuals should receive major emphasis,* the counselor-trainee will be expected to participate in a wide range of guidance activities, including some group counseling wherever possible and appropriate.

Agreement should be reached with the school authorities about allowing the trainee to secure audiotape recordings (or videotape, if possible) of some of his interviews and group sessions, which can be critiqued by his host counselor and his university supervisor. In this regard, it might be added that there is no such thing as a "good" or "bad" interview, student feeling to the contrary. Every interview can be learned from and has value. The point is to systematically and intensively explore all the behavior of the trainee and all his interactions with his counselees.

In addition to counseling with individuals, the trainee must be given an opportunity to assist in the development of ways (since these have not been established) of working with teachers on different approaches to instruction and to assessing classroom climates, and of working with administrators in an examination of the constraints placed upon the personal development of students by the organization, structure, and operations of the enterprise. These last two activities could well prove to be the mainsprings of what is termed developmental guidance, as distinguished from remedial emphases. For it is still true today, protestations notwithstanding, that the twin processes of instruction and guidance remain separate programs in schools, and that the interrelationships and interrelatedness between these processes are alarmingly minimal.

The key to the success of the practicum is supervision. Immediate supervision has to come from the host counselor since he clearly would know more and best about the students and the particular school context than anyone else involved. The trainee should meet with his host counselor continuously to discuss his interviews and his experiences in the school. At the university, the trainee will participate in a weekly seminar with his fellow trainees and will also receive some individual supervision at least weekly.

TRAINING AND SCHOOL PRACTICE

It must be openly acknowledged that the practicum training discussed above, like most contemporary training programs, has only a minimal relationship to current practice. For what most school-counselors now do, they need little graduate work or specialized training; on-the-job training would more than suffice. Counseling in schools is not considered to be separate from instruction, but rather is regarded as supportive of the administrative aspects of the instructional process. This fact helps to explain why teachers are preferred by administrators for these positions and why easy access to these positions is maintained for teachers; in many states provisional certification is obtainable by teachers with the satisfaction of very minimal requirements. If the function of counseling is as described, it also helps to explain the felt irrelevance of graduate courses, which is experienced by many students.

In many schools where we have arranged practicums (especially so in southern California), the trainees have been the envy of the regular staffs because they have been protected from administrative and clerical duties and allowed to focus on counseling. Many regular staff members express regret at not having undergone a similar training experience. At the same time they admonish the trainees to "enjoy this privileged status while they can," since they will be engulfed by other demands when they assume a full-time position. Small wonder that our graduates have often been disenchanted with the opportunities offered by regular school employment, not because they were overwhelmed by large caseloads, but because of the myriad of other duties ascribed to the position of school-counselor, which are unrelated to basic guidance work or to their basic professional preparation.

Who then decides the duties of a counselor? It is clear that the building principal has much to say in this regard (e.g., Liddle & Kroll, 1969; Herr & Cramer, 1965). Despite formal administrative arrangements and despite the development of assistant superintendencies related to the various functions, such as pupil personnel services, the building principal still retains direct and unencumbered access to the superintendent. Evidence indicates that the principal usually has little question about the role and function of "his" counseling staff, and his ideas are often quite divergent from those held by counselor-educators. Further, the differences among principals who have some training and experience in guidance positions are quite minimal (Hart & Prince, 1970).

Thus, the question of maximizing the relationship of graduate training to school practice is a bit more complex than "exposing the principal to a guidance point of view." The development of the counseling function is inextricably related to the organization, structure, and processes of schooling, and any change in it has implications for the whole.

SUMMARY

This essay began with a consideration of the present status of counseling-in-education and moved to a description of a proposed redirection of the function of counseling in schooling. Research on training practices was examined, and attention was then directed to the practicum experience. Finally, the relationship between graduate training and actual practice was examined.

REFERENCES

Arnold, D. L., & Hummel, D. L. Follow-up of graduates of the counselor training program at Kent State University. Kent, Ohio: Kent State University, 1958. (Mimeo.)

Baker, R. L. Differences between guidance workers and teachers in knowledge of human behavior. *15th Yearbook, National Council on Measurements Used in Education,* 1959, 71–79.

Brayfield, A. H. Counseling psychology. *Annual Review of Psychology,* 1963, **14**, 319–350.

Cash, W. L., Jr., & Munger, P. F. Counselors and their preparation. *Review of Educational Research,* 1966, **36**, 256–263.

Hart, D. H., & Prince, D. J. Role conflict for school counselors: Training versus job demands. *Personnel and Guidance Journal,* 1970, **48**, 374–380.

Herr, E. L., & Cramer, S. H. Counselor role determinants as perceived by counselor-educators and school counselors. *Counselor Education and Supervision,* 1965, **5**, 3–8.

Hill, G. E., & Green, D. A. The selection, preparation, and professionalization of guidance and personnel workers. *Review of Educational Research,* 1960, **30**, 115–130.

Kehas, C. D. Guidance-in-education: An examination of the interplay between definition and structure. In V. F. Calia & B. Wall (Eds.), *Pupil personnel administration: New perspectives and foundations.* Springfield, Ill.: Charles C Thomas, 1968.

Kehas, C. D. Toward a redefinition of education: A new framework for counseling in education. In S. C. Stone & B. Shertzer (Eds.), *Introduction to guidance: Selected readings.* Boston: Houghton Mifflin, 1970.

Liddle, G. P., & Kroll, A. M. *Pupil services in Massachusetts schools.* Boston: Massachusetts Advisory Council on Education, 1969.

Munger, P. F., Brown, D. F., & Needham, J. T. NDEA Institute participants two years later. *Personnel and Guidance Journal,* 1964, **42**, 987–990.

Patterson, C. H. Counseling. *Annual Review of Psychology,* 1966, **17**, 79–110.

Sorenson, G., & Kagan, D. Conflicts between doctoral candidates and their sponsors: A contrast in expectations. *Journal of Higher Education,* 1967, **38**, 17–24.

Stoughton, R. W. The preparation of counselors and personnel workers. *Review of Educational Research,* 1957, **27**, 174–185.

Stripling, R. O., & Lister, J. L. Selection, preparation, and professionalization of specialists. *Review of Educational Research,* 1963, **33**, 171–178.

Whiteley, J. M. Counselor education. *Review of Educational Research,* 1969, **39**, 173–188.

Training for the Applied Psychologist in a University Psychological Services Center

Paul T. King and Janet P. Wollersheim

University of Missouri

Like all professions, psychology is increasingly becoming a field of subspecialities. Bordin's essay in this volume presents coverage of the field of counseling psychology in considerable breadth. The present essay delimits the area of coverage to that of the Ph.D.-level applied psychologist working within the setting of a university psychological services (counseling) center. As Bordin notes: "The mainstream of counseling has from the beginning been located within educational systems." Thus, discussion in some depth of the role and training of the psychologist in such a setting can be expected to highlight many of the issues involved in the training of counseling psychologists.

To discuss the training of such psychologists in some detail, it will first be necessary to make some general comments concerning the changing roles and functions of the psychologist in a counseling center. Next, the training of the psychologist will be viewed both from the academic and from the experiential perspective. Then will come the topic of supervision, followed by a more detailed analysis of appropriate role behaviors and expectations. Finally, some recommendations pertaining to training will be presented.

The writing of this essay in some ways recapitulated the struggles that are going on in the training of psychologists at the present time. The two authors are relatively far apart on the experiental-didactic training model discussed. We did our best to integrate our points of view, feeling that integration and compromise represent a higher-order adjustment than separation and division. To the extent that the reader is able to identify certain passages as emphasizing the didactic, the ideas more closely represent the junior author (Janet P. Wollersheim), while the passages highlighting the advantages of experiential methods more closely represent the thinking of the senior author (Paul T. King). Both authors agree that each kind of training has value. Also, in the sections discussing therapy and supervision the junior author is more strongly identified with the more direct, cognitive-behavioral approach, while the senior author's identification lies more with the less direct, affective, experiental approach. Again, both authors believe that each approach has merit; their divergence lies more with the relative merit of the two approaches and consequently the emphasis each should receive in training.

CHANGING ROLE OF THE PSYCHOLOGIST

The counseling psychologist has undergone quite a change in the past 30 years. He is not perceived as doing the same sorts of things he did in the early 1940s, and he also views himself differently. Prior to the Rogerian era, counseling was almost exclusively seen as a process between two individuals. The client often came to the counselor in a passive frame of mind, consulting with an expert, who he hoped had some answers. This is perhaps why Rogerian therapy caught on as well as it did. It reversed the old process of clients putting the responsibility for their improvement on the counselor.

Until recently, the mechanics of the counseling interview were well standardized. Clients came in for a 50-minute hour and talked to a counselor who most probably was warm, accepting, and nondirective in his interaction with the client. The atmosphere of the interview was generally one of quiet respect between counselor and client. The atmosphere of counseling centers was only slightly removed from that of a doctor's office, which was one of observable professionalism.

The problems that clients brought with them most often pertained to palpable anxiety over such things as lack of success, sexual impulses, and uncertainty about control of hostile impulses. The counselor tended to deal with repressed material, and fostered insight either by interpreting to the client the nature of his problems, or by allowing him to come on such insights himself. Almost all counseling was done within the interview room, and it was unthinkable to consider doing it anywhere else.

Today, counseling wears new faces. One-to-one counseling, although still important in most counseling centers, is giving ground to group processes, which come under many labels: sensitivity groups, microlabs, encounter groups, confrontation groups, and so on. Traditional psychotherapy and insight methods are seen less frequently, and behavioral-modification approaches are increasingly more common.

At the same time that modern theologians have been insinuating that God is dead, and that there has been a progressive deemphasizing of man's soul, there has been a corresponding decrease in the attention paid to basic personality theories that purport to explain the prime motivating impulses of mankind.

Students are not as concerned with the basic "essence" of man, which exists inside his skin, and with what man thinks and feels. Rather, they focus their attention outward onto what man does, and how he behaves. This state of affairs has resulted in a reversal of applied psychology's former trend of delving into the unconscious mind and exploring hidden feelings.

Students now come to counseling centers with a host of problems radically different from those of students in the 1940s and 1950s. Nowadays, students are concerned with problems of personal values and who they are as persons. Many are tired of the system or social structure, which is producing crisis children by the millions, a commercialism that is out of touch with their needs, and an ecological system that seems to be making the planet unfit for human habitation. Guilt and anxiety are less noticeable now than indications of confusion, hollowness of values, and an aimlessness in the overall business of living.

The counseling psychologist today, more than at any time before, must be a generalist in orientation rather than the possessor of a narrow set of professional skills. Present-day centers are "chock-full" of counseling-related activities, such as educational-skill laboratories, group and dialogue sessions, and workshops for academic advisers, all of which give a distinct cast of busyness and activity to the average counseling center. Many centers are heavily involved in internship training programs; in addition, practicum experience for academic credit also is being offered to graduate students in the field. The concept of a multipurpose center has been gradually developed, and this has done much to displace the atmosphere of remote professionalism to which we alluded previously.

Many students now come in under the influence of drugs, or are worried about how to break the drug habit. Psychologists must know how to deal with such problems. Students seem to be looking for something to give meaning to life, and for an answer to the complexity of the current pace of living. The flood of stimuli impinging on students is driving many of them to make an effort to simplify their environment, and to find something to make life less intricate. Under this sort of relentless pressure, students may turn to cults or escapisms for asylum. Traditional methods of psychotherapy may be ineffective here.

The contemporary psychologist is spending more time in doing institutional research as an essential part of his professional duties. Demographic studies on various student populations, or studies on perceptions of various agencies within the university, are now within his bailiwick. Centers are involved in studying themselves, asking questions relevant to the planning of future operations, or to publicizing what they do. Center personnel are interested in general questions related to student perceptions of offered services, or to the image students have of the center. For example: Are females more likely than males to bring problems to the center? Do students feel that their problems are apt to be handled confidentially? Do students who have already been counseled at the center feel different than noncounseled students about taking problems there? What type of professional persons do students expect to encounter at a center: psychiatrist, counselor, counseling psychologist, clinical psychologist? Knowledge about such questions helps centers educate their clientele to use their services more effectively.

We are not comfortable about predicting what the clients of the future will be like. It seems likely that they will be saddled with a greater feeling of responsibility for human suffering and misery than clients are now, for there is already a noticeable trend in that direction. The psychologist of the future will be dealing with problems based on social issues, as opposed to more individual worries. There will be a continuing concern with understanding personal values, and possibly much effort will be spent upon simplifying personal existence in an era when the individual is flooded with instant information from all over the world, and relentlessly bombarded by the electronic media with forecasts of disaster.

An unfinished piece of research on the values of college students by the senior author and his colleagues indicates that a large percentage of students, when asked about their main concerns, focus on issues such as war, hunger, environmental pollution, and the hypocrisy rampant in our social structure.

TWOFOLD TRAINING

Educational programs endeavoring to produce applied psychologists usually see their task as that of turning out those curious beings referred to as "scientist-professionals." Although the desirability and feasibility of such a training model is an issue that elicits much debate, a more appropriate model for the applied psychologist has been hard to come by. Furthermore, one might go so far as to suggest that, generally speaking, the scientist-professional model has not failed our educational and training programs, but, rather, these programs have failed the model. Just as the concepts of balance and temperance are important in helping clients maintain stability in their lives and achieve their goals, so too these concepts are important for programs that endeavor to train applied psychologists. More often than not, a training program lacks quality because it is lopsided, stressing one aspect of training to the neglect and deemphasis of the other aspect. A good training program—one that produces applied psychologists who are maximally effective and efficient—must provide an education that helps students to appreciate their field as both a science, committed to research concerning behavior, and a profession, which responds seriously to its responsibility for the application of scientific knowledge to the solution of human problems.

Admittedly, this is not an easy task, but promoting a balanced perspective in education, like all desirable objectives, requires effort. Without a proper balance between the applied psychologist's scientific education and professional training, one runs the risk of producing either the soft-hearted, but equally soft-headed, psychologist, who operates under the fallacious assumption that the only factors involved in good professional service are a love of mankind and good intentions, or the hard-headed, but snobbish and myopic, psychologist, who worships at the altar of science (spelled with a capital *S*), while viewing his main professional responsibility in the social realm as that of sneering at the inefficiency of applied methods, and berating his colleagues who take seriously the social responsibilities of their profession.

To work, the scientist-professional educational model must be flexible. Flexibility means that the student, having satisfied basic standards by completing a core curriculum of courses and applied experience, is allowed considerable diversity in the program. Some may concentrate on research while others focus on advanced skill in the area of application. Most likely, this model will produce some true scientist-professionals, that is, psychologists whose major activities involve research and professional service. However, the greater number of psychologists emerging from this program will be more highly identified with one or the other of the dual roles of research and service. We do not believe this state of affairs to be undesirable, because the pure researcher, having completed basic training in professional application of psychological knowledge, will be aware of significant research problems and less prone to "hide his head in the sand" regarding relevant clinical variables. Likewise, the psychologist who focuses his major efforts in the area of professional service will have a healthy respect for the limitations of psychological knowledge, and, by being a good consumer of research, he will hopefully make a contribution in the upgrading of techniques of application.

Let us now turn to the didactic, or more traditionally academic, side of the applied psychologist's education. Here it is proposed that the most desirable objective is to produce a psychologist first and a specialist second. Accordingly, we would expect the core curriculum to include courses in basic psychology, such as might be offered by proseminars, or a series of courses covering such areas as learning, social and developmental psychology, personality, and the like. The attempt here would be to educate the student broadly in the field of psychology. Study of statistics and research design would also be included, as would the experience of doing a research dissertation. Courses in occupational and educational information, personal adjustment, assessment, counseling, and behavior change would give the student depth in his area of specialty. Then, too, a good program would allow students a number of electives. A basic program along the lines delineated would provide breadth, depth, and a degree of personal freedom for the student and his adviser to tailor the program to particular needs and interests. Some students feel more comfortable with formalized, didactic instruction, while others prefer the unstructured, teaching approach. We now look at some of these considerations.

There are several clear-cut levels of training that every psychology-degree candidate must master. Some of these levels have traditionally been taught in a didactic manner, while others have employed a more experiential technique. We are beginning to find in psychological training what educational researchers have known for a long time—that some students learn better under didactic methods, and others fare better with experiential training. The same is true of practicum teachers. It is almost impossible for some teachers to adopt experiential techniques and be effective with them in their interaction with their students.

This raises the question whether all counseling is not more experiential in nature than didactic, and many applied psychologists would answer that negatively. They say that present trainees are really not mastering the "hardware" of the profession sufficiently to do a good job with a client. They would contend that students are not being taught, for example, the ability to discriminate a well-constructed test from a poor one, or the ability to decide which test will answer the clients' questions most effectively, and are not learning some of the more traditional methods of psychotherapy. The "nitty-gritty," factual, material of the training process is best taught by the didactic process, its proponents say. This point of view holds that basic concepts and skills in counseling must be made a part of the counselor's armamentarium early in his training, and that it is delinquent professional behavior to simply try anything that works on the client. Counseling is perceived as basically a learning process, as is learning how to counsel, so it makes sense to those who hold this position that the methods which have been effective in other basic learning situations should be applied to practicum teaching.

Traditionally, most of the experiential training has been carried on in internship training programs run by counseling centers, but many practicum and prepracticum classes have begun to have this emphasis.

The avowed purpose of practicum is to enable the student to combine his knowledge of theory with the actual practice of counseling. Practicum may have two or three levels: prepracticum, beginning practicum, and advanced practicum. Typically, prepracticum is the time when students are instructed further in the selection and interpretation of tests, observe seasoned counselors doing counseling, role-play with simulated clients, and observe videotapes of themselves and other class-members in action. Beginning practicum initiates counselors into the real counseling process, under close supervision of a senior practicum supervisor. Clients are carefully screened, and are usually educational-vocational in nature. In the advanced practicum, clients with more difficult problems are worked with, and the nature of the supervision tends to be more self-exploratory for the student, with less structure evident in the supervisory relationship. Laboratory experiences may accompany the lecture in the more formal course work, such as a lab section involving the administration of intelligence tests in a course in the theory of intelligence. Field experiences are designed for those students who come to a program at an advanced level but whose work experience has been judged inadequate or inappropriate. In the case of lab experiences and field training, experiential training has not been focused upon to the extent that it has in the more central practicum sequence.

As we mentioned above, implicit in the sequence of practicums is the notion that certain skills and capabilities must be developed in the student before he is loosed on the client. This makes for a situation in which students go through a considerable amount of course work before they ever see a client, with the possibility that the ultimate sensitivity and awareness of counselors may be partially closed off by the prior conceptualizing forced on them by their teachers and readings.

If cognitive learning is the goal of certain levels of practicum, then perhaps didactic training is the method of choice, but even then, perhaps not for everybody. If empathy is a critical variable in counseling, and if the ultimate goal for each psychologist is to learn how to utilize feelings in himself and in his client in a constructive way, an experiential method that promotes the most expanded use of the counselor as a person and as an instrument of change may be called for. Johnston and Gysbers (1966) found that supervisors actually preferred a democratic, unstructured interaction with the students. On the other hand, students did not want the supervisor to act as if he were doing therapy with them (Miller & Oetting, 1966).

Experiential training attempts to accomplish specific things with the student, although the paths to these goals are not as neatly marked as in the case with more formal instruction. For example, a student undergoing experiential training in practicum would experience more of a peer relationship with his supervisor, and the supervisor would ordinarily attempt to be as democratic as possible in his relationship with the student. The atmosphere during the supervisory session would be therapeutic-like, but would fall short of the actual therapeutic process. The supervisor would help the trainee learn how to separate his own conflicts from those of the client, and to see the similarity in his relationships with his supervisor and with his clients, revealing a habitual way of being with people in serious settings. The supervisor would not make an effort to get the student to adopt a certain style of counseling, but would expect this to grow and develop in a unique and personal way, as the student has more experience with clients. It is anticipated that the student will appreciate his own stimulus value as a counselor and become attuned to those things in himself that expedite the greatest personal growth in the client, as well as those things that prohibit it.

The value of experiential training has an inherently strong pull with certain types of psychologists, and they believe it is clearly the best kind of training. However, the evidence about its superiority is cloudy. A colleague of the authors, Parry (1969), found that students trained with the experiential method did not raise the level of therapeutic conditions to a significant degree as determined by the research of Truax and Carkhuff (1967).

A note for the integration of didactic and experiential methods was heard from the research of Gysbers and Johnston (1964), which found that students undergoing practicum experience initially preferred structured help from the supervisor, but wanted increasing freedom and less structure during the latter stages of training. Silverman (1969) discovered that clients tend to feel emotionally closer to counselors who have received experiential training. Blane's research (1968) revealed that supportive supervision produced greater empathy in the counselor, apparently because of his increased feelings of security in the interview. Students have rated the most significant things in their supervisors to be concreteness, personal support by him, and constructive criticism (Miller & Oetting, 1966). Jan Birk at the University of Missouri is presently researching the effect on the practicum student when his training expectations are fulfilled—that is, when he expects didactic training in counseling and receives it, as compared with those who expect didactic and receive experiential training. Other combinations in this same vein are also being investigated. Perhaps one's desires and expectations are crucial variables in determining how the training is perceived.

SUPERVISION

It can be confusing to counselors in training when their supervisor adopts what seems to be a frankly therapeutic attitude with them; many students are frightened by this approach and resent it. The confusion for the students arises because the supervisor is not sure of his supervisory goals, and is uncertain of the distinctions between therapy and supervision.

Therapy, depending on the type, will often be an effort on the part of both therapist and client to work through general problems, making use of self-understanding, eliciting feelings and insights, and promoting more adjustive behavior. The relationship is not ordinarily seen as having a specific time for termination. The client is allowed to develop strong personal feelings; these may even be fostered by the therapist, and the focus of the dyad is almost exclusively on the concerns, emotions, and behaviors of the person in therapy. The therapist will usually show a willingness to accept client-chosen goals and will give the client considerable freedom in choosing topics of discussion. There may or may not be instructional or pedagogical material in the interview.

Experiential supervision is often perceived as being closer to therapy than didactic supervision. However, experiential supervision still differs from therapy in many ways. Supervision will most often be a triadic relationship rather than dyadic. The supervisor not only must observe the productions of the client, but must also focus on the responses of the counseling student to them. This immediately makes things more complex. Much of supervision involves the supervisor's getting the student to understand how his responses are affecting the general direction and attitude of the client, making the student aware of his impact as a counselor.

Supervisors are often eager to serve as models for their supervisees, but most are unwilling for the students to become personally attached to themselves, as in the development of strong positive or negative transference. Most supervisors think such feelings cannot be worked through in the less intense supervisory relationship. Modeling usually takes the form of the supervisors demonstrating how certain things are done, or how particular aspects of a counseling situation are handled. The student, usually in a mildly anxious state anyway because of the newness and threat inherent in this situation, will tend to copy the competence he sees in the supervisor, and will feel better because of having some guidelines for action. Supervisors have the responsibility of showing students how to listen to the feelings of the client as well as to their own feelings. This ability to listen on dual channels is hard for some students to achieve, especially when the client is talking about material that is threatening to the student counselor, as it produces regression and avoidance behavior in the student. Teaching the student how to maintain an integrated ego position while doing such dual listening will be the goal of many supervisors.

Supervisors are perhaps more free to bring up topics for discussion in supervision than they would be in a counseling situation, and strong emotional feelings on the part of the student, if they are persistent, would not generally be dealt with in the supervisory session (unlike therapy), but the student would be referred to another psychologist for more intensive intervention. The bringing up of instructional material is obviously not rare in supervision.

One of the trouble spots in the supervisory situation is the student's knowledge that he is being evaluated, and that he will be given a rating or assigned a grade on the basis of his performance. This understandably creates tension in both individuals (supervisor and student) and should be talked about at the outset. It is upsetting to students, who cannot help being aware that the supervisor, in spite of his acceptance and warmth, still must be a critical observer of what the student does.

The supervisor has the responsibility, during the interaction, of creating an atmosphere in which the student feels reasonably comfortable and emotionally free enough to talk about the aspects of the counseling relationship that are giving him trouble. Often, in their effort to be kind and to promote a democratic atmosphere within the supervisory session, supervisors are reluctant to provide the feedback and criticism that is needed for their supervisees' development. Counselors seem to find it particularly difficult to allow anything to arise within the supervision hour that implies negative feelings, evaluation, or disagreement. This is perhaps a carry-over from their normal approach to the therapy or counseling hour. Some counseling supervisors find it comfortable to structure at the outset that supervision is different from the therapy process, although acknowledging that there are similarities. Then, pointing out some of the ways in which the supervisor will work with the supervisee, and mentioning some of the things he will not be doing, tend to reduce tension and eliminate uncertainty for the supervisee.

Ideally, the supervision of the counselor should fit his individual needs. For example, a counselor who works almost exclusively in the cognitive domain should have the opportunity under supervision to use his affective life in his interaction with his clients. Or the counselor who is on good terms with his own hostility, but is unable to express affection for others, might be urged by his supervisor to actualize this part of himself. Supervisors quite often will take the approach of explaining to the counselor the effect his behavior has on the client. This does not mean saying to the student-counselor, "Stop that behavior!", but allowing him to make a judgment whether he wishes to elicit such feelings and behavior in the client.

Supervisors run into the particularly unpleasant problem of having to decide whether a counselor-in-training has a personality and manner of relating to people that will allow him to be an effective counselor. Often a practicum student will have the intelligence to make satisfactory grades in his course work, but is unable to offer constructive help in the counseling situation because of a character trait, or because his interpersonal relationships are not conducive to growth and development in the client. This puts the supervisor in the unpleasant position of having to make a decision, on the basis of a subjective judgment, that will seriously affect the future of the student.

The variables that make an effective counselor have not been satisfactorily researched and postulated. Sometimes the student himself realizes that he is not "cut out" to be a counselor and eliminates himself from the field, but this does not always occur. Procedures that will help supervisors decide early which students should be counseled out of applied professional work include introducing practicum courses early in graduate training, obtaining representative samples of the student's performance over a broad range of counseling roles, and exposing the student to as many different supervisors as possible. The latter procedure insures that such a decision will be a consensus of several supervisors, and hence there is a greater chance for correcting erroneous subjective judgments.

ROLE BEHAVIORS AND EXPECTATIONS
FOR PSYCHOLOGISTS

The twofold training program outlined above should prepare the applied psychologist for the role behaviors and professional expectations he will encounter. It is doubtful whether anyone can precisely define the many specific facets that the psychologist's role will assume ten years from now. However, we may be confident that transfer of learning will be manifested by the products of an educational program that trains psychologists first and specialists second. The specific problems to which the applied psychologist addresses himself may change, but his methods of approach and operation, and his knowledge concerning models of human behavior (which he will presumably keep updated), should be applicable.

The applied psychologist working in a university counseling center will probably continue to make his greatest contributions in the areas of assessment and behavior change. Admittedly, what is assessed and what is seen as needing change will show considerable variation during our era of rapid social change. The psychologist's assessment role is expanding. While the evaluation and understanding of problems presented by the client in individual counseling continues to capture considerable attention, psychologists are becoming more and more involved in evaluating problems in a broader social context, such as black-white campus relationships, or student body–administrator conflict in such areas as housing. Psychologists are being asked to work with deans, housing officials, and student leaders in evaluating what aspects of college life engender conflict and frustration in the members of the college community.

In the realm of behavior change, individual and group counseling still occupy central positions, but here too the trend is toward expansion beyond exclusive concern with traditional problems and traditional sources of remediation. Walk-in counseling services are being set up in places where students congregate, such as student-union centers. Psychologists work with groups in dorms on problems such as developing effective study skills or overcoming shyness in social situations. On one campus known to the authors, students with certain emotional problems and students with good adjustment are living together in a wing of a dormitory, with psychologists helping members of both groups of students to interact in such a way that the experience becomes one that fosters emotional and social growth.

As the social climate of our campuses change, the psychologist is finding that client problems are changing. Subsequently, new ways to approach problems must be found. For example, on some campuses students themselves have set up so-called crash pads, which are devised to give aid to students with drug problems, who, for one reason or another, are reluctant to route their concerns through traditional channels. Consulting with these students regarding methods of helping these drug-users can contribute significantly in the area of treating problems.

More than ever before, psychologists are becoming involved in social-action movements. In such situations, issues of social values are involved, and two or more groups are usually in conflict because of different values on the issue. In such situations it seems important to remember that it is not necessarily appropriate for the psychologist, *acting in his role as psychological consultant,* to take a position on the values in question. More often, the psychological consultant can be of benefit by acting as a communication catalyst, with the objective of helping the opposing parties resolve their conflicts. Then, too, the applied psychologist's knowledge of human behavior and behavioral change can be used much more extensively in the area of problem prevention. In our concern with helping to remedy the problems at hand, it is too easy to forget the important contribution that can be made by working with college administrators on the specific issue of making the university community a health-engendering environment.

Psychologists are recognizing that we have too long committed the "organism error" (Peterson, 1968) of focusing our attention almost exclusively upon the individual, forgetting that behavior occurs in a larger social context, and that changes in this milieu can do much to promote better adjustment. In sum, then, it is the psychologist concerned with assessment and behavior change, not only as related to the individual and small groups, but also as related to the broader social environment, who is likely to make the greatest contributions to the university community.

RECOMMENDATIONS

In concluding this essay, the following recommendations are made regarding the education and training of applied psychologists:

1. The scientist-professional–training model seems to deserve better implementation in our educational programs. Applied psychologists should meet basic standards in the scientific-research aspects of psychology and in the applied-skill aspects. These basic minimal standards can be insured by requiring the student to complete a core curriculum. The remaining part of the program should allow considerable diversity in breadth and depth, recognizing that some students will be more the "research type" and others more the "professional type."

2. If the scientist-professional–training model is to be successful, it must be strongly supported by the academic department in which the educational program is offered. This involves more than merely offering the

scientist-professional program to students, and includes hiring faculty who can serve as models along the continuum of roles offered by the training model. Thus, some faculty members would be very invested in both research and applied functions, while others would concentrate their efforts much more in one activity than in others. Departmental support means that faculty members would receive recognition with corresponding raises in pay and rank, achievable not only by research, but by competent teaching and professional work as well.

3. Training psychologists first and specialists second means to train broadly, and is seemingly one way of insuring that such psychologists will be able to readily adapt their knowledge and skills to changing problems and role expectations.

4. While training in assessment and behavior change will continue to focus on individuals and groups, courses and practicum experiences should reflect the expansion of the terms *assessment* and *behavioral change* by including attention to the broader social context. Accordingly, concerns with community mental health and psychological ecology would be appropriate.

5. Students need more training in the role of consultation and in the function of prevention. Again, course work and practicum experiences should make some offerings along this line, rather than leaving these functions to be learned in a nebulous, on-the-job fashion, as is presently the case.

6. The study of personality theory in our graduate schools should be emphasized more than it has been recently. Students should be given more training and should become conversant with our more important theories of personality. This would enable them to conceptualize the personality dynamics of clients and to formulate their problems in a meaningful way. In turn, this emphasis would offset our present trend of overfocusing on peripheral behavior to the extent that counselors fail to adequately conceptualize their client's behavior.

7. We must look closely at the professional personnel who are training our counseling psychologists. Too many of our counseling educators immediately become engaged in training other counseling educators upon receiving their doctorates, without acquiring full-time applied experience in the field. Occasionally, the extent of their experience has been only an internship or a practicum sequence. Supervisors and teachers provide better models for student psychologists if they remain active in their profession by continuing to see clients, or if they have had a considerable amount of full-time applied experience. We should like to avoid the situation of counselor trainers, who do not see clients, training other counselor trainers, who do not see clients, ad infinitum.

REFERENCES

Blane, S. M. Immediate effect of supervisory experiences on counselor candidates. *Counselor Education and Supervision,* 1968, **8**, 39–44.

Gysbers, N. C., & Johnston, J. A. Expectations of a practicum supervisor's role. *Counselor Education and Supervision,* 1964, **12**, 68–74.

Johnston, J. A., & Gysbers, N. C. Practicum supervisory relationships: A majority report. *Counselor Education and Supervision,* 1966, **6**, 3–10.

Miller, C. D., & Oetting, E. R. Students react to supervision. *Counselor Education and Supervision,* 1966, **6**, 73–74.

Parry, K. A. The effect of two training approaches on counselor effectiveness. Unpublished doctoral dissertation, University of Missouri, 1969.

Peterson, D. R. *The clinical study of social behavior.* New York: Appleton-Century-Crofts, 1968.

Silverman, M. S. Effects of differential practicum experiences on client and counselor perceptions of initial interviews. Unpublished doctoral dissertation, Northwestern University, 1969.

Truax, C. B., and Carkhuff, R. R. Toward effective counseling and psychotherapy: Training and practice. Chicago: Aldine, 1967.

A Two-Year Program of Counselor Education

David Donald Malcolm

San Diego State University

The role of the school-counselor is not always clearly understood. Even though there seems to be agreement about the need for the counselor, there is confusion about how best to make use of his potential. To understand the rationale for the program of counselor education described in this essay, one must first understand the concept of counselor role implicit to it. We view school counseling as a career commitment, not as a temporary or occasional assignment. We believe that the needs of the school require the counselor to have a special professional expertise, and that this expertise cannot be acquired without extensive and intensive training.

Our approach to the problem of defining counselor role has been to search first for that which is unique in the contribution the counselor is expected to make to the school. His contribution can be unique only to the extent that he acquires special expertise, which makes it possible for him to do more than other educational personnel towards the achievement of certain important goals of the school. In this essay, we first point out where we think the unique contribution of the counselor is made, and then attempt to describe the professional expertise we think he needs to make this contribution. Next, we show where our thinking has led us regarding similarities and differences between elementary-school and secondary-school counseling. Finally, we describe briefly a four-semester instructional program designed in accordance with our particular set of beliefs.

THE COUNSELOR AND LEARNING EFFICIENCY

The work of the classroom teacher is thwarted daily by children who are too immature to assume responsibility for their own learning, or who are totally uninterested because they cannot see the relevance of school learnings to things

109

they value, or whose minds are so preoccupied with fears and anxieties and personal concerns as to preclude learning. Every teacher knows how little is accomplished by the child who comes to the classroom with his learning efficiency thus impaired. Every teacher welcomes help in this area. It is precisely here that the school turns to the counselor. Part of the counselor's task is to help every child to achieve greater learning efficiency so that he can benefit more fully from the offerings of the school.

There are at least three ways in which the skilled counselor can help children to come to the classroom more ready to benefit from the offerings of the school. First, the counselor can help each student achieve as smooth a transition as possible through the normal sequence of developmental stages from childhood toward adulthood. Only if the student successfully moves into maturer stages of development will he be able increasingly to assume responsibility for his own learning; not until he does can he take full advantage of the educational opportunities offered by the school. Second, the counselor can help each student with both short-term and long-term decision making and planning, thereby promoting the more efficient learning that results from goal-directed behavior. The counselor helps each student to invest significance into the learning activities in which he takes part by helping him to recognize relevance to valued goals. Finally, the counselor can help each student to be reasonably free from, or at least able to control, distracting needs and problems, so that he is able to give attention in the classroom to the learning activity in which he is involved.[1]

The school-counselor we envision promotes learning efficiency by working with the child in (1) the developmental aspects, (2) the decision-making aspects, and (3) the crisis aspects of his life. His contribution is unique, not because he alone has concern for these matters, but because he has acquired special expertise that enables him to do more than other educational personnel in working with students in these areas.

THE COUNSELOR AS THE GUARDIAN OF INDIVIDUALITY

Someone has said that every institution carries the seeds of its own destruction. In a sense, the school is no exception. For many reasons, the school, by its very nature, is an institution that must too often reward conformity, risk the dampening of creativity, and place concern for the mass above that for the individ-

[1]Much of this paragraph, and of the three that follow it, has been lifted virtually verbatim from *A Joint ACES-ASCA Policy Statement for Superintendents of Schools and School Boards Concerning the School Counselor* (David D. Malcolm, ACES, and Donald G. Hays, ASCA, Co-Chairmen), adopted, Dallas APGA Convention, March 1967.

ual. It is our contention that the school in a democratic society must therefore make special provision to build into its structure some compensatory mechanism, lest in the long run it defeat its own ends. Obviously this must be a concern of all educational personnel. At the same time, the special expertise of the counselor makes him the one to whom the school logically turns as the special guardian of individuality and of the individual.

There are several things the counselor can do in fulfilling this, the second major part of his role. First, he can provide each student who so desires with an opportunity for self-exploration and self-discovery of his own innermost feelings and personal values in a nonthreatening relationship with a mature adult. Second, he can work directly with teachers and other significant adults to help them to understand and foster the unique individuality of each student. Finally, he can participate in curriculum construction and other school policy-making activities, with special responsibility for insuring that the guidance point of view permeates the total activities of the school. In this part of his role, the counselor works (1) directly with the child himself, (2) through the significant adults in the child's life, and (3) through the pervasive climate of the school.

COUNSELING AS "INTERVENTION"

We now turn away from counselor role per se to look at the special professional expertise that makes the counselor's contribution to the school unique. To do this, we must first introduce certain formulations, which we have found to be helpful to us in our thinking.

The basic formulation is the concept of intervention. We use *intervention* in the broad sense of the word. In this sense, counseling by its very nature is intervention. The counselor is making some sort of intervention into the life of the student simply by virtue of being involved at all. In the sense in which we are using it, the concept of intervention is broad enough to include such diverse types of counselor behavior as environmental manipulation, exhortation, help in decision-making, "shaping" through positive reinforcement, and the close human relationship of the basic encounter. Intervention can be direct, either individual or in groups; intervention can be indirect, either through other persons or through things. In any case, intervention always involves two separate aspects of counselor behavior: (1) the decision regarding the sort of intervention to be made, and (2) the program of action that carries it out.

Let us now follow this thinking a little further. Any person can make an intervention of some sort into the life of the child. The point is, the choice of one from among the variety of possible interventions should not depend on whim or be left to chance. It is our contention that determination of the intervention most appropriate in any given instance requires special expertise. To make a conscious, cognitive determination of this sort, a counselor must possess (1) understanding of the dynamics of human behavior, including his own; (2) knowledge of the institutional settings that influence the life of the student; and (3) ability to see the world through the student's eyes. It is to these three essential ingredients that we believe the counselor-education program should be directed.

NEED FOR THE SECOND-YEAR PROGRAM

Throughout the 1960s there appeared in the professional literature a series of position papers, committee reports, policy statements, and other pronouncements overwhelmingly supporting the two-year program as the minimum preparation for counselors. Impressive as this consensus among professionals may be, perhaps even more compelling is empirical evidence from our own experience. This evidence is of two kinds. First, we have been impressed by the number of students who, after having completed a one-year program and fully satisfying certification requirements, have voluntarily returned in search of further training that might help them in their work. The second source of evidence has been our experience in year-long NDEA Institute programs. Even given a hand-picked group of students, ample financing, sufficient staffing, and the best curriculum we were capable of designing, we still found ourselves with "unfinished business" at the end of the academic year.

What we seem to be finding is that in one year our students reach the point of having the technical competence to make an effective intervention, but they still feel inadequate as far as knowing how to determine what sort of intervention should be made. The first graduate year typically brings the student just to the point where he is really ready to zero in on the process of intervention. This, in our eyes, is the unfinished business at the end of the first year of counselor education, and, consequently, the central thrust of the second year in our program.

COUNSELOR ROLE AT DIFFERENT LEVELS

Up to this point, we have felt no need to make distinctions between counseling at the elementary-school level and counseling at the secondary-school levels. Certainly, concern for increasing learning efficiency and for preserving individuality from the crush of the forces for conformity is common to both levels. Certainly the concept of intervention is as valid at one level as the other. Certainly there is much that is common to the education of prospective elementary-school and secondary-school counselors.

At the same time, it is important to stress that differences in age group and differences in institutional settings will often be the critical factors in determining the sort of intervention to be made. Over a two-year period, we believe, more of the experiences of counseling students should be differentiated than common. Most of the common experiences come during the first year as both groups of students are establishing initial technical competence. Differentiation increases during the second year as both groups focus more directly on the process of intervention.

COUNSELING IN THE ELEMENTARY SCHOOL

In the literature, and in the school districts with which we are familiar, at least three different concepts of the elementary-school counselor are beginning to emerge: (1) the visiting teacher, or school social-worker, model; (2) the diagnostic psychometrist-psychologist model; and (3) the learning-consultant model.

In the *school social-worker model,* the elementary-school counselor works for the most part with children with school-related difficulties, and he places his primary emphasis on working directly within the family situation in cooperation with other community agencies.

In the *psychometrist-psychologist model,* the elementary-school counselor likewise works chiefly with children with school-related difficulties, but he emphasizes diagnostic case-study as a vehicle for making specific recommendations for remediation when indicated.

In the *learning-consultant model,* the elementary-school counselor is first of all a learning specialist who works through the significant adults in the child's life rather than directly with the child himself; he is concerned with the learning climate of the whole school more than he is with the school-related difficulties of individual children.

We maintain that none of these models is the exclusive answer, and that the definitive model for the counselor in the elementary school has yet to evolve. The effective practitioner, to intervene successfully on behalf of the learning efficiency and individuality of the elementary-school child, must draw heavily from all three models. Moreover, in actual practice none of these models is completely pure. There is considerable overlap between them, regardless of the particular title preferred in any given school district, and we anticipate that counselors of all three types will eventually tend to become increasingly alike. The objectives are much the same regardless of the particular pattern or title, and in the long run the broadly educated counselor is more likely to achieve these objectives than one whose preparation has been more narrowly focused.

COUNSELING IN THE SECONDARY SCHOOL

The voices that led to the creation of Title V (B) when NDEA was passed in 1958 are still with us. Manpower needs in time of crisis require that an effort be made to assist every individual to achieve his full potential. In a complex society, an ever-increasing number of persons need specialized help in their search for information and self-understanding. The conflict, change, and confusion that characterize the adult world are reflected in the emotional storms faced by youth in search for a meaningful place in that world. In an age in which so many forces conspire toward the alienation of the individual, society has turned to the counselor in its search for an antidote.

At the secondary-school level, the voices calling for counseling are sometimes primarily concerned with the precollege counseling of college-bound youth, sometimes with youth out of school or about to leave school to enter the job market, sometimes with minority-group or otherwise disadvantaged youth. The one thing all seem to have in common is an abundant faith in counseling. To the counselor and to the counselor-educator, the challenge posed presents both opportunity and danger. The danger is that expectations will be placed unrealistically high.

In the long run, we believe, those calling for more precollege or vocational or minority-group counseling will be less likely to find their high expectations dashed by the broadly educated counselor committed to a career of lifelong learning than by the counselor limited by specialization to working only with certain groups. As counselor-educators, we believe that we serve the needs of the secondary schools best by dedicating our energies to improving the professional preparation of the broadly educated career counselor. To conclude this essay, we turn now to a brief description of the sort of two-year program we would find consistent with our particular set of beliefs.

FIRST-YEAR PREPARATION

Didactic Instruction

In the fall semester of the first year, we believe, the thrust should be toward experiences which combine to make the semester intensely personal, sometimes painfully so. The emphasis should be on understanding the dynamics of human behavior, including the enrollee's own.

All courses should emphasize personal implications. Extensive use should be made of small groups as an instructional method. Materials presented in one course should be subjected to analysis in others. Each enrollee should seek to work out his own individual reconciliation of divergent theoretical points of view and should be expected to participate in group-therapy sessions. Individual counseling should be available for those who seek it. In a very real sense, the chief subject matter studied during the first semester is the enrollee himself.

In the spring semester, the tone should gradually change. The courses should shift attention from the dynamics of the individual's inner world to the forces at work in his environment. Independent and individual study should begin to replace the cooperative group activities that predominated during the first semester, with enrollees now working on problems and projects of special personal interest. Tutorial study should be available to accommodate individual needs. In other words, the second-semester program should be designed to capitalize on the motivations built up during the first semester. Each enrollee who is ready to do so should be expected increasingly to assume responsibility for his own personal and professional development.

During the fall semester, when the focus is so much on the enrollee himself, little differentiation need be made between those preparing to work in elementary schools and those preparing to work in secondary schools. By contrast, in the spring the two groups should be separated for perhaps half of the formal instructional program.

Practicum

Practicum experiences during the first year should be closely integrated with didactic instruction and consequently should reflect the same shifting emphases. Thus, during the first semester, critiquing of counseling sessions should tend to focus first and foremost on the behavior of the counselor, and during the spring semester should gradually place more of the emphasis on understanding the student's problems. During the first semester, enrollees should handle a small number of cases and be closely observed and supervised; during the spring direct observation and supervision should be more and more replaced by opportunities for consultation and advice. During the second semester, differentiation between elementary-school and secondary-school enrollees becomes marked in terms of both practicum subjects and activities.

SECOND-YEAR PREPARATION

Didactic Instruction

The focus of the didactic part of the program during the second year should be on the advanced study of the dynamics of human behavior. Didactic instruction should be interdisciplinary in nature, combining advanced tutorial study and elective course work. Ordinarily, elective courses will be course offerings in such departments as anthropology, economics, philosophy, psychology, and sociology. The heart of the didactic instruction, however, should be a tutorial plan designed to provide an approach to the study of human behavior that is truly interdisciplinary in nature.

Although the most common type of tutorial activity might well be special reading assignments, tutorials should also include such activities as preparation of formal or informal reports, auditing lectures or parts of courses, field observations, interviews with prominent authorities, and experimental or other types of research projects. Tutorial reading can and should range from technical articles to popularizations; from the physical and behavioral sciences to the arts and humanities, including poetry and fiction; from exciting contemporary writing to the great landmarks of the past. Selection of tutorial activities should be at the discretion of the enrollee and tutor, guided only by the criterion that the activity selected is believed likely in some way to enhance the enrollee's understanding of human nature and human behavior.

Practicum

To the second-year practicum should be assigned the twofold task of (1) developing in each enrollee increasing technical competence, and (2) serving as the basic integrative experience. Practicum should continue to include direct observation and supervision with extensive use of videotapes, tape recorders, and one-way glass. The central focus of the practicum, however, should be on the concept of intervention, particularly on the process of making a conscious, cognitive determination of a choice from among the variety of interventions possible in each case under consideration. Practicum critiquing sessions, which during the first year dealt predominantly with technical competence, should turn more and more to focusing the insights gleaned from tutorial experiences on this one central task. In this way, the concept of intervention becomes the unifying principle for welding didactic and practicum into a meaningful four-semester learning experience, the justification for a two-year program of counselor education.

SUMMARY

The position of school-counselor can be justified only to the extent that the school-counselor possesses special expertise that permits him to make a unique contribution to the school. Counselor-educators must identify as precisely as possible this special expertise and then offer an instructional program designed to develop it. Such an instructional program will ordinarily require a minimum of two years of full-time study. In this essay we have attempted (1) to give our reasons for holding these beliefs, and (2) to show the directions in which these beliefs seem to be leading us.

REFERENCES

Arbuckle, D. S. Counselor, social worker, psychologist: Let's "ecumenicalize." *Personnel and Guidance Journal,* 1967, **45**, 532–538.

Association for Counselor Education and Supervision. Committee on Professional Preparation and Standards. Standards for the preparation of secondary school counselors—1967. *Personnel and Guidance Journal,* **46**, 96–106.

Brammer, L. M. Eclecticism revisited. *Personnel and Guidance Journal,* 1969, **48**, 192–197.

Bruce, P. Sources for personal validation. *Counselor Education and Supervision,* 1969, **8**, 327–330.

Carnes, E. F. A parting shot. *Counselor Education and Supervision,* 1966, **5**, 226.

Expectations and commitments: A joint ACES/ASCA policy statement. Washington, D.C.: American Personnel and Guidance Association, 1969.

Malcolm, D. D. On becoming a counselor. *Personnel and Guidance Journal,* 1968, **46**, 673–676.

McCully, C. H. Professionalization: Symbol or substance. *Counselor Education and Supervision,* 1963, **2**, 106–111.

Ofman, W. The counselor who is: A critique and a modest proposal. *Personnel and Guidance Journal,* 1967, **45**, 932–937.

Sorenson, G. Pterodactyls, passenger pigeons, and personnel workers. *Personnel and Guidance Journal,* 1965, **43**, 430–437.

Issues

1. Is it possible to provide an adequate, much less a quality, program of counselor education without a specific role description involving different settings?
2. Are there concepts in the educational philosophy and practice of medically oriented counseling programs that would be of value to other programs?
3. Clearly the emphasis is toward increased specialization; how can the broad base of knowledge be protected, and indeed should it be?
4. Regardless of discipline, practicum and supervision seem to be the key elements of professional education in practice (versus theory). The professional competence and personal security of counselors are clearly essential components of this phase of education. How do educational programs develop such competence and security?

Annotated Readings

Rioch, M. J. Changing concepts in the training of therapists. *Journal of Consulting Psychology,* 1966, **30**, 4, 290–292.

Many professionals in the mental health field recognize the ability of nontraditional workers with relatively little training to produce good therapeutic results. The question is raised and discussed as to why the guardians of our present system are slow to use fully new resources the effectiveness of which has been demonstrated. The suggestion is made that professionals with extended traditional training should identify themselves with the advancement of knowledge and leave more of the practice of crafts to new categories of workers.

Spilken, A. Z., Jacobs, M. A., Muller, J. J., & Knitzer, J. Personality characteristics of therapists: Description of relevant variables and examination of conscious preferences. *Journal of Consulting and Clinical Psychology,* 1969, **33**, 317–326.

Recent studies of the significance of the psychotherapist's personality are summarized and discussed with the aim of developing measures for clinical research. Ten variables are described, comprising a relatively comprehensive and discrete list of potential importance. They include: objectivity, dependability, sincerity, sureness, directiveness, empathy (both affective and cognitive components, i.e., responsiveness and understanding), respect, interest, and warmth. The measurement of conscious attitudes toward these variables in 54 psychiatrists, 77 psychologists, and 78 social workers is described. The method uses a questionnaire requiring forced choices between paired adjectives and provides rankings among the variables. The results indicate both similarities and differences among therapist groups in relative preferences for these characteristics.

Webb, W. B., Goldstein, S. G., Bordin, Edward S., & Bard, M. Viewpoints on the new California school of professional psychology. *Professional Psychology,* 1970, **1**, 253–264.

The four viewpoints were stimulated by the new California training program as described by Karl Pottharst in the February 1970 issue of *Professional Psychology.* The authors come from both clinical and academic settings and are all involved in some phase of professional preparation of students. Wilse Webb is a professor of psychology at the University of Florida and was formerly a member of APA's board of directors. Steven Goldstein is an assistant professor of psychology at the University of Oregon Medical School and newsletter editor of both his state psychological association and the Corresponding Committee of Fifty of Division 12 (APA). The third contribution is from Edward S. Bordin, who is professor of psychology and chief of the Counseling Division, Bureau of Psychological Services, at the University of Michigan. He is also a consulting editor of *Professional Psychology.* The last statement comes from Morton Bard, professor of psychology and director of the Psychological Center at the City College of the City University of New York.

Suggestions for Further Reading

Albee, G. W. The uncertain future of clinical psychology. *American Psychologist,* 1970, **25**, 12, 1071–1080.

Baron, J. Is experimental psychology relevant? *American Psychologist,* 1971, **16**, 713–716.

Bennett, V. D. C. Doctoral school psychology training program at Rutgers. *Professional Psychology,* 1971, **1**, 298–300.

Boxley, R., & Wagner, N. N. Clinical psychology training programs and minority groups: A survey. *Professional Psychology,* 1971, **1**, 75–81.

Cass, L., Cain, A., & Waite, R. American Association of Psychiatric Clinics for Children training standards for predoctoral internship in clinical child psychology. *Professional Psychology,* 1970, **1**, 170–174.

Dinkmeyer, D. Elementary school guidance: Principles and functions. *School Counselor,* 1968, **16**, 11–16.

Division of Psychotherapy, American Psychological Association. Recommended standards for psychotherapy education in psychology doctoral programs. *Professional Psychology,* 1971, **2** (2), 148–154.

Fine, R. Training the psychologist for psychotherapy. *Psychotherapy: Theory, Research and Practice,* 1966, **3**, 184–187.

Finney, B. C. Some techniques and procedures for teaching psychotherapy. *Psychotherapy: Theory, Research and Practice,* 1968, **5**, 115–119.

Fox, R. E., & Weiner, I. B. Uniform dates for announcing internship awards: A goal of the APIC. *Professional Psychology,* 1971, **2**(2), 199–200.

Golann, S. E., Breiter, D. E., & Magoon, T. M. A filmed interview applied to the evaluation of mental health counselors. *Psychotherapy: Theory, Research and Practice,* 1966, **3**, 21–24.

Hyman, I. A. The traineeship in school psychology: A report on growth and growing pains. *Professional Psychology,* 1970, **1**, 351–353.

Jacoby, J. Training consumer psychologists: The Purdue University program. *Professional Psychology,* 1971, **2**, 300–302.

Kurz, R. B. New committee on professional training. *Professional Psychology,* 1970, **1**, 131.

Mahrer, A. R. Adding the clinic to clinical training. *Professional Psychology,* 1970, **1**, 191.

Noble, F. C. The two-year graduate program in counselor education: A reexamination. *Counselor Education and Supervision,* 1965, **4**, 160–162.

Rosenbaum, M. Some comments on the use of untrained therapists. *Journal of Consulting Psychology,* 1966, **30**, 292–294.

Saretsky, T. Transference and countertransference problems of the candidate analyst. *Psychotherapy: Theory, Research and Practice,* 1966, e. 188–189.

Schneider, S. F. Reply to Albee's "The uncertain future of clinical psychology." *American Psychologist,* 1971, **26**, 1058–1070.

Vollmer, H. M., & Mills, D. L. (Eds.) *Professionalization.* Englewood Cliffs, N.J.: Prentice-Hall, 1966.

Webb, W. B. The practice of psychology and the university training program. *Professional Psychology,* 1970, **1**, 253–258.

Willower, D. J., Hoy, W. K., & Eidell, T. L. The counselor and the school as a social organization. *Personnel and Guidance Journal,* 1967, **46**, 228–234.

CHAPTER 4

Theoretical Approaches to Supervision

Practicum supervision, for most practitioners (student and supervisor alike), occasions both personal trauma and exhilaration. For some, the mere fact of having to be judged or to judge is either too threatening or too authoritarian to have any personal value or educational gain. Others feel that the process of supervision is analogous to pleasing someone rather than creating new learning. Only a few eagerly approach clinical supervision with a positive expectation. With this as an almost universal experience, it is of interest to note that the process somehow manages to be perpetuated with very few changes or innovations, if any.

Ideally, the practicum should be a point of culmination for the professional-in-training—an opportunity to apply techniques and methods, to create facilitating relationships, to experiment, and to benefit from expert feedback, all within the safe boundaries of supervision. To further complicate the issue, it is probably also safe to assume that the vast majority of supervisors feel that practicum supervision is the one most important episode in the total professional learning process. Assuming that in very few instances neither the commitment to teach nor the commitment to learn falters, what is it that happens to such a potentially positive situation?

One possibility is the model itself. Practicum supervision is traditionally a dyadic interaction between the counselor-in-training and someone who has already achieved a level of proficiency. Seldom are the members of this pair matched on any of the variables we might consider to be crucial for a therapeutic dyad, such as sex, compatability, and problem intent. All too often the supervisor knows very little about the student, whose methods of responding, of changing, and of developing are already fairly well established. This is a decided handicap in creating an individualized learning situation. The actual interview being supervised is seldom observed by the supervisor, and therefore either written or verbal reports by the student, or taped excerpts, also chosen by the student, are used. The bias such a sampling introduces is clear, and it is further compounded by the student's felt need to be seen as capable. If the supervisor is a member of another discipline, the interaction may be strained even more by differences in expectations, method, and goals, which may not be discussed. Sometimes the personal conviction of the supervisor about his own method of doing therapy can be so great as to reduce his effectiveness in presenting the favored approach to a supervisee who has tentatively adopted another method, or who wishes to try a variety of methods.

Finally, the key element in the practicum—the client—is almost never involved in the supervisory task.

Perhaps there is a need to revise the model for supervision to take into account some of the variables and values that are clinically known to facilitate human growth and potential, and that are necessary to create a climate where experiential rather than rote learning can take place.

Each author in this chapter presents a partisan and discrete theoretical framework for doing clinical supervision; also included are the practical steps needed to implement the method(s). The final essay, however, is a joint effort to integrate the theories. Walz develops the self-theory model, Gysbers and Ronnestad do the same for the learning model, and Roeber defines the trait-theory model. The integrated paradigm is clearly a thoughtful and viable approach to strengthening a crucial professional experience without reducing the essentials of the component theories. This is clearly an ambitious task. Whether it achieves its aims should be an empirical question.

Practicum Supervision: Self-Theory*

Garry R. Walz

University of Michigan

Self-theory can be thought of as one of the major conceptual foundations of counseling. Basic to this theory is the idea that the major determinants of behavior are an individual's perceptions and conceptions of his self and his environment. "We see things not as they are but as we are [Gibson, 1951, p. 98]." Self-theory, or phenomenological psychology, has made comparatively little impact on an American psychology, which is dominated by behaviorism and psychoanalysis. Applied workers, however, have found it particularly useful for developing rich conceptual models, which have provided a means for meeting their problems. Combs and Snygg's work on understanding individual behavior and Rogers's client-centered therapy are two of the more notable implementations. Also, the work by Combs, et al. (1971) furthered the focus on human relationships.

It would seem appropriate to look at the implications of self-theory for supervision, if for no other reason than that it has so greatly influenced contemporary counseling.

Let me say at this point that I am not at all sure, as seen from the vantage point of self-theory, that there is such a thing as counseling supervision. *Supervision* is an ill-defined term adopted from other work areas. It is usually associated with terms like *direction, training, standards,* and *evaluation.* None of these terms is appropriate to the relationship between counselor-candidate and counselor-educator, which I will describe in this essay. Since *supervision* is the generally adopted term, however, I will continue to use it as a label for a concept that we have yet to define.

*Paper originally presented at the annual convention of the American Personnel and Guidance Association, Boston, April 9, 1963.

PRINCIPLES OF SELF-THEORY

It may be appropriate to begin this essay by reviewing the basic rationale of self-theory. In this review I have made particular use of the work of Combs and Syngg (1959) and a paper on self-theory by Patterson (1962). For ease of review I have expressed self-theory as a series of principles.

1. There is no reality for an individual other than what he perceives. "What is perceived is not what exists, but, what one believes exists . . . [Combs & Snygg, 1959, p. 84]."

2. A person acts on the basis of his perceptions. "People can behave only in terms of what seems to them to be so [Combs & Snygg, 1959, p. 5]." It is a person's perception of activities, and not the activities themselves, which determines behavior. His present perceptions include his views of both the past and the future.

3. We can only infer the nature of a person's phenomenal field. It cannot be observed directly. We can develop these inferences by: (1) observing a person's behavior, (2) questioning him about his behavior, (3) testing him, and (4) unstructured interviewing.

4. The appropriate vantage point for the study of behavior is the internal frame of reference. This approach is similar to someone asking, "Under what circumstances would I have done that? [Patterson, 1962, p. 5]." Structuring, questioning, and evaluating are avoided. The observer attempts to place himself in the person's place so he can view the world and the person as the person does.

5. We can predict a person's behavior when we know his phenomenal field. "Understanding of the inferred field makes possible the prediction of future behavior [Patterson, 1962, p. 5]."

6. The self-concept "includes all the perceptions and conceptions a person has about himself, his attitudes and beliefs [Patterson, 1962, p. 5]." "What a person thinks and how he behaves are largely determined by the concepts he holds about himself and his abilities [Combs & Snygg, 1959, p. 122]."

7. To change behavior, we must first change perceptions, particularly perceptions of the self.

8. There are certain conditions under which perceptions change.
   a. A person has an experience that relates to the self-concept.
   b. The experience is not only relevant to the self-concept, but is also inconsistent, or in some way raises a question or poses a problem.
   c. A person, however, may resist change as a means of preserving his self-concept. Thus, experiences inconsistent to the self-concept may not be perceived by the individual.

d. The less important an aspect of self is, the easier it can be changed.
e. Experiences perceived as threatening will result in the person's adopting restrictive, obstructing behavior or acquiescing behavior. The choice will be dependent upon which behavior is perceived as the best way to enhance the self.
f. Voluntary changes in behavior are most likely to occur when the individual is in a situation where he does not feel the need to defend himself.

What can we say in summary regarding change in perception and, hence, change in behavior? It would seem that there must be an experience that is both clear and relevant to the self-concept, but inconsistent with existing perceptions. The experience must also be relatively free of threat to the self.

IMPLICATIONS FOR SUPERVISION IN SELF-THEORY

It would seem that self-theory has a number of implications for supervision. Let us look at a few of them.

If we wish to promote growth we should concentrate on the candidate's perception of his experiences and not that of the supervisor. This is close to the time-honored saying, "We should begin where the student is, not where we want him to be." The essential element here is that we must adopt a form of supervision that allows for the candidate to express his perceptions so we may *know* how he sees things. The supervisor and the candidate may well be exposed to the same stimulus (interview), but their perceptions of that interview can differ greatly. If we are truly interested in the real learning of the candidate, we must work at his level of perception and see things as he sees them. This is akin to the process in counseling where the counselor attempts to put himself in the place of the client. Operationally, this may have some implications for a supervisory focus on expression and communication rather than evaluation and the dispensing of information. The latter may work to retard rather than facilitate a mutual examination of the candidate's perceptual field.

A candidate's perception of a given counseling experience is only partially determined by present stimuli; both past and future will affect his perception and hence his behavior. Thus it would seem that we can only understand the candidate's behavior by relating it to past experience, his interpretation of this experience, and his perception of present activities. Perhaps a supervisor's greatest contribution here is to assist the candidate to examine his perceptual field and consider the implications inherent in his perceptual structuring.

One merit of such an approach is that it could meaningfully illustrate the counseling process to the candidate. It is probable that many elements in the supervisory process are basically similar to the counseling process. This would seem to argue for an emphasis on perceptual change as a forerunner to behavior change, rather than an emphasis on information giving. Perhaps most basically of all, the supervisor is a model to the candidate in the truest sense of the word. Unquestionably the process-relationship associated with the supervision will transfer to the counseling situation. The relationship with the supervisor may well be more important than what the supervisor says or does. Example is mightier than precept.

A further reason for an emphasis upon candidate perception rather than performance is that we wish to concern ourselves with his basic counseling behavior, not his actions in a given interview. A focus on how a candidate saw a client, and how he perceived his role with that client, would provide a more useful vehicle for assisting the candidate than a focus upon his behavior (and technique) in a single interview.

Implicit in what we have said is the idea that we must know the candidate as well as his work. Counseling style must be viewed with reference to the counselor using that style. Knowledge of the candidate will stem most directly from the relationship between the supervisor and the candidate. Other sources, such as tests, observations, and peer reactions, should also be of use to the supervisor in making inferences about the candidate's behavior.

The question, "Under what conditions would I have done that?" is an appropriate guide for the supervisor to use in trying to adopt the counselor-candidate's frame of reference. In fact, the supervisor's task is compounded by really having to adopt two frames of reference, the client's and the counselor's. It may be that the supervisor would do well to focus his attention on the client so that the two can share their perceptions of the client's behavior and discuss how his needs might best have been met. This approach would seem to provide for an easy movement to alternatives available to the candidate and how he might have best assisted the client.

It is apparent that a counselor-candidate might change his behavior for many reasons. Threat, competition, fear, understanding, or reward could all serve as motivators. It would seem equally clear, however, that only voluntary changes based upon understanding are desirable. Changes induced as a function of threat are likely to last only so long as the threat persists, and may inhibit all behavior rather than promote the desired behavior. There are perhaps even greater objections to the use of fear and threat to promote learning. If this is the way counselors learn, then may they not transfer these procedures to their relationships with clients and peers? On neither logical nor operational grounds may we say in this case that the ends justify the means. Threat may cause a counselor to change his behavior, but if it undermines his faith and belief in the counseling process, he has paid too high a price for what he has learned.

It would seem appropriate for a supervisor to concentrate on how a counselor-candidate "sees" his counseling, rather than on how he "does" his counseling. Changes in perception precede changes in behavior. Tyler's review of counseling research (1961, p. 238) would suggest that we can expect more changes in perception than in behavior as a result of counseling. Can we expect more of supervision? The supervisor's role would seem to be that of clarifying perceptions so that the counselor-candidate can implement his new perceptions in his own unique way.

It is probably true that the counselor behavior that makes a difference in the interview is a function of the counselor's self-concept. Therefore, we must deal with a counselor's behavior as we deal with a client's behavior, and not as something to be changed through advice and admonition. Changes in the candidate's self-concept are most likely to occur when the change is not seen as a threat.

We would seem to need a variety of counseling experiences so that the counselor-candidate will have clear and relevant experiences on which to develop his own counseling philosophy. Perhaps we also need a more definitive way of defining the interaction between counselor and client so that we can describe the range of experiences in which a counselor-candidate has participated.

PURPOSE OF THE COUNSELING PRACTICUM

Running through our discussion so far has been the central question, "What is the purpose of a practicum?" We must first answer the questions: "*What* is a practicum for? What are its *content* and objectives?" Then we will be able to provide an answer to the questions: "*How* is a practicum to be conducted? What should be the organization and *process* of supervision?" In a progress report on counselor-education standards, Roeber (1962) suggests that the objective of supervised practice in counseling is "to effect the transformation of a counselor-candidate to an independently functioning counselor [p. 25]." "The counseling practicum must be a growth experience for the candidate ... [p. 26]." "The counseling practicum represents the major practical experience in any program ..." "The counseling practicum is virtually a tutorial form of instruction ..." [p. 28]."

Implicit in these and other discussions of the practicum is the idea that the practicum serves as both an agent for developing working skills and a "growth experience" for the candidate, where all of his previous learnings and experiences come to fruition.

It may be of interest at this point to look at what might constitute an average practicum experience. This indubitably is not what each of us does in our own institutions, but we probably can agree that something quite like this goes on at other institutions.

Counselor-candidate Bill Williams has completed 15 semester hours of graduate course work in guidance. As an experienced social-studies teacher he has had many personal conferences with students. He willingly, however, accepts the policy of the program that candidates cannot see "live students under glass" (counsel students under supervision) until they have finished their formal course work. He has done well in his courses, but he is not at all sure how he will use what he has learned in his counseling courses with a student. It has not gone unobserved by him that the authorities in the field disagree, and that even members of the department are unable to get together on what they believe. The environment is totally new—one-way vision mirrors, tape recorders, small groups of other graduate students, and clients who seem much more formidable than the high school students he knew. *He does not know* whom he will see, what his problem is, how the client will react to him, or how he will react to the client, what they will do, or when he is finished, or whether it was a "good" interview or a "bad" interview. *He does know* that a supervisor is watching, that everything he says is being recorded on tape, that others will critique his interview, that he cannot get a counseling certificate unless his supervisor says so, that he is expected to make use of what he learned in class, and that the supervisor, in one way or another, *will* tell him whether it was a "good" or a "bad" interview.

That there may be some generally common elements in this description of supervisory practices is shown by a study of North Central Region practicum supervisors by Walz and Roeber (1962, pp. 2–7). They found practicum supervisors to be primarily cognitively oriented, seeing their role as that of instructing and raising questions, and focusing on "undesirable" rather than "desirable" counselor behavior. Generally, attention was devoted to specific counselor actions, rather than the interaction between counselor and client.

SELF-THEORY SUPERVISION

What would be the difference between supervision as we have described it and the supervisor who operated on a self-theory framework? As a general statement, there would seem to be several points of disagreement. The self-theorist supervisor would emphasize the relationship between himself and the candidate. He would seek to understand how the candidate saw himself rather than evaluate his performance. His major goal would be to create a climate in which the candidate could view his behavior without fear of disapproval or rejection. Through his relationship with the candidate, and in the accepting climate created between them, the natural growth processes would exert themselves.

The candidate would be stimulated to develop a personally appropriate counseling style.

All but the most ardent must find this self-theory approach incomplete. It may be more meaningful to define a self-theorist approach through a series of working hypotheses. Any approach to supervision at this point might best be thought of as a series of hypotheses that would provide a rationale and a systematic approach to dealing with the candidate in a wide range of learning situations.

WORKING HYPOTHESES

Significant learning by the counselor candidate will be greatest when the supervisor uses a self-discovery supervisory approach. Significant learning is here defined as learning that makes a difference in a person's behavior or perceptions. This is *not* intended to suggest that *all* materials may best be learned this way (e.g., statistical procedures). It is intended to convey the idea that learnings about self and changes in counseling behavior are most effectively learned this way. To try to teach a person counseling is either to concentrate on that which has little influence on his behavior, or to cause him to accept what you think is important, and hence to come to depend upon others to decide what he should learn. This is probably what Rogers had in mind when he said, "I have come to feel that the outcomes of teaching are either unimportant or hurtful [1961, p. 276]." I would suggest that the appropriate role of the supervisor is not instruction, but the creation of a climate in which the candidate's drive for self-improvement may assert itself.

The supervisor will make his greatest contribution to candidate growth when his relationship with the candidate is as a fellow learner. Significant learning will be facilitated when the supervisor tries to understand what meaning an experience has for a candidate and attempts to clarify that experience for himself and the candidate. Attitudes here are crucial! The trying to understand may be more important than the understanding.

Supervisory evaluation of candidate performance is not conducive to candidate growth. We have often written of the inconsistencies inherent in the teacher-counselor role. An equally large inconsistency is present in the notion that a supervisor can be in both a helping and a judgmental relationship with a candidate. It must be one or the other. Evaluation should be a part of the counseling practicum, but it should be divorced from the responsibilities of a supervisor. The supervisor's role should be that of helping the candidate to see what the requirements of being a proficient counselor are, and what he can do to meet them. Evaluation of a counselor's performance could well come from a "jury" of supervisors, who observed a candidate's counseling but were not in a helping relationship with him. The "verdict" of the jury could then be used by the supervisor and candidate together to review progress and plan for future interviews. In this relationship the supervisor helps the candidate to clarify his responsibilities, and provides resources the candidate can use in learning to meet his responsibilities.

Candidate learning is facilitated when the candidate clearly perceives his task. It is to be expected that learning will be facilitated when the candidate sees the task of becoming a counselor as involving certain problems and issues. "Significant learning occurs more readily in relation to situations perceived as problems [Rogers, 1961, p. 286]." The practicum experience should be so designed that early in his preparation the candidate is involved in actual counseling situations so he is able to *perceive for himself* the problems he faces. The supervisor can be of real assistance to the candidate at this point by identifying with him the problems he faces. The practicum should be so designed and conducted that it is perceived by the candidate as a means of meeting the problems he faces in becoming a counselor. A frequently displayed sign reads, "Are you helping or are you part of the problem?" Do we as supervisors sometimes become "part of the problem" by confusing the candidate as to what it is he is to learn and how he can go about learning it? Clarity of the task and the means to accomplish it is essential.

Congruence between a supervisor's feelings and behavior towards a candidate heightens their relationship. Sincerity and truthfulness are important in all interpersonal relationships. They are especially important in a relationship that exists to free another person from the need to defend himself from threat and rejection. Only if the supervisor is able to accept his feelings can he enter into a real relationship with the candidate. His feelings and behavior toward a candidate must be one. It destroys the meaning of a relationship if a supervisor is perceived by a candidate as feeling one way and acting another. It would seem appropriate for a supervisor to say, "I've found myself irritated with you for not listening to your tapes." As supervisors we may occasionally bemoan our human inclination to grosser emotions. But better express it than repress it. Joy, sorrow, anger, pleasure—they are part and parcel of human relationships.

Supervisory warmth and understanding foster a candidate's capacity for dealing effectively with new situations. I hope I will be pardoned for again expressing the old educational truism, "We must begin where the student is and not where we would like him to be." Even the best program of counselor education will present people at the practicum gates who seem deficient in the basics— perhaps worse yet, who have developed sufficient security in our permissive grounds to question our most cherished ideas. We must accept the candidate as he is and try to understand his feelings. Rogers's call for unconditional positive regard, empathy, and warmth are as appropriate for the counselor-candidate as the client. Above all we need to be "with" the candidate as he experiences feelings of joy, sorrow, and discouragement. When we are "with" the candidate during his "gut" learning experiences, we get a glimpse into his perceptual world, which will bring us closer to mutual respect and understanding. Shield him we can't, empathize we must!

A wide variety of instructional resources facilitates candidate learning. A particularly crucial role of the supervisor is assembling a quantity of instructional materials sufficient to meet the particular needs of a given candidate. Ideally, he will have "programmed" the materials so he can offer a candidate appropriate instructional materials at each stage of his development. It would be important, however, that they be perceived as offers that the candidate can choose if they seem useful to him. The candidate should not feel the need to use them, nor should they impose an arbitrary structure on his learning experiences. New media-instructional devices would seem to hold particular merit as providing a means for learner choice of materials and rate of progress. The supervisor would be able to make the new media devices available, indicate for what problems they would be useful, and discuss with the candidate his (the candidate's) reactions to them. Thus the resources would be available when the need was perceived.

CONCLUSION

Basic to all that we have said is a reliance on the self-actualizing tendency in counselor-candidates. If they are actively involved in helping others to grow, and have identified the problems and issues they face, then they will hasten to learn. The supervisor, through his personal relationship with each candidate, will provide the buoyancy needed to move beyond disappointments and depressions. The end-product will be a climate in which the candidate is both learner and helper, in which he can pick and choose resources as needed, and in which what he can be, he will be.

REFERENCES

Combs, A. W., & Snygg, D. *Individual behavior.* (Rev. ed.) New York: Harper & Row, 1959.

Combs, A. W., & W. F. *Helping relationships.* Boston: Allyn and Bacon, 1971.

Gibson, J. J. Theories of perception. In W. Dennis (Ed.), *Current trends in psychological theory.* Pittsburgh: University of Pittsburgh Press, 1951.

Patterson, C. H. Phenomenological psychology: An approach to human behavior. Paper presented to American Personnel and Guidance Association, April 17, 1962.

Roeber, E. C. Practicum and internship. In Association for Counselor Education and Supervision,

& American School Counselor Association, *Counselor Education—A Progress Report on Standards.* Washington, D.C.: American Personnel and Guidance Association, 1962.

Rogers, C. R. *On becoming a person.* Boston: Houghton Mifflin, 1961.

Tyler, L. E. *The work of the counselor.* (2nd ed.) New York: Appleton-Century-Crofts, 1961.

Walz, G. R., & Roeber, E. C. Supervisors' reactions to a counseling interview. *Counselor Education and Supervision,* 1962, **2**, 2–7.

Practicum Supervision: Learning Theory

Norman C. Gysbers

University of Missouri—Columbia

Michael Helge Ronnestad

University of Oslo

Practicum supervision has emerged as a focal point of professional research and discussion. According to the American Personnel and Guidance Association (1967, p.), supervised counseling experience is considered "an integral part of the total counselor education program." The Committee on Counselor Effectiveness of the Association for Counselor Education and Supervision concluded that supervision of counselor-trainees was necessary to reach the objective of counselor effectiveness (1969).

This essay examines the implications of selected learning-theory concepts and principles underlying the process of practicum supervision. More specifically, learning-theory concepts such as performance objectives, modeling, and types of reinforcement are discussed, and recommendations to facilitate counselor-candidate learning are made.

PERFORMANCE OBJECTIVES

In recent years, increased concern has been expressed in educational literature about the importance of specifying performance objectives to facilitate learning. This concern is reflected in behavioral-counseling literature by an emphasis on observable, measurable outcomes. As Bandura has commented, "In developing and implementing programs for modifying behaviors, the specification of goals is of central importance (1969)."

A recent expression of this movement is the development of taxonomies of counselor competencies (Dagley, 1972; Springer & Brammer, 1971) and of competency-based certification plans in several states (Brammer & Springer,

133

1971). Winborn, Hinds, and Stewart (1971) discussed the advantages of using performance objectives in counselor preparation. They pointed out that when performance objectives are used, instructors and students know what is required for completing a course or a program, and students can focus on completing these requirements rather than on competing with fellow students for grades.

When used in counselor-education programs, performance objectives are found most frequently in content-oriented courses. We feel that performance objectives must also be developed for practicum. Too often, practicum supervision generally, and the supervisory relationship specifically, is viewed as a mystical and unspecifiable happening. By stating performance objectives, structure and direction are provided for supervisors and counselor-candidates. Performance objectives provide a common focal point for supervision sessions, and direction for activities to meet the individual needs of counselor-candidates.

Counselor-candidate evaluation in practicum is a frequent topic of concern and discussion in the literature and at professional meetings. Evaluation is perceived as threatening by many counselor-candidates, and may be potentially damaging to the supervisory relationship. To specify performance objectives may not completely eliminate feelings of threat. It is expected, however, that specification of performance objectives may reduce the threat, in that this procedure would help separate subjective assessment of counselor-candidate personality characteristics from objective counselor-candidate behavior. Since counseling can be divided into subcomponents, which constitute specific skills or behaviors, the efficacy of the supervisory process might be enhanced by the supervisor focusing not so much on the personality characteristics of the counselor-candidate, but on the specific counseling behaviors of the candidate. Counseling deficiencies can be viewed as learning deficiencies. An ineffective counselor-candidate is one who has not been exposed to the appropriate learning conditions. From this perspective, the supervisor's task is to provide appropriate learning experiences, and reinforcement for appropriate counseling behaviors.

Evaluation of counselor behavior should be based on the degree to which specific objective criteria have been met. Supervisors should be aware of two types of evaluation. The first type is tied to certification. It is typically done at the end of the practicum in the form of a grade. The second type, more important from a learning-theory point of view, involves the evaluation inherent in providing counselor-candidates with information about their performance. Feedback, in the form of positive or negative reinforcement provided by the supervisor throughout the practicum experience, serves a pedagogical function by helping counselor-candidates to reach the required competency level.

TYPES OF REINFORCEMENT

Little research has been done on the effects of conditioned verbal reinforcement on supervisory outcomes. Research reported in educational and psychological literature generally favors positive control in changing behavior (Loree, 1970, pp. 252–259). Conditioning using aversive stimuli following the occurrence of an operant has been found to be highly susceptible to extinction. "Unless the punishment is very severe, it is effective only as it is continued [Reynolds, 1968, p. 112]." It is likely that if the supervisor attempts to emphasize appropriate counselor responses, the effects will be different than if he reacts primarily to errors that are made.

From a learning-theory perspective, we would suggest that the initial behavior of the supervisor has implications for the supervisory relationship and for counselor-candidate learning. Frequently, counselor-candidates approach supervision with the anticipation of fear. In fact, for some counselor-candidates, a supervisor-candidate relationship seems to pose an even greater psychological threat to personal security than does the counseling interview itself. Robinson (1936) suggested that these anticipatory feelings of fear in counselor-candidates concerning supervisor-candidate relationships occur because supervisors are perceived as being representatives of authority. She suggested that candidates also fear the supervisor because they feel he will have knowledge of their reactions before they have control and possession of them.

This same theme was reiterated by Sanderson in his book *Basic Concepts in Vocational Guidance* (1954) when he suggested that supervisors usually are perceived as threatening figures who challenge candidates' habitual modes of adjustment, self-perceptions, and attitudes toward others. Robinson (1936) pointed out that these attitudes of fear may not be conscious. "They may be covered by the conventional eagerness to learn and the assertion that learning is under one's own voluntary control; but underneath they operate in every person who attempts to work under supervision [p. 46]."

Consequently, as a result of these anticipatory feelings of fear concerning the supervisory relationship, many counselor-candidates at first exhibit defensive behavior in a supervisor-candidate conference. Unfortunately, for some this defensive behavior persists. It may be that these candidates are unable to effect changes in their own need patterns. Apparently, this inability to effect changes makes it difficult for them to function effectively in either a counseling relationship, where the needs of someone else are handled, or a supervisory relationship, where this inability to operate in a counseling relationship is considered.

On the other hand, for others, while a supervision conference is at first an occasion of anxiety, it later becomes a more hopeful occasion—an experience during which appropriate kinds of learning seem to occur. In these cases, it may be that a supervision conference is no longer perceived as threatening, but as a meaningful relationship, which is helpful in securing more effective counseling behavior. Apparently, these candidates are able to effect whatever changes are necessary in their need patterns to function effectively in counseling and supervisory relationships.

Mowrer's two-factor learning theory (1960a, 1960b) is used to explain these contrasting reactions to supervision, and to draw some parallels between supervision and learning theory. When beginning candidates interact with supervisors, the language of these supervisors becomes the equivalent of a buzzer signifying either that the loss of personal security anticipated as a result of counseling behavior will not occur, or that what they had anticipated is in fact a reality.

Suppose that the words of supervisors (external stimuli) are perceived as hopeful—hopeful in the sense that they signify the end of a threat to personal securities. If this occurs, it increases the probability that counselor-candidates will either consult further with supervisors to obtain more of these hopeful words, or will approach another counseling-interview situation with the anticipation of hearing more of these hopeful words afterwards.

At the same time, suppose that these hopeful feelings also become attached to internal stimuli resulting from certain kinds of interview behavior—behavior which the supervisor suggests is appropriate. If this occurs, there is an increased probability that in later interviews, candidates will repeat this same appropriate counseling behavior in an attempt to obtain more of the same type of satisfying internal feedback.

During future interviews, even though an internal buzzer signifying fear may be momentarily turned on again upon seeing a new client, the counseling-interview situation will recall to candidates who perceived the supervisor's language as hopeful, that no loss of personal security (shock) actually occurs. This realization turns the buzzer off, causing feelings of fear to subside. As this occurs, candidates experience the emotion of relief—relief at knowing that counseling and supervisory relationships no longer need be perceived as threatening.

On the other hand, suppose that the language of a supervisor is perceived by candidates as threatening. This kind of perception increases the probability that ineffective counseling behavior of the same type that occurred in the initial interview will continue in future interviews. The continuation of fearful feelings in candidates who perceive the supervisory relationship as threatening also produces feelings of disappointment—disappointment based on the fact that a threat to personal securities did not end.

An emotion of disappointment, acting as secondary reinforcement, usually causes two types of reactions. For some candidates it seems to produce an emotion not unlike sorrow. Apparently, even though feelings of fear concerning the supervision conference produced an anticipated loss of personal security, some hope was present to suggest that this would not happen. Thus, when these candidates perceive an actual loss of personal security occurring as a result of the supervisory relationship, the emotion of disappointment (type 1, sorrow) causes withdrawal and inhibition, increasing the probability that ineffective counseling behavior will continue.

For other candidates, however, an emotion of disappointment seems to produce an opposite reaction—a reaction of anger. In this case, again, even though feelings of fear concerning a supervision conference produced an anticipated loss of personal security, some hope was present to suggest this would not occur. Thus, when these candidates perceive that a supervision conference actually did cause a loss of personal security, the emotion of disappointment (type 2, anger), instead of producing withdrawal and inhibition tendencies, seems to motivate more aggressive (defensive) action in counseling and supervisory relationships.

Supervisory behavior creates specific emotional reactions in counselor-candidates. Also, overt counselor-candidate behavior is similarly influenced. Research has suggested that both negative and positive types of reinforcement, administered by supervisors, influence counselor-candidate behavior. Davidson and Emmer (1966), investigating the effects of supportive and nonsupportive supervision behavior, found that counselors who received the latter tended to shift the focus of their interview from the client to themselves, more so than did counselors receiving the supportive supervision. Blane (1968) investigated the effects of positive supervision, negative supervision, and no supervision on counselors' empathic understanding, and concluded that positive-supervision exposure resulted in the highest level of counselor empathy. Neither of the above studies dealt with types of reinforcement in a strict theoretical sense. Both studies, however, may be regarded as practical applications of positive and negative reinforcement principles to the supervisory process, and as such they support empirical research on types of reinforcement.

MODELING

Does the supervisor serve as a model for the counselor-candidate? If so, is this desirable? It would seem that the degree to which candidates model the behavior of the supervisor is a function of characteristics of the supervisor as well as of the candidate.

It is hypothesized that the more anxious, less confident, and less experienced counselor-candidate may attempt to model the supervisor more than the less anxious, more competent, and more experienced counselor-candidate. We also expect that modeling in supervision may be a function of the degree to which "matched-dependent" behavior (Miller & Dollard, 1941) has been conditioned previously. It appears likely that someone previously reinforced for imitative behavior, is also more likely to emulate a model in supervision.

The behavioral literature suggests that certain characteristics of the model have been found to influence the modeling process. Models who are perceived to be experts (Mausner, 1953), who have demonstrated a high level of competence (Rosenbaum & Tucker, 1962), and who are regarded as having social power (Bandura, Ross, & Ross, 1963) have been found to be more influential modeling agents than persons without these characteristics.

It is probable that some degree of modeling takes place in supervision whether or not it is encouraged by the supervisor. Excessive modeling may inhibit the counselor-candidate from finding a mode of functioning or a counseling style that is personal and natural. The supervisor should be on guard against any strained, unnatural counselor-candidate behavior that seems to be expressing an attempt to imitate the supervisor's style of counseling. However, a unique, personal, and natural candidate style should not be emphasized to the exclusion of considerations of effective counseling. The focus should always be, not on a personal and unique style of counseling, but on an effective style. Ideally, of course, we would like to see the counselor functioning naturally *and* effectively.

We are suggesting that modeling is desirable if two conditions are met. The first is that the supervisor's style of counseling be demonstrated to be effective; the second is that the style to be emulated be congruent with the mode of operation of the counselor-candidate.

Modeling may be used in the acquisition of response patterns that were not previously in the behavioral repertoire of a counselor-candidate. An example of this may be counselor-candidates learning to use confrontive responses. Through observing or listening to the supervisor demonstrating confronting responses to client statements, this behavior may be learned.

Observation of modeled actions and subsequent consequences may also have an inhibitory or disinhibitory effect on observer behaviors (Bandura, 1969, p. 120). In supervision we can evidence this when we see an increase in the occurrence of a certain behavior in the counselor-candidate after this behavior has been elicited by the supervisor (in a demonstration of test interpretation, for example) with positive outcomes. Similarly, it can be observed when noticing a decrease in the occurrence of certain behaviors observed to have punishing consequences. Listening to other candidates' tapes of counseling interviews provides another example of vicarious learning. By listening to the consequences of counselor-candidates' statements, counseling behaviors may be learned. The supervisor should be aware of the dangers of indiscriminate adoption of vicariously learned behavior, in that behaviors learned to be appropriate in one situation may be highly inappropriate in another with different dynamics operating. Only through exposure to a variety of problem situations can adequate discrimination and generalization learning take place.

RECOMMENDATIONS

On the basis of the preceding discussion, we make the following recommendations for practicum supervision:

1. Positive means of behavior change in counseling supervision should predominate over negative means of behavior change in modifying candidate behavior.
2. Supervisory competencies should be stated in the form of performance objectives, and processes to teach these competencies should be delineated and incorporated in counselor-education programs.
3. Supervisors should focus on counselor-candidates' observable behavior in supervision.
4. Supervisors should have a thorough knowledge of the performance objectives counselor-candidates are trying to meet, so that appropriate learning experiences can be designed and appropriate behaviors can be reinforced when they occur.
5. Modeling in supervision may be desirable if the model's counseling style has been demonstrated to be effective, and the style to be emulated is congruent with the mode of operation of the counselor-candidate.
6. Modeling in supervision should be applied to teach specific counseling behavior, or to inhibit or disinhibit certain counseling responses.

REFERENCES

American Personnel and Guidance Association. *Standards for the preparation of secondary school counselors—1967.* Washington, D.C.: American Personnel and Guidance Association, 1967.

Association of Counselor Education and Supervision, Committee on Counseling Effectiveness. Commitment to action in supervision: Report of a national survey of counselor supervision. Paper presented at the meeting of the American Personnel and Guidance Association, Las Vegas, March 31, 1969.

Bandura, A., Ross, D., & Ross, S. A. Imitation of film-mediated aggressive models. *Journal of Abnormal and Social Psychology,* 1963, **66**, 3–11.

Bandura, A. *Principles of behavior modification.* New York: Holt, Rinehart and Winston, 1969.

Blane, S. M. Immediate effects of supervisory experience on counselor candidates. *Counselor Education and Supervision,* 1968, **8**, 39–44.

Brammer, L.M., & Springer, H. C. A radical change in counselor education and certification. *Personnel and Guidance Journal,* 1971, **49** (10), 803–808.

Dagley, J. *A taxonomy of counselor education objectives.* Unpublished doctoral dissertation, University of Missouri—Columbia, 1972.

Davidson, T. N., & Emmer, E. T. Immediate effect of supportive and nonsupportive supervisor behavior on counselor candidates' focus of concern. *Counselor Education and Supervision,* 1966, **11**, 27–31.

Loree, M. R. *Psychology of education.* (2nd ed.) New York: Ronald, 1970.

Mausner, B. Studies in social interaction: III. Effect of variation in one partner's prestige on the interaction of observer pairs. *Journal of Applied Psychology,* 1953, **37**, 391–393.

Miller, N. E., & Dollard, J. *Social learning and imitation.* New Haven: Yale University Press, 1941.

Mowrer, O. H. *Learning theory and behavior.* New York: Wiley, 1960. (a)

Mowrer, O. H. *Learning theory and the symbolic processes.* New York: Wiley, 1960. (b)

Reynolds, G. S. *A primer of operant conditioning.* Glenview, Ill.: Scott, Foresman, 1968.

Robinson, F. P. *Supervision in social case work.* Chapel Hill: University of North Carolina Press, 1936.

Rosenbaum, M. E., & Tucker, I. F. The competence of the model and the learning of imitation and nonimitation. *Journal of Experimental Psychology,* 1962, **63**, 83–190.

Sanderson, H. *Basic concepts in vocational guidance.* New York: McGraw-Hill, 1954.

Springer, H. C., & Brammer, L. M. A tentative model to identify elements of the counseling process and parameters of counselor behavior. *Counselor Education and Supervision,* 1971, **11**, 8–16.

Winborn, Bob B., Hinds, William C., & Stewart, Norman R. Instructional objectives for the professional preparation of counselors. *Counselor Education and Supervision,* 1971, **10**, 133–137.

Practicum Supervision: Trait Theory

Edward C. Roeber*

Indiana State University—Terre Haute

During the past five years, the number of practicums has increased significantly, and this in itself has been no small achievement. A practicum has long been recognized as an integral part of a counselor-education program. Several conditions, especially those having to do with staff, facilities, and equipment, inhibited their development. Various factors, such as the NDEA of 1958, influenced the upsurge in the number of practicums. Special facilities, sufficient equipment, and an adequate number of qualified supervisors are now becoming accepted as minimum standards for a counseling practicum (ACES & ASCC, 1962; APA, 1952). As a next step in the maturation process, we are faced with the question of how best to utilize our practicum resources. How can we, for instance, begin to develop a rationale of practicum supervision? What issues are associated with such a task? Which learning, personality, or other theories have some application to supervision of a counseling practicum? It is the purpose of this essay to examine these questions.

ISSUES IN PRACTICUM SUPERVISION

Very little professional literature has been given over to the actual processes of practicum supervision. Either supervisory rituals have been passed by word or demonstration from one generation to another, or each supervisor has had to develop by trial and error his own repertoire for supervision. Perhaps we have even assumed that development of an adequate counseling repertoire transfers automatically to development of an equally adequate supervising repertoire. Such an assumption may well represent one of the major issues in

*After writing this essay while at the University of Michigan, the late Professor Roeber served as Distinguished Professor of Education at Indiana State University, Terre Haute. Permission for use of this material was granted by Professor Roeber's widow, Maybelle Roeber, whom we wish to thank.

practicum supervision. Can we, for instance, assume that a "good" counselor will ipso facto be a "good" supervisor? Or should we expect that a "good" supervisor will need competencies beyond those normally associated with a "good" counselor? Some other time, explorations into such questions might lead to a stimulating discussion, but I intend herein to concentrate upon issues of supervision and only indirectly on issues having to do with supervisors' competencies.

READINESS FOR PRACTICUM EXPERIENCES

Whenever practicum supervisors congregate, attention invariably turns to a discussion of individuals who enroll in practicums. Who are these enrollees? What kinds of background do they bring to a practicum? Is there a state of readiness that portends "success" for a practicum enrollee? What kinds of prepracticum experience are prerequisite to entry into and "success" in a practicum?

Presumably, selection of counselor-candidates is a process (Hill, 1961) beginning with, or in some cases prior to, first exposures to formal preparation, and continuing throughout a program of counselor preparation. As an integral part of such a program, a practicum provides another set of checkpoints in a selection process. Whether or not there should be any prepracticum selection is a matter of controversy because, except for obviously "sick" counselor-candidates, no one has shown much evidence regarding characteristics that portend "success" in a practicum. Thus far, at least, we probably can distinguish gross interoccupational differences (a counselor from a mechanic) more efficiently than we can intraoccupational differences (a "good" counselor from a "fair" or even "poor" counselor)—a phenomenon corroborated by Thorndike and Hagen's research (1959). Our problem is complicated by the number of characteristics that seem to have some relationship to a counselor-candidate's development during a practicum. Recognizing our inefficiencies, we acknowledge the need for further research regarding selection criteria, "success" criteria, and relationships of counselor characteristics to practicum outcomes.

METHODOLOGY AND TECHNIQUES

Practicum supervisors daily encounter a variety of attitudes and behaviors during practicum. Fear, hostility, withdrawal, and apathy are not uncommon, and, at least in mild forms, are probably the norm for counselor-candidates rather than the exception. Especially designed to assist a counselor-candidate, practicum in actual practice forces him to look at himself and his relationships with other people. He may become fearful that a practicum will reveal personal inadequacies, and that he will be exposed as a fraud in the eyes of peers and supervisor. It is little wonder that he devises new defense mechanisms or calls up old ones to cope with threat. Instead of perceiving one-way-vision glass, television, recording machines, or a supervisor as facilitators to learning in a practicum, he may view them as obstacles and wish to fight or flee them. Until he sees them as helping media, he probably will experience disruptive discomfort. Contributing to possible discomfort are the motivations an enrollee may bring to a practicum—that is, he may see a practicum as an obstacle to obtaining a degree or certification as a counselor, or he may already feel competent and see a practicum as a means of obtaining "a seal of approval," à la *Good Housekeeping,* or he may see a practicum as a means of satisfying personal needs through vicarious relationships with counselees. Until extrinsic motivations give way to intrinsic motivations, his development in a practicum will be superficial at best.

We are confronted with many questions regarding our application of methodology and techniques during a practicum. To what extent do different characteristics distinguish counselor-candidates who are rendered helpless by threat during practicum experiences from those who are stimulated by threat to strive for higher levels of development? To what extent can manipulation of environment, such as coached clients, regulating the number of clients for counseling, or prepracticum experiences, be used to bring counselor-candidates to a level at which they function independently? Or is this latter goal realistic? Which is more potent in a counselor-candidate's development, a supervisor-candidate relationship, or manipulations of the practicum environment, or cognitive learnings? Which methodology and techniques increase or reduce threat? Can we differentiate among these approaches? Does a practicum have to replicate in facilities, clients, and organization the probable employment setting of counselor-candidates? Can supervision itself be adapted to the characteristics of counselor-candidates? Is there more or less one approach to supervision? To what extent can supervision create a dependency role for certain counselor-candidates? What criteria can we use to determine a counselor-candidate's development during a practicum? These questions are obviously a sample of many possibilities. In essence, they stress the relationship of differences among counselor-candidates to possible variations among approaches to practicum supervision.

TRANSFER OF LEARNING

Supervisors, if they have taken time to investigate, have probably encountered practicum enrollees who give superficial evidence of progress, or who "go through the motions" of learning their lessons well, only to revert on the job to a previous form of inadequate performance (Tyler, 1961, pp. 257–58). Such counselor-candidates develop or call up old adjustive mechanisms during a practicum, and then readily slough off any learnings when they leave the practicum. Several questions are readily apparent. In any given period of time, how much transfer can we expect from practicum to job? Which characteristics of counselor-candidates portend ready transfer of learnings from practicum to job? Which practicum experiences tend to facilitate transfer? Which experiences weaken or interfere with transfer? Is it possible that learnings, although not apparent in a practicum, may become evident on the job? These questions are closely related to previous issues of practicum readiness and methodology. The backgrounds of counselor-candidates, and the manner in which candidates are treated in a practicum, cannot be divorced from immediate practicum outcomes and job performance. In a sense, the problem of transfer does not present isolated issues. On the other hand, the importance of transfer may well transcend all other "success" criteria.

So much for this sampling of issues. It is also my task to introduce a possible theory of practicum supervision.

BASIC CONCEPTS OF TRAIT THEORY

Several years ago, Thurstone (1947) commented upon the role of theory in science. His remarks are appropriate as a prologue to my discussion of theory in practicum supervision: "To discover a scientific law is merely to discover that a manmade scheme serves to unify, and thereby to simplify, comprehension of a certain class of natural phenomena. A scientific law is not to be thought of as having an independent existence. . . . A scientific law is not a part of nature. It is only a way of comprehending nature." A theory of practicum supervision, therefore, must be concerned with a principle (or group of principles) that explains phenomena observed, experienced, or felt by counselor-candidates and supervisors during a series of practicum activities. It must presuppose several ways of describing the same phenomena and that we are searching for comprehensive descriptions, which can be applied to the largest possible number of instances or situations. Although there are an infinite number of possibilities, three ways to examine supervision immediately come to mind: trait-, learning-, and self-theories. It is my intention to examine the implications of trait theory.

In a sense, trait theory is limited in its description of phenomena that occur during a practicum. It is especially effective in describing counselors before, during, and after practicum experiences; and this should not be depreciated. Because of its historical significance (Pepinsky & Pepinsky, 1954, pp. 22–26), as well as its relevancy to several facets of practicum activities, it serves as a proper beginning in our search for a practicum rationale. Certainly, on the basis of research efforts to date, trait theory has contributed more than any other theory to our perceptions of individual differences among counselors, if not to our insights into how we deal with these individual differences. Although not always explicit in the literature, the following concepts have nevertheless been associated with trait theory:

1. On the basis of measurable differences among traits,[1] one individual can be distinguished from other individuals.
2. Intraindividual differences loom nearly as large as interindividual differences, suggesting that the variability within an individual is nearly as large as the variability among individuals.
3. On the basis of measurable differences among traits, or among trait patterns, it is possible to predict the performance or behavior of an individual or group of individuals.

In each of these concepts, stress has been placed upon the word *measurable.* This idea was expressed by Thorndike (1959) when he said, "Whatever exists, exists in some amount [p. 16]," and has led to a wide range of studies designed to establish the existence of human traits. Research has fairly well documented the fact that measurable differences do exist among individuals and also within a single individual. (Perhaps the greatest problem has been one of semantics; i.e., what names should be attached to these traits.) Research has at least partially demonstrated that many kinds of behavior, such as school achievement and work performance, are related to individual traits, although we must confess only moderate success in defining performance criteria.

TRAIT THEORY AND PRACTICUM SUPERVISION

In spite of weaknesses sometimes attached to trait theory, it still provides valuable hypotheses related to an understanding of practicum enrollees. Although considerable emphasis has been placed upon a holistic understanding of individuals, and this would apply to counselors as well as to the individuals they counsel, there are also practical limitations to understanding the whole counselor-candidate. Ideally, we hope, as we attempt to understand a practicum enrollee, that we can develop a comprehension of his total behavior transcending his independent characteristics.

The following series of hypotheses—and I emphasize the fact that they are

[1]For the purpose of this discussion, the term *trait* has been defined broadly and includes attitudes, interests, abilities, values, etc.

hypotheses and not theories in a technical sense—has been developed on the assumption that there is little to be gained from discarding what we already know about individual differences. Perhaps, as we develop a rationale for supervision, we can also learn how to apply our knowledge about individuals.

1. In a practicum, counselor-candidates, who reach a stage where they function independently and effectively, exhibit more than one pattern of traits.

An emphasis upon trait patterns for counselor selection does not represent a novel concept. As a matter of fact, Jones, some 20 years ago, concluded, "It seems probable that we shall find not a single pattern that indicates a successful counselor, but different patterns equally good and equally effective in different situations (1942)." And recently this same idea has been expressed by Tyler: "Perhaps it would be better if we all assumed that any personality pattern which permits rich and deep relationships with other human beings to develop is satisfactory [1961, p. 246]." They are both saying that we must give up the idea that there are one or two dimensions or a single pattern of many dimensions (Tuma & Gustad, 1957), which will predict success in a practicum or on the job, and that we might more profitably strive to identify differential patterns, all of which under different circumstances may lead to successful performance in a practicum and on the job. It even seems possible that a counselor-candidate, though deficient in some characteristic, might be able to compensate appropriately for some kinds of handicaps and thus develop into a "successful" counselor.

There are even nagging questions regarding the feasibility of prepracticum selection. To what extent will it ever be possible to find trait patterns, excluding those individuals who are obviously ill, that are not amenable to change, providing a counselor-candidate is willing to experience discomfort and actively seek change? Self-selection for a counseling work takes place whenever a counselor-candidate decides whether he can tolerate and is willing to commit himself to change—not change imposed upon him but change for which he takes responsibility (Arnold, 1962). The decision points may come at any time, but presumably during a practicum they will be accentuated and more frequent in number.

In this hypothesis, trait patterns, by the nature of work performed in a practicum or on the job, will involve both cognitive and affective factors. For many years, and quite understandably so, counselor education has placed a heavy emphasis upon cognitive factors in the selection process and cognitive learning in didactic courses; but research does not vindicate our reliance upon cognitive factors in isolation from conative factors; for example, Joslin (1961) found some positive relationship between growth in knowledge and interview performance, but with hardly better odds than flipping a coin. Practicum supervisors also react strongly to cognitive stimuli from typescripts of counseling interviews—at least this emphasis was one of the conclusions from a study involving 18 supervisors of the North Central Region (Walz & Roeber, 1962). Although research has been tending toward a study of affective factors and their relationship to counseling performance (13), it has not established whether affective factors in isolation from cognitive factors can improve the odds of our predictions. We can only conclude that our research has not yet established the relative significance of cognitive and affective factors. Man is a thinking, feeling organism. We might better turn our efforts toward discovering patterns that combine cognitive and affective traits, patterns that portend movement toward successive stages of development (Embree, 1951; Hunt, 1962; Super & Bachrach, 1957).

2. During a practicum, differential trait patterns call for the use of differential criteria of development for counselor-candidates.

From the first hypothesis, we assume that individuals who complete didactic counselor-education courses, especially those courses that are prerequisites for a practicum, exhibit a variety of trait patterns. And if counselor-candidates are selected according to a set of fixed criteria, they still show significant interpersonal and intrapersonal trait differences. This second hypothesis merely acknowledges these individual differences as inescapable, and places considerable stress upon the identification of developmental criteria appropriate to the trait pattern of each counselor-candidate. Developmental criteria are day-to-day, week-by-week behavior cues, which indicate whether a counselor-candidate is effecting desirable changes in trait patterns—desirable in the sense that they increase his effectiveness in interpersonal relationships, and are so satisfying to him that they are likely to become permanent parts of his behavior repertoire. This hypothesis further assumes that these criteria, although they overlap somewhat from one individual to another, are so unique for each counselor-candidate that it is impossible to postulate a global set of criteria for groups of candidates.

In order to understand the intent of this hypothesis, let us take the case of a fictitious counselor-candidate by the name of Mr. Bill. Having progressed through didactic courses with much higher than average marks, Mr. Bill enrolls in a practicum. In a seminar-type group with five other enrollees, Mr. Bill does not contribute to discussions; the supervisor becomes concerned about his aloof lack of interest and his failure to participate. In a coached-client interview, Mr. Bill again seems aloof and unable to express warmth or affection. In a conference with his supervisor and from test results, Mr. Bill indicates a pattern of behavior marked by the attitude that "any show of affection or feeling toward another person is a sign of weakness." In his teaching experience, Mr. Bill's major concern was control of students. He felt that a teacher should be respected, but not necessarily liked, by his students—this style of teaching was a natural one because it fit well into his style of living. Developmentally, self-control seemed to have been a family pattern, for his father, mother, and siblings led a Spartan-like existence. What can we postulate as some immediate and long-range criteria for Mr. Bill's personal and professional development in a practicum? Some of us might raise questions regarding his selection as a counselor-candidate—but the deed is done and what criteria should we use? Can we expect that he will ever become a gregarious, outgoing person exuding warmth and readily expressing affection toward other persons? (There are serious questions that might be raised about counselor-educators developing images of an ideal counselor as someone similar to their real or ideal perceptions of themselves—and then permitting these images to govern selection and methodology.) Should he first be referred to a psychological service for counseling? There are some among us who advocate and others who question such a procedure for counselor-candidates (Arbuckle, 1961, p. 67; Tyler, 1961, p. 248). What if we assumed that we were not going to require a complete change of personality, but rather would work toward slight modifications that might accommodate a few visual cues of understanding and affection? Here there might be two schools of thought, one emphasizing personality change first, followed by a counseling practicum; the other assuming that a practicum, by small increments of change, can affect personality and make whatever adaptations are necessary to develop an acceptable style of counseling. Recognizing the danger of generalizing from insufficient data, we might tentatively postulate that Mr. Bill is progressing in a practicum if we were to observe the following behavior cues:

    a.   An increasing amount of small-group participation—and a continued trend toward participation, perhaps slow at first. His increasing participation in the small group will be transferred to other groups.

    b.   An increasing amount of visual, nonverbal acceptance cues in interviews—and an easier reading of these cues.

    c.   During interviews, an increasing indication of visual, nonverbal cues at the time of critical incidents, such as unexpected counselee behavior, direct questioning, rejection of counseling or testing, expressions of hostility or rejection by a counselee, etc.

    d.   During interviews, Mr. Bill does not retreat into intellectualism or technicalities of tests or other information whenever a client expresses affection or positive regard toward him.

    e.   During conferences with his supervisor, Mr. Bill evidences an increasing desire to discuss his feelings about interpersonal relationships and certain adaptations which he feels he can accommodate.

In an actual situation, these criteria may be stated in terms of more specific practicum activities. These statements then become immediate criteria. It is also self-evident that these criteria are working hypotheses, which can be altered as new insights are gained into Mr. Bill's development. These criteria may be developed by supervisor and/or counselor-candidate in many ways, such as conferences, self-reports (Chenault, 1962), and so forth.

The formulation of differential criteria seems to be a reasonable approach on two counts: (1) counselor-candidates differ with respect to the motivations they bring to a practicum and, therefore, their development will not be identical; (2) these complex motivations, when coupled with differential patterns of other traits, preclude identical rates of development for all enrollees. Differential criteria can account for individual differences and form a rationale for eventual endorsement of enrollees as independently functioning counselors, assuming that enrollees perceive endorsement as worth the time and effort it takes to reach this level of personal and professional development.

3. Differential criteria of development call for the use of differential patterns of practicum experiences and practicum supervision.

If we are able to identify trait patterns and also unique criteria for each counselor-candidate's projected development, it then follows that we can identify unique patterns of practicum experiences and supervision by which we hope to transform a counselor-candidate into an independently functioning counselor. The concept of a tailor-made practicum for each candidate is not a new idea. Its antecedents can be found in any practicum where a supervisor (or a group of supervisors) designs differential experiences in order to effect changes in an enrollee's counseling repertoire. "Counseling repertoire" is expected to encompass not only mastery of substantive knowledge, but also conative learning, such as a candidate's respect for, acceptance of, and approach to others individually and in groups. (And it might also be important to assume that a respect and acceptance of himself undergirds his relationships with others.) Again, these differential experiences may have some similarities from one individual to another and yet not be common as a whole to a group of counselor-candidates.

For a practical application, let us look again at Mr. Bill's situation. His supervisor can choose from a number of practicum experiences (APA, 1952; Williamson, 1948, pp. 299–305) and supervisory relationships (Arbuckle, 1961, pp. 72–76; Demos & Zuwaylif, 1962). Practicum experiences come in many forms, such as observation of other counselors, listening to tapes of other counselors, counseling with coached clients, role playing, reading case histories, and counseling with "live" clients. Supervisory relationships have at least two dimensions: (1) roles, such as variations among paternalism, laissez faire, and permissiveness, played by supervisor; and (2) major thrusts or themes during supervisory sessions, such as emphases upon the counselor's behavior during interviews, upon an understanding of the client, upon cognitive material that the counselor-candidate has not mastered as yet, or upon the supervisor's relationship with a counselor-candidate. In Mr. Bill's case, what differential experiences might help him to relate more warmly with his clients? It is at this point that we must look elsewhere for clues regarding differential approaches to supervision. Trait theory can help us to understand counselor-candidates, their trait patterns, and hopefully what they need in order to become independently functioning counselors. Other theories will have to supply a rationale for integrating these understandings with practicum resources for the development of each counselor-candidate.

In summary, a counselor-candidate's development in a practicum is directly related to his discovery and development of a style of counseling that is consistent, within professional limits, with his present and developing style of life. Such a goal assumes that counselor development and personal development go hand in hand; and that superficial change in one, as a result of a practicum, is not likely to effect permanent change in the other, nor is either one apt to transfer to work on the job. It furthermore assumes that development in a practicum is dependent upon (1) understanding a counselor-candidate's pattern of traits, (2) setting up differential criteria for assessing his progress, and (3) designing practicum experiences and supervision that expedite his personal and professional development. Trait theory can help in the first two understandings, but differential practicum supervision and experiences are dependent upon other theories. Although perhaps idealistic, these hypotheses nevertheless provide a framework around which we may eventually develop a rationale for practicum supervision.

REFERENCES

American Psychological Association, Committee on Counselor Training, Division of Counseling Psychology. The practicum training of counseling psychologists. *American Psychologist,* 1952, **7**, 182–188. (a)

American Psychological Association, Committee on Counselor Training, Division of Counseling Psychology. *Counselor training; Methods and procedures.* Columbia: University of Missouri Press, 1952. (b)

Arbuckle, D. S. *Counseling: An introduction.* Boston: Allyn and Bacon, 1961.

Arnold, D. L. Counselor education as responsible for self development. *Counselor Education and Supervision,* 1962, **1**, 185–192.

Association for Counselor Education and Supervision, & American School Counselor Association. *Counselor education: A progress report on standards.* Washington, D.C.: American Personnel and Guidance Association, 1962.

Chenault, J. A. The diary report in counselor education. *Counselor Education and Supervision,* 1962, **1**, 193–198.

Demos, G. D., & Zuwaylif, F. L. H. Counselor attitudes in relation to the theoretical positions of their supervisors. *Counselor Education and Supervision*, 1962, **1**, 8–13.

Embree, R. B., Jr. The use of practicums and internships in counselor training. *Educational and Psychological Measurement*, 1951, **11**, 752–760.

Hill, G. E. The selection of school counselors. *Personnel and Guidance Journal*, 1961, **39**, 355–360.

Hunt, C. M. Developmental phases of counselor growth. *Counselor Education and Supervision*, 1962, **1**, 45–51.

Jones, A. Preparation of teachers and specialists for guidance service. *Review of Educational Research*, 1942, **12**, 127.

Joslin, L. C., Jr. Knowledge and counseling competence: An investigation of two outcomes of a counselor education program. Unpublished doctoral dissertation, University of Michigan, 1961.

Kazienko, L. W. Self-description of good and poor counselor trainees. *Counselor Education and Supervision*, 1962, **1**, 106–123.

Pepinsky, H. B., & Pepinsky, P. N. *Counseling theory and practice.* New York: Ronald, 1954.

Super, D. E., & Bachrach, P. B. *Scientific careers and vocational development theory.* New York: Bureau of Publications, Teachers College, Columbia University, 1957.

Thorndike, E. L. Measurement in education. *Teachers College Record*, 1921, **22**, 379.

Thorndike, R. L., & Hagen, E. *10,000 careers.* New York: Wiley, 1959.

Thurstone, L. L. *Multiple factor analysis: A Development and expansion of the vectors of the mind.* Chicago: University of Chicago Press, 1947.

Tyler, L. E. *The work of the counselor.* (Rev. ed.) New York: Appleton-Century-Crofts, 1961.

Tuma, A. H., & Gustad, J. W. The effects of client and counselor personality characteristics on client learning in counseling. *Journal of Counseling Psychology*, 1957, **4**, 136–141.

Walz, G. R., & Roeber, E. C. Supervisors' reactions to a counseling interview. *Counselor Education and Supervision*, 1962, **2**, 2–7.

Williamson, E. G. Supervision of counseling services. *Educational and Psychological Measurement*, 1948, **8**, 297–311.

Practicum Supervision: Integrated Theory of Supervision

Garry R. Walz

University of Michigan

Edward C. Roeber

Indiana State University—Terre Haute

Norman C. Gysbers

University of Missouri—Columbia

Michael Helge Ronnestad

University of Oslo

If one were to poll counselor-educators, beginning counselors, and experienced counselors as to what experience in their preparation had the most meaning for them, the result would be near unanimous—practicum! Needless to say, such unanimity in education is rare. It is all the more unusual when we consider that the practicum is a relatively new experience on the educational scene, and that differences in practicum organization and content are many and run deep. The experiences an individual has in a practicum in one institution may differ considerably from what he might have in another. Seemingly, though, the experience would be highly valued wherever it was taken and however it was conducted.

There are those who would question any intellectual tampering with so flourishing an educational enterprise, asserting that the very diversity of approaches, and of opportunities for individual creation, may be the secret of the potency of this experience. However correct these feelings may be, there would seem to be a larger consideration. We are no longer just preparing counselors. We are preparing counselors for a "changing world," and such counselors must be dynamic changers themselves if they are to even come near satisfying societal expectations. But our concern goes beyond the expectations of others. One overriding factor haunts all our endeavors: the demands on counselors, and public expectations of what counselors can do, have multiplied out of all proportion to the resources provided for counselor preparation. NDEA, improved counselor-education programs, and an expanding body of research notwithstanding, the time and resources available for counselor preparation are still limited. The challenge would seem to be what we can do now, given the same or even reduced resources—not what we could do if we were given greatly expanded resources. However successful we have been in the past, we must do even better in the future.

In the preceding essays by the authors of the present essay, the implications for supervision are considered from three theoretical positions: trait and factor, learning, and self. In each essay the aim is to develop recommendations for supervisory practices that stem logically from each position.

Throughout these essays the objective is the development of an integrated theory of supervision. The authors hope that such a theory would assist all of us in self-examination and research on our supervisory practices. Lest we seem presumptuous or even naive, we wish to make it clear that we see this as a beginning rather than an ending. We are mindful of the salutary effect that Callis's integrated theory of counseling (1960) has had on both practice and research. Perhaps most of all we were motivated by a conviction that only by making specific and concrete what we felt, would it be available for examination and use by others. Therefore, we have tried to bring our thoughts together in a way that would provide testable propositions—if not testable, then at least readily understandable.

It is our hope, à la Hall and Lindzey, that the worth of these efforts will be judged by the research and discussion they provoke, rather than by the intrinsic merit of the theory. If the results of the theory are such that others are stimulated to raise questions or to undertake research, we will feel we have made our mark. We invite you to be our fellow travelers in exploring the process of supervision.

OBJECTIVES AND RATIONALE

It is noteworthy that none of the recent professional documents dealing with the practicum concern themselves specifically with objectives. Usually, reference is made to a global objective, such as "to effect the transformation of a counselor candidate to an independently functioning counselor [Roeber, 1962]." Some concern for objectives is implicit in the distinction made between laboratory experience, counseling practicum, and internship. Useful as these statements are, there would still seem to be a need for clarification regarding the major thrust of the counseling practicum.

The learnings in a practicum seemingly are of three kinds: cognitive, skills, and professional and self-development. Cognitive learnings emphasize information and concepts, such as counseling theories and occupational information. Skills learnings are acquired through practice, such as test interpretation and some aspects of interviewing. Professional and self-development are expressed in concern for confidentiality and congruence between counseling style and life-style.

THEORETICAL FOUNDATIONS

In the three theory essays by the authors, an attempt is made to understand supervision from the perspective of trait theory, learning theory, and self-theory. The integration of these positions is presented below as a series of 13 propositions.

PROPOSITIONS

An attempt is made here to distill the insights from the separate theoretical position-papers into an integrated whole. To assist in this integration, the propositions have been combined under four descriptive headings: The Development, The Learner, Facilitating Relationships, and Learning Experiences.

Development

1. Candidate learning is greatest when professional competencies and self-development are experienced by a candidate as coordinate emphases of the practicum.

Self-development is a necessary part of all professional development. Relationships are lived, not taught. But self-development is not in itself sufficient development. There is a professional core of knowledge, which may be stated in terms of performance objectives, that must be learned if the candidate is to realize the counseling potentials of his self-development.

The Candidate as a Learner

2. Significant learning by a candidate necessitates both self-discovered and directed learning experiences.
3. Learning is dependent upon self-understanding; that is, upon under-

standing one's unique characteristics as they relate to perceptions of self and others.

4. Learning is enhanced when performance objectives are stated for one's personal and professional development.
5. Candidate learning is facilitated when objective evaluation is made as to the degree to which performance objectives are met.

We should clearly distinguish between the candidate as a learner, assuming responsibility for resolving his own needs, and the candidate as a "learnee," assuming that we, as his teachers, undertake the responsibility of instructing him. It would be folly to suggest that all candidate learning must be self-discovered. Much of the cognitive material would never be learned if left to self-discovery. The crucial decision is determining what is most appropriate for this candidate at his level of development.

Facilitating Relationships

6. The supervisory relationship is that of both learner and helper.
7. The supervisor is characterized by feelings of warmth, acceptance, and positivism.
8. The supervisor is a spontaneous, open, and congruent person.
9. The supervisor's tasks include understanding individual differences among candidates, recognizing differential rates of candidate development, and providing learning experiences to help candidates reach the competency-level specified.

We have posited what we believe to be important dimensions of the supervisory relationship. There is little professional literature on the characteristics of a practicum supervisor. Typically, many assumptions are made regarding the relationship of counseling effectiveness to supervisory performance, even to the point of assuming that development of an adequate counseling repertoire transfers automatically to development of an equally adequate supervisory repertoire.

The propositions presented above describe the supervisor in terms similar to those used to describe a counselor. This seems appropriate. It is doubtful whether anyone could operate effectively as a supervisor unless he had experienced at least a degree of success as counselor. There is a need, however, for a further distinction. Demonstrating the capacity to form quality relationships with a student is no guarantee that an individual can form equally good relationships with counselor-candidates. We see evidence of this in the school-counselor who relates well with students but is at loggerheads with members of the faculty. Seemingly, relatability is a more specific concept than commonly assumed.

Learning Experiences

10. A wide range of instructional resources for both self-learning and directed learning is conducive to candidate growth.
11. Continuous and relevant feedback concerning the attainment of performance objectives is conducive to rapid and significant personal growth and acquisition of counseling skills.
12. Learning experiences should be adopted to the competency levels and the specific needs of counselor-candidates.
13. Candidate progress is promoted when disruptive emotions are absent from the practicum experiences and supervision.

In a study of university programs, Hatch (1962) identified variety of instructional procedures as one of the major criteria of a superior program. This finding would seem to have relevance for practicum. When the range of experiences and learning rates is considered, it is apparent that individual learning needs can only be met by a wide variety of instructional resources. Of particular importance is the need for greater depth and breadth of self-instructional materials. Such materials run the gamut from annotated bibliographies to counseling simulators.

Teaching machines hold particular promise. Such machines do not really teach, but they enable the candidate to come into contact with the supervisor through the mediation of the equipment. Much material of a cognitive, factual nature could be programmed. This would release the supervisor from the repetitive aspects of his teaching so he could concentrate on interpersonal relations and the inquiry phases of learning. It would also reduce the authoritarian aspects of his role. Most of us have the best of intentions with regard to promoting individual development, but our "needles are worn out" from playing the same record so many times.

It is a general concern that the practicum should provide adequate means of reinforcement. The reward may be so delayed ("Let's go over your tapes next week") and so diffuse ("That was a good interview") that reinforcement may operate only in a very broad sense. We need specific criteria with an immediate means of reinforcement.

In summary, from the perspective of an integrated theory, supervision may be viewed as the growth-enhancing, individualized process whereby experiences and feedback are provided to educated counselors capable of functioning independently and effectively.

REFERENCES

Callis, R. Toward an integrated theory of counseling. *Journal of College Student Personnel*, 1960.

Roeber, E. C. Practicum and internship. In Association for Counselor Education and Supervision, & American School Counselor Association, *Counselor education—A progress report on standards.* Washington, D.C.: American Personnel and Guidance Association, 1962.

Hatch, W. R. What standards do we raise? Report of meeting of Directors of National Defense Counseling and Guidance Training Institutes, U. S. Office of Education. Counseling and Guidance Institutes Branch, 1962.

Issues

1. Is the value of including the client in the supervisory situation outweighed by any practical problems, or are the practical problems a convenient rationale for not changing the model?
2. Should individual counseling or therapy be a required part of professional preparation? Would the requirement be more appropriate at the doctoral level, or would it have equivalent value at the master's?
3. Do some models of supervision require more capabilities of the supervisor than other models? If this is so, are there any implications for counseling education?
4. What should be the general basis for making a referral (with allowances for the fact that different instances may require different bases), and how can a practitioner determine the qualifications of the person *to* whom he makes the referral?

Annotated Readings

Pierce, R. M., & Schauble, P. G. Follow-up study on the effects of individual supervision in graduate school training. *Journal of Counseling Psychology.* 1971, **18**, (2) 186–187. (b)

The subjects were 14 counselor-trainees who had been part of an earlier study assessing the effects of high- and low-functioning supervisors on their supervisees. The results of the study indicated (1) that the supervisees of the high-level supervisors continued to function more effectively on the measured dimensions than the supervisees of the low-level supervisors; (2) that neither the supervisees of the high-level supervisors nor the supervisees of the low-level supervisors tended to change significantly on the measured dimensions.

Pierce, R. M., & Schauble, P. G. Toward the development of facilitative counselors: The effects of practicum instruction and individual supervision. *Counselor Education and Supervision,* 1971, **11**, (2) 83–89. (a)

The functioning of 22 counseling and therapy practicum students on the dimensions of empathy, regard, genuineness, and concreteness was assessed over a 20-week period. Predictions of growth were made on the basis of the level of functioning of individual supervisors and practicum instructors. It was found that students with high-level practicum instructors and low-level individual supervisors also showed significant gains, but took a longer period to do so. Students with low-level practicum instructors and low-level individual supervisors showed no growth on these dimensions.

Suggestions for Further Reading

Bandura, A. Psychotherapy based upon modeling principles. In A. E. Bergin & S. L. Garfield, (Eds.), *Handbook of psychotherapy and behavior change.* New York: John Wiley, 1971.

Eysenck, H. J., & Beech, R. Counterconditioning and related methods. In A. E. Bergin & S. L. Garfield (Eds.), *Handbook of psychotherapy and behavior change.* John Wiley, 1971.

Krasner, L. The operant approach in behavior therapy. In A. E. Bergin & S. L. Garfield (Eds.), *Handbook of psychotherapy and behavior change.* New York: John Wiley, 1971.

Murray, E. J., & Jacobson, L. I. The nature of learning in traditional and behavioral psychotherapy. In A. E. Bergin & S. L. Garfield (Eds.), *Handbook of psychotherapy and behavior change.* New York: John Wiley, 1971.

Ruble, R. A. Student-centered approaches to practicum supervision. *Counselor Education and Supervision,* 1968, **7,** 143–144.

Rychlak, J. F. A question posed by Skinner concerning human freedom, and an answer. *Psychotherapy: Theory, Research, and Practice,* 1973, **10** (1), 14–23.

Seaman, E. H., & Wurtz, R. E. Evaluating the practicum: Whither or wither? *Counselor Education and Supervision,* 1968, **7,** 282–285.

Skinner, B. F. *Beyond freedom and dignity.* New York: Alfred A. Knopf, 1972.

Strickland, B. The philosophy-theory-practice continuum: A point of view. *Counselor Education and Supervision,* 1969, **8,** 165–175.

CHAPTER 5

Theoretical, Professional, and Ethical Issues Involved in Preparation Programs

Virtually the entire scope of educational practice and research is subsumed in the topics of theoretical, professional, and ethical issues. It is probably true that these issues are so much with us that we take them for granted and do not reevaluate them. Their value is as much in provoking speculative thought and encouraging investigation as in providing structure and guidelines for the profession. If a service-oriented profession is to develop and grow, and at the same time to maintain a firm structure and cohesiveness, it must constantly develop and revise its theoretical foundation, which contributes so much to the direction of its educational programs, and determines to a large extent the vitality of the group as a whole. Constantly changing mores, service demands, and opportunities create issues, which can be ignored, or can be modified so as to be accommodated by already existing policies. The result of either approach is undoubtedly a static, somewhat lifeless organization, whose attractiveness to potential members is minimal and whose service to society might be questioned. What can be hoped for is the development of the profession through evaluation and subsequent change based on empirical data.

Finally, a profession is trusted by society in general, as well as by related professions, because of its ethics. If theoretical issues sustain the dynamism of the profession, and professional issues assure the continued growth of the profession, then ethical issues are essential to the effective delivery and reception of professional services to society.

Familiarity with the state of these three areas should be part of the fundamental and continuing professional education. They are, after all, the issues that affect us most directly, whether or not we involve ourselves. Familiarity and involvement are the chief means by which we experience our corporate professional identity and actualize our individual responsibility.

The first two authors in this chapter begin with similar statements indicating that the theoretical, professional, and ethical issues overlap considerably. They then proceed, with great clarity, to separate the issues; while each author approaches the task quite differently, their conclusions and recommendations are compatible. Arbuckle, with characteristic concern for the "larger" picture,

161

takes a more global approach. For example, he questions what the impact of federal funding will be on the future of the profession; he is concerned about how programs in counselor education may be mass-producing graduates who are alienated from their constituents and perhaps from themselves; and he urges a revamping of educational philosophy to reduce emphasis on "right" and "wrong" ways to practice.

Livers speaks to these three issues from the explicit perspective of those specifically concerned with implementing and developing an educational program geared to meet the needs of the profession. He discusses curriculum in terms of the specific demands of settings and populations; he explores the possiblity of defining counselor function by way of both field evaluation and analysis of the purpose of education in general. And finally he asks, since the counselor performs so many tasks, "to whom is he ultimately responsible?"

In the third essay a case is made for "ethical concern" on the part of the counselor-candidate. Farwell argues that a self-search for values is basic to effective operation within professional ethical guidelines. He offers the further argument that a study of the ethical positions of professional associations assists the counselor-in-preparation to understand some of the "what" and "why" of the experiences offered by preparation programs.

Theoretical, Professional, and Ethical Issues in Counselor Education

Dugald S. Arbuckle

Boston University

The division of the issues discussed in this essay into theoretical, professional, and ethical is somewhat artificial, since in a way it is obvious that all of these issues are theoretical, professional, and ethical. For ease of discussion, however, let us look first at what might best be described as theoretical issues, then at professional issues, and finally at ethical issues.

THEORETICAL ISSUES

The Functions of the Counselor

The two major theoretical issues, I would think, are those dealing with two obviously related problems—the functions of the counselor, and the effectiveness of the counseling process. One can hardly talk about professional education with any degree of understanding unless he knows whom he is educating and for what he is educating him, and these questions, as yet, are far from answered (Arbuckle, 1968a). It would probably be correct to say that the job of the counselor, over the years, has gradually evolved as a response to specific needs of children in school, needs that were not being met by other staff members. This is probably one of the reasons for the line that unfortunately continues to separate those who practice counseling in schools from those who educate counselors, and the difference sometimes makes communication difficult. This high level of sensitivity is beautifully illustrated in a published reaction, appropriately titled "Riposte," by Blanche Paulson (1967), who is the Director of the Bureau of Personnel Services for the Chicago Public Schools. This was a response to an article in which I suggested there ought to be an ecumenical movement encompassing counselors, psychologists, and social workers in schools (Arbuckle, 1967). The sensitivity was especially apparent in such statements as "One wonders if the school really exists for Arbuckle . . .," and "Apparently in an effort to emphasize the distinctness of his point of view . . .," and ". . . if the professors have not been talking with each other they should begin, for their graduates have been holding dialogues at the operational level for years," and "In the section on background only the psychologist escapes some derogation," and "It is doubtful, however, whether he needs to repeat his generous offer of the proud name 'school counseling psychologist.' School-counselors and school social workers are justly proud of their own names."

These statements reflect a suspicion, particularly of "professors" and "psychologists," which, while by no means totally unjustified, is, nevertheless, regrettable. The other side of the coin was reflected in other communications regarding the same article, which in effect chastised the author for suggesting that the good name of school psychologists should be sullied by comparing them with school-counselors. This, in turn, reflects the attitude of a special committee of the Division of Counseling Psychology of the American Psychological Association (1962), whose published scope and standards of preparation in psychology for school-counselors reads almost like a complete education program at the doctoral level for a category of professionals who might be called something like "school-counseling psychologists."

This lack of communication and understanding between the practitioners of school counseling and the educators of school-counselors continues, and any broad agreement as to the functions of counselors is extremely difficult as long as this gap exists.

In addition to the gap between the school-counselor and the educator of the school-counselor, there continues to be a misunderstanding, which is more than ideological or methodological, among those who educate school-counselors. It is the concept that there is a right way and a wrong way, and this attitude is illustrated, ironically enough, in a book called *Revolution in Counseling*. McDaniel (1966), one of the authors of the book, says:

To oversimplify, the revolution has overthrown the "um-humm" and "you feel," replacing them with "that's good: and "try this." The counselor not only listens— attentively, empathetically—but also talks and does—even thinks and plans. What the counselor does *outside* of the office—in developing curriculum, in modifying teacher behavior, in building a better learning environment—is important.

Surely all would agree that any effective counselor does, and has been doing, what McDaniel suggests, but this does not mean that those who talk in terms of psychotherapy, and individual counseling, those who work for long periods of time with children where the stress is on affect rather than cognition, must be thrown out. "That's good" and "Try this" make good sense for some children some of the time, but the "um-humm" and the "you feel" also make good sense for some children some of the time. Thus, among counselor-educators and school-counselors, there continues to be a wall of misunderstanding, and until this is broken down, the functions of the school-counselor will continue to be vague and unclarified.

The issue of counselor functions is also being affected by the recent stress on behavior therapies. The extent to which the counselor is a conditioner and manipulator of the human individual is a problem that has been with us for a long time, but the behavior therapies are receiving particular stress today, and many see conditioning and manipulating and modifying the behavior of the client as the logical function of the counselor.

The issue, probably, is not so much whether the counselor is a conditioner or a modifier of behavior. Of course he is; no one could be in intimate and personal contact with a person without having some impact or effect on him. The basic issue concerns the extent to which the counselor aids the individual to determine for himself, accepting the responsibility of his own decisions about the direction in which he chooses to go. This, in turn, is determined by the degree of the counselor's personal freedom. Is he free enough to allow the client to be who he will, or must he, subtly or otherwise, impose upon the client his own version of the culture's version of the good life. Thus the issue for the counselor-educator is simple: how much do you impose upon the student counselor your version of the right way, conditioning him to become the sort of counselor you wish him to become, with the consequence that he, in turn, will condition his clients to become the sort of persons he wishes them to become? Again, this is not a black and white issue. As counselors and counselor-educators, we condition and we impose. The issue is: How much?

The Effectiveness of Counseling

One might assume that as a profession ages, it develops more precise answers to the question, "What is the result of what you do?" In the case of counseling, however, we might wonder whether we have more evidence now that questions the effects of counseling than supports the positive effects of counseling!

In many ways Rogers was one of the first to challenge and question the effectiveness of traditional psychotherapy, and those who attacked him indicated rather clearly that they had little in the way of empirical evidence to back up their statements about the effects of their particular brand of psychotherapy. It is likely that at least part of the violence of the reaction against Rogers was due to the fact that he was presenting some evidence as to what happened to clients with whom he was involved, whereas his opponents could give little other than their opinions.

Probably the major thorn in the side of all counselors and psychotherapists, however, was Eysenck. In an article published some years ago (1952), he presented evidence supporting his flat statement that "the figures fail to support the hypothesis that psychotherapy facilitates recovery from neurotic disorder." A few years later, Levitt (1957) presented evidence that led to a similar conclusion regarding children. He said, "It is concluded that the results of the present study fail to support the view that psychotherapy with 'neurotic' children is effective."

In more recent years, two of the more questioning voices regarding the effectiveness of counseling and psychotherapy have been those of Bergin and Carkhuff. Bergin (1967) presents compelling evidence questioning the efficacy of psychotherapy. Summarizing his presentation, he says, "Meat controlled studies of psychotherapy reveal no significant effect of treatment." Carkhuff does much the same thing in a book edited by himself and Berenson (1967), and their statement is that "there are no professional training programs which have demonstrated their efficacy in terms of a translation to constructive behavioral gains in clients."

While there is increasing evidence that the effective practice of counseling and psychotherapy is related to such factors as congruence and genuineness, nonpossessive warmth, and empathic understanding, there is also evidence that at least implies that most programs of counselor education do not consider these as the basic ingredients around which a counselor-education program should be built. Studies by Bergin and Solomon (1963), and by Melloh (1964), for example, indicated no relationship between the level of empathic understanding provided in counseling and such measures as grade-point average and practicum grades.

Adding to the skepticism about the effectiveness of counselors and counselor-education programs is the fact that there is evidence indicating that lay personnel are just as effective, or ineffective, as professionally trained counselors and psychotherapists. Golann and Magoon (1966), for example, described an experiment from which they concluded that psychotherapeutic services can be provided in a school setting by carefully selected and specially trained individuals who do not have professional degrees. Carkhuff (1966) concludes that the evidence available today "indicates that the primary conditions of effective treatment are conditions which minimally trained non-professional persons can provide."

The various studies reported above do not, of course, refer only to the effects of psychotherapy in a clinical or medical setting. They hold just as true for schools and the children in them. Hill and Grieneeks (1966), for example, reported a study from which they concluded, "If academic counseling is positively affecting performance it is not being reflected when the criterion measure chosen is grade point average." In a study which won a research award from the American Personnel and Guidance Association (APGA), Gonyea (1964) indicated that there was a negative relationship between the extent to which counselors developed the "ideal therapeutic relationship" and the degree to which their clients reported themselves to be improved.

Traditional university programs of all kinds tend to stress the intellectual, the cognitive. The scholar is one who knows, more than one who does, and the "publish or perish" philosophy is generally interpreted to mean that advancement in a college or university is more dependent on one's ability to write about what he knows than on his ability to communicate in some meaningful fashion to students—i.e., to teach what he knows. Thus it is not unreasonable that the traditional counselor-education program tended to stress what one knew about people, the culture, and behavior and change, and minimized the place of the counselor in effecting change in the behavior of the individual. There was maximum stress on what the student-counselor knew about the client, minimum stress on what he knew about himself. There was an imposition on the student-counselor of what others felt to be effective means of learning; there was little opportunity for the student-counselor to develop what for him might possibly be effective means of learning, and helping others to learn. There was a stress on understanding the theory of counseling, rather than on the ability to practice counseling. In a sense, an experience was provided for the student-counselor that was quite contrary to the experience he was supposedly learning to provide for future clients. It was a case of "Learn what we are telling you to do, in terms of a relationship with future clients, even though this is quite contrary to the behavior you are experiencing with us."

It would seem reasonable enough to conclude that a major issue today for counselors and the educators of counselors is the question or whether or not counseling does what it is supposed to do. If some of the evidence is correct, it would at least seem possible that counselor-educators are educating student-counselors in unverified ways to have unknown effects on clients.

PROFESSIONAL ISSUES

There are many issues and problems in counselor education, but two would appear to stand out. These are the *involvement*, or lack of involvement, of state departments of education and professional bodies in the accreditation of counselor-education programs, and the federal government's influence on and control of counselor-education programs.

State Certification and Professional Accreditation

The legal determination of what is required to educate a counselor continues to be controlled by state departments of education, and thus in the United States there continue to be fifty versions of what is necessary to educate an individual for "certification" as a counselor. It is obvious that one may question the professional status of any occupation when the criteria for certification vary drastically from state to state, and when the determination of professional adequacy is made by state officials, some of whom would have little professional standing in the very field whose workers they certify! Equally distressing, of course, is the fact that certification is generally not acquired by graduation from an accredited program, but rather by an official determination, usually person by person, as to whether the applicant has satisfied an individual official's interpretation of state requirements for certification. While the official requirements change with painful slowness, interpretations of these requirements vary as the certifying personnel vary, and when personnel turnover is high, so is the level of confusion.

Thus, on the basis of state certification, the position of the school-counselor is not a definable position, at least on the national level, and the student who sees counseling in the schools as his future occupation will immediately note a wide divergence as to the criteria for the professional education of counselors.

Dissatisfaction with this individual, state by state pattern of counselor certification was evident well over a decade ago, and various members of the APGA began to press for professional approval or even accreditation of programs of counselor education by the appropriate professional body. A major step came in 1962, with the publication by APGA of six position papers recommending standards that should be developed for the selection and professional preparation of secondary-school counselors (1962). In the same publication it was indicated that a revised statement would be published by January 1964, thus "allowing time for further consideration before action is taken by the 1964 Senate [1964]." A revised set of standards was voted upon and accepted by the Association for Counselor Education and Supervision (ACES) at its 1967 convention in Dallas (1967).

Whether the results of all of this activity are worth the effort is questionable, since the standards suffer from two overwhelming flaws. The first is that they are based on opinion, rather than the evidence of empirical research. Scores of grass-roots committees over the years have contributed their opinions through various questionnaires, and the majority opinion has eventually appeared as a "standard." This might be considered the democratic approach to research, but it is somewhat akin to having the teacher determine the "right" answer by having the students vote on what they consider to be the "right" answer. The "opinion" procedure would be questionable even if it were the opinion only of those persons who have shown over the years that they have a high level of understanding in the field of counseling and counselor education. This, however, has been anything but the case. Thus the second major flaw is that the opinions are not even valid as expert opinion. A recent U.S. Office of Education directory (1964) lists some 325 institutions as having programs of counselor education, and this is to be expected, since the way an institution gets listed is to say that it has a program of counselor-education! Nor does an institution have to have much involvement in counseling and counselor education in order to become a member of ACES. Thus, an opinion from one who has little or no involvement in counseling and counselor education becomes just as valid in determining a "standard" as the opinion of one who has spent his life in the field. Hill (1967) bemoans the fact that only one-third of some 2000 members of ACES bothered to answer a 10-minute check list, and questions their level of professionalism. A more logical answer might be that those who were most professionally involved in counseling and counselor education could see no sense in having standards for a profession determined in this way, and simply refused to play the game.

Thus the standards, whatever they might be, might be questioned from a research point of view, and a perusal of them tends to buttress the fact that they represent opinion rather than evidence. It is not so much that there is anything questionable about the standards as such; rather, the standards do not get at what would appear to be the crucial elements of a counselor-education program. Thus it could well be that two programs could be rated as acceptable on the basis of the standards, yet one might prove to be quite ineffective, the other quite effective. Much stress is placed on the cognitive aspects of the program, and much of it reads somewhat like a program for the education of chemists. The standard referring to the self-understanding and self-evaluation of the student counselor is dealt with rather casually, the statement being that "opportunities . . . are provided." More important would be the extent to which the opportunities were used, and what was the result of their use. After all, the provision of a gymnasium in a school is not necessarily any indication of top physical condition among the students! The practicum experience, of necessity, is described in a cognitive sense, and a top-ranked practicum, according to the standards, could very easily prove to be totally meaningless to a group of students. In a similar manner, the qualifications of the "well-qualified" staff are described in the usual terms of degrees and experience.

Thus it would seem that APGA, at the present time, feels that it can go no further than providing sets of standards for a quality program of counselor education (1967). It has, as yet, refused to accept the responsibility of becoming the accrediting agency of school-counselors, as have its two most involved divisions, ACES, and the American School Counselors Association. Thus, the certification of school-counselors continues to be an issue, but for at least some time to come, it would appear that state certification, varying from state to state, on a person-to-person basis, will continue in effect. A program of counselor education that might be totally inadequate on the basis of professional standards will continue to produce individuals who will be certified as counselors in various states, and a person who is regarded as a legitimate "counselor" in one state will have a status of illegitimacy in a neighboring state.

The Influence and Control of the Federal Government

Federal involvement in public education has, of course, been an issue for many decades, but one decade ago it was a minor issue as far as counselor-education was concerned. Recently, it has been, without doubt, a major issue, and it may well again become *the* major issue. Money represents power and control, and the more federal money is poured into the education of counselors, the more the federal government can exercise control over the direction of counselor-education, and thus over counseling. The major involvement of the federal government in counselor-education began with the passage of the National Defense Education Act of 1958 (NDEA), and that involvement increased tremendously in subsequent years, although in 1972 it waned considerably. There is always the possibility of a resurgence. It is surely crucial that when federal funds are provided for professional purposes, the direction of the use of those funds be determined by those who are professionally most competent in the field. This, in turn, should be determined by their professional peers, and not by federal bureaucrats who have little or no professional competence in the particular area. While in the heyday of NDEA activities there was criticism of the activities of the U.S. Office of Education by individual members of APGA, there has been little sign of action by APGA against bureaucratic control of federal funds assigned for the purpose of counselor education. If federal funds are provided so that quality programs of counselor education can become available, it would seem logical that those involved in counseling and in the education of counselors should be the determiners of the criteria for excellence in counselor education, as well as for those institutions that should have such programs. As a case in point, the Director of the Division of Educational Personnel Training made several basic changes in the criteria for the determination of quality in counseling and guidance institutes that ran counter to the recommendations of APGA.

Although at the present time federal monies for the support of counselor education have waned, there is always the proposition that we should learn from experience. There was, during the heyday of NDEA, considerable evidence of bureaucratic control. Members of the profession, both as individuals and through professional associations, must insure that credibility gaps do not persist between counselors and counselor-educators and various offices of the federal government, particularly in reference to agencies or units that exercise control over the issuance of training grants. It is possible for one or two bureaucrats to hold very real power, and until professional bodies take action, the direction of counselor education may be determined by a few individuals of questionable competence. The determination of what constitutes a "good" program is particularly intriguing when one considers the increasing evidence that raises serious questions as to the efficiency of any of the current training programs for counselors.

It would probably be quite safe to say that the proposals for counselor education already funded by the federal government have hardly satisfied a criterion of counselor-education effectiveness based on empirical evidence. In all, the objectives were broad and human and highly desirable and bookish, but there is serious question as to the extent to which the programs were built around the objectives, as contrasted with the objectives being fitted to the program. The programs that were offered were still primarily cognitive in nature, with the stress on knowledge and knowing. The offering was still overwhelmingly through courses, for which semester-hours of credit were offered, and in which, we can assume, the student had the usual experience of being evaluated and judged on the basis of someone else's version of what he knew. It would appear that the major stress was on the development of knowledge in the broad area of the social sciences; it was to a lesser degree on knowledge about the client, and it was to a still lesser degree on knowledge about the counselor. A planned no-credit experience of self-understanding and self-appraisal rarely appears in program proposals. There is minimal evidence of any belief in the concept that the major resource the counselor brings to counseling is himself, at least in the sense that minimal stress is placed on the self-development and self-understanding of the counselor. All these things, of course, might have happened in these programs, but there was no way of telling this from the written proposals. In program proposals the most important ingredient in any program—the staff—remained generally little more than unknown names to the evaluators. We know little more than that most of the staff had doctorate degrees and a few years of experience in counseling or teaching, which may mean much, or little. Thus, the U.S. Office of Education was, in a way, playing a game of blind-man's buff with the professional education of school-counselors, as well as with the American taxpayer's dollar. Many of the proposals that were funded might well have provided effective experiences in counselor education, but the odds are that many that were not funded might have provided even more effective experiences. On the whole, the proposals that were funded do not appear to be too different from most standard counselor-education programs around the country; they were no more effective than most standard programs; and few, funded or not, would appear to be closely geared to the criteria that have been discussed.

It is of interest, and some concern, to note the recommendations made by the Special Subcommittee on Education of the House of Representatives after its investigation of the Division of Educational Personnel Training. The recommendations, three in number, said little or nothing, and no statement was made regarding the control and direction of counselor-education programs by the Division of Educational Personnel Training. From this we may reasonably enough assume that the committee approved of the degree of control and direction of professional programs by the federal government.

ETHICAL ISSUES

Three issues, which are primarily ethical in nature, would appear to stand out. These have to do with the broad question of change, the problem of the alienation of the student-counselor from the program, and the values of the counselor (Arbuckle, 1968b).

The Question of Change

There is little argument that the major function of the counselor is to help the client to change in some way. The change may, of course, be very minor, but the very fact that the client comes to the counselor means that he is saying, "I want to know something, or do something, or in some way have something happen to me, so that I will be not quite the way I am now." It may be a student simply asking about information on several colleges, or it may be an individual caught on drugs, seeing nothing ahead but the choice of slow destruction by drugs or more immediate death by suicide. In both cases, the counselor becomes involved with the client in the process of change—and both cases pose an ethical dilemma, a very minor one in the first case, a major one in the second case. What are some of the facts of this dilemma of change?

Tremendous as our powers of change may be today, those who are involved in operant conditioning assure us that they are nothing compared with what lies just around the corner. Bijou (1966) sees the counselor of the future as a behavorial engineer, and a rather routine problem brought to such a counselor might be the predetermination of the sex of a planned child. Somewhat more complicated, but quite within the realm of the reality of the not too distant future, would be the request for counseling in the determination of whether or not a planned child should be a genius or a person of low-level intelligence, or possibly one able to withstand unusual environmental stresses and strains. At such a stage, of course, sexual involvement for the purpose of reproduction would be distinctly old-fashioned, and too risky, since one would not know in advance what kind of child was going to be born. One would not even know the sex of the child until it was born! Even now scientists can put together a simple form of deoxyribonucleic acid (DNA), the chemical that determines the bodily form of every organism on earth, with full biological power. The goal ahead is to rewrite the genetic code, and thus redesign the bodily form of organisms. Men might then take direct command of the evolution of their own bodies, right from the very creation of life itself.

Thus the power of the manipulation and the direction and the control of one human by another is, without doubt, going to increase tremendously in the very near future, and Vance (1967) puts it modestly when she says, "Certainly man's understanding of technique in the behavioral sciences far surpasses his understanding and commitment to certain goals." If this poses something of an ethical problem now, it will soon pose a question of the very survival of the members of the human race as individual human beings possessed of individual rights and individual dignity. Even today we all know counselors who are so fascinated by technology that their mode of operation differs not at all from that of the experimental psychologist in his rat laboratory. Whether the creatures being experimented with are rats or humans is of no particular concern; the fascination is the ability of the counselor to modify and change the "other" almost as he wishes. Tillich (1961) was certainly correct, at least for some counselors, when he said that "technique has become not merely a means to an end, but an end in itself."

May (1961) felt this pressure when, in talking about existentialism, he said, "It seemed to many observers to be ineffectual against the onmoving lava of conformism, collectivism, and the robot man." But he also voiced the feeling and the faith of the existentialist, as well of as those who would distinguish individual man from a random collection of behaviors, when he added, "No matter how great the forces victimizing the human being, man has the capacity to know that he is being victimized, and thus to influence in some way how he will relate *to* his fate. There is never lost that kernel of the power to take some stand, to make some decision, no matter how minute." But the hard fact of life, neither moral nor immoral, is that the power to change grows daily. This reality must be faced by the counselor, and he must raise for himself the question of where he stands, today and tomorrow, rather than looking wistfully backward at a yesterday that is gone.

As the power to change grows, the more serious becomes the simple question, "Who determines who will be changed and what will be the direction of the change, for what purpose?" Our Western civilization is based, in general, on the supremacy of man over the state, and this shows in the political concept that the government is our voice, not our master, and when it no longer is our voice, then we change it. While most Americans would still hold to this concept in theory, its practice has often been, at best, rather half-hearted. Counselors, as any student knows, show a wide variance in their practice of the concept of "individual rights," especially the rights of the young as contrasted with the old. Van Kaam (1967), for example, is very much on the side of the individual when he says:

> ... when I am acting as an authentic counselor I want the unique personality, the freedom, the spontaneous initiative of my counselee: I want him to grow in his own independent being. . . . Therapeutic care does not want to force, to push, to impose, to seduce. What is more, as soon as the counselor tries to overpower the counselee, if only by suggestion, his activity is no longer therapeutic care.

Williamson (1967), however, shows some doubts about the capacities of the individual when he says, "Does he [the individual] have the right to become less than he could become? . . . unfortunately . . . many of us are inclined to let the individual make his own choice in a simplistic misunderstanding of freedom within democracy." Moser (1962) seems to attribute a somewhat questionable capacity to the clergyman, while giving no credit to the client, when he says, "Since God is able to direct the clergyman in other areas, the same power will abide in advice giving." This attitude is apparently ecumenical, since Saalfield (1958), a priest, reflects somewhat similar feelings when he says, "The Catholic counselor should ask the pupil 'How often do you go to Mass and confession?' Catholic counselors must create right attitudes." Many students in schools and colleges will attest to the wide divergence between the supposed acceptance of the theory of individual rights and the actual practice of this belief. It is unfortunate that counselors are among those who show a high level of distrust in the capacity of the young, or, for that matter, of anyone other than themselves, to determine the direction in which one might go.

The feeling that "I know better than you what is the best direction for you" is all too common when the old are with the young, when parents are with their children, when teachers are with students, and even, alas, when counselors are with clients. Shoben (1966) points to the major flaw in this attitude when he says, "It is equally a mistake to assume that predictive success or the power of behavioral control somehow reveals the normative ends toward which conduct may properly be directed." Van Kaam (1966), addressing himself to the same issue in talking about the teacher, says, "He should create the ideal conditions in which the child himself can awaken to these values; and the most ideal condition for this awakening of a spontaneous insight and estimation is not to force such ideals upon him. In that case we prepare him only for hypocrisy or an uncreative mechanized life or even neurosis."

But man in a sense is conditioned not to believe in himself, he is conditioned away from himself. He learns all too frequently, from his parents, his teachers, his clergymen, how not to become the authentic person, how never to experience the ecstatic thrill that comes only to those who are free—free to live and free to die, but never to be chained. The respect that one has for his own freedom and rights is usually reflected in the respect he shows for the rights and the freedoms of others. The autocrat is always a slave, since his continuing lack of trust in others is merely a reflection of his lack of trust in himself.

The counselor too, of course, is a conditioned product of his society, but the counselor should be different. He should be the one who has somehow intervened, with help or on his own, and cut into the bland and painless process that is manipulating and modifying and molding him into an faceless image. He is the one who somewhere has said, "Wait. What is this? Must I do this? Must I become this person? Why?" He has assumed control of his own destiny, and he has accepted responsibity for the direction in which he might go. He is a free man, and he expects neither a kindly God nor a kindly nature to lead him by the hand, and accept responsibility for his life and his living. Nor is he fearful of what a vengeful God or a vengeful nature might do to him. He can accept the risks of living the free life of the free man.

The Alienation of the Student-Counselor

Programs of counselor education, like other forms of human conditioning, all too frequently tend to enlarge the area of alienation of the student-counselor. A student's professional program frequently teaches him that there is a great deal he must not believe, very little he can believe. Rather than help him to open and enlarge his area of potential experiencing, it restricts him even further. Dreyfus (1967) expresses this feeling when he says:

In many ways schools of psychotherapy tend to reinforce man's alienation from man. The therapist, like the physician, keeps his therapeutic armamentarium between himself and the patient, preventing real inter-human contact. . . . Helping would-be therapists to be more human with freedom to respond should be the goal.

An excellent example of this restricting of the freedom of the student counselor, and of the pressure on the student *not* to experience and *not* to question, but rather to think as he is told to think, is indicated by this comment, written by a counselor-educator of some renown, on the paper of a student:

Crap. . . . your first big problem will be to bury this self-concept junk on the high school level particularly in the educational-vocational level. Counselors should be expected to know, offer alternatives based on accurate and current information. Then they can save the foot-and-mouth game of reflection for those students who need support and can't be hurt too much by ineptness in training and technique.

The attitude behind this comment is very clearly, "Do it my way, because my way is the right way." It is little wonder that students who are the products of such programs are alienated not only from other professional ideologies and values, but probably from most of their fellow humans who do not think as they think. In a sense, then, they become the conditioning agents of the culture, and the repression of the individual, under the guides of a professional relationship, is continued. This was illustrated recently in a videotape of a discussion among a group of students who were involved in clinical practices. One member of the group described herself as holding to a psychological orientation, spent the whole time defending her position, and appeared to be totally closed to any individual who did not hold to her concept of orientation. Another student described himself as holding to a physiological orientation, and he was as defensive and as closed as the first student. It is distressing at the professional level, among those who at least wear the garments of the learned, to find this same narrow indoctrination, this "We have the answers," this learned alienation of self from others, and of self from self.

The Values of the Counselor

The reaction of the counselor to ethical issues would appear to be a reflection of the values that differentiate him as a human being (Arbuckle, 1970). The counselor can be a powerful instrument in helping an individual to move and to change, and movement and change usually imply change in values. The values of the counselor, then, as one who has potentially such a powerful effect on the lives of others, are obviously of critical importance. Dare one suggest that there are certain values that should be a part of the counselor, and that there are others that should have no part in his makeup?

Counselors with different values do apparently differ in what they do well and what they do poorly, as one would expect. In a study by Watley (1967), for example, counselors with a trait-and-factor orientation differed significantly from those with a client-centered orientation in their ability to predict freshmen grades and persistence and success in an educational major. Thus, if the ability to predict is considered to be an important aspect of counseling, it would appear that counselors whose values reflect a trait-and-factor orientation would be a better bet than those whose values reflect a client-centered orientation. A study by Bare (1967), on the other hand, tended to indicate that both clients and counselors agreed that counselors who showed achievement needs, high original thinking, high vigor, and low-order needs, are rated as being more helpful, as facilitating a closer relationship, and as showing empathy for their clients. Thus, if a close, empathic counselor-client relationship were considered to be critical, then counselors of this kind would be a better bet. In a study of general counseling effectiveness, Whiteley, Sprinthall, Mosher, and Donaghy (1967) found a high relationship between the effective counselor and cognitive flexibility, which refers to dimensions of open-mindedness, adaptability, and a resistance to premature closure in perception and cognition. In this study, at least, the counselor who had a higher level of individual freedom, and was less of a conditioned product of his culture, would appear to be more effective.

Thus, one might at least theorize that if we hold to the importance of individual freedom, and if we believe in a society in which the dignity and the rights of individual man are the only reason for the existence of the state, then the values of the counselor might at least be characterized by some of the following:

Openness and flexibility, which means that the counselor is not the slave of any dogma—religious, secular, professional, or personal. The belief of a person is a part of his experiencing and his living, and his beliefs and values are open to change as circumstances and people change. The counselor does not believe because he has to, and he accepts personal responsibility for his beliefs. All his beliefs are thus laced with rationality, and he does not continue to believe what has intellectually been shown to be false.

The counselor accepts belief as an area in which we do not know, in an empirical sense, and thus sees it as irrational to argue that one person's belief is right and another's is wrong. In a religious sense this would mean that one could be devout and still accept the possibility of error, and this, in turn, would of course mean that religion would be an area of uncertainty rather than an area of certainty. "I believe" would never be confused with "I know," and there would be little point in closing one's mind to a colleague, or killing one's fellow-man, because of a differing belief, since one would accept the possibility that the colleague or the fellow-man might be right.

Since belief is a matter of faith, it would seem logical to suggest that the counselor, at least, should believe positively. Why not hold to the belief that man *can* grow and develop, and that he has within him the seeds of self-actualization, rather than hold to the belief that man is vicious and evil, and must spend his life battling the evil forces that reside within him? A belief is not factual, but it is a fact that one believes. When one views the other person and feels, "You *can* do it, you *can* stand up straight and tall, you *can* experience freedom," then what happens in the human relationship *is quite different* from what happens when one views the other person as evil and hopeless and condemned. This latter statement is a statement of fact, not of belief.

The counselor will personally exemplify a high level of personal freedom and self-actualization, and he will thus have no need to impose on others. He may serve as a model, not one to be imitated and followed, but rather a model from which the other person can draw strength and gradually develop his own concept of self, his own person, and thus become capable of experiencing a high level of personal freedom.

REFERENCES

American Personnel and Guidance Association. *Counselor education: A progress report on standards.* Washington, D.C.: American Personnel and Guidance Association, 1962.

American Personnel and Guidance Association. *Manual for self-study by a counselor education staff.* Washington, D.C.: American Personnel and Guidance Association, 1967.

Arbuckle, D. S. Counselor, social worker, psychologist: Let's ecumenicalize. *Personnel and Guidance Journal,* 1967, **45**, 532–538.

Arbuckle, D. S. Current issues in counselor education. *Counselor Education and Supervision* 1968, 7, 244–251. (a)

Arbuckle, D. S. Values, ethics and religion in counseling. Paper presented at the National Catholic Guidance Convention, April 1968. (b)

Arbuckle, D. S. *Counseling: Philosophy, theory and practice.* (2nd ed.) Boston: Allyn and Bacon, 1970.

Bare, C. E. Relationship of counselor personality and counselor-client similarity to selected counseling success criteria. *Journal of Counseling Psychology,* 1967, **14**, 158–164.

Berenson, B. G., & Carkhuff, R. R. (Eds.). *Sources of gain in counseling and psychotherapy.* New York; Holt, Rinehart and Winston, 1967.

Bergin, A. E., & Arbuckle, D. S. *Counseling and psychotherapy: An overview.* New York: McGraw-Hill, 1967.

Bergin, A. E., & Solomon, S. Personality and performance correlates of empathic understanding in psychotherapy. Paper presented at American Psychological Association Convention, Philadelphia, September 1963.

Bijou, S. W. Implications of behaviorial science for counseling and guidance. In J. D. Krumboltz (Ed.), *Revolution in counseling,* Boston: Houghton Mifflin, 1966.

Carkhuff, R. R. Training in the counseling and therapeutic practices: Requiem or reveille. *Journal of Counseling Psychology,* 1966, **13**, 360–367.

Directory of Counselor Educators, Washington, D.C.: U.S. Office of Education, December 1964.

Dreyfus, E. A. Humanness: A therapeutic variable. *Personnel and Guidance Journal,* 1967, **45**, 573–578.

Eysenck, H. J. The effects of psychotherapy: An evaluation. *Journal of Consulting Psychology,* 1952, **16**, 319–324.

Golann, S. E., & Magoon, T. M., A non-traditionally trained mental health counselor's work in a school counseling service. *School Counselor,* 1966, **14**, 81–85.

Gonyea, G. The ideal therapeutic relationship and counseling outcome. *Journal of Clinical Psychology,* 1964, **19**, 481–487.

Hill, A. H., & Grieneeks, L. An evaluation of academic counseling of under- and over-achievers. *Journal of Counseling Psychology,* 1966, **13**, 325–328.

Hill, G. E. The profession and standards for counselor education. *Counselor Education and Supervision,* 1967, **6**, 130–136.

Levitt, E. E. The results of psychotherapy with children. *Journal of Consulting Psychology,* 1957, **21**, 189–196.

McDaniel, H. B., Krumboltz, J.D. Counseling perspectives: Old and new. (Ed.) *Revolution in counseling,* Boston: Houghton Mifflin, 1966.

May, R. (Ed.) *Existential psychology.* New York: Random House, 1961.

Melloh, R. A. Accurate empathy and counselor effectiveness. Unpublished doctoral dissertation, University of Florida, 1964.

Paulson, B. B. Riposte. *Personnel and Guidance Journal,* 1967, **45**, 539–540.

Moser, L.E. *Counseling: A modern emphasis in religion.* Englewood Cliffs N.J.: Prentice-Hall, 1962.

Saalfield, L. J. *Guidance and counseling in catholic schools.* Chicago: Loyola University Press, 1958.

Shoben, E. J. Personal worth in education and counseling. In J. D. Krumboltz (Ed.), *Revolution in counseling.* Boston: Houghton Mifflin, 1966.

Standards for counselor education in the preparation of secondary school counselors. *Personnel and Guidance Journal,* 1964, **42**, 1061–1073.

The scope and standards of preparation in psychology for school counselors. *American Psychologist,* 1962, **17**, 149–152.

Tillich, P. Report of a speech given at M.I.T. *Time,* April 21, 1961, **77** (17), 57.

Van Kaam, A. *The art of existential counseling,* Wilkes-Barre, Pa.: Dimension Books, 1966.

Van Kaam, A. An existential view of psychotherapy. In D. S. Arbuckle (Ed.), *Counseling and psychotherapy: An overview.* New York: McGraw-Hill, 1967.

Vance, B. The counselor—an agent of what change? *Personnel and Guidance Journal,* 1967, **45**, 1012–1016.

Watley, D. J. Counseling philosophy and counseling predictive skill. *Journal of Counseling Psychology,* 1967, **14**, 158–164.

Whiteley, J. M., Sprinthall, N. A., Mosher, R. L., & Donaghy, R. T. Selection and evaluation of counselor effectiveness. *Journal of Counseling Psychology,* 1967, **14**, 226–234.

Williamson, E. G. Youth's dilemma: To be or to become. *Personnel and Guidance Journal,* 1967, **46**, 173–177.

Theoretical, Professional, and Ethical Issues in Counselor Education

David L. Livers

Illinois State University

The title of this paper epitomizes the three issues that influence and provide direction to the contemporary counseling scene. The word *issues* implies that we are concerned with matters about which there is no universal agreement. In essence, then, we are dealing with a comprehensive collection of problems, which when resolved will represent the line of development we may expect for the future of counseling and of counselor education. It is a foregone conclusion that problems afflicting counseling in general are inherently matters of concern to counselor education and to counselor-educators.

There is overlap in the use of such terms as *theoretical, professional,* and *ethical.* On the other hand, the root differences are sufficient so that each can be operationally defined in a way that exposes some of the most critical problems we are facing. The terms are treated in this essay in the same order in which they appear in the title. The operational definitions are presented first, and each is then discussed separately in terms of specific issues.

ISSUES DEFINED

Theoretical issues are here identified as ideal standards, which serve as models of excellence to be sought in counseling and counselor training. Such standards are sometimes hypothetical or "pie-in-the-sky" types of things, as opposed to practical or possible practices for the rank-and-file counselor or counselor-education program. The connotations of the word *theoretical* indicate that such standards are considered to be ideal because there is strong supportive evidence of their desirability. It does not imply that there is an established ordinance demanding conformity.

Professional issues here refer to the more esoteric problems unique to the counseling field. Concerns in this area have their greatest implications for those

180

within the field. It is also acknowledged that counseling has indeed become a mature area of specialization, and that participating practitioners have developed sufficient expertise to have progressed from amateur standing to what may truly be regarded as professionalism. Issues in this area will not be as readily apparent or important to the layman, to society in general, or to the neophyte or would-be counselor. They are the kinds of issues, however, which are highly critical to members of the profession and particularly to counselor-educators.

Ethical issues are seen as standards of conduct that constitute a basic moral code for the counseling field. Herein lies the crux, perhaps, of that which is ultimately most critical. Issues in this area are deemed more important because the standards that are developed spill over into society and are interpreted and judged by the lay public. Ethical standards are subject to interpretation and to evolutionary change. To further compound the problem, the moral code that governs practitioners in the field is largely unwritten, and in practice, what is right and what is wrong are not always clearly discernible.

THEORETICAL ISSUES

Just as the distinguishing characteristics used to identify the theoretical, the professional, and the ethical are somewhat arbitrary, so also is the selection of topics covered in each category. The issues selected, however, are without question among the most critical faced in counselor education and in the counseling field. Two basic theoretical concerns are the enrichment of counselor training and the selection of counselor-trainees.

Enrichment of Counselor Training

To reach a point at which no further enrichment seems necessary is an unattainable goal for almost any training program. Certainly the counselor-education field is no exception. The only questions might be: (1) what should be done? and (2) how can it be accomplished? In answering these questions, two basic approaches merit consideration. One has to do with enrichment through a longer training program. The other approach is concerned with revitalizing the curriculum.

In the early 1960s there was a movement to extend the master's degree program in guidance and counseling to a minimum of two years (Wrenn, 1962). The timing was unfortunate. The demand for any kind of counselor was so great that longer programs were not feasible. Now, perhaps, would be a more logical time to reevaluate program length, for in the 1970s, we suddenly have an oversupply of counselors. The reversal in traffic of employees versus employers at the placement service of an American Personnel and Guidance Association convention dramatically illustrates the turn-around that has occurred in only two years. Whereas we should not let supply and demand totally dictate the length of training programs, demand presents an element of reality that cannot be ignored.

There is, of course, no assurance that longer training programs will guarantee a better product. Indeed, we can even say there is efficiency if an incompetent counselor-education program turns out its products in a shorter time. On the other hand, there is every expectation that the graduates of the typical counselor-education program would be more competent, more confident, and more capable of performing effectively on the job if they spent a little more time in preparation.

Neither is there anything sacred about a two-year training period. It is unfortunate that we have fallen into the habit of determining worth along traditional lines, such as specified times or credit-hours. Our concern should not be for one year or two years of training time. Rather, we should ask whether the product is adequately prepared for the job. Programs should be flexible enough to add and delete course work according to current needs in the field.

While longer training programs with built-in flexibility are desirable in theory, there are some complications. One of the most serious problems would be to establish minimum requirements for recognition as a qualified counselor. Should we require a two-year master's or a one-year program? Should we have two or more counselor-preparation levels, such as a paraprofessional, intern, counselor, and/or specialist (30 hours past a one-year master's), with certification based on degree of sophistication in training? Should we have something like the Washington State Plan (Brammer & Springer, 1971) and base certification on the attainment of behavioral objectives or performance standards, disregarding credit-hours and degrees? There are probably as many options as there are units having the power to issue certificates.

Theoretical considerations dealing with certification and length of program can only be determined by states and/or by institutions training counselors. There is a trend toward some form of institutional approval for certification in several states. Any such plan offers a better opportunity to build a flexible program designed to train counselors according to current needs in the field. The only legitimate criterion for lengthening a program, however, is whether the change is essential to accommodate training needed to assure the development of a more competent counseling practitioner.

One need only scan the contents of a few of the periodicals in the counseling field to see countless suggestions—each deemed a panacea for the improvement of the counselor-education curriculum. It is not possible to please everyone, but everyone should approve a search for improvement. There is little doubt that most programs tend to be theoretical, traditional, and slow to change (even though change is inevitable). What kinds of changes should be made? Maybe the most important criterion for such decisions should be whether they ethically, morally, and legally help counselors work more effectively as facilitators of problems and decisions faced by counselees. Two kinds of curriculum change seem most imminent.

First, there is a need to learn about current problem emphases, and areas of insecurity, identified by the neophyte counselor. This can best be learned, perhaps, by conducting an on-going follow-up program of graduates in guidance and counseling after they are out in the field. Of course it is not enough to simply be aware of needs. Changes must be made in the content of courses in accordance with the results of the study that reflect inadequacies in training.

For example, on the basis of published articles written by counselors in the last two years, there is a concern for a better understanding of the youth culture. If a follow-up study confirmed this, then the typical counselor-education program should include in its course work an explanation of the youth culture, their values, objectives, vocabulary, and what is happening. I am not suggesting that counselor-educators take a stand on either promoting or discouraging the youth culture. I am suggesting, however, that as long as it is a significant issue with the potential clientele of graduating counselors, we must help our graduates to gain an understanding of it.

There are many such issues that need to become part of a counselor-education curriculum. There is a need for constant revision, deletion, addition, and change of courses. Most important, the curriculum should be current, relevant, and constantly changing. The basis for such change should come from counselors "on the firing line," who forward their information through the follow-up study.

A second basic curricular need is to offer more experiential opportunities to counselors-in-training. There is no substitute for experience in helping the would-be counselor gain a better perspective of his job as a counselor and an understanding of whether he belongs in the profession. Theoretical approaches to counseling and vicarious experiences through textbooks are helpful, but only the confrontation of the real world can give insight into how one actually establishes counseling relationships, or what kind of impact one has on others in those relationships.

Most counselor-training programs currently offer a practicum course to provide the real-life atmosphere subsequently found on the job. At best, the one-semester practicum class is too artificial to accomplish its ambitious purpose. Some form of internship or expanded practicum would provide a better opportunity to learn the responsibilities one assumes as a counselor. It is likely that an internship would automatically lengthen a program, although we should not be compulsive about an exact one-year internship because we know it is being done in other training programs.

Selection of Counselor Trainees

Literally hundreds of articles have been published on the subject of selection, but it still remains an unresolved theoretical issue. From the work of Bailey (1940) to the present time, there has been a steady flow of literature dealing with factors thought to assist in predicting counselor effectiveness. The results have been disappointing. Over 30 years of research has added little to help us understand which applicants should be approved for study in counselor education.

Major criteria currently used in selection focus on intellective factors. Counselor educators, however, agree that such factors are far from adequate. On the other hand, directors of quality programs will be desirous of finding candidates who can complete the academic requirements for a graduate degree. The use, then, of undergraduate grade-point average and perhaps of standardized scholastic-aptitude tests is valid, the same as it is for any graduate program. While such criteria are valid, however, they are not sufficient. The biggest problem still remains unsolved. How can we identify the nonintellective factors that seem to be associated specifically with counseling effectiveness?

While the major part of the research of the past 30 years has been directed toward intellective factors, a considerable number of studies have used a variety of tests purporting to measure variables such as personality, values, maturity, interests, attitudes, and "counselor aptitude." Unfortunately, the results of the studies are inconclusive, and none of them indicate that counselors can be characterized according to any kind of standard profile. Testing of any kind, then, adds little predictability as to which applicants should be selected.

Letters of recommendation are also used by some counselor-educators to help evaluate candidates. The results generally are positively skewed, however, as might be expected. When the prospect can select his evaluators he will not often pick someone who will appraise him unfavorably. Perhaps a personal telephone interview of one or more listed references would yield more candid responses.

Another selection procedure, which in one form or another may offer some promise, is the interview. Many schools currently require an interview, although relatively few seem to have a structure for it. While the interview is at best a subjective evaluative procedure, there is more opportunity to explore flexibility, values, attitudes, maturity, and personality. Whereas the interview has not yet been widely researched as a screening procedure, it may be a key part of future evaluations, particularly if it is combined with some of the philosophies of Carkhuff.

A basic principle of selection proposed by Carkhuff (1969) is that "the best index of a future criterion is a previous index of that criterion." As it applies to the process, Carkhuff says: "Under optimum conditions the most desirable approach to selecting a helper, whether professional or subprofessional, would be to cast him in the helping role." In other words, if the prospective major in guidance and counseling were to participate in a brief sample experience resembling the role we would expect of him after training, we could get some index of his effectiveness. Carkhuff further suggests that the prospect be cast in the role of both a helper and a helpee with some representative of a relevant population.

Even if Carkhuff is correct in assuming that sample pretraining behavior is indicative of future professional performance, there are still some problems. First, can we reach general agreement regarding the identification of the future role and function of the practitioner? Second, can we set up appropriate samples of helping roles that would supply us with comparative norms that might serve the screening purpose? Finally, in the proposed procedure, could the personal biases of the evaluators be minimized to assure a fair screening device?

Obviously there are still no "pat" answers, which would offer conclusive methods of differentiating between desirable and undesirable applicants. Operationally, the quality counselor-education programs will probably carry on a continuing selection process, beginning with the candidate's application and carrying through a probationary period. A common core of beginning course work might allow opportunity for assessment of nonintellective factors that seem to be indicative of counseling effectiveness. Perhaps more comprehensive follow-up studies of counseling graduates would yield additional information concerning our selection of candidates.

Counselor-educators in every existing training program must not only be aware that selection is a problem, but must actively move to improve their own procedures. Thirty years of failure is no excuse for complacence. Better selection methods are a challenge—a challenge no professional counselor can choose to ignore.

PROFESSIONAL ISSUES

Of many professional issues that might be treated, none seem more critical than (1) the role and function of school-counselors, and (2) evaluation.

Counselor Role and Function

This issue is being treated in the professional category because it is seen as a responsibility of those in the field. Decisions about what a group of confused "professional helpers" identify as basic responsibilities should not come primarily from co-workers outside the immediate field, who have not assimilated the variety of proposals and theories vying for consensus approval. Decisions should come, though, as soon as possible. Lack of agreement on the role and function of school-counselors may well be at the heart of all the other issues being discussed.

The existence of controversial issues can be a stimulating thing for any field. That is not true, however, in the controversy over the role and function of school-counselors. No problem in the whole field is as frustrating and disruptive! School-counselors are often rendered ineffective because they are unsure of what their role should be. Lacking the necessary conviction, they are too often manipulated, by boards of education, superintendents, principals, teachers, and even students, into doing a variety of tasks that further distorts their image and purpose. School-counselors unwittingly and undeservedly become the scapegoat for many of the ills of education in our time, and counselor-educators subsequently become the scapegoats of disenchanted school-counselors. Most critical is the fact that students across the United States are not receiving badly needed help, which school-counselors can and should provide.

Shertzer and Stone (1971) provide a comprehensive review of models and theories that have been proposed during the short history of the guidance and counseling movement. The review also provides some clues as to why the field is somewhat disoriented.

In the discussion of models, it seems evident that some feel an urgency for the development of theory for the sake of theory rather than for the sake of the students involved. "Social reconstruction" and "science of purposeful action" are good examples of models developed by those who are out of touch with what is happening in schools across the nation. The "developmental," "decision-making," and "personal-development" models all propose theories that tend to be both overlapping and incomplete. Either there is an ego-involved need to apply one's name to a theory, or there is an urgency to submit another name of a model to the semantic contest of "What shall we call it?" The "constellation of services" of Hoyt (1970) is acknowledged to be the most prevalent model, but is criticized for being "atheoretical." Such criticism should be regarded as a compliment.

The authors of the above review ask what can be made of all of these models. If we have a compulsive need to state a theory, perhaps an acceptable one can be developed through a process of selecting commonalities and compromising disagreements. It is not an either/or proposition.

Should counselors endorse a developmental approach and provide for personal development? Should they assist with decision-making and student appraisal, providing informational materials and counseling? Should counselors be prepared to offer assistance to students for educational, vocational, social, and personal problems? Most would agree to these basic elements. Again there is the possibility that the composite model would be "atheoretical." Does that really make any difference? School-counselors are not necessarily asking for a theory. They are asking for agreement on what their role and function should be.

Perhaps the key to the whole problem of role is to reconsider why we have counselors in schools and why we have schools. The basic purpose of schools is to provide instruction. That point should not be too controversial. Why the counselor? A counselor in a school should be seen as a staff member who has a role that is obviously different from that of either instructor or administrator. His basic responsibility is to help students who need assistance, whose instructors and administrators either do not or cannot assist them. The role and function of school-counselors, then, should be predicated on the needs of students rather than on a set of principles predetermining what the needs of students should be.

The next step in role definition is to sort out the administrative and instructional duties so the counselor can supply his intended function. Meting out discipline, for instance, is an administrative function. Much of the clerical-detail paperwork should be handled by qualified secretaries. A counselor's training does not include preparation for clerical work, and counselors are notorious for their ineptness and error in performing such tasks. A school cannot financially justify paying a counselor's salary for secretarial performance. Tutoring D and F students, substitute-teaching, and providing work for homebound students are clearly instructional duties. Agreeing on what counselors should *not* do is an important part of role definition.

One more perturbing feature that needs to be acknowledged is the element of change. The concerns of students can be expected to change, as can the procedures for dealing with student problems. Currently, students are concerned about problems with drugs, ecology, and so forth. In five years there may well be new concerns. Currently we are seeing the development of peer counseling. Hopefully we will find new and even better means of helping students, using methods that have yet to be discovered.

These few brief words are not expected to be an elixir to heal a basic ailment of the profession. They are only a beginning. The key would seem to be that we should seek to identify role and function, using points of agreement between counselors and counselor-educators, instead of fragmenting our approach and dwelling on where we differ. Also, counselors must recognize that they have a heavy responsibility to interpret counselor role and function in their local schools, and that to a great extent no one can tell them how to get that message across.

Evaluation

The real impetus for the growth in the number of guidance workers can easily be traced back to the NDEA Act of 1957. For several years guidance flourished, and no one questioned whether it was accomplishing its goals or even if it had any. Toward the end of the 10-year reign of NDEA legislation in the mid-1960s, questions were increasingly being asked about the effectiveness of guidance services. We did not have the answers.

Two major difficulties seem to impede the evaluative efforts of most practitioners even if they are given time, money, and opportunity. Perhaps most basic is the first issue discussed relative to role and function. It is difficult to evaluate something that has not been adequately defined. The other problem is one of criteria. Assume that guidance and counseling is a profession that helps students with problems of personal, social, educational, and vocational adjustment. A completely satisfactory evaluation would involve an assessment of change in behavior, attitude, self-concept, values, or some other personality dimension. Neither available test instruments nor operationally defined criteria lend themselves to a ready acceptance of results indicating either success or failure of guidance and counseling programs. The experimental approach, then, is severely hampered in key areas where a program needs evaluative data.

Even though evaluative evidence is essential to help plan appropriate programs for the future, most programs have done little over the years to collect evaluative data. The advent of the accountability era and the passage of the Vocational Education Act (VEA) Amendments of 1968 have renewed our attention to evaluation. The VEA amendments specifically state that any school district whose vocational-education program is sharing in the reimbursement from that bill must conduct a follow-up study and indicate what happens to students who participated. VEA programs (which include vocational guidance by definition) are further instructed to set up measurable behavioral objectives so that meaningful results will be obtained. It is very unfortunate that legislation must get us to do things that are such obviously desirable practices.

The new career-education concept, coupled with the accountability era, clearly identifies the necessity for demonstrating the success of a given program. The budget cutbacks experienced by many school districts further demonstrate the need for justifying the existence of guidance and counseling services.

Admittedly there are some practical considerations regarding availability of time, money, and research-trained practioners. There are also the theoretical problems of criteria and identification of role and function. However, the real world is no longer going to accept apologies and excuses. We should conduct satisfaction studies and follow-up studies, and to the best of our ability should furnish evaluative data demonstrating our accomplishments and needs. Research does not have to be a high-powered statistical analysis of mystical variables. The simple follow-up study can provide a wealth of evidence, which may serve as a basis for changing the guidance service or justifying current practices. Practicing school-counselors cannot wait for role definition or for someone with more expertise to conduct research projects. The evaluative function is a necessary professional part of the job of every practicing school-counselor.

ETHICAL ISSUES

Two major ethical issues seem to lie at the heart of many problems in the counseling field. One is concerned with "responsibility," which in this essay encompasses confidentiality. The other closely associated ethical issue is value system.

Responsibility

The key problem, in considering "ethical issues" in counseling, centers on the word *responsibility*. What is the counselor's responsibility to his client and to the client's parents, teachers, principal, institution, and institutional governing board, or to society in general? What is the counselor's responsibility regarding requests for personal data from parents, colleges, business and industry, law-enforcement officials, referral sources, the federal government, or even from the local school data-processing center. So far the counselor's responsibility seems almost synonymous with confidentiality—but there is more. What is the counselor's responsibility to a client who comes in with questions about where to get birth-control pills, where to get an abortion, or use of drugs? How does a counselor work with a client who is pregnant, spaced out on drugs, or homosexual? Today the counselor's work is a complex responsibility involving the rights of the client, the attitude and judgment of the counselor, and the trust of society in its institutions and their representatives.

Can we legislate for the portion of responsibility that deals with confidentiality? At this time only Michigan, Indiana, Wisconsin, and North Dakota have enacted such laws (Pardue, Whichard, & Johnson, 1970). There is good evidence that legislation alone does not significantly help the counselor in this respect. It even "ushers in new responsibilities and challenges (Gade, 1972)." The counselor having privileged communication becomes the judge. With or without privileged communication, it is likely that an occasional counselor may be drawn into a lawsuit on charges that he has behaved "in a careless, negligent, or stupid manner; [and] that he could have and should have known better (Beymer, 1971)." Even legislation does not seem to have the potential for affording complete protection to counselors regarding responsibilities that also involve professional risks.

The counselor is placed in the unique position of making judgments based more on conscience than on either precedent or law. The consequences of those judgments have a potential for causing reactions ranging all the way from nothing to legal action, which could cost the counselor his job. A convenient conclusion (particularly if you are not a counselor-educator) is to fix the responsibility on counselor-education programs and simply say that counselors must be trained to cope with these problems. Admittedly, counselor-educators should do a better job. On the other hand, to place the entire blame on counselor-educators is to employ a type of scapegoating that both oversimplifies the problem and ignores some basic facts that reveal some of the challenges of being a counselor.

Why are counselor-educators not more effective in affording assistance to counselors in practice? First, it is impossible to formulate a set of guidelines that will universally apply to any and all local environments and situations. The individual merits of any counseling case necessarily require individual judgment on the part of counselors. Second, any guidelines that might be promulgated relative to counselor actions do not carry the impact of law and sometimes not even the endorsement of the general public. Guidelines help to show direction, but are in no way to be seen as commandments from which there may be *no* deviation. Incidentally, just as there is some misunderstanding by the general public of the role and function of counselors, so there is some misunderstanding of actions and decisions counselors may make. A third built-in problem counselor-educators contend with is the limited ability to train people to make judgments. The ability to make appropriate judgments comes in large measure from experience in making judgments, gaining confidence in good decisions, and learning from poor decisions. Within some limits, counselor-educators can give assistance during training—but to a large degree the artificiality of any training program prevents the feeling that can only come with full responsibility, on the job, sometimes under fire. Then, too, there is doubt as to whether some people have the perceptual sensitivity to become good "judgment makers." There is doubt, too, whether such people should be training to become counselors—if we can identify them.

At first glance the preceding paragraph may sound like a colossal counselor-education "cop out." Perhaps an example would add perspective. Let us take an actual case of a counselor who has worked with students who had questions about where to get the "pill," and with students who had experienced "bad trips." In some way it leaks back to the principal or the board of education that students have been seen about such problems. Assume further that the case occurred in one of the 46 states where counselors do not have privileged communication. The board of education calls the counselor to the next board meeting, informs him of the information it has, and demands that the counselor furnish a list of students he has seen relative to sex and drugs, or be fired.

The counselor is confused, disillusioned, perhaps embittered. In training he learned that the counselor's basic responsibility was to the client. Now, simply because he is doing what he learned in graduate school, he faces the threat of losing his job. Perhaps his first reaction is that those guys in the ivory tower just don't understand reality.

The principal in his training learned that he was the boss in his building, and that he would be held responsible for all that occurs there. He feels on that basis that he should know what transpires between the counselor and the students. The board of education, sensitive to the concerns of the community, feels an obligation to investigate to see if there is any wrongdoing, and if so to whom, by whom, and whether it in any way casts some reflection on the board. If there is criticism, on whom should the board members put the pressure—the principal, the counselor, or both?

Now, in summarizing, the counselor-educator knows that the counselor cannot reveal the names of his clients as requested. It is not only a breach of ethics, but it would eliminate every possibility in that school for counselors to work effectively with problems of sex, drugs, or perhaps anything else. The counselor should resign rather than break such a confidence. Confrontations leading to such crises should rarely occur, however, as counselors are inculcated with a theory that will provide a basis for judgments, along with experience that will enable them to prevent such eruptions.

The counselor should uphold the laws of society and the regulations of the school. He should be supportive of his fellow staff members and the administration. He must also maintain his clients' confidence and handle information discreetly. The counselor's whole modus operandi and philosophy should be thoroughly discussed and agreed upon at the time he is interviewed for the job. Institutional policies should be established regarding confidentiality, as suggested by Marsh and Kinnick (1970). It is a little late to talk about shaping policy and procedure when a crisis arises. Guidelines should be established at the outset. The counselor must be able to be honest and sincere with all of those with whom he has a working relationship.

The principal must hire only those counselors in whom he feels he can place complete confidence, regardless of what counseling problems are discussed or who is involved. The board of education should have confidence in its administrators' ability to carry out all policies established and to supervise all staff members in the performance of their responsibilities in their areas of specialization. The community should feel confident they have elected a board of education that will satisfactorily represent them in establishing the policies for the school and its staff.

Obviously, the preceding paragraph oversimplifies a very complex theoretical framework. It does not tell a counselor how to establish relationships, trust, and confidence. It does not give a counselor a basis for making judgments and decisions. It does not tell how to resolve differences and explain confidential obligations. How do you teach responsibility? The question is open-ended. Perhaps that is why it is an ethical issue.

Value System

Closely related to responsibility is the issue of value system. A basic precept taught counselors is that they should respect the value system of the client and not inflict their own values on him, even if they feel their goals are rationally and logically superior. Obviously it would be easier, take less time, and to some seem to "make sense" for us as counselors to use a "process of rational persuasion" in our "efforts to facilitate healthy development," as suggested by Rousseve (1971, p.). But who are we to play God and decide what is superior and what is healthy development?

While counselor-educators, counselors, and counselors-in-training all sanctimoniously subscribe to a philosophy of respect for the values of all clients, there is evidence that their homage is actually little more than lip service. There seems to be a pronounced disparity between theory and practice.

Most of the May 1971 issue of *Personnel and Guidance Journal* was devoted to a variety of groups who attest to a disbelief that counselors effectively "keep the faith" with respect to values. The message is that counselors do not typically have the trust of minority groups (Smith, 1971; Ward, 1970; Russell, 1970; Banks, 1970; Spang, 1971; Vontress, 1969), the drug culture (Ream, 1971), feminist advocates (Eyde, 1970; Gardner, 1971), homosexuals (Killinger, 1971), pacifists (Kincaid & Kincaid, 1971), ecologists (Herbert, 1971), the non–college-bound (Betz, Engle, & Mallinson, 1969), and others. We know that counselors are guilty of being so turned off or uninformed about the above groups that they are minimally effective in their counseling efforts. We know that most counselors grew up in an environment that embraced the virtuous, chauvinistic, upward-striving, white-middle-class societal value system. The fault is not in the values of counselors. The fault is in basking in a false sense of security that we respect each person in the above categories as a worthwhile individual, and that we are doing everything in our power to merit the trust of those who are in those categories. The fault is in the difference between our verbalized theoretical intentions and what we do as counselors in practice.

These introductory comments on values are not be construed as an unequivocal endorsement of liberal counseling activists. There is more hypocrisy and danger in the intent of a radical-activist counselor, who proposes to change the system into one in his own image (Dworkin & Dworkin, 1971), than there is in most of their less active colleagues in counseling, whom they criticize. Obviously, when there are so many divergent groups demanding change according to their own plans, someone will have to compromise. To attempt to please everybody is to guarantee failure. As counselors who wish to effect change, one of our top priorities for progress must be to be honest and to put into practice the theoretical ideal of open acceptance of other's values. As Dr. Kenneth Hoyt said, "The most effective agents of change will be those who are evolutionary, not revolutionary (1970)."

For the sake of clarification, let us take the example of a counseling case demonstrating both a variety of biases a counselor might have, and a rationale the client may have for being apprehensive about talking to a counselor. Suppose an unwed pregnant girl comes to a counselor for some assistance. She should not have to question whether the counselor is Catholic, Protestant, atheist, male, female, black, white, or what have you. She should not have to question whether the counselor is competent to give assistance with her immediate problems. She is looking for capable, understanding, unbiased help. She wants to know all the alternatives for her next step—not the ones the counselor thinks are right for her. The same kind of logic applies to any of the above-mentioned groups. They are all looking for fair and open treatment. Each wants to be seen in the same way we should view all counseling cases —as unique, important, worthwhile, with a problem to be resolved, not judged.

It is little wonder that counselors are criticized for being discriminatory or ineffective with some of the subgroups urgently needing assistance. Counselors must take steps to bridge the credibility gap that has developed. Unfortunately, there are no patent cure-alls which will guarantee acceptance of counselors by all clients. The suggestions that follow are not the only possible solutions, but perhaps they will furnish a point of departure for remedial action.

First, counselors must be committed to carrying out the theoretical position of assisting clients in behavioral changes without inflicting counselor values. The disparity between theory and practice must be narrowed. Perhaps the supervised counselor internship proposed above is a means of helping to bridge the gap. Lip service is not good enough. Some means must be found to help counselors internalize respect for the individual's right to his own value system.

Second, while the theoretical position in the preceding paragraph is desirable, it cannot be completely attained. Many counselors will have particular biases, which, try as they may, cannot be held back. In such cases it is not appropriate for the counselor to work with a client who evokes his bias. The counselee should be referred to another counselor if at all possible. Counselor-education programs have a heavy responsibility to follow the advice of Socrates and help a would-be counselor to "know himself." In order to make appropriate referrals a counselor must know where he does not work fairly. Evidence suggests that most of the better counselor-education programs are making progress with helping counselors understand their biases, but we have a long way to go.

Third, counselors and counselor-educators must read their professional literature and look for constructive articles suggesting methods other counselors have found effective in helping clients who have previously been victims of discriminatory counseling. Many recent articles (Anderson, 1971; Aubrey, 1971; Brazziel, 1970; Dahl, 1971; Eyde, 1970; Haettenschwiller, 1971; Hott, 1969; Hurst, 1971; Proctor, 1970; Smith, 1970; Vontress, 1970; Washington, 1970) suggest positive approaches to breaking the bias barrier.

While the above suggestions are not offered as a panacea for a critical counseling ill, they are a start. If they do nothing more than call attention to the problem they will serve a useful purpose. Counselor-educators must find better ways to deal with the problem of "value" in their training programs.

REFERENCES

Anderson, S. Group counseling in drug awareness. *School Counselor,* 1971, **19**, 123–126.

Aubrey, R. F. School-community drug prevention programs. *Personnel and Guidance Journal,* 1971, **50**, 17–24.

Bailey, R. J. The preparation, certification and selection of personnel workers for the secondary schools of the United States. Unpublished doctoral dissertation, New York University, 1940.

Banks, W. M. The changing attitudes of black students. *Personnel and Guidance Journal,* 1970, **48**, 739–745.

Betz, R., Engle, K. B., & Mallinson, G. G. Perceptions of non-college-bound vocationally oriented high school graduates. *Personnel and Guidance Journal,* 1969, **47**, 988–994.

Beymer, L. Who killed George Washington? *Personnel and Guidance Journal,* 1971, **50**, 249–253.

Brammer, L. M., & Springer, H. C. A radical change in counselor education and certification. *Personnel and Guidance Journal,* 1971, **49**, 803–808.

Brazziel, W. F. Getting black kids into college. *Personnel and Guidance Journal,* 1970, **48**, 747–751.

Carkhuff, R. R. *Helping and human relations.* New York: Holt, Rinehart and Winston, 1969.

Dahl, S. Who is building the bridges? *Personnel and Guidance Journal* 1971, **49**, 693–697.

Dworkin, E. P., & Dworkin, A. The activist counselor. *Personnel and Guidance Journal,* 1971, **49**, 748–753.

Eyde, L. D. Eliminating barriers to career development of women. *Personnel and Guidance Journal,* 1970, **49**, 24–28.

Gade, E. M. Implications of privileged communication laws for counselors. *School Counselor,* 1972, **19**, 150–152.

Gardner, J. Sexist counseling must stop. *Personnel and Guidance Journal,* 1971, **49**, 705–714.

Haettenschwiller, D. L. Counseling black college students in special programs. *Personnel and Guidance Journal,* 1971, **50**, 29–35.

Herbert, R. Ecology: A shared journey. *Personnel and Guidance Journal,* 1971, **49**, 737–734.

Hott, I. The school counselor and drugs. *School Counselor,* 1969, **17**, 14–17.

Hoyt, K. B. This I believe. In W. H. Van Hoose and J. J. Pietrofesa (Eds.), *Counseling and guidance in the twentieth century.* Boston: Houghton Mifflin, 1970.

Hurst, F. W. A university drug education project. *Personnel and Guidance Journal,* 1971, **50**, 11–16.

Killinger, R. R. The counselor and gay liberation. *Personnel and Guidance Journal,* 1971, **49**, 715–719.

Kincaid, J., & Kincaid, M. Counseling for peace. *Personnel and Guidance Journal,* 1971, **49**, 727–735.

Marsh, J. J., & Kinnick, B. C. Let's close the confidentiality gap. *Personnel and Guidance Journal,* 1970, **48**, 362–365.

Pardue, J., Whichard, W., & Johnson, E. Limiting confidential information in counseling. *Personnel and Guidance Journal,* 1970, **49**, 14–20.

Proctor, S. A. Reversing the spiral toward futility. *Personnel and Guidance Journal,* 1970, **48**, 707–712.

Ream, C. Youth culture: Humanity's last chance. *Personnel and Guidance Journal,* 1971, **49**, 699–704.

Rousseve, R. J. Toward an epitaph for the non-judgmental educator-counselor. *School Counselor,* 1971, **19**, 6–9.

Russell, R. D. Black perceptions of guidance. *Personnel and Guidance Journal,* 1970, **48**, 721–728.

Shertzer, B., & Stone, S. C. *Fundamentals of guidance.* (2nd ed.) Boston: Houghton Mifflin, 1971.

Smith, P. M., Jr. Men who think black. *Personnel and Guidance Journal,* 1970, **48**, 763–766.

Smith, P. M., Jr. Black activists for liberation, not guidance. *Personnel and Guidance Journal,* 1971, **49**, 721–726.

Spang, A. T. Understanding the Indian. *Personnel and Guidance Journal,* 1971, **50**, 97–102.

Vontress, C. E. Cultural barriers in the counseling relationship. *Personnel and Guidance Journal,* 1969, **48**, 11–17.

Vontress, C. E. Counseling black. *Personnel and Guidance Journal,* 1970, **48**, 713–719.

Ward, E. J. A gift from the ghetto. *Personnel and Guidance Journal,* 1970, **48**, 753–756.

Washington, B. B. Perceptions and possibilities. *Personnel and Guidance Journal,* 1970, **48**, 757–761.

Wrenn, C. G. *The counselor in a changing world.* Washington, D.C.: American Personnel and Guidance Association, 1962.

Ethics and the Helping Professional

Gail F. Farwell

University of Wisconsin—Madison

Why ethics? As helping professionals we are engaged with other persons, with behaviors, with the larger society, and frequently with an institution that provides the sanctions for our work.

Students undertaking study in the helping professions must face up to their own ethics as well as to the ethical standards of the profession. The brief presentation that follows includes references to, as well as reprints of, codes of ethics developed by two major associations—the American Personnel and Guidance Association and the American Psychological Association.

There are some basic questions for the counselor to consider when he thinks about his functions and purpose as a helping professional.

1. What constitutes ethical behavior?
2. What criteria should be used to determine what is ethical?
3. Why is a code of ethics helpful for counselors? Indeed, is a code of ethics helpful?
4. What are some of the basic ethical issues in counseling?
5. Why be ethical? Whose code shall I follow?

The counselor is accountable for his actions. Because a considerable portion of his work is done in private, he has great potential for being powerful. He can be manipulative, intervening in such ways as to meet his own needs more than those of the client with whom he is working. He has access to professional information, instrumentation, and tools, and to the most personal experiences of another individual (the client). What he does with these tools and with the information solicited or given is of critical concern.

The counselor, in his movement toward professionalism, knows his own stance. He is aware of his need for competency in both generating and handling information about his clientele. There is a need for the helping person to communicate his ethical stance to his publics—clients, sanctioning agency, and referral resources. Dynamic interaction is the key to the counseling, consulting, and group work implemented by a counselor. Human values come into play; the dynamic tension created is basic to relationships of all types, and certainly of tremendous importance in a helping relationship. Every individual who would presume to counsel with others must face this truth and deal with it, not by assuming the values of his professional colleagues, or by absorbing society's values, but through a constant and determined inner struggle of facing his own "self," and from that confrontation a unique and personal value system. Within a preparation program, and specifically in supervised experiences, a candidate can expect his value-ethical system to come under close scrutiny. The persons responsible for recommending degrees, licensure, and certification have a right to expect candidates to reveal, explicate, and demonstrate their own systems. One's value system—the basis for all action, all ethical and unethical behavior—must be formulated and experienced before one assumes the adoption of a professional society's code of ethics.

Primarily, a value system can be reduced to the question of what is right and what is wrong for a person. The competency to distinguish between right and wrong, and then to act in accordance with the "right," is characteristic of a moral person. Therefore, it seems to this writer, a counselor is moral when he chooses right from wrong in human relationships and he is ethical when the "right" he selects conforms with the ideal "right" as described by his professional colleagues. Here, we go back to Webster. In his definitive study and codification of the meaning of terms, he states that to be *ethical* "implies conformity with an elaborated, ideal code of moral principles."[1] Ethical behavior is based upon a conscious knowledge of right and wrong, arrived at through self-analysis translated into action consistent with what one sees to be right and conforming with a code of ethics.

How do we determine what is ethical? From what has gone before, the reader, utilizing the definition given above, can identify behavior in reference to a code of ethics. Carried to its logical conclusion, the criteria used to determine what is ethical would be contained in an official, elaborated, and ideal code. (Note appended codes.) However, it seems apparent that some criteria other than those contained in the official code must be considered.

In searching for answers to the question of when behavior is ethical, it may be desirable to substitute other terms to describe the action (asking, for example, whether the behavior is *consistent, logical, right, helpful, expedient,* or *good*). Here we get into the phenomenon of "situational ethics." It appears that the connotation each of the above terms adds to the definition is worthy of consideration. Behavior must be viewed in a manner other than merely checking

[1] *Webster's New World Dictionary* (Cleveland: World Publishing, 1957), p. 956.

whether or not it conforms with the code. Thus, in addition to the criteria specified in various codes, these standards might well be added:

1. Does the behavior help the counselor?
2. Is the behavior morally "right"?
3. Is the counselor's behavior fairly consistent?
4. Is the counselor's response basically rational?
5. Is the behavior properly motivated?

In addition to these points the reader should refer to the specifics in the codes of ethics appended to this essay.

In finding an answer to the question about *the helpfulness of a code of ethics,* a definition of *helpful* must be sought. To be helpful is to be useful. With this arbitrary conclusion, a code of ethics might be considered useful in the following ways: as a guide to neophytes through the perilous maze of becoming counselors, as a means of drawing attention to the rules of the game, and as a means of enhancing professionalism.

One cannot have all the experiences desirable before entering a preparation program. Most agree, therefore, that it is necessary to include practical experience in preparation programs. This experiential route has many implications for the counselor-in-preparation, as well as for clients being interacted with. The neophyte can be introduced to sensitive areas and basic issues, and can experience insight in counseling situations. A review of a code can assist the beginning counselor in his understanding of why certain study and assignments are given within the content of course work, practicums, and the internship.

There are many people employed in the helping professions. In a large vocation there naturally arise multiple problems, which can be faced and solved if those involved refer to the rules of the game. In this sense, a code of ethics, containing ideal answers to real problems, can prevent misunderstandings between professionals and serve as a kind of basis for relationship and mutual assistance. A code of ethics can serve as more than a rule book; it can be the *common tie* that binds counselor to counselor, providing a real basis for relating. In addition, a code of ethics enhances a profession; by definition, a profession assumes responsibility for disciplining and improving itself, and an ethical code is inherently a core element in this process.

Is a code really helpful? It can be; it can also be a crutch or an escape. Since every human being must ultimately be responsible for his actions irrespective of laws or codes, standards are not needed to assure that society or the individual act ethically, nor does the existence of a code truly affect the behavior of individuals—personally held moral values determine one's behavior. This behavior is learned, and through a preparation program, which includes the facing of behavioral issues and dilemmas and encounters through supervision, the candidate can come to a stance that will serve him in his professional interactions. A code of ethics does not in fact modify one's behavior; the code may reinforce one's decision to act one way or another, but it does not determine that action. The person determines the action. A code of ethics is a guideline; it is a tool. The counselor's perceptions and competency are at the root of ethical practice and implementation.

The counselor's ethical system develops out of his commitment to a concept of man and how man grows, develops, and changes. Whose or what code should I follow? My final answer is "my own." Since behavior follows a value system, and since a value system must be one's own, one is ultimately responsible only to himself as to what course of action he takes; but he will also be responsible to his client, to the persons with whom that client comes in contact, and to the whole sphere of influence pervading the counselor's domain.

It is essential that counselor-candidates undertake critical self-search in order to seek out and firm up where they stand in relation to their fellow men and to the intervention strategies they will employ as counselors. This may imply a need for "counseling" of the counselor-in-preparation, for in my definition of counseling the central theme is *the integration of personal experience* so that effective *decision-making* and *accommodation* can result. After all, counseling is a relationship that enhances the systematic information-processing of a client so that he moves toward self-competency in dealing with life, which is in a continual state of flux.

REFERENCES

American Personnel and Guidance Association, Committee on Ethics. Code of ethics. *Personnel and Guidance Journal,* 1961, **40**, 206–209.

American Personnel and Guidance Association, Ethical Practices Committee. *Ethical standards casebook.* Washington, D.C.: American Personnel and Guidance Association, 1965.

American Psychological Association. *Casebook on ethical standards of psychologists.* Washington, D.C.: American Psychological Association, 1967.

American Psychological Association. Ethical standards of psychologists. *American Psychologist,* 1968, **23**, 357–361.

American Psychological Association. *Ethical principles in the conduct of research with human participants.* Washington, D.C.: American Psychological Association, 1973.

Ethical Standards*

American Personnel and Guidance Association

PREAMBLE

The American Personnel and Guidance Association is an educational, scientific, and professional organization dedicated to service to society. This service is committed to profound faith in the worth, dignity, and great potentiality of the individual human being.

The marks of a profession, and therefore of a professional organization, can be stated as follows:

1. Possession of a body of specialized knowledge, skills, and attitudes known and practiced by its members.
2. This body of specialized knowledge, skills, and attitudes is derived through scientific inquiry and scholarly learning.
3. This body of specialized knowledge, skills, and attitudes is acquired through professional preparation, preferably on the graduate level, in a college or university as well as through continuous in-service training and personal growth after completion of formal education.
4. This body of specialized knowledge, skills, and attitudes is constantly tested and extended through research and scholarly inquiry.
5. A profession has a literature of its own, even though it may, and indeed must, draw portions of its content from other areas of knowledge.
6. A profession exalts service to the individual and society above personal gain. It possesses a philosophy and a code of ethics.
7. A profession through the voluntary association of its members constantly examines and improves the quality of its professional preparation and services to the individual and society.
8. Membership in the professional organization and the practice of the profession must be limited to persons meeting stated standards of preparation and competencies.
9. The profession affords a life career and permanent membership as long as services meet professional standards.
10. The public recognizes, has confidence in, and is willing to compensate the members of the profession for their services.

The Association recognizes that the vocational roles and settings of its members are identified with a wide variety of academic disciplines and levels of academic preparation. This diversity reflects the pervasiveness of the Association's interest and influence. It also poses challenging complexities in efforts to conceptualize:

*Personnel and Guidance Journal, 1961, **40**, 206–209.

a. the characteristics of members;
b. desired or requisite preparation or practice; and
c. supporting social, legal and/or ethical controls.

The specification of ethical standards enables the Association to clarify to members, future members, and to those served by members the nature of ethical responsibilities held in common by its members.

The introduction of such standards will inevitably stimulate greater concern by members for practice and preparation for practice. It will also stimulate a general growth and identification with and appreciation for both the common and diverse characteristics of the definable roles within the world of work of Association members.

There are six major areas of professional activity which encompasses the work of members of APGA. For each of these areas certain general principles are listed below to serve as guide lines for ethical practice. These are preceded by a general section which includes certain principles germane to six areas and common to the entire work of the Association members.

SECTION A

General

1. The member exerts what influence he can to foster the development and improvement of the profession and continues his professional growth throughout his career.

2. The member has a responsibility to the institution which he serves. His acceptance of employment by the institution implies that he is in substantial agreement with the general policies and principles of the institution. Therefore, his professional activities are also in accord with the objectives of the institution. Within the member's own work setting, if, despite his efforts, he cannot reach agreement as to acceptable ethical standards of conduct with his superiors, he should end his affiliation with them.

3. The member must expect ethical behavior among his professional associates in APGA at all times. He is obligated, in situations where he possesses information raising serious doubt as to the ethical behavior of other members, to attempt to rectify such conditions.

4. The member is obligated to concern himself with the degree to which the personnel functions of non-members with whose work he is acquainted represent competent and ethical performance. Where his information raises serious doubt as to the ethical behavior of such persons, it is his responsibility to rectify such conditions.

5. The member must not seek self-enhancement through expressing evaluations or comparisons damaging to other ethical professional workers.

6. The member should not claim or imply professional qualifications exceeding those possessed and is responsible for correcting any misrepresentations of his qualifications by others.

7. The member providing services for personal remuneration shall, in establishing

fees for such services, take careful account of the charges made for comparable services by other professional persons.

8. The member who provides information to the public or to his subordinates, peers, or superiors has a clear responsibility to see that both the content and the manner of presentation are accurate and appropriate to the situation.

9. The member has an obligation to ensure that evaluative information about such persons as clients, students, and applicants shall be shared only with those persons who will use such information for professional purposes.

10. The member shall offer professional services only, through the context of a professional relationship. Thus testing, counseling, and other services are not to be provided through the mail by means of newspaper or magazine articles, radio or television programs, or public performances.

SECTION B

Counseling. This section refers to practices involving a counseling relationship with a counselee or client and is not intended to be applicable to practices involving administrative relationships with the persons being helped. A counseling relationship denotes that the person seeking help retain full freedom of choice and decision and that the helping person has no authority or responsibility to approve or disapprove of the choices or decisions of the counselee or client. "Counselee" or "client" is used here to indicate the person (or persons) for whom the member has assumed a professional responsibility. Typically the counselee or client is the individual with whom the member has direct and primary contact. However, at times, "client" may include another person(s) when the other person(s) exercise significant control and direction over the individual being helped in connection with the decisions and plans being considered in counseling.

1. The member's *primary* obligation is to respect the integrity and promote the welfare of the counselee or client with whom he is working.

2. The counseling relationship and information resulting therefrom must be kept confidential consistent with the obligations of the member as a professional person.

3. Records of the counseling relationship including interview notes, test data, correspondence, tape recordings, and other documents are to be considered professional information for use in counseling, research, and teaching of counselors but always with full protection of the identity of the client and with precaution so that no harm will come to him.

4. The counselee or client should be informed of the conditions under which he may receive counseling assistance at or before the time he enters the counseling relationship. This is particularly true in the event that there exist conditions of which the counselee or client would not likely be aware.

5. The member reserves the right to consult with any other professionally competent person about his counselee client. In choosing his professional consultant the member must avoid placing the consultant in a conflict of interest situation, i.e., the consultant must be free of any other obligatory relation to the member's

client that would preclude the consultant being a proper party to the member's efforts to help the counselee or client.

6. The member shall decline to initiate or shall terminate a counseling relationship when he cannot be of professional assistance to the counselee or client either because of lack of competence or personal limitation. In such instances the member shall refer his counselee or client to an appropriate specialist. In the event the counselee or client declines the suggested referral, the member is not obligated to continue the counseling relationship.

7. When the member learns from counseling relationships of conditions which are likely to harm others over whom his institution or agency has responsibility, he is expected to report *the condition* to the appropriate responsible authority, but in such a manner as not to reveal the identity of his counselee or clients.

8. In the event that the counselee or client's condition is such as to require others to assume responsibility for him, or when there is clear and imminent danger to the counselee or client or to others, the member is expected to report this fact to an appropriate responsible authority, and/or take such other emergency measures as the situation demands.

9. Should the member be engaged in a work setting which calls for any variation from the above statements, the member is obligated to ascertain that such variations are justifiable under the conditions and that such variations are clearly specified and made known to all concerned with such counseling services.

SECTION C

Testing

1. The primary purpose of psychological testing is to provide objective and comparative measures for use in self-evaluation or evaluation by others of general or specific attributes.

2. Generally, test results constitute only one of a variety of pertinent data for personnel and guidance decisions. It is the member's responsibility to provide adequate orientation or information to the examinee(s) so that the results of testing may be placed in proper perspective with other relevant factors.

3. When making any statements to the public about tests and testing care must be taken to give accurate information and to avoid any false claims or misconceptions.

4. Different tests demand different levels of competence for administration, scoring, and interpretation. It is therefore the responsibility of the member to recognize the limits of his competence and to perform only those functions which fall within his preparation and competence.

5. In selecting tests for use in a given situation or with a particular client the member must consider not only general but also specific validity, reliability, and appropriateness of the test(s).

6. Tests should be administered under the same conditions which were established in their standardization. Except for research purposes explicitly stated, any departures from these conditions, as well as unusual behavior or irregularities

during the testing session which may affect the interpretation of the test results, must be fully noted and reported. In this connection, unsupervised test-taking or the use of tests through the mails are of questionable value.

7. The value of psychological tests depends in part on the novelty to persons taking them. Any prior information, coaching, or reproduction of test materials tends to invalidate test results. Therefore, test security is one of the professional obligations of the member.

8. The member has the responsibility to inform the examinee(s) as to the purpose of testing. The criteria of examinee's welfare and/or explicit prior understanding with him should determine who the recipients of the test results may be.

9. The member should guard against the appropriation, reproduction, or modifications of published tests or parts thereof without express permission and adequate recognition of the original author or publisher.

Regarding the preparation, publication, and distribution of tests reference should be made to:

"Tests and Diagnostic Techniques"—Report of the Joint Committee of the American Psychological Association, American Educational Research Association, and National Council of Measurements used in Education. Supplement to *Psychological Bulletin,* 1954, **2**, 1–38.

SECTION D

Research and Publication

1. In the performance of any research on human subjects, the member must avoid causing any injurious effects or aftereffects of the experiment upon his subjects.

2. The member may withhold information or provide misinformation to subjects only when it is essential to the investigation and where he assumes responsibility for corrective action following the investigation.

3. In reporting research results, explicit mention must be made of all variables and conditions known to the investigator which might affect interpretation of the data.

4. The member is responsible for conducting and reporting his investigations so as to minimize the possibility that his findings will be misleading.

5. The member has an obligation to make available original research data to qualified others who may wish to replicate or verify the study.

6. In reporting research results or in making original data available, due care must be taken to disguise the identity of the subjects, in the absence of specific permission from such subjects to do otherwise.

7. In conducting and reporting research, the member should be familiar with, and give recognition to, previous work on the topic.

8. The member has the obligation to give due credit to those who have contributed significantly to his research, in accordance with their contributions.
9. The member has the obligation to honor commitments made to subjects of research in return for their cooperation.
10. The member is expected to communicate to other members the results of any research he judges to be of professional or scientific value.

SECTION E

Consulting and Private Practice. Consulting refers to a voluntary relationship between a professional helper and help-needing social unit (industry, business, school, college, etc.) in which the consultant is attempting to give help to the client in the solving of some current or potential problem.[1]

1. The member acting as a consultant must have a high degree of self-awareness of his own values and needs in entering a helping relationship which involves change in a social unit.
2. There should be understanding and agreement between consultant and client as to directions or goals of the attempted change.
3. The consultant must be reasonably certain that he or his organization have the necessary skills and resources for giving the kind of help which is needed now or that may develop later.
4. The consulting relationship must be one in which client adaptability and growth toward self-direction are encouraged and cultivated. The consultant must consistently maintain his role as a consultant and not become a decision maker for the client.
5. The consultant in announcing his availability for service as a consultant follows professional rather than commercial standards in describing his services with accuracy, dignity, and caution.
6. For private practice in testing, counseling, or consulting the ethical principles stated in all previous sections of this document are pertinent. In addition, any individual, agency, or institution offering educational and vocational counseling to the public should meet the standards of the American Board on Professional Standards in Vocational Counseling, Inc.

SECTION F

Personnel Administration

1. The member is responsible for establishing working agreements with supervisors and with subordinates especially regarding counseling or clinical relationships,

---

[1]This definition is adapted from R. Lippitt, "Dimensions of the Consultant's Job," *Journal of Social Issues,* 1959, **15** (2).

confidentiality, distinction between public and private material, and a mutual respect for the positions of parties involved in such issues.

2. Such working agreements may vary from one institutional setting to another. What should be the case in each instance, however, is that agreements have been specified, made known to those concerned, and whenever possible the agreements reflect institutional policy rather than personal judgment.

3. The member's responsibility to his superiors requires that he keep them aware of conditions affecting the institution, particularly those which may be potentially disrupting or damaging to the institution.

4. The member has a responsibility to select competent persons for assigned responsibilities and to see that his personnel are used maximally for the skills and experience they possess.

5. The member has responsibility for constantly stimulating his staff for their and his own continued growth and improvement. He must see that staff members are adequately supervised as to the quality of their functioning and for purposes of professional development.

6. The member is responsible for seeing that his staff is informed of policies, goals, and programs toward which the department's operations are oriented.

SECTION G

Preparation for Personnel Work

1. The member in charge of training sets up a strong program of academic study and supervised practice in order to prepare the trainees for their future responsibilities.

2. The training program should aim to develop in the trainee not only skills and knowledge, but also self-understanding.

3. The member should be aware of any manifestations of person limitations in a student trainee which may influence the latter's provision of competent services and has an obligation to offer assistance to the trainee in securing professional remedial help.

4. The training program should include preparation in research and stimulation for the future personnel worker to do research and add to the knowledge in his field.

5. The training program should make the trainee aware of the ethical responsibilities and standards of the profession he is entering.

6. The program of preparation should aim at inculcating among the trainees, who will later become the practitioners of our profession, the ideal of service to individual and society above personal gain.

Ethical Standards of Psychologists*

American Psychologist, May 1968

The psychologist believes in the dignity and worth of the individual human being. He is committed to increasing man's understanding of himself and others. While pursuing this endeavor, he protects the welfare of any person who may seek his service or of any subject, human or animal, that may be the object of his study. He does not use his professional position or relationships, nor does he knowingly permit his own service to be used by others, for purposes inconsistent with these values. While demanding for himself freedom of inquiry and communication, he accepts the responsibility this freedom confers: for competence where he claims it, for objectivity in the report of his findings, and for consideration of the best interests of his colleagues and of society.

SPECIFIC PRINCIPLES

Principle 1. Responsibility. The psychologist[1] committed to increasing man's understanding of man, places high value on objectivity and integrity, and maintains the highest standards in the services he offers.

a. As a scientist, the psychologist believes that society will be best served when he investigates where his judgment indicates investigation is needed; he plans his research in such a way to minimize the possibility that his findings will be misleading; and he publishes full reports of his work, never discarding without explanation data which may modify the interpretation of results.

b. As a teacher, the psychologist recognizes his primary obligation to help others acquire knowledge and skill, and to maintain high standards of scholarship.

c. As a practitioner, the psychologist knows that he bears a heavy social responsibility because his work may touch intimately the lives of others.

Principle 2. Competence. The maintenance of high standards of professional competence is a responsibility shared by all psychologists, in the interest of the public and of the profession as a whole.

*Reprinted with permission from *Casebook on Ethical Standards of Psychologists* (Washington, D.C.: American Psychological Association, 1967).
[1]A student of psychology who assumes the role of psychologist shall be considered a psychologist for the purpose of this code of ethics.

a. Psychologists discourage the practice of psychology by unqualified persons and assist the public in identifying psychologists competent to give dependable professional service. When a psychologist or a person identifying himself as a psychologist violates ethical standards, psychologists who know firsthand of such activities attempt to rectify the situation. When such a situation cannot be dealt with informally, it is called to the attention of the appropriate local, state, or national committee on professional ethics, standards, and practices.

b. The psychologist recognizes the boundaries of his competence and the limitations of his techniques and does not offer services or use techniques that fail to meet professional standards established in particular fields. The psychologist who engages in practice assists his client in obtaining professional help for all important aspects of his problem that fall outside the boundaries of his own competence. This principle requires, for example, that provision be made for the diagnosis and treatment of relevant medical problems and for referral to or consultation with other specialists.

c. The psychologist in clinical work recognizes that his effectiveness depends in good part upon his ability to maintain sound interpersonal relations, that temporary or more enduring aberrations in his own personality may interfere with this ability or distort his appraisals of others. There he refrains from undertaking any activity in which his personal problems are likely to result in inferior professional services or harm to a client; or, if he is already engaged in such an activity when he becomes aware of his personal problems, he seeks competent professional assistance to determine whether he should continue or terminate his services to his client.

Principle 3. Moral and Legal Standards. The psychologist in the practice of his profession shows sensible regard for the social codes and moral expectations of the community in which he works, recognizing that violations of accepted moral and legal standards on his part may involve his clients, students, or colleagues in damaging personal conflicts and impugn his own name and the reputation of his profession.

Principle 4. Misrepresentation. The psychologist avoids misrepresentation of his own professional qualifications, affiliations, and purposes, and those of the institutions and organizations with which he is associated.

a. A psychologist does not claim either directly or by implication professional qualifications that differ from his actual qualifications, nor does he misrepresent his affiliation with any institution, organization, or individual, nor lead others to assume he has affiliations that he does not have. The psychologist is responsible for correcting others who misrepresent his professional qualifications or affiliations.

b. The psychologist does not misrepresent an institution or organization with which he is affiliated by ascribing to it characteristics it does not have.

c. A psychologist does not use his affiliation with the American Psychological

Association or its divisions for purposes that are not consonant with the stated purpose of the Association.

  d. A psychologist does not associate himself or permit his name to be used in connection with any services or products in such a way as to misrepresent them, the degree of his responsibility for them, or the nature of his affiliation.

Principle 5. Public Statements. Modesty, scientific caution, and due regard for the limits of present knowledge characterize all statements of psychologists who supply information to the public, either directly or indirectly.

  a. Psychologists who interpret the science of psychology or the services of psychologists to clients or to the general public have an obligation to report fairly and accurately. Exaggeration, sensationalism, superficiality, and other kinds of misrepresentation are avoided.

  b. When information about psychological procedures and techniques is given, care is taken to indicate that they should be used only by persons adequately trained in their use.

  c. A psychologist who engages in radio or television activities does not participate in commercial announcements recommending purchase or use of a product.

Principle 6. Confidentiality. Safeguarding information about an individual that has been obtained by the psychologist in the course of his teaching, practice, or investigation is a primary obligation of the psychologist. Such information is not communicated to others unless certain important conditions are met.

  a. Information received in confidence is revealed only after most careful deliberation and when there is clear and imminent danger to an individual or to society, and then only to appropriate professional workers or public authorities.

  b. Information obtained in clinical or consulting relationships, or evaluative data concerning children, students, employees, and others are discussed only for professional purposes and only with persons clearly concerned with the case. Written and oral reports should present only data germane to the purposes of the evaluation; every effort should be made to avoid undue invasion of privacy.

  c. Clinical and other materials are used in classroom teaching and writing only when identity of the persons involved is adequately disguised.

  d. The confidentiality of professional communications about individuals is maintained. Only when the originator and other persons involved give their express permission is a confidential professional communication shown to the individual concerned. The psychologist is responsible for informing the client of the limits of the confidentiality.

  e. Only after explicit permission has been granted is the identity of research subjects published. When data have been published without permission for identification, the psychologist assumes responsibility for adequately disguising their sources.

f. The psychologist makes provisions for the maintenance of confidentiality in the preservation and ultimate disposition of confidential records.

Principle 7. Client Welfare. The psychologist respects the integrity and protects the welfare of the person or group with whom he is working.

a. The psychologist in industry, education, and other situations in which conflicts of interest may arise among various parties, as between management and labor, or between the client and employer of the psychologist, defines for himself the nature and direction of his loyalities and responsibilities and keeps all parties concerned informed of these commitments.

b. When there is a conflict among professional workers, the psychologist is concerned primarily with the welfare of any client involved and only secondarily with the interest of his own professional group.

c. The psychologist attempts to terminate a clinical or consulting relationship when it is reasonably clear to the psychologist that the client is not benefiting from it.

d. The psychologist who asks that an individual reveal personal information in the course of interviewing, testing or evaluation, or who allows such information to be divulged to him, does so only after making certain that the responsible person is fully aware of the purposes of the interview, testing, or evaluation and of the ways in which the information may be used.

e. In cases involving referral, the responsibility of the psychologist for the welfare of the client continues until this responsibility is assumed by the professional person to whom the client is referred or until the relationship with the psychologist making the referral has been terminated by mutual agreement. In situations where referral, consultation, or other changes in the conditions of the treatment are indicated and the client refuses referral, the psychologist carefully weighs the possible harm to the client, to himself, and to his profession that might ensue from continuing relationship.

f. The psychologist who requires the taking of psychological tests for didactic, classification, or research purposes protects the examinees by ensuring that the tests and test results are used in a professional manner.

g. When potentially disturbing subject matter is presented to students, it is discussed objectively, and efforts are made to handle constructively any difficulties that arise.

h. Care must be taken to ensure an appropriate setting for clinical work to protect both client and psychologist from actual or imputed harm and the profession from censure.

i. In the use of accepted drugs for therapeutic purposes special care needs to be exercised by the psychologist to assure himself that the collaborating physician provides suitable safeguards for the client.

Principle 8. Client Relationship. The psychologist informs his prospective client of the important aspects of the potential relationship that might affect the client's decision to enter the relationship.

    a.   Aspects of the relationship likely to affect the client's decision include the recording of an interview, the use of interview material for training purposes, and observation of an interview by another person.

    b.   When the client is not competent to evaluate the situation (as in the case of a child), the person responsible for the client is informed of the circumstances which may influence the relationship.

    c.   The psychologist does not normally enter into a professional relationship with members of his own family, intimate friends, close associates, or others whose welfare might be jeopardized by such a dual relationship.

Principle 9. Impersonal Services. Psychological services for the purpose of diagnosis, treatment, or personalized advice are provided only in the context of a professional relationship and are not given by means of public lectures or demonstrations, newspaper or magazine articles, radio or television programs, mail, or similar media.

    a.   The preparation of personnel reports and recommendations based on test data secured solely by mail is unethical unless such appraisals are an integral part of a continuing client relationship with a company, as a result of which the consulting psychologist has intimate knowledge of the client's personnel situation and can be assured thereby that his written appraisals will be adequate to the purpose and will be properly interpreted by the client. These reports must not be embellished with such detailed analyses of the subject's personality traits as would be appropriate only after intensive interviews with the subject. The reports must not make specific recommendations as to employment or placement of the subject which go beyond the psychologist's knowledge of the job requirements of the company. The reports must not purport to eliminate the company's need to carry on such other regular employment or personnel practices as appraisal of the work history, checking of references, past performance in the company.

Principle 10. Announcement of Services. A psychologist adheres to professional rather than commercial standards in making known his availability for professional services.

    a.   A psychologist does not directly solicit clients for individual diagnosis or therapy.

    b.   Individual listings in telephone directories are limited to name, highest relevant degree, certification status, address, and telephone number. They may also include identification in a few words of the psychologist's major areas of practice; for example, child therapy, personnel selection, industrial psychology. Agency listings are equally modest.

    c.   Announcements of individual private practice are limited to a simple statement of the name, highest relevant degree, certification or diplomate status, address, telephone number, office hours, and a brief explanation of the types of services rendered. Announcements of agencies may list names of staff members with their qualifications. They conform in other particulars with the same standards as individual announcements, making certain that the true nature of the organization is apparent.

d. A psychologist or agency announcing nonclinical professional services may use brochures that are descriptive of services rendered but not evaluative. They may be sent to professional persons, schools, business firms, government agencies, and other similar organizations.

e. The use in a brochure of "testimonials from satisfied users" is unacceptable. The offer of a free trial of services is unacceptable if it operates to misrepresent in any way the nature or the efficacy of the services rendered by the psychologist. Claims that a psychologist has unique skills or unique devices not available to others in the profession are made only if the special efficacy of these unique skills or devices has been demonstrated by scientifically acceptable evidence.

f. The psychologist must not encourage (nor, within his power, even allow) a client to have exaggerated ideas as to the efficacy of services rendered. Claims made to clients about the efficacy of his services must not go beyond those which the psychologist would be willing to subject to professional scrutiny through publishing his results and his claims in a professional journal.

Principle 11. Interprofessional Relations. A psychologist acts with integrity in regard to colleagues in psychology and in other professions.

a. A psychologist does not normally offer professional services to a person receiving psychological assistance from another professional worker except by agreement with the other worker or after termination of the client's relationship with the other professional worker.

b. The welfare of clients and colleagues requires that psychologists in joint practice or corporate activities make an orderly and explicit arrangement regarding the conditions of their association and its possible termination. Psychologists who serve as employers of other psychologists have an obligation to make similar appropriate arrangements.

Principle 12. Remuneration. Financial arrangements in professional practice are in accord with professional standards that safeguard the best interest of the client and the profession.

a. In establishing rates for professional services, the psychologist considers carefully both the ability of the client to meet the financial burden and the charges made by other professional persons engaged in comparable work.

He is willing to contribute a portion of his services to work for which he receives little or no financial return.

b. No commission or rebate or any other form of remuneration is given or received for referral of clients for professional services.

c. The psychologist in clinical or counseling practice does not use his relationships with clients to promote, for personal gain or the profit of an agency, commercial enterprises of any kind.

d. A psychologist does not accept a private fee or any other form of remuneration for professional work with a person who is entitled to his services through an institution or agency. The policies of a particular agency may make explicit provision for private work with its clients by members of its staff, and in such instances the client must be fully apprised of all policies affecting him.

Principle 13. Test Security. Psychological tests and other assessment devices, the value of which depends in part on the naiveté of the subject, are not reproduced or described in popular publications in ways that might invalidate the techniques. Access to such devices is limited to persons with professional interests who will safeguard their use.

a. Sample items made up to resemble those of tests being discussed may be reproduced in popular articles and elsewhere, but scorable tests and actual test items are not reproduced except in professional publication.

b. The psychologist is responsible for the control of psychological tests and other devices and procedures used for instruction when their value might be damaged by revealing to the general public their specific contents or underlying principles.

Principle 14. Test Interpretation. Test scores, like test materials, are released only to persons who are qualified to interpret and use them properly.

a. Materials for reporting test scores to parents, or which are designed for self-appraisal purposes in schools, social agencies, or industry are closely supervised by qualified psychologists or counselors with provisions for referring and counseling individuals when needed.

b. Test results or other assessment data used for evaluation or classification are communicated to employers, relatives, or other appropriate persons in such a manner as to guard against misinterpretation or misuse. In the usual case, an interpretation of the test result rather than the score is communicated.

c. When test results are communicated directly to parents and students, they are accompanied by adequate interpretive aids or advice.

Principle 15. Test Publication. Psychological tests are offered for commercial publication only to publishers who present their tests in a professional way and distribute them only to qualified users.

a. A test manual, technical handbook, or other suitable report on the test is provided which describes the method of constructing and standardizing the test and summarizes the validation research.

b. The populations for which the test has been developed and the purposes for which it is recommended are stated in the manual. Limitations upon the test's dependability, and aspects of its validity on which research is lacking or incomplete, are clearly stated. In particular, the manual contains a warning regarding interpretations likely to be made which have not yet been substantiated by research.

c. The catalog and manual indicate the training or professional qualifications required for sound interpretation of the test.

d. The test manual and supporting documents take into account the principles enunciated in the *Standards for Educational and Psychological Tests and Manuals.*

e. Test advertisements are factual and descriptive rather than emotional and persuasive.

Principle 16. Research Precautions. The psychologist assumes obligations for the welfare of his research subjects, both animal and human.

a. Only when a problem is of scientific significance and is not practicable to investigate it in any other way is the psychologist justified in exposing research subjects, whether children or adults, to physical or emotional stress as part of an investigation.

b. When a reasonable possibility of injurious aftereffects exists, research is conducted only when the subjects or their responsible agents are fully informed of this possibility and agree to participate nevertheless.

c. The psychologist seriously considers the possibility of harmful aftereffects and avoids them, or removes them as soon as permitted by the design of the experiment.

d. A psychologist using animals in research adheres to the provisions of the Rules Regarding Animals, drawn up by the Committee on Precautions and Standards in Animal Experimentation and adopted by the American Psychological Association.

e. Investigations of human subjects using experimental drugs (for example, hallucinogenic, psychotomimetic, psychedelic, or similar substances) should be conducted only in such settings as clinics, hospitals, or research facilities maintaining appropriate safeguards for the subjects.

Principle 17. Publication Credit. Credit is assigned to those who have contributed to a publication, in proportion to their contribution, and only to these.

a. Major contributions of a professional character, made by several persons to a common project, are recognized by joint authorship. The experimenter or author who has made the principal contribution to a publication is identified as the first listed.

b. Minor contributions of a professional character, extensive clerical or similar nonprofessional assistance, and other minor contributions are acknowledged in footnotes or in an introductory statement.

c. Acknowledgment through specific citations is made for unpublished as well as published material that has directly influenced the research or writing.

d. A psychologist who compiles and edits for publication the contributions of others publishes the symposium or report under the title of the committee or symposium, with his own name appearing as chairman or editor among those of other contributors or committee members.

Principle 18. Responsibility toward Organization. A psychologist respects the rights and reputation of the institute or organization with which his is associated.

a. Materials prepared by a psychologist as a part of his regular work under specific direction of his organization are the property of that organization. Such materials are released for use or publication by a psychologist in accordance with policies of authorization, assignment of credit, and related matters which have been established by his organization.

b. Other material resulting incidentally from activity supported by any agency, and for which the psychologist rightly assumes individual responsibility, is published with disclaimer for any responsibility on the part of the supporting agency.

Principle 19. Promotional Activities. The psychologist associated with the development or promotion of psychological devices, books, or other products offered for commercial sale is responsible for ensuring that such devices, books, or products are presented in a professional and factual way.

a. Claims regarding performance, benefits, or results are supported by scientifically acceptable evidence.

b. The psychologist does not use professional journals for the commercial exploitation of psychological products, and the psychologist-editor guards against such misuse.

c. The psychologist with a financial interest in the sale or use of a psychological product is sensitive to possible conflict of interest in his promotion of such products and avoids compromise of his professional responsibilities and objectives.

Issues

1. What is the mechanism by which significant research findings—those with definite educational implications—can be effectively and quickly incorporated into programs of professional education?
2. By what means and at what stage is it possible to identify, for purposes of admission to professional programs, the nonintellective factors associated with success in counseling and/or therapy?
3. What are the minimum requirements that should be used as a standard to determine whether someone is qualified as a professional? Who should be responsible for establishing these standards? Are there any advantages to the current disparate situation?
4. Since it is not possible to provide in advance for every situation involving questions of values and ethics, what can programs and supervisors do to prepare professionals for meeting these situations when they arise?

Annotated Readings

Duncan, J. A., Gazda, G. M., & Sisson, P. J. Professional issues in group work. *Personnel and Guidance Journal,* 1971, **49** (8) 637–643.

This article first describes the explosion of interest in and practice of group work, with the resultant lag between the development both of standards for training and practice and of a code for ethical behavior/practice. A questionnaire is used to fill in some gaps regarding the number of cases of unethical behavior/practice in group work and the respondents' recommendations for dealing with the problems raised both externally by the public media and internally by professional association members. The data from the questionnaire are summarized, analyzed, and made relevant to the problem of ethics for group practices. Conclusions are drawn from these data, from others who have addressed themselves to the problems, and from the authors' own experiences in the group field. From these conclusions the authors list recommendations for alleviating the problem. (Entire issue of *Journal* is devoted to group process. Some articles relate to innovative techniques.)

Heath, B. R. G. Needed a professional identity: Aces or jokers? *Counselor Education and Supervision,* 1970, **9**, 126–131.

The ASCA statement on the role of the school-counselor is a reification. As a generalist the counselor dissipates his professional identity. Institutional restraints on the job and on the campus lead to incompetence in counseling practice and a pervasive belief that counseling is ineffective. A suggested alleviation of this problem specifically involves the abandonment of the teaching-experience requirement, increasing counselor–education–staff commitment to counseling, and the introduction of a paid internship for counselor-candidates. Two specialists are recommended to replace the present guidance model: A counselor-consultant and a career-information specialist.

Killian, J. D. The law, the counselor, and student records. *Personnel and Guidance Journal,* 1970, **48**, 423–432.

The counselor's legal responsibilities in the release of information about students involve matters of parental rights to information; possible defamation, libel, and slander; and privileged communication. The counselor, however, has little to fear from legal actions, provided that he performs in a professional and ethical manner and follows certain basic principles. When in doubt, he should feel free to consult with the judge in the case, and even at times with the attorneys involved. Relevant statutes and judicial rulings are cited to illustrate these various points.

McGreevy, C. P. Factor analysis of measures used in the selection and evaluation of counselor education candidates. *Journal of Counseling Psychology,* 1967, **14**, 51–56.

A factor analysis was performed of data commonly used to select counselor-candidates, together with three types of evaluative criteria. Data were gathered from the 86 enrollees of three NDEA Institutes held at Arizona State University. Fourteen factors were extracted, which were interpreted. Results support the use of the Miller Analogies Test for identifying academically able candidates. Faculty ratings of candidates made at the conclusion of the Institutes were not found to be highly related to any other selection or evaluation data. The findings suggested that more research is necessary to determine the characteristics and

217

qualities that counselor-educators feel counselor-candidates ought to possess before and after the candidates' formal preparation.

Thoreson, R. W., Krauskopf, C. J., McAleer, C. A., & Wenger, H. D. The future for applied psychology: Are we building a buggy whip factory? *American Psychologist,* 1972, **27**, 134–138.

Amid growing patient disenchantment there has emerged concern over the relevancy of the methods of applied psychology. A survey of 200 doctorate recepients randomly sampled from our 1000 graduates of programs in counseling psychology, indicates that the role of the counseling profession is ill-defined. Academicians have been hastening a widening gulf between the scientist and the practitioner, which, however, is not formally reflected in separate training programs. Moreover, the failure of most academicians to recognize the dynamic character of knowledge has resulted in outmoded overviews and, inversely, retreat into specialization.

In a compensatory push toward relevance, there has been a rising trend of community involvement and, particularly, service for the disadvantaged. But inasmuch as these new programs tend to operate from inappropriate traditional paradigms, they are largely disorganized and ineffective.

By way of remedy, the role of the professional psychologist might be redefined as translator-teacher-evaluator, serving as a mediating link between scientist and practitioner. This could promote a desirable dynamic equilibrium between investigation and application.

Suggestions for Further Reading

Ames, K. A. The development of an instrument for assessing the philosophical positions of school counselors. *Counselor Education and Supervision,* 1968, **7**, 335–339.

Clark, C. M. Confidentiality and the school counselor. *Personnel and Guidance Journal,* 1965, **43**, 482–484.

Clinebell, H. J., Jr. *Basic types of pastoral counseling.* Nashville: Abingdon Press, 1966.

Cox, R. F. Confidentiality—Where is our first obligation? *School Counselor,* 1965, **12**, 153–161.

Daubner, E. V., & Daubner, E. S. Ethics and counseling decisions. *Personnel and Guidance Journal,* 1970, **48**, 433–442.

Gutsch, K. U. Counseling: The impact of ethics. *Counselor Education and Supervision,* 1968, **7**, 239–243.

Heayn, M. H., & Jacobs, H. L. Safeguarding student records. *Personnel and Guidance Journal,* 1967, **46**, 63–67.

Schmidt, L. D. Some ethical, professional, and legal considerations for school counselors. *Personnel and Guidance Journal,* 1965, **44**, 376–382.

CHAPTER 6

What the Counselor Needs to Know

What doesn't the counselor need to know? This question would probably be more to the point than the one in the title, considering the experiences, behaviors, and problems—individual, situational, familial, and societal—that confront clinicians in schools, colleges, hospitals, community mental-health centers, family clinics, head clinics, outpatient units, residential treatment centers, rehabilitation services, rap centers, church agencies, and private practice. The complexity of life in the third-last decade of the twentieth century literally "blows one's mind." What follows from this is obviously the need for updating programs of graduate education. But what might be less obvious, though equally significant, is the need for firmer grounding in the basic skills that serve as foundation for the more specialized skills. In other words, the total repertoire of abilities must of necessity be increased—and this should not be at the expense of fundamentals. There is no research indicating that marathon therapy sessions are more skillfully conducted by persons who have *not* had considerable experience in basic group therapy—quite the contrary—and, of course, more and more such examples could be offered. Basic skills are important.

How then can counselors-in-preparation cover all the material that is expected of them? One obvious answer, perhaps, is that programs must be expanded—or perhaps specialization at an earlier stage of education is necessary—or perhaps something else is needed. Clearly, demands are being placed on counselors to go into settings that until recently did not include them, or did not even exist. Enthusiasm is not a substitute for competence. There must be a sound base—a development, if you will, of something very much like a role description of the counselor in the myriad of new settings—which can serve as a guide for program development and student selection.

Opportunities are growing at an almost geometric rate. If they are to strengthen the profession and increase leadership, educational programs and professional organizations must determine guidelines for acceptable preparation. Included in this concept of total preparation would be "continuing" education.

Fortunately for the reader, the essayists in this chapter have interpreted in

221

the broadest sense—i.e., theoretically—the task of exploring what the practitioner should know, in addition to dealing with more limited questions of specific program recommendations.

By way of paraphrasing Tiedeman: with rank come responsibility and privilege. He asserts that the true professional, in the fullest sense, should be allowed to do what he believes is right and called for. This is far from being a simple acknowledgement, because his conceptualization of "professional" places great emphasis on *knowledge, responsibility, competence, creativity, leadership,* and *continuing education*— all these terms are developed and criteria for evaluating them are included.

Writing in a very different style and describing separate issues and objectives, Wolleat communicates an equally meaningful sense of the functions of the clinician. She provides a framework for considering not only curriculum, but such hard-to-pin-down aspects as the self-knowledge of the practitioner and the development of value systems. The attention she directs to the importance of the facilitative relationship as a very explicit part of the professional curriculum makes it less likely that the implications for change in programs will be avoided.

What the Counselor Needs to Know, Do, and Be*

David V. Tiedeman

Northern Illinois University

THESIS

What does the counselor need to know?
Everything necessary!
What does the counselor need to do?
"Counsel" under educational conditions!
What does the counselor need to be?
Professional!

Obviously the counselor cannot know everything. Therefore, I qualify my answer to the first question by the judgment of the counselor. This may seem circular, but it is necessary.

Obviously, counseling is not a universally appropriate technique or set of duties. Therefore, I qualify my answer to the second question by noting that counseling can exist under educational conditions only if both teachers and counselors are truly able to manufacture that educational condition.

Obviously the counselor must be something, and I contend that he must be a professional something. Further on in this essay, I qualify this to indicate that the counselor as a professional merely professes. This is a different definition of the term *professional* from the one sociologists are inclined to use. The sociologist is interested in professionalism from the standpoint of the status of the occupant of a position. I am interested in the professing of counseling because, I believe, it is the only way to protect the freedom of students in an educational condition in which there is public and professional expectation and sanction for growth in wisdom and responsibility on the part of every student.

There are senses in which my answers to the three questions are not facetious. Explore these nonfacetious senses with me in this essay. See if I can bring you to understand the senses, their necessity, and their potential value. However, note that I consider what the counselor should be, do, and know—not the reverse, as I did above.

*This essay is based on an article of similar name published in *Notre Dame Journal of Education*, 1971, **2**, 101–122.

WHAT SHOULD THE COUNSELOR BE? A PROFESSIONAL AT PRACTICE IN GUIDANCE

We stunt the growth of professional practice in guidance by an inordinate primary concern for the courses we offer in the education of a counselor. This concern ordinarily arises from the blinders we counselor-educators wear as psychologists dedicated first to behavioral science and then to practice (see Thompson & Super, 1964). "Tell me what behavior *you* want and *I* will tell you how to get it," therefore, dominates the education of counselors, where it is inappropriate, as well as our research, where it is appropriate. Unfortunately, this attitude even spreads to counselors in practice. Counselors are now prescribing the education of those who will follow them (Hill, 1967). The result is that we are now in a stalemate. On the one hand, the counselor wants to be a professional. On the other hand, his education is not yet fully geared to letting him become professional.

How come? I contend it is because we are not yet fully sure of what we want the counselor to *be*. Therefore, I first describe who and where the counselor ought to be. In two subsequent sections I consider what the counselor should do and what he should know.

Practice in guidance aims at leaving each person with a sense of control over part of his environment (whatever that environment may be) sufficient for him to experience self-esteem in the circumstances he wants to create. The practice of guidance, in which I am interested and in which I hope my students will be similarly interested, takes place in the educational condition. The educational condition is sometimes available in schools and colleges, as we expect it to be. However, the educational condition can also occur in private, at home, at work, in community service, or at play. (Gains seem to be rapid when they occur at play, whether the play goes on in schools and colleges or outside of them.)

In the educational condition, the student comes to know the "known," and to practice in the unknown as well as the "known." The "known" is offered students in our schools and colleges as something originally external from them, but expected to be internalized by the conclusion of "education"—a course, a year, or a degree, whatever the case may be. Inherent in my statement of the educational condition is the relationship of the knower to the "known." Also inherent in my statement is the relationship of the present knower, the student, to the "prior" knower, the teacher. In the educational condition the teacher brings the student into relation with the "known" so that the student comes to know it. The counselor observes and helps in the process of internalization, so that the student also has opportunity to examine and work through the matter of authority for the "known" in the process of his getting to know it. The counselor also stands ready, at those teachable moments, to help in the unraveling of such a process to generalize the emerging understanding of personal responsibility for knowing to goal-determination and means-selection in realms of existence outside of "courses." In this generalization process the counselor attempts to insure that goal-determination and means-selection take place, have the cast of the possible, seem accurate and explicit, and are pursued and/or revised in awareness.

I presume a need for both teacher and counselor in my model of knowing. The teacher deliberately introduces the "known" and works with both its staging and the student to anticipate and guide its internalization. In the course of this practice, the teacher works intuitively with the processes of discovery and insight, which set the stage for understanding and possible appreciation —not mere recall of the "known." I contend that the counselor, for his part, deliberately brings the issues of *responsibility* and *projection* into the educational condition, and works with the "known" (in only the very general terms of a subject's structure, not its specific context) and the teacher's staging of discovery and insight. The counselor does so expecting that awareness of the issue of authority for the "known," under requirement of future action with the "known," will generalize in ways such that the student will come to understand his own possibilities and responsibilities in relation to future activity.

When teacher and counselor are both present in the educational condition, as modeled above, the student "enjoys" two external sources of expectation, which are not fully congruent. The student is therefore in the best position possible to experience expert but separate powers from dual sources. The student thereby assumes the traditional position of the citizen in our democracy: namely, a position that faces him with the necessity for integrated but free activity while the activity arises from two expert but only partially understanding sources.

I find the above framework necessary to handle an issue vital in guidance: namely, how to be definite in professional action without original logical contradiction of the fact that teacher and counselor both want the student to become responsible for his own education, to make up his own mind, and to act without erroneous projection of his mistakes on others and without self-deception as to causal connections among sequences of events. In short, I believe I can help a student, but not inordinately affect his choice of specific goals or selection of specific means for goal pursuit.

As a professional counselor, I am definite about my actions in relation to responsibility and projection, which I dedicate myself to help bring into the awareness of those I help. However, as a professional counselor, I also guarantee free goal-determination and means-selection to my students by working in an educational condition. In the educational condition there is public sanction for the teacher to present goals and means. In this same educational condition there is also traditional public expectation, but less present public sanction, for the counselor to face the student with his responsibility and authority for goal-determination and means-selection. Although I want to permit individual goals and means, I do not want such pursuit to emerge in ignorance of biological, psychological, sociological, and cultural influences on the selection of goals and means. By having both a teacher and a counselor as professional helpers, the student is exposed to the "known," which helps him to lay out both his civilization, in which he takes his place, and his aspirations and deterrents, in which his responsibility supposedly emerges without occurrence of too much projection. Because he is exposed to the separate but equal powers of organized understanding and individual action, the student becomes able to set his own vector in this field of dual forces.

In short, I am arguing that teacher and counselor both do, and ought to, treat the student as a whole. However, the professional role of each of these practitioners is different. The differences between these roles create distinctions in the ways the two practitioners see the "known." Both practitioners must be secure enough to know that their "known" is not the totality of the person they help. When this simple fact is not only known, but is always consistently acted upon, teacher and counselor become interdependent in the educational condition. When both in turn work as professionals, not technicians, the student can in turn become independent, but without escaping attending to reciprocity, that condition so necessary for the limitation of man's independence in his social existence.

I am also arguing the ideal realization, the fully developed appreciation of tentativeness and commitment in living. Obviously, the developed condition does not spring full-blown like Minerva from Jupiter's forehead. The evolution of independence, because of appreciation of the predicament of the "known" and the knower in knowing, is long and undoubtedly never completed. I wish I could offer the stages of that evolution in full detail. I cannot because they are not known. Perry started to lay bare these stages (see Wise, 1966) in relation to liberal education. Kohlberg (1964) postulated similar but not identical stages in the evolution of moral judgment.

I content myself with stating the ideal condition because it is all I need here in order to establish belief in the necessity for professional practice in guidance. If we as counselors are to leave the selection of goals and means to students, we must be behavioral scientists with regard to responsibility and projection. However, we must concurrently act with full and unfettered intuition as professionals when we counsel. Otherwise we will seriously limit the emergence of the ideal condition, which I have outlined, by transgressing the rights and obligations of students in ways I do not want the sanction to do.

WHAT SHOULD THE COUNSELOR DO? PROFESS GUIDANCE

I have argued that the professional practice of guidance in complement to teaching is required to educate for freedom in expectation of reciprocity during social interactions. The doing consequence of this statement of what the counselor should be is that the counselor should profess guidance.

Do not lightly turn your mind from my passive noun *professional* to my active verb *profess*. To *profess* a practice is to commit yourself to the *doing* of that practice. Such a commitment is necessary if the practice is to have integrity. However, concomitantly with commitment must come the perspective of tentativeness about goals and procedures. When the paradox of commitment and tentativeness is not alone understood but also appreciated, the professional has attained the mature condition of his profession (Tiedeman, 1967). Such a mature condition in turn gives the professional complete opportunity to doubt within a continuity of belief in his capability to do the difficult. The condition also permits the professional to know that he must know everything *and* that he cannot know everything. This allows him to expect excellence, but to understand that perfection is ever attainable but never realized.

He who would profess guidance, therefore, must work himself free of the bounds of the disciplines as they exist if guidance is to be the profession it would like to be rather than the technology it now is. This is the premise on which my entire argument rests. It is not my purpose to argue that *all* who practice guidance either are or must be professional. That line of reasoning leads to matters of economics, which I prefer to avoid while considering the ideal as I am now doing. Neither is it my intention to concern myself with issues of status between technology and profession. The unearned reputation gains no more respect from me than it does from you. Rather it is my purpose to examine the necessary conditions of professionalism and to propose the further elaboration of a program of preparation and later practice, which is designed to provide, ultimately at least, those conditions deemed necessary for professionalism. After we know that we can and do prepare professionals, we can trouble ourselves with issues of quantity, authority, responsibility, and status. Then we can learn to use the capacities of the professional to the advantage of our several desires. In fact, I argue, of course, that the true professional should even be accorded the right to do what *he* thinks is best.

To be free of the bounds of the disciplines as they now exist in no way implies that the professional has the right to be ignorant of any aspect of a discipline that is of immediate use in the solution of problems he elects to pursue. I do not advocate license, merely freedom with respect for the problem and those affected by it. In fact, the professional, as well as the students I consider in the second section, in relation to the attainment of purposeful action through education must accept responsibility for the actions he causes to occur and, in so doing, must accept criticism if he fails in an endeavor because of ignorance. The "ignorance" noted here is, of course, that stemming from failure to consider a procedure that might have been successful and was available in print. The professional just has to be learning continuously from his own experience and from the experience of others. Otherwise the quality of his effort will deteriorate.

Although the professional is responsible for keeping himself informed, his purpose is different from that of the scientist or scholar, who also keeps himself informed—about some things, that is—namely, those things needed for the development of *his discipline*. The professional keeps himself informed in order to solve the problems *he* elects to consider. Furthermore, the professional assumes no obligation either to provide solutions of so-called general utility (although his solutions may well be of that nature) or to inform others of his solutions. The professional must provide explanations when demands are legitimate, of course, but he need not seek his recognition from a more general audience, as does the scholar. The professional is accountable only to those he elects to serve, so long as he also remains within the bounds of propriety while he strives to find the solution to the problem he pursues.

My contention, then, is that the professional must be free of the past at the same time that he has a true appreciation of that past and of his desire now to solve problems of a particular nature. The aspiring professional is a professional only when he convinces himself pragmatically that he can solve those problems with a reasonable degree of consistency in his successes. Let us now examine how this process occurs in the creation of those who would solve problems in guidance.

WHAT SHOULD THE COUNSELOR KNOW? EVERYTHING

I have argued that guidance must be conceived as a professional practice in complement to teaching in education for freedom in expectation of reciprocity during social interaction. I have then argued that the counselor must profess in order that this condition of freedom and responsibility may arise in educational context. Here I want to limit my argument about counselors professing in order to consider the main part of my argument, namely, what should the counselor know?

I have made my statements of what a counselor should be and do in order to have an ideal that a counselor might keep in mind at all stages of becoming a counselor. There are compelling economic and human grounds, which suggest that an entire counseling staff need not, and probably never can, be fully working at the professional level I advocate. However, I contend that an educational institution, which incorporates the profession of guidance, must have *at least one member of the staff* who is professional in my ideal sense. I am willing to take this stand on grounds that my conditions for freedom and responsibility can be met if there is at least one professional in an entire service who professes as I recommend. This implies that all other members of the counseling staff should consider themselves journeymen under loose but not lax supervision of the professional. It also implies that journeymen counselors counsel by virtue of the responsibility *shared* with them by the professional counselor. This responsibility should be considered as a "loan," as is the case in all line organizations. The system will function best if the professional counselor does not have to give much attention to "withdrawing his loans." However, the system will collapse if the professional counselor does not consider himself responsible in this ultimate sense, and if his journeymen counselors do not accord the professional either the right to that expectation or the opportunity to oversee its application.

In taking the position I do, I want it clear that I do not necessarily link my recommendation for authority concentration in a professional person with his possession of a doctoral degree. Not all persons who hold the doctorate are professional in my above sense of the ideal. Also, many who are professional do not hold the doctoral degree. I attempt below to give further indication of what I think it takes to be a professional. I particularly attempt to separate the professional from the professor, with whom, I think, we and our graduates have unwittingly tended to identify him.

In taking the position I do, I also ask you to remember that the education of a professional has no strongly fixed required pattern in my judgment. I am talking about a well-educated person who is willing to act as if he knows, while knowing that he never fully can know. The attainment of the well-educated condition is a lifelong matter halted at death, but it might well be associated with a good secondary and collegiate education. For me it is irrelevant whether this well-educated condition has been attained with collegiate concentration in psychology or not. I have found that persons who concentrate in English and history in college bring a great deal to the study of guidance. Their problem is in understanding science and professionalism. Ordinarily the problem with the psychology concentrator is the contrary one of understanding humanism and professionalism. Hence either type of person can be off to an equal start in a guidance program that wants humanism and science to be welded by students into professionalism before considering the student's capability for professing to have matured. This is the "known" part of guidance, which I consider first in the following sections. I relate the needed understanding to that of appreciating science, applied science, and purposeful action.

You will find that I also expand upon my belief that professionalism is bound up with learning while experiencing. I argue that this arranged experience under supervision must be part of the education of a counselor. However, I trust it is understood that experience occurs throughout life. Therefore, relevant experience is acquired before graduate study in guidance, which forms the knowledge and intention the guidance program attempts to coalesce into confidence in professing guidance. Relevant experience is also acquired upon graduation from graduate programs in guidance. I hope that the initial part of that experience is under the supervision of a professional. However, as my journeyman graduate practices, he might well achieve professional status in his own eyes and those of relevant colleagues, and/or he might return for further graduate study and experience. I consider this experience and practice part of the counselor's education in the second of my major subsections below.

First I turn to what the counselor needs to know about the science of guidance.

WHAT SHOULD THE COUNSELOR KNOW? SCIENCE, APPLIED SCIENCE, AND THE SCIENCE OF GUIDANCE

Thesis. I contend that we are presently almost devoid of theory *in* guidance. I do not like to be a prophet of doom and gloom; I *am* convinced that we must daily *continue* to practice guidance with what little theory we have. Neither do I like to seem falsely erudite by expressing a meaningless platitude as an inflammatory opinion. Hence, I shall seriously attempt justification of the conclusion I have just expressed.

Please note my stress upon "in" when I conclude that we are almost devoid of theory *in* guidance. There must be either a theory *of* guidance or a theory *for* guidance before there can ever be a theory *in* guidance. My opinion is that we do not have a theory *of* guidance, and that even the little theory available *for* guidance is not yet *in* guidance. We are almost without theory in guidance because (1) we have tended to rely upon others for theory; and (2) we have been relatively uncritical of our practice. Neither of these conditions favor the development of theory.

Science and Scholarship. The fruits of a scientific procedure are well known. In fact those fruits are presently so prestigious that they themselves are frequently made coextensive with the entire meaning of the word *science*.

Public impressions notwithstanding, there is a distinctive meaning of *science* that is importantly different from the product of being scientific. Think of the process of science, not the products of that process. The process of science is best known in terms of effort to make a prior implicit understanding explicit. Polanyi (1966) and Schwab (1962) deal with these parts of the scientific process. The process of making something explicit can itself be dealt with logically because it has prior existence. We know this logic as the scientific method.

The scientific method is not the be-all and end-all of being scientific. How does the implicit understanding given explicit existence by the scientific method itself appear? Polanyi found himself infected with that question after he wrote *The Study of Man* (1959). The explicit product of his "infection" proved to be *The Tacit Dimension* (1966). In this book Polanyi makes explicit the origination of tacit understanding from the interchange of conscious and unconscious activities, an interchange in accord with Kubie's idea (1958) of the preconscious and Koestler's idea (1964) of the play-like bisociations that are the turning points in productive creativity.

Although I have noted above that both Polanyi and Schwab deal with the process of science, they do so in different ways. Polanyi is interested in the process as it takes place in the individual scientist. In this case, one becomes interested in the origination of tacit understanding, and in the processes of making that tacit (implicit) understanding explicit. Schwab is interested in another aspect of the process of science, namely, (1) the origin of a *line* of inquiry, and (2) the follow-on activities, in which *many* scientists, not one scientist, later engage in making an earlier discovery even more explicit, and eventually in making that discovery come to the end of its usefulness as an explanatory device because its explanatory power becomes overloaded with detail. Schwab refers to this duality as that of fluid research on the one hand and of static research on the other. Static research *accepts* the general restraints of an explanation and secures finer and finer empirical observations and organizations *within* those restraints. Fluid investigations, on the other hand, bring the restraining conditions of static research into question, doubt, reinvestigation, and ultimately reformulation. Ordinarily it is in fluid investigations that tacit understandings of individual scientists become more salient, and in which reorienting discoveries of potentially higher value are achieved. Static investigations, on the other hand, elaborate a fluid understanding and thereby make the understanding have greater power in its domain.

Explicitly stated theories and statically investigated theories result in an accretion of data that ordinarily earn credibility from large numbers of people. An explicit theory and static investigations of it are bound, however, by the restraints of the theory. A theory only applies in its own domain. Thus, in the realm of physical objects, where the objects can have no knowledge of the scientist's explanation of their activity, explicit theories and tacit investigations come to be valued highly. Note well, however, that an explicit theory with high accretion of static investigations is bound within the restraints of the theory. These restraints mean that the failure of a higher-order conception or structure can be understood within the circumscribed restraints of the theory in order to tell where a part of the whole has failed. However, an explicit theory and static investigation do not enter the realm of thought, speculation, or possibility in relation to variation of the restraints of the theory. In this regard, an explicit theory and static investigation are able to explain failure in a hierarchic structure of those parts. However, not one explicit theory and supporting static investigation is able to explain or to create the whole; that is, the entirety of parts and their hierarchy. The explanation and/or creation of the whole involves mentation that is not resident in science. The required mentation, however, is resident in the scientist or in some other person who uses some part, but not all, of a science's explicit statements.

Science and Applied Science. In the physical sciences, studies devoted to the application of general theory are called "applied" sciences. Engineering is an applied science, for instance. Applied sciences are ordinarily accorded a lesser status in our society than are the so-called pure sciences such as physics. This is presumably because an applied science requires merely the application of general laws available elsewhere. As one stereotyped perception sees it, the pure sciences represent the inventory of available ideas; the applied sciences merely "merchandise" those ideas. The pure scientist can always do *if* he wants to; the applied scientist can *only* do. The pure scientist is a scholar; the applied scientist a technician.

Unfortunately, such a conception of applied science, even in the physical sciences, ignores (1) the intelligence and creativity frequently required in the simultaneous use of at least two principles, to say nothing of the simultaneous use of several principles; and (2) the possibly unknown interactive effects that can only be *discovered* in the simultaneous application of several principles, each of which had been previously studied in only an isolated way. The first cantilever bridge that performed as expected was a real engineering feat, after all! We did not discover how two different metals affected each other as they weathered until we actually studied them when joined. Even in the physical sciences, then, there perpetually are frontiers of doubt, of discovery, and of potentially expensive and dangerous trial, all of which are an ordinary part of the mastery of new applications. Furthermore, after applications have been mastered, repetitions may still be difficult. The creation of the continuously proper adjustment of the chemicals required in the refining of petroleum is no easy matter, and mistakes can be dangerous and expensive. Many engineering and other professional schools realize these facts about applied science, and aim their instruction, development, and research primarily at such ever-evolving frontiers. Such schools thereby offer a liberating education; students must master known principles and must also learn how to know and to act while being doubtful.

Guidance as Applied Behavioral Science. An adult becomes an active agent in the life of another person during the process of guidance. Principles must be intelligently used by a professional agent in situations relevant to the purpose of bettering the life of the person who is to be helped. Guidance is therefore an *applied* field. Unfortunately, we in guidance tend to commit two errors in responding to this realization. One error is to consider guidance a mere technology, a bag of rules. The other error is to consider the behavioral sciences to be identical in nature to the physical sciences, a set of principles unshared with the intellect to which applied.

Our mistake in considering guidance a technology is apparent in many ways. We offer instruction only in the *principles* and *practices* of guidance, seldom in the *theory* of guidance. Few good books on theory in guidance are available. We are frequently required by academic councils to turn to a department of psychology for our theory. Most of our scholars prefer to identify themselves as psychologists rather than as educators or personnel workers. We readily accept the value premises of the lay public (e.g., economic demands for manpower) and scamper to offer the demanded practice. A review of guidance-personnel work by Barry and Wolf (1957) was deliberately cast in a historical mold because the authors confessed an inability to frame a theory of guidance. We still have college guidance, educational guidance, vocational guidance, and the like. In short, we have usually acted like technologists and we are largely known as technologists. We lay claim to a few techniques and a sphere of limited activity, but not to a theory. Is this condition even *logically* sound?

As noted earlier, commitment to apply the theory of the physical sciences ordinarily is a commitment to operate with inanimate objects in combinations in which they are not necessarily considered in the original framing of theory. An engineering application may require simultaneous use of physics, chemistry, psychology, and law, for instance. Thus, applied physical sciences can easily be difficult, require ingenuity, and lead to discovery of new relationships in the operations of inanimate objects. To be sure, a commitment to make application of the theory of the behavioral sciences, as in the case of guidance, involves these same considerations. However, an important element differentiates applied behavioral science from applied physical science. In those applications of the behavioral sciences where the intellect of the subject is directly involved in the course of the application, the application, if it is to be at all effective, cannot ignore the meaning system of the individual. The commitment espoused in guidance thereby places an unusual demand upon theory in behavioral sciences. Guidance must have a theory that not only predicts, but also permits control of some aspects of the behavioral repertoire of the subject *without threat to his freedom.* Guidance needs a theory, then, which deals with change in the idiosyncratic systems of meaning of each person. But what changes in personal meaning are to be sought and will be tolerated?

The Purpose of Guidance. Usually, purpose, theory, and practice improve apace and remain consistent, as they should be. The unusual divorce of practice and theory in guidance, which I have been noting, means that the practice, theory, and purpose of guidance are presently not well articulated. In fact, I have been alarmed by our lack of clarity even as to purpose. Yes, we *do* have the "guidance viewpoint"; we *are* interested in the "whole" child. I am amazed, however, by our sensitivity to repeated questioning about purpose. We quickly turn from such questions and get back to doing. We know what we are up to, but we are not very articulate about our purpose as a result.

Practice is one avenue to assimilation and socialization. There are appropriate ways to encourage one type of response rather than another. Rules are learned by such means. Learning solely by this means subjugates a minor intellect to that of a master, however. Furthermore, it limits the repertoire of appropriate responses to only those learned.

Man is capable not only of being taught *how* to do something; he can also be taught *why* he should do it. Furthermore, man is capable of placing ideas in familiar and unfamiliar juxtapositions and of reflecting upon the consequences of such juxtapositions. Finally, man can symbolize the stimuli he receives and perceives. These cognitive capabilities of man, when cultivated, greatly enlarge his potential for assimilation and socialization. Furthermore, they enable the exercise of wise judgment when information is incomplete.

The course of life in our society is to move from dependence to independence, by at least the transitions from home to school to work and back to home. A number of identity crises are encountered in this course, and the aftereffects of these crises gradually solidify in an attitude toward self-in-world. The purpose of guidance is to insure that this attitude toward self-in-world be both realistic and hopeful. Otherwise the transfer from infant dependence to adult independence will not be effected without withdrawal or projection. In short, then, the purpose of guidance is to place the keystone of responsibility for being into the arch of self-determination, as that arch is constructed within the broad strategy of education from childhood to mature adulthood. Furthermore, this is to be done by scientific facilitation of the evolution of an idiosyncratic system of meaning.

Guidance is practiced within the framework of education by making each person aware of the process of becoming as the process may be available to him. The premises about self-in-world that a person has experienced with feeling are aspects of ego that guidance seeks to bring into awareness. So is cause and effect; the means-ends linkages that one establishes in his enhancement of self are important for his eventual position in his society as it exists. Of considerable relevance is implantation of the concept that education is not an end in itself. Education and teachers are to be outlived. Living and life are the more ultimate ends. Living and life require the *use* of knowledge in novel ways, and the evaluation of the experience from use in relation to one's gradually crystallizing organization of self.

Mathewson notes that the purpose for the practice of guidance is "beyond systems (1960)." By this Mathewson means that guidance, by attempting to establish a hopeful and effective attitude toward self-in-world, lays the foundation for relatively significant action in time of doubt, with well-founded reliance upon self in cooperation with others and upon one's intellect as trained through education. Only thus does education become truly liberating and man become *for himself* (Fromm, 1947).

The attitude toward self-in-world is idiosyncratic, of course. Hence, primary attention in guidance is individually centered, and counseling is one of its prime media. Counseling brings the self into awareness by creating a nonjudgmental focus upon anger, fear, doubt, guilt, shame, joy, and so forth. These are windows through which we may peer into self; the windows by which we can know identity. The circumstances in which we experience these emotions can be examined to reveal fundamental premises by which we organize our relationship to things, ideas, and people in the world. These are the "anchors" of our attitude toward self-in-world, our psychological life-space, the meanings of our existence.

With my admission that counseling is a function of guidance, you may begin to doubt my opinion that we are practically without theory in guidance. Yes, a lot of attention *has* been given to the study of counseling during the past several decades. We *are* making headway in developing a theory of counseling. Our difficulty has been that we have assumed that we are also thereby making headway in developing a theory of guidance. This I doubt. Otherwise I would not have framed such a severe indictment of the current state of guidance.

Counseling is an effective means of focusing upon psychological defenses. The awareness gained from these peeks into one's self can have the generalized effects both of freeing psychological energy and of acquainting the subject with the influence of emotion upon establishing the premises of his psychological life-space. Furthermore, counseling can have some influence in establishing a realization of the importance of self in one's life. Controlling emotion through ego, while honoring and intensifying emotional experience, represents the ultimate experience of freedom in our political system. Although these advantages *can* accrue from counseling, they are not now really an integral part of a theory of guidance.

In guidance we aim to strengthen the ego. This means that we are dealing with an attitude about self-in-world that forms over *a lifetime*, not just during an interview. It is a fundamental belief in guidance that this attitude embodies a strong belief in self when an elaborated system of choice is available to each person. It is further believed that each of these choices must be effected in awareness and hope, but with a confrontation both of the reality of self and opportunity and of the responsibility to choose and to accept the consequences of choice. These conditions require that a period both of anticipation and of adjustment must be associated with each choice. Furthermore, the conditions require that there must not only be a striving for identification with group or cause, but also reciprocation of the wish for identification, which eventually leads the person to feel accepted and potent. In any period of any choice, counseling can be of help for a myriad of reasons. Guidance, however, is interested in the science relating this network of choices and its difficulties and their treatment to the strengthening of ego. Hence a science of guidance must be developmental. Any science presumes diagnosis and prescription. The science of guidance must embrace the nourishing of a responsible acceptance and honoring of self as it is reflected in the attitude toward self-in-world. It must consider the implantation and metamorphosis of motivation. Guidance is interested, then, in attitudes that are acquired over a lifetime. These attitudes establish the uniqueness of personality. Guidance attempts to keep the character of personality productive. Obviously, a theory of counseling is insufficient. In fact, a theory of counseling intended only to provide a window for self has no necessary connection with anything; such a theory relies only upon the possible pervasiveness of knowledge of self. Guidance is more purposeful. *It needs a more elaborated, interconnected, and directed theory,* a "self-situational" theory. Field and I have, therefore, created the language of a guidance theory, namely a science of purposeful action applied through education (Tiedeman & Field, 1965).

Idiosyncrasy and Science. This is a good place to pause and to consider a major concern in guidance, namely, whether we can promulgate idiosyncratic meaning in a scientific way. In other words, are idiosyncrasy and science incompatible?

For me, idiosyncrasy and science become incompatible only if we specify a *kind* of idiosyncrasy rather than *that* one develop idiosyncratic meaning for life. With specification of a *kind* of idiosyncrasy it is possible to favor, to require, and even to condition. Guidance then becomes noneducative, nondevelopmental. This is not true, at least of *the* idiosyncratic meaning actually achieved, if one only specifies that a person develop the convictions that bind and support his life. Hence we bind an applied science of guidance only to the goal of fostering the responsible pursuit of idiosyncrasy. It is to this purpose that we must write the examinable and later examined propositions of a science, which permit a practitioner to work with a little confidence. Obviously the examined life is attained only developmentally, never fully and never ultimately elaborated. However, guidance must be prepared to note the development it fosters, and to elaborate the consequences of one form of pursuit and the other at each developmental stage. This is the science of guidance. As noted, the ultimate concerns of the science of guidance must be with (1) the stages *required* for the maturely examined life; (2) projection and withdrawal in the mastery of each stage; (3) fixation at lesser stages; and (4) information in the meaning system of every individual of relevance for development. These are the propositions that must be developed for the needed self-situational theory of guidance.

Finally, my friend and astute critic, Professor Mathewson, has privately noted for me that I have specified theory in developing my position *about* theory. I prefer to say, as I did with Field (Tiedeman & Field, 1965), that I have merely specified the linguistic pattern necessary for a science of guidance and highlighted the concerns that must be explored in developing theory. In this sense I have specified theory, and we presently have in guidance a linguistic framework compatible with our requirements for theory. The details of the developmental process, and the diagnostic and prescriptive linkages of relevance to the nurture of that process, are far beyond my present power to specify, however. In this sense, I have *not* specified a theory of guidance, and, as I have contended in this essay, we do not have theory in guidance.

Criticism in Guidance. In the thesis of this section, I noted that we are impoverished for theory in guidance both because we have relied upon others for theory and because we have been relatively uncritical of our practice. I have written enough of our expectation that others will provide theory. I now write a bit now about our general lack of criticism.

Barry and Wolf (1957) were the ones who directed my attention to our usual avoidance of criticism. After I read their suggestion I began to devote more thought to the subject.

In guidance we tend to practice alone. Even if others are on the same staff with us, we manage to stay so busy that we do not have many case conferences with colleagues, as the psychologist attempts in the clinic. We do not tend to create records of our actions, to be examined carefully later on when we know the consequences of our intervention. We do not tend to argue about publications, to take stands, to explore issues again and again. In short, we do not tend to take those steps specifically designed to help us learn professionally. Yes, we do return to school now and again, and we do attend many professional meetings. These activities are intended to help us pick up ideas. However, there is a relative lack of "putting oneself on the block," so to speak. Hence, there is not much effort to establish oneself among colleagues solely by virtue of the excellence of one's own ideas. Rather, we tend to rely more upon sociability and congruence of ideas to establish ourselves with colleagues.

In stating these opinions I do not intend to advocate ruthlessness. I have experienced ruthlessness and have no liking for it. We must continue to let others know that we like and accept them, particularly if we want to criticize them. Acceptance provides room in one's psychological life-space for one to benefit from criticism. The impression I do intend to leave, however, is that we must believe that to disagree is not to be disloyal, and we must become more critical of our practice. We must stop just demonstrating what we do, and turn more frequently to asking critical questions about that practice. These questions, our answers, and our responsibility must be more public.

Theory and practice ordinarily advance together. Intensive analysis of theory suggests ways that theory can be translated into practice and thereby subjected to verification; these are the rudimentary ingredients of a science. It makes little difference, then, whether we develop a science from theory or from the criticism of practice, just so long as neither is neglected. It does make a difference when both theory and criticism are neglected, as we have been doing in guidance. The present existence of these conditions causes me to conclude that we are essentially without theory in guidance.

Theory for Guidance. Although my indictment is essentially pessimistic, I am not. When I note that guidance is almost without theory at this time, I speak only of a practice that has largely been content to emphasize technique without much concern for theory. This practice has mainly focused upon social pressures; it has lacked an interest in a psychosocial theory of identity formation. The profession of guidance would advance a giant step if it were to admit that the focus of its practice should be upon the self-in-situation. This is essentially to admit that a counselor must be primarily a psychologist *and* an educator.

Although there is not much of a theory *in* guidance, there is psychological theory available *for* guidance. The difficulty lies in the fact that guidance cannot just borrow psychological theory. Much of psychological theory merely describes past events. Such descriptions are not sufficient for a practice intending to *promote* ego-strength and outlook. As I have said, the commitment of guidance to affect action makes guidance need a theory that psychology has been without—namely, a theory of controlled change of idiosyncratic meaning systems such that the orientation of everyone towards self-in-world would be relatively productive. Psychologists have made a start. We must borrow what they have available. However, let *our* purpose guide *our* development of *our* theory and lead to the training of *our* people, as has been the case so far. In the long run, the resulting guidance psychology will probably be achieved more rapidly and less expensively. Furthermore, the training of future guidance psychologists will be more efficient because we will train for a limited goal.

Although the goal of theory in the guidance psychology I envisage is rightfully limited, we should not underestimate its importance. We aim to nourish ego-strength by enhancing the rationality of choice within a system of choices, as such a goal can be achieved through application of a psychosocial theory of identity formation without limiting statutory rights to self-determination.

I am sure the values of appraisal, implanting of hope, counseling, opportunity, placement, acceptance, and adjustment are very evident if such a purpose is to be obtained. The task before us today is to formulate an appropriate developmental theory that will not be just a responsive theory, as is true of so much theory in psychology. Our theory must be a theory aimed at the generation of ego-strength, not just its repair. Therefore, our theory must be intertwined with education, the institutionalized means of becoming. I am very hopeful that if we only agree upon this goal, we will be able to achieve it in a reasonable time. Many of us must change our attitudes if we are to pursue such a goal. This is what the counselor must know in the fundamental sense of truly *appreciating* it.

WHAT SHOULD THE COUNSELOR KNOW? LEARNING AND EXPERIENCING

My answer to the question of what the counselor needs to know has so far been presented in terms of the counselor (1) ultimately aspiring to be a professional person, (2) engaging in a professional practice, and (3) having a theory of guidance at the core of his practice. I here expand slightly on (1) the concepts the counselor needs to acquire, (2) a process of education that embodies learning by experiencing, and (3) the reorganization of authority in education, which will be required for the professional practice of guidance.

The Acquisition of Concepts. The appreciation of the past, which is relevant to a problem under consideration by the professional counselor, requires familiarity with and understanding of a wide variety of concepts as these are specified in existing disciplines. Freedom from the past, which is also needed, requires an attitude toward knowledge that accepts knowledge as the best explanation now available, but not necessarily as valid forevermore. This attitude is cultivated in liberal education, but not all liberal education so liberates, because some who teach in liberal education unfortunately fail to give the goal-setting problem to their students. The blame does not entirely rest with the teacher, however, because many students do not arrive at a valid attitude of mastery of the past, which also seems to be necessary for freedom in the present.

The fact that the setting of goals must rest with the professional means that his education can never be completely specified, even if it seems reasonable to hope that we might approach that condition of understanding necessary for providing and requiring acquisition of an exhaustive set of solutions for all the problems a professional will ever encounter. The education of the professional, therefore, cannot rest upon his acquisition of the presently known. Rather, it must rest merely upon the delineation of the currently known, the provision of a continually modified catalogue of correct knowledge, the development of the capacity to use the currently known, and the acceptance of the responsibility to know as exactly as possible when needed. The management of time, then, becomes critical in the decisions of the professional. As he deals with the means-ends issues of the problems he elects to solve, he must keep the power ordinarily attributed to his capacity to solve problems. This requires acceptance of that capacity by those with whom he is in contact, in order that he will be accorded the time necessary to effect solutions. As a result, prompt recall, efficient solutions, and frequent success are generally helpful in his work. The professional must have confidence and skill in dealing with matters both of recall and of use if he is to remain powerful among those he attempts to serve.

Here then are the implications in encapsulated form: (1) nothing needed should be too difficult for ultimate mastery by the professional; (2) the library must be his open book; (3) he must have the habit of using that library; and (4) he must manage his time so that he maintains a reputation for efficient problem-solving. Such is the type of liberal education our professional needs. It is immaterial whether he gets that education before, during, or after his experience as a professional. It is very important that he have such an education, however, before he maintains a practice of his profession.

Learning while Experiencing. The reputation of the scholar rests in his capacity to present and to develop his *discipline*. Similarly, the reputation of the professional rests in his capacity to present and to develop his *service*. The latter activity involves the use and invention of concepts and the maintenance of reputation in continual use.

The scholar ordinarily teaches by taking his audience through a definite sequence designed to maximize the possibility that his view will be believed. The attainment of this aim generally means that the presentation is limited and has a high degree of internal consistency. There will be an effort to admit what one does not know, but there will also be an effort to seek belief of, and the attribution of value to, what is considered to be accurate. The scholar expects, however, that his audience will maintain perspective, placing his contribution in relation with those of others and with what must be used if the student is to reach his own objective. The scholar makes little effort to see that members of his audience evolve objectives, put his contribution in perspective, or use it accurately, except for the responsibilities of this nature that he adopts for the purpose of his own teaching. In fact, the scholar may even be bothered by matters of use, both because he has no intention of offering his contribution for that purpose, and because such insistence brings into question the beliefs that have caused him to invest his own time as he has done. The scholar naturally expects that his contribution is of value; how else can he maintain his insistence on the support of his endeavor? After all, his contribution is his talent.

The professional experiences difficulty when he is enlisted to prepare others to be professional. His value as a professional lies in his having insights that are powerful in enabling those he serves to delineate and to secure their objectives. But insight is a personal matter; *you cannot teach insight!* This problem has plagued, plagues, and will plague professional education. A professional can do; he can watch another do and offer criticism; but he cannot guarantee that his student will himself do. In fact, if the professional educator tries to guarantee that his student will do as he has done, he is doomed to failure from the outset. The only way a professional can guarantee the actions of his students is to condition them, and the very nature of conditioning removes the problem of goal-setting from the student. Hence, a conditioned student can never be a professional in my sense of that word.

What, then, are the implications for professional education? The first is that professional education ought to be largely a matter of opportunity for practice under the supervision of a professional able to win the respect of his students. The student must have opportunity to set goals, elect means, and act with responsibility for the outcome. All this must be done with opportunity, obligation, and authority for observation and criticism on the part of the professional. The student must be free to leave, however, so that the professional is put on his mettle in keeping his students under his guidance. I presume it obvious that this argument may be extended to my kind of practice, not just practice arranged during graduate study. In such an event, however, the reputation and wisdom of the counselor must be called into account.

The Apportionment of Authority. The professional we are considering needs the freedom both to elect his goals and to choose his means. The attainment of this condition requires that the resources of an organization be generally available to the professional with not very much delay or doubt. The professional should be examined closely when he is hired, and his practice should remain under constant scrutiny. Resources must be made available to him, however. In addition, his authority to decide on means and ends should remain beyond question. Otherwise, an employee may be accepting responsibility without the needed authority. In this case he is definitely not a professional as we define one, even though he may long to be held accountable and may believe that he can do the job without authority. Unfortunately, some aspirants to the status of professional do delude themselves in this way. They seek the reputation of professional without realizing where the power of such work actually rests.

School departments are largely organized at present so that only one of their employees can be a professional in our terms. The only professional employee of school departments is the superintendent. Ordinarily, it is the superintendent who allows his school committee to give him ultimate responsibility for determining the goals of instruction. The superintendent ordinarily accepts this charge, and does not in turn try to give this responsibility to his teachers. In his effort to keep teachers from blame, he places them in relation to himself as technicians. The superintendent merely lets teachers decide on means to attain *his* ends. He does not let them stand accountable before their publics —parents and colleagues—for the definition of goals and the investment of resources in the pursuit and presumed attainment of their goals.

You may contend that the case is overstated, that at least principals of schools are also professionals in the organization of authority in the school at the present time. There may well be cases in which this is so. In fact there may even be a smaller number of cases in which the authority and responsibility for goal-setting and investment of resources are actually well established in the position of the teacher or possibly the counselor. My contention is that such cases are the exception to the rule, however. Such a state of affairs should not be so; it just is.

As I indicated in one of the preceding sections, the capacity to operate as a professional will ordinarily require the aspiring specialist, if he is not the superintendent, to realign avenues of authority in the organization of the school system he elects to serve. The trick is to insure that education, if it occurs at all, occurs as the *collaborative* endeavor of a group of aspirants each of whom acts as a professional. The problem in the education of those who would profess education is to bring such aspirants to realize this condition, to gain confidence in operating within its responsibilities and restraints, and to become competent as professionals, either *before* their experience in a program of graduate studies terminates, or before they are promoted from journeyman counselor to professional counselor. When this problem is adequately passed on to a student in a graduate school, he becomes a powerful agent for modification of authority and responsibility for teaching when he is employed.

HOW MIGHT THE COUNSELOR BE EDUCATED? A CASE IN POINT

The Committee on Professional Preparation and Standards, American Personnel and Guidance Association (APGA), has recently brought to successful conclusion the effort of APGA to create a consensus on the needed education of the counselor (see Hill, 1967). The statement covers the type of education that has ordinarily been offered to the counselor, at least for the past decade or more. The statement indicates the resolve of APGA to make programs for the preparation of counselors more permanent and more fully staffed in universities, more coherent in philosophies and implementations, and more inclusive of supervised practice as a primary means for the education of the counselor. However, the statements on what the counselor should know, and how he should be helped to know those things, are in general stipulated as lists, not as sequences in which an overall design can be shown.

My experience in the education of counselors has indicated that an overall design is helpful. It gives me and my students a perspective of what is expected of them as it is happening to them. Because of this, and at the risk of criticism, I discuss only one graduate program in this essay—the one that my colleagues and I conduct at the Graduate School of Education, Harvard University. It is the program I know best and can address from my experience with its operation. It is no paragon of virtue. It is constantly in revision, incorporating suggestions from student and faculty alike.[1]

The Harvard Graduate School of Education is content to recruit students with bachelor's degrees who have prepared in any number of majors while in college. We frequently admit students with majors in English, education, history, mathematics, natural science, psychology, or sociology. We have also been known to admit students with preparation in anthropology or foreign languages. Since the number of college students who major in either of the latter fields is small, we get very few applicants from them who might have an interest in guidance.

Our admissions policy reflects our belief that the admitted student should have a strong undergraduate preparation, which has been as "liberating" as possible. Because of the fact that the elective may be taken in our preparation of counselors, adviser and student have opportunity during the course of graduate education to augment the understandings of our students. In general, the expectation of the faculty is that a student with appreciation of the sciences, but not of the humanities, will study a little bit in the humanities while at Harvard. The faculty holds the contrary expectation regarding those with appreciation of the humanities but not of the sciences. Obviously these expectations put the adviser on his mettle. When we offer a student an elective, we intend that he be free to elect. Also, when students have electives they are inclined to opt for specialization over perspective. Therefore, the carrying out of the expectation of the faculty is left as an individual matter between adviser and student. The adviser advises and uses the power of his position of sponsorship of his blooming protégé. However, final choice is granted the student. In general, the faculty has proven willing to go with the student on his decision. However, adviser and student have a fine opportunity in the course of the discussion to examine whether the student is afraid of a particular sector of man's epistemology. Why is more specialization better than perspective, or vice versa?

[1]The program has since been discontinued.

When the student arrives at the Harvard Graduate School of Education with admission in the area of guidance, program in guidance delineated in Table 1 becomes available to him.

The program in Table 1 represents a pattern from which the student can emerge with either the master of education or the doctor of education. If a student becomes a candidate for the master of education, he pursues the program recorded as the first year. This requires that he present 10 half-courses of study and practice. Study is largely in human development and the humanistic foundations of education along with the philosophy of guidance.

Table 1. Guidance Program at Harvard Graduate School of Education

Year	Term		Subject and/or Practice
1	summer	1	Observe teaching; practice teaching
		2	Human development: teaching and learning
1	fall and spring	3–4	Counseling: theory, laboratory, and practicum
		5–6	Assessment: achievement, aptitude, interest via structured test interviewing and group testing
		7	Human development: language-arts development for elementary-school counselors; career development for others
		8–9	Directed electives: humanistic foundations of education and guidance, and the philosophy of science
		10	Elective
2	summer	—	Independent study and/or work
2	fall and spring	11–12	Assessment: theory and laboratory in personality testing
		13–16	Counseling: practicum in counseling disturbed students with emphasis on kind of practice elected
		17	Directed elective for doctoral students: intermediate statistics
		18	Elective
3	summer	—	Independent study and/or work
3	fall and spring	19–22	Internship in assessment, counseling, or administration
		23–26	Independent study
4	summer and spring	—	Project or dissertation

Practice is linked with study as one practices and offers supervised experience in teaching, assessment, and counseling.

The Ed.M. student has an option during his second year, a year required before he can qualify for the degree. The student must present an internship to qualify for the degree. The option is that the student can intern full-time or half-time. If the student interns half-time, he normally studies and practices in personality assessment and counseling at the same time that he performs as a journeyman the usual duties of a counselor, be they in elementary, secondary, or tertiary institutions.

The candidate for the doctor of education plans his program in consultation with his adviser. He must present at least one course in two of the school's three professional areas, teaching, guidance, and administration, and at least one course in each of two of the school's three disciplinary areas, history and philosophy, psychology, and social sciences. However, for the most part the Ed.D. student develops a pattern like the one recorded above. He essentially needs the first-year preparation, which overlaps with that of the Ed.M. During his second year he studies and practices in personality assessment and counseling. He is also strongly urged to see that he is prepared at the level of intermediate statistics. The third year for the Ed.D. candidate is again devoted to a half-time internship. During the third year the internship is specialized. Specialties may include more intensive study and practice in personality assessment and school consultation, which is ordinarily associated with the position of school psychologist. Specialties may also include the more intensive study of personality assessment in the normal range of behavior as those assessments have direct relevance to education and ego-development. This study and practice are ordinarily associated with the position of counseling psychologist. Finally, specialties may include more intensive study of organizational assessment and practice in administration for reason of creation of an educational climate appropriate for the cultivation of individuality within organization. This study and practice are ordinarily associated with the positions of assistant superintendent, coordinator of pupil personnel services, or dean of students. A few students are also helped to specialize in administrative practice appropriate for the cultivation of individuality through business organizations.

The above practice under supervision means that the Ed.D. has accumulated more than he would have in the year of supervised practice prescribed by the American Psychological Association before he is awarded the degree. Furthermore, the year and more of supervised practice is distributed among teaching, counseling, and probably administration. In addition, it is likely to be at several levels of education. It is also likely to include collegial arrangements with principals, psychiatrists, psychologists, social workers, and teachers. In the instances of a few students, there will be collegial arrangements with businessmen.

The Ed.D. student is also required to submit a qualifying paper, which must meet the approval of three members of the faculty. In addition, the student may opt to write a dissertation or to do a project. The dissertation is ordinarily in the usual pattern in psychology. However, the faculty in guidance encourages students to deal with the philosophy of science, which involves the study of persons who are able to know what the student knows about them. The project requires a year's work in relation to the candidate's job. The project must demonstrate the student's capacity to carve out a limited area, in an educational practice in which he can exert leadership among colleagues and other relevant publics, for the reason of achieving an improvement in the ordinary practice of the group. The student is judged in terms of his capacity to think as he acts, and to draw his plans and their consequences into coherent wholes that have important bearing on his intentions for the project. Three members of the faculty have cognizance in the project while it is going on. All three members must be satisfied that the student has done a satisfactory job in keeping his goals in mind and in choosing and pursuing means for their attainment in the course of the active life of the project.

I deliberately present the Ed.M. and Ed.D. programs at Harvard as a unit. I have previously argued that the counselor, who ordinarily holds only the master's degree, should be considered a journeyman until checked out by his counseling colleagues over several year's of closely supervised field experience. At the conclusion of that check his colleagues may consider the journeyman a master counselor and relax the requirements for his supervision. The program at the Harvard Graduate School of Education represents the essence of this plan, in my judgment. Should a student take the Ed.D. rather than the Ed.M., he accumulates at the university the supervised experience necessary to test his status as master counselor or administrator. It is true that even the Ed.D. student may actually have his first job as an assistant, particularly if he has not worked prior to his graduate study. However, the progress of the Ed.D. toward the status of master counselor is ordinarily quickened by his completion of the doctorate prior to work in counseling. This does not mean to deny the Ed.M. that status over a longer period of time. If the Ed.M. fails to achieve that status, it is probably because we lack mechanisms to certify it for him, not because he has failed to educate himself as he experiences the duties of counseling.

NEEDED EXPANSION OF OPPORTUNITY FOR PROFESSIONAL PRACTICE UNDER SUPERVISION

A major problem in the setting of goals, and the selection of means to attain those goals, is the need to accomplish the feat (1) in collaboration with *diverse* specialists who have the obligation to comment in relation to what they know and think; and (2) in a limited interval of time, with a public in which the decision is to be implemented, and with the effects available for observation, review, and criticism by professionals and others. When that feat is accomplished to the satisfaction of respected professionals, he who tried and succeeded becomes more confident of his capabilities and commitments, and is more likely in the future to act with the habits of our professional, provided he is able to work in a position in which authority and responsibility for the management of means-ends sequences are both to be his.

The programs for graduate study available at schools of education do not now provide the opportunity for this ultimate chance to test oneself as professional. Such chances have been available in the doctoral programs for those who become *scholars,* because these students could read papers before their peers and superiors. The chances available to the aspiring professional are more limited, however. The aspiring professional has courses available in which he can tell professors who work independently what he thinks, but neither student nor professor has a common context of use for immediate validation. Furthermore, he can practice under supervision with those *limits on practice* in accord with those he plans to accept. It is my contention that the training of the aspiring professional at a university should be freed with deliberate speed from these limits, which are only formal and economic rather than rational. All who aspire to profess education need the opportunity to work as professionals under supervision for a concentrated and extensive period of time, and in a context in which they have both responsibility and criticism from the variety of specialists practicing in a school organization.

The disparity between this ideal and the present condition of professionalization through education is obvious, I am sure. We presently have a system of professionalization which (1) is not generally accepted as being necessary; (2) is not enough even when provided; (3) does not offer practice under the supervision of a *complex* of professionals; and (4) does not insure competence and confidence before ultimate licensing for professional practice.

THE PROSPECTS FOR MY BELIEFS

I have argued that education consists of a substance and a process, which youth are encouraged to unite in their own interest through mastery of the process of becoming purposeful. I have further argued that the officers who profess education within the organization of the school must monopolize authority for problem-solving with regard to the education of youth. This monopolization, if it is also to be rational, must be accompanied by proof of excellence in (1) what is known to be of relevance to a problem, and (2) in the use of what is known. In order that youth can remain free to attain individuality through organization, the professionals monopolizing authority, as I want them to do, must use their authority so that youth *are free* to set their own goals. To accomplish this feat, my professional must be free of any scholarly discipline, for every discipline contains in itself restraints, which are necessarily accepted as goals by any who accept the tenets of the discipline.

My opinion is that professionalization through education requires liberation through education, as well as extended and elaborate practice in problem-solving under supervision. It is important that the practice both be under supervision and take place at the inception of, not during the later course of, growth in confidence. The provision of an apparatus for professionalization through education, as I envision it, will require an expansion in the liberal education of practitioners. The expansion is now occurring rapidly in California and New York and more slowly elsewhere. However, an expansion of practice under supervision is *also* necessary, in my judgment. The necessary expansion is in the quantity and quality of the supervision available when practice is underway, as well as in the context of problems the embryo professional is responsible for solving under supervision. However, nothing I seek can be realized unless education is conceived as profession, rather than as technology, by *three* different *kinds* of officers in a school department, namely teacher, counselor, and administrator.

Unfortunately, the climate is not now propitious for the recognition of education as profession rather than as technology. In the first place, liberal education is frequently conceived and practiced as a training rather than a liberating experience. Secondly, practice in education is largely conceived as training to the goals of the professor, rather than as practice under observation and with responsibility for criticism, at the same time that the student is required to engage in goal-determination and the use of resources. Thirdly, there is a tendency to confuse learning with teaching, and to believe that education can be achieved through the mechanization of teaching, not just through mechanization of access and display of the known. Finally, there are compromises in the quality of those who are permitted to practice in education. The insidious effect of this last condition is that, because the less well educated become subservient to a few who have more education, responsibility for the setting of goals gets removed from teachers or counselors. When responsibility for the setting of goals is not a part of the job of a teacher or counselor, there is little or no hope that such responsibility can or will be passed along to youth, which is the ultimate objective I have set forth.

You can see that I am essentially pessimistic. I find that the issue of the expansion of opportunity for education to individuality through organization is definitely in doubt. The challenge to those of us who care is that the tide of mechanization, which I have just sketched, can be halted and turned. I do not despair, however, because I believe that there *are* professionals in education. They are supposed to be experts in the solving of problems. I have just sketched a problem that I would like to solve. I would welcome help.

As we act to solve the dilemma I have noted, however, let us acknowledge that the required solution is going to cost more money than is presently provided for education. We are not going to achieve individuality through structure, in excess of that now achieved spontaneously, until we set our minds to pay what it will cost to achieve real liberation through education. Men really liberated through education paradoxically stand alone *with* their fellow men. Such a state will be sorely needed in all of us, for we must each attack my problem while being a part of the condition that we wish to modify.

REFERENCES

Barry, R. E., & Wolf, B. *Modern issues in guidance-personnel work.* New York: Teachers College Bureau of Publications, 1957.

Fromm, E. *Man for himself.* New York: Holt, Rinehart and Winston, 1947.

Hill, G. E. (Chm.) Standards for the preparation of secondary-school counselors, a report of the APGA Committee on Professional Preparation and Standards, Sub-committee on Standards for the Preparation of Secondary School Counselors. *Personnel and Guidance Journal,* 1967, **46**, 96–106.

Koestler, A. *The act of creation.* New York: Macmillan, 1964.

Kohlberg, L. Development of moral character and moral ideology. In M. L. Hoffman and L. W. Hoffman (Eds.), *Review of child development research.* New York: Russell Sage Foundation, 1964.

Kubie, L. S. *Neurotic distortion of the creative process.* New York: Noonday Press, 1958.

Mathewson, R. H. Beyond systems. North Eastham, Mass.: Author. 1960. (Mimeo.)

Polanyi, M. *The study of man.* Chicago: Phoenix Books, 1959.

Polanyi, M. *The tacit dimension.* Garden City: Doubleday, 1966.

Schwab, J. J. *The teaching of science as enquiry.* Cambridge: Harvard University Press, 1962.

Thompson, A. S., & Super, D. E. (Eds.) *Professional preparation of counseling psychologists: Report of the 1964 Greystone conference.* New York: Teachers College Bureau of Publications, 1964.

Tiedeman, D. V. Predicament, problem, and psychology: The case for paradox in life and counseling psychology. *Journal of Counseling Psychology,* 1967, **14**, 1–8.

Tiedeman, D. V., & Field, F. L. Guidance: The science of purposeful action applied through education. In R. L. Mosher, R. F. Carle, and C. D. Kehas (Eds.) *Guidance: An examination.* New York: Harcourt Brace Jovanovich, 1965. (First published in *Harvard Educational Review,* 1962.)

Wise, W. M. Counseling individuals in liberal arts colleges. In E. J. McGrath (Ed.), *The liberal arts college's responsibility for the individual student.* New York: Teachers College Press, 1966.

What the Counselor Needs to Know: Dimensions of Counselor Behavior

Patricia L. Wolleat

University of Wisconsin—Madison

Counseling, as a socially sanctioned process of changing human behavior, has gained its legitimacy through an emphasis on the development of the potential of individuals. This individual focus historically has rendered counseling an effective form of help-giving for an ever-increasing number of persons within an ever-widening sphere of their lives. Beginning with a narrow focus on the development of vocational potential in adolescents, through the making of wise occupational choices, the domain of counseling is now extending both up and down the age ladder, and into many other aspects of human growth and development as well—social and interpersonal, moral and ethical.

The consequences of this expansion and diversification are evident not only in the numbers and types of clients with whom counselors work, and in the variety of settings in which counselors are employed, but also in the proliferation of counseling methods, techniques, and approaches. As attempts to define professional behavior have increased, so has the set of functions to be defined, such that at present no one definition or description of counseling is universally accepted by those who consider themselves professional counselors. Counseling, within a broad field of helping relationships, accommodates a tremendous variety of theoreticians and practitioners, whose views of counseling, assumptions, goals, and methods differ widely, and there is every indication that what we now see is but a glimpse of what the counseling of the future will be.

The goal of meeting individual developmental needs through the counseling process, and the differing missions of the institutions that support counseling services, requires a high degree of flexibility and adaptability in the profession itself and from its individual practitioners. Thus the traditional one-to-one, face-to-face model of counseling is being questioned as the only approach to help-giving. Many counselors are seeing the benefits of applying their behavior-change technology to small groups, to natural groups such as families and classrooms, and even to larger systems, such as the educational institution itself.

250

The recognition that the effectiveness of counseling as a help-giving behavior-change process depends upon the preparation of counselors who possess the necessary skills to be effective with a wide range of clients in a wide range of settings and circumstances, poses a serious challenge to counselor-educators, who are responsible for designing learning experiences that will turn out practitioners competent to cope with both current and future realities. In confronting the question of what a counselor needs to know now, and what he will need to know in the unknown and unpredictable future in order to be a responsible and competent intervener in the lives of others, the counselor-educator is faced not only with transmitting a relevant body of knowledge and teaching a set of essentially undefined skills, but with the realities of the training situation as well. Time, staff, and resources are not unlimited. The counselor-in-training contracts with the preparing institution for only a limited amount of time. Moreover, the individuals who present themselves and are selected for formal training vary considerably in their level of professional development, experience, and potential. The educators themselves often are not involved directly in training on a full-time basis, since they must also respond to expectations of scholarship, institutional service, and continuing development of the profession. The restraints surrounding the preparation of counselors demand that time and resources be expended judiciously and efficiently with the full recognition that what a counselor needs to know will be constantly increasing.

To answer the question of what a counselor needs to *know* depends to a large degree on being able to specify what it is that he is to *do.* However, the specific things that he will be doing are not and cannot be known during preparation. What is needed, therefore, is a formulation of the counselor's role that transcends the specifics, which inevitably will vary from counselor to counselor, client to client, and situation to situation. The key to such a conceptualization lies in the recognition of the fundamental principles that counseling behavior is purposeful, and that its primary purpose is for the counselor to behave in ways that facilitate behavior change in clients toward the end of maximizing their individual potential. Consider for a moment the implications of this statement.

For the counselee, behavior change may mean a variety of things. It may involve some observable difference in the way that he interacts with some aspect of his environment, such as relating to others or coping with school. For another client, behavior change may entail viewing himself and his experiences from a new and different perspective. For still another, change or growth may be observed in the feelings he holds toward himself and others. Thus, any change in an individual's thinking, feeling, or acting behaviors may be considered as evidence of behavior change.

The counselor effects change through the impact of his own behavior, which is observable to the client. The only access the client has to the help-giving process is through the overt behavior of the counselor, or those whom the counselor enlists to assist in the behavior-change process. From the point of view of the client, what is happening inside the counselor's head matters little, since he can respond only to the counselor's manifest behavior. In the immediacy of the counseling interaction, it is not what the counselor thinks, believes, or feels that directly produces an impact on the client, but rather what he does or communicates. The counselor's realization and complete acceptance of the impact of his behavior on the client is a critical prerequisite to any further learning that can take place.

Recognition of the impact of behavior leads to a second consideration in determining what a counselor needs to know—namely, whether or not the impact he has on the client is facilitative. Not all of the behavior in the typical counselor's repertoire is necessarily productive in facilitating change or growth in clients. Reviews of research on traditional counseling and psychotherapeutic practices have in fact concluded that counseling and psychotherapeutic interventions resulted in positive outcomes for only about one-third of the clients, no impact for another third, and destructive consequences for still another third (Bergin, 1963). If such conclusions have any validity whatsoever, it is imperative that counselors have the skills both to precisely assess the impact of their behavior and to modify it if necessary. The primary task of a counselor-education program, then, is to teach counselors not only how to behave in facilitative ways, but also where and how to look for the impact of their behavior.

The effectively functioning counselor operates at a high level of awareness in his professional behavior. The ends toward which his behavior is directed, his behavior itself, and the impact his behavior has on the client or institution are all directly accessible to him. He is constantly and actively engaged in a process of evaluation. His behavior is purposeful, and its effects are measured against those purposes. If one of the desired outcomes of training, then, is that the counselor learn to view his behavior in relation to the purposes it is intended to serve, we can begin an examination of what the counselor needs to know with a consideration of what those purposes are. Focusing on the purposes or functions of the counselor's behavior provides a framework from which to view the content of his preparation.

Whether the target of the behavior-change process is an individual, a group, or even a system, all behavior of the counselor is intended to serve one of the following functions: (1) establishing goals for the behavior-change process, (2) setting conditions where behavior change can occur, (3) designing and implementing strategies of intervention to meet the established goals, and (4) evaluating goals, processes, and outcomes.

Effective functioning in each of the above roles presupposes that the counselor has a supply of relevant information and a means of processing that information in order to make appropriate decisions regarding his behavior. Good decisions are not made in a vacuum, but in the presence of the most valid information that can be assembled. In gathering information for his decision-making, the counselor draws upon three primary sources—himself, the client or target, and the accumulated body of theory and research in the area of human behavior. Proficiency in using these sources of information constitutes another goal of counselor preparation.

Certain portions of the total amount of information available to the counselor tend to assume particular utility within each of the four functions. In the following discussion, an attempt is made to examine the types and sources of information that are especially relevant to the behavioral decisions the counselor makes in the contexts of establishing goals, setting optimal conditions for behavior change, designing and implementing interventions, and evaluating the goals, processes, and outcomes of the interventions.

ESTABLISHING GOALS FOR THE BEHAVIOR-CHANGE PROCESS

The counselor's task in the goal-setting process is to establish, with his clients, goals for behavior change that are both desirable and feasible. The first of these dimensions, desirability, is primarily a value question, and the second, feasibility, is related to the probability of successful attainment.

The Client's Values. The client, of course, is the final arbiter of the goals of the counseling process. From the standpoint of preserving the dignity of the client, this is an absolute necessity. On a practical level, it is insurance that the client will be motivated to participate actively in the counseling process. Seldom, however, does a client know, when entering a counseling relationship, exactly what the goals of his involvement should be. Indeed, the reason that he may have sought the assistance of a counselor at all is that he cannot on his own determine the direction his behavior should take. Thus the client may need assistance not only in achieving goals, but in defining or establishing them as well. In order to determine with the client what would be desirable outcomes for him, the counselor must demonstrate a high level of proficiency in communicative skills—the ability to listen actively and to communicate back to the client that he has understood, and to help the client clarify areas where he may be experiencing confusion.

In addition to knowing and understanding what changes would be desirable from the client's standpoint, the counselor must also be aware of his own values, and particularly how they are likely to affect his interaction through the things he communicates. Furthermore, the counselor must have an informational base related to the kinds of behavior valued in the society or culture in which the client functions.

The Counselor's Values. Why is it important that the counselor be aware of his own value system? It has been established that the direct impact of the counselor is through his behavior. However, the counselor's behavior is determined by mediating mechanisms, which reflect his past learning—his assumptions, beliefs, and values. These mediating mechanisms, to a certain extent, define the limits of the counselor's behavior. Just as the client is seldom aware of the goals toward which his behavior should be directed, so the beginning counselor is seldom aware, at any meaningful level, of precisely what his own values, assumptions, and beliefs are. If the counselor is to exert control over his behavior within the counseling interaction, he must have an understanding of the determinants of his own behavior. This understanding can be achieved through bringing his belief system to a high level of awareness where if necessary, it can be examined and modified.

Cultural Values. In addition to knowing his own value system and that of the client, the counselor can also benefit from an understanding of the society or culture of the client. Every culture or subculture defines for its members the limits of acceptable behavior. Sociologists refer to these definitions as norms. An examination of the norms of a social group will permit the counselor to determine which client behaviors are likely to be rewarded and which will be punished. Since norms differ from culture to culture and over time, it is necessary that the counselor possess tools for analyzing them. The bases for understanding the values of a social group can be attained through a familiarization with the disciplines of anthropology and sociology.

Every individual, within his own life-space, is a member of many different systems or subcultures. Some of these subgroups may reflect or magnify the values and attitudes of the general culture, while others may tend to reject or disconfirm them. The family, as the chief mediator of the general culture, is instrumental in providing the first and perhaps the most permanent foundation of value orientation. However, as the child moves from the shelter of the family into a broader spectrum of associations, with peers and teachers, for example, he will likely be exposed to new value systems, which may challenge his existing orientation. Thus, the counselor must be particularly sensitive to the unique set of influences that governs each client's life, and especially attuned to the discontinuities that may result from the juxtaposition of conflicting value orientations.

Sociological studies of norms and of cultural values converge in descriptions of the healthy or effectively functioning human being. Such descriptions can provide the counselor with an integration of concepts from philosophy, psychology, and sociology, which give him another informational base from which to judge the desirability of counseling goals. Among the several descriptions of the healthy personality are Maslow's *self-actualizing person* (1954), Allport's *mature personality* (1963), Rogers's *fully functioning person* (1962), Shoben's *normal personality* (1957), Heath's *reasonable adventurer* (1964), and Blocher's *effective personality* (1966).

Although the client is the final authority on what constitutes desirable behavioral goals, the counselor is an integral agent in the process by which those goals are decided. The values he holds influence the kind of information he seeks from clients in ascertaining what the client's values are. In addition, the counselor's values determine the goals he is willing to set with his clients. No counselor is expected to work with a client toward goals he himself cannot accept. A counselor may refuse to work with a client either because a mutually acceptable goal cannot be negotiated, or because the negotiated goal is contrary to his own value system, or because it is not considered to be in the best interests of the client as defined by the client's value system or that of the larger society.

In summary, in determining the desirability of behavior-change goals, the counselor draws upon an informational base, which includes the client's value system, his own values, the norms of the larger society, and the convergence of all of these as represented in the various descriptions of the effectively functioning person.

Feasibility of Counseling Goals. Whereas the desirability of a counseling goal is primarily a value question, feasibility is defined in terms of probability of successful attainment. Some goals would be desirable for a client to attain, but cannot be attained through the counseling process. Although counseling is becoming more and more sophisticated, and is applicable to an increasing number of clients and behaviors, it is not yet at the point where it is the answer to all of an individual's concerns. Thus, in the determination of goals, it is important that their feasibility, as well as their desirability, be examined.

If the counseling process is limited, it is limited by the capabilities of the individuals involved, as well as by what the client's environment will permit. It would be very unwise for a counselor and client to undertake a counseling goal that has very little probability of success. Not only would this be a waste of time and effort, but the failure to negotiate reasonable goals may cause aspersions to be cast on the counseling process as an ineffective form of help-giving. Here it is important that the counselor know the capabilities of the client for reaching a given goal, his own competencies, and what the system, or the client's environment, will permit or sustain.

Judgment of an individual's capabilities for reaching a given counseling goal rests upon the counselor's understanding of the stages of human development from both a nomothetic and an idiographic point of view. The concern of the nomothetic approach is the formulation of generalizations, which reflect the commonalities and comparabilities across individuals. Each human being, however, is unique. The counselor, therefore, must acquire the tools to gauge the applicability of these generalizations as they are integrated into the idiosyncratic self-structure of each individual client. An individual's potential for growth is associated with his stage of development, as well as with a variety of other factors, which may be subsumed under the label of "motivation." While the counselor can exert some influence to change the client's motivation, he must recognize the restraints imposed by the various stages of development and accurately assess the possibilities for growth within this developmental framework and the client's special place in it.

A second consideration in the determination of feasibility is the counselor's assessment of his own competency. Counselors differ in their interests and abilities. Some of these differences are reflected in the ages or types of clients with whom they are most effective, as well as in the approaches they can use most comfortably. As the beginning counselor gains experience, he may broaden the domains in which he is effective; however, there is very little likelihood that he will ever be equally effective with all potential clients. Thus the counselor must be open to examination of his own particular strengths and weaknesses, and must make intelligent decisions based on accurate self-knowledge.

A third dimension of the feasibility issue is related to assessment of the systems within which the client functions. As noted above, the norms of the culture, social groups, and institutions determine which behaviors are likely to be rewarded and which are likely to be punished. The success of a counseling intervention is dependent upon the new behaviors, acquired in the safety of the counseling relationship, being transferred into the client's operational environment. In order to assess the behaviors a system will support and maintain, the counselor must be prepared with the analytical tools to examine the characteristics of the many systems and subsystems that make up the client's life space; for example, the educational system, the classroom, the family, peer groups, place of employment, and so forth. These tools are necessary not only to assess the systems, but also to identify nonsupportive elements of the client's environment, which may become the targets of further interventions by the counselor.

The counselor's observational capabilities can be enhanced through the informed use of a wide variety of psychometric and sociometric instruments designed to assess individual, group, and system dynamics. Among these observational aids are standardized tests, inventories, rating scales, and sociograms. Informed use of these systematic observation tools rests on a thorough understanding of the principles of measurement as they are applied to the selection, administration, and, especially, the interpretation of counseling instruments.

SETTING CONDITIONS UNDER WHICH BEHAVIOR CHANGE CAN OCCUR

Behavior change, whether at a crisis point or as a natural concomitant to the developmental process, is seldom unaccompanied by resistance to change for both individuals and larger systems. Change embraces the unknown and therefore involves an element of risk. The unknown outcomes of changing behavior can indeed present overwhelming obstacles to the behavior-change process. This resistance, however, can be reduced if the change process occurs under conditions minimizing the risks associated with it. One of the functions of the counselor is to arrange for these conditions to be present.

The Facilitative Relationship. One set of conditions favorable for inducing behavior change comprises the qualities of the interpersonal relationship between the counselor and the client, which the counselor, through his behavior, communicates to the client. These qualities characterize the "facilitative" relationship. As the medium through which behavior change is effected, the facilitative relationship is primarily the reciprocal communication of trust between counselor and client. When an individual places himself in the hands of a counselor, it is of utmost importance that he have assurance that the counselor is both concerned about him as an individual and competent. In other words, the client must trust the counselor, even if the changing process is at times painful. If the counselor fails to communicate this basic trust, the counseling relationship will not provide the supportive atmosphere necessary to reduce the threat of change.

Rogers (1957) postulates that the qualities that generate trust between counselor and client are both necessary and sufficient conditions for behavior change. Although the sufficiency of these qualities has been questioned, there is general agreement that certain conditions are at least facilitative in the behavior-change process. The facilitative conditions are both specifiable and measurable. Rogers, in his clinical observations, identified at least three of them—congruence, empathy, and positive regard.

The technology of the facilitative relationship has two related aspects— sensitivity and communication. Relative to the sensitivity dimension, the counselor-in-training must learn how to "read" the client; that is, he must be able to understand how the client views himself. Such an understanding depends heavily on the counselor's ability to listen actively to the client's verbalizations and to recognize nonverbal cues as well. Active listening involves far more than just hearing the client's words. It requires an active stance toward understanding and interpretation. In active listening, the counselor is not only following what the client is saying, but is tuned into the affect that accompanies the verbal content of the client's communication. The counselor's sensitivity in understanding the client is incomplete unless he also has the ability to communicate back to the client that he has understood. Skill in unambiguously communicating the facilitative conditions is rooted in a thorough understanding of the variables entering into the interpersonal communication process. These variables must be comprehended at a level of understanding that permits the counselor to manage his own communicative behavior in a conscious manner toward the ends he regards as facilitative of the client's goals.

There are an almost infinite number of response alternatives in an interpersonal interaction. Some of them serve to open or expand opportunities for further communication; others tend to limit further interaction or close communication. In a counseling relationship, it is usually desirable to strive for open communication. Every counselor must find for himself the ways in which he can keep communication open; i.e., he must develop an idiosyncratic empirical system for assessing the effects of his communication patterns. This is a conscious and deliberate process for most beginning counselors, and requires a willingness to experiment. Initially, the counselor may relate in such a way that open communication is thwarted; thus, the training process is a time when inappropriate behaviors can be unlearned, and new, more appropriate ones added. The foundational bases of the facilitative relationship are found in counseling theory and theory of interpersonal communication. The counselor must have a firm grounding in both of these.

DESIGNING AND IMPLEMENTING STRATEGIES OF BEHAVIOR CHANGE

The development of the facilitative relationship is the first stage in the counseling process. However, in some cases the relationship itself is not sufficient to effect the desired goals. Thus, the counselor must have at his disposal a number of strategies, which he can use as means to the goals. Developing specific plans for behavior change is a third function of the counselor.

Prior to the counselor's designing a behavior-change strategy, he must have a conceptualization of how human behavior is changed; that is, he must have a theory of behavior change. Behavior-change theories serve as the science underlying counseling theory and practice. Every theory is based on different assumptions about the human organism, and postulates certain mechanisms that account for behavior changes. In spite of vast differences among the assumptions and predictions made, however, there is evidence that counseling strategies based on a number of these theories result in positive outcomes for the client. A theory is nothing more than a means of organizing observations, and should not be construed as some ultimate truth. Most theories demonstrate the capability to adequately explain a portion of the vast universe of human behavior, but none of them adequately accounts for all of it. Thus it is important that the counselor be conversant with a number of behavior-change theories, so that he can construct a framework for viewing the totality of the behavioral phenomenon that he confronts in practice.

Behavior-change theories fall into one of three broad categories: relationship, cognitive, and behavioral. Briefly, the relationship theories begin with the assumption that man has an inherent tendency toward self-actualization, and that these inherent growth tendencies are released within the safety of a trusting human relationship. The cognitive theories are based on the assumption that intervening between the environment and the individual's behavior are a number of conceptual mechanisms, which, in a sense, provide meaning to the world. The individual processes information coming to him via these constructs. In order to change behavior, then, one must first modify the way in which the client thinks about himself or his situation by changing the construct system or set of assumptions from which he operates. In the behavioral models, behavior is thought to change according to the consequences it receives from the environment. If an individual receives reward or positive reinforcement for his actions, he is likely to repeat them; if, on the other hand, he is punished or no reinforcement is forthcoming, the behavior is likely to disappear. Thus, in changing behavior one works on the basis of setting the conditions for certain behaviors to occur and manipulating the environment to produce the desired consequences.

Once the counselor knows some of the mechanisms by which behavior can be changed, and has a goal in mind, he is in a position to integrate the two by designing a procedure that will efficiently move toward changing behavior in the desired direction. Just knowing how behavior changes is not sufficient, however; the counselor must also know how to manage his behavior so that these principles can be put into operation.

A very tempting answer to the question of what a counselor needs to know to effectively design and implement a behavior-change strategy is "everything." The effectiveness of the counseling process at this point depends heavily on the counselor's creative use of himself and the environment. He must be open to all the sources of gain surrounding him. To illustrate, many clients are concerned about making decisions related to undertaking a major role change in their lives—moving from one level of education to another, entering the job market, getting married, and so forth. In such cases, the counselor needs information above and beyond that which he can obtain from himself and the client. He must, for example, be familiar with sources of information about the world of work and various educational alternatives. Certainly, there is no expectation that the counselor will have all of this information stored in his memory. In fact, those who think that they do are probably not giving their clients the benefit of exposure to all the alternatives possible. What the counselor must know, rather, is where to find the information the client needs to make good decisions.

Awareness of the resources in the environment extends beyond merely knowing where to turn for information. The counselor must also know how to mobilize other human resources. In implementing certain strategies based on the behavioral model, for example, the counselor may find that the most effective reinforcers for a client are not under his direct control, but rather lie with significant others in the client's environment—parents, family, peers, teachers, and so forth. In such cases, the counselor acts as a consultant, enlisting the cooperation of others and teaching them new ways of behaving toward the client.

The counselor's consultant role is not always directed toward the attainment of an individual's goals. When the counselor works within an institution where other professional personnel share responsibility for the individual's development, he may choose to work indirectly through other staff members to effect changes in the organizational structure and climate to better meet the developmental needs of all its members. Essentially the counselor performs the same four functions as in the direct counseling model, however his "client" is not an individual, but rather the institution itself. In school settings this approach may be considered in terms of dispersing the guidance and counseling functions throughout the system. The counselor brings his expertise as a consultant to bear upon training other personnel in such areas as career development and the creation of a positive learning environment through the formation of facilitative interpersonal relationships among all members of the institution. In order to effectively change an institution, the counselor must have the tools and skills to understand its dynamics, analogous to those needed for understanding an individual. Such understanding includes knowledge of organizational structure, leadership patterns, communication networks, and group dynamics.

EVALUATING GOALS, PROCESSES, AND OUTCOMES

Systematic evaluation is an extremely important function of the counselor. Continued improvement of the counseling process requires that the counselor receive constructive feedback regarding his performance. Enhancement of the counselor's professional growth is sufficient justification, in itself, for ongoing attention to evaluation; however, it serves other purposes as well. The growing tide of consumerism in this country demands that publicly supported programs demonstrate results commensurate with financial outlays. Increasingly, educational and other public agencies are being called upon to provide evidence of their effectiveness. Continued support for counseling services depends upon the counselor's ability to communicate the importance of his role to interested publics, and to present data attesting to its effectiveness in meeting the needs of clients. Thus the counselor must constantly be engaged in an evaluation of goals, processes, and outcomes.

The training program performs two essential functions in regard to evaluation. First, it must instill an attitude that evaluation is an indispensable activity in the counselor's professional behavior. Second, it must provide a methodology by which evaluation can be carried out. During the training process the counselor's behavior is continuously under scrutiny. As he proceeds through a variety of learning experiences, he systematically receives feedback from professors, supervisors, and peers. Once he leaves the training institution, however, these built-in sources of evaluation become increasingly less available, and he must learn to accept responsibility for this process himself. That is, he must become less dependent on outside sources of evaluation and learn to engage in self-evaluation.

Much of what the counselor needs to know in order to be proficient in self-evaluation has been implicit in the discussion of the other three functions performed by counselors. He is engaged in a process of evaluation as he makes decisions regarding the desirability and feasibility of counseling goals and whether or not these goals were attained. Evaluation is inherent in the personal feedback system that he develops to assess both the immediate and long-range impact of his behavior on his clients. Insofar as the counselor is aware of the purposes of his behavior in relation to the client's goals, he is attending to evaluation of the behavior-change process. The system of self-evaluation developed by the counselor is essentially idiosyncratic. Although he may learn to use observational instruments relevant to the process of counseling to anchor his self-observations, one of the goals of training is to help him develop a personally meaningful empirical system for self-assessment. In addition to developing a system of self-assessment, the counselor must also know how to employ an evaluation methodology that is communicable to those whom he depends upon for support.

SUMMARY

Counseling is a systematic, goal-directed form of help-giving. In assisting the development of each individual client toward utilization of his maximum potential, the counselor engages in four fundamental functions—establishing goals, setting up a supportive environment, designing and implementing interventions to accomplish the goals, and evaluating the goals, processes, and outcomes. The purpose of counselor preparation is to provide the candidate with the basic skills and informational bases to operate effectively within each of these roles. The well-prepared counselor should possess the competencies to assess and understand himself and the impact of his behavior, the counselee, and the environments in which they both operate.

REFERENCES

Allport, G. W. *Pattern and growth in personality.* New York: Holt, Rinehart and Winston, 1963.

Bergin, A. E. The effects of psychotheraphy: Negative results revisited. *Journal of Counseling Psychology,* 1963, **10**, 244–250.

Blocher, D. H. *Developmental counseling.* New York: Ronald Press, 1966.

Heath, S. R. *The reasonable adventurer.* Pittsburgh: University of Pittsburgh Press, 1964.

Maslow, A. H. *Motivation and personality.* New York: Harper & Row, 1954.

Rogers, C. R. The necessary and sufficient conditions of therapeutic personality change. *Journal of Consulting Psychology,* 1957, **21**, 95–103.

Rogers, C. R. Toward becoming a fully functioning person. In A. W. Combs (Ed.), *Perceiving, behaving, becoming.* Washington, D.C.: Yearbook Association for Supervision and Curriculum Development, 1962.

Shoben, E. J. Toward a concept of the normal personality. *American Psyhcologist,* 1957, **12**, 183–190.

Issues

1. How much of what constitutes the sense that one is a "real" professional comes from specific technical capabilities, and how much comes from the clear and communicated acceptance of responsibility? Can one ever be substituted for the other? What specific elements of each are necessary to achieve the sense of being "professional"?
2. Should experiential learning be exclusively associated with clinical issues, or is there a wider possible application in graduate education?
3. Can the use of paraprofessionals eventually reduce the professional role to one of administration?
4. Should professional function determine curriculum or should curriculum affect function?

Annotated Readings

Bard, M. Relevancy in clinical training. *Professional Psychology,* 1970, **1**, 263–264.

> Discusses the value of separating a clinical degree from an academic degree at the Ph.D. level. Argues for a doctor of psychology as a clinical degree and doctor of philosophy in psychology as an academic degree clearly requiring more scholarly work.

McClain, E. W. Sixteen personality factor questionnaire scores and success in counseling. *Journal of Counseling Psychology,* 1968, **15**, 492–496.

> The Sixteen Personality Factor Questionnaire (16 PF) was administered to 91 men and 46 women high-school counselors in five NDEA Institutes. Supervisor ratings in counseling practicum were correlated with raw scores on the 16 PF. The correlation coefficients were used as weights for standard scores on the 16 PF in separate specification equations for men and women to differentiate various levels of counseling competence. Application of the specification equation differentiated levels of competence in four out of six tests. Scores of the most successful men counselors tended to reflect masculine characteristics, and scores of the most successful women tended to reflect feminine characteristics.

Ohlsen, M. M. Evaluation of education for the professions. *Counselor Education and Supervision,* 1969, **9**, 30–40.

> All who educate for the professions share certain common problems: (1) defining the professional's role in precise terms, (2) identifying the essential components to prepare him to function in that role, (3) developing these into an adequate program, (4) selecting good prospects for the profession, (5) appraising the adequacy of the program, and (6) encouraging the growth of professionals in practice. Because instruments available for screening prospective professionals are far from perfect, and using the data obtained from them tends to involve tough decisions, too many who educate for the professions tend to rely primarily on candidates' earlier academic records and measures of scholastic aptitude. Instead, they must continue to try to identify the unique factors that contribute to success in practice, and to develop measuring instruments, observation techniques, and /or standard interviews, which can be used to predict success prior to admission to professional preparation programs. Finally, there is no substitute for committed staff members who can teach, who care about their students as persons, who can encourage and excite learning, and who can do the necessary research to improve the quality of professional services.

Robb, J. W. Self-discovery and the role of the counselor. *Personnel and Guidance Journal,* 1967, **45**, 1008–1011.

> The major thesis of this philosophic treatise is that unless the counselor realizes in his own life the full import of the search for meaning and self-understanding, he will be unable to empathize adequately with the struggles of another human being who likewise seeks to realize his highest potential. Hindering our self-discovery are the problems of meaninglessness, alienation, and the loss of freedom. The path toward breaking out of our insulated selves is (1) to accept fully, on a personal level, a sense of responsibility for what we are, and (2) to realize that self-fulfillment occurs within a social context. The former involves a sense of

personal integrity, and the latter gives a contextual frame of reference to our search for meaning. The path to self-understanding is difficult and threatening, but as the counselee perceives—on both the intuitive and operational levels—the counselor's sincerity in his own quest for fulfillment, the goals we seek to achieve in the counseling relationship will be facilitated.

Suggestions for Further Reading

Counseling Psychologist. New directions in training—part 2. 1972, **3**(4), 1–102.

Kaswan, J., Siegel, S., Mattis, P., Mirels, H., Nolan, J. D., Pepinsky, H., & Weaver, T. A different approach to clinical training. *Professional Psychology,* 1970, **1**, 287–288.

Lister, J. L. Theory aversion in counselor education. *Counselor Education and Supervision,* 1967, **6**, 91–96.

Livingston, I. B. Is the personnel worker liable? *Personnel and Guidance Journal,* 1965, **43**, 471–474.

Lloyd-Jones, E. M., & Rosenau, N. Social and cultural foundations of guidance. *Personnel and Guidance Journal,* 1970, **49**, 324 & 327.

Richardson, H. D. Preparation for counseling as a profession. *Counselor Education and Supervision,* 1968, **7**, 124–131.

Roberts, R. D., & Solomons, G. Perceptions of the duties and functions of the school psychologist. *American Psychologist,* 1970, **25**, 544–549.

Rousseve, R. J. Counselor, know thyself! *Personnel and Guidance Journal,* 1969, **47**, 628–633.

Schlossberg, N. K. Sub-professionals: To be or not to be. *Counselor Education and Supervision,* 1967, **6**, 108–113.

CHAPTER 7

The Counselor as a Person
The Role of His Experiences, Personality, Philosophy, and Values in His Total Preparation Program

At one point in recent memory, there was a not too flattering saying among psychotherapy process researchers to the effect that you could always identify the therapist: he was the one who moved the least on a process continuum during a therapy hour. Since that time there has been a noticeable shift in focus among those responsible for preparing counselors, from one of solely academic preparation to one that includes personal suitability and development. The suspicion that people with personal problems tend to go into mental-health fields has often been borne out in fact, and more often to the detriment of both the client and the counselor. The concern with the counselor as a person has gained strength from a variety of sources, including practicum supervisors who heard about maladaptive counselor behavior in sessions with clients, from fellow students, from professional colleagues, and from counselees. The structure of graduate education very often works contrary to the spirit of the educational discipline—in this instance, if a student successfully passes his academic courses, there is often no means of dismissing him from a program. All too often the practicum situation sheds very explicit light on the questionable stability of a student—but at a time when the greater part of his work for the degree is over—thus the student gets "pushed up," with the hope, but seldom the conviction, that time will bring about changes.

What exactly should be the role of graduate preparation in the development of values, personality, and philosophy? One response is that the role should be, on the one hand, as great as is needed to remedy deficits in the individual already accepted, and on the other hand, as cautious as possible about encouraging candidates whose deficits may be symptomatic of more pathological problems. Surely it is reasonable to expect that the more complete the individual, the greater will be his capacity to fully utilize his personal resources in all aspects of his professional life and to continue personal and professional growth. This would seem to many to be a definition of superior performance.

267

Implicit in this postulate is the commitment to individual needs by the departments educating counselors, for idiosyncratic needs cannot be met unless they are first recognized—and that usually occurs only by personal interaction.

Each of the authors in this chapter responds to the basic question of what it is that the counselor needs to know, and they do this from the perspective of what he ought to be doing. There is great value in this health model because the steps to implement each set of ideas are unambiguously set forth. That the practitioner must be a person committed to personal growth and continual development is a prerequisite for each of these position papers. The mandate to screen candidates for professional education and to evaluate programs is clear.

Gendlin proceeds at length to analyze the current model of scientific knowledge and specificity of constructs in terms of (1) their helpfulness in achieving the desired ultimate goal of client change; (2) their destructive capacity in the process of bringing about change; and (3) the implications for theory, practice, professional preparation, and personal growth of the clinician. He offers an alternative to the scientific knowledge model: experiential knowledge.

Hosford presents a compelling argument as to why the true humanist must employ behavioral methods. The multiple applications of method present a broader view of this approach than has been available; the many detailed examples and specific recommendations for programs makes his an essay of genuine practical importance.

Riccio challenges the complacency of the counselor about issues affecting the population he is working with and himself; and he exhorts professionals to be congruent—i.e., to reconcile discrepancies between what is done and what is professed. The implications for what must be done by the individual represent personal and professional risk, but the value in terms of the significance of the changes is clearly supported.

The Role of Knowledge in Practice

Eugene T. Gendlin

University of Chicago

Certain uses of knowledge are detrimental to practice and some are helpful. I will try to specify these uses exactly. We need knowledge. The spirit of research, and of commitment to theoretical universals, may seem the opposite of what is needed in being deeply sensitive to a given human being or group with whom one is uniquely interacting. Nevertheless, I plead for both. It is a problem in our field today, that good, subtle, intuitive practitioners are often both unaccustomed and hostile to careful formal thinking. Conversely, much research and theory in the field comes from persons who lack the direct experience for which they devise concepts. Naturally, such research and theory cannot be very successful. Practitioners reject such research and theory, the kind that is distant from the powerful and rich experiential complexity of practice. Unfortunately, they think of that as the only kind. In rightly rejecting poor and useless theory, they believe they must reject theory altogether.

So long as our practice lacks good concepts, the lifelong learnings of the relatively few who can practice successfully must always be lost again with them, when they die. Worse, even while they are here, practicing, they cannot train others. What they say is understood only by those who already sense and know it. Their experiential knowledge remains locked within them. They must be personally invited to come and give workshops; those with whom they personally interact are lucky ("He was analyzed by—himself"). This means that while a few can practice effectively, the field as a whole remains ignorant.

But is a science of practice even possible? Again, do not take the word *science* to mean what now passes for science. Rather, the question is: What sort of quite different-looking science would be a science of practice? Is such a very different science possible? Or is there something about practice that would make knowledge of any form impossible? (For *science,* after all, is only derived from *scientia,* the Latin word for knowledge.)

In the following, what I say about how concepts do and do not apply to people refers equally to one's own struggle with oneself in regard to working with others. I am concerned with how concepts are used in regard to people —myself as much as anyone else. The crucial factor is the relationship between concepts and direct experience.

HARMFUL USES

Should one, for example, have diagnostic test results about a person one is going to work with? Does it help? My answer is that it can help only if one uses such knowledge in a very special way, otherwise not. I want first to show the kinds of uses that obstruct rather than help.

There is, in our field, a silly tendency to want to turn the persons we work with into knowledge—I mean that we make our main task to *know* what is wrong with them. We think that if we can only say what is wrong, we will have done our work. But the objective is not to know what is wrong, or to know anything; the objective is to aid the person to change and resolve what is wrong. The diagnostic work-up points us in this false direction of trying to know what is wrong. The diagnostic work-up makes us believe that we may have gotten it—this and this must be what is wrong. We only need some sessions with the person to confirm and specify the diagnostic impression. And then—when we can triumphantly confront our client with the correct explanations and definitions—what do we have? Usually a stuck case, because now that we know what is wrong, there are no procedures for fixing it.

There is a false assumption that, if you know the cause of psychological, emotional, or behavioral trouble, all you have to do is tell it to the person and he or she will change. But it is not so; all of us know much about ourselves, which we understand very well and in its origins, and still it does not change. What changes people are certain processes of experiencing and interacting, not mere knowings.

There is in our field much foolish practice consisting entirely of the professional person telling the person seeking help certain abstractions, which do a minimum of good. ("My counselor told me I was very hurt when I was two years old, when my sister was born and took up all my mother's attention." I ask, "Do you remember how that felt?" "No, I don't remember it, but I think my counselor is right, she convinced me." It is clear that this case will take quite a long time to get very far, if that sort of thing is all that is happening!)

To turn the client into some theoretical concepts, and then deal with the concepts rather than the client, that is the key way of misusing knowledge in practice. In such a use of knowledge, the knowledge makes the practitioner less sensitive than would be if there had been no knowledge or concepts of this kind. If he had none, he would have to deal with the person directly, listening and interacting with the person's feelings and not clearly formulated experiences. The practitioner would have to take in everything possible. The practitioner would have to consult his own global and not yet clear sense of what is happening in the person and between them. The practitioner would have to respond honestly, not from sharp and sure concepts, but rather from that shaky personal sense that is as likely to be wrong as right at any given time. Few know it, but to give this of oneself is to give oneself as a person, and that is very much more than to give a few abstractions, however correct they may be.

In such an interaction, not guided by concepts, the practitioner is not only giving to the interaction the person he or she is—which is unutterably more than a few concepts—but also the client's actual, confused, but concrete experience is enabled to interact with the practitioner in small steps, as both travel not yet charted terrain. Nothing but the real terrain guides them, and the real terrain is the client's concretely sensed, albeit confused, feel of what he is up against in himself. Diagnostic tests may give us some answers faster, but they cannot give us the actual process of working through. Even if we knew everything, the process would still have to be done. It would still require the very personal and open presence, sensitivity, and response of the practitioner at many, many tiny steps into concretely felt, unclear, experiential material. Not through the knowing, but through these experiential steps, is anything resolved.

Would the experiential interaction be aided, or hampered, if one also had knowledge? Suppose we pass by the number-one pitfall of knowledge: *to attend to and be guided by concepts and to skip the essential experiential process.* Let us say we know this, and we will at all costs get our client to engage in such a process with us. Cannot knowledge help us in this process?

Yes, for if we stay anchored, every moment, to some directly felt sense of some person, then all that we know—diagnostic knowledge and life experience—can make us *more sensitive* to recognize what we are directly encountering. By this I do not mean that we will swiftly find some category into which to put what we are hearing. We must let what we are hearing emerge and articulate *itself.* We must let our guide be the person's felt experience, the struggles to point specifically to it and articulate it. If we make someone's feeling and its articulation our constant reference point, then all the patterns and concepts we ever learned can help us help people. But this assumes that we go many small steps with people into what they feel, which is not at first clear. We will discard with ease the various successive conceptualizations the person and we try out, and sensitively use as our criterion whether the person feels a slight movement, a direct signal from the knot in the stomach that something we said is pertinent. Without such very sensitive steps, bit by bit, into what is directly felt, any use of concepts and patterns we have learned must stop the person's progress. People must let go of what they feel in order to think our concepts with us. Then they must still tell us why our concepts do not apply. All this takes a lot of time, during which people lose hold of the directly felt edge on which they should be working.

I will say more below about the positive use, in which all knowledge makes us more sensitive. Now I want to return to discuss a second detrimental effect of knowledge.

Suppose we are committed not to substitute knowledge for the concrete experiential process, and suppose we go with the person, step by step, into his or her concretely felt sense of what is wrong. The knowledge of the diagnostic tests may still hamper us in a second way: the biasing effect. Whether we choose so or not, what we "know" will dispose us to hear and construe the person's unclear feelings in certain ways. We will hear something that sounds a great deal like one of the abstractions in the diagnostic, and get a knowing feeling that includes whatever we associate with it. Even trying not to have it so, our minds will be occupied with that way of looking at it. Thus, even if we do engage in an experiential process with the person, we will hear and respond in a biased way.

We can overcome the biasing effect by listening much harder and more specifically to the exact, finely differentiated spot the client is now speaking from. We can refer directly to that felt but not yet clear "something," and what the client now says exactly. Even so, it takes extra effort to hear beyond what we "know." If we always listen beyond what we know, we will see, in a step or two, both how different and how more detailed is the matter the client is struggling with. We will feel the "knowledge" dropping away again, in favor of a grasp of just what, exactly, the client has there. Thus, although we will experience our biases, we can hold out until they are overcome by the further steps of detailed process.

It must be emphasized that what persons struggle within themselves, and interact from, is experience, not concepts. They struggle with concretely felt and not yet clear senses of living in various ways. If troubled persons do not do this, but talk and ramble without letting their attention go down into their felt sense of what they are talking about, they should be stopped. What they say must be taken in, accepted, and responded to as exactly as possible, but then they should be asked to let themselves stay quiet for a little time, and let their attention down into how the whole thing feels now, and what feels like the crux of it. And they should be told that this "crux" need not be clear, it will be a feeling sense of what is really wrong. This will always reveal detail beyond our biases.

We must therefore know that diagnostic and conceptual structures are always false, because they are thin stick-figure patterns. If used as thin patterns, they can be highly useful! They are like words—they can aid us to articulate what we feel, and to live forward on the plane of speaking and thinking what cannot be lived in life as yet. As aids to dealing directly with what we feel, concepts help. But if we take them as telling us what the person is, then we necessarily distort the person, however correct a given application of a pattern or concept may be. No diagnosis is correct. All concepts may help if viewed as articulating aids for the much richer and moving flow that constitutes a person.

There is always the danger, if the pattern fits at one moment in some way, that we will let it bias us the rest of the way, so that we hear subsequent moments through its perspective. *It would be better, therefore, if we assumed from the beginning that all possible diagnostic concepts may apply to the same person at different times and in different ways, than that we keep viewing him or her through one particular set.*

It is the same with other types of knowledge about the person. If you are practicing in a hospital or agency, and the person you are working with has a record folder—should you read it? Will it not dispose you to view the person in certain ways? And what ways? In reading the record you would view the person through the eyes of others in his life. But the patient is here for help. Obviously those other persons were not able to help him. Why put yourself into their set? It is bound to be an unhelpful one. The patient's record is the record of those who did not understand him!

What if there is one main thing to worry about with this person—suicide or a psychotic break, for instance? Shouldn't you know it? Again, a focus on a specific symptom is most likely to have been in the way of others trying to help and hear the person. You want to overcome such a tendency to hear everything a person is saying through a single focus. It is hard to overcome. But don't we need to know such factors so that we can be careful? What does "careful" mean? How, knowing this, can we be careful in ways we shouldn't always be careful anyway? There is no specific way to be careful, only a generalized way of being tense and somewhat worried with the person, something that is not likely to be much help. Let the person be with you in a new way free of the old rut and roles. Let the old bad fact come up in this new context so it will change.

Suppose the person tells us about some events in his life, and we doubt if they really happened. Need we know? Does it matter that they did not happen exactly as now reported? Again, we must keep it clear to ourselves that we are trying to aid change and resolution, we are not detectives trying to unearth a static truth. What matters is not what happened as such, but what it did to this person, who is still troubled by it and stuck in. *So we need more knowledge of how the events make the person feel. What people do to themselves because of what happened is more important than what happened. The more personal account of the events is as useful as a factual one.*

Even if the client is speaking quite psychotically, saying, for example, "The

Austrian army stole all my possessions," we can understand that as meaning, "Someone did me dirt and took everything away from me." "The FBI is after me," or "The Cubans will get me," means, "I am afraid," or "Some people want to hurt me." Such feelings can be responded to also in the normal distortions most people make when they tell their side of a conflict. We know that the spouse will tell the other side of the story, which will of course sound different. If the relationship is to be saved, the spouse must come to the interview as well. But right now this person is here, and so we must go into his feelings. We move away from the events into the part of this person's experience that hurt him, and into what exactly about it still hurts.

In this process of experiential work, knowing the facts would, if anything, dispose us to an external, biased view of our person. To be sure, objectively the person may have acted badly—but there are always enough people around to point that out. The labels and categorizations we apply in ordinary life, like those of diagnostics, are external. By "external" I mean that if someone calls you passive-agressive or whiny, you cannot from this go in any very useful direction. You have been given a signal that your behavior is wrong, which you may already know from the bad results you obtain. But the label does not tell you how to get into what is wrong in you. Someone will have to go with you into the felt but not yet clear detail—somewhere in how you feel is a good life-force getting lost in some bad pattern; we will have to inquire what it feels like to you when others call you whiny. This is best done not by viewing your feelings as already condemned and defined, as that is likely to lead even you yourself to misinterpret and shut off your feelings. You should not feel this way, so you try not to. Instead, you ought to welcome the feeling, so that it can unravel, and you may then see that you have both a right push to take up for yourself, and some fear about doing just that, which makes you try to come on softly when you are angry. You may find, when you feel this way, that you are afraid you will cry. Your hurts and despair at being unable to be effective may become open for you to explore. None of this can happen if your counselor—and you—take the perspective of "whiny" or "self-pity" or "passive-aggressive," or any such externally descriptive label. Therefore it is best to hold off using such concepts, and to let the working-through process move beyond the biases our concepts give us.

Now I may seem to have contradicted myself. Did I not say that concepts could make us more sensitive to what we hear and sense in the person's working-through? Did I not then say that concepts may bias us to hear what fits them? Isn't this the same thing, said once with the laudatory word *sensitive* and the second time with the condemning word *bias*? Am I not saying that if your concepts dispose you to hear in a certain way, which turns out to be right and helpful, you are "sensitive," but if it turns out to be a wrong direction, then the concepts "biased" you?

The answer lies in the relationship you maintain between the concepts and the actual felt experiential process and its articulating steps. What the concept disposes you to hear may turn out to be right or wrong—either way it makes you "sensitive" if you receive whatever is articulated experientially, and use it to correct what you thought. On the other hand, even if you are right, you are what I call "biased" if you do not continue further to correct and alter your right conception by the subsequent steps of experiential articulation. This brings me to the third pitfall I want to discuss.

This is the pitfall of using concepts *logically* (rather than, as I will call what I advocate, *psychologically*). I mean by "logically" the assumption that if some concepts fit a person, then whatever else is true of him should be logically consistent with these concepts. If the given category holds, other diagnostic categories and all they imply should be excluded. The details and further steps should be those that would be predicted from the concepts. All this is not so, and to expect it is a pitfall.

For example, suppose you have given an interpretation that actually aided a person to get into direct touch with the lived, felt version to which your interpretation pointed. Now you might consider your interpretation correct (and in some respects, of course, it was). But the person's very next step in articulating his directly sensed feelings may reveal further details, which are rather different from what would have been logically consistent with the interpretation that was just so helpful.

Our concepts may fit at one point and not at other points; they may fit at one level of generality but not in the details; they may fit in certain respects, and quite other categories may fit in other respects. To avoid the pitfall, it is not enough to know this; one must allow and encourage the person to pursue his concretely felt and articulated details just as he actually finds them. The attitude I recommend is: "Now that our interpretation has aided you in getting in touch with the actual feeling, let's see just what really is in that feeling, and just how it is there. It is bound to be somewhat different than we think." If this is the method, our concepts can often aid us in suggesting tentative possibilities, which may be close enough to aid the person to tap directly into what he actually does have there. Then we and the person must both be open to it, however it shapes up.

A fourth pitfall is the *differential* use of our diagnostic concepts to infer from them different ways of treating people.

The diagnostic concepts we have today do not have differential procedures attached to them. The diagnosis does not tell us anything to do with "schizophrenics" that we do not also do with "manic-depressives," and the same is even more true with various neurotic types. Some people claim to have invented such differential ways of acting with differently categorized people, but these are artificial, unfounded ways of acting. For example, at one hospital I know, schizophrenics are said to have difficulty "distinguishing between themselves and others," wherefore the staff is instructed to "set limits" for patients categorized as schizophrenic. The idea is that a person can experience the separateness of another person through that other person's defining her or his own limits. But the result of this staff policy is not the intimate personal relations in which an honest, helpful person is encountered as a separate person. That would be desirable with any patient. Indeed, it may be more necessary with schizophrenics than with others, but it is not a differential procedure—*everyone* is most aided by another person who will do that! The result in the hospital, however, is that staff-members rather artificially become very hard and incommunicative about shutting the T.V. off at 8:30, or they deny the patient a drink of water. The policy makes all members of the staff treat the patient in a peculiar way, and the patient cannot know why.

There is no tightness between diagnostic category and a supposedly indicated treatment. If the latter is imagined to exist, it makes the counselor act artificially in a way that is unrelated to the patient's behavior or feelings.

The differential procedures are anybody's guess, and are in no way established. We have not even crude reports of such ways having been tried out, with the results observed. Therefore, I say that our diagnostic concepts have no differential procedures attached to them, and if some people use concepts that way, so much the worse. They will act in some nonhuman, artificial, unresponsive way towards a person because of the category into which the person has been placed.

It is best to behave as openly, responsively, and humanly as possible toward anyone, so long as nothing clear is established about differential treatments.

A fifth pitfall of knowledge is that the psychological concepts we now have, both diagnostic and common-sense, are *static* concepts. I mean by this that they are concepts of what is wrong, of what happened, of what personality structure or character structure the person has. But we want that to change! Therefore we do not want concepts that will help stabilize it in its present condition! What matters is not how he now *is* and *has been,* or why. What matters is how he can change. We need concepts for the change forces in the picture! We need concepts for what is trying to happen, and can't. We need to think about what positive life-process is being frustrated, but is trying to happen in this bad structure. We do not want concepts only to clarify and harden-in that bad structure.

Anyone caught in self-defeating patterns, malfunctioning character structures, pathological repetitions, and so forth, feels these as painful. Such pain is not a mere extra, a bad result—rather it is the very living of the organism not able to proceed. Right in the midst of how pathological patterns are experienced (but not in our concepts of them) are the felt life-forces tending toward resolution. But I am not saying that people should focus on the positive. *I am saying that in the experiencing of what is wrong, positive forces are involved, whether noted or not; whereas in the concepts of what is wrong, no change-avenues are given.* From our concepts of pathology, nothing follows but discouragement. If that is how a person is, what can change it? We don't know. The type of concepts we have do not tell us. But in experiencing oneself in these structures, there is always the sense of pain and incompleteness, frustration and desperation, and not only in the abstractly general terms I have used here, but in very, very specific senses of what is wrong and why it feels wrong. These very specific senses, when found, lead to steps. When a person is trying to sense exactly what is wrong, he is sensing with his organism, and an organism is an organized adaptive system. From conceptual knowing of what is wrong, nothing follows. But a directly felt sense of a felt trouble, when the person has just gotten hold of it and does not know what it is—at that moment organismic body life has moved a step. When one gets hold of the feeling that is the crux of a trouble, tension reduces. If one loses this precarious direct hold on the trouble spot, tension rises again. If one can keep a hold on it for a minute or so, a next step will emerge, one that no one could have predicted in advance. Another "thing" will arise, another edge will come into view, everything will feel just a little different.

We talk about "integration," but that is just another abstraction. People cannot lay all their pieces out on a table, like jigsaw puzzle pieces, and then integrate them into one picture. People are not made of pieces. The body as one living system "integrates," and we do not see the "pieces." To live with one's body, while attending specifically to the felt sense of a trouble, is the integrative process, because the body is one process. A living body moves with an adaptive tendency. Just as hunger is not a thing or a state, but a tending toward eating, so also psychological contents are not really "contents," but tendencies toward living processes that are stuck or have not happened yet. To "find" a trouble-spot is not like finding a thing or an object, but like finding a hunger, a process that should be happening or continuing, and is not. To attend or find or focus attention is itself a special way of living that process forward; hence, after a minute of that kind of attention, a new step emerges that could not emerge previously. And these steps, stemming from the person's directly felt experiencing, constitute therapeutic change.

I have discussed five misuses of knowledge: (1) concepts as substitutes for the experiential process of the person; (2) concepts as biasing us to construe what we experience along the lines of the concepts, instead of in its own different specificity; (3) logical uses of concepts; (4) differential uses of concepts; and (5) the tendency of current concepts to keep things static, as is, when the inherent nature of bodily experience is really a pushing toward something further—the change we should be working for.

HELPFUL USES

Now, in contrast, how should we use knowledge to aid practice?

If one anchors oneself always to a directly felt experiential sense, either one's own or another person's, then and only then can knowledge be used helpfully. One can then use every kind of knowledge and concept, however correct or wild, for one is not putting the concept into the experience to distort it, or, worse, to replace and lose the experience in favor of the concept. There is therefore no risk in using any concept—one does it to see if the concretely felt experience will respond in some new way. The felt experience itself may become sharper as a result of saying that concept (it may become sharper, not only because something about the concept is right, but also sometimes because something about the concept is importantly wrong!). We are glad we used the concept, when the experience is now felt in some way more clearly, or some new aspect arises from it, or some other *directly felt effect* is had. A concept or interpretation is helpful when it produces some directly felt effect in the very specific felt sense one was working with and anchored in.

A second key rule of using concepts helpfully is that once a felt effect occurs, *it is that effect which must be followed* and allowed to articulate itself. We will have lost all the good the concept did us, if we lose hold of that directly experienced effect, and instead say, "Since it aroused that effect, the interpretation must be right."

Recently, a very competent and sensitive psychoanalyst presented excerpts from three of his cases. In each instance the excerpt ended when he had shown that his interpretation of the case was correct. Since the patient assented to his interpretations with a great flow of feeling, I asked, "Didn't you pursue this into what got released for the patient, and see, into the details, what new experiential steps could now emerge?" I don't think the psychoanalyst knew what I was talking about. This is again the pitfall of letting knowledge substitute for the experiential process so that it does not occur at all. This pitfall threatens us every time we use a concept effectively, because we then come to be impressed with the concept. Instead, we must follow the experiential difference it has made, the new or slightly altered felt aspects now directly there for the person. If we do this, the process will move into concrete steps, and a new, specific, but not yet understood, felt sense will be gotten at.

When another felt sense also opens up, what we then say in concepts may well contradict what we said so successfully earlier. Even if we contradict it later, however, we will be glad we said it because, had we not, we would not have gotten to the later step.

I have added a second and third characteristic to our discussion of how to use concepts and knowledge helpfully in practice: We had (1) always be anchored to some specifically felt experiential sense; and (2) pursue the effects of the concept. We now add: (3) allow concepts to be contradicted by a later step of feeling, however effective and right the concept may have been earlier.

That these characteristics are essential can be understood from the fact that we are engaged in a problem-resolution process—that is to say, in a change process! Naturally, then, we are not desirous of having our concepts remain consistent! We do not want our efforts to end in a consistent, stable, noncontradictory system; that would mean the person was not changing! Instead, we want to use concepts as links in a change process. If at some time the concept fits so perfectly as to release the client into newly felt aspects of himself, this very effect of the concept would lead to changes such that the concept would soon no longer apply.

We want to use our concepts always to point to some directly felt experiential sense, or to seek such a direct sense if the person does not have one. This means that we always have more than concepts—always have at least the pointing to some experiential sense, however vague and difficult-to-get-hold-of it might be. This means that we must always use concept *and* experience, never just concepts. We must never let experience go in favor of concepts, but must always keep both.

We need something like the attitude of a chemist testing some unknown white powder to find out what it is. Suppose that if the addition of given acid produces a smoke reaction, the white powder is identified as one thing, and if not, that it must be something else. If the chemist pours the acid all over the white powder, and there is no smoke reaction, what can he use for his next test? The powder will have the acid in it. So he uses only a tiny bit of the white powder for his test, and has most of it left to take other bits for other tests.

Never let go of the experiential sense you have, and also show the client how to hold on to it while trying to see if a given interpretation does anything. Many people all too willingly let go of what they sense, or never even begin to look at it. Instead, they take your interpretation (or their own), and go from it in the many directions one might think from it. This makes for a long rambling thinking process quite unrelated to personal change and growth. The person must attend directly to the felt sense of what is wrong, and must take the concept or interpretation to that felt spot, and see if it has any directly felt effect there. If not, it is useless right now, however correct it may be. But we may try other concepts and interpretations at that same spot—as well as always letting that spot speak from itself, of course.

With this method of always referring concepts to the felt sense to see the effect they have, if any, one can use all manner of concepts. *One can use not just one theory, but many*—as many as one can learn. One need not either forgo another theory, or lose one's own favorite theory. Many ways to sense relations and structures, forms, and connections are more likely to help us find some form that will have a felt effect. The experiential method (Gendlin, 1968a) enables one to use well all theories, however inconsistent they are as pure theories.

In this way we can use all knowledge helpfully in practice, and the more the better. Personal learnings function in the same way as theories. If I impose on my client the idea that she is like my Aunt Linda, surely that will be poor. But if, from knowing Aunt Linda, I have experienced some pattern of human feeling, it may make me more sensitive to what this client's very specific and different felt sense now is. *The key to a safe and helpful use of any and every kind of knowledge lies in the reference to, and criterion role of, the directly felt sense and its steps.* Of course it is foolish to identify this unique person with either Aunt Linda, or with one of Freud's cases, or with one of his abstractions. But it is not foolish to say that all the knowledge and observation I have ever garnered makes me both more sensitive to, and more able to articulate, this very different, finely complex "funny feeling" my client is now pointing at and attempting to make a step into.

Among Dostoevski's characters there is a gushy lady who identifies the living people around her with characters in novels and plays. "You are Tchatsky, and she is Sofiya, in the last scene of . . ." But do not think that the formal practitioner telling the client, "You are Hilda in Freud's case . . ." is any more helpful, nor is it helpful to follow the "You are . . ." with an abstraction from these cases.

I propose that we constantly seek an experiential felt sense, that we try to find something to say that touches upon a felt sense, or will make it move, shift, or open up. If this is constantly our criterion, so that we cheerfully throw away concepts that have made no difference, and try further concepts, then indeed, instead of having too many conflicting theories and possible interpretations, we have too few. But if one is mired in the notion that the person must be translated into concepts, one seeks only one set. Then to use a concept is a great risk, and there are too many conflicting interpretations. But if we seek concepts, sophisticated or commonplace, which will resonate with a felt sense, and will have a felt effect, then we always know too few. Most of what we try out fails at this exacting test. We do not mind a concept failing in such trying out. The ease with which we can let a concept fail is crucial here. When there is no effect, we cheerfully throw the concept away, rather than get stuck with our good reasons for saying it, the endless implications. Then there is room a second later for another sounding, into the felt sense. There is room and time for other concepts to be tried out as well. At no cost, one can try out many different things. The absence of cost, however, depends on keeping the directly felt rather than the thought-about. We keep the concrete sense of the spot a person has felt into, just as the chemist keeps his powder.

Interpretations and concepts must be checked against the person's experientially direct feel of what is talked about. It is not enough to find some concepts reasonable, or even to be able to prove them as logically what must be so. When a person says of himself that something "must be" a certain way, that shows he has no direct touch with it. He is inferring, perhaps correctly, but has not directly encountered the feeling. In our use of knowledge in practice, this direct encounter is like the empirical findings for the researcher. No amount of reasonable deduction can replace an empirical test. No amount of "it must be so" can take the place of instituting a direct empirical study that actually finds it so. Similarly, when I say something and the client agrees, I always say, "Well, you haven't looked yet. See if that's right." I mean that even though we both agree it must be so, he must stop thinking and begin to sense how it is in him in a directly felt way. If he finds it there, then we were right, and also, he will have fresh detail emerging. Nothing we figure out about ourselves is ever right in its details.

Quite often the good results of good use of knowledge in practice come not from the rightness of what we thought, but from its wrongness. In response to some concepts, the sensing into the as yet vague feeling can often be a quite definite no, which is an advance. "I don't know why, but that isn't right," he may then say. The person has a hold now on a directly felt facet, which was not there before, and consists in that much clarity: this, what we said, is wrong in this specifically felt way. Now we must pursue this quite specific but as yet unknown sense, and soon the felt sense opens up into more clarity.

It is essential always to ask the other person (or oneself, if you are working on yourself) to sense directly what, in whatever was just said or thought, is right.

Knowledge is like a map—it is not equivalent to the terrain. If you are driving to New York, and the road before you veers to the left, you go with it, even if there is a straight line on your map. You know the real terrain will have many turns, and the map is a simplification. In a misuse of knowledge, you would drive on straight ahead into the cornfield because the line on your map is straight.

Similarly, when you use a map, if you see something on the map that ought to appear pretty soon, you look for it. If it never appears, you will not get too confused with the fact that it is marked on the map. You do not say, "Well, it's here, we don't need to see it, it's on the map." At most you say, "It must be somewhere around here," and you know quite clearly that you have not found it yet.

However, in using knowledge in practice, many practitioners confuse the differences between what "must be," according to their cognitive map, and what is actually encountered in direct experience. This is our first pitfall again —that of forgetting even to engage in an experiential process of looking for it directly, and letting a concept of it replace the experience. But now we are talking not of letting go of the experience and substituting concepts for it. We are talking about the more important case where one has not yet had the experience. Then it is most important, when thinking something, to check it, to seek into experience and see if one finds there what one surmised.

In direct experiential checking, one will never merely find what one expected, but always much more, usually something somewhat different, and certainly something much more detailed.

A counselor talking to a client, therefore, must always invite the client to check into himself to determine whether anything either person says is so. The counselor must think of the client's experiential terrain as concretely real and capable of being attended to, and as a place in which to look for anything that we surmise might be there. It is like being on the telephone with someone, and looking for something in his room. From our end we cannot see it, we can only surmise it. We ask him to look under the radiator, but we cannot fix it from here that the thing be there. Either it is found directly, or it is not found. (We can still maintain, for future reference, that we think something like it might be found sometime, but that is another matter.)

In this process of aiding the person to get further into his felt sense and to sense what it is, everything we have ever experienced helps us. We can recognize a person's feeling much faster if we have known many people who had —not quite this—but similar feelings. The more of the range of human feeling we have experienced, heard about, and read about, and the more unique variants of it we have encountered, the more quickly we can sense this next unique one now being shared with us. If you have never heard that people who fear some harm happening to a person close to them often find they themselves have hostile feelings for that person, it will take you much longer to aid such a person to find his anger in the middle of his overconcern. If you have never heard of projections, it will be a longer struggle for you, and the person you are aiding, to sense that some way the person feels belongs to different times and people than those present now. It is often very helpful to ask a person, "Does this way you feel belong somewhere in your past—was there a time when you felt this way and it fit the situation?"

Such knowledge is really valuable, and no one would want to be without it! Not that any particular bit of it will necessarily be right or helpful, but rather that the totality of your experiences and what you are capable of thinking and understanding is vastly enhanced by this body of knowledge. Not to have it would be like choosing not to have traveled widely, or not to have known or heard about many different kinds of people. Of course, the more you have seen and heard, the more sensitively and swiftly you can receive the next person's unique ways of being.

I am not saying that conceptual knowledge is as good as personally having accompanied someone into his actual feelings and experiences. But it can help one do the latter. Of course, from statements alone one cannot understand what is involved, what it is like to be that way. For example, I may know that overconcern can be defended-against hostility, but I will not know whether and how such an opposite effect occurs unless someone who has it, shares it with me, in the small steps necessary to grasp it, or unless I myself have discovered and worked through something like it in myself. However, to have heard of it even in the simplest, most mechanical way, as I phrased it here, can aid one in first hearing or finding it. Then, after the actual experiencing has been worked through, I will know not only that category or concept, but also what it is really like in at least one version of unique living detail.

Therefore, however poor our knowledge may be, we want it, such as it is, very much indeed.

However, unless one is able to use it in the ways I am trying to delineate, it is better not to have such knowledge. The basic characteristics of using knowledge helpfully in practice are:

1. To keep every bit of use of it anchored to a specific way a person directly feels, and to let the criterion of the knowledge be whether there is a response of the felt sense to that concept. If there is no response, then the concept must be discarded, and swiftly, before we become mired in some lengthy abstract discussion of why the concept is or is not correct.
2. If there is a response, again the concept must be dropped in favor of pursuing directly whatever felt sense or edge the concept helped one find.
3. This may change that very concept.

With many people, this experiential level is not easily had, since they pay little or no attention to it. They must first be shown this mode of experiencing. In order to be able to show it, we ourselves must have it very clearly. I will therefore say more about it, and how it differs from, and relates to, thought, observation, and emotions.

The essential characteristic of directly felt experience is that it is always *multiple,* always very many facets all in one felt sense. This makes a directly felt sense *conceptually* vague (we do not know all that is involved in it), while yet it can be *felt* quite clearly. An example of this is one's sense of what I call the "spot": something is wrong; one does not know just what, but can feel it quite distinctly. Another example: When people have bad situations, they often wake in the morning feeling fine, and then the "whole thing" comes back to them as they recall it. In such an experience they have the feel of the "whole thing" rather than thinking this or that facet.

Thought, on the other hand, is specific, about just this or that facet. Thought can be viewed as a special sort of experiencing; it too involves some feel of what one is thinking, but it is specific and objectified, so to speak, in verbal or other symbols.

Thought can be unrelated to directly felt experiencing, as when we try to think objectively or logically about something other than what we feel. We often need objective and logical thinking. However, thought may also be closely related to directly felt experiencing, as when we seek to articulate the crux of what we feel in a specific thought sequence. I call it "articulating" when thought has this close relation to directly felt experiencing. Articulation always proceeds in steps. As I have already said, a step of thinking articulation may lead to a change in feeling, which in turn may lead to a second and different step of thinking, which in turn may somewhat alter the feeling, and so on.

External observation is not really as different from directly felt experiencing as one might at first suppose. If we did not accept how external observations are already cut up into common-sense units and into social roles and recognizable events, if we took the whole of what we observe, our observation would be a directly felt sense of a complex whole, which would be conceptually vague, though definitely sensed. However, most of the time we observe windows and tables, or teachers and students, and so forth. Only when a situation is unclear, when something not yet known is wrong, or when there is a problem, do we have a "sense of" the situation without clear, conceptually defined units.

A directly felt experiential "sense" is nothing subjective, it is one's bodily felt sense of living in a given situation. There is no internal/external split; we feel internally our living in the external situation.

However, since external events are so often already defined, people often report, "He did this, and she said that . . . ," and they must be invited to sense into what the whole thing feels like, to them, rather than only the defined events.

Thus, both thought and observation, in usually being already cut up into specific units, differ from directly felt experiencing. However, both thought and observation can be closely related to directly felt experiencing: thought can articulate what one directly feels. What one directly feels is always the living in some situation or situations which are or were observable.

Directly felt experiencing is also always differentiated from emotion by its characteristic of multiplicity.

An emotion like anger, depression, or joy is a tonality, a certain uniform quality. However much one focuses one's attention on an emotion, it remains the same quality and may increase in strength. To focus on anger makes one angrier, to focus on how depressed one feels makes one more and more depressed. Focusing on an emotion like anger is often not helpful. Focusing on a felt sense, on the other hand, includes all the implicit complexity of what has made one angry. One can say much about this. These and those people have done this and that wrong. Suppose I am angry at myself because I did this and that wrong. We might speculate as to what traits of mine made me particularly vulnerable to getting mad about what happened. But instead of all this event-reporting and speculating, instead of the emotion of anger, I want to sense directly the *feel of all that,* which has made me angry. There and only there is movement and resolution possible. Let me sense what all that, together, feels like. Now I am focusing not on the emotion of anger, but on my feeling of that whole maze of felt complexity, which makes for my anger. Where does all that get to me? Now I am focusing not on the emotion, which is one, and will not change but only increase, but rather on a felt sense of very many things together. I am sensing into that feel of it all, to sense where I am stuck in it; thereby I may soon refer directly to some specific sense, which is still unresolved for me. *This* (I may not know yet what is in it) is my sense of what is wrong. As I feel into "this," I may soon find myself with newly clear aspects. I will find out which aspect of the situation, or of me, is most involved —and what is difficult about it. "Oh," I may then say, "it isn't so much what they did, it leaves me not knowing what to do back. *That's* what it is. And so I am collaborating with them if I don't get mad. It's that I am always likely to go along and talk myself out of any conflict and even help them, that's what I'm fighting against doing again." And later I might go further in: "Something seems so impossible about taking care of myself in the first place, so I never say what I need until everything is done and it's too late. It's that feeling that I can't say what I need. Now what is *that?*"

So it must be emphasized that the felt sense I am talking about is not emotion, but that feeling of the complexity of circumstances and personal aspects that may make for a given emotion at a given juncture.

Many people seem to know only about thinking, observation, and emotions. They seem never to let their attention into a sensing of a whole complexity, although this is available to any person.

People must often be asked to stay quiet, not only not to speak to us, but also not to make words at themselves. In such a quietness they must be asked to let themselves feel "that whole thing" about which they were just then talking. This might have been a broad problem, or a specific aspect. They should be asked to sense "whatever the crux of it is," or "whatever is still wrong," or "where you are still hung up in it," or some question that asks for a felt response in them. They must be instructed not to answer this question in words, although of course they could. Everyone knows a great deal, and could answer in words. "Don't answer it yourself, let the answer come from how it feels. Wait."

Very often, an immediate deepening of the counseling process occurs when one asks a client to perform these very simple instructions. I call the process "experiential focusing (Gendlin, 1969)."

The key characteristic of the directly felt experiential sense, with which concepts must interact in practice, is that such a sense is multiple although felt as one feeling. Even if what was being talked about is very specific, the feel *of it* will be multiple. It is a feel of "that whole thing," or "whatever is still wrong." It is always a feel of a whole, however specific. Conceptually, very many facets *could* now be said from it, even though it seemed simple and specific before. This differentiates it from emotions, which are simple, and do not contain many facets under them.

Body (and bodily felt sensing) is not only a whole, but also a moving living process. Therefore, when a person senses such a whole, a further step will form. Such a step, if not imposed but allowed to form, to "come," is made by the whole, and is a specific further *movement*. Whereas concepts are static, implying only what is logically consistent, the movement from felt wholistic sensing is, as it were, biologically moving. Whatever specific sense one thereby gets, words or other symbols can then articulate it. This makes the characteristics "steps" of movement in articulating. Both directly felt sensing and concepts change.

The five characteristics we have so far for using knowledge helpfully in practice are:

1. Always refer to some person's specifically felt experiential sense of what is being talked about and consider what is said as pointed there. The person must be invited to check directly and see if he can feel what the interpretation refers to, and whether it is right. This means never using concepts as universals, with the individual merely falling into the classification the concepts define. It means always checking the concepts against direct feeling and its differentiation, and considering the concepts as possible pointers and perhaps openers of what is felt.
2. If the concepts make no felt difference, they can be dropped easily and smoothly, without getting involved in why and how they should have been right. Others can be tried immediately. Or, if they have made a felt difference, that difference must now be pursued, not the concepts. The direct working with what they have roused or sharpened will lead to problem-resolution, not the concepts as such.
3. Understand from the start that the concepts now effective in making an experiential difference will very likely be contradicted by subsequent concepts that will later make such a difference, since the person is hopefully changing.
4. A directly felt experiential sense is always multiple, though felt as one.
5. Sensing into one's directly felt feeling makes for a movement of steps.

Let me now generalize about this use of knowledge. It means that we radically change what we have usually thought concepts to be. Instead of viewing some statement as a sharp rendition of a structure in experience, we view it as possibly effective in dealing with really-lived experience that is never only one single structure. For example, let us say that the client finds himself with some jealous feeling, and we refer to it and try to get its worst edge. He feels a certain way he cannot name. We arrive, after a while, at the formulation that it makes him feel small and left out. My own knowledge of the Oedipal theory has aided me in aiding him; not that I imposed the theory on him, that would take too long for the little likelihood that it would fit now. The theory aided me in being sensitive to such edges of feeling as "small" and "left out"; the client is the child, and the other two are adults making adult love. Thus he has hold of the feeling now, and the Oedipal theory had only sensitized me so I was better able to hear the "small and left out." We pursue, not my theory, but this felt sense, which he has directly.

The Oedipal theory may help me further. In my own mind, without interrupting the client's process, I ask myself: "If the Oedipal theory fits, what would follow?" That the client would also feel that he could not as easily go out and find other adults, that he has, as it were, to stay in his room. I ask him, "Does it also seem you can't step out very easily?" Again, whether this is helpful or not depends entirely on whether some further directly felt aspect can be got hold of by the client, not whether he says yes or no to this. If so, the aspect might lead to steps that would change this.

Now even if right again, still I will not assume that there exists somewhere in the client a structure—made of hard bones, as it were—which might be called the Oedipal structure. Even if the client likes and uses psychoanalytic language and himself calls it his Oedipal structure, I would not assume such a structure. Instead, what I assume is that his rich and complexly textured experience is such that his child and family complexity is aroused by the events, and that this more global experiential mass is what we are really dealing with, rather than any given way of patterning it. Thus, even when the sharpest theoretical patterning works at its best, I will still consider the experiential reality to be not the pattern but the experiencing. I will consider that this pattern helped get certain facets, and in a minute other patterns and theories may help us get other facets.

Because of this translation I make from sharp conceptual structure to more broad experiential process, I can also use theories as above, without telling them. I can ask myself what it would feel like, if a given theoretical connection obtained, and then ask the client directly if he finds a feeling like that. It saves the time of talking the theory at him, which is very complicated, and instead asks a question that is very simple. If he finds nothing, we lost little time and did not get embroiled in intellectual complexity.

I may thus add characteristics 6 and 7:

6. Let every theory and conceptualization be a thin cognitive pattern, which might be part of, but never equivalent to, the globally felt texture of living. In this way you do not reify concepts and identify the person

with them, but allow the same experience already having one set of concepts fitting to it, to still be there for other concepts as well.

7. In using theories in practice, translate them into what one might feel-ingly find directly. Permit yourself any amount of complex reasoning privately, but make the intervention be a simple question, whether the person feels something like—some way of feeling you can imagine he might find. (Again, what he actually finds may be different and more specific, and we pursue that, not my inferences.)

This way of using concepts and theories changes them drastically. No longer would human nature or personality be conceived as made up of the kinds of patterns the different theories seem to hold. Neither Oedipal structure, nor Anima, nor anxiety bonds, nor any of the varying conflicting renditions of personality, is to be taken literally. (All give us terms and patterns with which sensitively and helpfully to search into ourselves, and we may use all, not just one of them. Often, as the client is trying to sense into a given felt sense, a number of theories may go through my mind, from Freud to Jung to my Aunt Linda. Any edge I can ask about can help, and if not, will not make us lose hold of where we are. But I must ask for a feeling edge, do you feel "something like this . . . ?" If I tell my reasonings, he must let go of his directly felt sense, in order to follow me, and we will be lost.)

This means conceiving of human nature as fundamentally experiential and preconceptual—as not this or that structure, but a texture and a flow. At a given point some pattern or order is effective for an experiential step, but soon a quite different pattern or order may aid us. Human personality is neither this nor that patterning, but the life process—more than conceptual patterns, but *responsive to them*. It is beyond the scope of this essay to explain this respon-siveness, except to say that our conceptual patterns do, of course, come from experience, and themselves constitute a way of continuing experience where it is blocked. Of course, conceptualizing is to continue living on another plane, but one can often continue it there (symbolically) when one cannot yet do so in life.

To say what some experience is, is itself a living process. One seems to be merely saying about, but much is changed in the very moments when one says something with reference to experiential felt sense, and if effective there is a sense of relief of the "knot" in the stomach, a release and the freeing feeling of at last knowing what that is, which one focally felt. One thinks one merely knows what that was, but in fact it has also just changed. Thus, rather than view concepts as *of* static objects the concepts represent, we view concepts as patterns capable of bringing about that kind of continuation of experiencing where it was stopped.

The continuation of experiencing on the symbolic level, via the conceptual pattern, is good only if it is actually felt as an experiential effect. Only then is it effective. Of course, such continuation of concrete living in a symbolic field is not always enough. Quite often a bit of action or interaction is needed for certain changes to take place. For example, one attendance at an encounter group can be worth many therapeutic sessions, if it enables the client safely *to act* his next step, rather than talk it. Similarly, the therapist must be available for concrete personal interaction, and not just experiential differentiation. One actual fight with the therapist may be worth many sessions of feeling into the client's difficulties around conflict confrontations. But during or immediately after such interaction, it will again be important to aid the client to feel directly what the interaction has stirred or changed.

If we take the position I have outlined, then we can be strongly in favor of knowledge of any sort, and the more the better. But there is very little knowledge in our field. You can appreciate that fact especially when you experience a deep resolution of some difficulty. Then you notice that there are no concepts to formulate it! Our science or knowledge lacks concepts very badly.

We cannot expect a much better therapy without better concepts than we now have. These must come from articulating what we at first know experientially, as in the example above, when you have had a resolution experience. Now you no longer need concepts, but as a field we need them badly! Had we had them before you resolved your problem, they might have aided you.

DISCARDING PRETENDED KNOWLEDGE

Now that we have discussed three pitfalls, or misuses of knowledge, and seven criteria for a helpful use of knowledge, let me raise a somewhat different question. I want to discuss our field's pretense of possessing a knowledge that does not exist. This is the pretense to scientific, established knowledge on which authoritative judgments can be based.

The public does not know how little we know. They should be told. Whenever you notice people relying on your supposed expert knowledge, you should tell them that, as a field, we know very little. We are experts in the process of resolution, but not in any of the content! I "know" that if you focus on the feeling of all this, and get to where it is now still unresolved, then we will resolve it. But I know little else. Psychiatry and clinical psychology are not like medicine, and the public should be protected from the false analogy. A psychiatrist is a doctor of medicine, and if he still recalls what he learned but never used, his *medical* judgments are based on knowledge. His *psychiatric* judgments simply are not. It takes many people a long time to face this flatly, because they wish there were some knowing authority somewhere. The psychiatrist is the duly authorized representative of society insofar as taking responsibility is concerned. But insofar as knowledge is concerned, that person knows the most who best knows this individual with whom we are working.

Everyone knows himself best. After that, the counselor who has spent the most time with him will know best. To go by a psychiatrist's judgment, if he is not the counselor who has spent the most time with the client, is to rely on a social ritual in a false way. The social ritual concerns responsibility, not knowledge. There is no knowledge in our field, as there is in medicine, such that a consultant can be brought in and the facts laid before him.

Similarly, supervisors are foolish if they tell the therapist-in-training about the patient. I am often impressed by the spectacle of a therapist playing five minutes of tape to a supervisor, or even just telling about the case, after which the supervisor asserts a good many abstractions supposedly about the client, whom he has never even met. The therapist, having spent 20 or 40 hours with the client, listens respectfully, and may even comply and act in certain artificial ways suggested by the supervisor. What use of "knowledge" is involved here?

It is again a social ritual. The person socially placed in the more *responsible* position is confused with a person *knowing* more. Actually, it is obvious that this person knows less—about this patient. He may also know less about people in general. Most of what we learn about people in general comes from our own experience, our own struggles, our own being in therapy. A very few but precious bits of knowledge may come from books. The supervisor may have much less from all these sources than the beginning therapist, and all of them may have less than the patient. Why then is he the supervisor? It is because of age, seniority, years of schooling in medicine, statistics, and animal psychology, agency structure, theology, and so forth. The supervisor may be more skilled as a therapist and may know more than the starting therapist. I am only saying that it is just as likely not so.

How then is such a supervisor able to say so much that sounds quite likely about a patient who is not here? It is again because of misuse of knowledge, which substitutes it for experience, rather than placing it in interaction with experience at every step.

It is obviously easier to read a map when one is sitting at home than when using the map on some real terrain. If we have a little bit of information about someone, we can say a lot, and the less concrete information we have, the more we can say. We can invent typical syndromes and draw logical inferences in a vast number of directions, as long as there is no concrete person there to react to it with confusion, tightness, and a stopped process. Were the person there, most of these thinkings would soon be found useless in the present concrete juncture. Then still to think of something helpful would be hard.

Of course, if the supervisor can listen sensitively, and if there is a tape recording, the supervisor can help the counselor hear better what the client is saying. Supervisors ought to concentrate on aiding the person who is present in front of them. Everyone working with troubled people runs into trouble. One's own weak points are called out; one runs into one's own typical difficulties. The therapist being supervised is the experiencing person on whom supervision should focus. Where does the case give him trouble, and what are the personal meanings and feelings this rouses? This may seem exactly like therapy for the therapist, but it takes its rise from the difficulties made by the case in question.

We must also face the simple truth that we have no knowledge concerning the goals and proper end-points of psychotherapy. "My therapist thinks I should keep coming," is a statement of a poor therapy, in which the client has no direct feeling of help happening, but believes (on the false medical analogy) that his "doctor" is continuing a medicine he still needs. No knowledge exists to base such a judgment on. Similarly, if the therapist says, "With this person our goal is support, rather than exploration," something foolish is happening. If the counselor avoids what the client feels, the client is left alone with the most threatening aspects of his experience. Those who distinguish between "supportive" and "explorative" therapy, probably do the exploring so badly that it requires a very healthy patient to bear up under it. Therefore they consider some patients too ill or weak for it, and of course it is just as well to spare anyone that kind of exploration. What is usually meant is that the therapist throws the wildest and most insulting abstractions at the patient, and they then see what happens. "Supportive" therapy, in contrast, means the counselor avoids what the client brings up. Neither should ever be done.

Anchoring very specifically in the person's own felt sense of what he is up against, never does anything except help. The more upset, borderline psychotic, or disturbed someone is, the more one should respond gently and exactly, without shying away from anything that is being expressed. Anything so bad that a person is thought not able to take it, so that we avoid it when we are with him, is there anyway for him to deal with all alone when we are not there. If we avoid referring to his feeling of panic or despair, of suicidalness, or whatever, our not speaking to it when we hear it does not make it safer. It does not make it not be there. Better keep it company and bring it into interactive space.

Thus the misuse of knowledge—its use in practice without constant anchoring and checking—is also an unsafe procedure, whereas constant sensitive asking as to how it really is, and very carefully taking experiential facets as they come, is safe with anyone. There is no sound basis for claiming that therapy should have different goals for different types of patients.

It is essential to let go of pretended but nonexistent knowledge, both with regard to our own judgments and also in regard to those we wish others could give us. To let go of the pretense will generate the very spirit with which what we say must be taken. Knowing that we do not know whether what we say is right, the client cannot help but look into himself to see if it is, and this will make for constant connection between concept and experience. The same is true for the practitioner. Once freed of the illusion that only you are unsure —that you ought to be able to come up with some sure interpretation—you can then sense into yourself, into your own felt impression of all you have experienced, and you can share tentatively from this much more personal level.

To give up the pretense of possessing knowledge in our field that does not yet actually exist, is to be able to laugh and say freely: "I don't know that, because no one does. Dr. X may have called you 'schizophrenic,' but no one is agreed on what that word means, and it gets used a lot of ways. Everyone has some schizophrenic aspects, yet some people are in the hospital and we don't know why. You might be crazy, but Dr. X wouldn't know. I guess you're scared of some of the ways you feel? Do you want to say what they are?"

To give up such pretended knowledge means knowing not to send a person to a hospital or psychiatric service because you think someone there will know more than you. The supposed knowledge of the people in such places is not a reason for hospitalizing someone. There is no such knowledge there.

Of course, if we give up pretended knowledge, then we must use any knowledge we do have in a helpful way. It will help to tell people that you have heard of what they are describing, that you have seen it before, or whatever is true. It will help to say what you know, together with where you know it from and the doubt and confusions surrounding it. You might well say: "Oh yes, I have heard of that happening. People know about a thing like that. But they don't understand it very well. It's supposed to have something to do with such and such, but I'm not sure that's right. Does it go anywhere for you to look for such and such?" Here you are sharing, not some supposedly sharp and reliable knowledge, but exactly what you do and do not know.

Also implied in giving up pretended knowledge is the recognition that the ability to help others is independent of status and nonrelevant education. If others work under you who can help better than you can, enable them to work. Your status is a social power and responsibility. Use it as well as you are able to give the go-ahead to those who can work best. Your judgment is wanted, society has put you in the position of judging. Do not think, therefore, that because certain people work under you, you must be able to work better than they. Again, it is only in terms of responsibility that you are placed above them, to decide who should function, and in what ways.

Our field needs theory *and* practice, both together in interrelation. If you yourself do not do counseling well, but have much abstract knowledge, learn the process. The best way is to find someone who can counsel you, and in such a way that you can feel more than words happening in you. Then you will also know what your knowledge refers to, and you will be able to make it pay off. You need not remain in the anxiety-producing position of using only abstract knowledge to cover for you. We have only one life each—therefore, why accept an end of its expansion?

Most of counseling and psychotherapy is learned by being a client or patient in a counseling that works—one that is more than words. Most of the rest of the learning occurs, and can occur, only in practice—with the chance of talking intimately about it as one practices. Only a very small percentage of what one must know comes from books and theory. Yet that small amount is very precious, and we must make it grow.

If you yourself are a sensitive practitioner, develop your knowledge and thinking side. Obtain for yourself such little knowledge as we do have. Stop thinking of it as a separate, essentially unreal, matter of academic publishing. Instead, help make new concepts of the kind that emerge from practice. Articulate your experience, at first merely describing what you do and experience. Of their own accord, such articulations form into clearer and clearer assertions of your experience. Concepts are, and inherently come from, experience—to articulate experience *is* concept-formation. Of course, for a time such work may seem very private, and you may get little understanding from others; certainly such work seems unrelated to the academic and publishable. But so little of that is genuine knowledge, why make it a standard? Rather, let new concept-formation develop over some years' time. Do it just for yourself; eventually just this will have the most significance for others. The more unique and close to your own experience your thinking is, the more universal significance it has for others when it becomes articulated.

Our field needs a thinking top. We cannot make advances, cannot even teach what is now achieved by some, if we cannot devise concepts for our practice. However, this can be done only from practice.

We must overcome the seeming split between research and theory on the one hand, and practice on the other. Only both together can advance the field.

But to move toward the kind of knowledge and use of knowledge we need, we must give up the harmful uses of knowledge and the pretensions to knowledge we do not have.

SUMMARY

I have discussed the following pitfalls, or misuses of knowledge:

1. Substitution of concepts for experience, thus skipping the necessary experiential process.
2. Predisposing to a way of hearing experiential expressions, rather than staying open to their inevitable detailed difference from what we could predict.
3. The tendency of concepts to be about a static pattern and thus keep the person static. Concepts do this by drawing in, in heavy lines, so to speak, the way the person is rather than the way he would be changing if he could.

The helpful use of knowledge in practice, as I have sketched it, consists in:

1. Keeping all verbalizations in constant reference to some directly felt aspect of some person (it might be ourselves if we are exploring ourselves).
2. Pursuing the felt difference concepts make, rather than the concepts' implications, and discarding concepts if they make no felt difference that can be worked with directly.
3. Letting our conceptualization of a person or a problem change, so that what we said, which was so helpful and led to real experiential movement at an earlier step, might be contradicted by what we say at a later step, which has a felt effect there. After all, change is what we want.
4. Remaining aware that a directly felt sense is always multiple, and although felt as one it is a rich whole.
5. Remaining aware that this, in due course, will result in a step of movement.
6. Letting all real persons and experiencings be forever different from conceptualizations and structures and patterns of theory, so that even when the pattern fits most strikingly we will still know that the experience and person is a rich texture and flow, not the pattern.
7. Permitting oneself any theory and line of reasoning, knowing that at most it may be a lead to some feeling the person might actually find, directly, in himself. (Similarly, if we are exploring ourselves, we may think anything, but even so, do not forget to become quiet and feel into your direct sense of the trouble to see if something like you thought is directly there to be found.)

REFERENCES

Gendlin, E. T. A theory of personality change. In P. Worchel and D. Byrne (Eds.), *Personality change*. New York: John Wiley, 1964.

Gendlin, E. T. Experiential explication and the problem of truth. *Journal of Existentialism,* 6, (22), 1966.

Gendlin, E. T. The experiential response. In E. F. Hammer (Ed.), *Use of interpretation in treatment: Technique and art.* New York: Grune & Stratton, 1968. (a)

Gendlin, E. T. Focusing ability in psychotherapy, personality, and creativity. In J. M. Shlien (Ed.), *Research in psychotherapy.* Vol. 3. Washington, D.C.: American Psychological Association, 1968. (b)

Gendlin, E. T. Focusing. *Psychotherapy: Theory, research and practice,* 1969, **6**, 4–15.

Gendlin, E. T. *Experiencing and the creation of meaning.* New York: Free Press, Macmillan, 1962 (reprinted 1970).

Gendlin, E. T. Experiential psychotheraphy. In *Current psychotherapies,* R. Corsini (Ed.) Itasca, Ill.: Peacock Publishers, 1973.

Behaviorism Is Humanism

Ray E. Hosford

University of California—Santa Barbara

I have often been asked, "Why are you a behaviorist?" In many cases the questioner seems to imply that there may be some underlying "need" or predisposition in my personality, which caused me to adhere to the behavioral counseling point of view, as opposed to the client-centered, Freudian, trait-factor, or some other theoretical approach. On one occasion, one of my graduate students in counseling at the University of Wisconsin told me that she was surprised to find me so open to students, even to being in some respects more "client-centered" than supposedly client-centered counselors. I thanked her, and asked why she was surprised. She replied that she and the other graduate students, upon hearing that I was a behaviorist, had just assumed that I would be, as she put it, "cold and only interested in research and manipulating people." She implied that she had assumed from reading the literature, that behaviorists as counselors either did not care to, or really could not, establish warm, personal counseling relationships.

I have on many occasions thought about the popular conceptions, or rather misconceptions, about behavioral counseling, which, I am certain, many unfortunately share with this graduate student. Undoubtedly one of the reasons that such distortions arise stems from the predisposition of many to judge behavioral counseling before they fully understand it. The coldness and impersonality wrongly attributed to behavioral counseling are not so much the consequence of a mechanistic application of its principles, as they are the result of the mechanistic accusation made by many uninformed persons after only a limited exposure to behavioral theories and procedures. Perhaps more important, however, has been the fact that, in our emphasis on determining essential elements of the counseling process, which lead to demonstrable changes in client behavior and thereby establish scientific respectability for what we do as counselors, we have not discussed sufficiently the importance of other aspects of counseling—which for us often appear to be common sense—integral and necessary in the total counseling process. Thus, many persons

295

assume that the totality of behavioral counseling consists only of some "conditioning" process. In this essay—which is, in effect, a combination of two speeches, "Behavioral Counseling," given at the 1969 state convention of the South Dakota Personnel and Guidance Association, and "The Behavioral Approach to Counseling and Guidance," given at the Devereux Schools—Santa Barbara Campus, in September 1970—I would like to illustrate and discuss some of the problems and issues with which behavioral counselors are concerned, and why I personally believe behaviorism is indeed the most humanistic approach to counseling. Along the way, as we examine those things that led me personally to become interested in and finally to practice from this point of view, perhaps we can clear up some of the typical misconceptions about this approach.

During the past two decades we have witnessed the emergence or reemergence of several counseling theories. Many of these arose because of the ineffectiveness of Freudian and other dynamic approaches. Counselors and psychotherapists were searching for more adequate ways to help people solve the problems for which they sought counseling. Although some of these approaches were received enthusiastically by the profession, they soon lost much of their appeal when they could not hold up under the test of empirical research. Many of these theories fell into the same trap as the ineffective psychoanalytic approach that preceded them. Instead of growing out of systematic research and new breakthroughs in knowledge, which we equate with any scientific inquiry, they evolved more from the therapist's own needs and preferences, and from his reflections of what he believed to have occurred. In effect, the outcomes of therapy were visible only to the therapist, and could only be described in his therapeutic terminology. Furthermore, since he started out from a set theory, and classified and explained all observations only within that frame of reference, his results could only serve to confirm what he believed at the outset. In other words, he determined beforehand what he would find, and then forced every explanation to fit his initial theory. What could be more mechanistic? No wonder such inadequate procedures soon lost their appeal within the profession. No wonder clients received little in the way of satisfactory assistance under such conditions.

I have no quarrel with philosophy, but we are in the business of helping people find solutions to problems they encounter in life. To talk about humanism is one thing; to practice it is another. If a counselor is a humanist, it should be evident in his *behavior,* and by what he has done to help people solve problems for which they sought counseling, not in what he claims to be his philosophy of life. If today we are talking about humanism (I thought we always were), we are talking about helping our fellow man realize out of life his greatest potential. To rely on counseling techniques that have only philosophic rather than scientific foundation as their base is, to me, completely antithetical to the true principles of humanism. What we think is good for others may not be what we would want for ourselves or our loved ones if we were faced with similar critical problems in our lives. We would want the counselor to use counseling techniques that have been scientifically tested and applied in the marketplace of counseling. The fun and games of many new "counseling procedures" for which only a philosophic foundation exists, may be very worthwhile for many people—at least for those who enjoy the experience and who do not get worse because of it. However, until the therapist can put into operational terms what he is doing, why he is doing it, and what outcomes usually occur—so that I or any other counselor can employ the same procedure and achieve generally the same result—I have to say that the approach is not scientific, and that any therapeutic change reflected in the counseling outcome results mainly from the personalities of the therapist and the client and the interaction between them. Undoubtedly, it is more the way in which the therapist is structuring the relationship—i.e., "helping the client to express verbally his concern, providing the conditions under which anxiety and stress are gradually extinguished and systematically reinforcing the client to talk positively or more positively about [himself] [Hosford, 1969b]"—that determines the effectiveness of the treatment.

Another reason why our counseling practices stem principally from philosophy rather than science is the fact that our research has been irrelevant to what we do as counselors. The gap between the research laboratory and the counseling office has been too great for the results of the research to affect counseling practice. In my opinion, the trend we see occurring—one in which counseling research is becoming more pragmatic—has been brought about both by behavioral counselors and by others as well who became disenchanted with the limited effectiveness and replicability of traditional counseling research.

It was just this kind of growing disenchantment with traditional counseling that prompted me to seek more effective means of helping people achieve the desired changes in their lives—changes that would be observable not only to me, the counselor, but, more importantly, to the client and those around him. Early in my counseling career it became clear to me that all too frequently such changes were simply not achieved—largely because of the tendency for too much diagnosis and too little prognosis in the counseling process. I recall, for example, an experience I had as a junior-high-school counselor a few years ago. The science teacher sent a student to me and asked that I do a referral to psychological services on the boy. Bob was a 6-foot eighth-grader who scored somewhere between 135 and 140 on a Stanford-Binet. According to the teacher, Bob was "not doing a dang thing." For example, the teacher related that Bob neither entered class discussions nor attempted class or homework assignments. He had noted these and several other behaviors as the reasons for referring Bob. Since he had requested a psychological referral, I referred the student on to the school district's psychological services. After the school psychologist had worked with him for quite some time, she sent back a confidential report (stamped "Highly Confidential," I might add). This was the type of report counselors often receive from referral agencies. After the confidential report had been routed to the various teachers who had this student, it was returned to me and on it was written in large red letters "SO WHAT!" Well, because school psychology and school counseling are (or should be) the same profession, I was more than a little disturbed, and I quickly asked the science teacher if I could sit down and talk with him about it. When we met, he said, to my best recollection: "I am sick and tired of sending people to you counselors and psychologists; all you are doing is telling me in fancy psychological terms exactly what I said in common sense. I didn't refer Bob to you only to find out that he is preschizophrenic, I referred him because I wanted to see him change. Now he is still in my class, behaving the same way, doing the same things, and you haven't helped him a bit." Besides labeling Bob "preschizophrenic"—whatever that means—the psychologist had also attributed to him such classificatory terms as having "low affect," "feelings of inferiority," and an abnormal Rorschach profile. It was quite clear that we had been of little or no help to this teacher, let alone to the student. Bob was still completely uninterested and unresponsive in the classroom. What is worse, the diagnosing and labeling, which had been done under the guise of assistance, had precisely the opposite effect. Teachers began seeing and responding to Bob as if he were emotionally disturbed. This is but one case in which teachers, parents, and students themselves expected changes, which did not occur; there are many more.

The more I was exposed to such traditional counseling practices of spending so much time and energy trying to diagnose and find a "cause" for the client's behavior, rather than using the same time and resources in helping the child to change, the more I became completely disillusioned with the whole profession of counseling. I personally was experiencing very realistically what so many parents and teachers must feel about counseling when they are frustrated in their attempts to get the help they need. Too, I often felt at a loss, not knowing what to do to help clients change some behavior for which they sought counseling. At this time I had had two years of graduate training, principally in clinical psychology, and could, from the feedback I received, develop an excellent relationship with nearly all of my clients. In fact, on numerous occasions, I had received verbal and written reinforcements from parents and students relative to my counseling. Clients returned in large numbers. I felt good about that, but I felt very ineffective. My main interest has always been to help people, but I felt I was not accomplishing much. I counseled clients only to find that two months later they were still doing, or unable to do, the very behavior for which they had sought, or were referred to, counseling in the first place. My disenchantment became such that I was planning to ask to be relieved of my duties as a counselor and return to teaching. Fortunately for me, however, 'during that same year I started a doctoral program at Stanford University, where I was exposed to behavioral counseling and finally received training in a systematic approach to helping people change their behavior.

Training in behavioral counseling provided me with much more than the learning of specific counseling techniques, such as reinforcement, modeling, desensitization, behavior rehearsal, and the like. Most important, I feel, is that it provided me with a way of conceptualizing client problems in ways that enabled me to do something about them. I no longer looked for sickness; I looked at what the client could do, what he wanted to do, and what it was in his environment that was maintaining his present behavior. In addition, I learned that my role as a counselor carried with it the responsibility of helping to prevent problems from occurring, as well as that of improving the decision-making skills of our clients.

We must look very closely at what we are doing in society and in education to promote the very behaviors that we, as counselors, are asked to change! In other words, we must ask ourselves how it is that kids learn that they do not have self-worth, that they are "emotionally disturbed," and that they are "dummies." We cannot follow the examples of our predecessors in psychology and psychiatry, who emphasized diagnosing and locking up the individual rather than trying to do something about those practices in society that promote these and a multitude of other deviant outcomes.

We can all profit from rereading some of the ideas of John Dewey, who put great emphasis on the child's environment—that which the individual is allowed to do is what he learns. To paraphrase Postman and Weingartner (1969), in their provocative book, *Teaching as a Subversive Activity,* each of us learns to see, learns to feel, and learns to value. What perceptions we hold, what attitudes we assume, and what sensitivities we develop are learned because our environment permits or encourages or insists that we learn them.

PREVENTING PROBLEMS

Does our environment encourage a love of learning, or do we quickly extinguish the inquisitiveness and explorative behaviors of children? To tell a child he should enjoy learning is silly; any sensible person knows it is how and what you have a child *do* that will determine his attitude and feelings for learning.

Much that is done in our schools in the name of education, for example, constitutes a far greater crime than anything done by individuals who react against those practices, or who fail to respond to them at all. We are constantly diagnosing students in our grouping practices. We are grouping kids in special education; we are now even grouping kids who are "emotionally upset" or "emotionally disturbed." We are even grouping kids in the first and second grades! Contrary to a vast amount of evidence (cf. Bandura, 1969) indicating that such practices do more harm than good (if you want kids to learn to behave "normally," you expose them to normal behavior), we still diagnose and group kids—probably more for the sake of ease in school management than for increasing the learning of the students. Too often, I think, we *make* our "dummies" and our "emotionally disturbed" children. We teach them to behave in abnormal ways because those are the models to which we expose them, and all too often it is only the deviant behavior we reward by attention. If we exposed such children to normal behavior, treated them as "normals," and expected normal behavior from them, they would more often behave normally.

Most of us are no doubt familiar with the Rosenthal studies (1969), in which teachers at the beginning of the year were given very positive impressions of some students (higher IQ's, etc.) and actual information for other students, who had been previously matched by such factors as IQ's and achievement levels. At the end of the year, all students were retested, and those for whom teachers had been given higher expectations demonstrated significantly higher IQ's and achievement levels than did the other students, for whom teachers had correct information. Remember, they were matched at the beginning! It seems to me that the principle involved here is very important to preventing problems. If we give teachers and others positive expectations of children and then find subsequent positive changes in the students' behavior, what happens when we group kids into classes such as "mentally retarded," "socially and emotionally disturbed," and the like? The power of positive thinking, as Maltz points out so well in his book *Psychocybernetics* (1960), is indeed powerful.

A good illustration of this can be seen in an experience that I had in the same junior high school I mentioned in the case of Bob. Before Rosenthal's study was published, another counselor and I carried out a study very similar to his. Because we were upset over the grouping practices set up by the district, we wanted to obtain some data from which to argue against the prescribed policy. During my first year of counseling at this school we had 13 levels, in which students were grouped according to IQ and achievement scores. One day a teacher came to me and said, "Ray, you have Joe _____ in my class and he is an 8-8 and you have him in 8-7." When I asked what the difference was, she could not tell me; all she knew was that he did not belong in the 7's. This experience prompted me to test out some of the same hypotheses that Rosenthal subsequently tested. In this particular area of California it was not unusual to have 5 or 10 new students every day, and on the opening day of this particular year we had 115 new students who had not been previously registered. The usual procedure was to give each new student an intelligence test and an achievement battery in addition to a half-hour individual interview. After testing each of these students and matching them as closely as possible in terms of IQ and achievement, we raised the data on one group and placed them in classes three levels higher than they normally would have been programmed. At the end of the year, the students whose test data had been so raised scored as a group significantly higher on the reading section of the California Achievement Test than did the other students, who were matched but whose test data were not changed.

Another example of what can occur when we stereotype students by grouping is an experience rather close to home for me. My wife and I invited her sister to stay with us for a semester. Linda was a junior in a large high school in Seattle, and we thought that a semester in California would be an excellent experience for her. Linda had been receiving B grades in English, but after coming to California she began getting D's. Because I had told her parents that we would supervise her schoolwork, we were more than concerned with the low grades she was receiving in English. First I did the "normal" thing; that is, what most of us do. I lowered my own anxieties by "getting after her" for not working. It failed to help. I then tried to help her in the way parents often do; I took over. The course was in writing themes, and I began correcting any mistakes and making suggestions. Still the grades she received on her themes were D's. The next theme I did completely myself, and if anything got me through graduate school it was the fact that I got my highest grades on term papers. Anyway, Linda got a D— on the paper I had written. That minus really did it. Getting a little more than upset, I had Linda rewrite the paper three times exactly as she had handed it in. I then took a copy to each of three teachers in a different school. One was Phi Beta Kappa in English and was teaching the subject at the time; one had been an English teacher; the third was an English major in her first year of teaching, but not teaching English. I asked each teacher to read and grade the paper. I told them only that a junior in high school had written the paper and that there was a disagreement as to its grade. One teacher scored the paper A+, one A, and one A—. In fact, one teacher said, "I don't see how a junior in high school could have written such a sophisticated paper." This was the same paper that Linda's teacher had graded D—. I made an appointment with the teacher and proceeded to confront him with the situation. As I recall, he said something like, "It's not my fault, Mr. Hosford, it's the counselors. Linda was programmed into this class and I thought she was also a Track-3 student." I said to myself, and wished I had said it out loud, "My God, what happens to other students in Track-3 who try and do not have parents or others concerned enough to attempt to change the situation." The teacher went on to tell me that these students cannot learn. He had a set about these students before they ever set foot in his classroom. If we as counselors remain passive about such practices, we are doing little in the name of preventing problems.

We live in a society that relies too much on grouping individuals into manageable units. We group the Negro, the Chicano, the culturally deprived. In other words, we stereotype them. We tell them, in effect, we know all about you from the group to which you belong. Somewhere in all of this grouping the individual gets lost. Or, what is worse, he begins believing that what is thought to be true of the group is also true of him. Is it any wonder that students often give up before they even start?

Not too long ago funds were made available by several states to set up special and separate programs for the "emotionally disturbed." From what we know in research in learning, much of what we learn is acquired through imitation —in other words, learning by emulating the behavior of others. Nonetheless, we take "emotionally disturbed" kids, separate them from those who demonstrate normal behavior, and then expect them to learn normal behavior. Even mental hospitals are finally learning that placing "well" individuals in with others who demonstrate psychotic behaviors serves to create more "psychotic" behaviors rather than to help the persons act normally.

I often recall my first experience with group counseling, which serves as a case in point. The school district in which I worked was launching a program of group counseling. I was asked to sit in with a psychologist and observe his group counseling, and then to implement a similar program with our counselors. What the psychologist did, I'm afraid, was and is all too typical. With the help of classroom teachers he identified some students as "emotionally disturbed" and put them in a group. (Most of us now realize this does not work in groups. One cannot put all "emotionally disturbed" or academic under-achievers in a group and expect them to learn to achieve and behave normally.) As the group started out, I was somewhat dismayed. The counselor was very permissive—to the extent that I saw students get up and pull down the blinds in the room, turn off lights, and perform other behaviors of a similar nature. One student even got on top of the table and walked around. All of this did not take place the first day, of course, but things got progressively worse. Now as I look back on what was happening, it is evident to me that each of these students was learning from the others atypical or deviant behaviors that they had not learned beforehand. What they learned from the group counseling was how to become more and more "emotionally disturbed." Near the end of the year, I was observing a greater frequency and variety of deviant behaviors and hearing four-letter words that only a few years ago would have shocked most of us. I decided to question the psychologist about what I perceived as a gradual worsening of the situation. On the contrary, I was told, these students had these aggressions within themselves and the free atmosphere of the group counseling served as a way of getting them out. Furthermore, he related, letting the students perform as they felt was an excellent method of diagnosing their problems. I had thought Freud's hydraulic-energy model was shown to be erroneous years ago. Rather than serve as a therapeutic release valve, the group sessions were helping the students to learn a few four-letter words heretofore not in their vocabularies as well as to perform a greater variety of deviant behaviors. In order to get the reinforcement from the others in the group, members had to display a more deviant behavior than those performed by the other members.

The medical model of viewing behavior in terms of sickness, and proceeding by means of diagnosis, labeling, and treatment, is not only inappropriate for psychological behavior, but has served to keep counseling from being the effective service it ought to be. Far more important than diagnosing is helping a client determine where he wants to go, what he wants to change about his behavior. We may explore for weeks, even months (psychoanalysts prefer years!), and perhaps still not discover why an individual behaves the way he does. We can, of course, put together a lot of psychological gobbledygook to "explain" a client's behavior—and believe me, this is done every day—but such "diagnoses" and classifications are usually little more than educated figments of the counselor's imagination. Instead, we should help clients set up a model for themselves in terms of what they would like to be like, and what they would like to be able to do differently, as a result of our counseling. We often spend more time trying to show ourselves and the client that he is sick than we do in helping him learn not to be sick.

Another area in the schools which needs the attention of counselors and those concerned with preventing psychological problems is that of grading practices. I wonder why we have to grade students relative to some group. Our objective in education should be to help students learn to learn and get the most out of their education. If we were to take each child where he is, set up objectives with him that he needs to accomplish, utilize strategies and experiences specifically designed to help him achieve these objectives, then arrange for periodic success and reinforcement as he makes progress toward these outcomes, and evaluate his performance in terms of charting his progress, he would not only learn a lot more—he would enjoy doing it. An example of what can happen when students are rewarded for any improvement, rather than compared against a group norm, is another case that is rather close to home for me. When my daughter Jackie was in kindergarten, her teacher wanted to hold her back because she was not ready for the first grade. The main problem, according to the teacher, was that Jackie was not well coordinated and therefore too immature to learn to read in the first grade. The teacher did not know at the time that my daughter had a "lazy" eye, which in combination with her left-handedness made it almost physically impossible for her to see what she was drawing as she drew it. The teacher did have some dissonant information, something to which I usually pay little attention; Jackie had had an intelligence test, and the teacher could not understand why a girl with such a high IQ did not have better coordination. We were moving across town and decided to let Jackie go on to the first grade without mentioning any of this to her new teacher. This teacher had a program wherein she sat down with each student once a week to set up objectives that the student was going to work on for that week. Some would work on behavior, while others chose academic improvement or one of a multitude of other areas. My wife and I encouraged Jackie to work on some objective in reading. For motivation, the teacher had a treasure chest in the back of the room. A big gold key was required to open it. Every student who showed evidence that he had achieved some success towards his objective was given the key by the teacher, and was able to pick out anything he liked from the treasure chest. Jackie, who a few months earlier was to have remained in kindergarten because she was not ready to read, completed the first-, second-, third-grade readers and was into a fourth-grade text before her first year of school was over. Why? I think it was because this teacher set up some objectives with Jackie and then Jackie was left on her own. She was not compared to the rest of the group. The success she got was relative to her own progress. Any work she did was rewarded if she improved from where she was before. She did not encounter the aversive experience of working hard only to find out that she was not to be rewarded because she did not do as well as some of the others in her class.

I think there is an important point here for counselors. We must look closely at what we are doing in the schools, in the name of grading and in the name of learning, that does not foster learning and certainly does not foster good mental health. We are all too often guilty of making our dummies in the schools just as much as we make our achievers. Few of us would like to "bang our heads against the wall" day in and day out and never see anything but a D or F. Yet we wonder why such kids are not motivated to want to learn.

These examples have illustrated but a few of the practices in counseling and education that often promote rather than reduce anxieties, tensions, aggressions, and other maladaptive behaviors. There are many others. One-third of the behavioral counselor's job is committed to this area—changing practices in society in general, and in schools in particular, that promote feelings of inferiority and limit progress toward self-realization.

DECISION MAKING

A second area with which behavioral counselors are concerned is that of decision making. I think we would all agree that one of the major problems for which people need and seek counseling is that they cannot make decisions in a wise and rational way. Many people make their decisions haphazardly, without any consideration of the process involved. Some go about the process impulsively, without any thought to possible other actions they might take that could bring about more positive consequences. Nor do they take the time to consider the potential consequences of any alternatives they do consider. A good decision is one that is made with knowledge of facts and one's values, along with the consideration of possible alternatives and the consequences of each course of action. For quite some time, counselors have heard that one of the major purposes of guidance and counseling is to assist students in making educational and vocational decisions. At the same time, counselors, parents, and, above all, students are beginning to question the efficacy of what we call traditional counseling. Most of us have read Scott's pamphlet *So You Are Going to College* (1967), in which he cautions parents and students not to rely on high-school counselors, since about two-thirds of the students in a survey of opinion about preparing for college named their counselors as the person who gave them the worst advice, indicating that their counselors were, among other things, generally ill informed. We could, of course, argue the design and validity of Scott's study; it does have flaws. But that is not the point. More important are the reasons why Scott was able to get this type of response in his study, and it seems to me that the answer lies in the fact that for far too long we, as counselors, have been product-oriented rather than process-oriented. That is, we have been concerned with the client's making the "right" decision, and have done little to involve him in the important experience of learning the steps involved in making wise decisions.

Here again, if we accept Webster's definition of *humanism* as referring to the "dignity and worth of man and his capacity for self-realization through reason," the behavioral approach offers the most humanistic solution to the problem of decision making. If, as Ivey (1969) suggests, the self-actualized person is one who "can generate alternative behaviors in a given situation and can 'come at' a problem from different vantage points or theoretical views as he receives environmental feedback," then the self-actualized person has a maximum choice of alternatives for his behavior. This is the goal of the behavioral counselor.

An illustration of a man who had good counseling and learned how to make rapid decisions can be seen in this often-quoted example. Once a married man took his mistress into the woods, where they dallied a while to do the things that married men take mistresses into the woods to do. Unfortunately, he was seen by the village gossip. The man's immediate reaction was to define his problem. He said to himself, the gossip will surely tell my wife so I must stop the gossip. However, he knew that to stop her was impossible, short of murder, because she would spread the word regardless of anything he could do. Because he had had good counseling and had learned how to make decisions, he surveyed all the alternatives available, considering the possible consequences of each until he arrived at a workable solution. He quickly sent his mistress away. He raced home and took his wife for a walk in the woods, at the very same place, for the very same purpose. And the next day, when the village gossip ran into his house to tell his wife what she had seen, his wife just smiled and looked away. The implication is, of course, that counselors should be more interested in helping patients learn how to solve problems for themselves than in reaching some broad, undefined goal.

We have a very complex theory of guidance, but we need some new practices that are based on research and learning. I have been counseling a man and a woman who are about at the point of divorce. During our first interview, all the wife could talk about was the fact that her husband did not demonstrate to her that he loved her. And in the course of the interview it became very clear why he did not love her any longer. She was engaging in all of the behaviors that would make anyone not love another person. She was trying everything in her power to get him to say that he loved her, when what she needed was some good old-fashioned learning: learning of what behaviors to engage in, learning how to behave in the ways that would result in the kind of love she wants. What I am attempting to do now is to help her learn how to engage in the behaviors that will lead to the type of response she wants from her husband so that, in time, she will have a better image of self. That is, instead of simply giving advice, instead of simply being prescriptive, I am attempting to help her learn and put into practice the behaviors necessary to solve her problem.

The same holds true in any kind of counseling, including counseling in the schools, where our concern should not be focused on the product, not on making sure that Johnny goes to Stanford or Harvard, but on making sure that John has learned how to make his own decisions. And there are many things that a counselor can do to help people acquire the behaviors involved in good decision making. Systematic positive reinforcement (see, for example, Krumboltz & Schroeder, 1965; Krumboltz & Thoresen, 1964; Ryan, 1963, 1968; Thoresen & Krumboltz, 1967), social modeling (cf. Krumboltz & Thoresen, 1964; Krumboltz, Varenhorst, & Thoresen, 1967; Thoresen & Krumboltz, 1968; Thoresen, Hosford, & Krumboltz, 1970), experience tables and knowledge of success probabilities (cf. Yabroff, 1969; Gelatt, 1964), simulated vocational problem solving (Krumboltz & Sheppard, 1969; Varenhorst, 1969), and self-directed decision-making programs (Magoon, 1969) are all procedures that have been shown to be highly effective in helping clients learn more effective methods of making life's decisions.

What we need to do is to move ahead. We need some innovation in the new revolution of counseling. And we need to get back to some good common sense, systematically applied. We need more focus on helping people learn the behaviors necessary for functioning as happy and successful individual human beings, and less focus on worrying about the "sicknesses" that have led them to us for help.

CHANGING BEHAVIOR

The third job of a behavioral counselor is changing behavior—i.e., behavior modification. We now have procedures available that are not just based on philosophy, but have been scientifically demonstrated as effective in helping clients change a variety of behaviors. As I pointed out above, I was first exposed to these techniques in the doctoral program at Stanford. Since then I have tried them out with elementary, junior-high, and high-school students, with youngsters in a guidance clinic, with college students, and with adults in my private practice. And I have found that they work.

During one of my first years in elementary-school counseling, we had a little boy who threw tantrums on the playground. Whenever Bobby did not get his own way, he would start kicking, yelling, and screaming. When his teacher came to see me to ask what she or I could do to help him, I asked if I could observe him on the playground and in class before we decided on a course of action. I went out on the playground and observed Bobby while the same teacher was on yard duty. It was easy to see what was maintaining Bobby's behavior. Whenever Bobby was not fast enough to get the ball, or when someone took it from him, he refused to play and often started crying, yelling, and/or kicking people. Each time his teacher went over very quickly, and very lovingly got Bobby to quiet down. Although this sounds good, all the teacher was doing was reinforcing the very behavior she wanted to get rid of. Because the teacher requested my help, she was, in effect, my client. Thus I sat down with her and explained in terms of learning how this boy was learning to throw tantrums. We also got the mother in. She was divorced (which is usually enough to establish the "cause" for many counselors). We discussed Bobby's tantrums, and it became evident that the mother was also reinforcing him in a manner similar to that of the teacher. She could not get him to go to bed at night with the light off and was lying down with him until he fell asleep. When I asked her if she wanted to do this, she replied, "No! Of course not." When I asked why she did it, she said, "Well, he yells and screams." I explained to both the teacher and the mother how we might arrange the environment in such a way that Bobby would not gain attention when he displayed inappropriate behavior. I asked her to go into his room each night, turn out the light, tell him that he was a big boy now and could sleep with the light off, and then go out and close the door. I even suggested that she turn the television or stereo up if Bobby's yelling upset her. What had been happening was that when the mother had tried similar procedures, Bobby would yell loud enough and long enough to make her call his father, who lived several miles away, to help her do something with Bobby. The boy had had some psychiatric help, but the mother said she gave up when she did not see any change. When the teacher asked what she might do, I suggested that she ignore his antics on the playground by busying herself with others and just ask him to wait when he approached her crying or screaming. But I also suggested that both his mother and his teacher reward him with attention (pats on the back, smiles, and hugs) when he played well, went to bed without yelling, and so on. I suggested that the teacher just ask him to leave the classroom and signal the office for one of us to come down and get Bobby. He was then to sit in the counselors' or nurse's office with no punishment. Within a very short time Bobby changed remarkably. Again, we might ask if Bobby were emotionally disturbed or upset. I don't think so. I think he had just learned that throwing tantrums paid off more for him than behaving in other ways. This example shows one way a behavioral counselor might proceed. In this case we merely changed the contingencies of reinforcement, which were maintaining the behavior. By changing the behavior of the teacher and the mother, we in effect changed Bobby.

In a second case, the student sought my help. Mickey was a shy girl, who came to me because she "froze up" while speaking before the class. She related that she had been asked to give a book report, and when she got up in front of the class her mouth opened and closed but nothing happened. I noticed from reading her cumulative folder that one teacher had written, "Do not ask Mickey to speak in front of the classroom; she gets very anxious and tense." When I observed her in class, I noticed that she spoke up very well while sitting in her seat. The problem had been going on for three years, and no teacher had asked her to give any oral reports because of her anxiety. After discussing the problem with Mickey and asking her what she would like to be able to do (which, she said, was "not to get so nervous"), I met with her and her father to explain our course of action. In counseling we refer to the process as "systematic desensitization." To her father I related that we were going to practice in my office, step by step, each part of giving oral reports. Then we would try it on a graduated basis in the classroom. At no time, I related, would Mickey be asked to talk before any group if she felt anxious. I arranged with her teacher to assign Mickey to a small social-studies group, which was to give its presentation orally to the class. In this case, however, Mickey was only to point on a map to those areas about which the group members were talking. She did not have to talk. Gradually, over a period of time, the teacher and two students intentionally involved her more and more in the discussions. In my office Mickey practiced systematic relaxation and the imagination of progressive steps involved in speaking in front of the class. I did not have her imagine herself speaking before the class until she was able to imagine a variety of other, less anxiety-provoking behaviors associated with speaking before groups. At the end of the year, Mickey was one of the few students in her class who volunteered to give a speech for parents who would be at the school and in the classroom for the culminating activities. Again, I would like to make the point that Mickey was not ill in any sense. She had just learned some inappropriate behavior in the same way that others learn appropriate behavior. My role as the counselor was to help her unlearn the inappropriate behavior and learn what she needed to solve her problem.

The reader might think me emotionally involved, and I am! So often is behavioral counseling contrasted with other approaches, which are called humanistic. Similarly, the words *manipulative* and *mechanistic* are referents used by some counselors to describe behavioral counseling, particularly with regard to the third area of concern for the behavior counselor, behavior modification. I doubt if I could do better than to repeat Ullmann's answer (1969) to the use of such adjectives to describe the behavioral approach. He suggests that the problem is caused more by "a mechanistic, uninsightful view of the application of behavioral concepts" than by any simplistic or mechanistic aspect of the counseling procedures utilized. To equate the characters in Skinner's *Walden II,* Orwell's *1984,* or other such fascinating works with the end-products of behavior modification is to look at only one extreme of such procedures. Such an analogy is not unlike those used by extremist groups in equating sex education with fornication in the classroom. As a behavioral counselor I am an applied behavioral scientist. This does not mean that I have to negate any humanistic qualities. As Woody (1969, p. 95) says, "Quite the contrary. Rather [I] must strive systematically to integrate behavioral science principles as manifested in behavior modification techniques into [my] previously established human relations context."

Any treatment, however, if potent enough to begin with, can do damage. I cannot deny that behavioral counseling is manipulative. Nor can others refute the same charge for their counseling approaches. As I have said before (Hosford, 1969a, p. 26):

Rogers' phenomenology is just as manipulative as Krumboltz's or Skinner's behaviorism. None of us is beyond the reach of controlling techniques; people constantly control and manipulate each other by words and gestures. The techniques used by governmental, religious and educational institutions to control human behavior are powerful indeed. The by-products of such control, much of which is accomplished by aversive means, can be very detrimental, causing such negative responses as fear, anxiety, depression and anger, to name a few.

The important point is not whether counselors should manipulate clients—all forms of counseling are manipulative—but rather that counselors should constantly be aware of the fact that, by the very nature of counseling relationships, they are manipulating their clients, and therefore should use this manipulation to achieve the goals desired by their counselees.

Many other misconceptions about behavioral counseling need clarification, and an adequate discussion of each would merit a separate essay. While I think many misconceptions may be justified, if only by lack of knowledge, others are tied to issues that are nothing more than semantic word games for which answers cannot be gained. To waste our time debating whether it is a "symptom" or behavior with which the behavioral counselor is dealing is irrelevant. Proof one way or another is impossible, and for counselors to dwell on such issues is to keep us from finding new and more effective ways for helping people. Nevertheless, some clarifications of points of view are needed lest we reject something before we understand it. Probably the most misunderstood is the importance of the relationship to the total counseling process. Some counselors believe that the use of external reinforcements is often the extent of behavioral counseling. In reality, the use of a variety of reinforcements, counselor- and self-administered, may represent only a small part of the behavioral counselor's involvement (see, for example, Krumboltz & Thoresen, 1969). Just as behavioral counselors do not have exclusive rights to systematic reinforcement or other behavior-modification techniques, Rogerians and other evocative counselors do not have sole title to the behaviors associated with establishing a close counselor-client relationship. Behavioral counselors can be, and often are, just as warm and accepting as counselors utilizing other modes of counseling. Indeed, we are naïve if we think clients will relate their problems to counselors who are cold and unaccepting in the relationship. How else can we learn and understand what it is that the client desires to change about his life? The fact that the counselor often serves as an important model for the client would also suggest that he should demonstrate many of the behaviors associated with a good relationship if any emulation on the part of the client is to occur. On the other hand, we are equally naïve if we believe that the establishment of a warm, accepting relationship is sufficient in itself to bring about the change in the client's behavior for which he sought counseling. It is better, I believe, to view the relationship not as counseling or psychotherapy per se, but as one ingredient, and an important one, of the total counseling process.

It would be well for all counselors to be cognizant of the contingencies of warmth, acceptance, and similar counselor-relationship behaviors, and how they influence the client's subsequent verbalization and other behaviors. Few events are as reinforcing for many people as the finding of persons who listen and respond warmly to their concerns. To use accepting responses indiscriminately may well serve to promote the very behavior that the client needs to extinguish. A warm, positive relationship, in which the counselor is ignorant of his controlling effect on the client, represents potentially greater manipulation, less humanism, and possibly greater detriment to the achievement of the client's desired goals than do techniques used openly and specifically to achieve a solution to the client's problem. On the other hand, a warm, positive relationship, in which the counselor is aware of his controlling effect and uses it to reach goals both he and the client have agreed upon, constantly evaluating results and adapting procedures as needed, represents a powerful means in helping the client acquire the behavioral change he desires. I often wonder how many people develop cases of hypochondriasis because some accepting counselor or medical doctor responded more warmly to their complaints and "sick talk" than to client discussions of what they could do to overcome their problems! Similarly, how many individuals in group counseling engage in "emotional pornography" (taking off their "emotional clothes," i.e., defenses) for the reinforcement they get from other members in the group.

It has not been possible to consider fully all the jobs of a behavioral counselor as I see them. Nor have we more than touched on the basic issues and misconceptions which some raise about the approach. I do think it is important to realize, however, that behavioral counseling does not replace traditional counseling. Rather, it supplements it. The behavioral counselor is, in effect, "a scientific humanist concerned with theory but more concerned with determining effective procedures for helping people [Hosford, 1969a, p. 95]." Indeed, as Krumboltz points out (personal communication, 1970): "We are all after the same things—helping people do what they want to do. While some may call it self-actualization, we may prefer to look at it as helping clients acquire (i.e., learn) a maximum choice of alternatives for their behavior."

The business of helping people find solutions to problems they encounter in life is too important for us to rely solely on philosophic principles. To the behaviorist, it is not the theory, but the techniques and procedures the counselor uses, that in the end must account for any changes in behavior demonstrated by the client (Hosford, 1969a). Demonstrated effectiveness of a procedure is the main criterion determining whether it is used. Any technique "advocated without scientific evidence as to its merits and without constant efforts to improve upon it [is not behavioral] [Krumboltz & Thoresen, 1969, p. 4].

The old cliché, "Actions speak louder than words," is applicable. If I am a humanist, I am concerned about and committed to employing the most effective procedure for helping people solve the problems for which they seek counseling. And that is what behavioral counseling is all about.

REFERENCES

Bandura, A. *Principles of behavior modification.* New York: Holt, Rinehart and Winston, 1969.

Gelatt, H. B. *The influence of outcome probability data on college choice.* Unpublished doctoral dissertation, Stanford University, 1964.

Hosford, R. E. Behavioral counseling—A contemporary overview. *Counseling Psychologist,* 1969, **1**(4), 1–33. (a)

Hosford, R. E. Some reactions and comments. *Counseling Psychologist,* 1969, **1** (4), 89–95. (b)

Ivey, A. E. The intentional individual: A process-outcome view of behavioral psychology. *Counseling Psychologist,* 1969, **1** (4), 56–59.

Krumboltz, J. D., & Schroeder, W. W. Promoting career exploration through reinforcement. *Personnel and Guidance Journal,* 1965, **44**, 19–26.

Krumboltz, J. D., & Sheppard, L. E. Vocational problem-solving experiences. In J. D. Krumboltz and C. E. Thoresen (Eds.), *Behavioral counseling: Cases and techniques.* New York: Holt, Rinehart and Winston, 1969.

Krumboltz, J. D., & Thoresen, C. E. The effect of behavioral counseling in group and individual settings on information-seeking behavior. *Journal of Counseling Psychology.* 1964, **11**, 324–333.

Krumboltz, J. D., & Thoresen, C. E. (Eds.) *Behavioral counseling: Cases and techniques.* New York: Holt, Rinehart and Winston, 1969.

Krumboltz, J. D., Varenhorst, B. B., & Thoresen, C. E. Non-verbal factors in effectiveness of models in counseling. *Journal of Counseling Psychology.* 1967, **14**, 412–418.

Magoon, T. M. Developing skills for educational and vocational problems. In J. D. Krumboltz and C. E. Thoresen (Eds.), *Behavioral counseling: Cases and techniques.* New York: Holt, Rinehart and Winston, 1969.

Maltz, M. *Psycho-cybernetics.* New York: Essandess Special Editions, 1960.

Postman, N., & Weingartner, C. *Teaching as a subversive activity.* New York: Delacorte Press, 1969.

Rosenthal, R., & Jacobson, L. *Pygmalion in the classroom.* New York: Holt, Rinehart and Winston, 1969.

Ryan, T. A. The influence of counselor reinforcement on client decision-making and deliberating behavior. Unpublished doctoral dissertation, Stanford University, 1963.

Ryan, T. A. Effect of an integrated instructional counseling program to improve vocational decision-making of community college youth. U.S. Dept. of Health, Education and Welfare, Research Project No. HRD 413–655–0154, Grant No. 6–85–065. Bef., 1968.

Scott, J. F. So you're going to college. Public Affairs Pamphlet 394. (Obtainable from 381 Park Avenue South, New York, N. Y. 10016.)

Thoresen, C. E., Hosford, R. E., & Krumboltz, J. D. Determining effective models for counseling clients of varying competencies. *Journal of Counseling Psychology,* 1970, **17**, 369–375.

Thoresen, C. E., & Krumboltz, J. D. Relationship of counselor reinforcement of selected responses to external behavior. *Journal of Counseling Psychology,* 1967, **14**, 140–144.

Thoresen, C. E., & Krumboltz, J. D. Similarity of social models and clients in behavioral counseling: Two experimental studies. *Journal of Counseling Psychology,* 1968, **15**, 393–401.

Ullmann, L. P. From therapy to reality. *Counseling Psychologist,* 1969, **1**, 68–72.

Varenhorst, B. B. Learning the consequences of life's decisions. In J. D. Krumboltz and C. E. Thoresen (Eds.), *Behavioral counseling: Cases and techniques.* New York: Holt, Rinehart and Winston, 1969.

Woody, R. H. Behavioral counseling: Role definition and professional training. *Counseling Psychologist,* 1969, **1**, 84–88.

Yabroff, W. Learning decision-making. In J. D. Krumboltz and C. E. Thoresen (Eds.), *Behavioral counseling: Cases and techniques.* New York: Holt, Rinehart and Winston, 1969.

The Counselor as a Social Reconstructionist

Anthony C. Riccio

Ohio State University

The notion has prevailed for some time in educational circles that it is extremely important to know the *why* of things as contrasted to the *how* of things. Theory has been deemed far more important than practice. Status has been accorded to theoreticians; scorn has been heaped upon those members of the campus community—except for physicians of one kind or another—who are essentially concerned with practice. As an exercise in the pursuit of academic snobbery, the stress on theory has had few negative consequences. But as members of the campus community have become involved far and wide as consultants on the social problems besetting the nation, the focus on theory at the expense of practice has had consequences that are potentially damaging, especially in view of the national effort to improve the economic potential of disadvantaged youth in an attempt to win the war on poverty.

It has always seemed to me that far too many professorial types are primarily concerned with theory, and express little interest in applying their theories to the problems confronting mankind. They are involved in academic gamesmanship; they are not especially concerned with alleviating human misery or elevating the human spirit.

If these assertions have any validity, and I believe they do, then an interesting problem confronts counselor education. What relationship should exist between the theoretical postures of counselor-educators and the counseling practices of the students whom they prepare to work in school and agency settings?

Several sociologists, who have looked at the development of the guidance movement, have come to the conclusion that the preoccupation of counselor-educators with the individual qua individual, as contrasted to the individual as a member of a complex societal situation with a demanding and sanctioned set of circumstances, is close to being irrelevant in contemporary America. The basic criticism of these sociologists appears to center on the notion that guid-

313

ance personnel should be essentially concerned with the individual in *situation*, rather than with the individual in isolation.

A developing body of literature suggests that counselor-educators and the counselors they prepare must become agents of social reconstruction. For by attempting to alter society in terms of what they know to be the persistent needs of youth, they will make it much easier for the counseling process to be effective. How effective is counseling that assists a youth to arrive at a course of action that dooms him—because of societal sanctions—to a life of continual frustration? On the other hand, if the counselor helps to bring about a society in which due cognizance is given to the characteristics and legitimate needs of counselees, there is every reason to believe that the outcomes of counseling activity will be aided and abetted.

In fact, the theoretical orientation of a counselor-educator and the disciplinary components of his own preparation—both preservice and inservice—will in no small measure influence, if not determine, the manner in which he defines the problems he deems worthy of attack. As Haberman (1966, p. 48) has noted:

Researchers and writers define the disadvantaged using a variety of conceptual schemes. Sociologists concerned with group behavior and interaction tend to use concepts related to the process of alienation. The means by which selected individuals become detached from their primary groups and the processes by which subgroups become disaffected and move into conflict with the majority group are a major emphasis of those who study alienation. Psychologists and others whose major unit of study is the individual rather than the group are more likely to utilize the concept of dependency than alienation in delimiting the disadvantaged. Educators, forced to focus on symptoms rather than causes, will more likely use a term like "nonachieving."

A relevant concern dealt with in this essay, then, is the determination of an appropriate posture for the counselor-educator interested in having his students function as counselors who will help disadvantaged youth to become advantaged youth—youth for whom success in contemporary America will be a reasonable probability rather than an undreamed-of goal.

As I have thought about my responsibility to help my students become agents of social reconstruction, I have decided that I must find answers to two questions:

1. What assumptions must I make if I decide that counselors should become agents of social reconstruction?
2. Is there any evidence that counselors can indeed be successful agents of social reconstruction?

ASSUMPTIONS

The adoption of such a significant posture—that the counselor should indeed become an agent of social reconstruction—forces the counselor-educator and the counselor to challenge some basic notions, which have prevailed in the field of guidance and counseling for some time. For example, since the period of dominance of Rogerian thought in guidance and counseling, the notion that one set of values might be superior to another set of values has been a repugnant thought. At the same time, however, that leaders in guidance and counseling have blanched at the notion that some values were far superior in twentieth-century America to other values, they have conducted themselves in an entirely different manner from their preachments. Counselor-educators, by and large, have done what most middle-class Americans have done. They have attempted to work diligently, to get as much education as they are able to master, to earn as much money as possible so that they might reside in attractive homes in an outer city or suburban environment with good schools, which, in turn, might enable their children, early in life, to be exposed to and become enamored of the basic middle-class values, which counselor-educators have been pursuing for some time. The difficulty, of course, is that counselor-educators, especially Rogerians, have for some time been leading an incredibly schizoid existence. They have spent much of their professional time railing against the harmful aspects of the imposition of middle-class values in America, and have spent the remainder of their time striving mightily to lead middle-class lives. They have done this at the same time that they have preached the necessity of congruence between thought and action for the well-adjusted personality.

The first assumption I have to make, when discussing the possibility of the counselor-educator becoming an agent of social reconstruction, is that it is possible for the counselor-educator to be congruent, to establish a definite and demonstrable relationship between what he preaches as a counselor-educator and how he lives as a human being. I realize that this is a massive assumption. It certainly cannot be verified unless the counselor-educator is capable of conducting a thorough examination of conscience—with or without assistance.

I have conducted such an examination of conscience—without assistance—and have come to the conclusion that certain things I believe in, I believe in so thoroughly that I cannot do otherwise than attempt to communicate the importance of these beliefs to my students. For let us never forget that the counselor is simply a teacher with specialized training beyond the level of teacher certification—and that both are agents of socialization. I further concluded that to have an impact on my students, I must indeed demonstrate to them that the life-style I am recommending to them is one I am capable of following and indeed am following myself.

What are these values I believe in so strongly? *Essentially, they are middle-class values!!!*

I believe that every American should get as much education as he can possibly profit from. I believe it is the job of the counselor to help every youth share this belief and to help every counselee get as much education as possible. Clearly, education is relevant to our increasingly technological society.

I believe that every American should prefer working—if possible—to doing something other than work. I believe that counselors should focus much of their activity on helping counselees to share this belief, and further should help the counselee to acquire the experiences necessary for securing a productive position in our employment structure.

I believe that every American should prefer to be healthy to being other than healthy. I believe that counselors should support, for example, hot lunch programs for needy youth, as well as tax-supported programs for dental and medical care.

I believe that positions on social issues should be based on hard research data whenever possible. This belief implies that I must share with my students data I have gained from relevant reading. For example, do not the increased educational requirements demanded by industrial concerns have implications for counselees who are contemplating early marriage? Is there any relationship between age at time of marriage and the level of occupational placement of one or both marriage partners? If there is, does the counselor have an obligation to communicate the relationship to his counselees?

I believe that human misery and social injustice should be obliterated in America, the most bounteous nation on the face of the earth. I believe that counselors should do their utmost to alleviate human misery and correct social injustice in their work settings and in their local communities.

I believe that the individual as individual is becoming less important in contemporary America, and that man must be able to get along with his fellow man if he is to be relevant in modern society. The counselor, if he is to have an impact in his work setting, must learn to relate effectively with his co-workers. I do not believe that it is necessary for him to dilute his personal or professional integrity to achieve this end.

I believe that people involved in such helping relationships as counseling and teaching have a calling that is comparable to a divine calling. I believe it is their solemn duty to help improve society by being in the vanguard of society—not by simply performing what they perceive to be the will of a majority of their constituents, who are essentially concerned with preserving the status quo.

Finally, I believe that all Americans must regain a vision of the tremendous importance of the public school as the single most important vehicle making it possible for downtrodden groups to find their place in the sun, and in so doing acquire their rightful share of the bounty of this land.

The second assumption I must make is that my colleagues and my students are at least willing to listen to my arguments that the counselor can become much more effective if he participates in social reconstruction. Few people who have listened to my arguments that the counselor become an agent of social reconstruction have disagreed with my contention that, as our society becomes more open with respect to such things as increased career opportunities for minority-group youth, many more alternatives become legitimate outcomes of the counseling process. Many, on the other hand, have disagreed with me on the matter of the inculcation of the beliefs I have expressed above. In fact, on several occasions individuals have demanded: "Who do you think you are—God?" I really hate to have such questions asked, since I have a tendency to answer in the affirmative. But do we really believe, when we work with youth who are perhaps 15 or more years younger than we are, that we have not learned anything in these years that should be communicated to our counselees? Are we not fooling ourselves when we maintain that we do not really care what course of action a counselee decides upon, just so long as he has made his own decision? Certainly, the final decision on any matter is going to reside with the counselee, but I think a counselor is guilty of negligence if he fails to share with the counselee data relevant to a counseling concern that he has acquired from reading and from his own personal experience. Let us be honest with ourselves and with our counselees. We do care what kind of decisions they make. And further, we each have a notion of what is a more desirable or less desirable solution to a problem presented by a counselee.

The third assumption I must make is that the setting in which the counselor works, and the community in which he lives, will permit the counselor to function as an agent of social reconstruction. In the not too distant past, this would have been an invalid assumption. But in view of recent Supreme Court decisions, teacher militancy, and clerical concern with the Social Gospel, more counselors will indeed be permitted, if not encouraged, to become agents of social reconstruction. For the beliefs listed above in this essay are certainly in harmony with basic historical documents and social legislation in our country. In fact, it is somewhat amusing to watch the scurrying efforts of professors and school administrators, interested in presenting a favorable image to funding agencies, as they hasten to hire minority-group members to fill slots with some visibility attached to them. How can a work setting punish a counselor who is attempting to live up to the work setting's own expressed goals or operating policies?

EVIDENCE

Many of the recent decisions that have come forth from the Supreme Court have been objected to by some people, who felt the decisions were influenced strongly by evidence presented and witness given by social scientists rather than by legal experts. In fact, it has become commonplace for social scientists and educators to be in the forefront of much of the recent social legislation in this nation. On the local scene, school-counselors and counselor-educators have helped to bring about many social changes, which have increased broadly the quantity and quality of counseling alternatives now available to counselees. The examples cited below all deal with Central Ohio because I am most familiar with the situation in this setting, and have been intimately involved, as Chairman of the Education Committee of the Columbus Urban League, with bringing about some of these changes.

One of the most significant educational developments in Columbus in recent years has been the development and use of the Columbus Testing Profile (CTP). This profile makes it possible for school-counselors to share with interested parents a graphic portrayal of the student's performance on standardized measures. When parents have this knowledge, they are in a position to work hand-in-glove with the counselor in determining and reinforcing what the counselor, counselee, and parents believe to be legitimate expectations of the counselee. The CTP was developed by counseling personnel in the Columbus public schools after a group of parents became quite concerned that they had relatively little knowledge about the educational potential and performance of their children, and about how their children might best be encouraged to prepare themselves for meaningful participation in the American Dream. The parents were supported by social-work personnel in neighborhood groups, who aided in the presentations of their concerns that were expressed to the Columbus Board of Education.

The Columbus Leadership Conference, a group of downtown business and professional men, was concerned that many students were leaving school without an adequate appreciation of the employment opportunities that prevail in Central Ohio and the requirements for taking advantage of these opportunities. A counselor-educator worked with this conference in setting up and meeting with appropriate board of education members and school officials, and a plan now in operation in the Columbus public schools introduces students, by group-guidance methods, to a consideration of local employment opportunities and the requirements of same. Materials for this program were also developed by guidance personnel. The only reservation I have about this program is that many classroom teachers view it as simply another burden placed upon their already weary shoulders. Ideally, to my mind, such a program should be handled by the counseling personnel in the several schools. By virtue of their special training, they should be more qualified than the teachers to handle this task.

Another example of effecting social reconstruction is the work being done jointly by vocational educators and state-guidance supervisors in establishing and publicizing the need for increased opportunities in vocational education for Ohio youth. Members of these two divisions of Ohio government have in no small fashion made it possible for a curricular choice in vocational education to become one alternative to be considered in a vocational-counseling session. (Parenthetically, I might also note the fine work being done by our guidance supervisors in teaching school-counselors how to administer and use the General Aptitude Test Battery.)

One of the most impressive aspects of guidance programming in Central Ohio is the exceptionally comprehensive presentations made in Career Days and Higher Education Days. Counselors and counselor-educators in our region have done a good deal to help secondary-school students in Central Ohio become aware of many careers of possible interest to them. Many of these programs have former students of the school make career presentations to show that such careers are certainly within the realm of possibility for students attending these programs.

The most dramatic example of effecting social change in our area did not involve, to my knowledge, either a school-counselor or a counselor-educator, but rather, of all things, a researcher at the Vision Institute at Ohio State. This professor was shocked that minority-group members were not employed on a construction project at the university. He played a major role in filing a suit to halt construction until the discrimination was halted. A number of university personnel testified that minority-group youth, knowing they would have difficulty being employed as construction workers, could not entertain such careers as viable alternatives. The suit was won—despite the strong opposition of labor forces—and construction work is now an alternative that all youth might consider in counseling sessions.

The incidents related above all give positive testimony to the fact that social change can be brought about by interested people—but there is still room for much improvement in our metropolitan community. Let me cite a couple of examples. The Columbus Urban League, as one of its major functions, helps youth to secure employment. Yet we have a list many pages long of recent high-school graduates in our community who have been unable to pass the simple employment examinations administered by industries in our communities. What is most distressing about this list is that the Urban League comes into contact with only a small percentage of the graduates of our high schools. I am certain that counselors at the Ohio State Employment Service have also come into contact with many high-school graduates who cannot pass simple employment examinations. The matter, of course, is compounded by the evidence cited in the Motorola Case that there is little relationship between performance on employment examinations and ability to perform on the job. I am not interested in finding fault with our schools and teachers in this matter. I want to know why counselors have not established programs to coach students to pass these examinations. Certainly, we all know enough about testing to know that students can learn to become test-wise. Would not such coaching increase the effectiveness of counseling in both our schools and our employment agencies?

Another area in which much work remains to be done in our community centers on the concept of providing quality education for all of our students. Since almost every piece of educational legislation passed in the last 10 years has made some provision for the use or preparation of counselors as vital instruments in the war on poverty, it appears clear to me that the Congress of the United States sees counselors as being agents of change. I am not only talking about school-counselors, but also about counselors who work in state and federal agencies. What is the obligation of the counselor who finds his agency accused of racial discrimination in counseling and placement functions? What is the role of the school-counselor who realizes that programs of compensatory education have been abysmal failures, and that the results of experiments in which inner-city students have been transported to outer-city schools on a quota basis have been unbelievably promising? Should he exercise any pressure or give any testimony as to what kind of programs are needed to provide the quality education or counseling his school or agency should be involved in? I think so. In fact, to do otherwise is to deny himself the right to be called a professional.

In the preceding two paragraphs, I have tried to outline briefly some of the work that can be done locally by counselors who view themselves as agents of social reconstruction. But reality demands that we recognize that social reconstruction does not come about overnight. One of the major differences between the educational researcher and the educational practitioner is that the researcher can wait for all the data to come in before he makes recommendations, but the practitioner cannot put his clients on ice until he has sufficient data in terms of which to act. He must engage in action at the same time that he is gathering data, acquiring insights, or attempting to reconstruct society. The counselor must continue to work with individual clients while he is engaged in social reconstruction. Such being the case, what is the legitimate posture of the individual counselor who is interested in helping disadvantaged youth to become advantaged? Does any counseling approach offer much hope for success in this quest? I think one does. I have been tremendously impressed by the work being done at Stanford by Krumboltz (1966) and his students. These people have attracted a considerable amount of attention because in their research and writing they have emphasized doing something about specific counselee behaviors, have focused upon observable behaviors, and have compelled us to examine some of the treasured shibboleths that have been with us for a number of years (Burck, in press). They have studied test-anxiety, decision-making behavior, and information-seeking behavior. They have insisted that we demonstrate conclusively that counseling can make a difference. Krumboltz has stated that "counseling goals need to be stated as those overt behavior changes desired by the client and agreed to by his counselor. The counselor has an obligation to share in the determination of the client goals and would not be expected to work toward goals which were outside his interests, competencies or ethical standards [1967, p. 222]." It is readily apparent that Krumboltz expects the counselor to assume much more responsibility for what transpires in counseling sessions than have many other writers in the field. It is my belief that Krumboltz is terribly relevant to the needs of twentieth-century American youth, and to all recent federal legislation calling upon the counselor to help make our society a great society.

Let me explain. It seems to me patently clear that some of our youth appear destined to be losers in contemporary society; others appear to be almost certain winners. A relevant question for counselors is what can be done to help almost certain losers to become probable winners. I think that we must examine the differences between probable winners and probable losers, and then try to eradicate the differences between the two groups by remaking the probable losers to the image of the probable winners. The question, to my mind, is not whether we should do this, but rather *how* we can do it. This is what Krumboltz and his students have done. They have focused their work on how the laws of learning might be applied effectively to the specific problems defined by the counselor and his client. They appear to have restricted themselves to trying to produce specific changes in the behavior of clients—changes, however, that are requisite to becoming more relevant in contemporary society.

Effecting change in the behavioral patterns of counselees is, in a way, social reconstruction in microcosm. The counselor is in effect reconstructing the phenomenal field of the counselee. But before the counselor can even think of becoming a social reconstructionist in the broader sense, he must be convinced that change is necessary in our society. This conviction must involve more than an intellectual commitment—it must be a gut-level commitment acquired by personal experience with the children of the poor in their own community setting, as well as in the school or agency setting. For when the counselor experiences the lives of the poor, he can then and only then be willing to make sacrifices to help them desire to improve their condition. It is only then that the counselor will give personal witness to the need for change; only then that he will be able to say, with DeMott (1968, p. 65):

There are some things on earth that must be changed and that will be changed. They simply must and simply will . . . You know for the first time that certain events must occur and that you and others are going to make them occur, or at least are going to work to make them occur. You see that revolution is not a word but a pointing toward what obviously, absolutely must happen, and you are lifted up by this sight, by the freshening awareness of how criminally wrong a wrong can be *known* to be . . . .

If counselors are indeed to help shape the great society, they must be capable of feeling for their counselees what DeMott felt for his students.

REFERENCES

Burck, H. D. The counseling revolution: Promises and problems. *Guidance Journal,* in press.

DeMott, B. Encounter in Mississippi. *Saturday Review,* Jan. 20, 1968, p. 65.

Haberman, M. Guiding the educationally disadvantaged. In C. E. Beck (Ed.), *Guidelines for guidance.* Dubuque, Iowa: W. C. Brown, 1966.

Krumboltz, J. D. (Ed.) *Revolution in counseling: Implications of behavioral science.* Boston: Houghton Mifflin, 1966.

Krumboltz, J. D. Changing the behavior of behavior changers. In A. C. Riccio and G. R. Walz (Eds.), *Forces for change in counselor education.* Washington, D.C.: Association for Counselor Education and Supervision, 1967.

Issues

1. What would be the impact on the mental-health professions and their clientele if Gendlin's proposed use of conceptual knowledge were to be broadly practiced? What are the obstacles to such an acceptance?
2. Will behaviorism become the method of the future, thereby further technologizing (in contrast to professionalizing) practitioners, or does it have the potential for something else?
3. If one accepts the need for social reconstruction in areas particularly related to school populations, and if one further accepts the appropriateness of the counselor as an activist, how, where, and when does the professional acquire the judgment to distinguish between the role of provocateur and that of leader? Where, how, and when does the practitioner develop the skills for the role he chooses?
4. How does the concept of professional responsibility to the client relate to the concepts of behavioral manipulation, experiential therapy, and social reconstruction? When are these concepts related constructively? Is there a time when any or all of them are related destructively?

Annotated Readings

Bohn, M. J., Jr. Therapist responses to hostility and dependency as a function of training. *Journal of Consulting Psychology,* 1967, **31,** 195–198.

Therapist responses to a typical client, a hostile client, and a dependent client were studied as a function of the Ss' training. Ss were 18 advanced graduate students in a course in theories and techniques of psychological counseling. The course included didactic material with supervised experience in the form of role-playing, structured interviews, and practice counseling. Responses to tape recordings of these clients were obtained before and after the course and were scored for directiveness. Results showed Ss to be increasingly directive to the typical, hostile, and dependent clients, respectively on both administrations, and showed Ss to be less directive to all three clients on the second administration. The decrease in directiveness to the dependent client, however, was not significant. Implications suggested were that different clients elicit different responses from the same therapist, and that training may affect responses to hostility more than it affects responses to dependency.

Howard, K. I., Orlinsky, D. E., & Trattner, J. H. Therapist orientation and patient experience in psychotherapy. *Journal of Counseling Psychology,* 1970, **17,** 263–270.

The Therapist Orientation Questionnaire and the AB Scale were completed by 21 experienced psychotherapists. Scores based on these instruments were correlated with patient-experience-factor scores, derived from the Therapy Session Report questionnaire. Little relationship was found between these measures of therapist orientation and patient experience for the total sample. However, when patients were separated into more homogeneous diagnostic groups, some significant relationships emerged. Schizophrenics and anxiety reactions were most responsive, and personality disorders and depressive reactions least responsive, to the different therapist orientations. The element of therapist orientation that had most impact on patient experience was therapists' acknowledgement of countertransference potentials.

Stubbins, J. The politics of counseling. *Personnel and Guidance Journal,* 1970, **48,** 611–618.

The career of the counselor is influenced by the bureaucratic structure of his institution, whether secondary school, university, or public agency. Important elements in the client-counselor interaction are found in the limitations imposed upon the counselor by the values and modus operandi of the institution and its preconceptions of the client's problem. To cope effectively with such matters, counselors should be trained as social critics and should develop a greater awareness of how their professional roles are shaped by institutional power structures.

Woody, R. H. Psychobehavioral therapy in the schools: Implications for counselor education. *Counselor Education and Supervision,* 1969, **8,** 258–264.

Article develops two propositions: (1) counselors should be doing psychotherapy, and the most efficacious therapeutic approach for counselors is the integration of conditioning-based behavioral modifications and insight-oriented procedures—i.e., psychobehavioral therapy. Suggests a minimum two-year program, including self-understanding counseling—therapeutic experience.

Suggestions for Further Reading

Allen, T. W. Effectiveness of counselor trainees as a function of psychological openness. *Journal of Counseling Psychology,* 1967, **14**, 35–40.

Babbott, E. F. Counselor interns and sabbatical leaves. *School Counselor,* 1969, **16**, 398–401.

Bare, C. E. Relationship of counselor personality and counselor-client personality similarity to selected counseling success criteria. *Journal of Counseling Psychology,* 1967, **14**, 419–425.

Chenault, J. A proposed model for a humanistic counselor education program. *Counselor Education and Supervision,* 1968, **8**, 4–11.

Delaney, D. J., Long, T. J., Masucci, M. J., & Moses, H. A. Skill acquisition and perception change of counselor candidates during practicum. *Counselor Education and Supervision,* 1969, **8**, 273–282.

Gough, H. Some reflections on the meaning of psychodiagnosis. *American Psychologist,* 1971, **26**, 160–166.

Grossman, D. Of whose unscientific methods and unaware values? *Psychotherapy: Theory, Research and Practice,* 1968, **5**, 53–54.

Johnson, E. L. Existentialism, self theory and the existential self. *Personnel and Guidance Journal,* 1967, **46**, 53–58.

Kemp, C. G. *Intangibles in counseling.* Boston: Houghton Mifflin, 1967.

Lowe, C. M. The need of counseling for a social frame of reference. *Journal of Counseling Psychology,* 1968, **15**, 485–491.

Ofman, W. The counselor who is: A critique and a modest proposal. *Personnel and Guidance Journal,* 1967, **45**, 932–937.

Pietrofesa, J. J., & Van Hoose, W. H. Participant change during an EPDA institute: Personality, attitudinal, and learning dimensions. *Counselor Education and Supervision,* 1971, **11**, 147–152.

Pohlman, E. Counseling without assuming free will. *Personnel and Guidance Journal,* 1966, **45**, 212–216.

Thoresen, C. E. The systems approach and counselor education: Basic features and implications. *Counselor Education and Supervision,* 1969, **9**, 3–17.

Vontress, C. E. Cultural barriers in the counseling relationship. *Personnel and Guidance Journal,* 1969, **48**, 11–17.

Ward, E. J. A gift from the ghetto. *Personnel and Guidance Journal,* 1970, **48**, 753–756.

CHAPTER 8

Procedures in the Preparation Process

The process of learning to be a counselor or therapist is too often overburdened with tedium. Traditional methods of transmitting knowledge, in this field as in others, are too often prized without evaluation, and at the expense of innovation and improvement. On the other hand, change for the sake of change is equally likely to yield poor results. Energy is almost exclusively confined to the master's and doctoral programs, implying either that once a person has successfully completed a program he is educated for all time, or that his appetite for further professional growth has been so stimulated that no amount of service demands and/or human lethargy can deter him from further self-education.

There has been a great deal of concern in the field about ways to increase professional competence, and at the same time to provide opportunities for personal growth during the formal learning process and after. The availability of closed-circuit television has added enormous possibilities to the range of educational formats. So also have the treatment modalities themselves: group therapy, encounter groups, co-therapy, and so forth. The increase in types of professional placement opportunity has led many M.A. and Ph.D. graduates to seek further learning in specialized areas. The wealth of new societal complexities has greatly affected the quantity of material to be integrated and assimilated by today's mental-health professional.

This chapter brings together many suggested methods for preparing counselors and continuing their professional development. Hopefully the content will generate new interest and ideas.

The innovations in transmitting professional material detailed in this chapter are practical and therefore possible. They do much to involve the student in the process of acquiring learning—both experiential and theoretical. Cody details a variety of ways to utilize role playing in graduate preparation. Cottingham makes a point of stressing the great adaptability of case materials to suit a range of explicit needs. Gross maintains that the advantages to multiple supervision are both qualitative and quantitative. Kurpius cites significant research as the basis for the myriad uses of videotape, as both direct and supportive learning media. Lee suggests new ways for groups to be involved in both experiential and theoretical foundation building. Mowsesian proposes a program of continuing education that would sustain professional growth in the field and at the same time provide essential feedback to ongoing programs. Finally, Thrush recommends contemporary literature as an interesting, constructive, and enjoyable way to give practitioners an awareness of specific kinds of influences that the culture exerts on clients, and of a range of experiences and behaviors common to "real" people as well as fictitious characters. He includes topic references and a selected bibliography.

Role Playing with Stimulated Recall

John J. Cody

Southern Illinois University—Carbondale

Programs in counselor education face many problems. Perhaps none of these surpasses in importance the need to provide beginning counselors with practice in dealing on an individual basis with those who seek help. It is not unusual to find courses in counseling techniques, counseling theory, and counseling methods offered in a counselor-education program. What is unusual is to find a counselor-education program in which students have the opportunity to develop their counseling skills to a reasonable level through interaction with others in real or mock counseling settings. As might be expected, there is no cure-all for this dilemma. However, several proferred alternatives seem to provide a situation that will help students become better acquainted with the conditions of counseling. One such solution is role playing, accompanied by stimulated recall of the events in the practice counseling session.

PREPARATION FOR ROLE PLAYING

The term *role playing* is used in this essay in a very specific sense. It is intended to convey the idea that an individual assumes the role of another person and responds in that assumed role in a practice counseling setting. It should be noted that *role playing,* as used here, does not carry many of the psychological ramifications attached to it when attempting to modify personality through the utilization of the technique of having the counselee play another person's role. As described herein, the role-playing procedure is a technique employed to facilitate the counselor's learning in a practice counseling situation. In order to be effective, it must be combined with positive information based on experience and knowledge gained through course work. Role playing is not simply "I feel and go." It requires the individual to know something about human behavior, to be able to predict how people, given certain kinds of previous behavior, will perform under specific situations. Since none of us is born with

329

the knowledge of how others are likely to behave, we learn it from living, from observing, and from formal study. Role playing, in order to be effective, should be prepared for from the beginning of the counselor-education program. Students involved in developmental psychology, learning courses, and courses in personality should be made aware that these academic experiences give them a rich background for developing roles that can be portrayed in a practice counseling session. Nothing defeats role playing as quickly as the unprepared and untutored use of the method. A similar circumstance can be found in the use of films. Films may be a very effective means of helping students to learn in a classroom situation. It is unlikely that students are going to learn much from films unless they have been prepared to receive the film, and unless the instructor has gone over the film and can use some specific incidences from the film as a teaching aid. The teacher should also have a good idea of the concepts involved in the film, and either the recognition of agreement or disagreement between the concepts he wishes to get across and those touched on by the film. A similar situation exists in role playing. If a role playing situation is determined on the spur of the moment, or with little preparation on the part of the participants or the instructor, little value can be expected. Typically, people look to the role-playing technique as a quick means of providing instant subjects for counseling. This is far from true. If a counselor-education program intends to employ role playing, it must build it in as an integral part of the program from the very beginning of a student's course work. As an example, a person in a child-psychology course, a learning course, or a course in adolescent development might be required to develop two or three roles based on the principles or knowledge gained through his psychology-course experiences. One might take a course such as personality theory and devise a role based on course content. Personality theory affects a person's growth, as it affects the way a person thinks and behaves. A student might draw out of such a course a role or roles to be portrayed in a counseling-like setting. Perhaps an example will serve to illustrate this point more effectively.

A neophyte counselor might use information obtained from a course in learning. Having been exposed to the proposition that people may be a product of their reinforcement history, a student may decide to develop the role of a client whose specific behaviors can be attributed to his reinforced past experiences. Say that Mary, a 14-year-old high-school student, refuses to make choices between alternatives when requested to do so by her teachers or her parents. She responds only to direct questions or directions accompanied by some contingency related to failure to follow the directive. When Mary is asked to complete an assignment in her text, it is not even partially completed. When queried about the situation, she indicates that the task was not required. Similarly, when asked how she evaluates World War II and its effect on trade with England, her response is, "It was terrible." In order to get a response relative to trade with England and World War II, questions specific to relationships between identified aspects of the war and England are required. The student may develop a hypothetical situation of reinforcement of how such behavior began and how it is maintained. Principles such as extinction, competing stimuli, satiation, and schedules of reinforcement may be brought to bear on how Mary should and will behave in a counseling session.

With such information in mind, the counselor-student may begin to draw some inferences about Mary's behavior based on answers that might be drawn from questions similar to those that follow. How might Mary react to a query about what she thinks about her social-studies teacher? What kinds of behavior would Mary require of the counselor as reinforcement in order to produce the kinds of verbal or related behavior desired? In order to portray such an individual, would the role-player have to have some idea about what makes a human being tick? These three questions, and perhaps others as well, will require a good deal of thought and practice if the role of Mary is to be portrayed in a practice counseling session.

In another role, a counselor, Bob, has refused to follow any explicit directions. He apparently prefers to be directed by reason to nearly every activity. Before beginning work assignments in school, he wants reasons for the assignment and a description of how the assignment has meaning for life. From all indications, Bob requires a free atmosphere and a wealth of information before he begins work or makes a decision. His behavior was in this same pattern when he was asked to register for the courses he was to take in his junior year. The counselor-student learned through studying personality theories that an individual may become most productive if he is freed from threat in his environment. It is of greatest consequence to him as a role-player to require the counselor to provide that threat-free situation. In this, as in any other case, threat-free is interpreted by the client, and as a consequence almost any procedure the role-player might consistently require would be reasonable. In addition, the student may identify other aspects of Rogers's theory that would give him some guides to behaviors. For example, he would have to grapple with the question of defining positive regard. Perhaps some thought and clear writing would evoke a clearer depiction of the differences between understanding and empathy. Actualization and reacting as a whole organism could take on more precise meaning as the students tried to explore them in a role.

Given this state of affairs, the beginning student (role-player) should have some idea of how such an individual came to behave in this manner. Some inferences could be made about the way his parents acted toward or with him. The student role-player might want to ask such questions as: What kinds of friends would this individual be likely to have? What makes a person like this continue to behave in this way? What kind of atmosphere will be demanded from the counselor? These are just some of the questions that will enable a role-player to practice and perform consistently in a practice counseling session.

IMPROVEMENT OF COUNSELING SKILLS

Up to this point, role playing has been described in relation to a student employing knowledge gained in course work to formulate a behavior-set to be employed in practice counseling settings. Perhaps the fact that no research is available to either support or reject the notion that such practices aid the learning of subject-matter content reflects the state of empirical findings in this area. Although much has been said about role playing, little has been done to validate the outcomes claimed for it. It seems reasonable to contend that using information, even in a mock-up situation, provides an opportunity to test the learned notions against something other than claims of an author. Further, if there is anything to learning through concrete examples, role playing may have a good deal to offer. Even if this claim is sound, this specific outcome of role playing is secondary. The primary intent of such a practice is to provide practice counseling for beginning students in a counselor-education program. Pancrazio and Cody (1967) investigated one facet of this problem and concluded that this variety of role playing did little to affect beginning counseling students in recognizing appropriate counseling procedures.

In a practicum conducted by the author, counselors were found to lack skills in handling simple dialogue in counseling situations. As an example, most of the analyzed counselor-client excerpts depicted clearly that counselors tend to ask questions and then provide a set of answers for the subject to consider. In many cases the client picked a response indicated by the counselor apparently just to make his counselor feel good. Another area in which counselors were found lacking was the ability to make a clear statement to the client. It took as many as six restatements by the counselor each time he wished to communicate. An example was:

You really wanted to make your girlfriend jealous—*(pause)*—I mean you didn't want your girlfriend to take you for granted—*(pause)*—I guess you really want to hurt her —*(pause)*—you want to treat her as a friend, not a girl, or you treat her like any other girl—I guess I mean she really isn't your girlfriend in the sense of engaged, etc.

Among other results, one common peculiarity rising from the newest generation of counselors is the phrase "O.K., you know what I mean." In many cases this response follows a break in the counseling session, a direct question on the part of the counselee, or even a nonsense statement on the part of a counselor. This kind of "wastage" in a counseling session was overcome with practice gained by practice counseling with role-players. In other words, it seemed clear that many counseling skills are developed through supervised practice. In a simulated counseling session, a beginning counselor can develop a repertoire of responses that he might wish to employ. It also enables the counselor to gain confidence in his ability to respond to common or unusual events in the counseling session.

It was not uncommon to find serious errors in test interpretation, statements concerning legality of acts, and interpretation of institutional policies and requirements. This observation suggests that supervision and some assurance that the counselor can respond responsibly in a counseling session are essential before real clients are exposed to their practice.

STIMULATED RECALL

An additional feature employed with role playing to aid the neophyte counselor is stimulated recall. Kagan and Krathwohl (1967) employed the technique with live counselors using a videotape arrangement. Bloom (1954) employed a similar technique with beginning instructors. It is not a new approach to counselor education, but it does add a new dimension to role playing.

Stimulated recall is a technique that employs either audiotapes or videotapes to record (in this case) a role-playing session. A recaller, usually the practicum supervisor, queries the role-player and the counselor in separate sessions to ascertain in each instance the exact feelings and intent of both counselor and counselee during a counseling session. In order to save time, a sampling of parts of the interview seems most convenient. For effective change or even consideration of change on the part of the practicing counselor, review of selected samples of the interview seems most useful. One experienced supervisor can note quickly those areas where it is felt that the counselor has a weakness. This part of the interview can be the centrix of a supervisory session.

For another situation the supervisor might wish to bolster the counselor's confidence and select only those sections of the tape in which a reasonable degree of agreement will be found between counselor and role-player. The ultimate goal is to develop a counselor's skills to the point where his perceptions and intent are in agreement with what the role-player indicated were his expressed feelings or the intent of his statements. It should be noted that both the person playing the client and the counselor practice listening, restatement, and interpretation skills.

Once the students become acquainted with the recall technique, they can participate in the total process by going over tapes and stimulating recall of the situation with other role-playing clients and/or counselors. Through involvement of the students in the recall procedures, they receive the added experience of learning how others respond to specific situations. The recall technique adds another dimension to role playing, and together they provide a realistic substitute for the counseling of people genuinely seeking help.

The stimulated-recall procedure can also be used with genuine or role-playing counselors to investigate the process of counseling. One interesting approach, using genuine clients and stimulated recall, was conducted by Seymour Bryson (1972) in a study of the relationship of race to counselor and client understanding. Whenever a teaching technique can be employed as a research tool as well, the balance among practice, inquiry, and teaching has approached an optimal level.

It seems appropriate at this point to stress that all substitute procedures for the actual practice of interacting in the real situation fall short of perfection. However, since so little is known about the true impact of counseling on real clients, it seems imperative that the client be protected from possible harmful effects of interacting with an inept counselor. The hope is that counselors, upon completion of their program, would indicate that they had enough or more than a sufficiency of laboratory experiences in counseling. As it stands now, nearly all follow-up studies of counselor-preparation programs indicate that the student was shortchanged in this aspect of his program.

THEORETICAL REFERRENT FOR COUNSELING

In many situations, claims about one counseling methodology or another being reasonable for a training procedure, while others are not, detract from the usefulness of a training innovation. This should not be the case with role playing and/or stimulated recall as they are portrayed here. Whether or not a program is directed toward a Rogerian, behavioral, Adlerian, ecclectic, or other theoretical or practical point of reference should make little difference. It is not critical whether the program is structured to involve what has become for some the prestige level—personal counseling—as opposed to the supposed mundane level—educational and vocational counseling (or guidance, as others would have it). This outline of activity seems reasonable for each. No matter what counseling referent a program purports to emphasize, the student must be aware of its principles before it can be implemented. If a student is required specifically to identify in writing his frame of reference and the behaviors he will engage in as a result of his position, then the role-playing stimulated-recall procedure can have meaning. Supervisors and students will then know what is being attempted in the counseling session and how well the student implements his identified intent.

One important value of utilizing the student's statement about what he perceives to be counseling is that it provides a basis for evaluating this section of the training program. If a student identifies an acceptable or feasible method of interacting in a counseling session, it seems reasonable to infer that such statements can be used to determine whether or not the student is performing as indicated. A criterion of acceptable counseling skills can be identified by the supervisor, a supervisor and the student, or the student as to what will indicate the development of sufficient skill to complete a program. In this era of performance-referenced criteria as indicators of professional competence, the role-playing stimulated-recall techniques, along with predetermined behavioral reference-points, can constitute a formidable evaluation paradigm. If used along with grades in academic courses and the professional judgment of the supervisor, such an evaluation scheme would have few rivals.

A CAUTION

One exposure to a single form of role playing is not intended to make a counselor-in-training a person experienced in all forms of this art. A great deal of caution must be exercised so that students do not become bewitched by a limited use of this method and assume that they are now qualified to engage in the free use of the many forms of role playing. If anything, students should learn through personal experience that only with considerable preparation and cautious introduction can role playing be of much value. Perhaps such experiences will lead to the extinction of the notion that any class in the public schools is a suitable laboratory for experimenting with this activity. Counselor-students may learn on their own that attempting to depict another person may have negative as well as positive results. As an example, if a child finds himself unable to accept the behavior of another whose role he has assumed, he may reject this individual or individuals like him as a result of this experience. He may also grow to know the complexities of feelings and how these relate directly to behavior. However, such outcomes are not easily predicted. It is hoped that counselors-in-training will explore in detail the experiences they find beneficial and exciting. Programs that cannot offer such in-depth exploration, at both the academic and the experience levels, should be especially cautious about how role-playing procedures are introduced and how they are carried out.

SUMMARY

Role playing, supervised and based on a sound academic background in the behavioral sciences, is a reasonable experience for counselors in a professional preparation program. Such an opportunity would provide the experiences of developing, interpreting, and playing roles, as well as practice in counseling. By using stimulated-recall techniques, role-playing experiences can be made to resemble more closely the skills required in real counseling situations. Add to these procedures a precise statement of a counseling "position" and procedures related to it, and the basis for evaluation of this aspect of the program has been established. Similarly, a first step in developing performance criteria for professional activities will have been taken. Each of these recommended procedures is couched in a caution—role playing as it is described in this essay is only one aspect of the art. Such experiences are not intended to qualify counselors as experts in the use of role-playing procedures in anything other than practice counseling settings.

REFERENCES

Bloom, B.S. The thought process of students in discussion. In S. J. French (Ed.), *Accent on teaching: Experiment in general education.* New York: Harper & Row, 1954.

Bryson, S. Relationship between race of counselor and race of clients with level of understanding in an initial interview. Unpublished doctoral dissertation, Southern Illinois University, 1972.

Kagan, N., & Krathwohl, D. R. Studies in human interaction. U.S. Dept. of Health, Education and Welfare, Office of Education, Bureau of Research, Final Report, Project No. 5–0800, Grant No. OE 7–32–0410–270, 1967.

Pancrazio, J. J., & Cody, J. J. A comparison of role-playing and lecture-discussion instructional methods in a beginning course in counseling theory. *Counselor Education and Supervision,* 1967, 7, 60–65.

Using Case Materials in Counselor Preparation

Harold F. Cottingham

Florida State University

INTRODUCTION

The term *case materials,* as used in this essay, includes both written and taped materials that describe or illustrate counseling cases. In addition, materials that present the theoretical bases for selected practices with cases are identified. Reference to role-playing sources is not included since this topic is treated elsewhere.

This essay is organized into three major parts, treating, respectively, descriptive case materials, application of case materials to counselor education, and selected aspects of case materials use in training counselors. Descriptive case materials are classified by written and taped sources. The section on application of case materials considers the didactic, practicum, and experiential phases of counselor-preparation programs. Finally, the section on selected aspects of case material use examines briefly some theoretical, ethical, and practical problems.

DESCRIPTIVE CASE MATERIALS

Written Case Materials

The Case Study. *Case study* is a term used to describe the systematic organization of personal information describing an actual or hypothetical individual's involvement in a helping situation. In the preparation of counselors, case-study materials from both textbook and local sources are used. Typical of compilations of case studies in book form are publications by Rothney (1953), Lloyd-Jones (1956), Adams (1962), Callis, Polmantier, and Roeber (1955), and Dreikurs (1968). While these references contain some questions and discussion topics, their substance is mainly detailed case studies per se, selected to represent a variety of cases at different educational levels. Some references give greater emphasis to the construction of case studies and/or their use in counselor-preparation activities. Illustrative of this practice are books by Tollefson (1968), Rothney (1968), Bucheimer and Balogh (1961), and Ullman and Krasner (1965). The latter work is restricted to behavior-modification approaches. In the area of pastoral counseling, Aldrich and Nighswonger (1968) have developed a casebook.

Many single references, restricted to an individual case and developed in literary rather than academic style, are also available for instructional use. Titles that serve this purpose are Baruch's *One Little Boy* (1952), Green's *I Never Promised You a Rose Garden* (1964), and Axline's *Dibs: In Search of Self* (1966). In some instances, single case studies are designed to illustrate different educational problems, such as Gannon's *The Many Faces of Kevin Michael Pullen* (1968). For parents of exceptional children, useful case studies are found in Ross's *Exceptional Child in the Family: Helping Parents of Exceptional Children* (1964).

The Case History. The case history, rather than being composed of selected personal data, normally includes relatively complete historical information under several categories. Generally the case history is designed as a summary account of an individual's development to date, rather than for focus on a current situation or problem. Since most case histories are compiled with the needs of a specific individual in mind, the use of illustrative case-history materials in counselor-education instructional settings is limited.

Using case histories in the preparation of counselors may involve the discussion of anonymous or disguised local case histories taken from laboratory or practicum files. A modification of the approach is a case-history analysis proposed by Swenson (1968), who suggested a formula for looking at deviant behavior as equaling the ratio between one's stress and maladaptive habits and his strengths and adaptive habits. In turn, this formula, when applied to case-history data, permits a counselor to decide upon a level of therapeutic assistance. The use of literary sources describing actual case histories in life is illustrated in MacIver's *The Frog Pond* (1961).

Problem Cases. Problem cases are generally designed for instructional purposes, and consist of typical student cases built around types of problems or kinds of information. One feature of problem cases is the focus on specific aspects of the situation through questions or discussion points. Although these may be derived by counselors from local data sources, several published case collections are available. One such casebook is that of Womer and Frick (1965), who developed 25 cases illustrating various aspects of test-data use in counseling. Current journals such as *Elementary School Guidance and Counseling* occasionally have columns devoted to problem cases. Lloyd McGehearty is listed as the editor of the case-analysis materials in the March 1969 issue of this journal.

The case conference is a modification of case-study methods in which the emphasis is on treatment or change, as well as upon the grouping of historical data for diagnostic purposes. Case conferences also involve the physical meeting of individuals who confer regarding future action or problems of a particular individual. Case conferences may be limited to staff discussion for consultation, or may involve other school personnel or community agency representatives. On occasion the student or counselee may be asked to sit in on the case conference. Procedures for developing case conferences are described by Tollofson (1968).

Prepared Typescripts. In counselor-education programs, typescripts are literal transcriptions of tape-recorded counselor-client interviews. While they may include only actual conversation, they may also contain symbols used by the counselor in training to evaluate his responses. This may be done with a local system of coding for classification purposes, or may refer to such scales as the Porter or Truax classification schemes. While few, if any, published typescripts are available, many counselor-education programs make available model or sample typescripts in laboratory manuals or in practicum instructional materials.

Simulated Counselor Problems. Of a more innovative nature for counselor-preparation purposes are guidance (or counseling) procedures designed for use in classroom or laboratory settings. Although these may be locally developed, one collection is available commercially. Dunlap and Hintergardt have compiled *A Counselor's Week* (1968), consisting of 10 workbook-type trainee exercises. These exercises include a variety of lifelike situations in a typical school; moreover, pupil data, a master class schedule, and some community information are provided as background. A modification of this technique, focusing on exercises in awareness and sensitivity, is illustrated by Gunther's *Sense Relaxation: Below Your Mind* (1968).

Role Characterization. Under this heading are included materials that make use of skits or dramatic presentations to illustrate principles useful in counseling or guidance activities. One such approach is described by Kelz and Trembly in *Supervised Counseling Experiences* (1965), a manual for use in counseling practicums. A complete series of some 33 sociodramas or playlets is published by Methods and Materials Press (circa 1955). These range from social problems to cheating and discrimination situations in school settings. At a broader level, for use at PTA or faculty meetings, Hopke's skit (1963), *A Look in on Guidance,* might be helpful. '

Specialized Casebooks. Some casebooks are compiled with specific purposes in mind. One such collection is the *Ethical Standards Casebook* (1965) issued by the American Personnel and Guidance Association. Its primary function is to illustrate problem cases and approaches that are representative of various types of ethical and legal issues arising in personnel work. A similar publication is offered by the American Psychological Association (1953).

Literary Fiction as Source Material on Group Dynamics. Of increasing use in providing counselors-in-training with background reading on group dynamics are paperback fictional writings. Many of these are rich in color, interpersonal communication, and realistic group experiences, and at the same time provide challenging cases for class discussion. Typical of the publications having application to group work are Nathanson's *The Dirty Dozen* (1965), Kesey's *One Flew over the Cuckoo's Nest* (1962), Adleman and Walton's *The Devil's Brigade* (1966), and *The Little Prince* by Saint-Exupéry (1968).

Taped Materials

Counseling Theory. Taped materials are becoming increasingly available as aids in counselor preparation, for both practice and demonstration purposes, as well as for presenting substantive material of a more theoretical nature. With the improved methods of recording, both local and commercial tapes are resources. McGraw-Hill, for example, makes available lecture tapes describing the theoretical positions of such men as Ellis and Williamson. Other tapes dealing with Adlerian approaches, psychoanalysis (Mowrer), and behavioral therapy (Stampfl) are also marketed. With portable transistorized recording equipment, many counselor-education programs have developed their own tape collections of well-known lecturers on counseling taken from workshops, conferences, and conventions.

Counseling Practice. Illustrative of tapes devoted primarily to demonstrations or examples of counseling practices are commercial tapes presenting specific approaches to counseling. Only a limited number of such tapes present actual counseling sessions, for obvious reasons. Two tapes of this type are available from McGraw-Hill (Sound Seminar Series, 1968): Dreikurs, *A Mother with Two Sons,* first and second counseling session. McGraw-Hill also issues demonstration tapes showing the application of rational-emotive therapy (Ellis) and client-centered counseling (Webster & Miller).

Local or institutional tapes are often provided for counselor-education students. These tapes may be developed from actual counseling sessions by faculty members who have counseling responsibilities. In this process, efforts are often made to organize these materials by general approaches or theoretical positions for more effective student listening. To provide anonymity, only tapes on which names and facts are unidentifiable are used.

Class Tape Critiques. In conjunction with courses in counseling theory, students often tape role playing or, in rare cases, actual counseling sessions. These are then played before the class for critiquing purposes. In addition, students may combine this activity with the making of a typescript of segments of the taped interview, which they evaluate themselves. In turn the instructor may critique the students' own evaluation, as well as the actual interview, using the typescript as a medium for his red-pencil comments.

A variation of the student role-playing tape procedure is the superimposing on the tape or adding to it of questions or issues by the instructor. This subsequent tape can then be used for discussion purposes in class. Still another technique is the development of model tapes by students or faculty with unfinished interviews so that students can suggest various types of counselor responses to client expressions.

Group Process Tapes. Similar in nature to tapes dealing with one-to-one personal interviews are tapes that illustrate group-counseling methods. One of the few actual counseling "demonstrations" is the one by Dreikurs, which involves a group of eight preadolescents. This Sound Seminar tape (McGraw-Hill, 1968) is titled *Counseling Demonstration with Preadolescents. The T-Group Movement: Its Past and Future* (McGraw-Hill) is an example of group-process methodology rather than pure demonstration. A somewhat similar combination of methodology and demonstration is the tape by Blinder and Kirschenbaum, *Married Couple Group Therapy* (McGraw-Hill).

On a different educational level, and stressing general purposes rather than application to specific cases, is the tape by Downing, *Group Counseling in the Elementary School* (McGraw-Hill). From a very functional basis, a series of Personal Growth Encountertapes by Human Development Institute (Bell & Howell, 1968) offers practical, expert, supervised directions for encounter groups. This collection of tapes, consisting of ten 1½-hour sessions, provides complete instructions for self-directing small groups, interspersing directions with time for group interaction. The emphasis is upon releasing "here-and-now" feelings and receiving member feedback, with each tape identifying a separate session goal.

APPLICATION OF CASE MATERIALS IN COUNSELOR PREPARATION

Didactic Work

The use of case materials in the didactic or cognitive-theoretical aspects of the counselor-education program can do much to enhance the comprehension of basic principles underlying guidance and personnel work. Not only do case materials, written or taped, offer a multimedia approach, but they provide reinforcement learning in combining theory with practice to supplement text-book sources. The flexibility offered by these case-oriented resources can offer the individual student a means to reapply basic theory to situations or problems beyond the traditional text offerings.

Case materials can be used in many courses in the counselor-education sequence, although their potential value is perhaps greater in certain course areas. For example, in such courses as counseling theory, behavior assessment, group process, and guidance management, the opportunity for use of case materials is obvious. As the knowledge areas expected of counselor-education students become more available in programmed form, an even greater use can be made of supplementary case materials for individual use.

The actual use of case materials in counselor-education didactic experiences will vary with many factors. However, the primary value of case studies or problem cases will be to augment or illustrate principles or theories presented in the more formal aspect of instruction. If a variety of case materials reflective of different student needs and goals can be maintained, the course content can have greater personal relevance to each student. By interspersing case material with theoretical knowledge, the course format can be flexible as well as more appealing to students. Another feature of case-study instructional sources is the potential for development of creative and locally applicable materials. These can be representative of typical clients as well as local situations that counselor-education students may encounter in the field. Similarly, as use is made of case data from local or regional sources, community contacts and the skills of the graduate students are both enhanced.

Practicum—Laboratory Experiences

The process of providing practicum experiences offers rich opportunity for the use of case materials. Since this broad area stresses the application of theory to practice, the development or integration of actual or simulated case-data situations is highly important. These applications can serve to strengthen the student's field or laboratory learnings, but can also add new kinds of vicarious settings for the translation of theory into practice.

In the counselor-education sequence of activities, laboratory experiences are seen as either part of some course experiences or as separate units of the program. Within a class having some didactic elements, such as counseling approaches, the use of case materials is frequently appropriate. Particularly in this course do students need actual or case-study examples of different counseling orientations, since the subtleties of various positions are not easily discerned from textbook materials.

Field-work experiences and counseling-laboratory procedures may well depend heavily on case-study media. For example, some authorities strongly recommend a careful review of case studies or analyses, representing a variety of client needs and situations, before any actual clients are interviewed in the laboratory. Students too, in most instances, feel more comfortable if they have stronger background preparation for dealing with live counselees. Fortunately, with the flexibility built into most practicum experiences, ample opportunity for developing student readiness through case-study activities is available: variable student needs must be determined, however.

Another feature adding to the significance of case-material use in the practicum is the assumption that its empirical-pragmatic nature requires tailor-made experiences for students, insofar as possible. With the proper collection of case-study resources, differential student needs can be met. It may be necessary to develop a combination of local and commercial materials, but this condition can well strengthen the quality of cases available for meeting specific educational plans of students. The actual operational procedures followed for the full use of case materials are a vital factor. It is assumed that in order to integrate the students' learning experiences, the case-study collection is built into practicum work, but is also open to student use on a self-programmed basis. For example, students should have free access to the file of materials, as their needs vary from laboratory and practicum experiences on through any internship that may be required. This usage of case data will be enhanced by the opportunity for peer-group discussions among students.

Experiential Aspects of Counselor Education

This relatively new aspect of counselor education, while a component of selected programs for some time, has only been given formal recognition in recent years. Essentially, the nature of this phase of the program focuses on the improvement of interpersonal relationships through such activities as encounter or sensitivity groups and individual growth experiences. Rather than being a standard unit in the counselor-education sequence, this stress upon immediate and intuitive learnings will vary greatly with the individual student's strengths and limitations as a facilitator of change in others.

Although the experiential portion of an educational program is somewhat informal as well as individual, the use of case materials in course work can lend emphasis to the concepts and methods for arriving at greater interpersonal growth. Needless to say, the philosophy of the instructional staff, as its members interpret and apply case materials to instructional settings, will have a bearing on student insights and viewpoints. In programs where little or no opportunity is available for group experiences formally sponsored by the department, students can use case materials for self-initiated personal-growth groups.

With the advent of group process as an accepted and variable method of behavior change in a variety of settings, both printed and audiovisual materials for group development are now available. Reference was made above to Encountertapes, marketed by Human Development Institute and developed by the Western Behavioral Sciences Institute. In addition to literature sources of a fictional nature, such organizations as the National Training Laboratories (NEA) have issued handbooks for professionals responsible for group activity. One such publication is entitled *Handbook of Self Development and Human Relations Training* (Nylen, Mitchell, & Stout, 1967). A good portion of the book consists of descriptions of training exercises, along with objectives, plans, materials, and methods for group development. Time schedules and case materials are also provided.

SELECTED ASPECTS OF CASE MATERIAL USE

Theoretical

In viewing the theoretical aspects of case materials as an instructional tool, several concerns may arise. The primary question is one of identifying various types of case material as being illustrative of certain theoretical positions. Unfortunately, case studies, case analyses, and role characterizations are not often designed to portray explicitly stated theoretical approaches. Tapes, on the other hand, are frequently developed intentionally to demonstrate a fairly well-defined set of principles or concepts.

Since counseling theory is currently in an emergent state with no clear-cut process orientations related to specific outcomes, it is difficult to use case materials, particularly in written form, to clarify basic assumptions. On the contrary, with results apparently obtained often by composite or hybrid methodological approaches in case studies, the student could easily become confused as he seeks to find examples of particular positions. This raises a serious question as to the value of some case materials in extending a student's knowledge of theory. While some case data on behavior modification, for example, do adhere to a single philosophical and operational approach, many case materials do not. A related aspect of this problem is the need for faculty agreement on the type and number of case-material collections that will effectively supplement classroom instruction on theoretical orientations.

Ethical

Various ethical issues may tend to limit the full use of case materials in the counselor-education process. While no problem is faced with commercial case problems or analyses, the identity of the participants may prove an ethical matter if the case materials are developed locally. Even though the counseling situation being recorded is useful for instructional purposes, of greater importance is the anonymity necessary if such materials are reproduced. Still another factor is receiving permission for release of such recordings from the parties involved; if an alternative is sought, can some portions of the tape, on which situations or personalities are unidentifiable, still be used for teaching purposes?

Ethical issues may develop in another respect when case materials are used by faculty or students. Particularly when written case materials are used, if no firm theoretical assumptions are clearly stated, improper inferences may be drawn from the actions portrayed by the participants. The question must also be raised, for similar reasons, as to the advisability of permitting students to use such materials in an unsupervised manner. This same limitation might appear in connection with the use of taped directions for self-initiated encounter groups.

Other ethical concerns may arise as students are asked to develop typescripts, or as such typescripts are used for class purposes. In the former instance, the feasibility of asking students to be responsible for preparing complete typescripts of a 45-minute interview, as opposed to selected segments, raises several questions. For example, what criteria are suitable for identifying the portions of the interview to be reproduced in typscript form? Should these be applied by student or instructor, or jointly? Further, during a practicum course, how much typescript material can reasonably be expected from a student, as representative of his typical skills? In the use of typescripts for instructional purposes, the question of simulated versus actual cases must be raised. If genuine client-counselor scripts are employed, the elements of confidentiality and client identity must be considered.

Practical

In spite of the merits of using case materials in counselor education, several practical considerations must be recognized. As with other supplementary instructional resources, the matters of initial cost, recency, and maintenance cannot be ignored. Since some case materials require not only filing or storage space, but also electronic equipment, these factors may determine the extent of the original investment.

Other difficulties may arise as the case materials are integrated into the various curriculum experiences. Initially, the value of the case materials depends on whether the range or variety of resources is adequate to strengthen all aspects and different viewpoints in the curriculum. The extent of faculty agreement on relevancy of the materials to departmental philosophy may require discussion before purchase or actual use. Again, as viewpoints change, the question of updating materials to supplement other teaching aids must be periodically answered.

In the actual instructional setting, the effectiveness of the transfer of concepts and methods from simulated to live clients is difficult to assess. This problem is often compounded if students use case materials with minimum supervision and show little initiative to obtain faculty assistance. Another practical consideration is that uncritical students may set too serious a value upon a case study. This, of course, might be offset by an evaluative review or critique file for the departmental collection of case materials. Presumably some sort of monitoring system for student and faculty use of case data would be advisable.

SUMMARY

This essay has identified various types of written and taped case materials. These have been briefly described, with illustrations of typical case data in each category. The second section was devoted to the application of case data to three aspects of the counselor-education program: didactic, practicum, and experiential. The final portion of the essay examined some of the problems associated with the use of case materials in three categories: theoretical, ethical, and practical.

REFERENCES

Adams, J. F. *Problems in counseling: A case study approach.* New York: Macmillan, 1962.

Adleman, R. H., & Walton, G. *The devil's brigade.* Philadelphia: Chilton, 1966.

Aldrich, C. K., & Nighswonger, C. *A pastoral counseling casebook.* Philadelphia: Westminster Press, 1968.

American Personnel and Guidance Association. *Ethical standards casebook.* Washington, D.C.: American Personnel and Guidance Association, 1965.

American Psychological Association. *Ethical standards of psychologists* Washington, D.C.: American Psychological Association, 1953.

Axline, V. *Dibs: In search of self.* Boston: Houghton Mifflin, 1966.

Baruch, D. W. *One little boy.* New York: Julian Press, 1952.

Bucheimer, A., & Balogh, S. *The counseling relationship: A casebook.* Chicago: Science Research Associates, 1961.

Callis, R., Polmantier, P., & Roeber, E. *A casebook of counseling.* New York: Appleton-Century-Crofts, 1955.

Dreikurs, R. *Psychology in the classroom.* (2nd ed.) New York: Harper & Row, 1968.

Dunlop, R. S., & Hintergardt, B. C. *The counselor's week: A simulation for counselor trainees.* Scranton: International Textbook, 1968.

Gannon, F. B. *The many faces of Kevin Michael Pullen: A guidance case study.* New York: College Entrance Examination Board, 1968.

Green, H. *I never promised you a rose garden.* New York: Holt, Rinehart and Winston, 1964.

Gunther, B. *Sense relaxation: Below your mind.* New York: Collier-Macmillan, 1968.

Hopke, W. *A look in on guidance: A skit. Counselor Education and Supervision,* 1963, **2**, 152–153.

Human Development Institute. *Encounter tapes for personal growth groups.* Atlanta, Ga.: Bell & Howell Co. 1968.

Kelz, J. W., & Trembly, E. L. *Supervised counseling experiences.* Boulder, Colo.: Pruett Press, 1965.

Kesey, K. *One flew over the cuckoo's nest.* New York: Viking Press, 1962.

Lloyd-Jones, E., Barry, R., & Wolf, B. (Eds.) *Case studies in college student–staff relationships.* New York: Bureau of Publications, Teachers College, Columbia University, 1956. (a)

Lloyd-Jones, E., Barry, R., & Wolf, B. (Eds.) *Case studies in human relationships in secondary school.* New York: Bureau of Publications, Teacher's College, Columbia University, 1956. (b)

Lloyd-Jones, E., Barry, R., & Wolf, B. (Eds.) *Guidance in elementary education: A casebook.* New York: Bureau of Publications, Teacher's College, Columbia University, 1958.

MacIver, J. *The frog pond.* New York: George Braziller, 1961.

McGehearty, L. (Ed.) Case analysis: Consultation and counseling. *Elementary School Guidance and Counseling,* 1969, **3**, 217–222.

Nathanson, E. M. *The dirty dozen.* New York: Random House, 1965.

Nylen, D., Mitchell, J. R., & Stout, A. *Handbook of staff development and human relations training.* Washington, D.C.: National Training Laboratories for Applied Behavioral Science (NEA), 1967.

Ross, A. O. *The exceptional child in the family: Helping parents of exceptional children.* New York: Grune & Stratton, 1964.

Rothney, J. W. M. *The high school student: A book of cases.* New York: Dryden Press, 1953.

Rothney, J. W. M. *Methods of studying the individual child: The psychological case study.* Waltham, Mass.: Blaisdell, 1968.

Saint-Exupéry, A. de. *The little prince.* (Trans.) New York: Harcourt Brace Jovanovich, 1968.

Socio-Guidrama Series. Springfield, N.J.: Methods and Materials Press, circa 1955.

Sound Seminar Series. New York: McGraw-Hill, 1968.

Swenson, C., Jr. *An approach to case conceptualization.* Boston: Houghton Mifflin, 1968.

Tollefson, N. F. *Counseling case management.* Boston: Houghton Mifflin, 1968.

Ullman, L. P., & Krasner, L. (Eds.) *Case studies in behavior modification.* New York: Holt, Rinehart and Winston, 1965.

Womer, F. B., & Frick, W. B. *Personalizing test use: A counselor casebook.* Ann Arbor: Bureau of School Services, University of Michigan, 1965.

The Supervisory Process: Multiple-Impact Supervision

Douglas R. Gross

Arizona State University

If one were to single out the aspect of counseling practicum that has received the most emphasis in recent literature, it would certainly be the supervisory process. Even though this emerging emphasis is quite noticeable in a perusal of the literature, it is interesting to note the seeming lack of agreement when one attempts to discuss the supervisory process in terms of goals and procedures. Only one aspect of this process is the subject of considerable agreement —namely, the belief that the supervisory process should be a learning experience. Beyond this basic assumption, the motto seems to be, "Every supervisor for himself."

Basically, the supervisory process is defined in terms of the relationship between the supervisor and the counselor-candidate and the steps taken by the participants in the learning process. While this relationship, for many supervisors and supervisees, may continue to resemble the traditional teacher-student model, except in usually being on a one-to-one basis, no one seems to be defending this model openly in print these days (Koile, 1967).

Arbuckle (1965), among others, held that the supervisor should be more like a counselor than a teacher, but acknowledged that the counselor-client model is not adequate for conceptualization of the supervisory process.

Patterson (1959, 1962), on the other hand, contended that supervision is neither teaching nor counseling or psychotherapy. It is, or should be, a learning situation, but the type of learning is closer to that which occurs in counseling and psychotherapy than to classroom instruction. He felt that the supervisory situation should be more like counseling and psychotherapy than like didactic teaching. He stressed that the conditions of supervision that appear to achieve the desired results in student growth appear to be the same as those conducive to client growth in counseling. The supervisory relationship should be one in which the student is not threatened.

The limitations of the teacher-student model and the counselor-client model

348

for supervision are well known. Basically, the teacher-student model seems to provide the counselor with too little opportunity for learning how to understand and change his counseling behavior, and gives too little attention to the complex dynamics of counselor-client interaction and of supervisor-counselor interaction. The focus seems to be primarily on content, cognitive learning, didactic procedures, and domination of the process by the supervisor. The counselor-client model, on the other hand, implies that the focus is essentially on process, emotional, and experiential learnings—that the supervisee identifies the problem, which the supervisor treats or deals with on a counseling basis (Koile, 1967).

Roeber (1962), in a position paper on practicum and internship, stated that programs of practicum supervision are inhibited by a combination of factors. He stressed aspects of terminology, staff, facilities, equipment and materials, and conditions, and set forth the hypothesis that the real question surrounding the supervisory process is, "Can the supervised practice bring counselor enrollees to such a level of competency that they can without further supervision provide professional helping relationships for pupils, parents, teachers, administrators, and other adults [p. 3]?"

The literature indicates that the experiential and conceptual aspects of the supervisory process currently are not too well defined. It seems that a point has been reached, however, where those involved in the supervisory process are beginning to apply their knowledge and experience to the development of a theoretical base. The works of Walz (1963), Roeber (1963), Gysbers (1963), Ekstein and Wallerstein (1958), Kell and Mueller (1966), Wolberg (1954), Sanderson (1954), and Hansen (1965) are illustrative of this point. Inherent in all of these writings is the striving for a rationale for what is done in the area of practicum supervision.

Ekstein and Wallerstein (1958) and Ekstein (1964) examined the functions of supervision, and stated that the supervisor is a therapist, a teacher, and an administrator, who by shifting his identity among these three functions forms a new gestalt, a new identity with a focus on learning for the student-therapist. The point is also made that the supervisor must keep his identity with the setting in which he conducts his supervision, and in this sense he is an authority responsible for evaluation, granting of credit, and assignment of grades.

Walz, Roeber, and Gysbers (1963), in the preparation of three papers dealing with theory development, attempted to come to an understanding of supervision by looking at it in terms of how a supervisor would operate using trait-factor, learning, or self-theories. They formulated 13 hypotheses regarding supervisory behavior and the supervisory process. In summary, the hypotheses stress the concepts of self-learning based upon increased self-understanding initiated through the supervisor-supervisee relationship. This relationship is characterized by the clarification and reclarification of counselor-counselee goals and tasks, in the context of a nonthreatening, warm, accepting, and positive atmosphere. They stress the utilization of a wide range of instructional resources and of continuous and relevant feedback. Self-learning seems to be the end-goal of the supervisory process, regardless of the means by which this learning is gained.

Kell and Mueller (1966) described the supervisory relationship as an important human encounter, which has similarities to counseling, and they took the position that the task of the supervisor is to facilitate the objectives and processes that the counselor himself wants to pursue, even if the client-counselor goals and approaches may not be those the supervisor would choose for himself. The supervisory process develops primarily from the dynamics of the interaction between the counselor and his clients, with both the supervisor and the counselor focusing on the counseling relationship and aiding the counselor to differentiate his own feelings and conflicts from those of the client.

Wolberg (1954), in discussing the supervisory process in the area of psychotherapy, characterized it in terms of beginning, middle, and latter stages, and stated that the supervisory relationship is one to which the supervisee reacts with mingled attitudes of admiration, jealousy, fear, and hostility. Wolberg contended that admiration and jealousy are usually inspired by the supervisor's superior knowledge, education, and status. Fear of the supervisor is often the product of the therapist's helplessness in the face of an authority who, he feels, may judge him unfairly and destroy his career and livelihood in the event he fails to live up to expectations. Hostility issues from many sources.

Sanderson (1954) stated that supervision, if conceived as a helping process intended to promote the student's professional growth, is predicated on a relationship between two persons. He also inferred that there can be little question that supervision which attempts to penetrate beyond the cognitive or intellectual acceptance of facts is also a helping phenomenon.

Hansen (1965), in an article dealing with candidates' expectations of the supervisory process, stated that the essence of supervision comes in the conference between candidate and supervisor as they discuss both the client and the candidate's skills, sensibility, and understanding. He felt that supervision is instructional, but that it goes beyond that to focus on the personal feelings of the candidate. To Hansen, the effective supervisor is one who is able to establish a one-to-one relationship conducive to self-development of the candidate.

As indicated from this discussion, the supervisory process is above all else a learning experience; therefore, the following paragraphs attempt to synthesize what various authors state to be the learning stages experienced by counselor-candidates as they begin, move through, and complete the experiential program termed supervision.

Hogan (1964) identified four stages through which the clinician goes in his development as a therapist, and suggested appropriate supervisory procedures for each. At the first level, the therapist is highly motivated, but dependent, insecure, and lacking in insight. For this level, Hogan argues for much straight teaching, information giving, interpretation, support, exemplification, and efforts to help the therapist-trainee become sensitive to his own feelings in relations with the client.

The second stage is exemplified by the candidate making attempts to involve his own personality in the process even though he is conflicted over his dependency-autonomy needs. He is both overconfident and overwhelmed; he feels committed to the profession, but has doubts about himself. Supervisory methods proposed include exemplification—i.e., the supervisor sharing what he would do in order to support and assist the therapist in clarifying his ambivalence.

The third stage is characterized by greater confidence and less dependency-autonomy conflict; there is greater differentiation between unhealthy and healthy motivations, and a greater commitment to the profession. Supervisory processes include sharing, exemplification, and confrontation.

In the fourth stage, the development of the counselor-candidate is characterized not only by more personal autonomy and security, but also by the awareness and acceptance of some insecurity, along with his own professional problems, and by insight. The supervisory approaches at this stage are sharing and confrontation; the peer-supervisor model replaces the control-supervisor model.

In discussing stages of counselor-candidate learnings, Altucher (1967) set forth certain basic assumptions regarding both supervision and its participants, supervisor and supervisee. Supervision initially assumes that the counselor-candidate is interested in improving his skills and is capable of doing so. In the beginning, the difficulties the counselor encounters in his work may arise from lack of experience. Persistent difficulties are more apt to arise from his characteristic way of meeting situations. The goals of supervision are to help the counselor remain open to his own experiences.

In Altucher's terms, the beginning counselor is in a state of discomfort at being confronted by a bewildering array of stimuli. He brings this discomfort with him to the supervisory sessions. The stages of learning revolve around the movement that takes place within the counselor-candidate in replacing the initial discomfort with increasing degrees of comfort. This movement along a discomfort-comfort continuum marks the types of learning, or stages of learning, experienced by a counselor involved in a counseling-practicum experience. The role of the supervisor in this experience is that of relationship building, providing the type of relationship that will allow for this type of progressive change.

Kell and Mueller (1966) did not discuss counselor learning in terms of various stages, but emphasized the role of the supervisor as a model to be emulated by the supervisee. They stated that the need for the counselor to emulate the supervisor may be one part of the process of identification as the counselor moves along the developmental continuum.

Clark (1965) conceptualized supervision and its inherent learnings as a continuum, along which candidates are assisted in moving from low differentiation, and integration of a relatively small number of processes, attitudes, skills, and techniques involved in counseling, to the high differentiation of all of these various elements. Through the use of diagrams, Clark showed how the candidate moves from a point of low differentiation and integration to a point of high differentiation and integration. This movement seems to depend upon the focus of the supervisor and the aspects of the resulting relationship. As the counselor moves along this continuum, more and more emphasis is placed upon the person of the counselor and his interaction with the client, and less on what Clark calls the "it" factors involved in the counseling process.

The preceding information gives credence to the idea that the process of supervision and concepts regarding supervisee learnings are in a state of flux. There are few definitive answers to questions as to which are the most operative methods of conducting supervision, or the most beneficial types of learning. Even though such a flux seemingly exists, there seems to be a theme of consistency with regard to certain factors incorporated within the process of supervision and the learnings inherent therein. Based upon this contention, it would seem warranted to list the following:

1. The supervisory process is an individual type of instruction with large degrees of variability among supervisors.
2. The supervisory process is a learning experience with heavy emphasis on self-learnings.
3. The supervisory process is generally discussed in terms of the supervisor-supervisee relationship.
4. The functions of the supervisor in the supervisory process generally fall into one of the following categories: (a) teaching, (b) counseling, (c) administration, and (d) evaluation.
5. Techniques utilized in the supervisory process stress the importance of one-to-one confrontation between supervisee and supervisor, peers, self, and counselee.
6. The learning stages of the supervisory process are generally viewed as a continuum characterized by increasing degrees of security, self-assurance, self-understanding, and movement from high structure to low.
7. The learning environment of the supervisory process is generally stated in terms of supervisory, institutional, or supervisee goals and expectations, and characterized by degrees of warmth, acceptance, and lack of threat.

8. Supervisory learnings generally emphasize the development of a repertoire of skills and knowledge useful in relationship building.
9. The goals of the supervisory process can generally be classified in three somewhat distinct but interrelated categories: (a) cognitive, (b) experiential, and (c) integrative.
10. The degree to which the goals of the supervisory process are met is directly proportionate to the degree of relationship impact available in the supervisory encounter.

The true significance of these patterns of emerging consistency is open to much conjecture and interpretation. It would seem warranted to conclude, however, that the learnings that take place in the supervisor-supervisee encounter are based upon a myriad of relationship variables stemming from the interaction between the supervisor, supervisee, and counselee.

The methods utilized within this relationship to bring about supervisee learnings are legion. They run the gamut from group discussions, role-playing, audiovisual techniques, and case reports to readings. Each has its merits; one method, which seemingly has had little emphasis, is that dealing with the concept of "multiple-impact supervision," the multiple-supervisor–multiple-supervisee method. This method, if the contention regarding goal achievement being directly related to relationship impact is correct, would offer depth and meaning to the learning situation called supervision. Such a method would increase the dimensions of the supervisory relationship providing for greater interaction and feedback from a multiplicity of sources.

Figure 1 represents the author's conceptualization of the relationship variables inherent in the traditional approach to the supervisory relationship; that is, supervisor, supervisee, and counselee. This traditional one-to-one or one-to-two relationship would be expanded under the concept of multiple-impact supervision. By increasing the number of supervisors to two or more per supervisory group, and in turn increasing the number of supervisees per group, one automatically increases the supervisee-counselee contact. Therefore, the threefold interaction pattern, as represented in Figure 1, is no longer one-to-one or one-to-two, but increases according to the numbers included in each of the three designated areas. The underlying concept of multiple-impact

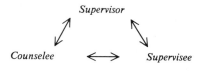

Figure 1

supervision is increased exposure for the supervisee in the area of relationship-impact variables. The proposed concept for multiple-impact supervision could be expanded to include three or more supervisors and increasing numbers of supervisees.

To show how the proposed concept of multiple-impact supervision might work in an actual setting, suppose that a practicum program is set up to handle 50 practicum students during the course of one semester. There are 10 supervisors employed to work with the practicum enrollees. Each supervisor is assigned five enrollees and the 10 supervisors are divided into teams of two. This brings about the situation of two supervisors for every 10 practicum students. Working as a team, the supervisors observe and interact with each of the 10 enrollees either on a group or an individual basis. Situations are structured so that the 10 supervisees observe one another during the semester, and sessions are established whereby each supervisee receives feedback from each of the other nine enrollees. Tape exchange (audio-video) is required in which each supervisee is required to listen to and critique a tape from one of his fellow enrollees and give feedback, either in a one-to-one or a group situation. The concept of teams might also be applied to the 10 supervisees, dividing them up in pairs for the purpose of observation and interaction. This can be done on a rotating basis throughout the semester so that five different pairings occur during this time period.

The supervisors conduct their observations and supervisory sessions both individually and as a team. The team approach provides an avenue for a three-way dialogue between the supervisee being observed and the two supervisors. This can also be expanded to include the supervisee's team partner.

Counselee involvement adds yet another dimension. The program can be structured in such a way that immediately after the counseling session the counselee could interact with either of the two supervisors or with the supervisee's team partner. This could be done on a one-to-one basis, or perhaps a group of counselees could be brought together for their reactions to the counseling session, with the purpose of providing feedback for the supervisees involved.

The inherent purpose of such a proposed program is to provide greater person-to-person contact. The program as proposed expands the traditional supervisor-supervisee-counselee concept by increasing the numbers involved in each of these three categories, thereby increasing the relationship variables at least twofold. Figure 2 represents the new relationship structure.

The benefits of such a conceptualization as multiple-impact supervision are multidimensional and therefore difficult to enumerate. The greater the variety in the composition of the supervisory teams, the more varied the total supervisory experience. In conclusion, multiple-impact supervision would place greater emphasis on the following, which are offered for the reader's consideration:

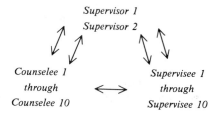

Figure 2

1. Through the pairing of supervisors with differing theoretical approaches, supervisees receive a wider range of information dealing with theoretical approaches to the counseling process, and a variety of methods and techniques to be utilized in working with both individuals and groups.
2. Through the pairing of supervisors with differing experiential backgrounds—i.e., educational, clinical, and agency—supervisees are provided with a diversity of conceptualizations as to the nature and circumstances surrounding the problem areas presented.
3. Through the process of bringing together supervisory staff to work as a team, the knowledge and skill of each member of that team are enhanced through the sharing of ideas, methods, and approaches not only in terms of the counseling process, but also in terms of effective instructional techniques.
4. Through the process of bringing together teams of supervisors across the entire practicum program, the chances for the development of more consistant goals, purposes, evaluative techniques, and supervisory procedures are greatly enhanced.
5. Through the pairing of supervisees into teams, each individual member of a team is given the responsibility for observing his fellow team member, critiquing his counseling sessions and providing feedback. Through the process of peer observation and feedback, the supervisee is exposed to a wider range of counselee types and a variety of counseling styles.
6. Through the process of bringing together groups of counselees for evaluation of individual sessions, the supervisees are provided with a dimension of feedback not often found in the "typical" practicum program.
7. Through the process of multiple-impact supervision, a counselor-education program is able more effectively to utilize its supervisory staff and provide an "in-depth" supervisory experience for a larger number of students.

REFERENCES

Altucher, N. Constructive use of the supervisory relationship. *Journal of Counseling Psychology,* 1967, **14**, 165–170.

Arbuckle, D. S. *Counseling philosophy theory and practice.* Boston: Allyn and Bacon, 1965.

Clark, C. M. On the process of counseling supervision. *Counselor Education and Supervision,* 1965, **4**, 64–67.

Ekstein, R., & Wallerstein, R. *The teaching and learning of psychotherapy.* New York: Basic Books, 1958.

Ekstein, R. Supervision of psychotherapy: Is it teaching? Is it supervision? Or is it therapy? *Psychotherapy: Research, Theory and Practice,* 1964, **1**, 137–138.

Gysbers, N. C. Practicum supervision: I. Theory, learning theory. Paper presented at the annual convention of the American Personnel and Guidance Association, Boston, April 1963.

Hansen, J. C. Trainees' expectations of supervision in the counseling practicum. *Counselor Education and Supervision,* 1965, **4**, 75–80.

Hogan, R. A. Issues and approaches in supervision. *Psychotherapy: Research, Theory and Practice,* 1964, **1**, 139–141.

Kell, W., & Mueller, W. *Impact and change.* New York: Appleton-Century-Crofts, 1966.

Koile, E. A. Counseling supervision: Models to choose from, models to move from. Paper presented at the annual convention of the American Personnel and Guidance Association, Dallas, Tex., March 1967.

Patterson, C. H. *Counseling and psychotherapy: Theory and practice.* New York: Harper & Row, 1959.

Patterson, C. H. *Counseling and guidance in schools.* New York: Harper & Row, 1962.

Roeber, E. C. Position paper—practicum and internship. In *A Progress Report on Standards.* American Personnel and Guidance Association, April 1962.

Roeber, E. C. Practicum supervision: I. Theory, trait theory. Paper presented at the annual convention of the American Personnel and Guidance Association, Boston, April 1963.

Sanderson, H. *Basic concepts in vocational guidance.* New York: McGraw-Hill, 1954.

Walz, G. R. Practicum Supervision: I. Theory, self theory. Paper presented at the annual convention of the American Personnel and Guidance Association, Boston, April 1963.

Walz, G. R., Roeber, E. C., & Gysbers, N. C. Practicum supervision: II. Synthesis, integrated theory of supervision. Paper presented at the annual convention of the American Personnel and Guidance Association, Boston, April 1963.

Wolberg, L. R. *The technique of psychotherapy.* New York: Grune & Stratton, 1954.

Objectives, Theories, and Methodologies for Video Application in Counseling and Counselor Training

DeWayne J. Kurpius

Indiana University

INTRODUCTION

The results of the use of videotaped feedback in teaching individuals and groups about the impact their behavior has on others are positive, regardless of whether those involved have been psychiatric patients, counselor-trainees, or supervisors. The factors that contribute to these results are varied, but they tend to cluster into two prime categories. The first category relates to the stimulus impact created by viewing a playback sample of one's own behavior. This process creates a type of stimulated awareness of self and others, which includes (1) one's physical features, i.e., recognizing how one looks to others in a particular setting; (2) self-image confrontation, meaning the process dealing with the immediate introspection caused by the playback; and (3) the general viewing and critiquing of verbal and nonverbal behaviors related to the learning objectives specified. The second category of factors contributing to positive results with the use of videotape is perhaps even more important from a training point of view. It includes the playback processes and procedures followed, which in turn contribute to the positive results related to utilizing videotape feedback.

CATEGORY I

The first category, concerned with viewing one's own behavior, has been the topic most prominent in the literature; and although various approaches to looking at playbacks have been described by different writers, these descriptions tend to take on similar meaning. For example, Wilmer (1968a) defined the response to viewing one's own tape as "self-awakedness." In the playback process, the individual experiences "a sudden turning-on of the self [p. 21]" being viewed on the monitor. This phenomenon has been similarly described by Alger and Hogan as "image impact [1967, p. 24]." In both cases, the individual is focusing on physical features, nonverbal behavior, verbal behavior, and the general interaction which is taking place.

A vivid illustration of the insight that can be gained from observing oneself on video playback follows from Rogers (1968):

Once you have seen what you have been doing you can begin behaving in new, more satisfying ways. For example, a young woman viewed herself on a videotape with the sound turned off. Her gestures were alternately wide open, with hands extended to people, and closed off and restricted (all within the course of a few minutes of speech). "That's it," she said when she was shown what she was doing, "I don't know whether to be open or closed." She chose openness, and the change in her in the course of a very short time has been remarkable [p. 39].

Wilmer (1968a) tells of a questionnaire given to both patients and staff after two months of videotaping on the ward. "The patients," he says, "correctly perceived that many of the staff were being stiff, impersonal, and unresponsive and were hiding behind clichés and psychiatric jargon [p. 10]." The observations made by members of the staff point to the types of behaviors which students could work toward correcting in their training:

A staff member said, "I became painfully aware of qualities I don't like, but maybe with time can change—especially rigidity of posture, lack of spontaneous movement, and a monotonous verbal quality that seems rehearsed." Another commented, "During one particular community meeting when I thought I was listening to someone objectively, I discovered on replay that I had a very tight-lipped, disapproving expression on my face [p. 133].

One of the early feedback processes using videotaped self-image in counselor training was that of Kagan, who in 1966, in a seminar at Michigan State University, introduced a technique called Interpersonal Process Recall (IPR). The IPR process was created to provide interview data to both the client and the counselor immediately following the interview. The rationale for developing IPR has been described by Kagan and Krathwohl (1967, p. 5):

Because it is difficult for a person both to introspect and to interact with another person in a normal manner at the same time, we wondered if there were a way of permitting the mind to interact with a situation at one time and to introspect concerning the reaction at another. We concluded that if we could give a subject enough clues and cues to help him relive the experience, we could explore in depth at a later time various points in the interaction, the thoughts, feelings, changes in thoughts and feelings, and the meaning of various gestures and expressions.

The results of using this structured approach assisted the trainee by providing him with maximum feedback based on stimulated recall of what he and the client were actually thinking, feeling, and doing at specific periods during the interview. The unique experience of seeing himself on the screen and pursuing specific events enables the trainee or his supervisor to become more objective and systematic in the learning process. Observation has indicated that those in a supervisory capacity are not immune to the effects of self-confrontation and feedback. Wilmer (1967a) emphasizes the positive results for those who function in the supervisory role and participate in the openness of videotaping:

Videotaping is stressful for the patient but more so for the therapist. Mistakes of any kind are indelibly recorded. Jargon or cliches, "canned lectures," lack of spontaneity and disguised feelings are revealed. The effect of seeing one's errors in the presence of others is shattering only if one cherishes unrealistic illusions. It is a healthy experience to be humbled now and then, but it is not healthy to be humiliated. But to counteract these unpleasant experiences the psychiatrist also sees and hears himself when he is skillful, incisive, witty, intelligent, clear and efficient [pp. 126–127].

Although research studies utilizing video technology have been limited, a few have been completed, as was indicated in a review by Danet (1968). One study, made by Boyd and Sisney (1967), attends to the concerns of "immediate self-image confrontation by videotape and its impact on the self-concept [p. 247]." Each person in the experimental group was exposed to "replay of a standardized 10-minute interview covering the S's reactions and feelings about other patients on the ward, himself, and his family." Instead of being shown tapes of themselves, the control group saw "a 10-minute taped segment of a daytime television comedy." In addition, Leary's Interpersonal Check List "was administered several days before, immediately following, and two weeks after the self-image confrontation experience [p. 248]." As a result, those in the experimental group who were exposed to the immediate self-image confrontation by videotape, and its impact on the self-concept, displayed and maintained less pathology than the control group did for "at least" a period of two weeks. As reported in the original study by Boyd and Sisney, the "ideal self" concept and the "public self" concept "moved closer together for the experimental group than they did for the control group [p. 248]." The author did state, however, that the findings are based upon the validity of the instrument and that other studies are needed.

In a study by Geertsma and Reivich (1965), repeated self-confrontation through videotape was used. Following an initial evaluation, a therapeutic interview of 45 minutes was taped, with the individual subject also completing a "rating scale to describe herself as she thought she was at that time [p. 249]," afterwards filling out another to describe herself as she saw herself on the tape.

For the next six weeks, she returned, first to watch her session from the week before and then to tape her new session. In order to use an additional outside appraisal of this subject's performance, eight student-nurses viewed the tapes in order and rated them. Since the suggestion of this study was that the subject learned to look at herself more realistically, Danet (1968) quoted the authors, who believe "that self perception and its related phenomena (for example, body image, self-concept, self-regard) occupy a position of central importance in our understanding of personality functioning in both normal and disturbed states [p. 249]."

Family counseling, as suggested by Berger (1969–1970), also points up the particular usefulness of video playbacks in that they can "demonstrate the patterns of unconscious arrangements as well as the responses of family members to each other," which, he says, "can expedite insight, understanding and motivation to change better than any previously used modality." He indicated that "typical repetitive, regulating patterns which may be revealed and played in a focused feedback are":

1. Placate—"You're right," or "Yes, I'm wrong about that."
2. Blame or provoke guilt—"But you made me do it that way," or "It's your fault because . . . ."
3. Preach—"When I was a child . . . ," or "I can't understand how a child who's been given everything like you have can sit there and say that to me . . . ."
4. Change the subject to something irrelevant—"I'll get back to that but I want to point out that the other day . . . ."
5. Withdraw—into silence, resignation, and a "What's the use? It won't make any difference anyway" attitude.
6. Use denial—"It may have looked that way, but you just don't understand."
7. Respond psychosomatically—"Since I've been sitting here, my heart is pounding like it's going to break," or "I'm getting a splitting headache now—you get me upset when you say those things."
8. Discount—a family member uses a dismissing type of head nod to the side and down or a hand movement with palm down to indicate that what is being expressed by another family member is being "put down" or "discounted."
9. Be realistic—when a family is open, truthful, and conscientiously attempts to truthfully recognize and accept and resolve realistic conflicts of interest or problems while being congruent in communicating or relating [pp. 80–81].

In addition to making it possible for clients to see themselves, such playbacks assist the trainee in learning to recognize specific patterns and roles, such as:

"help-rejecting complainer, injustice-collector, pollyanna, virtuously honest sadist, compulsive helper, teacher's pet, guilt-provocateur, victim, doctor's assistant, Don Juan, C. T., Mama, manipulator, etc. [p. 81]." Berger also mentions that playback of tapes fits in with any therapeutic approach based on personality theory, which includes:

subconscious or hidden motivation for one's behaviour or attitudes; the significance of signs and symbols which regulate and arrange relationships; resistance; transference and the impact of the concomitant communication of emotion, behaviour and thoughts through multiple levels and multiple channels in human relationships [p. 79].

In addition, "Therapists interested primarily in modifying behavioural states by suggestion, direction, education or desensitization methods can also utilize video constructively [p. 79]."

In his literature review on the use of videotape to effect self-confrontation, Danet (1968) mentions several studies, by authors such as Cornelison and Tausig (1964), Moore, Chernell, and West (1965), Geertsma and Reivich (1965), Kagan (1967), and Boyd and Sisney (1967), which suggest the practical value that video feedback may hold for counselor training. A summary of the stimulated awareness associated with video usage suggests that video utilization is a necessary resource for training counselors. For example, if, as part of his training, the supervisee learns the process for examination of the impact his own behavior has on others, as well as its reciprocal effects, he can accelerate his development and better critique his interviews with clients, both during and following training.

The second category contributing to the positive results of video feedback is found in the purposes and procedures followed while engaging in video-assisted training.

CATEGORY II

Although more complex approaches will also be described in using videotape, the simplest technique is to record and critique the initial behavior of the student, followed by subsequent sampling over time so that developmental comparisons are possible. Ideally, sequenced tape samples during the training period would give the trainee more to build on, particularly if he reviews the earlier tapes each time he makes a new one. This simple approach, in order to provide an initial self-image experience for purposes of later comparison, has been refined and modified in several studies, most of which, though they have been carried out within a psychiatric context, have implications for counselor training and other nonpsychiatric preparation programs.

Stating objectives and following a systematic plan are prerequisites to using video as an effective teaching aid. Wilmer (1968b, p. 1157) suggests that

The technical aims of television learning techniques are: (1) to raise the amount and level of interactional discussion; (2) to avoid passive teaching roles of conventional television; (3) to stop, start, and reverse the machinery so that all participants can ask questions; (4) to promote active probing and creative thinking; and (5) to dampen authoritarian elements of teaching and foster learning dialogues in which the machine is an active participant.

One of the most significant results of an instructor's systematic use of video-tape is that "television learning techniques allow the teacher to have programs entirely under control. What is shown, when, and how are the basic questions that are now being asked in television learning [p. 1157]."

In the *"participant recorder"* quality of television Wilmer (1968b) saw several advantageous results for the teaching of interviewing techniques, for in many ways videotape is superior to a human observer:

First, the observer is no longer the sole instrument of thought from which phenomena are selected; second, there is no time lag interval between the event and the final recording; third, by immediate or repeated replay to all the participants, retrospective evaluations can be corrected from the recorded audiovisual evidence. Fourth, machinery does not have to be in a prepared state of mind, has no psychologic constellation, no given biases, no emotional involvement, and no unconscious; and fifth, television plays an invariably formal role and its feedback is total and unedited [p. 1158].

Although nearly every experiment incorporating videotape indicates positive results, the study by Logue, Zenner, and Gohman (1968) would seem to suggest that systematic use over a period of time is a significant variable; for a brief nonsystematic exposure probably would not bring about change in trainees any more than it did in the patients who were given "practice job interviews using a video tape recorder for the shaping of behavior [p. 436]." In their discussion, the authors suggested a reason for the lack of significant results, which may also be applicable to counselor training (p. 438):

It has been noted at this hospital in other uses of the video tape in group therapy that self-confrontation which is intrinsic in the playing back of the therapeutic encounter is quite anxiety producing and may contribute to a temporary regression in terms of efficiency of behavior. In other words, what one may be dealing with in the attempt to increase efficiency by single-practice interview and subsequent group and individual replay is this anxiety effect. Whatever positive features might be gained from the attempted modification of specific bits of behavior is nullified by the self-conscious anxiety which might contribute to less able performance. . . . The breaking of old

habits of behaving in any organism is usually initially characterized by lower performance and greater variety of response. Later research into this area might well use more
than a single interview and confrontation to not only desensitize the person to the
anxiety-producing situation but also to allow greater reinforcement of the suggested
new behavior.

Since sequenced time samples are recommended for the best training, the
probability remains that most trainees will gain more from a program of
videotaping if it is spread out over much of the training period. As students
become more sophisticated in the technology and process for using videotaped
sessions, more and more peer and self-study become evident.

As pointed out by Danet (1968), a review of videotape research indicates
that questions of the following type must be asked:

For which individuals and under what conditions is exposure to one's self-image in this
manner a beneficial experience? What is the optimal period of time and the right
number of times to provide this experience? When and under what conditions will
self-viewing produce negative or harmful results [p. 256]?

Results of some of the experimental teaching that has incorporated the use of
videotaping have suggested different systematic approaches for individual and
group sessions, indicating direct implications for the use of videotape techniques in counselor training. Also, as discussed in the literature and in many
institutions, there are instructional programs that include recorded monologues in training. In addition, researchers have explored simulation as a
training aid and video-computer assistance, as well as the impact of nonverbal
behavior and body language. The most important aspect for the daily user of
videotape is the technical quality of the recorded session. Because of the
importance of these topics, separate subsections have been developed for each
area.

TECHNICAL ASPECTS OF RECORDING INDIVIDUAL
SESSIONS IN LABORATORY SETTINGS

As anyone who has worked with videotape realizes, the content and quality
of the recording must be adequate if those studying it are to benefit from its
use in supervision. For this reason, the technical aspects of recording a counseling interview are mentioned here to suggest ways in which tapes can be used
systematically as a part of entry, advanced, and renewal counselor-training
experiences.

A number of writers—Wilmer (1967b), Kagan and Krathwohl (1967), and

Berger (1970)—have described the technical aspects of video usage for training purposes. The most common equipment required is a video recorder, camera and tripod, microphone, and monitor. Both portable and fixed equipment are important for meeting multiple needs. The following description presents a laboratory setting utilizing remotely controlled equipment operated by a technical assistant; however, many of the techniques are applicable to portable equipment also.

Having worked on films and a television documentary of a "therapeutic community," Wilmer (1967b) stresses the necessity of "skills in direction and camera work to enhance the artistic, dramatic impact, the visual cue discrimination, and memory recall [p. 210]." In order to focus the attention of the viewers, whether they be supervisors, counselor-trainees, or clients, he formulated a sequential approach to recording the basic interview.

First in this sequence is a "wide-angle shot" including "the entire bodies of both participants and the room furnishings [p. 210]." Wilmer suggested that the student conducting the interview choose whatever furniture he wants as well as its arrangement. Following this establishing shot, "the camera lens zooms in, 'tightening' on the upper portions of [p. 210]" interviewer and client.

Next, the complete face of the person who is considered "the primary object of interest," whether client, counselor, or supervisor, is focused on by another camera as the second step in the sequence. Third should be the entire face of the other person in the interview. Each of these shots is important, especially during first-session recording, since it shows one person in the interview how he appears to his companion.

At this point, a camera is at the back of each person: "Although they are not necessarily close, by zoom lens they can bring the subjects as close as the director wishes. For a variable period of time, depending on the nature of the evolving transaction, these two camera shots alternate [p. 210]." Switching from interviewer to client and back again when appropriate, "the camera is now telling the story from the point of view of each participant." By this time, if "two cameras are being used the participants are not aware of which camera is recording or what special effects are being used":

The camerman shooting over the shoulders of the individuals is directed to include in these pictures a portion of the head of the person from whose perspective he is photographing. The purpose of this is to photographically reinforce the impression of a relationship, to portray the image of seeing oneself as another sees one. When one sees oneself all alone on the screen all the time, the narcissistic investment vitiates the purpose of videotaping, namely to see ourselves as others see us. The solitary face on the screen is a familiar image to the viewer, one that he knows from any mirror, but the inclusion of the part of the other "mirror" person is a totally new psychological experience [pp. 211–212].

Fifth in the sequence, "A split-screen effect" (made possible by an attached component called a synchronizing generàtor) "with the two faces side by side is recorded [p. 212]." First, the "full face" of the person being concentrated on, either supervisee or client, is shot, "to convey the image of one person as the primary object, being seen by the other." The other half of the split-screen shows the second person in a "side view" as he looks at the first. Then, each is shown from the opposite view:

The impression is of one person looking at another who is looking at the viewer. If split-screen effects are used with two full-face pictures looking at the camera, the viewer is confronted with a decision as to which of the two faces looking directly at him he will look back at.

Sixth, "various zoom lens closeups are made," in order to emphasize whatever the instructor thinks pertinent, such as "the hands, the feet, or any portion of the body or face [p. 212]." A "horizontal split-screen effect" may come after closeups of the eyes, with those of the client shown on top and those of the interviewer on the bottom. In order to counteract the movement of the individuals' heads,

the camera moves slightly to keep their eyes in the picture as much as possible. Hence we see head movement as well as eye movement. Eyes are the most expressive portion of the face, as all artists, photographers and lovers know, and their reciprocal interactional relationship is dramatized in this split-screen picture.

This technique provides "a striking picture of eye contact, eye movements, and," as pointed out by Wilmer in reviewing Hess and Polt's work, changes in the size of the pupils, indicating emotional and attitudinal responses.

Last in the sequence is a shot of both client and interviewer. As the taping nears completion, the camera is focused to show "the entire bodies of both participants . . . exactly as they were at the beginning of the interview." Although this sequence records the essentials of an interview, whoever acts as cameraman may include closeups of telling movements and when appropriate "a 'two-shot' of both participants in full view to remind the viewer of the total relationship [p. 213]."

Other comments on techniques of using equipment in closed-circuit television teaching were pointed to by Trethowan (1968), who used "three miniature transistorized cameras [p. 517]" arranged in the following way:

Two are mounted on wall-brackets, the third, which is mobile, is mounted on a tripod and dolly. The wall-mounted cameras each carry a single lens; the mobile camera is fitted with a lens turret carrying three lenses (1-inch, 2-inch, and wide-angle). All are easily interchangeable [pp. 517–518].

Arranged in this way, such equipment provides several possibilities for camera work, if camera angles and lenses are adjusted properly.

For example, when observing a two-person interview, one camera may be positioned to give a sitting view of the patient (i.e., lap to head), the second a close-up of his face, while the third may be focused on the interviewer. Alternatively, one camera may be set to view both interviewer and patient together, the other two being used to view each separately in close-up. Larger groups may be observed by positioning the cameras so that those which are wall-mounted are placed in diagonally opposite corners of the studio, each viewing the one half of a group over the heads of the other half, the third mobile camera being focused on those not easily included within the viewing ambit of the two wall-mounted cameras [p. 518].

Although more diversification in the types of shots could be achieved with "a remotely controlled zoom lens and a pan-and-tilt mechanism," the nature of therapeutic interviews is such that more expensive equipment is not required. For this reason, fixed and prefocused cameras are considered adequate as well as less obtrusive than moving cameras would be during an interview.

The studio Trethowan (1968) described is 20 by 12 feet and does not require special lighting in addition to the regular "six overhead 4-foot flourescent tubes" and a 200-watt lamp. In regard to regulating the light in the room, he found that during videotaping, when camera sensitivity may need to be delicately balanced, drawing "blackout blinds and curtains" will keep the intensity of light constant so that "the automatic sensitivity control can be switched off and each camera adjusted as desired [p. 518]." Except for avoiding white clothing, persons can wear any other color without causing difficulty.

In order to provide proper acoustical background for sensitive sound equipment, this studio "contains a fitted carpet, fairly heavy curtains, and walls made of partially sound-absorbent material. A double entrance door with a hanging curtain over it helps to reduce extraneous noise [p. 519]." The sound is transmitted by

two sensitive cardioid microphones and a high fidelity stereophonic amplifier giving up to 10 watts in either channel. The microphones are suspended well above eye-level and are sensitive enough to pick up sound from anywhere in the studio. Two channels are used to enhance reproduction, but may be used independently for certain research purposes [pp. 518–519].

In addition to recording specific events for teaching purposes, other techniques may be used to record certain aspects of the interaction in order to aid recall during the replay. Three of these reviewed by Wilmer (1967b) are "feeding light signals into videotape," "silence, behavior and inner dialogue," and "feeding written messages into the videotape [pp. 218–220]."

A videotape technique to record "the unspoken thoughts" of an interviewer, which may overcome the distortion that recalled thoughts are subject to, has been devised. In order to make light signals part of a tape, a light signal board can be constructed and placed behind the client. By pulling one, or possibly two, levers, the interviewer can operate this mechanism. As an alternative, signals may also be superimposed:

A videotape may be made either showing the total scene or use of split-screen effect placing the two figures side by side. The light board may be set in another room before a camera and the light signals superimposed on the picture of the participants. The control box with levers is beside the doctor and below the desk top. The lever is connected with a rheostat. The further down the lever is pulled, the brighter the light becomes, until at maximum position it triggers a switch which causes the light to blink. The light is covered with red plastic to prevent glaring on the camera [p. 219].

Such signals have been used to record "the time, intensity, and duration of a doctor's 'inner dialogue.'" Since controlling such a technique is difficult, usually a single lever is used.

A "light signal" may also show "how an individual uses his silence in relation to speech." "the preverbal, internalized precursor of vocal speech." As a symbol of thinking, speech is preceded by a "form of preparatory internal speech," "the preverbal, internalized precursor of vocal speech."

It often takes the form of a fantasied, incredibly quick and condensed "conversation." As a guide to what, when and how to speak, it takes place as the therapist is listening for cues as to whether to correct, rephrase or reject his contemplated speech [p. 219].

Use of a light signal can point up "various patterns of meditative silence and contemplative inner dialogue [p. 220]." By watching a replay, interviewer and client may both learn what their silences mean. They may "learn more about listening to one another, and that silent listening involves highly active mental work [p. 220]."

Another light may be used to indicate one particular client behavior per session, emphasizing for the counselor-in-training such signals "as significant metaphors . . . halting or blocked speech, unusually strong affect, transference, counter-transference, fantasy, intellectualizations and symbolic gestures [p. 220]."

Although the taking of notes is usually considered to be a distraction during an interview, some instances seem to require doing so. An interesting technique involves superimposing notes written by the interviewer which pertain to the moment. To carry out this procedure, he

writes with a white charcoal pencil on a large pad of black paper held on his lap. A camera behind and at the side of the interviewer focuses on the notes. This picture is superimposed on the portrait of the interview. . . . The writing appears instantaneously across the screen. Watching this live, one is struck with the incredible slowness of writing notes (in contrast with the speed of thought) as well as the patient's behavior which the note-taking doctor does not see. The difficulty of performing two complex skills at the same time is obvious: note-writing occurs after thoughts are formulated while the attentive interviewer is already thinking ahead.

If both persons watch the replay, the client may be helped to

see the interview as a thoughtful, living relationship. Awareness of the doctor's un-spoken observations, reasoning, self-questions and speculations can give a new kind of usable insight to a patient with good ego strength. Replay, thereby, reconstructs and reinforces effective interpretations and illuminates off-target interpretations [p. 221].

Being involved in viewing the replay, the client is a part of "the learning experience, adding dignity and importance to his role [p. 221]."

Another method of transcribing notes instantaneously on the screen is the Victor-Electro-Writer. The interviewer "writes with a pen connected to an electronic transmitter which sends the messages to a receiving unit." Of course, the client cannot see the transmitter, which is within reach of the interviewer, and "the electronic receiver is in another room before a camera. By use of split-screen effect, the lower portion of the final picture shows the notes as they are written [p. 221]."

RECORDING GROUP SESSIONS IN LABORATORY SETTINGS

Just as the well-taped individual interview can accelerate counselor training, Wilmer (1967b) says, a videotaped group session replayed immediately can aid "understanding, observation, and decision-making [p. 214]" within a group and on the parts of group leaders if definite objectives and expected outcomes of videotaping are known ahead of time. In addition, the issue of time utiliza-tion is often mentioned by trainers and students in regard to the relationship between time used for playback and learner outcomes. Wilmer recommends that putting the beginning 10 minutes of a group session on tape "is adequate, and 20 minutes seems to be the maximum, if the tape is going to be replayed immediately and understood by members [p. 215]." As he cautions, tapes that contain "45–60 minutes are too long for ordinary teaching [p. 214]." Of course, capturing the total group process on tape is impossible, but "if one accepts the principle that videotape is useful for highlighting selected elements of the group process, it can be an invaluable tool [p. 215]." Although explicit statements describing microcounseling and counselor training in group work have not been made, even more brief time samples have been utilized by Ivey (1973).

Wilmer (1967b) continues that in order for trainees to see everyone at once, a "split-screen with half of the group on the upper and half on the lower portion" can be used, though "splitting undermines the feeling of circular encompassment [p. 215]." Several other techniques may be used, however; for example, keeping the whole group on camera 1, and picking up just part of the group, moving from face to face with camera 2, is one approach.

If more than two cameras are available, an assistant can keep one on the person speaking and another on group members who are responding. As he does so, he can alternate closeups. In addition, he may even superimpose the image of one person's face in full over other figures forming a part of the group. The advantage of this approach is that it "graphically reproduces one of the cognitive perceptual mechanisms of the therapist—seeing and hearing one person clearly" and being "simultaneously attentive to the others [p. 215]." Another technique, which Wilmer (1967a) called "ghosting," is based on a superimposed image, which involves placing "the main figure in the center of the screen and a reacting secondary figure at the side [p. 126]."

In setting up a design to train group leaders, Wilmer (1967b) describes the process of recording six trainees in a group experience for 10 weeks. The first week, students reviewed a videotaped therapy session. During the next five weeks he played the tapes back to the group while recording the group reactions to the original tapes. In setting up the playback, he used an elaborate process, which is described below, beginning with the first playback session following the original ten group sessions.

First, an establishing shot shows the entire group sitting in U shape. A second camera then picks up a full-face view of each person, with the picture of the entire group alternating between every two persons. After this sequence has been followed, one camera can stay with speakers, and the other can pick up a few persons together, the entire group, or a member who is responding. Closeups may be used for "unusual movement" and the last frame will be the whole group, the same "picture which was interspersed during the entire videotaping [p. 217]."

Becoming attuned "to the non-verbal gestures by which individuals reveal their intention to speak," the closeup cameraman "often has a person on the screen just before or at the moment he speaks." As a result, "the dramatic impact of the final production often conveys the group drama almost as if the director had a prepared script." The systematic use of such a teaching tape is described here:

During the replay discussion a monitor is placed in the open end of the group. On another monitor, in the control room, the videotape is replayed before another camera. By use of a split-screen the original group videotape is inserted into the lower right-hand quadrant of the videotape. The second videotape picture shows a group within a group. Because of the small dimensions of the insert, closeup pictures are seen more clearly [p. 217].

Of course, anyone can ask to have the replay stopped at any time so he can discuss the spot he has interrupted or have an earlier portion played again: "During the discussion of replay, the studio microphones are switched on and the still picture at the point they are discussing is held in the corner of the new recorded picture [pp. 217–218]." The discussion of the replay is paced in order that what is said about the 10-minute segment is completed within 50 minutes. Then the group watches a replay of this 50 minutes without any interruptions. Three hours are needed for each session if this procedure is followed. The end-result is the group members watching themselves watch the initial tape:

From a theoretical and practical point of view, this is a fascinating phenomenon. Its emotional impact stems from the novel effect on the group members who see themselves acting, then reacting, and finally reacting to the reacting. Thus they experience three levels of self and group participation: (1) original group; (2) group discussion as they watch the original group; and (3) re-experience both groups by viewing the final tape [p. 218].

During the remaining four weeks, the class reviews the tapes in order.

[They] are usually amazed at how vividly they re-experience the group feeling; their memories of the groups having blurred, they are often astonished at what they see and hear. The group interaction of the final replays is the fourth exposure of the group to themselves in action and has powerful teaching impact, for they now have some distance and are not concerned with any more videotaping. The videotape is reinforcing, clarifying, and correcting impressions and distortions by solid information feedback to the viewers. This self-study in depth is a form of sensitivity supervision, or more correctly, *sensitivity-revision*. It can be used in modified form for interviews or small group seminars. It has the unique effect of holding life still, so that one may look closely at segments of a human drama again and again [p. 218].

In his review, Danet (1968) reported his experiment of "submitting video-tape feedback to the scrutiny of research methods and employing an out-patient group therapy population." Attempting "to study the impact of video-tape feedback on both individual group members and on group processes under relatively controlled conditions," he based the study on "two outpatient, coeducational, co-therapist psychotherapy groups," one experimental which "received 10 consecutive minutes of videotape playback (the same 10-minute period from the end of the previous week's session) at the beginning of nine weekly sessions [p. 253]." The control group, on the other hand, was also taped, but did not view its playback.

In this study, as well as in the others reported by this author, "playback made denial extremely difficult, carrying the weight of innumerable verbal confrontations for some patients. It confronted them with the reality of how they presented themselves." Although results indicated that use of videotape affects group process, "when playback was introduced in the group's history" and "how the therapists handled the playback material" were important variables. Danet stresses the importance of Stoller's (1967) approach of " 'focused' feedback [p. 254]," for, as he cites from Stoller:

Unless there is some way of highlighting certain information, the value of that information decreases. It is out of this requirement that the concept of focused feedback grew: the centering of participant's attention on that aspect of the videotape feedback which would seem to be most relevant for beneficial behavioral change [p. 255].

The significance of Danet's "experimental finding lies in the suggestion that even a relatively brief (10 minute) segment not handled sensitively and skillfully by an alert therapist can overwhelm individual group members and disrupt the progress of the group-as-a-whole [p. 255]."

Speaking from the point of view of the therapist, Everett L. Shostrom (1968) emphasizes the influence that conducting group sessions for commericial television broadcast had upon his own functioning. The " 'pressure to be authentic' before a large T.V. audience," he stated, forced him to perform "much more effectively," an observation supported by the complaints of "back-home group members," and resulting in his additional depth of participation with home groups. Another observation based on his early T.V. sessions was his "lack of self-disclosure," which prompted his becoming more open in subsequent sessions. In addition, his co-therapist said that for her, too, the commericial T.V. group work "was a self-revealing experience, since she saw herself as much more incongruent and hostile on T.V. than she had ever experienced herself in back-home groups." As a result, she has become "much less strong and hostile in general [p. 208]."

The broad area of confrontation and feedback has not been adequately researched to objectively state the outcome effect on the persons involved. There is agreement, however, that video playback is a powerful process when used in group work since many groups report about complex interactions, which occur but are not fully understood and utilized by group members and leaders. If videotaped, these sections can be replayed and the interview analyzed and utilized more productively.

NONVERBAL BEHAVIOR AND BODY LANGUAGE

Research concentrating systematically on nonverbal behavior has been some-what limited until recently, in spite of the fact that the significance of body language has long been recognized in therapeutic interaction. Ekman and Friesen (1968) attributed this lack of emphasis, first, to the inability of research-ers to agree on the criteria for labeling affect as acted out in nonverbal language, and, second, to the fact that during the early research stages, persons viewing and analyzing film versions of an interview felt they gained little useful informa-tion for assisting the person requesting help. Finally, as a third factor contribut-ing to the weakness of the research findings, Ekman and Friesen named "the problem of obtaining permanent records of the behavior, determining an appro-priate unit of measurement, and devising analytic methods which will reveal the meaning of the nonverbal activity."

More recently, however, there has been increased recognition of the impact that nonverbal behavior has on accurate communication. Perhaps a prime contributor to this situation is the influence that group process, humanistic education, and affective education are having on the teaching-learning process. Related to this is a statement by Ekman and Friesen (1968) suggesting that most of the work in nonverbal communication has been in the area of affect. They believe that the cue one concentrates on determines one's judgment of the type of affective message as communicated by the nonverbal behavior. As carried out by the authors,

[The] difference between the information provided by head and body cues was refor-mulated to take account of distinctions between four types of nonverbal cues (body acts, body positions, facial expressions, and head orientations) and two types of information about emotion (the nature of the emotion, including inferences about both gross affect state and specific emotions, and the intensity of the emotion) [pp. 182–183].

Ekman and Friesen assume

that the face is an affect display system while the body shows the person's adaptive efforts regarding affect, or pictorial illustrations of some aspect of an affective experi-ence. Information about the nature of the emotion can involve only impressions as to gross affective state (e.g., pleasant versus unpleasant) or it can also include inferences about specific emotions (e.g., happy, sad, angry, disgusted, afraid, etc.). Specific emo-tions can frequently be perceived from facial expressions and from body acts, while both head orientation and body positions will most frequently only allow perception of gross affective states, and observers may not always agree about that [p. 183].

Since the facial expressions change more rapidly than body movements, perceiving head cues as indicators of "specific emotions" is done more often than perceiving on the basis of body cues.

Various degrees of intensity of affect can be discerned by studying facial expressions as well as the orientation of the head. In some cases, "facial expressions will not show the cues relevant to perceiving either extreme or intensity [p. 183]." "Body acts," however, "usually convey from moderate to high intensity, while body positions can convey the full range of intensity." Although we may be inhibited in showing an extreme of emotional intensity in facial expressions, "body acts and positions" are not under the same strictures. As a result, the body may provide more cues to reading an extreme of affective intensity than the face or the head (Kurpius, 1968).

This hypothesis is supported by a brief case study associated with a postdoctoral seminar in counselor supervision conducted by Kagan at Michigan State University during the summer of 1966. In this seminar, doctoral students were randomly assigned as supervisees to visiting professors who functioned as supervisor-trainees. Early in the first session of one supervisor-supervisee dyad, it was noticed on the videotape that the supervisee had slowly turned his body away from the supervisor, but was still maintaining eye contact by looking over his shoulder. Even though both members of the dyad were aware of the supervisee's body position, neither was able to focus on the meaning of the position until a second session had been completed and a third person assisted the dyad in a focused playback process. The outcome of the playback analysis was that the supervisor was confused, since eye contact was maintained and the supervisee's facial expressions were friendly and receptive. When the issue was directly confronted by the third person, a considerable amount of data was shared verbally, which was needed to renegotiate their working relationship.

In this brief case study, two factors related to the literature are supported. First, research on nonverbal communication and body language is in an infant stage of development and can be utilized only as general information for exploring relationship language; and second, total body communication must be considered a part of the general information acquired if we are to include all the meaning of a given act.

Wachtel (1967) says that in his work with videotape, "each movement or position is conceived of as having adaptive, expressive and defensive functions, some conscious and some unconscious [p. 97]." Since the additional experimentation and learning that can be achieved through study of the nonverbal language present on tape is important to counselor-educators in their work with trainees, Wachtel's approach is of interest. At first, leaving the audio on during their viewing, he and his associates "were interested not so much in what is communicated by the body alone, but in how addition of the body observations to the verbal data provided richer understanding of what was happening in the interview." By observing a client's gestures and positions, as well as his own, a student's attention may be drawn to particular verbal content in the interview since "one way in which the body and verbal material enrich each other is in pointing out where to look more carefully." For example, "an observation about" a person's "gesture" can bring "to light an important distinction occurring entirely in the verbal realm [p. 98]." This implies that we tend to focus on the language we understand best and avoid attending to the potential messages embedded in the nonverbal behaviors.

Wilmer (1967b) supported this with examples of nonverbal behavior relating to the eyes. For example, persons "commonly 'roll their eyes up and back' when they are thinking back on their life or searching their memories." Movements such as these may not be noticed until a tape is reviewed. Some individuals may "reveal characteristic eye movement patterns when discussing the same issues, e.g., rivalry with a brother." Of course, the movement of the interviewer's eyes is also important. They sometimes "telegraph their intention of speaking by characteristic premonitory eye movements, which sensitive" persons "probably detect subliminally." Other "interviewers have roving eyes, some mostly downcast, others more or less fixed, with patterns of quick side or upward glances." According to Wilmer, "it usually is possible to relate eye movements to the momentary elements of the interview [p. 213]." This type of observation, which may be gained from close study of tapes, aids the trainee in changing his own patterns of behavior to those which may be more effective in working with a client. Through watching tapes, a student can observe for himself that "one of the characteristics of a good interviewer seems to be a constant slow weaving eye movement as he continually scans" his client. "Awareness of what the eyes say is usually a part of preconscious thinking. It is instructive to bring this to consciousness, and it is fascinating and useful to speculate on its unconscious significance [p. 214]."

On a more descriptive level, another way in which replaying a videotape can call attention to nonverbal messages and their meanings was described by Alger and Hogan (1967) as aiding consensual validation in conjoint marital therapy. Their emphasis upon the clients' "increased awareness of the multiple channels of communication, many of them contradictory, between themselves [p. 1425]" was supported by the clients' insightful observations as they watched a tape of the first 10 minutes of their session.

Having recovered from "image impact," individuals "begin to pay attention to other aspects of the playback, especially in connection with their own activity and the reactions of the other persons. The authors state that during the remainder of the playback session, members are better able to focus on how they feel, how they interact verbally and nonverbally, and the complexity of the overall communication network. These authors believe that videotape is the most vivid way to make people aware of the "multiple channels" used in communication.

With the desire to help the client "get more insight into what he and the analyst were doing," Alger and Hogan (Alger, 1967) used videotape with family-counseling groups, which may be generalized to include communication between a counselor and client, or between a supervisor and student, in that

more messages are conveyed kinetically than verbally. Hundreds of these "gesture signals" are captured for immediate review on videotape. "We're more interested in these than in verbal content. In fact, verbal content is frequently only a metaphoric way of expressing feelings people cannot convey directly [p. 25]."

With the use of videotape, we are reminded of the value of a picture over words:

"Every one of us has been puzzled about what there is in our behavior that other people are reacting to," Dr. Alger says. "With this videotape we can now see for ourselves. It is a case where one look at the video screen is worth a thousand interpretations [p. 25]."

As Wachtel (1967) reminds us, "We have difficulty understanding the nonverbal communications of people of other cultures (Hall, 1959), and we probably make many more such errors among our own people than we realize." Since "the success or failure of an interaction may well depend on" our understanding of what we do nonverbally, we need to train ourselves to pick up the subtle quality of "such unconscious behavior [p. 97]."

Another advantage of making observations of the nonverbal and the verbal aspects of videotapes, according to Wachtel (1967), is that "new interpretations of those observations [p. 98]" may be conjectured as a result:

Noting, for example, a pattern of movements associated with aggressive comments and then observing a similar pattern occurring when person A's name was mentioned might lead to the hypothesis that the patient had aggressive feelings toward person A. Clearly, one must be cautious in this type of interpretation, but its potential seems considerable [p. 98].

This sort of analysis would be helpful in working with beginning students if the supervisor wanted to illustrate how particular mannerisms of the trainee might be associated with apprehensive, distorted, or irrelevant responses to his client. Supervisors should be cautious with such interpretations by allowing the trainee to apply the concept if, on repeated samples, similar patterns occur.

Even with the mention of caution, videotape provides the best possible device for educators, students, and clients to study the complex interaction between verbal and nonverbal communication during both the counseling and the supervision sessions.

SIMULATION AS A TRAINING AID

Another way in which videotape is used systematically for training purposes is simulation. Medical students, for example, have been videotaped in the role playing of case studies. In this way trainees may overcome the limitations of role playing, as described by Ramey (1968):

Many people are embarrassed by "acting out" in front of their classmates. (The prospect causes some students to drop a course.) The class, in turn, reacts adversely to a face-to-face confrontation, hesitating to criticize the players or probe the situation they are enacting in more than token fashion. Participants are handicapped because they cannot step out of the role and react to what is happening while it is happening. Finally, it is not possible to go back and repeat something just as it happened before [p. 55].

Although simulation of a client-counselor interaction would not involve as many role-players as a situation in which a doctor might find himself, such as telling a patient or a family that an individual is nearing death, this approach has been used most successfully to depict a case study of an individual as he might appear when talking with a client, or as a practicum student might communicate himself when in a supervisory session.

In the training of counselors, as well as of teachers and medical students, Kagan (Kagan & Krathwohl, 1967) used coached drama students to simulate responses with which clients may confront counselors. This technique of showing the taped simulation to a group of trainees or to an individual, which actually has the effect of bringing about a response in the persons watching, is a simple, but powerful, training device. Adapted to a class situation, this approach might include a supervisee reacting to the role-playing of a practicum student, or, as is often done, a beginning student role-playing for a practicum student or on tape with another student acting as counselor. According to Ramey (1968), one of the main strengths of videotaped simulation is that

disassociation of the television image from the actual persons seated in the group takes place. Class members feel free to tear the situation apart without regard for personalities, something they could never do if their classmates were performing in person. Fortunately, however, the disassociation is not complete, for involvement remains. Experimental use of tapes produced by a number of classes using the same hypothetical situation indicates that even if the students know the people who made the tapes, they do not seem to get as much from these tapes as from those produced by their own group [pp. 56–57].

If persons from within a training group were used for simulation tapes, those persons could also react to themselves on tape.

In one simulation, experienced students played the roles of a doctor, a dying patient, and his family:

The goal for this demonstration was to give students an opportunity to relate theory to practice by letting them experience such situations at depth level. In the judgment of the author and the faculty this goal was achieved.

The student who had played the part of the doctor ended the session by saying, "I can't tell you how glad I am to have had a chance to have a dry run on this kind of problem."

For demonstration purposes the class reactions were also videotaped and have been electronically spliced into the problem tape at the points at which classroom discussion interrupted the playback. Thus, a complete teaching demonstration of the use of this method with a group of first-year medical students is available on Ampex 600 tape [p. 58].

Since many settings in the helping professions require a team approach, simulation on tape has possibilities for training counselors for many of the environments in which they might work eventually, such as public schools, clinics, and universities.

Using the guidelines of the Missouri Diagnostic Classification Plan, Thayer, Peterson, Carr, and Merz (1972) developed a *Critical Moments in Counseling* videotape of 35 portions of simulated interviews, which last 30–70 seconds each. The clients role-play "a number of distinctly different problems which counselors and other personnel involved in the helping relationships face at various times in their respective careers [p. 188]." In addition to representing different types of problems and ways of responding to them, this tape can provide prepracticum students, as well as trainees in other helping professions, with the stimulus for learning communication skills. Another use might be as an evaluation tool throughout a training program, with emphasis during practicum. Along with these uses, such a videotape might play a part "in the selection or self-selection processes for counselor education programs at all levels [p. 190]."

Froehlich (1970) emphasizes that "on-the-job training has the problem of giving the student responsibility" when he has "neither extensive experience nor legal backing." For this reason, he thinks that the use of videotape simulation provides the student with an ideal preliminary experience and one which is commensurate with instructional theory:

When we recall that the students learn best when they know what they are looking for, when they dig for themselves, and when they go at their own pace, we realize that videotape simulation provides a process which can fulfill all three requirements for efficient student learning.

Videotape simulation gives the student the opportunity to learn information in such a way that he will use it in later life. In addition, he is learning information associated with a problem-solving situation which will act as an organizer of the information. As we learned earlier, this coupling of information to the problem-solving activity will lead to greater retention [p. 61].

Perhaps the most interesting aspect of simulation, however, is the view that it may bring about an experience that corresponds with reality more accurately than the sort of experience received during training on-the-job:

The re-enactment of scenes is true-to-life because the role players can be themselves without censoring their own behavior since they can hide behind the rationalization that they were just playing the role to please or to bring out a viewpoint as they were directed to do in their sealed envelope. In some respects, videotape simulation approaches reality more closely than does the recording of actual events because of the third person intrusion of the recording devices as discussed earlier in this chapter [p. 61].

An additional advantage is the fact that these experimenters "have not found any teaching method that creates as much student participation or involvement as does videotape simulation [p. 61]."

THE USE OF RECORDED MONOLOGUES IN TRAINING

Still another creative video process is the utilization of "television monologue." Wilmer (1970) notes ways that videotaped monologues have been used for supervision and consultation purposes. He includes several suggestions for taping such monologues. Having been told that what he does during the 15 minutes is up to him, and that after watching his tape by himself he can request that it be erased, the client (or trainee) is asked to sit in a chair in a familiar setting, and the camera is put in front of it. A boom microphone is used so that he is free of equipment. The technician leaves and does not return until it is time to turn off the camera at the end of the taping, at which point he leaves the client alone again to watch the rewound tape. After this exposure, the tape is erased if the client requests it. If the tape is not erased, client and therapist usually look at it together in a couple of days. An alternative way of handling the monologue is to tape for 10 minutes, have the client view himself, then tape him for another 5 minutes reacting to his replay or going on with his monologue, and finally to have the client look at his own responses.

In addition to the opportunities for supervision implicit in the replay with the client, his therapist, and other members of the therapeutic community, Wilmer (1970) describes another experiment, which contains potential instructional value. It involved simultaneous recording of interviews with four cameras, one at each corner of the room, while the same patient was interviewed serially by five different persons in ten-minute sequences. The identity of the interviewers was not known to the patient before. Each interviewer asked the same four questions in his own words and style. The interviewers were a professor of criminal law, a psychoanalyst, a newspaper reporter, a policeman in plain clothes, and a policeman in uniform [p. 1761].

Following 50 minutes of taping, four playbacks were shown "simultaneously in a block of four monitors" to all those participating. Of course, the client responded differently to the various interviewers; but in addition, the angle of the camera made the same dyadic interaction look different in the four monitors:

The same transaction appeared strikingly different from each camera angle, as well as with each interviewer. The patient behaved and responded in a significantly different manner, either conforming to, in subtle defiance of, or resistant to the interviewer's manner, style, and person. . . . In all instances, it was obvious that both people were interviewing each other, a fact that Sullivan noted long ago. . . . These findings are significant for clinical psychiatry as well as forensic psychiatry, now that television is being used in courts of law [pp. 1761–1762].

These differential responses and varied perceptions based on camera angle led to the attempt to "obtain reliable, replicable audiovisual records of an individual" by taping him "talking to the television camera with no one else in the room [p. 1762]." For purposes of supervision, videotaped monologues may be regarded as useful for instruction according to Wilmer's classification. Concerning practical considerations, he says, monologues may be regarded as "(1) predictive, diagnostic; (2) informational, historical; (3) behavioral representation of self; (4) psychotherapeutic effect; and (5) record of the patient at a given time and place [p. 1765]."

VIDEO-COMPUTER ASSISTED TRAINING

A relatively recent and more sophisticated process focusing on "continuous immediate feedback" (Semmel, 1972) has been developed by the Center for Innovation in Teaching the Handicapped at Indiana University. The system producing the data is referred to as a "closed-loop cybernetic system." It "consists of three interdependent stations: Teaching Station, Observation-Coding Station, and Analysis-Encoding Station [p. 8]." The Teaching Station at this time consists of a room equipped to receive audio and/or video transmissions. The Observation-Coding Station represents a typical one-way-glass observation room, which adjoins the teaching room. In this room, trained observers code the "teacher and/or pupil behavior [p. 10]" under the classification system specified. "At present, the coding terminals used to input observations data consists of ten mechanical push-buttons mounted on a metal box—a configuration similar to a touch-tone telephone [p. 11]."

"The Analysis-Encoding Station consists of a small computer (PDP-12) and the associated computer hardware required for the on-line processing of coded input data which is gathered and transmitted from the Observation-Coding Station." This set-up will produce "hard copy printout, storage, and transfer of the analyzed data [pp. 11–12]."

These three stations are linked together so as to provide immediate feedback to student teachers on a T.V. monitor in the classroom ranging from "simple frequency counts of desired behaviors, to abstract representations of sequential interaction patterns [p. 12]."

As computers become more available at schools and universities, both training and service components of counseling ought to consider systematic instruction in how to use computers on the job. Trainees, for example, should be aware of how to go about using stored data to aid in making more systematic decisions about their consumers.

Gluech and Stroebel (1969) reported that in their experience users' responses to receiving information from a video screen have been good. The system they describe could be used in a number of settings: "Using a security code system to activate a terminal at any location, any member of the clinical staff may interrogate the computer for any piece of patient information which he is authorized to obtain [p. 3]."

Of course, possible drawbacks to computer use do exist, such as "interrogating the computer file hundreds of times for past case histories to identify previous patients with similar problems to determine how various treatment alternatives have succeeded." This sort of search formerly was the area of clinical research. Since the 1950s, however, as Mechl has indicated (Gluech & Stroebel, 1969):

Once behavioral data are in a quantitative format, many decisions could better be made using actuarial techniques. He proposes the development of a "cookbook"—a set of simple rules which could be used to classify patient profiles into different categories or groups. Examples might be "automatic diagnosis" of "treatment assignments." The idea is to use a simple set of rules to scan all previous cases in the computer memory, thus freeing the clinician from this tedious effort and providing him with a distilled group of patient records which pass the specified criteria. He can then use his unique skills to evaluate this data subset, which is of high relevance for the care of his patient [p. 4].

The point here is that individuals training to work in settings in which they will be responsible for making decisions about people, and in which they will have access to stored data about a particular population, should learn how to use the computer as part of their instructional program. Such training would involve teaching students to make hypotheses, which could subsequently be submitted to the computer. Some of these hyptheses would be "in the form of intuitive hunches which would be difficult to derive in the tightly logical sense of the decision tree or rule book. With his hunch in mind," a clinician may take "15 minutes at the terminal setting up guidelines for establishing categories and assigning cases."

He then requests classification analysis and is informed in minutes if quantitative information about previous cases is sufficiently discriminative to substantiate his hypothesis. If the optimal weights calculated possess reasonable predictive validity (indicated by the computer program), he may immediately ask for a prediction about potential decisions on a current patient of interest. By providing clinicians with access to an "instantaneous," interactive computer system, an important step has been taken in extending the domain of clinical research into the day-to-day workings of the clinical decision process [p. 7].

Miller and Turpin (1972) described how use of other media may be combined with the use of interviews on videotape to bring about effective instruction with second-year psychiatry students. The Systems Analysis Index for Diagnosis (SAID)

consists of an inventory of 40 items . . . and a diagnostic chart with six broad categories. . . . The diagnostic chart is arranged as a matrix so that each diagnostic category is compared with every inventory item. The significance of each item is then indicated for each diagnostic category. The inventory, diagnostic chart, and instructions for using them are contained in the *SAID Handbook* [p. 1219].

Since this package was developed for 20 hours of teaching time, instruction is divided into 10 blocks of two hours each. The sequence, which is covered in five days, is as follows:

1. Observation of a videotaped interview.
2. Rating of the videotaped interview by students who use the SAID inventory and diagnostic chart.
3. Comparison of the students' ratings with consensual ratings by the faculty.
4. Discussion of the syndrome and how it was differentially diagnosed.

5. Brief lecture on the syndrome that the videotape illustrated.
6. General discussion [p. 1221].

Approximately 25 minutes of a two-hour segment is taken up with the video-tape presentation. How the remainder of the time is used varies.

First in the schedule, however,

the computer printouts of the previous day's ratings are handed to the students. These printouts list the distribution and mean of the students' ratings and the mean of the faculty's ratings for each of the 40 inventory items. Thus the student can compare his own ratings with the ratings of faculty and peers. At the end of the course each student's ratings are collated in a computer printout and given to him so that he can trace his progress from rating to rating.

According to the developers of the SAID approach, "It incorporates the application of learning theory to education by making the student an active participant in his learning and by giving him frequent immediate feedback." They have also stated "two major goals: to provide basic skills in symptom recognition and evaluation, and to illustrate how symptoms cluster in the major diagnostic categories [p. 1222]." Student evaluations of the program have been positive since the purpose of the process is preparation for future real-life clinical training experiences.

LIMITATIONS AND SUMMARY

Chodoff (1972) has warned against relying too much upon videotape for training purposes. He points to the frustrations involved first in obtaining fairly expensive equipment and subsequently in maintaining it, scheduling its use, and moving it around, as well as producing tape of sufficient audio and video quality to be used effectively for instruction.

In addition, selecting the segments of a tape most useful for trainees takes up valuable time of an instructor, who may make decisions based on "factors of conscious and unconscious selectivity present in conventional supervision [p. 822]." Also, if insufficient background is provided before selected sequences are shown to students, they may not be able to follow adequately, or "to identify with the participants in the therapy." Then, too, if observers ponder over too many details, "the overall strategy of the therapeutic encounter becomes obscured [p. 823]." Of course, the supervisor himself should be the first to refrain from concentrating on too much detail and to keep other observers from the same error.

In summary, however, one must say that the known results of video usage in counseling, counselor training, and related disciplines are impressive. By its very nature, the medium provides for openness of participants via immediate and delayed playback, for storage of videotape data for research purposes, and for self-instruction and acceleration of the development of objectivity in the counseling and training process.

Although there are questions to be answered about the objectives, theories, and methodologies of video application, the process is already sufficiently developed to suggest that it is probably the single greatest technical resource available for preparing counselors and other persons who work in applied fields. Perhaps computer-feedback via video will also become more common in the not-too-distant future; however, the complexity and cost of computer assistance will probably delay the immediate implementation of its potential.

REFERENCES

Alger, I. Video gives patients clearer view of themselves. *Journal of Rehabilitation,* 1967, May-June, 24–25. (Originally published: *Medical World News,* 1966, **1**, 1–2.)

Alger, I., & Hogan, P. The use of videotape recordings in conjoint marital therapy. *American Journal of Psychiatry,* 1967, **123**, 1425–1429.

Berger, M. M. Integrating video into private psychiatric practice. *Voices: The Art and Science of Psychotherapy,* 1969–1970, **5**(4), 78–85.

Berger, M. M. (Ed.) *Videotape techniques in psychiatric training and treatment.* New York: Brunner/Mazel, 1970.

Boyd, H. S., & Sisney, V. V. Immediate self-image confrontation and changes in self-concept. *Journal of Consulting Psychology,* 1967, **31**, 291–294.

Chodoff, P. Supervision of psychotherapy with videotape: Pros and cons. *American Journal of Psychiatry,* 1972, **128**, 819–823.

Cornelison, F. S., & Tausig, T. M. A study of the self-image experience using video tapes at Deleware state hospital. *Deleware Medical Journal,* 1964, **36**, 229.

Danet, B. N. Self-confrontation in psychotherapy reviewed: Videotape playback as a clinical and research tool. *American Journal of Psychotherapy,* 1968, **22**(2), 245–257.

Ekman, P., & Friesen, W. V. Nonverbal behavior in psychotherapy research. In J. M. Shlien (Ed.), *Research in psychotherapy.* Washington: American Psychological Association, 1968.

Froehlich, K. E. Teaching psychotherapy to medical students through videotape simulation. In M. M. Berger (Ed.), *Videotape techniques in psychiatric training and treatment.* New York: Brunner/Mazel, 1970.

Geertsma, R. H., & Reivich, R. S. Repetitive self-observation by video-tape playback. *Journal of Nervous and Mental Disease,* 1965, **141**, 29–41.

Gluech, B. C., Jr., & Stroebel, C. F. The computer and the clinical decision process: II. *American Journal of Psychiatry,* 1969, **125**, 2–7.

Ivey, A. E. Microcounseling: The counselor as trainer. *Personnel and Guidance Journal,* 1973, **51**(5), 312–316.

Kagan, N., & Krathwohl, D. R., et al. *Studies in human interaction: Interpersonal process recall stimulated by video tape.* (Education Research Series RR-20) East Lansing: Michigan State University, 1967.

Kurpius, D. J. Post-Doctoral Seminar in Supervision, Conference Summary, July, 1968.

Logue, P. E., Zenner, M., & Gohman, G. Video-tape role playing in the job interview. *Journal of Counseling Psychology,* 1968, **15**(5), 436–438.

Miller, P. R., & Turpin, J. P. Multimedia teaching of introductory psychiatry. *American Journal of Psychiatry,* 1972, **128**, 1219–1223.

Moore, F. J., Chernell, E., & West, M. J. Television as a therapeutic tool. *Archives of General Psychiatry,* 1965, **12**, 217–222.

Ramey, J. W. Teaching medical students by videotape simulation. *Journal of Medical Education,* 1968, **43**, 55–59.

Rogers, A. H. Videotape feedback in group psychotherapy. *Psychotherapy: Theory, Research and Practice,* 1968, **5**(1), 37–39.

Semmel, M. I. *Toward the development of a computer-assisted teacher training system (CATTS).* (U.S. Office of Education Tech. Rep. No. 7.2) Bloomington: Indiana University, 1972.

Shostrom, E. L. Witnessed group therapy on commercial television. *American Psychologist,* 1968, **23**, 207–209.

Stoller, F. H. Group psychotherapy on television: An innovation with hospitalized patients. *American Psychologist,* 1967, **22**, 158–161.

Thayer, L., Peterson, V., Carr, E., & Merz, D. Development of a critical incidents videotape. *Journal of Counseling Psychology,* 1972, **19**(2), 188–191.

Trethowan, W. H. Teaching psychiatry by closed-circuit television. *British Journal of Psychiatry,* 1968, **114**, 517–522.

Wachtel, P. L. An approach to the study of body language in psychotherapy. *Psychotherapy: Theory, Research and Practice,* 1967, **4**(3), 97–100.

Wilmer, H. A. Practical and theoretical aspects of videotape supervision in psychiatry. *Journal of Nervous and Mental Disease,* 1967, **145**(2), 123–130. (a)

Wilmer, H. A. Television: Technical and artistic aspects of videotape supervision of psychiatric teaching. *Journal of Nervous and Mental Disease,* 1967, **144**(3), 207–223. (b)

Wilmer, H. A. Innovative uses of videotape on a psychiatric ward. *Hospital and Community Psychiatry,* 1968, **19**, 129–133. (a)

Wilmer, H. A. Television as a participant recorder. *American Journal of Psychiatry,* 1968, **124**, 1157–1163. (b)

Wilmer, H. A. Use of the television monologue with adolescent psychiatric patients. *American Journal of Psychiatry,* 1970, **126**, 1760–1766.

Group Counseling: From Research to Training and Practice

James L. Lee

University of Wisconsin—Madison

INTRODUCTION

Group counseling is taking its place among the techniques of practicing school-counselors; at least one no longer hears continued argument that group counseling is an anomaly. At the same time, the efficacy of groups is under considerable question because of the lack of research and adequate standards (Back, 1972). While there are several excellent theoretical and practical statements on groups (Gazda, 1971; Glanz, 1962; Lifton, 1961; Kemp, 1970; Ohlsen, 1970), few of these have generated much research, with the possible exception of the behavioral approach. Present group-counseling theories are based on group-dynamics theory and research, but there still remains the uncertainty as to the efficacious application of these principles to the practice of group counseling in schools.

FROM RESEARCH

As a basis for both training for and use of groups in schools, a major portion of the existing group-counseling research was reviewed and classified to identify patterns in the findings. Such patterns led to a series of generalizations relating to practice and outcomes of groups in counseling. Two criteria were used to select studies for review: (1) the problems or goals dealt with by subjects in the studies were similar to typical problems dealt with by counselors in schools; and (2) the length of time for group meetings (individual sessions of 50–60 minutes and group sessions no longer than several weeks) was similar to the time restrictions of school-counselors. A third criterion was used as much as possible—that the subjects in the study be in the same setting and of the same age as those with whom school-counselors normally work. This third criterion could not be adhered to strictly because it would have eliminated the majority of the studies.

Several terms used to describe concepts common to the studies are defined below.

Internal Tasks: Tasks that focus on behavior, skills, habits, attitudes, or ideals within the group or its members; e.g., improving interpersonal skills through group interaction, improving self-concept or self-esteem, self-other awareness, and so on.

External Tasks: Tasks that focus on individual behavior, skills, habits, attitudes, or ideals outside the group's interaction; e.g., improving grade-point average (GPA) and/or classroom behavior, making realistic vocational choices, improving interpersonal relationships with teachers, and so on.

Transfer: Transfer of training refers to the application of knowledge, skills, habits, attitudes, or ideals acquired in one situation—such as the physics laboratory or counseling—to another situation—such as the kitchen, the farm, the machine shop, or interpersonal relationships and achievement in the classroom.

Counselor-Centered Group: A group in which the counselor assumes leadership in facilitating group establishment of goals and group interaction to accomplish goals. This is similar to Goldman's (1962) Level II process.

Student-Centered Group: A group in which the counselor participates, but makes no direct attempts to influence. He acts as a sounding board for members through reflection, questioning, and clarifying. He attempts to provide an atmosphere for expression of feeling but does not assume leadership, preferring to let it evolve among members. This is similar to Goldman's (1962) Level III process.

Generalizations extrapolated through the review and classification process are presented below with a brief description of a portion of the research they are based on.

Generalization 1: Change will occur, but transfer is less likely in student-centered groups with internal tasks.

Caplan (1957) used student-centered groups with "problem" junior-high-school boys—the counselor acted as a nonevaluating sounding board. The group's task was internal—problems and concerns of individuals were used as topics of discussion, with focus on interpersonal relations within the group. Measurement of change for subjects was both internal (self-concept) and external (favorable change of GPA). There were significant changes within experimental subgroups, and between them and noncounseled controls, when compared on self-concept. Changes measured using GPA were not significant within subgroups or between experimentals and controls.

Similarly, Broedel and his colleagues (1960) used student-centered groups with both internal tasks (acceptance of self and others as measured by the Picture Story Test, and interpersonal relationships within the group measured by students themselves and an observer team) and an external task (GPA). The subjects were junior-high-school gifted underachievers. Experimental groups gained significantly more in self-other acceptance than non-counseled controls. There were significant, healthy behavioral changes for subjects within the groups; but there were no significant changes in academic achievement.

These studies and others (Baymur & Patterson, 1960; Clements, 1966; Speegle, 1962) have used student-centered groups with internal tasks, and have produced significant changes on internal measures but not on external measures. These studies have proceeded on the assumption that group counseling, within the parameters in Generalization 1, would increase student self-acceptance and self-esteem, and that this increase is a necessary and sufficient condition for transfer of behavior change outside the group. In the studies reviewed this does not seem to hold true.

Generalization 2: Transfer is most likely to occur in a counselor-centered group with an external task.

Gilbreath (1967) used counselor-centered (CC) and client-centered (CLC) groups. The CC groups had an external task—relating personality traits to scholastic difficulties and achievement. The CLC groups had an internal task —free discussion with emphasis on a nonthreatening atmosphere for the expression of feelings. Internal measures (Dependency, Anxiety, Depression, etc.) and external measures (GPA) were used to compare experimental and control groups. Data reported on both achievement and personality measures indicated that CC groups with external tasks produced significant changes, whereas CLC groups with internal tasks produced no significant changes on either measure.

The review of the Gilbreath study and others (Hoyt, 1955; Spielberger, Weitz, & Denny, 1962; Krumboltz & Thoresen, 1964; Shaw & Winsten, 1965; Winborn, 1962; and Vriend, 1969) indicate that the likelihood of transfer is increased in CC groups with external tasks. There is also evidence within the studies reviewed that the group and task combination in Generalization 2 is highly related to significant changes on both internal and external measures.

Generalization 3: The likelihood of transfer in counselor-centered groups with external tasks will be increased if the counselor offers high degrees of the facilitative conditions.

Dinkenson and Truax (1966) used groups in which counselors offered various levels of therapeutic conditions by an "integrated didactic and experiential approach" (counselor-centered). The task of the groups was external—raising GPAs for underachievers. The level of therapeutic conditions was measured by the degree of counselor empathy, regard, and genuineness. There were no significant differences between the control groups and those experimental groups receiving moderate levels of therapeutic conditions. Experimental groups receiving high levels of therapeutic conditions increased GPAs significantly more than control groups.

Generalization 4: The likelihood of transfer in counselor-centered groups with external tasks will be increased if members communicate in accord with group norms.

Mezzano (1967) investigated the relationship between the degree of a student's investment in group counseling and change in academic achievement (external task). Degree of investment was defined as following established group-communication norms as inferred by participation, willingness to explore, and communication of feelings. Counselors initiated discussion topics, facilitated group discussion, and related personality patterns to scholastic skills (CC). There was a significant relationship between the degree of investment in group counseling (communication according to norms) and change in academic achievement.

Generalization 5a. On external tasks, both open-minded and closed-minded members have little difficulty communicating relevant to the task.

Generalization 5b: On internal tasks, open-minded members are more likely to communicate relevant to the task than are closed-minded members.

Personality factors, as they affect the communicative functioning of counselor-centered groups, were investigated by Kemp (1963). Communication of graduate students rated as having open and closed belief systems (Dogmatism Scale) in socio groups (external tasks) and psyche groups (internal tasks) was studied. The results indicated that there were no significant differences between "Open" and "Closed" individuals in the socio group sessions. In the psyche groups, those with "Open" belief systems initiated significantly more communication relative to the task than those with "Closed" belief systems. In the socio group, all members' responses were useful in attainment of group purposes.

It would be presumptuous to maintain that these generalizations are substantiated by the limited amount of research reviewed. However, the research is indicative, and provides a better basis for the practice of group counseling in schools than mere belief. As indicated in the generalizations, it appears that counselors can be more certain of facilitating change (transfer) if they carefully, with students' cooperation, establish specific external goals. Having established goals, the counselor then has the responsibility of designing tasks and group experiences, or facilitating the group's interaction with direct relationship to those goals. This means that the counselor, in an accepting, genuine, and empathic manner, must continually help the members relate group experiences to goals and purposes outside of the group.

TO TRAINING

Experiential learning—e.g., through counseling practicum—has always been thought essential in counselor training. It has been recommended that counselors, in addition to a counseling practicum, have a group-counseling practicum. This recommendation has generally not been fulfilled in training programs because of difficulties related to time, staff, setting, and other factors. There is another alternative, which incorporates the generalizations discussed above. This alternative is described below.

The University of Wisconsin—Madison counselor-education program is a full-time, two-year program. In place of the usual course sequence in counselor education, the program attempts to incorporate the material covered in several courses into a sequential whole. The students, during their first semester on campus, attend class in the counseling and guidance department for a full day twice a week. That day of instruction is divided into two parts—large-group instruction and small-group laboratory experience. The large-group instructional time is used for lecture, discussion, and presentation of material, as normally takes place in instruction. The small-group laboratory experience is organized so that groups of 10–12 students are assigned to one group for the semester. The small-group laboratory experience relates most directly to our discussion here.

The small groups serve three primary purposes: (1) learning, discussion groups related to large-group instructional input; (2) experience of group life and development under legitimate, organized, and facilitated conditions for an entire semester; and (3) learning of counseling skills related to both individual and group counseling. Specifically, in relation to purposes 2 and 3, tasks which relate to the external world of counselor practice are designed and used as a major portion of the group experience.

Examples of such learning-process tasks for groups are: *one-way versus two-way communication, listening triads* (Pfeiffer & Jones, 1969), and the *awareness wheel.* In greater detail, the awareness-wheel experience proceeds as follows. The instructor presents to the small group the framework shown in Figure 1 as a way to increase awareness of themselves and others as effective communicators. The presentation is made in the form of a wheel to underscore that one can begin anywhere in the wheel, with any level of awareness, and move back and forth to other dimensions to expand the information originally available to self and others. Thus, starting with a feeling, one can examine data

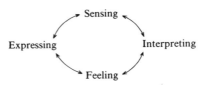

Figure 1. Awareness wheel.

and meanings associated with feeling. The students are then asked to use the wheel in slow motion; i.e., first describing what they sense ("I see you sitting back in your chair"), second adding their interpretation ("I think you're relaxed"), third adding their own feeling ("I'm comfortable too"), and so on. In discussing the experience, the instructor helps the members examine how they can use the wheel to analyze ordinary situations and gain information (awareness) about themselves (in perceptions, thoughts, feelings) in relation to others, in order to communicate more effectively, specifically as related to counseling. Students are also required to design tasks and lead their group as a basis for obtaining feedback concerning their own group-counseling skills. In this manner the student-counselor obtains experience as a group member on an ongoing basis, on a short-term immediate goal basis, and as a leader.

During the second semester, students participate in a practicum in a setting similar to that in which they wish to do their internship during the second year. They also spend one full day a week on campus in small-group supervision, experience, and instruction. In addition, each student has one hour a week of individual supervision. The second semester provides additional group experience, as well as the supervision of group counseling within the real setting, as part of the practicum experience.

The attempt within the program has been to provide an experiential model of both individual and group counseling. This model can then be applied to the students' work setting both during their internship, when there is the opportunity for practice, feedback, and evaluation, and after completion of their degree.

TO PRACTICE

In addition to using groups for intervention with the *usual* problems in the school (underachievement, disruptive behavior, test interpretation, vocational exploration, and so on), there are two other forms of practice implied through the generalizations.

The Counselor as a Group Consultant

There already exist in schools small groups with external tasks—student council, homecoming or prom committees, language and science clubs, and so on. Each of these groups has goals and functions that affect both individual members and the school environment as a source of academic and social learning. Counselors with group knowledge and experience can and should act as a valuable consultant to such groups. Through helping these groups focus periodically on interactions which help and/or hinder movement toward effective decisions or activities, counselors will promote understanding of effective group operation and individual growth and insight in a manner transferable to other forms of group or individual interaction.

The Counselor as a Psychological Educator

Many aspects of individual development can be directly taught and learned through experiential group interaction. Counselors can use microlab techniques with large classroom groups as an experiential mode of learning about self and basic principles of human relationships and communication. The effects upon individual and group relationships of such things as selective perception, one-way versus two-way communication, and hidden agendas, to name but a few, can be purposefully taught and experienced. Listening, speaking, and relating skills can be practiced. In this manner the counselors, as teachers, decide what outcomes, experiences, attitudes, or ideals are to be taught and experienced, and then use or design specific tasks or exercises to accomplish them.

CONCLUSION

The generalizations presented above imply some of the conditions within groups under which transfer is most likely to occur. There are large gaps between and among the generalizations. This results from the inconclusiveness of much of the research, and from a lack of sufficient descriptions defining either group processes (leadership) or types of group tasks. Nonetheless, these generalizations provide a basis for specific recommendations for both training and practice. The gaps between the generalizations also indicate directions for future research.

REFERENCES

Back, K. W. The group can comfort but it can't cure. *Psychology Today,* 1972, **6**(7), 28–35.

Baymur, F. B., & Patterson, C. H. A comparison of three methods of assisting underachieving high school students. *Journal of Counseling Psychology,* 1960, **7**, 83–88.

Broedel, J., et al. The effects of group counseling on gifted underachieving adolescents. *Journal of Counseling Psychology,* 1960, **7**, 163–170.

Caplan, S. W. The effect of group counseling on junior high school boys' concepts of themselves in school. *Journal of Counseling Psychology,* 1957, **4**, 124–128.

Clements, B. E. Transitional adolescents, anxiety, and group counseling. *Personnel and Guidance Journal,* 1966, **45**, 67–71.

Dickenson, W. A., & Truax, C. B. Group counseling with college underachievers. *Personnel and Guidance Journal,* 1966, **45**, 243–247.

Gazda, G. M. *Group counseling: A developmental approach.* Boston: Allyn and Bacon, 1971.

Gilbreath, S. H. Group counseling with male underachieving college volunteers. *Personnel and Guidance Journal,* 1967, **45**(5), 469–479.

Glanz, E. C. *Groups in guidance.* Boston: Allyn and Bacon, 1962.

Goldman, Leo. Group guidance: Content and process. *Personnel and Guidance Journal,* 1962, **40**, 518–522.

Hoyt, D. P. An evaluation of group and individual programs in vocational guidance. *Journal of Applied Psychology,* 1955, **39**, 26–30.

Kemp, C. G. Behaviors in group guidance (socio process) and group counseling (psyche process). *Journal of Counseling Psychology,* 1963, **10**, 373–377.

Kemp, C. G. *Foundations of group counseling.* New York: McGraw-Hill, 1970.

Krumboltz, J. D., & Thoresen, C. E. The effect of behavioral counseling in group and individual settings on information-seeking behavior. *Journal of Counseling Psychology,* 1964, **11**, 324–333.

Lifton, Walter M. *Working with groups.* New York: John Wiley, 1961.

Mezzano, J. A consideration for group counselors: Degree of counselee investment. *School Counselor,* 1967, **14**, 167–169.

Ohlsen, M. M. *Group counseling.* New York: Holt, Rinehart and Winston, 1970.

Pfeiffer, W. J., & Jones, J. E. *A handbook of structured experiences for human relations training.* Vol. 1. Iowa City: University Associates Press, 1969.

Shaw, M. C., & Wursten, R. Research on group procedures in schools: A review of the literature. *Personnel and Guidance Journal,* 1965, **44**, 27–34.

Speegle, P. T. The effectiveness of two techniques of counseling with students on academic probation. Unpublished doctoral dissertation, North Texas State University, 1962.

Spielberger, C. D., Weitz, H., & Denny, J. Group counseling and the academic performance of anxious college freshmen. *Journal of Counseling Psychology,* 1962, **9**, 195–204.

Vriend, T. J. High-performing inner-city adolescents assist low-performing peers in counseling groups. *Personnel and Guidance Journal,* 1969, **47**, 897–904.

Winborn, B., & Schmidt, L. G. The effectiveness of short-term group counseling upon the academic achievement of potential superior but underachieving college freshmen. *Journal of Educational Research,* 1962, **55**, 169–173.

Projected Planning for Innovative Techniques in the Counselor-Preparation Process

Richard Mowsesian

University of Texas—Austin

INTRODUCTION

Counselor-educators continue to be plagued by the issue of meeting the ever-changing needs of counselor-preparation programs—programs designed to meet the future needs of professional counselors expected to function in a variety of constantly evolving settings. In the past, the primary focus in preparing counselors was on placement in secondary schools, vocational rehabilitation agencies, and college counseling centers; a secondary focus was on preparation for other settings, such as child-guidance clinics. In the world of the 1970s and 1980s, the focus in counselor preparation will be on preparation of counselors to function in a wider variety of settings. Such environments as preschool, elementary schools, junior and community colleges, family consultation centers, neighborhood youth centers, and drug centers are representative of the broadening work setting of today's and, of even greater import, tomorrow's counselors. It is evident that the locus of a counselor's work is broadening to include almost every facet of American society, and it seems equally evident that this trend will not abate—we can expect it to continue.

The impetus for the diversification of counselor services comes from many sources. Federally and privately supported educational programs, the growing affluence of American society, the developing awareness that people need help to meet the demands of a complex society, and the revolutionary changes in the social, political, spiritual, and economic life of American society are all contributing to these demands for assistance. That these have affected and will continue to affect counselor education is perhaps an understatement.

An examination of existing counselor-preparation programs throughout the United States indicates that *most programs are educating today's counselors to be proficient in utilizing yesterday's tools to meet yesterday's needs.* Only a few

393

programs are making concentrated efforts to develop innovative programs to meet new demands—if not tomorrow's, then, at least, today's (see Thoresen, 1969; Loughary, Friesen, & Hurst, 1966).

One of the prime difficulties encountered in the development of new programs designed to educate the counselor for tomorrow is the curriculum-development lag. Regardless of how quickly one may wish to begin innovative counselor-preparation programs, there is a significant time lapse between the beginning and the end of the process of conceptualization, investigation, translation, and implementation. Generally, to shorten this time lapse, educators are apt to implement an idea prior to investigating its worth. Even with this questionable practice, it is an historical truism in curriculum development that new curriculums are usually far more advanced as models than in the forms they take when translated and implemented. There also seems to be a lack of desire in some quarters, or perhaps an inertia, about altering curricular programs to keep pace with new techniques and changes. Graduate-level education is perhaps more guilty of this mode of behavior with regard to curriculum change than are other educational levels.

It is not the purpose of the present essay to debate the curricular issues associated with the development of counselor-preparation programs. Rather, it is felt that the issue should be stated as an influencing factor for the discussion to follow. In an effort to provide a rich and constructive counselor-preparation program with a futuristic outlook, one may need to challenge the existing structure of graduate education. (The underlying assumption, though not necessarily advocated, is that all counselor-preparation programs find their locus in graduate education.)

Most graduate educational programs follow a fairly well defined course sequence. It is assumed that if one follows this sequence he is adequately prepared to function: in this case, to function as a counselor. It is the position in this essay that counselors, at the master's degree level, have barely mastered, or in some cases are not even aware of, the basic tools of their profession. They are barely sympathetic, much less empathetic; they are unsure as to the meaning of listening and hearing when counseling; they are unsure of the diagnostic tools available for their use, and generally use them improperly even if aware of their existence; and they have only a vague awareness of the body of available educational-vocational information and the rationale for their use, which are both so necessary in assisting the client at the decision-making points during the counseling process. In short, one may question whether such counselors know who they are, what they are about, or why they exist as counselors, and one may also well ask how they can function effectively. At the doctoral level, counselors are barely ready to begin to learn about their profession, since much of their preparation has been didactic. In some instances, they have had a modicum of supervised counseling experience, which, it is assumed, qualifies them to call themselves counseling psychologists. Obviously, these assertions do not apply to all counselors, but they do apply to many—perhaps to more practicing counselors than counselor-educators care to admit. An assumption implicit in much of graduate counseling education is that when one completes a given number of graduate courses at either the master's or doctoral level, he is qualified to be a counselor. For how much longer can we live with this kind of assumption? Experiential preparation is an important factor, and the planning for this is crucial.

SUPERVISION

The obvious goal of counselor education is to prepare individuals to function as counselors who will work with people in settings demanding the assistance of the counselor. It is expected that counselors will be able to assist others in coping with their exigent needs. Thus, *the counselor becomes a facilitator as well as an assistor in a client's self-confrontations with his exigent needs* (see Bernard & Fullmer, 1969, for a full discussion of this position). One may logically question the assumption that the counselor-education curriculum allows the counselor-in-preparation to truly develop the philosophy, tools, and skills needed to function effectively as a counselor—unless, that is, the preparation has been designed to help him learn how to be a facilitator as well as an assister.

Traditionally, counselor-preparation programs, especially at the master's degree level, are rigidly conceived as a sequential order of courses and experiences designed to meet state certification requirements, which are generally outmoded prior to implementation. Hence, counselor-preparation programs and counselor supervision are meeting state agency needs rather than those of counselors-in-preparation, society, or clients. In some instances, counselor-educators have attempted to modify their programs to adjust to changing conditions, but the constricting nature of state certification requirements has a tendency to impede modification, rather than to allow for innovation and change.

An assumption which is an attending factor in counselor preparation, and to which a considerable amount of time is devoted in supervisory experiences, is the personality of the counselor trainee (Berenson & Carthuff, 1967, Carkhuff & Berenson, 1967; Kell & Mueller, 1966; Kell & Burow, 1970). It is assumed that counselor trainees enter a counselor-preparation program, and especially practicum supervision, when they are reasonably well-integrated human beings, and have behavioral characteristics deemed mature and appropriate for working with people in the dyadic relationship called counseling. (The criteria for this view are generally subject to the whims and fancies of the evaluating counselor-educator or graduate program.) It is often assumed that because a person desires to be a counselor, "so be it."

It would seem that a future goal of counselor supervision ought to be the focus of more attention by counselor-educators on the personal variables of the counselor trainee with regard to their relation to counseling effectiveness. Admittedly, this is a difficult area to investigate. Research tools are generally poor or nonexistent, research in the area is fragmentary and often unrelated, and considerable research goes unpublished due to negative findings, which researchers and publishers are often reluctant to print.

There would seem to be an incongruity between what the goals of supervision are and what one hopes they are. One would expect that the intervention of supervision would effect both cognitive and affective changes in the trainee. Cognitive change is more discernible since it is here that the trainee's didactic experiences are implemented. The retention of the body of knowledge in counseling, such as it is, may be reasonably assessed. More difficult to assess is the impact of this knowledge as it is translated into practice. Affective changes are more difficult to perceive. Attempts have been made (Wildfang, 1969; Ward, 1971), but some follow-up studies indicate that the affective changes exhibited immediately following the total supervisory counseling experience are short-lived. The further removed the trainee is from the total supervised counseling experience, the more like his former self is his behavior (Munger, Brown, & Needham, 1964). What, then, must become the nature of the counselor-educator's supervisory responsibilities?

TERMINATION OF SUPERVISION

A question related to counselor preparation is, at what point should the supervision of a counselor-trainee be terminated? The paucity of the literature associated with this question is an embarrassment to counselor education. It is embarrassing because the process of termination is as crucial as any other phase of counseling, and should be conceived of as equally important in the supervisory process. Who should initiate termination? At what point in a person's preparation, and under what conditions should termination take place? Such questions require critical exploration. Termination should be considered within the total context of preparation, continuation education, and professional development.

Current counselor-preparation practices indicate that a trainee's supervision is terminated upon completion of a prescribed curricular sequence. This has been, and continues to be, the traditional mode of behavior of institutions committed to counselor preparation. Implicit in this pattern of behavior is the idea that both a counselor's education and the supervision of this education are terminal activities, the points of termination to be predetermined by the preparing agency. This notion assumes that the preparing agency has clearly defined the point of entry as well as the point of egress, with the trainee having no say in the matter. This seems quite incongruent with some basic assumptions about counseling. It has been advocated, in one form or another, that the process of termination has as much to do with successful counseling outcomes as does the process of counseling. If one accepts this notion, then *termination is not necessarily an end in itself, but a prelude to the future.* The entire concept of counseling is not a terminal activity, but a dynamic, lifelong activity, which is intermittently associated with a person's life space in a formal sense, but is in actuality a continual and growing part of the self. Should this be any less true of counselor supervision? Must we continually adhere to an archaic notion of termination of supervision as an end in itself? In the didactic sense termination of supervision may be interpreted as an end. This, however, need not be so. Just as in the modification of the counselor's existential self—which, I believe, is one of the true objectives of counselor education—so too can the didactic aspects of preparation contribute to a continual and never-ending change, growth, and development in the counselor trainee.

A major difficulty in defining the terminal point in a counselor's education and professional preparation is the ambiguity associated with the purpose of preparation. If, as some critics of counselor education have indicated, the purpose of counselor education is the training of technicians to perform given tasks and implement specific processes, then termination may be predicted as that time when the trainee demonstrates certain defined technical proficiencies, such as selecting correct counselor responses. (See the studies by Robinson [1950] and Snyder [1963] for a discussion of techniques of counselor response to client communications.) However, if this is the case, then counseling as such can never be considered a profession. It would, of necessity, be conceived of as a technical skill that could be taught to any willing individual. Termination of a counselor's education can be simply defined and identified. Once one completes a prescribed program of preparation and masters the necessary skills, he may be called a counselor. On the other hand, should counselor preparation find as its purpose the defining of a sequence of cognitive and psychological experiences, which are designed to assist the trainee to come to an understanding of his profession, thus freeing him to continue learning, growing, and developing beyond his formal education, then and only then will we have meaningful counselor-preparation programs. For too long, many counselors have been performing with a "bag of tricks," with little or no understanding of why these "tricks" are being used or of their effects on clients. *Some counselor trainees never learn from their counselor-education experiences; some learn about counseling; and some* (unfortunately, this group is relatively small) *learn from their experiences, and thus are enabled to go beyond the information learned.* In some way, counselor-trainees in the latter group come to understand counseling at a deep level based upon their experiences in counselor education. To identify the point of termination of formal education for this type of person is indeed a difficult task. Some may even feel it is impossible. However, the criterion variable for termination may be defined as a person's ability to go beyond his formal learning experience. In this way, we would no longer concern ourselves with the normative approach in counselor education, which is currently in vogue.

The idea presented above is obviously riddled with difficult questions, which must be resolved. However, most objections, if one logically pursues them to their origins, will find their locus in the structured requirements of graduate education, which was mentioned above. To alter this structure, much less change it, is in all likelihood impossible. A virtually insurmountable number of forces would interfere.

An alternative is to look within counselor-educators themselves. When this approach is followed, the entire question of termination must include ethical concerns. At what point in supervision does one say, "No, you don't seem to have the necessary characteristics to be a counselor"? Do counselor-educators have a right to terminate in such a manner? It is submitted that counselor-educators, by virtue of the very fact that they have chosen the profession of counselor education, have elected to assume the responsibility of deciding who should or should not be a counselor. Ethically, counselor-educators have a responsibility to the people who in the future will enlist the aid of counselors. That responsibility is to educate practitioners who will be facilitators and assistors, and will be able to minister to the psychological needs of clients without creating more traumatic psychological needs. Thus it behooves counselor educators to initiate the termination of a trainee's education program when this is deemed necessary. It is fully realized that this approach may be odious to many readers. However, it is felt that this is a viable position, one which, if debated, may lead to a more systematic approach in understanding the concept of termination in counselor education.

Another form of termination, which is more acceptable, is the self-initiated termination. In this case, the counselor-trainees have been aided in developing a deep self-understanding that the counseling activity is an inappropriate vocation for them; thus, termination is instituted in the form of withdrawal from the program, or transfer to a less self-threatening education program. This form of termination is, of course, most optimal, since the trainee has grown appreciably in self-understanding and realizes a more positive direction congruent with his self-initiated goals. One may also speculate that this avenue to termination also relieves the counselor-educator of the necessity for confrontation with the issue.

In the final analysis, the most acceptable form of a counselor-trainee's termination from a counselor-preparation program is, in fact, just a formalized experience, and not termination in the common usage of the concept. Counselor-trainees who have expressed in some fashion that they are able to learn from their experience, thus allowing themselves to go beyond the information learned, never in fact terminate their counselor education in the truest sense of the word. They do perhaps terminate the formal activity and experience of counselor education wherein they are evaluated by grades in the educative setting. In a very real sense, however, they never terminate their education. *They continually learn, and are willing to learn, from their experiences.* This, of course, follows the notions of counselor maturity and development that Bugenthal (1964) described. What we are saying here is that the counselor's learning experiences never in fact terminate. Thus, the notion of termination for people who have reached this level of sophistication in their education is inappropriate. A new concept of termination in counselor preparation must be explored.

Termination in the sense indicated above is in fact the prelude to learning. What we are saying is that the counselor-educator should be using criterion-reference variables (Popham & Husek, 1969), rather than normative variables, as a basis for his judgment regarding the state of self-understanding a trainee has reached. This would allow the trainee to learn from his experiences so he is free to go beyond the information learned. Then, and only then, should the trainee be allowed to proceed into the larger environment as a counselor. Thus, termination is a transactional activity, which begins at the onset of formal education, continues through the time of the process of education, and ultimately leads to independence as a counselor. Termination, if appropriately applied, should never be seen as a terminal event.

FOLLOW-UP IN SUPERVISION

If one accepts the thesis presented in the preceding paragraph, then concerns for outcomes in counselor education are inextricably related to the follow-up activity. Follow-up activities are grossly void as part of counselor-education programs. Since this is the case, one can only "armchair" the notion of expected outcomes as a result of the counselor-preparation experience. This, of course, is grossly inadequate for baseline conceptualization and innovative change in counselor-education programs. A viable and vital part of a counselor-education program should be a "built-in" requirement of follow-up as part of the educative experience for the counselor-trainee. If the notion of follow-up is included at the outset of a trainee's education, then, at the point at which he leaves the formal environment of counselor education, he will be conditioned to and ready for whatever follow-up activities the preparing institution wishes to initiate. It is through the follow-up activity that counselor-educators will be able to successfully evaluate the results of their efforts in preparing counselors to function in today's, and more important, tomorrow's society. If this notion is implemented, follow-up will indicate to the counselor-educator that what he did yesterday strongly influences what the trainee does tomorrow. Counselor-educators often give lip service to this concept, but make very little real effort toward implementation. What little follow-up is presented in the literature generally falls into the classification of "armchair" gathering of information. What is meant here is that the counselor-trainee generally receives a questionnaire in the mail; he responds to it, and the results are returned in the mail to the counselor-educator. This form of follow-up, no doubt, has value. However, one must question how much value it truly has if the purpose is to influence professional behavior. It would seem that a more viable follow-up program would have the counselor-educator periodically make visits in the field to talk with counselors, teachers, administrators, students, parents, and other significant people who are concerned with education and involved in the counselor's activities in his given environment.

One may justifiably argue that the form of follow-up activity recommended above is extremely expensive and time-consuming, and would never be implemented by institutions of higher education. All these arguments are accepted as valid. However, inactivity is not justified by the stumbling blocks placed in the path of counselor-educators by the higher-education structure. If, in fact, counselor-educators are truly disposed to follow the guidelines for counselor preparation set forth by the American Counselor Educators and Supervisors Association, then they must insist to the "powers that be" that they be allowed to dictate the total curricular structure of counselor education and supervision, which embraces the concept of continued education.

Conclusions

The following propositions are offered as conclusions.

1. The purpose of counselor education is to educate more effective human-interaction agents to function in today's and tomorrow's society.
2. The goals of counselor preparation are similar to counseling, and are thus related to the curriculum. The curricular structure of graduate counselor-preparation programs must be modified to (a) allow for individual trainee needs, (b) meet society's everchanging demands, and (c) create an attitude in counselor-trainees for lifetime growth and development.
3. Counselor education can never be conceived of as a terminal activity. It

is not an end in itself, representing the completion of a body of didactic experiences, but an experience point that allows the counselor-trainee to move toward the next stage of his development.

4. Follow-up in counselor supervision is part of the never-ending education of a counselor. Because of this, counselor-educators must incorporate, as part of the educational experience, continual involvement in the counselor-trainee's environment.

REFERENCES

Berenson, B. G., & Carkhuff, R. R. *Sources of gain in counseling and psychotherapy.* New York: Holt, Rinehart and Winston, 1967.

Bernard, H. W., & Fullmer, D. W. *Principles of guidance: A basic text.* New York and London: Intext Educational Publishers, 1969.

Bugental, J. F. T. The person who is the psychotherapist. *Journal of Consulting Psychology,* 1964, **28**, 272–277.

Carkhuff, R. R., & Berenson, B. G. *Beyond counseling and psychotherapy.* New York: Holt, Rinehart and Winston, 1967.

Kell, B. L., & Burow, J. M. *Developmental counseling and therapy.* Boston: Houghton Mifflin, 1970.

Kell, B. L., & Meuller, W. J. *Impact and change: A study of counseling relationships.* New York: Appleton-Century-Crofts, 1966.

Loughary, J. W., Friesen, D., & Hurst, R. Autocoun: A computer-based automated counseling simulation system. *Personnel and Guidance Journal,* 1966, **45**, 6–15.

Munger, P. F., Brown, P. F., & Needham, J. T. NDEA institute participants two years later. *Personnel and Guidance Journal,* 1964, **42**, 987–990.

Popham, W., & Husek, T. R. Implications of criterion-reference measurement. *Journal of Educational Measurement,* 1969, **6**, 1–9.

Robinson, F. P. *Principles and procedures of student counseling.* New York: Harper, 1950.

Snyder, W. U. *Dependency in psychotherapy.* New York: Macmillan, 1963.

Thoresen, C. E. The systems approach and counselor education: Basic features and implications. *Counselor Education and Supervision,* 1969, **9**(1), 3–18.

Ward, V. W. Potential client's perceptions of self versus the ideal therapist. Unpublished master's thesis, University of Texas at Austin, 1971.

Wildfang, P. Five groups' perceptions of self-ideal personality. Unpublished master's thesis, University of Texas at Austin, 1969.

Literature as a Sociocultural Encounter*

Randolph S. Thrush

University of Wisconsin—Madison

Books are the masters who instruct us without whip or rod, without harsh words or anger, asking naught in return.

Richard de Burg

The shibboleth that one person cannot help another unless he has had an identical experience probably stems from the fact that too many counselors have been so limited in their experiences that they are less than useful in too many instances. It is likely that this lack of effectiveness is more related to personal deficiencies and training-program inadequacies than it is to any basic theoretical dissonance. It does seem to be absolutely necessary, however, if there is to be any positive outcome, that the counselor be able to understand and emphathize with the individual who has come to him for help.

People acquire new behaviors and modify their existing behaviors through their experiences and interactions with their environment—either through the direct experience of encountering an ongoing situation, or by experiencing it indirectly through others. The argument that a counselor's relevance to client problems is related only to his direct experience with those problems is simplistic. It is impossible for a counselor to attempt to experience directly the full range of human behavior. Fortunately for the development of civilization and society, "time-binding" allows those human beings who come after to learn from those who went before. We accumulate knowledge without the necessity of having to rediscover all things in every generation. Through their interviews, counselors indirectly experience the behaviors related to them by the counselees. In so doing, the counselors gain experience and learn from their clients. One of the advantages of the experienced counselor is that he has lived through more situations with more clients than the beginner. By listening to

*The author is indebted to Jo Ann Poole, Judy Blackstone, and the staff of the University Counseling Center for technical assistance.

a number of people relate experiences relevant to a similar situation, the counselor can learn to understand that situation and to increase his range of utility.

The counselor can also learn from others by reading what they have written. There is an advantage to interacting with the person who is describing the situation, in that the counselor or learner can ask questions, clarify points, and validate his understandings. The counselor is thus able to learn in a more meaningful way because he can relate the experiences told to him to his own understanding and background. If neither direct experience nor interaction with the teller is possible, then using the written word is probably the next best alternative. Unfortunately, we do not know what books do what things to what people at what time and under what circumstances (Bryan, 1939).

Since the beginning of recorded history, written materials and books have been the freeway to knowledge for most people. From earliest times, human beings have used different kinds of written matter and storytelling to communicate their personal feelings, thinking, activities, and problems. Events from real life typically were presented, and the person's telling or writing represented actual life roles. The reader or listener was able to identify with the characters in the story. During the fifth century B.C., the Greek drama form developed. According to Aristotle, it had a cathartic effect upon its audience. Plato was talking about changing behavior when he suggested that the first stories people hear should be composed to bring the "fairest lessons of virtue to their ears." So we find that the Greeks were thinking about and using identification, catharsis, and behavior modification 2000 years ago.

Between the ancient Greeks and modern times, books have become as important as teachers, and writing has become our major permanent communication link. Sigmund Freud (1946) spoke of the creative writer as a valuable colleague, and in his own writings continually referred to characters and metaphors drawn from imaginative literature. He said of the imaginative writer (p. 70),

. . . in the knowledge of the human heart they are far ahead of us common folk because they draw on sources that we have not yet made accessible to science. The portrayal of the psychic life of human beings is his most special domain; he has always been the forerunner of science, and thus of scientific psychology too. For the borderline between normal and what are called morbid mental states is to some extent a purely conventional one. . . . The poetic treatment of a psychiatric theme may be perfectly correct without any loss in beauty.

Books, when properly used, may open up a new world of understanding and sensitivity to one's own problems, as well as to those of others. Stories can supplement real-life experiences, create new concepts and awarenesses, introduce new values, and change existing ones. Francis Bacon said that "reading maketh a full man," and Adler said, "Reading improves thinking."

Tucker (1905, p. 27) nicely summarized the importance of literature nearly 70 years ago when he said:

Literature enlarges our imagination; it expands our judgment; it widens our sympathies; it enriches the world to our eyes and minds by revealing to us marvels, delights, tenderness and suggestions which are all around us in man and nature; it keeps alive our better part in places and circumstances when that better part might perish with disease and atrophy; it continually irrigates with benign influences the mind which might grow arid and barren, and so it enables all the little seeds and buds of our intellectual and moral nature to germinate and produce some fruit.

As I talk with my colleagues, I find that quite often their learning, like mine, proceeded in step-wise fashion, or can be viewed as the blending of several significant (for each of them) areas. In my own case there seem to have been five quite distinguishable inputs. The first was general and liberal education. The second was specific learning in psychology and the study of the individual. The third was wide reading in the area of social and cultural anthropology. My understanding of the development of man in a variety of cultures helped me to appreciate the development of the individuals with whom I would be working. The fourth major input was a literary influence, which came from the written perceptions of a variety of authors in their quest to understand the nature of man. The fifth input actually is yet to be found, for it is the learnings of today and tomorrow, as I proceed with my inquiry, that provide the basis for my understanding of who I am and why men behave as they do.

When supervising psychologists-in-training in the early 1960s, I found that the assignment of a relevant literary work could quite often provide the insight necessary for the student to solve a counseling or therapeutic problem he was having. In the mid-sixties I began to use literature in a more formal way in counselor training.

In one summer course I was faced with the expectation of teaching something about counseling to people who had practically no behavioral-science background. We started out with Roy Heath's *The Reasonable Adventurer* to give them some understanding of personality theorizing. Each student then chose 6 to 8 novels from a list of 25 or 30. The assignment was arranged so that two persons would read each novel. The first reader had 30 minutes to report the content and impact of the book to the class, while the second reader had 10 minutes to present any information that had been omitted, or any contrary ideas or impressions that he had. We then spent about an hour discussing the novel, relating it to our own phenomenological field.

In the opinion of the students, this was one of the most meaningful educational experiences they had ever had, as well as a very efficient way to provide a tremendous range of ideas, descriptions, opinions, and contrary views. The general format was replicated twice with the same general evaluation.

It is really unfortunate that we know so little about the interaction of the learner with the material he is reading. We do know that this interaction is unique and is not easily generalizable. Lorang (1946) found, with only one exception, that no two children in any one room mentioned the same book to have changed their attitude or thinking. Weingarten (1964) found that 13 different books were valued by at least 10 persons of the 1256 college students studied. We have no conclusive knowledge as to the effect books have on different persons. We only know that the effects of a book are personal, and that the same set of materials may produce different effects on different persons.

Lorang also found that of 2308 students questioned about their reading, 53% reported having tried to act like a character they had read about in a book. Smith (1948) revealed that 60.7% of 502 respondents believed their attitudes had changed as a result of reading. One-third of the group believed that their thinking had been revised as a result of information that had clarified or corrected concepts or yielded new concepts. According to Lind's study (1936), reading influences people only when they make identification and sustain newfound attitudes in daily living. Weingarten found that 60% of the students felt that they had received help from reading in developing values for living or understanding life; 34% stated they had changed their behavior due to something read; and 20% indicated they had received help in solving problems through reading. Jackson (1944) indicated that reading can have a measurable positive social effect upon attitudes toward the black race.

Clear (1964) published a short description of a social-problems course in which half of the class read and discussed 13 books from a reading list of 26 contemporary novels, while the other half used a standard textbook on social problems. Pre- and post-attitude tests showed that the class members who read the novels became much more tolerant of people caught up in social problems than did those in the textbook section. The decrease in ethnic isolationism and prejudice was twice as large in the fiction section as it was in the textbook section. Clear (p. 73) concluded:

. . . with the almost unlimited wealth of material at our disposal in which one can live the life of the victim of a social problem sharing his frustrations, his fears, his hopelessness, his feelings of injustice through skillful artistry we can now teach social problems not with academic abstraction but with full emotional involvement.

Time (Anonymous, 1967) described the joint study of literature and theology spearheaded by the University of Chicago, which inaugurated its first course in this field in 1950. *Time* reported literature and theology courses being offered by eight other universities and divinity schools.

Fellner (1969) reported on an elective psychiatry course for University of Wisconsin sophomore medical students in which contemporary novels and plays were studied. His course had three basic objectives [p. 587]:

(a) to re-introduce the medical student to literature, to rekindle his interest in novels, plays and poetry; (b) to use play-reading and acting as a medium for teaching empathy, which, as had been noted, involves both self-awareness and an understanding of the emotions of others; and (c) to teach through direct involvement techniques of communicating that twofold awareness.

The books—all paperbacks—that he used over the six years since the initiation of the course and the time of his report are [p. 588]:

Albee, *The Zoo Story;* Anouilh, *Antigone;* Beckett, *Waiting for Godot;* Bellow, *Seize the Day,* Henderson, *The Rain King;* Camus, *The Stranger;* Dostoevski, *Notes from the Underground;* Faulkner, *As I lay Dying;* Hesse, *Steppenwolf;* Joyce, *Portrait of the Artist as a Young Man;* Kafka, *The Trial;* Lawrence, *The Man Who Died;* Mann, *Death in Venice;* Maugham, *The Servant;* McCullers, *The Ballad of the Sad Café;* Miller, *Death of a Salesman, View from the Bridge;* O'Neill, *Long Day's Journey into Night;* Rilke, *The Notebook of Malte Laurids Brigge;* Sartre, *No Exit;* Tolstoy, *The Death of Ivan Ilyich;* and Updike, *Rabbit Run.*

Weinberg (1967) provides an excellent short treatise on the function of the creative writer in the training of teachers. I urge you to read it in its entirety, because it provides a structure for the subjective side of knowledge that is very useful, although too long to be reviewed here. He points out that knowledge about persons—how they are motivated, how they are frustrated, how they suffer, how they become anxious and defensive, how they understand and what is important to understand—is presented to students as scholarly theory and empirical fact. He believes, however, that in the period following graduation and during their professional careers, a majority of students will spend their reading time with novels, rather than with scholarly dissertations, and much of their leisure time in attending plays and movies. If the student learns how and where to look for insights, all imaginative works of creative artists can contribute to his lifelong education. Weinberg suggests five ways to structure the reading of the student: (1) Develop the capacity to understand why fictional characters adopt certain attitudes and persist in certain behaviors; (2) look for the consequences of holding certain attitudes, values, or principles; (3) raise the question of how institutions interact to affect persons; (4) evaluate the consequences of teaching in schools steeped in the tradition of the Protestant ethic; (5) raise the question of how authors find important goals and lasting values, or the denial of these, for their characters. He also lists a number of books pertinent to each of the structures presented.

Spithill (1968) asks for the counselor to use fictional sources to understand adolescence, since novelists define this stage of life so well. She includes a cogent bibliography.

Riley and Standley (1968), from their experimental study, which used literary selections rated on the Truax scale for accurate empathy, unconditional positive regard, and therapist genuineness or self-congruence, concluded that literature offers richly subjective material for observing the qualities of helpful and damaging relationships. Selected readings can convey to the counselor the nuances of interaction more meaningfully than abstract categories, and literary material can supplement limited experience with counseling.

I conclude with a partially annotated list of books chosen by professional counselors as particularly significant in the understanding of human behavior. Many other books would be equally suitable. In each case I asked whether the book made a unique contribution or had a special viewpoint. From the books on this list, and from other books that are developmentally important to the reader, a reading list can be made that should increase the counselor's or trainee's understanding of human existence, and ultimately improve his counseling effectiveness.

SUGGESTED READINGS

Aldridge, J. W. *In the country of the young.* New York: Harper's Magazine Press, 1970.
A critical analysis of the values and feelings of the radicals and dropouts in the counterculture.

Algren, N. *Man with the golden arm.* Garden City: Doubleday, 1949.
Heroin addiction.

Axline, V. *Dibs: In search of self.* Boston: Houghton Mifflin, 1964.
Autistic children. Personality development in play therapy.

Bach, G. R., & Wyden, P. *The intimate enemy.* New York: Morrow, 1969.
Teaches people the principle of interpersonal confrontation. A "how-to" book with surface insights.

Baldwin, J. *Giovanni's room.* London: M. Joseph, 1957.

Baldwin, J. *Another country.* New York: Dial, 1962.
Struggle of men and meaning in the homosexual world. Dwells on ills of being outcast. Individual draws strength and power from social group.

Bandura, A. *Social learning and personality development.* New York: Holt, Rinehart and Winston, 1963.
A textbook. Probably the best application of learning theory to social development.

Banfield, E. *The unheavenly city*. Boston: Little, Brown, 1970.

Insight into the complex and overwhelming problems of the inner city. Discusses man's destructive nature and explores the causes and consequences.

Bellow, S. *Herzog*. New York: Viking, 1964.

Rebellion of middle-class Jewish male professor. One of the best descriptions of a relationship in our language.

Benjamin, H. R. *The saber-toothed curriculum*. New York: McGraw-Hill, 1939.

A classic treatise on educational philosophy.

Berne, E. *The games people play*. New York: Grove, 1964.

Methods of communication people use. Introduction to transactional analysis; easily understood, but reinforces cognitive processes.

Blocher, D. H. *Developmental counseling*. New York: Ronald, 1966.

An introductory textbook on theory and techniques of developmental counseling, based on belief counselor is a behavioral scientist and a change agent.

Brand, M. *Savage sleep*. New York: Crown, 1968.

If you see something, it is your responsibility. Trust yourself and your instincts.

Brown, C. *Manchild in the promised land*. New York: Macmillan, 1965.

Growing up black in the Harlem ghetto—socialization and education.

Brown, D. A. *Bury my heart at Wounded Knee*. New York: Holt, Rinehart and Winston, 1970.

Aids in understanding some American Indians. An Indian history of dealings of U.S. government with the Indian nations during 1870–1900, the years of the erosion of Indian autonomy.

Camus, A. *The stranger*. (Trans. S. Gilbert) New York: Knopf, 1946.

Struggle for meaning in an absurd world. Excellent literary statement of alienation.

Castaneda, C. *The teachings of Don Juan: A Yacqui way of knowledge*. Berkeley: University of California Press, 1968.

A young man's remarkable account of his experiences with hallucinogenic plants during five-year study with Indian teacher. The strange, frightening spiritual journey a man must undertake in order to become "a man of knowledge."

Castaneda, C. *A separate reality*. New York: Simon & Schuster, 1971.

Indian understanding.

Clavell, J. *Tai-Pan*. New York: Atheneum, 1966.

Helps to develop understanding of Chinese culture.

Davis, S. Jr. *Yes I can*. New York: Farrar, Straus & Giroux, 1965.

Self-made man. Not recommended for increasing black consciousness, but recounts the rise of a unique individual.

Denig, R. K. *The Manoe-Denigs*. New York: T. A. Wright, 1924.

Chronicle of a family

Dostoyevsky, F. *The house of the dead*. (Trans. C. Garnett) New York: Macmillan, 1915.

Remarkable reminiscences of the nightmare world of the Siberian prison-camp. First developed theme of spiritual regeneration through suffering.

Dostoyevsky, F. *Crime and punishment*. (Trans. C. Garnett) New York: Modern Library, 1950.

A man creates and executes a crime of reason (killing for the experience), then, overcome by emotions, confesses, and expiates his guilt through suffering. Points out man is not a completely rational animal.

Dostoyevsky, F. *The brothers Karamazov.* (Trans. A. R. MacAndrew) New York: Bantam, 1970.

Effect of sensuality and inherited sensuality on a family. Anguish caused by dual nature of man (both rational and emotional) recurs throughout.

Fairbairn, A. *Five smooth stones.* New York: Crown, 1966.

Demonstrates different perspectives of reality via skin color.

Farrell, J. *Studs Lonigan.* New York: Modern Library, 1938.

Trilogy portrays disintegration, physical and moral, of young Chicago Irishman, 1916–1931, because of spiritual poverty. Dated.

Faulkner, W. *The sound and the fury.* New York: Modern Library, 1946.

Commentary on Southern social scene.

Fowles, J. *The magus.* Boston: Little, Brown, 1966.

Eleventh commandment is not to use someone else for your own emotional satisfaction— don't hurt anyone. A man is taught to feel and to be sensitive to others through series of startling personal experiences manipulated by the magus.

Frankl, V. *Man's search for meaning: An introduction to logotherapy.* (Trans. I. Lasch) Boston: Beacon Press, 1963.

A man's feelings about the Nazi concentration camps. Strength to endure must (and can) come from within—from a belief in God and an inner decision that life is meaningful and has purpose.

Friedan, B. *The feminine mystique.* New York: Norton, 1963.

Early contribution to current women's movement. A landmark book. A beginners text on the psychology of women.

Fromm, E. *Escape from freedom.* New York: Farrar & Rinehart, 1941.

All three Fromm books deal with character structures and with interaction between man's psychological processes and his efforts to free himself from societal roles.

Fromm, E. *Man for himself.* New York: Rinehart, 1947.

Contribution toward self-theory, with compassionate dealings of outer and inner selves, and the pressures inherent in living.

Fromm, E. *The art of loving.* New York: Bantam, 1956.

Communal notions of giving up self in order to find happiness. How to give and receive love.

Golding, W. G. *Lord of the flies.* New York: Coward-McCann, 1962.

Something for everyone. Explores the destructiveness of human nature; suggests that positive change will only come from within oneself, and not from all the elaborate laws, political systems, and environmental manipulation man can devise. Young boys degenerating into adult society. Shows mass reduction in character and caring for others when survival is of prime importance.

Goodman, P. *Growing up absurd.* New York: Random House, 1960.

Psychological damage caused by current educational system. Points out societal pressures and messages given to youth.

Green, H. *I never promised you a rose garden.* New York: Holt, Rinehart and Winston, 1964.

True story of girl, returning from psychotic existence, and her therapist.

Greer, G. *The female eunuch.* London, England: MacGibbon & Kee, 1970.

A major but idiosyncratic book of women's movement.

Griffin, J. *Black like me.* Boston: Houghton Mifflin, 1961.

White man dyes his skin and lives as black man. He develops understanding of aspects of black experience and explores feelings of being black and discriminated against. Sensitizes the reader to the needs of oppressed people.

Hansberry, L. *A raisin in the sun.* London, England: Methuen, 1960.

Crisis in a black family of Chicago's South Side. The dream to rise from poverty is fulfilled, only to be slowly eroded by individual incapability and societal prejudice.

Harrington, M. *The other America.* New York: Macmillan, 1962.

Poverty in the U.S.; a part of America that may be close to us but is ignored or avoided.

Harris, T. *I'm o.k.—you're o.k.* New York: Harper & Row, 1969.

Explanation of transactional analysis and how it works. Easily understood book on interpersonal communications and relations.

Heath, R. *The reasonable adventurers.* Pittsburgh, Pa.: University of Pittsburgh Press, 1964.

The first personality theory developed from the study of normals rather than the study of deviants. A simpleminded typology that has tremendous practical application. A good first reader in the study of personality.

Heinlein, R. *Stranger in a strange land.* New York: Putnam, 1961.

Science fiction. We are viewed from the outside.

Hesse, H. *Siddhartha.* (Trans. H. Rosner) New York: New Directions, 1957.

A young man's search for meaning. Self-actualization from an Eastern point of view.

Hesse, H. *Peter Camenzind.* (Trans. W. J. Strachan) London, England: P. O. Wen, 1961.

Hesse, H. *Steppenwolf.* (Trans. B. Creighton) New York: Holt, Rinehart and Winston, 1963.

Hesse, H. *Demian.* (Trans. M. Roloff and M. Lebeck) New York: Harper & Row, 1965.

Difficult maturation in the face of upheaval and the loss of the established order and childhood values. Learning true self allows one to find his own answers to life. Discusses means by which modern man may recognize true self and use it to his advantage.

Hesse, H. *Beneath the wheel.* (Trans. M. Roloff) Farrar, Straus & Giroux, 1968.

How schooling (née education) destroys a person.

Huxley, A. *Brave new world.* Garden City: Doubleday, Doran, 1932.

Loss of individuality in planned society and man's search for humanity. Prophetic qualities make it valuable.

Jourard, S. *Transparent self.* Princeton, N.J.: Van Nostrand, 1964.

One of the "third-force" writers. Importance of self-disclosure. Psychological component of communication.

Kelman, S. *Push comes to shove.* Boston: Houghton Mifflin, 1970.

Autobiographical view of escalation of student protest. Of historical significance.

Kesey, K. *One flew over the cuckoo's nest.* New York: Viking, 1964.

Dehumanizing world of the modern mental hospital. Autonomous inmate tries to organize patients, but Big Nurse gets him. Sanity defined as whoever has the keys. Perceptive criticism of the philosophy of making mental patient "fit" into an unfit society.

Kesey, K. *Sometimes a great notion.* New York: Viking, 1964.

A family in conflict with itself and the outside forces trying to destroy it. America's need for, and inability to accept, traditional heroes.

Knowles, J. *A separate peace.* London, England: Secker & Warburg, 1959.

A boy discovering self and becoming a man.

Koestler, A. *Darkness at noon.* (Trans. D. Hardy) New York: Modern Library, 1941.

Man's endurance of stark fear, his strength, his winning over madness, demonstrates integrative self-theory, which remains intact. Insight into the feelings of hopelessness and despair in a Soviet prison.

Laing, R. D. *Knots.* New York: Pantheon, 1970.

Stark, simple expression of self caught in the increasingly complex conflicts of relationships. Poems.

Lederer, W. J., & Burdick, E. *Sarkhan.* New York: McGraw-Hill, 1965.

Influence of political ideology on individual and group behavior.

Lewis, C. S. *The Screwtape letters.* New York: Macmillan, 1945.

Problems and temptations of man from a Christian perspective. Explores the subtle rationalizations one generates in an effort to continue doing self-destructive acts and to alleviate ensuing guilt for doing wrong.

Lewis, C. S. *Till we have faces.* New York: Harcourt, Brace, 1957.

A myth retold—allegorical novel based on legend of Cupid and Psyche. A woman destroys those around her by her excessive love.

Lewis, C. S. *The great divorce.* New York: Macmillan, 1963.

One must be honest with himself and others or there will be undesired consequences. Individual sacrifice because of outside pressure leads to individual trauma.

Lewis, O. *La vida.* New York: Random House, 1966.

Won awards for research, validity, and good writing. A Puerto Rican family in Spanish Harlem.

Lewis, S. *Arrowsmith.* New York: Harcourt, Brace & World, 1945.

Triumph and tragedy in medical research.

Lewis, S. *Main street.* New York: Harcourt, Brace, 1948.

Blunt truths about the inadequacies of small-town life. Heroine finds Washington, D.C., no better than Gopher Prairie, Minn.

Lewis, S. *Babbitt.* New York: Harcourt, Brace, 1950.

A scathing denunciation of the materialistic culture that sacrifices individuals and individuality to Mammon.

Lewis, S. *Elmer Gantry.* New York: New American Library, 1967.

A powerful novel that focuses on a charlatan faith-healer and on his followers, whose human need to believe makes them gullible.

Little, M., & Haley, A. *Autobiography of Malcolm X.* New York: Grove, 1965.

Rich and painful chronicle of the best and worst aspects of growing up a black man in our century. Real life Madame Queen sounds frighteningly like fictional Big Nurse in Kesey's book.

Malamud, B. *The assistant.* New York: Farrar, Straus & Cudahy, 1957.

People can get together, but there are barriers.

Malamud, B. *The fixer.* New York: Farrar, Straus & Giroux, 1966.

Study of emerging political consciousness. It is not only how you define yourself, but also how others define you, that determines many things in life.

Matthiessen, P. *Sal si puedes.* New York: Random House, 1969.

Cesar Chavez and the new American revolution.

McCullers, C. *Heart is a lonely hunter.* Boston: Houghton Mifflin, 1940.

Describes the frustration and loneliness of a deaf mute, and sensitizes the reader to the needs of individuals with this handicap.

Mead, M. *Male and female.* New York: Morrow, 1946.

Sex-role differentiation in complex societies. Socialization and learning of role identity.

Michener, J. A. *Hawaii.* New York: Random House, 1959.

Social-psychological disintegration of one group and rise of others. Demonstrates power as opposed to trust and simplicity.

Michener, J. A. *Caravans.* New York: Random House, 1965.

Life in rugged and suspicious Afghanistani society.

Morgan, R. *Sisterhood is powerful.* New York: Random House, 1970.

An anthology of writings from the women's liberation movement.

Neill, A. S. *Summerhill.* London, England: Gollancz, 1962.

Opposite of *Beneath the wheel.* Explores an alternative method of educating children through a positive and more permissive approach.

O'Neill, E. *The ice man cometh.* New York: Random House, 1946.

If you take away someone's life meaning and show its fallacies, you may leave that person with nothing.

O'Neill, E. *Long day's journey into night.* New Haven: Yale University Press, 1969.

Drug addiction in the family and its consequences. Inability in family relationships for members to encounter each other openly.

Packard, V. *The hidden persuaders.* New York: McKay, 1957.

How we are motivated and manipulated by advertising principles. Views man as a reactive organism. Dated.

Paton, A. *Too late the phalarope.* New York: Scribner, 1953.

The battle of guilt and fear in man's conscience. What man does to the conquered (the black-skinned of South Africa in this book) destroys not only the conquered but also the conqueror. Paton's *Cry, the beloved country* is thematically similar.

Perls, F. S. *In and out the garbage pail.* Lafayette, Calif.: Real People Press, 1964.

Perl's autobiography of his struggle to grow as a person. Tends to receive polar responses from its readers.

Plath, S. *The bell jar.* London, England: Faber, 1966.

Excellent personal account of a woman dealing with societal expectations, disintegration of self, and eventual suicide. Theory and treatment well described. One sees through her eyes the cold, sterile, and insensitive way many mental patients are treated.

Potok, C. *The chosen.* New York: Simon & Schuster, 1967.

The painful process of making a scholar in the Jewish culture. A good view of a very strict Jewish sect and the development of two men—their commitments, and relations to each other and important other persons in their lives.

Puzo, M. *The godfather.* New York: Putnam, 1969.

A novel of the Sicilian-American Mafia, its control of the criminal, and its infiltration into "straight" American society. Its paradoxical concern for brotherhood and lack of concern for human life are amply illustrated.

Radcliffe, H. *Well of loneliness.* London, England: Hammond, 1956.

An early novel of lesbian experience.

Rand, A. *Atlas shrugged.* New York: Random House, 1957.

It really does feel good to get the world off your shoulders.

Reik, T. *Listening with the third ear.* New York: Farrar, Straus, 1952.

Provides the answer to the layman's question: "What is psychoanalysis all about?" *Masochism in modern man, A psychologist looks at love,* and *Psychology of sex relation* all by Reik, are also highly recommended.

Reik, T. *The need to be loved.* New York: Farrar, Straus, 1963.

Excerpts from the notebook of a man who not only explains behavior but truly understands it. Published to commemorate Reik's seventy-fifth birthday.

Rogers, C. *On becoming a person.* Boston: Houghton Mifflin, 1961.

Offers many personal challenges if read carefully. His ideas on development of total person.

Rolland, R. *Michelangelo.* (Trans. F. Street) New York: Duffield, 1927.

Salinger, J. D. *Catcher in the rye.* Boston: Little, Brown, 1951.

Holden Caulfield's classic search for identity sparks recognition in all who've made it to or through the late teen years.

Salinger, J. D. *Franny and zooey.* Boston: Little, Brown, 1961.

Holden all grown up. Identity crisis in young adults. Supersensitive souls try to make it in a world that seems stultifying.

Satir, V. *Conjoint family therapy.* Palo Alto, Calif.: Science & Behavior Books, 1964.

Excellent book on interpersonal communications.

Shostrom, E. *Man, the manipulator.* Nashville, Tenn.: Abingdon Press, 1967.

How-to book about therapy. Outlines man's efforts to satisfy needs through games.

Skinner, B. F. *Walden II.* New York: Macmillan, 1962.

A technically controlled society in which there is happiness. A planned Utopia based on behavioral principles.

Snow, C. P. *Strangers and brothers.* New York: Scribner, 1960.

Conflict with accepted social mores. Concern with justice and morality, with the relationship between loyalty and ambition, and with the nearly tragic conflicts between friends.

Solzhenitsyn, A. *One day in the life of Ivan Denisovich.* (Trans. M. Hayward and R. Hingley) New York: Frederick Praeger, 1963.

Study of compromises a human being makes for his survival when placed in a totally inhuman environment.

Solzhenitsyn, A. *Cancer ward.* (Trans. R. Frank) New York: Dial, 1968.

Reactions to death, hope, love, self, commitment to fellow man, and despair in a post–World War II Communist cancer ward.

Stalvey, L. M. *The education of a WASP.* New York: Bantam, 1971.

Malcolm X told white people to educate themselves. WASP housewife goes from middle-class serenity to awareness of American prejudice toward blacks.

Steinbeck, J. *The grapes of wrath.* New York: Viking, 1936.

Classic novel of the displaced people of the dust bowl. Steinbeck's insights into their plight make this a novel to help the reader understand the displaced of any time or place.

Steinbeck, J. *East of Eden.* New York: Viking, 1952.

Don't judge, it may not be as you imagined.

Steinbeck, J. *Sweet Thursday.* New York: Viking, 1954.

Life on skid row.

Toffler, A. *Future shock.* New York: Random House, 1970.

Influence of technology and changing society on man's life. Discusses physical and social disintegration in face of multiplication of social forms.

Tolkein, J. R. *Lord of the rings.* 3 vols. Boston: Houghton Mifflin, 1963.

Fantasy that illustrates need to reduce complexity to good and evil. Frodo lives!

Updike, J. *Rabbit run.* New York: Knopf, 1960.

Man caught between instinct and social custom, mood, and mind. Deals with the personal and moral consequences of life lived without a sense of direction or value.

Updike, J. *Rabbit redux.* New York: Knopf, 1971.

Rabbit faces the problems of a 36-year-old man threatened by the constant changes and insecurities of contemporary society. The inability to discover a personal sense of worth results in the destruction or uselessness of human relationships.

Voeks, V. *On becoming an educated person.* Philadelphia: Saunders, 1964.

Helpful tips for succeeding in college. Self-help book for college students. Psychological principles of self-modification.

Warren, R. P. *All the king's men.* New York: Modern Library, 1953.

Rise and fall of a demagogue. One of all-time great novels about politics. O'Connor's *Last hurrah* is another good one.

Watts, A. *The book: On the taboo against knowing who you are.* New York: Macmillan, 1967.

Pop mysticism.

Weil, A. *The natural mind.* Boston: Houghton Mifflin, 1972.

A new perspective on the drug scene from a young medical researcher.

Williams, T. *Cat on a hot tin roof.* New York: New Directions, 1955.

Patriarchal control immobilizes male offspring in this play set in South.

Williams, T. *Night of the iguana.* New York: New Directions, 1962.
    Fear and personality disintegration. Man not realizing himself.

Wolfe, T. *You can't go home again.* New York: Harper, 1940.
    Man cannot slip back into childhood patterns.

Wolfe, T. *The kandy-kolored tangerine-flake streamline baby.* New York: Farrar, Straus & Giroux, 1965.
    A series of essays and descriptions of American subcultures. A modern anthropology.

Wolfe, T. *Electric kool-aid acid test.* New York: Farrar, Straus & Giroux, 1968.
    An acid trip across the nation to survey the provinces and bewilder the natives.

REFERENCES

Anonymous. Theology: literature in the divinity school. *Time,* Dec. 22, 1967, p. 51.

Bryan, A. I. The psychology of the reader. *Library Journal,* 1939, **64,** 7–12.

Clear, V. Paperback pedagogy. *Saturday Review,* Feb. 15, 1964, p. 73.

Fellner, C. H. Paperback psychiatry. *Journal of Medical Education,* 1969, **44,** 585–588.

Freud, S. *Gesmammelte Werke,* Vol. 7. London, England: Imagos, 1946.

Jackson, E. P. Effects of reading upon attitudes toward the Negro race. *Library Quarterly,* 1944, **14,** 47–54.

Lind, K. N. The social psychology of children's reading. *American Journal of Sociology,* 1936, **41,** 454–469.

Lorang, M.C. *The effect of reading on moral conduct and emotional experience.* Washington, D.C.: Catholic University of America Press, 1946.

Riley, J. E., & Standley, F. L. Literature and counseling: The experience of encounter. *Counselor Education and Supervision,* 1968, **8,** 328–334.

Smith, N. B. The personal and social values of reading. *Elementary English,* 1948, **25,** 490–500.

Spithill, A. C. The valuable allies. *Personnel and Guidance Journal,* 1968, **46,** 879–883.

Tucker, T. G. *Literature and life.* Melbourne, Australia: Whitcombe & Tombs, 1905.

Weinburg, C. The function of the creative writer in the training of teachers. *Journal of Teacher Education,* 1967, **18,** 216–221.

Weingarten, S. Boundaries of reading in satisfying needs. *Education,* 1964, **84,** 480–489.

Issues

1. Can the stability associated with professional education be maintained without constant evaluation and change?
2. How explicit should professional organizations be with regard to continuing education as a factor in licensing, certification, job eligibility, and so forth?
3. What safeguards, if any, should be taken for the psychological safety of the individual members of counseling groups, therapy groups, learning-experience groups, encounter groups, and similar groups? Where does the mental-health professional acquire this sort of competency and sensitivity?
4. With any clinical material used for teaching there is always the danger of violation of confidence. The usual concern is that something about the material will enable someone listening to identify the client, but there are other sorts of concerns. For example, someone not in a professional school hears that case material is presented in a rather routine and not too safeguarded situation—this information acts as a deterrent to his seeking help through the university mental-health facilities out of concern for violation of confidence. What other sorts of situations could cause equivalent difficulty—i.e., inhibit someone who needs help from seeking it?

Annotated Readings

Ivey, A. E., Normington, C. J., Miller, C. D., Morrill, W. H., & Haase, R. F. Microcounseling and attending behavior: An approach to prepracticum counselor training. *Journal of Counseling Psychology,* 1968, **15**, (5, Pt. 2).

"Microcounseling" is a video method of training counselors in basic skills of counseling within a short period of time. This research studies the effects of microcounseling training procedures upon three groups of beginning counselors. Three different skills—"attending behavior," reflection of feeling, and summarization of feeling—were the focus of research. Central to all studies was attending behavior, which is the counseling skill of attending or listening to a client both verbally and nonverbally. These studies suggest that attending behavior and its related concepts may be described in behavioral terms meaningful to beginning counselors. Implications of the attending behavior and microcounseling frameworks are discussed.

Krumboltz, J. D., Varenhorst, B. B., & Thoresen, C. E. Nonverbal factors in the effectiveness of models in counseling. *Journal of Counseling Psychology,* 1971, **14**, 412–418.

The degree of model counselor attentiveness and prestige in increasing later information-seeking behavior (ISB) was tested experimentally. One of two videotaped interviews, in which the model counselor was either attentive or nonattentive, was presented to 56 female high-school juniors in seven schools. Four treatment combinations were arranged by introducing each of the two interviews with a statement attributing either high or low prestige to the model counselor. Active and inactive control groups ($n = 56$ each) were randomly constituted. Exposure to the videotaped model interviews produced more ISB than did either control procedure. Hypothesized differences attributable to levels of prestige and attentiveness were not found.

Martin, R. D. Videotape self-confrontation in human relations training. *Journal of Counseling Psychology,* 1971, **18**, 341–347.

Informational feedback, in the form of videotape self-confrontation, was presented to the members of three separate but essentially equivalent *T* groups. Dependent variables were (1) group variance in length and (2) frequency of individual verbal output. Maximum experimental control was achieved through the use of a time-series design, with each group serving as its own control. Changes in level and slope of the series were predicted contingent on videotape replay of past interaction to the groups. Results indicated that the effects of videotape feedback are not necessarily predictable, and may cause either beneficial or detrimental group-behavior change. Videotape feedback also seems to have markedly different effects on different groups. Conclusions are presented regarding the appropriateness of time-series research designs with such unique phenomena as *T* groups.

Monke, R. H. Effect of systematic desensitization on the training of counselors. *Journal of Counseling Psychology,* 1971, **18**, 320–323.

The purpose of this study was to determine whether the technique of desensitization would reduce the initial anxiety experienced by the beginning counselor-trainee before and during his first counseling session. Thirty counselor trainees in a NDEA Elementary Counseling and Guidance Institute were randomly assigned to either an experimental or a control group. The treatment consisted of two sessions of relaxation and five of desensitization. The criterion measures employed included (1) physiological measures using heart rate and skin resistance, (2) tape evaluations, and (3) self-reports. Analyses of the data revealed significantly less self-reported anxiety in the experimental group. No differences were found in heart rate, skin resistance, and tape-evaluation measures.

Suggestions for Further Reading

Betz, R. L. Effects of group counseling as an adjunctive practicum experience. *Journal of Counseling Psychology,* 1969, **16,** 528–533.

Beymer, L. Confrontation groups: Hula hoops? *Counselor Education and Supervision,* 1970, **9,** 75–86.

Eisenberg, S., & Delaney, D. J. Using video simulation of counseling for training counselors. *Journal of Counseling Psychology,* 1970, **17,** 15–19.

Foreman, M. E. *T* groups: Their implications for counselor supervision and preparation. *Counselor Education and Supervision,* 1967, **7,** 48–53.

Foreman, E., Poppen, W. A., & Frost, J. M. Case groups: An in-service education technique. *Personnel and Guidance Journal,* 1967, **46,** 388–392.

Hackney, H. L. Development of a prepracticum counseling skills model. *Counselor Education and Supervision,* 1971, **11,** 102–109.

Hansen, J. C., & Warner, R. W., Jr. Review of research on practicum supervision. *Counselor Education and Supervision,* 1971, **10,** 261–272.

Hountras, P. T., & Redding, A. J. Effects of training in interaction analysis upon counseling practicum students. *Journal of Counseling Psychology,* 1969, **16,** 491–494.

Hurst, J. C., & Fenner, R. Notes and comments—Extended session group as a predictive technique for counselor training. *Journal of Counseling Psychology,* 1969, **16,** 358–360.

Kagan, N., & Schauble, P. G. Affect simulation in interpersonal process recall. *Journal of Counseling Psychology,* 1969, **16,** 309–313.

Mahoney, S. C. The evocative value of fiction for psychotherapist in training. *Psychotherapy: Theory, Research and Practice,* 1965, **2,** 139–140.

Martin, D. G., & Gazda, G. M. A method of self-evaluation for counselor education utilizing the measurement of facilitative condition. *Counselor Education and Supervision,* 1970, **9,** 87–92.

Prescott, S. The value of postdoctoral institutes for practitioners. *Professional Psychology,* 1971, **2,** 259–261.

Reddy, W. B. Sensitivity training as an integral phase of counselor education. *Counselor Education and Supervision,* 1970, **9,** 110–115.

Taplin, J. R. Impression of the client as a function of perception mode and clinician experience. *Journal of Counseling Psychology,* 1968, **15,** 211–214.

Thompson, A. The Fairweather group program: Implications for counselor preparation and practice. *Counselor Education and Supervision,* 1968, **8,** 55–60.

Van Atta, R. E. Co-therapy as a supervisory process. *Psychotherapy: Theory, Research and Practice,* 1969, **6,** 137–139.

Zaccaria, J. S., & Moses, H. A. *Facilitating human development through reading: The use of bibliotherapy in teaching and counseling.* Champaign, Ill.: Stipes Publishing Co., 1968.

Zweben, J. E., & Miller, R. L. The systems games: Teaching, training, psychotherapy. *Psychotherapy: Theory, Research and Practice,* 1968, **5,** 73–76.

CHAPTER 9

The Relationship of Clients to the Clinical Setting

It is unlikely that a student at either the master's or the doctoral level knows precisely in what setting he will want to work after completing his education. For this reason, practicum assignments are designed to provide exposure in settings that present possibilities for the development and utilization of many different intervention strategies and competencies. Sometimes practicum placements are assigned on the basis of the personnel needs of the settings providing them, but caution should be exercised, because professional preparation may not be furthered in such situations, and as a result candidates will be short-changed in their development. Occasionally, however, and in fact more often than one could reasonably expect, the match works out well. Until recently one practicum setting would serve. However, the recent explosion in facilities and the accompanying specialization makes that no longer true. How then can a student gain professional experience that will help him choose a professional focus, and at the same time not risk becoming overly and prematurely specialized? What criteria are available to students in selecting a practicum location: Is an in-depth affiliation of greater value than several shorter-term affiliations? Are all settings equivalent, or do some have a basically broader training value? No, all these questions are not answered in this chapter, but the questions do form an interesting framework within which to read the essayists' descriptions and evaluations of the numerous practicum settings.

All the essays in this chapter describe in some detail specific settings for practicum. Some of these locations are relatively new in preprofessional placement. Each essay presents a description of the setting as it should be in order to provide a valuable clinical experience; in fact this constitutes the criterion by which the settings can be evaluated in terms of their suitability. Care is given to the level of professional performance expected of the students in the settings.

Boy provides a detailed picture of the school as a practicum placement. Dallis has a great deal of enthusiasm for the opportunities available in business and industry for clinical experience. Geller and Feirstein focus on the community mental-health center as a facility for providing new and direct methods of delivery of services, new roles, and new functions. Gust discusses new models such as the consultant role, which is available in many university counseling centers. Kirk and Chin also direct themselves to what university counseling centers can do for professional education, with an emphasis on shoring up the standards for professional practice.

Clients in the School

Angelo V. Boy

University of New Hampshire

If a school-counseling program is judged to be effective for a student clientele, it probably has a well-educated and professionally sophisticated counselor as its motivating force. He is one who has been able to internalize his professional preparation and translate it into a counseling program that accurately meets the basic needs of those whom it serves. That is, an effective school-counseling program is built with a sensitivity to the fact that the typical student possesses personal and developmental concerns that often inhibit his effectiveness as a person and as a learner. An ineffective school-counseling program is typically built around superficial activities, which have been conceived by adults who are unaware of the student's inner world and its accompanying frustrations and difficulties.

This essay examines some of the environmental variables that surround a school-counseling program, and the effect of these variables on the relationship of the student clientele to the counseling program. Once again, the degree to which these variables affect the client is proportionately related to the skill possessed by the school-counselor in positively affecting these variables so that they will contribute to the more effective personal functioning of the student.

PROGRAMS

In far too many schools, the counseling program does not possess a positive image among the students whom it is supposed to serve. Often this is so because the program is mechanistically inclined, rather than being person-centered. If a student senses that the counselor is only interested in him as a test profile, as a potential college freshman, as a potential electrician, as a career-day participant, as a follow-up-study statistic, or as a nonlearner, then he will not turn to the counselor when he is burdened by a personal problem that is shattering his existence. He comes into contact with the counselor only

423

when the counselor summons him to his office and indicates that the student is obligated to make a decision regarding some phase of his educational and/or vocational planning.

If a school-counseling program is truly to become professionalized, then it must be based upon a far more substantive rationale than has been offered in the past.

The substantive rationale upon which a school-counseling program should be based revolves around the concept of prevention. That is, school-counselors should possess adequate competence in dealing with the developmental concerns of youth. Professionals involved in the remediation of emotional disorders among adults have long realized that such emotional disorders can only be alleviated by a concentrated preventive effort among those involved with such individuals during the formative years. It is far better to render immediate treatment to an infected finger than to wait for the infection to reach a point where the amputation of an arm is the only possible recourse. The medical and dental professions are highly sensitive to the fact that better physical health can only be achieved when people seek out preventive assistance, rather than allowing their physical health to deteriorate to the point where remediation is the only possible solution.

The school-counselor has a potentially powerful contribution to make to mankind, but to make it he must move toward a professional rationale in which a preventive concept of counseling is the functional core of his existence. The school-counselor is in a uniquely strategic position because he deals with a clientele during the formative stages of their development. He deals with human problems as they begin to emerge. It is far more humane and logical for a school-counseling program to be involved during the formative years of youngster's development than to stand aside and watch the seeds of personal disintegration being sown.

The school's strategic position in the area of preventive mental health is expressed in the writings, among others, of Arbuckle, (1965, p. 141), Friedenberg (1959, p. 102), Boy and Pine (1963, p. 223), Berlin (1963, p. 414), Stiller (1964, pp. 236–237), Konopka (1966), Swartz (1965, p. 43), Frank (1963), Munson (1966, p. 22), Meeks (1963, p. 108), and Teigland, Winkler, Munger, and Kranzler (1966, pp. 950–955).

OPPORTUNITIES FOR INNOVATION

An effective school-counseling program innovatively meets two basic student needs:

1. The student's need for a therapeutically oriented counseling relationship in which he becomes voluntarily involved and feels free to discuss those personal dimensions of himself that hamper his effective functioning.
2. The student's need for nonacademic information that will enable him to make appropriate educational and/or vocational decisions.

The student's awareness of, and relationship to, a school's counseling program can be dramatically improved if the school-counselor is sensitive to the importance of having an effective program for orienting students to the program's rationale and its purpose in the life of the student. A meaningful orientation program would enable the student to perceive the counselor as a person to whom he can voluntarily turn when he feels the need to unravel a particular problem in his life. Some innovative orientation procedures, which have been well received by students and have resulted in increased student use of a school's counseling service, are as follows:

1. A homemade series of color slides depicting unidentified students in counseling relationships. Such slides are accompanied by audiotaped narrations by students, which indicate their reactions to the personally relevant dimensions of the counseling relationship (Boy & Pine, pp. 89–94).
2. An edited audiotape or videotape of a counseling session, which enables the student audience to better understand the verbal transaction between the client and the counselor.
3. A simulation of the counseling relationship before a group of students. That is, a student role-plays a fictitious problem with the counselor, and this simulation is followed by the "client" expressing his reaction to the counselor's counseling style (Boy, 1959, pp. 33–36).
4. A panel of students who have profited from counseling can orient peers to the value of counseling by discussing their reactions to counseling without revealing the confidences involved. Such panels, by demonstrating the positive attitude of peers toward the counseling program, can motivate students to seek counseling on their own volition.

Immediately following each of the preceding orientation procedures, the student audience becomes more knowledgeable about counseling by participating in a question-and-answer and discussion period.

Innovative procedures that would improve the relationship of the client to the informational phase of a counseling program are integrated with the current computer and technological revolution. Since increasingly sophisticated computers are part of our present and future, students are attracted to work with them in the process of making educational and/or vocational decisions.

However, a counselor cannot rely upon machines to do all of his work unless he conceives that work to be totally the gathering, collating, and dispensing of educational and/or vocational information, for, as Super points out, "The nature of vocational development is very similar to the nature of personal development, for the former is a specific aspect of the latter [1957, p. 192]." Moreover, Super adds, "That this [personal adjustment] may be a prerequisite to progress in vocational adjustment is suggested by cases in which progress with vocational problems was made after some time was spent, incidently to vocational counseling, in dealing with personal problems [1957, p.301]."

Loughary, Stripling, and Fitzgerald (1965) report on some research concerned with the process whereby a school-counselor provides educational information to students. They indicate that most of the counselor's educational information gathering and information-dispensing activities easily lend themselves to automation:

While their research is not complete, they estimate that they can account for and automate about 90 percent of the counselors preinterview behavior; while not as much work has been done on the interview behavior, they are tentatively estimating that for this particular counselor they can account for and automate approximately 75–80 percent of his interview behavior [p. 48].

With the advent of electronic data-processing equipment, school-counselors who function primarily as repositors and dispensers of educational and vocational information will find that they have been automated out of existence, since machines can perform such functions with a higher degree of skill than any human. The school-counselor who bases the rationale for his existence upon data collection and dissemination should begin to take a closer look at the implications of the continuance of such procedures.

Since computers can more effeciently house and dispense educational and /or vocational information, the school-counselor should turn to such hardware to handle the informational phase of a counseling program. If computers are used for such purposes, the student would then visualize the counselor as someone to whom he can turn when his problem is more affective than cognitive. Some innovative computer projects, which have and will improve the cognitive dimensions of the student's educational and vocational decision-making ability, are briefly noted below:

1. *Computer-Assisted Occupational Guidance.* Pennsylvania State University, Department of Vocational Education, 219 Chambers Building, University Park, Pa. Edward A. Campbell Research Associate.
2. *Information System for Vocational-Decisions Project. Annual report,* 1 June 1966–31 May 1967. Harvard University, Graduate School of Education, Cambridge, Mass. David V. Tiedeman, Project Director.

3. *San Diego County Career-Information Center.* Department of Education, San Diego County, San Diego, Calif. Martin Gerstein and Richard Hoover, Co-Directors.
4. Brewer, H. J. Automate your guidance office. *Canadian High News,* Canadian High News Ltd., 62 Shaftesbury Avenue, Toronto, Ont., Canada, Sept., 1967, pp. 3–5.
5. Loughary, John W., Friesen, Deloss, & Hurst, Robert. Autocoun: A computer based automated counseling simulation system. *Personnel and Guidance Journal,* 1966, **45**, (1), 6–15.

SUPERVISION

The successful administration of any school-counseling program is directly related to the administrator's sense of personal security in performing his job. A secure administrator has confidence in himself, and confidence in the ability of his counselors to carry on a successful program. He does not feel that his personal omniscience is essential to the operation of the program, his relationships with staff members are more human than professional, and he engages in administration within a truly democratic frame of reference.

In the name of so-called professionalism, many administrators have become more attuned to themselves than to the people with whom they work. Sensitivity to others is an important aspect of successful administration, since staff members have positive reactions to a supervisor who is aware of them more as human beings than as task performers. In other words, successful administration depends not so much on what the administrator knows, but on what he is. A staff will have a good response to a genuine person, whereas the pseudo knowledgeable administrator will find, if he is willing to investigate, that his staff is apathetic to the program because of the autocratic nature of his administration.

Counselors must feel that they are an integral part of a program, and they develop this feeling if they are involved in the major decisions related to the program. We often think of administration as coming from the top down—a vertical type of structure. Under this kind of administration, staff members do not activate themselves until someone at the top decides the direction of movement. Staff members are not able to become freely creative individuals, since creativity demands an opportunity to think for oneself rather than merely to carry out the directives of those above. Creativity on the part of staff members is the essence of a well-functioning and purposeful program. Unlocking the creative potential of staff members demands that the administrator achieve a relationship with his staff whereby they feel free to uncover new solutions to complex problems.

Any program becomes more meaningful to a staff when there is a horizontal type of administration. In this kind of administration the administrator does not view himself as being at the top of a hierarchy, but as a fellow-worker who is interested in bringing to the fore the full potential of each staff member. Nothing divides the democratic administrator from his staff, since there are no artificial barriers for staff members to scale in order to communicate. Staff members become actively involved in administering the program, since they are sharing with the administrator the responsibility for deciding the program's direction. The administrator in this type of relationship must be secure, since the staff has such a large voice in determining the program. He must have faith in the professional competence and decision-making ability of those with whom he works.

Some administrators fear allowing a staff to determine policy and run a program, since there is a possibility that a staff decision may not conform with the administrator's ideas on the matter. The secure administrator will evaluate his viewpoint in light of what the staff has decided, express his viewpoint, and encourage the staff to proceed toward a self-conceived, democratic solution. Under democratic administration in its purest form, staff members have a real voice in developing a counseling program. An autocratic administration is far easier on the administrator than a democratic one, since in an autocracy, with one person making decisions for many, things appear to run more smoothly. In this type of administration everything is spelled out in black and white by the administrator so that trouble can be avoided. Democracy is far more difficult to practice since the administrator may function in a sort of gray pattern, rather than administering from either a black or a white viewpoint. Democracy must be flexible, since people are flexible, and to the autocratic administrator flexibility is a sign of weakness.

A democratic administrator may have more difficulty in relating to the general public than his autocratic colleague, since often the public reacts more favorably to an administrator who has all the answers to all their questions. More often than not, the democratic administrator will find himself saying, "Frankly, I don't know—we'll have to look into it," but the "omniscient" autocratic administrator cannot bring himself to utter such a response since he feels it would be administratively unprofessional not to have answers at the tip of his tongue. A democratic administrator will be very much aware of possible answers to problems that arise, but since his attitudinal structure embraces the spirit of democracy, his staff must become involved in determining the answers to issues that affect their work. This respect for the dignity and worth of staff members is one of the basic principles governing the work of the secure administrator. He conceives the staff as a group of individuals who must be involved in the making of decisions if their work is to have some personalized significance.

Staff members thrive and grow with a genuinely human administrator who is one of them. They strike out on their own, discovering more meaningful ways to get a job done. They sift ideas in the process of reaching into the unknown, realizing that there is more unknown than known in the counseling field. These staff members are enthusiastic individuals, involved in their profession because of an administrator who reflects the truths of democracy in his attitude toward them and their work.

If the supervisor truly embraces the tenets of democracy, counselors will respond by being creative individuals who are concerned with continually evaluating the impact of the counseling program upon its clientele. Such counselors feel free enough to eliminate procedures within the program that interfere with the client's progress in counseling. Therefore, the more democratic the administrative atmosphere, the more imaginative are the counselors within that program, and the ultimate beneficiaries of such creative freewheeling are the students whom the program serves.

COMMUNICATION

Certain identifiable communicative characteristics, if possessed by the school-counselor, will result in the client feeling comfortable with, and profiting from, the counseling relationship. These counselor characteristics are (1) empathy, (2) acceptance, (3) faith and consistency, (4) sensitive listening, and (5) authenticity.

Empathy

Empathy means that the counselor puts himself into the client's being so that, in some way, he is the client. Instead of sitting back and sifting the rights and wrongs of the client's feelings, he experiences, however imperfectly, the same emotions and feelings as the client; he senses life from the client's internal frame of reference. The counselor's ability to feel the pain, the sorrow, the disgrace, the rejection, the threat that the client has felt, will, in turn, enable the client to perceive the dimensions of these feelings and move toward more self-enhancing attitudes and behavior. The counselor's empathic attitude will provide the client with a counseling relationship in which he can perceive why he acts and reacts as he does; he can move toward more appropriate behavior because he senses the inner need to move away from behavior that is not personally satisfying.

Behavior changes essentially because the client desires a change in his behavior. A counselor can assist clients to become if he is able to empathically absorb, and communicate to the client, the dimensions of the client's current state of being.

Acceptance

Acceptance means that the counselor respects the client's right to be—to be the owner of his current attitudes and behavior. The counselor is essentially transmitting to the client an attitude which says, "I respect what you are as a person, even though others may be dismayed by your existence." An acceptant counselor enables the client to feel comfortable with himself—to be! This right to be must be viscerally sensed by the client before he can begin to consider what he might behaviorally become. Too many school-counselors attempt to externally reconstruct what the client is, and are met by resistive and defensive reactions by the client. No client wants to be remade by the counselor; in fact clients resent such attempts! If there is any remaking to be done, the client, because of the natural tendencies toward self-determination that lurk in all men, wants to do it for himself. When the counselor accepts the client as he is, he is providing a counseling relationship to which the client can react positively as he moves toward the process of becoming.

Faith and Consistency

Too many counselors distrust man. They are prompted to mold their clients in their own image and likeness because they do not trust the client's ability to do this for himself. The counselor who manipulates the client shows a lack of faith in the client's ability to manage his own life and make his own decisions.

The counselor who trusts the decision-making ability of his clientele is one who trusts himself; he is secure enough in his own existence to transmit to the client an attitude of faith in the client's ability to shape his own life. Such a counselor proceeds in a consistent manner with his clientele, and is not warm and understanding in one counseling session, and moralistic and judgmental in a subsequent session.

When the counselor is consistent, he develops an expectancy on the client's part regarding the counselor's attitude and verbal behavior. When the client consistently knows what to expect from the counselor, he is able to comfortably unravel the nuances of his existence; he has nothing to fear in the counseling relationship and he senses the personal safety emerging from that relationship.

Many clients become confused when the counselor's behavior is inconsistent. They find it difficult to be themselves because the counselor, on the one hand, is the embodiment of all that is good in man, while, on the other hand, he exemplifies a negativism in the verbal interchange. It is no wonder that clients who are exposed to such contradictory counselor behaviors quickly terminate the relationship! If counseling is to advance itself as a communicating science, it must develop an identifiable consistency of procedure that significantly contributes to the self-emergence of clients.

Sensitive Listening

There is a socially acceptable way of listening that has no therapeutic value within a counseling relationship. This type of listening might be called judgmental listening, and it is characteristic of the type of listening that typically occurs in our society. We passively listen but we do not hear; we are quiet, not absorbing what a person is feeling, but waiting for him to be quiet so we can say, "Ah, yes, that is correct," or "No, I'm afraid you're wrong about that."

Sensitive listening demands that the counselor be attuned to the feelings that undergird the words being transmitted by the client. It requires that the counselor put himself aside so that he can internalize the feelings of the client. Such listening is not easy, because most people have been conditioned to render opinions rather than become involved in sensitive listening. When the youngster says, "I don't like science because of that Miss Jones, my science teacher," the counselor who is a sensitive listener responds to the feelings being transmitted by the client. The insensitive counselor might respond by saying, "You should be interested in science—we're living in a scientific age and it's going to be an important part of your future." The affectively insensitive counselor may be logically correct, but he did not possess an awareness that the youngster's negative attitude toward science may be largely based upon his negative feelings toward his science teacher! Feelings accompany statements made by clients, and the counselor who sensitively listens to these feelings is in the best position to be of assistance to the client.

Authenticity

Youngsters in school are so remarkably frank with each other that they develop a sixth sense, which enables them to viscerally know when they are in contact with a nonauthentic counselor. The counselor's authenticity as a person, or his caring attitude, will enable the troubled client to to feel, "At least here is a person who cares for me as a person—who isn't offended by me or my attitudes."

The school-counselor who plays a role, who goes through the motions of counseling without ever being emotionally present with the client, will soon find that his pseudo attitude is known to his clientele, and that they do not care to become voluntarily involved in a counseling relationship with him.

If the counselor is himself authentic, he will find that his clients feel comfortable enough to be authentic themselves; they can reveal their inner cores because they sense that the counselor himself is genuine. Clients respond to the authenticity of the counselor by pursuing personal dimensions of themselves which they have characteristically kept buried in the course of their existence. Facades by the counselor will be met with facades by the client; authenticity on the part of the counselor will be reciprocated with authenticity on the part of the client. In a very real way, the goal of counseling is to help the client move toward more authentic behavior, and this movement can be enhanced by the counselor who is himself authentic.

ASSESSMENT—EVALUATION OF THE SETTING

If a certain set of conditions exists in a school-counseling program, then specific outcomes should flow from that counseling program; there is a proportionate relationship between the existence of these conditions and the outcomes of a counseling service. If these conditions exist in a positive manner, the outcomes of the counseling program should tend toward the positive. If these conditions do not exist, the outcomes of the counseling program will tend toward the negative; when these conditions exist in either a positive or a negative manner, we can then draw a cause-and-effect relationship between the existence of these conditions and the outcomes of a counseling program.

The conditions that undergird an effective school-counseling program are (Boy & Pine, 1968):

1. The school-counselor is able to translate his professional education into practice—i.e., he is able to convert theoretical constructs into viable counseling relationships, which have significance and meaning for his clientele.
2. The counseling program has a rationale; it has a sense of purpose in the lives of students. It has a raison d'être that meets the basic needs of students.
3. The counselor has achieved a self-identity, which has been translated into a role definition. The counselor perceives himself essentially as a counselor, and not as an evaluator, administrator, information depositary, or loose-ends coordinator.
4. The counselor possesses a positive image among students. He is perceived as someone with whom students can communicate deeply in an atmosphere that poses no threat to the self.
5. The counselor motivates students to seek counseling of their own volition. He realizes that effective counseling occurs when the student voluntarily decides to involve himself in counseling and discuss problems that inhibit his functioning as a person.
6. The counselor provides orientations to the groups he serves—students,

parents, teachers, and administrators. He defines himself and counseling to these groups to help them understand the philosophical and empirical considerations undergirding his professional existence.

7. The counselor exists in a democratic administrative atmosphere. His professional knowledge and sophistication are respected in the building of a counseling program that has significance and meaning for students.

DEFICITS IN THE SETTING

Deficits in the setting exist when the above-cited seven conditions do not exist, or exist only at minimal levels.

VALUE OF EXPOSURE TO DIFFERENT SETTINGS

Within the total context of a school setting, different subsettings can have therapeutic value for students. These subsettings are as follows:

Individual Counseling. When the student is able to come to grips with himself and his behavior, his existence as a person is enhanced, and this leads to the student deriving more benefit from a school's educational offerings. Learning occurs because a student is psychologically free to learn, and individual counseling can assist the student to achieve this personally satisfying psychological freedom.

Group Counseling. A person's self-concept matures when the self is exposed to the external frames of reference provided in group counseling. Since youngsters in school value the opinions (external frames of reference) of their peers more than any other group (parents, teachers, etc.), group counseling contains much therapeutic potential. That is, as one journeys through life, his self-concept is shaped by an interplay between his self-perception and the external-to-self perceptions provided by others. Man achieves psychological balance when his self-perception becomes congruent with the perceptions provided by personally significant persons external to himself. Group counseling represents a reality setting, since no man is an island unto himself.

Informational Service. A school's nonacademic informational service has personal value to a student, especially when the student is psychologically free to absorb and make logical use of that information in the educational and/or vocational decision-making process. It logically follows that when a student has unraveled his own personal dimensions in counseling, he is ready to make rational educational and/or vocational decisions. An automated career-information center is a valuable adjunct to an effective counseling program; it represents a cognitively necessary culminating step for many students involved in an affectively oriented counseling program.

Instructional Program. Some teachers, by natural inclination, treat students as human beings and, therefore, have a positive therapeutic effect upon their existence. Such teachers realize that nothing can be taught unless the student is ready to learn, and they invest themselves in creating a learning atmosphere sensitive to the human needs of students. They possess a sensitivity to the fact that the cognitive wheels turn only when the student is psychologically comfortable enough in the learning relationship to allow them to turn. Students can achieve much personal growth when they have the good fortune to be exposed to such teachers.

Administrative Program. A school's administrator sets the tone of a school's atmosphere. If the administrator can create an atmosphere in which the dignity and worth of students are respected, he will make a very large contribution to the relevance of the educational experience for the students. A school is a microcosm of society, and it should be a model of democratic community living, which students can absorb and apply not only today but in the later stages of their lives.

The Curriculum. If the student feels that the curriculum is alive and meets his needs, he will tune in on the process of intellectual growth. If he feels that the curriculum is irrelevant and boring, he will engage himself in norm-violating behavior, which will capture his interest more than the curriculum. A vibrant curriculum is built around the needs of students, and has much therapeutic potential because it deals with issues touching the inner core of the student's needs and interests. The student's exposure to a relevant curriculum can produce an inner psychological satisfaction for the student, whereas an inappropriate curriculum will produce inner dissatisfactions and conflicts that can only find their expression in resentful and antagonistic behavior patterns.

REFERENCES

Arbuckle, D. S. *Counseling: Philosophy, theory and practice.* Boston: Allyn and Bacon, 1965.

Berlin, I. N. The school counselor: His unique mental health function. *Personnel and Guidance Journal,* 1963, **45** (5), 414.

Boy, A. V. Motivating students to seek counseling. *School Counselor,* 1959, **6** (4), 33–36.

Boy, A. V., & Pine, G. J. *Client-centered counseling in the secondary school.* Boston: Houghton Mifflin, 1963.

Boy, A. V., & Pine, G. J. *The counselor in the schools: A reconceptualization.* Boston: Houghton Mifflin, 1968.

Frank, J. D. *Persuasion and healing.* New York: Schocken Books, 1963.

Friedenberg, E. *The vanishing adolescent.* Boston: Beacon Press, 1959.

Konopka, G. *The adolescent girl in conflict.* Englewood Cliffs, N.J.: Prentice-Hall, 1966.

Loughary, J. W., Stripling, R. O., & Fitzgerald, P. W. (Eds.) *Counseling, a growing profession.* Washington, D.C.: American Personnel and Guidance Association, 1965.

Meeks, A. R. Elementary school counseling. *School Counselor,* 1963, **10** (3), 108.

Munson, H. L. *A rationale for elementary school guidance.* College of Education, University of Rochester, 1966. (Mimeo.)

Stiller, A. Social pressures and the guidance function. *School Counselor,* 1964, **11** (4), 236–237.

Super, D. E. *The psychology of careers.* New York: Harper & Row, 1957.

Swartz, H. Administrative aspects of the initiation of an elementary counselor program. *Report of the Fifth Annual All-Ohio Elementary School Guidance Conference,* Canton, Ohio, Nov. 19, 1965.

Teigland, J. J., Winkler, R. C., Munger, P. F., & Kranzler, G. D. Some concomitants of underachievement at the elementary school level. *Personnel and Guidance Journal,* 1966, **44**(9), 950–955.

Clients in Business and Industry

Constantine A. Dallis

Rohrer, Hibler & Replogle, Inc.

Business and industrial enterprises offer meaningful possibilities, both for practicum and internship as well as for future employment, to members of the helping professions, particularly those who are involved in counseling and clinical work. As always, the types of learning input provided in the academic setting must be adapted to the operational parameters imposed by the applied setting. It is the purpose of this essay to discuss the characteristics and factors that weigh upon the psychologist who conducts his practice in the business-industrial complex.

ENVIRONMENTAL VARIABLES

It is of the utmost importance that the psychologist with a corporation as a client should have an understanding of the industry in which the organization functions, the kind of product manufactured by the company and its financial condition, and the abilities of the personnel to function and successfully compete in the marketplace.

If one examines the individuals who constitute a firm, all the values of each person and each group can be seen coming into play with the values of others. In addition, needs differ somewhat as the level of management changes. For example, members of upper-level management are frequently concerned that the overall organization should continue to function smoothly after they have departed from the scene. Therefore, a primary concern for any executive group is the identification and development of those managers who can function as likely successors until such time as they assume a still more responsible role as members of the upper management group.

The general manager or president of a company is concerned about the competence of the people who work for his company. He would like to have the best people at the top show dynamic leadership. He would like younger

436

people to be eager to learn the business and to make it grow in a vigorous yet economically sound fashion. At the same time, the general manager is aware that he cannot have an ideal population.

One objective of a general manager or president is that of working himself out of a job, in a sense. If all the people in an organization are functioning well as a group, and as individuals, the top executive can relax. Needless to say, this phenomenon seldom occurs. When it does, the balance is so delicate that disequilibrium will certainly again set in from one source or another.

The upper-level executive is frequently ambitious and has a considerable amount of energy and drive. He is profit-oriented and realizes that company objectives can be accomplished only through the organized effort of people. It is important, therefore, that the upper-level executive work to establish a work climate in which people can feel that they are striving toward common objectives but in ways that preserve their individual personalities and meet their individual needs to a substantial degree.

Since managers must work through other people, they are concerned as to how they are perceived by others. In general, most people do not seem to know just how others view them. They do know how they would *like* others to perceive them, and that is in the success terms that they have defined for themselves. Generally, executives and managers who work in a corporation want to be seen as dynamic leaders and doers, both by those who sit in high corporate positions and by those whom they lead. Those in high corporate positions often want to be seen as capable businessmen by members of the board of directors, the financial community, and other responsible executives.

The life of a business executive is a difficult one because he is trying to satisfy the requirements of his superiors, his subordinates, and himself. He also tries to meet whatever demands are made on his time and energies by other civic leaders so that he can participate in the continuing development of the community in which he resides. He tries to find time to spend with his family, and if possible, he tries to find a few moments for himself. He is involved with many of the concerns of those who surround him, and he is expected to respond positively to all the demands made upon his time. Although these demands occasionally seem oppressive, he is rewarded many times by the people who turn to him for advice, counsel, and leadership.

Middle-level managers feel similar concerns. The criterion of success is to climb the managerial ladder. All eyes seem to be looking upward, for the rewards of success are greater position, responsibility, and remuneration, which yield greater status in the company, in the business community, and in the community at large.

The foreman is the one manager who differs from upper-and middle-level management. He is expected to represent management's viewpoint because he is on the first rung of the managerial ladder. He is generally perceived by others as being a member of the management team; yet, he is seldom consulted as to what ought to be done to solve the questions that confront him daily. Most foremen come from the hourly work force. They may try to get management's attention, but they frequently have little impact that they can see. They may attend seminars and try to improve themselves as much as possible, but this effort may still have little visible effect on those above them. One end result of this kind of situation can be that the foreman reidentifies with the hourly work force from which he moved upward. Then his objective may become simply to make it through the day with as little difficulty as possible, which may be counter to the objectives and expectations of upper management. To re-establish management identification on the part of the foreman, upper and especially middle management must take concrete steps to include him in efforts to cope with the problems, challenges and questions that arise in the everyday affairs of the business concern. It is not unusual to find that no one has taken the time to ask the foreman what he thinks. After all, many managers are busy themselves trying to cope with their own superior's expectations and objectives.

Each person operates in his psychological world, which comes in contact in some fashion with the psychological world of other people. These are not totally different worlds, but the values, experiences, and needs within each can differ with the level of management and with the particular background of the individuals under consideration. At the same time, one must be aware of the existence of various groups and sub groups, and the interplay among them. When all of this is superimposed onto the business objectives of a company, the work of the corporate psychologist takes on additional dimensions of interest and substantial challenge.

BACKGROUND

The psychologist who works with executives and managers in industry must be consciously aware of the economic, political, religious, and social values that appear to dominate the general scene. For these values, in all probability, will be dominant among managers. He must also be aware of the less predominant beliefs held by smaller groups, or subcultures, including those formed by age differences.

Needless to say, the psychologist must be sensitive to the changing business climate in general, as well as the fluctuations that occur within segments of business. He must be sensitive to the people who manage a business enterprise in terms of their psychological makeup, their philosophy of business, and their ability and style in relating to other people.

He must be sensitive to organizational structure or the lack of it. He needs to develop an understanding of various occupations at different levels and to learn what is required by each. He must learn that the same job or position title may not have the same meaning in two different companies and that both positions do not necessarily require persons of the same caliber or characteristics.

In the final analysis, the corporate psychologist must try to draw effectively from the pool of all knowledge being acquired in the social sciences; he must apply this knowledge to the community, the business enterprise, and the managers within these groups; and he must continue to assess variables that assume a high degree of importance in the decision-making process. His antennae must be "tuned in" at all times to environmental changes that may have an effect upon human behavior and, therefore, on the viability of his client, the organization.

WHAT DOES THE PSYCHOLOGIST DO?

Armed with all of the necessary information, how does a psychologist function in an industrial setting? As a corporate psychologist, he must gain an overview of need on the part of the client company. It is important to realize that no one person is completely armed with all of the needed expertise. One of the corporate psychologist's responsibilities is to recommend resources that can respond most competently to specific needs as they arise. For example, a compensation survey might be required. Organizations are available with the proper capabilities and personnel to complete such a survey, to collate the results, and make recommendations. The psychological impact of the recommendations can then be reviewed by the corporate psychologist and conveyed to the general manager with further recommendations and suggestions for selective implementation.

The use of an Assessment Center approach to evaluating and training managers in the basic skills of their work might also represent a resource recommended by the corporate psychologist to his client organization. While special expertise would be utilized in implementing such a programatic effort, the corporate psychologist would help formulate the job skills and psychological qualities to be dealt with by his client in their assessment center efforts.

Similarly, the corporate psychologist might recommend and help in obtaining special expertise such as that for validation of tests used in selection, study of consumer behavior, and the like.

Often the corporate psychologist is involved in the process of selecting managerial candidates and in the operation of the client-management development program. In the management selection process, the psychologist tries to obtain an understanding and psychological picture of the candidate as a person. Then he must make a judgment as to whether the candidate would be able to perform well in the position being applied for, as well as function appropriately with other managers in the company. Only then can the psychologist advise his client about hiring the candidate. Such an evaluation does not necessarily mean that one must totally conform to the viewpoints of the larger group. Frequently, fresh outlooks, new perspectives, and initiatives are needed to overcome complacency. There are times, too, when initial stress may have been placed on creativity, and what is now needed by the organization is a person able to organize people and ideas so as to provide a smooth, efficiently functioning structure within which ideas can be sufficiently harnessed for productive results.

The candidate should be able to work within the existing social-psychological structure. For example, a candidate for plant manager of a small manufacturing company had been highly recommended for the position. He was a highly intelligent person with a great deal of drive and ambition. Although his formal education was limited to high school, he had continued to educate himself through reading and thoughtful reflection about his experiences. He was imaginative, self-assured, emotionally stable, and dynamic. He was secure within himself and was able to rely on the abilities of the supervisors reporting to him. Because he communicated respect for them, they worked all the harder. His ambition was to assume the presidency of a firm some day. Although he joined the company as a manager, he did not remain very long. Dissatisfaction began to arise from a number of sources. What had been insufficiently considered was the manager's unwillingness to adapt to the kind of life-style dictated by the dominant ethnic group in the community. His uncomfortableness in the community became more apparent with time and played a major role in his departure from the company and the community scene. Although he was an outstanding manager, the locale was evidently inappropriate for him as an individual.

The psychologist many evaluate people who work in a firm for the purpose of identifying managerial potential. There are occasions when a person has been working for a firm in a rather inconspicuous position. If it appears, based on an assessment of his potential, that he is being underutilized or misused, the psychologist may make the necessary recommendations to higher management and bring this person to the attention of those concerned about the future development of personnel within the firm. The client management is thus further assured of not overlooking managerial potential that the client may wish to develop further.

The psychologist may work on an ongoing, developmental basis with managers in industry. He develops a counseling relationship with managers for the purpose of helping them to think through the decisions with which they are confronted regarding themselves, the use of personnel, and the future of the business. There is a great deal of satisfaction to be derived from this element of the practice, since one can evaluate the overall impact of one's work with hopefully positive and productive results.

PROGRAM

A practicum or internship program established in an industrial setting would provide experiences necessary for the development and growth of the neophyte-corporate psychologist. Initially he could speak with managers to obtain a feel for the company and its people. At the same time, he could begin looking over previous evaluations of current managers and could discuss his own general appraisals and written evaluations with the psychologist consulting with the company. When he and his supervisor feel he is ready, he might begin by evaluating personnel in low-management positions in a variety of departments after sitting with the supervising psychologist, observing him making several evaluations. Such evaluations could be discussed with both management and the psychologist. The neophyte could eventually be included in the ongoing program of counseling with managers at some higher level if the internship is for an extended period of time (one year). Time is important because managers do not want to jump from psychologist to psychologist. Conferences with the intern and supervisor, in addition to group meetings with the president and other manager, would provide further insight for the intern.

During the course of this time, regular meetings with the psychologist to discuss issues, feelings, views, and techniques should be held; for, in the early period, there is a great deal of uncertainty and questioning that should be handled by the supervising psychologist. Once familiarity occurs and a degree of certainty develops within the psychologist, he will become more free to assume responsibility in the program as opportunities arise.

OPPORTUNITIES FOR INNOVATION

Bonus Plans

Working in a business setting provides the psychologist with the opportunity of suggesting new approaches for dealing with people; e.g., bonus plans, stock-option plans, and profit improvement plans are only a few of the ways of considering money as an additional incentive. One must not assume that techniques are a panacea for motivating workers and managers. Plans of this type must be carefully thought out in accordance with the business and psychological needs of the company, the overall market conditions for the products produced, and alternative employment opportunities for the people under consideration. A bonus plan is good in the eyes of the receiver only as long as it generates bonuses. If, after several months of bonuses, the plan stops producing extra funds, the employees may become puzzled and wonder what the trouble is. As the frequency of the bonus failure increases, frustration sets in and productivity may well decline. This may be avoided if considerable time is taken in the initial phases to carefully think through the consequences of instituting such a plan. This means involvement by representatives of all groups as well as a careful examination of every variable used in the final formula. The utilization of outside consultants with specific expertise in the area of bonus plans is, of course, very helpful.

Social Changes

A business organization typically may be viewed as a microcosm of the larger society of which it is a part. Therefore, problems such as racial, religious, or sex discrimination may occur. As in the larger society, these problems, concerns, or needs may necessitate psychological counseling as managers and executives struggle to cope with these relatively new dimensions of responsibility, which are being assigned to them by the larger society of which they are inevitably a part.

Many students in higher education look upon the business world with a jaundiced eye. When asked why, they frequently give some substantially valid reasons. The business comminity has at times been accused of being so profit-oriented, so money-hungry that it would do anything for the sake of a dollar. One can cite the historical exploitation of workers in the building of some large empires in the manufacturing, construction, and transportation industries as evidence. Or one can cite the cases of price-fixing among several large corporations. A good case can be made that, all too frequently, too many companies think of themselves first and the larger society second. However, one must recognize that without profits, free enterprise cannot exist. A proper balance, therefore, between profit needs and societal responsibility is rather difficult to achieve but is necessary as an ideal to be striven for.

Most businessmen perceive themselves as good citizens. They work diligently and contribute to many civic causes; they are hard workers and loyal Americans. It must be stated at this point, however, that businessmen have contributed greatly only in their own spheres. Unfortunately, too few have taken a lead in moving into heretofore unplowed areas. Businessmen are, of necessity, realists. As they are beginning to recognize new roles they can fill, job-corps centers have been established for the disadvantaged and efforts to facilitate learning through the sale of programmed instruction have been undertaken, frequently resulting in the initiation of business enterprises.

The social problems that face urban areas are, of course, enormous. One can talk about what should be done, but the involvement of private enterprise and the capital that can be brought to bear are indeed vitally important. Although the federal government has taken the lead in establishing programs to help the poor, such attempts will not be enough unless there is a total commitment by people in the community and in the business power structure to face and solve the problems.

Many managers feel that something should be done, but they are somewhat at a loss as to what to do. When such attitudes are expressed, the psychologist is in an excellent position to help the executive explore not only how he can make a contribution, but also, if possible, to what extent the company can be of help. For example, with union approval and management cooperation, apprenticeship programs can be expanded to include the hard-core unemployed. Part-time jobs can be filled by mothers who need money but are able to work only a few hours a day. In short, the psychologist is in an excellent position to recommend to receptive executives programs of company involvement for the betterment of the community.

EDUCATION

Another area in which the psychologist can bring about change is in the field of education. Executives recognize that the future of any firm rests with the upcoming generation. It also recognizes that a better job needs to be done in explaining the position and needs of business students, as well as in listening to what students have to say. With managers who do express concern, involvement can be encouraged, such as speaking with high school or college groups, working closely with university officials, and making themselves visible to the student in a role other than parental or authoritarian. In other words, the psychologist can help the executive to bridge the gap between business and student bodies.

One executive has expressed mixed feelings about his managerial position. At times he is satisfied with his role in life; there are other times when he "champs at the bit." He is basically concerned about student–business relations and business–community relations. He would have made an excellent YMCA social director. But he reached the conclusion that to have any impact at all, one must have a power base.

He has become a successful businessman in the eyes of his fellow businessmen. With this power base established, he has involved himself in a number of projects in the schools and the community. He believes that he has a greater impact through his current managerial position than he would have if he were operating in a Community Chest Agency or an educational institution.

A second area of education in which the psychologist may be able to effect innovation is in bringing new programs to the attention of executives. Frequently, executives subscribe to the idea that competent people who work for them should upgrade themselves. This goal can be furthered by means of the subsidy of employee attendance at seminars, workshops, and regional meetings. It is obvious that when personnel improve, the company also improves.

SUPERVISION

To supervise a practicum student in the industrial setting is not ordinarily as easily arranged as in the usual counselor-education setting. However, the possibility exists that audiotape, videotape, or a third-party observor arrangement might be feasible.

Managers who are sufficiently self-confident sometimes do permit themselves to be taped under conditions of anonymity and guarantees that such tapes would be used for educational purposes only. The presence of a third person in the room will not disturb the individual being interviewed, provided that an explanation and introduction are made, coupled with the obtaining of permission from the client. Most adults accept the reasons for the presence of three persons or a tape recorder. The principal prerequisite is a brief but clear explanation as to why such steps are being taken with him; he also can refuse to cooperate without any derogatory effect. The client's degree of cooperativeness during the interview would soon bear out any suspicion on the psychologist's part that he might feel "trapped" and unable to walk out.

The primary difficulty is the length of time that a practicum-student would be involved with a company. Firms spend a great deal of money educating a new psychologist in terms of their business and personnel. It takes several months for a person to get the feel of a company. The injection of a new practicum student for no more than a year could be a stumbling block, but it is one that may be overcome.

For the most part, the presence of practicum students might be a bit more upsetting in industry than in universities or secondary schools, but if the relationship between top management and the psychologist is a sufficiently good one, and if the psychologist closely supervises the practicum student, obstacles may only be minor in nature.

COMMUNICATION

On the surface, the single problem most frequently found in the industrial setting is the apparent lack of communication. It is difficult for people to communicate their thoughts in a manner understood by the receiving parties.

There are certainly many reasons for this, and these reasons must be carefully examined.

Frequently, managers who do not communicate well are not aware of themselves with any degree of depth. They continue to pursue their lives, ignoring, misinterpreting, and distorting the cues that are fed to them daily. For example, a manager in a large firm was informed by his superior that he could apparently do a good job, provided that something was done about his communications problem. Puzzled, the manager, at the request of his superior, sought out the psychologist for the purpose of solving the problem. Obviously, it was not as easy as it seemed. This manager had ignored his own feelings and, in addition, had interpreted the behavior of others by placing them in stereotyped categories; i.e., if girls with red hair are thought to have tempers, he perceived any girl with red hair as having a bad temper. Operating under these assumptions usually leads to trouble in short order. But our manager evaded any cues that told him something different. He married a girl on the basis of this kind of stereotype; one could almost predict the outcome—divorce.

This manager's subordinates realized after a few months that they were unaware of what was happening elsewhere in the firm. Two subordinates and the psychologist met to discuss the situation. Weekly meetings of short duration were suggested, with each person (a total of four individuals) taking a maximum of 10 minutes without interruption to explain what had taken place during the week and what had been his successes and failures. At the conclusion, there would be a 10-minute discussion and a short summary. It was thought that such a procedure would begin to break the ice with the manager and accomplish several other goals as well. First, it would provide the manager with the structure needed to verbalize without too much threat. His anxiety level could be kept to a minimum, since he was in control of the material he was about to present. Second, presentations by others and the summary technique would force him to listen intently to what was being stated. Third, the discussion period would require him to involve himself in discussion. With time and clarification, his perceptions of those at the meeting might change. As he became more comfortable, the organized procedure would be relaxed and moved into a discussion session, followed by a summary. The manager would also see the psychologist after each weekly session.

Within two months, the subordinates became more acceptant of their superior, marveling at his technical knowledge and his suggestions as to what procedures might be followed. As their acceptance increased, he became more relaxed and, to some extent, began accepting each person in the group for himself. There were also two other changes. He began to introduce himself to workers two levels below him, who had never met him; he began to question the assumptions upon which he was operating. He began to understand that others liked him for what he was, and that he should not be afraid to let others see him through discussion. This manager still falls short of communicating well, but he has become more acceptant and more confident of himself. With these insights, he is becoming a more effective manager—he realizes what needs to be done, and he is pursuing the task with vigor.

A second kind of communication problem is caused by organizational structure. Managers like to feel needed and thus frequently find themselves responding to subordinates several layers below them. One may find an extraordinarily large number of people reporting to the president when, in fact, four or five key people would be sufficient.

Communication would be enhanced if subordinates would report their concerns to their immediate supervisors instead of circumventing them. There are many reasons why strict organizational lines are not followed. Supervisors frequently do not make good listeners. They often ignore concerns that are expressed to them and fail to tell their subordinates the results of their deliberations about the particular concerns over which they have control. In instances in which supervisors are good listeners, but have no authority to respond to a concern, the lack of communication is repeated with their own superiors, and so it goes.

This pattern of behavior can be broken. Managers responsible for their functional areas, such as sales and manufacturing, can get together to determine what questions should be discussed. They, in turn, can request that the appropriate subordinates, such as the customer service manager and the production control manager, or any others who would be involved in the question, get together to discuss possible solutions to that question. An action program can then be established with appropriate defined assignments to specific members of this subgroup. Cross-sectional meetings held for the purpose of meeting specific objectives frequently set the stage for cooperation and the general sharing of viewpoints. Not all problems can be easily solved, but new pathways of discussion can be established.

A third area should be mentioned. Many memos are written explaining and re-explaining policy. Errors occur frequently because the reader places his own interpretation on the printed words if such latitude exists. The written message should be conveyed clearly and simply to reduce error in understanding, for errors in interpretation can be costly to a firm.

PERFORMANCE APPRAISAL

A difficult question to answer in any setting is, "How much of an impact am I having and how good is my work?" It would be possible in some instances to make use of general questionnaires or Q sorts to reach determinations about one's effectiveness. However, there are more obvious ways of satisfying one's curiosity about one's own effectiveness.

If one works with the president of a firm, an obvious measure is whether he continues to make use of the psychologist's services. One may argue that retention of service is by no means a measure of effetiveness. All it indicates is that the president likes the psychologist. But the psychologist's function includes bringing to bear all the information and impressions that would be helpful to top management. Frequently, such information is not of a positive nature, i.e., the kind a senior executive wants to hear. Most executives who hire psychologists want someone who can, and will be, honest with them in their general appraisal of a situation. Therefore, the continuation of services can be used as a criterion for evaluation.

One can also make a determination of one's effectiveness in terms of the frequency with which executives ask his opinion about the use of personnel. Such use of the psychologist indicates confidence in him as a consultant. One can also make a determination regarding the frequency with which advice and counsel is accepted and implemented. The psychologist can observe the success or failure of his programs by observing how effectively people manage in their respective positions.

As mentioned above, the psychologist evaluates personnel within and out-side a company for managerial potential as well as for available managerial positions. The psychologist is in a position to follow-up his recommendations and is able to make a determination as to whether expectations have been met.

In these ways the psychologist determines his ability to do a good job. A program of following-up rejected candidates for managerial positions is usually extremely helpful in determining whether the psychologist has made accurate statements in his reports concerning this group as well.

EXPOSURE TO DIFFERENT SETTINGS

There is nothing more educational and, in some respects, more humbling than to move around through a variety of industrial settings. One can discuss the world of work and a variety of occupations, but experience in observing people operate in different positions is enough to cause the neophyte to have second and third thoughts about dealing with different companies. Once confidence arrives, one begins to understand not only the individuals who make up a company, but also the company itself as if it, too, were an entity.

The psychologist quickly reaches the conclusion that a knowledge of the general economic situation and its effect upon certain segments of industry is vitally important. A change in government fiscal policy can upset the best-laid plans.

The variety of settings gives the psychologist an opportunity to compare large and small firms and his own ability to comprehend the various mazes that exist. But most important, dealing in different settings provides the psychologist with the opportunity of relating to people from all socioeconomic levels, with all their diversity of educational backgrounds and political, social, economic, and psychological outlooks. There is a deep feeling of substantial involvement obtainable as one moves about, for the challenges for learning and understanding are immense.

The challenge of working with managers in the business arena can be even greater than working in an educational setting or even a therapeutic setting. First, the model that seems most appropriate is a health model. The company and those persons who comprise management are healthy (i.e., functioning) people who are working together to accomplish several tasks. The accomplishment of those tasks is relatively measurable. In addition, the impact of these accomplishments can be felt in terms of job satisfaction and personal growth as well as business growth and impact on the comminity. One need not wonder if the person will ever "cope" in the outside world, as may be the question in a hospital setting.

At the same time, the adult business community has control and power in their grasp. They can make things happen. The young man or woman in the educational setting may make things happen and can look forward to a great future. But they do not have total control over themselves; their parents still have a say in what they do. Nor do college students have an immediate potential for influencing the lives of others readily.

Therefore, the corporate psychologist must be astute, observant, willing to learn, and pragmatic in his approach. At the same time, the dynamics that he faces in the business–industrial sphere challenges him at every turn, for he is not only relying on what he has learned in psychology alone, but he is relying on all the social sciences. For the practitioner psychologist, however, this is a stimulating challenge.

Professional Training in Community Mental-Health Centers

Jesse D. Geller

Yale University

Alan R. Feirstein

Case—Western Reserve University

Since the passage of the Community Mental Health Centers Act of 1963, the National Institute of Mental Health has awarded grants to assist in the construction and staffing of over 400 comprehensive community mental-health centers, and by 1980 it hopes that 2000 will be in operation. While it is too early to evaluate the effectiveness of such a nationwide network of community facilities, it is clear that they are having far-reaching consequences for the training of mental-health professionals. It is our purpose in this essay to explore some of the challenges these centers pose for professional training. We have tried to present a balanced view of the strengths and shortcomings of mental-health centers as settings for the training of members of all the mental-health-related professions. The issues raised, although not equally applicable to all the professions, are nonetheless critical in the training of psychiatrists, clinical and counseling psychologists, psychiatric social workers, and psychiatric nurses. Some of the trends that have had great impact upon the training in mental-health centers are (1) the emphasis on comprehensive services and continuity of patient care; (2) the emphasis on social action and indirect services; (3) the utilization of indigenous nonprofessional workers; and (4) work in multidisciplinary teams.

Before turning our attention to the training issues raised by these trends, it is necessary to define explicitly the characteristics of community mental-health centers. This task is complicated by the number of radically different notions about what community mental health is, how it should operate, and what it could become.

449

WHAT IS A COMMUNITY MENTAL-HEALTH CENTER?

The burgeoning literature on community mental health, social psychiatry, community psychology, and community psychiatry is both highly polemical and confusing. Some authors speak of the community mental-health movement as if it represented the coming of a "therapeutic millennium." Bellak (1964), for example, believes that it represents "a third major revolution in the history of psychiatry." Others criticize it, on the other hand, as "the newest therapeutic bandwagon (Dunham, 1965)." Whittington, in fact, maintains that it is "a definitely conservative, and perhaps even reactionary, movement [1965, p. 76]." For still others, community mental health represents merely a new and possibly more efficient superstructure for the distribution of the same old services (Shatan, 1969).

Historical Antecedents

Despite this controversy and the uncertain meaning of the term *community mental health,*[1] there does seem to be general agreement concerning the antecedent forces and events that gave impetus to this movement. A detailed analysis of these various influences and historical developments is beyond the scope of this essay.[2] Nevertheless, it should be noted that the following historical precedents and advances in research have been incorporated into the design, organizational structure, philosophy, and objectives of mental-health centers:

1. The realization that large, geographically remote, custodial hospitals in many ways fostered the very processes they were designed to alleviate —intractable chronicity, apathy, extreme dependence, and loss of human dignity (Stanton & Schwartz, 1954; Goffman, 1961; Gruenberg, 1966).
2. The recognition of the success of medication in materially reducing the length of hospital stay, the clear demonstration that most mentally ill people could thus be treated in their own communities (e.g., Pasamanick, Scarpatti, & Dinitz, 1967), and the demonstration that socioenvironmental treatment programs hold great promise for patient care (e.g., Jones, 1953; Caudill, 1958; Cumming & Cumming, 1962).

[1]Goldston (1965) has assembled, from the literature, five different and contradictory definitions of "community psychiatry."
[2]For an extensive discussion of the development of the community-mental-health movement, see the reviews by Sabshin (1965), Ewalt (1969), Freedman (1967), and Hersch (1968).

3. The publication of the report of the Joint Commission on Mental Illness and Health (1961), which documented:

    a. The nationwide neglect of the mentally ill, particularly of certain groups, e.g., the poor and the uneducated.

    b. The insulation and rivalry that characterized the relationship between different social-welfare facilities.

    c. The acute shortage of trained manpower in mental health.

Definition

Given the above-mentioned definitional confusion, we have relied primarily upon the guidelines and regulations outlined in the 1963 Community Mental Health Centers Act (U.S., 1963) in arriving at the essential characteristics of community mental-health centers. The U.S. Department of Health, Education and Welfare offers the following definition of a community mental-health center: "Basically, the mental health center is a program of mental health services in the community, in one or more facilities, under a unified system of care."

Every community mental-health center must comply with these definitional requirements if it is to be eligible for federal matching funds. Yet for several reasons, no two community mental-health centers will be exactly alike. First, the guidelines for the administration of federal construction grants emphasize that services must be tailored to local needs and desires, and that the eventual consumers of the services must have a voice in policy-making and decisions. Obviously, the priorities of a mental-health-center program serving a metropolitan, low-income, minority-group community will differ from the treatment emphases of mental-health centers located in middle-class suburban or rural communities.[3] The differences among community mental-health centers further derives from the fact that some communities develop their centers by integrating previously separate agencies, while others achieve this goal by modifying and expanding the services provided by their state hospitals, and still others use psychiatric units in general hospitals as the fulcrum of the community mental-health program (Glasscote, Sanders, Forstenzer, & Foley, 1964).

Although the major emphases of comprehensive mental-health-center pro-

---

[3]Because the community-mental-health-center movement is so intimately related to changes taking place in the economic and sociopolitical sectors of society (e.g., the war on poverty, the civil rights movement), it is often forgotten that these programs are also developing in relatively affluent communities.

grams may thus vary considerably from one center to another, all, as the definition indicates, attempt:

1. To coordinate previously isolated or unrelated existing programs and to establish missing elements in a *comprehensive service* network.
2. To increase the availability of health services to all the people within the community ("catchment area") in which the mental-health center is located.

ATTRIBUTES OF COMMUNITY MENTAL-HEALTH CENTERS

Comprehensive Services

To qualify for federal funds, a center must provide at least five essential services:

1. Twenty-four-hour inpatient hospitalization.
2. Outpatient treatment programs for adults, children, and families.
3. Partial hospitalization services, such as day care, night care, weekend care.
4. Emergency services 24-hours a day to be available within at least one of the first three services listed above.
5. Consultation and education to community agencies and professional personnel.

A *comprehensive* community-mental-health-center program includes the following additional services:

6. Diagnostic services distinct from the evaluative procedures inherent in other services.
7. Rehabilitative services, including vocational, recreational, and resocialization programs.
8. Precare and aftercare services in the community, including foster-home placement, home visiting, and half-way houses.
9. Training for all types of mental-health personnel.
10. Research and evaluation.

The federal guidelines further specify that these services must be coordinated in such a way as to insure "continuity of care." The exact manner in which this goal is to be achieved has not been specified, however, and consequently there is no prescribed pattern or model for organization and administration. Mental-health centers across the country have therefore experimented with various organizational structures that allow patients to move easily from one type of treatment to another as their needs change.

Some centers are organized as a federation of semiautonomous specialized-treatment units, with staff working primarily within one unit. The centralized administration of these units hopefully facilitates transfer of patients between units, and also encourages closer communication between staff on different units. Other centers, most notably Fort Logan, are organized into small, semiautonomous, multidiscipline clinical teams, which receive all their patients from a specific geographic segment of the community and supply all necessary services to this population. They work with a patient, then, throughout his treatment course, even as the type of treatment (e.g., inpatient, outpatient) may change.

Whatever the coordinating mechanism, the provision of services under a single organizational system is more than a matter of organizational aesthetics, since even in communities with an unusually high concentration of professional resources the deployment of mental-health services has tended to be isolated and fragmented. Such organizational inefficiency led to problems in both intake and treatment processes. In the past, patients might receive evaluation by one agency, only to find that the evaluating agency did not have available the type of treatment appropriate to their needs. A unified system of patient care, on the other hand, should allow the patient easy access to all treatment modalities at the time of intake, or as his needs change in the course of treatment (e.g., where an inpatient is ready to be discharged to outpatient care, where an outpatient in psychotherapy could also use rehabilitation and resocialization services, etc.). Such continuity of service is especially important for people who might be reluctant to ask for help in the first place or for those who could become confused by contacts with multiple independent agencies (e.g., "multiproblem families").[4]

Community Responsiveness

In all likelihood, the most far-reaching changes in the delivery of mental-health services will result from the commitment on the part of community mental-health centers to provide comprehensive services to large numbers of people in the local community, and indirect service to still others through prevention, consultation, and mental-health planning.

To begin with, in order to provide whatever kind of treatment is needed at

[4]Overcoming the encapsulation of existing clinical facilities has been one of the most formidable and difficult problems confronting mental-health centers. Rivalries between agencies and disciplines, as well as commitment to short-term professional and organizational vested interests, have hampered the development of mutually acceptable and facilitating mechanisms of coordination. Thus, for many mental-health centers a comprehensive integrated program remains an ideal rather than an actuality.

the time it is needed and within the community where the patient lives, mental-health centers have:

1. Located their treatment facilities reasonably near the patients' homes.
2. Reduced the number of patients transferred to isolated mental hospitals.
3. Relied primarily on a variety of therapeutic activities that go far beyond the one-to-one doctor-patient relationship, e.g., group and milieu therapy, and home visits.
4. Made the widest possible use of volunteers, indigenous nonprofessionals, and paraprofessionals as therapeutic agents.
5. Emphasized crisis-intervention and brief rather than long-term programs of psychotherapy.[5]
6. Provided consultative services to the people who come into daily contact with members of the community—public-health nurses, physicians, teachers, the police.

Paralleling these developments are the innovative strategies that mental-health centers are using to widen the segment of the population that can be reached by mental-health services. Mental-health-center personnel are abandoning their traditional posture of "waiting" for patients to seek out their treatment programs. This shift has resulted in a significant increase in the time spent by mental-health practitioners in case-finding, as well as in such innovative settings as store-front clinics and neighborhood-based field stations.

Since the proponents of community mental health believe that various political, social, and economic forces existing in the community are inimical to mental health, mental-health-center programs are addressing themselves to issues that traditionally were not regarded as within the legitimate domain of psychiatric agencies. Thus, besides widening their clinical interests, mental-health centers are also actively seeking solutions to such problems as unemployment, poor housing, discrimination, and inadequate schools.

Finally, community mental-health centers have attempted to insure equal participation in the use of resources by involving local citizens in policy decisions and in the planning of services. This objective has frequently been painful to implement. Difficulties in assessing the qualifications of groups who claim to represent the community, and questions of how to negotiate between lay community representatives and community-mental-health-center professionals have been continuous sources of strain, especially within urban com-

---

[5]Although outpatient psychotherapy, as practiced within mental-health centers, has been modified to reach more persons through brief therapy techniques, and to appeal more effectively to blue-collar and low-income groups, most authors agree that such work still tends to be skewed in the direction of the analytic model (Zwerling, 1965; Pasamanick, 1967).

munities. At this point, there is little uniformity in the manner in which centers are dealing with this issue, and it remains unclear what direction "community participation" is taking. For these reasons we will only touch on this aspect incidentally in our discussion of training in mental-health centers.

IMPLICATIONS OF COMMUNITY MENTAL-HEALTH CENTERS FOR TRAINING

For purposes of presentation we discuss the impact of mental-health centers on training under the two major headings outlined in the preceding section—comprehensive services and community responsiveness. Of necessity, this format will, at times, result in an artificial splitting of essentially related issues.

Comprehensive Services

The diversity of the patients eligible for treatment, and the range of treatment modalities provided by a training institution, inevitably shapes and determines the nature of a student's educational preparation. Thus, while effective supervision is at the core of any clinical training program, it must also be recognized that the breadth and diversity of experiences to which a student is exposed profoundly influence the quality of his training. The limitations imposed on a trainee's experience by selective admissions policies, or by restricted treatment emphases, cannot be overcome by supervision, no matter how excellent that supervision might be. Since mental-health centers are obligated to provide comprehensive integrated services to all the patients from a defined catchment area, they are able to offer trainees a much broader range of experiences than are traditional facilities.

Range of Patients Seen

Working in a mental-health center, the trainee has the opportunity to observe and work with patients of all ages (children, adults, the elderly), of all socioeconomic levels, and of all degrees and types of pathology. The Conference on Graduate Psychiatric Education (1964) cited the availability of a wide range of psychiatric illnesses as a critical factor in judging the quality of an institution's training program. Obviously, unless a student has knowledge and familiarity with patients suffering from various types and degrees of psychopathology, the development and refinement of his diagnostic skills will be severely limited.

Equally important is the opportunity to work with different age levels and socioeconomic groups, since these experiences challenge students to critically examine their most basic concepts and standards of psychopathology and health. Only after seeing a wide variety of patients can the student clinician develop an appreciation of the special stresses and adaptive tasks faced by people at particular life-stages or from particular socioeconomic backgrounds. The development of both internal norms and realistic expectations about behavior regarded as "within the normal limits" is possible only to the extent that a clinician has an understanding of the average expectable environment and level of functioning of broad developmental and social groups.

Once the student has this understanding of the broad social matrix from which his patients come, he will be challenged to confront such issues as: What kind of behavior represents idiosyncratic pathology and what is normative for the particular group from which the individual comes? What and who should be diagnosed? Are the nonpsychotic Class IV and V patients "psychiatric" patients, or are they products of a social pathology that is amenable only to social and political action?

These questions about the very nature of health and illness represent an attempt by the clinician to understand the world in which his patients are enmeshed. This move, in turn, will encourage questions about whether an individual's pathology can be adequately understood or dealt with without taking into account familial and often broader societal issues. Zwerling (1965), in fact, maintains that the most basic contribution of community psychiatry promises to be a fundamental re-examination of our ideas regarding the diagnosis, etiology, and pathogenesis of mental illness. He anticipates that the community-mental-health movement will result in a "shift in focus from illness as a pathologic property of a sick patient to illness as an adaptive response to pathogenic forces in a sick environment [p. 12]." Zwerling predicts, furthermore, that with the decline in influence of the view of mental illness as residing entirely within an individual, there will be a study of the family *as a family*, rather than an emphasis on the uncovering of the noxious influence of various family members on the "patient."

The re-examination of these questions about the nature and etiology of mental illness is not merely an academic exercise, for, as Arnhoff (1969) has pointed out, attitudes towards these issues will "determine the scope of the problem, the differential roles and responsibilities of the 'mental health' professions vis-à-vis other groups and society in general, the manpower specifications and requirements to deal with the problems, and last, but by no means least, the underlying social philosophy guiding these efforts [p. 149]."

Besides helping students to broaden their bookish, class-bound, and culture-bound perspectives of health and illness, the variety of patients served by mental-health centers makes it possible for the trainee to begin to formulate generalizations about the efficacy of various modalities of treatment with different groups. In attempting to tailor treatment to the specific needs of their patients, therapists-in-training initially tend to rely upon a host of commonly held, although frequently unsubstantiated, beliefs regarding the prerequisites, requirements, and conditions necessary for successful and effective psychotherapy. From the literature they learn: that to benefit from insight-oriented psychotherapy a patient must be above average in intelligence, articulate, highly motivated, and capable of introspection; that the class-linked expectancies of blue-collar patients render them unsuitable candidates for intensive psychotherapy; that the acutely psychotic patient requires therapy that discourages free access to lurid fantasies, and instead focuses on helping him in testing reality and closing off access to fantasy; that patients must sacrifice money or its equivalent if they are to be successfully treated.

The student clinician can evaluate the merit of these guidelines only to the extent that he has contact with a broad range of patients and can experience for himself the relative usefulness of different types of interventions with patients with different intellectual capabilities, different expectations regarding psychotherapy, and different degrees of pathology. By actually working with members of groups alleged to be recalcitrant to psychotherapy—the indigent, the chronically ill, the addicted, the unmotivated—he can begin to evaluate assertions that "justify" not treating whole classes of patients psychotherapeutically. Only after he has judged the worth of these assertions for himself can the student begin to determine why a type of treatment successfully employed with one group of patients may not be effective with other groups.

Contact with many different types of patients, moreover, permits the student to assess his unique skills and strengths as a therapist, thereby possibly helping him to overcome what Fierman (1965) called "the general tendency of uncritical psychotherapists to characterize their own limitations in doing psychotherapy as being patient qualities which indicate poor prognosis [p. 409]." Such diversified patient contact also allows the student to learn about his preferences and to at least begin making important career decisions. Plans about specialized training (psychoanalysis, social psychiatry, community action, sociotherapy, etc.) can most meaningfully be introduced when the student has had contact with sufficiently diverse clinical problems to make some decision about the type of professional activity that best suits his temperament, skills, and interests.

Continuity of Care

Some of the major deficiencies in both the delivery of mental-health services and the training of mental-health professionals have grown out of the fact that psychiatric facilities, until recently, were not organized to provide a full and integrated range of treatment settings and modalities. Trainees in traditional agencies were forced to either refer many patients for intake to another agency, or to accept them into a form of treatment that was at best a compromise with the most reasonable treatment modality. In these traditional services, trainees lost contact with outpatients who had to be hospitalized, and sometimes even with inpatients who were ready for discharge but whose outpatient treatment could not be provided for by the agency.

Mental-health centers, on the other hand, are required by legislation to coordinate their comprehensive services in such a way that patients who are eligible for treatment in one service are eligible in any other, and may be transferred among the service components as their condition requires. The provision of unified comprehensive services thus potentially allows the student to follow a patient as he changes from one clinical setting to another (e.g., from inpatient to outpatient, or vice versa). Provision for such continuity of care makes it feasible for the student to follow the complete course of his patient's illness over time, rather than losing contact with patients as the treatment setting changes. Being able to follow the patient through various settings allows continual reassessment of goals and re-evaluation of diagnostic conclusions in the light of data obtained in different treatment settings. For example, the therapist who must hospitalize his outpatient can check observations and impressions obtained in office contact against the much broader range of behaviors that can be observed on an inpatient unit. This possibility of continued contact between patient and therapist, even when the patient must transfer from one clinical unit to another, also has important implications for the depth of the relationship that student clinicians can form with their patients. Kubie (1968) criticizes the mental-health-center movement for neglecting the student's need for intensive work over long periods with a single patient. He says that "the prolonged and intimate exposure to the struggles of the individual patient is the sine qua non of the student's evolution toward human and clinical maturity [p. 260]." While such criticism cannot be taken lightly (we will comment further later in this essay), it must be noted that the continuity of care and comprehensive services provided by mental-health centers need not preclude, but rather may facilitate, intensive personal involvement between patient and clinician. If the clinician is able to continue working with his patient, regardless of what treatment setting the patient is in, an intensive and long-standing relationship can develop and continue throughout the course of the patient's treatment.

Variety of Settings

By rotating through the various mental-health-center treatment settings (e.g., inpatient, outpatient, day hospital, rehabilitation), trainees have contact with a wide range of models of therapeutic intervention (e.g., supportive and insight psychotherapies, sociotherapy, etc.). This diversity of contact enables the student to learn how to make sophisticated judgments about the appropriateness of a particular type of therapy or treatment setting for a particular patient. By seeing the actual functioning of treatment units with widely divergent philosophies and tactics, the student broadens and sharpens his understanding of what treatment is and how it can best be tailored to a patient's individual needs.[6]

In addition to its impact on training for direct patient care, contact with multiple-treatment settings allows the student to observe both the regressive and integrative forces that a particular setting can exercise on patients, and enables him to see how the expression of psychopathology can be affected by social determinants (e.g., group norms on different wards, inpatient versus outpatient status, open versus closed doors, etc.). He can thus observe in microcosm the impact of different environments and organizations upon patient behavior. In addition, by having contact with wards run with different leadership styles, the student will be able to develop some understanding of how the organization of a ward (e.g., processes of decision-making, reward systems, interstaff and interdisciplinary relationships) can have a profound effect on patient behavior and on the quality of patient care.

This brings us to our last point in this section. While the community mental-health center's emphasis on a unified system of comprehensive services does seem to have several advantages for the broad-based training of mental-health clinicians, it is possible, as some have argued, that such diversity may dilute what is essential and distract the trainee from his core objective—the acquisition of basic clinical skills and the development of a professional identity. Early contact with so many different treatment modalities, concepts of mental illness, and supervisory views can confuse the student, who is probably still trying to develop a clear idea of what treatment is, or what he would like to do in his field. With so many different role models and such an expanded definition of clinical care, the student may, furthermore, become bewildered about the type of skills he should be developing, and may receive superficial experience in numerous areas but substantial training in none. We shall return to this controversy.

[6]Individuals who receive their training in centers organized into semiautonomous, multidiscipline clinical teams, which are responsible for all services provided to patients, are especially likely to be directly involved with their patients throughout all treatment areas and modalities. Pasamanick (1967) maintains that this organizational framework not only improves the quality of patient care, but is also, for several reasons, superior from a training point of view. For one, it avoids the confusion and waste that result when trainees rotate from one facility to another in order to be exposed to different settings and patient types. Second, he believes, trainees in such a system are more likely to develop a longitudinal view of the process of falling ill and getting well. Pasamanick has therefore proposed that we should abandon training programs in which blocks of time are devoted to specialty areas, such as mental retardation and addiction, and substitute a program in which trainees work with all types of patients from the beginning of their training, and carry them through for long periods or for as long as they remain in the training center.

The Implications of Community Responsiveness for Training

Probably the most controversial implications for the training of mental-health clinicians stem from attempts to realize the second major objective of the community-mental-health movement—increasing the availability of early treatment for people of all socioeconomic classes within the catchment area.

In order to be responsive to the immediate and pressing service demands of their communities, mental-health centers have sought to shorten waiting lists for services by establishing, for example, walk-in clinics, and have experimented with techniques that do not overload available treatment facilities. Crisis-intervention within the home, time-limited therapy, short-term inpatient treatment, group and milieu therapy are some of the treatment strategies used by mental-health centers to insure that treatment is available to people at the time they need it most urgently. Much of the work of mental-health centers is premised, to paraphrase Caplan (1964), on the belief that during the disequilibrium of a crisis the person becomes highly susceptible to influence by others, and a little help, rationally directed and purposefully focused at a strategic time, might be more effective than more extensive help given at a period of less emotional accessibility. Besides using brief, crisis-oriented modalities of treatment, there is a definite trend within the mental-health-center movement toward activities aimed at primary prevention of mental illness. More and more indirect and nonclinical services are being provided by mental-health professionals who believe that it is impossible to deal with urgent social and community problems from a traditional point of view. In fact, one of the major thrusts of the community-mental-health-center movement is a shift from a *clinical-medical* orientation to a *public-health* frame of reference. Thus, besides widening their clinical interests, mental-health professionals are now assuming such new roles as mental-health consultant, change agent participating in such areas as antipoverty programs, or even political lobbyist promoting new legislation in areas touching on the welfare of the community. As Rosenblum (1968) noted, these activities are no longer viewed by many professionals as insignificant ancillary services, peripheral to the "primary" functions of diagnosis and treatment. Hersch (1969) has observed, moreover, that professionals who have moved in these directions have little concern for the distinction between professional and citizen roles. There seems little doubt that these trends will continue, and that mental-health centers will serve both as focal point for new approaches to treatment and as setting encouraging new roles for professionals and nonprofessionals.

These developments bear upon such critical training issues as: What is the proper role of a trainee in the ongoing social change of an urban community? How can these changes be incorporated into our curriculum? Can intensive, exploratory psychotherapy, reflection, objective study, and the long view flourish in metropolitan health centers, where the central and urgent problems and tasks seem to be related to changes taking place more broadly in the political, economic, and social sectors?

Even the most conservative mental-health educators and advocates of intensive individual psychotherapy recognize that training programs must give due consideration to these present trends, and to future ones insofar as they can be envisaged. There seems to be widespread agreement that trainees must be prepared to assume a variety of roles, many of them not yet created. There remains, however, a great deal of controversy about how training for assumption of these new roles should be accomplished. It has been argued that the competent pursuit of new techniques, whether they be crisis-intervention or working for social change in a political way, must evolve from a firm clinical foundation that can only be provided by intensive, long-term focus on a few individual patients and intrapsychic phenomena. In his highly provocative article, "Pitfalls of Community Psychiatry," Kubie (1968) forcefully advocated this position and consequently recommended (p. 261) that:

If these young men do not allow themselves time enough to learn the inner nature of psychological illness, time enough to understand the processes of falling ill and of falling well, if they do not take time to learn how to deal with one patient at a time by learning how to recognize those unsolved inner problems which the psychiatric patient can stir in the therapist, then despite their goodwill they cannot expect to improve the lot of any. Their hopes to be able to help a thousand patients before they can help even one will remain naïve, and their good intentions will suffer the fate of all good intentions which are not guided by mature knowledge and experience. Instead of making psychiatry widely available, they will destroy it by truncating their own maturations as psychiatrists and that of countless others.

On the other hand, there are prominent psychiatrists who argue that early training in psychodynamically oriented long-term psychotherapy gives rise to the view in students that this model is the most desirable, and ultimately the ideal, form of treatment. This training focus, it is argued, seriously impairs the student's capacity to effectively learn other role models. Pasamanick (1967), for example, interprets the neglect of the mental subnormalities, the functional psychoses, and the organic psychoses of the aged—which from his point of view are the major problems of psychiatry in terms of suffering, disability, and social cost—"as a concomitant of the type of training which emphasizes the one-to-one relationship of middle-class therapist to middle-class responsive patient in intensive, long-term care as the most desirable and status invoking activity [p. 471]." He concludes that "in view of the obvious present need it would appear inappropriate, and indeed irresponsible, to continue to train physicians for lengthy dyadic relationship psychotherapy [p. 482]."

The present authors are reluctant to enter this controversy, for without careful research and study of the training and skills that facilitate performance in the newly developing roles and tasks, any assertion about training can have only the status of articles of faith. We note with interest, however, Sabshin's discussion (1965) of this issue. Sabshin (p. 49) cited statements in training brochures that affirm emphatically:

> You must first train the resident to conduct diagnosis and treatment in the dyadic relationship with the patient—to learn how to conduct psychotherapy is the core of the psychiatric residency. Everything else flows from this central process and can be generalized from it. Psychiatric residents are not adequately trained if they have not succeeded in mastering this particular core.

We agree with Sabshin that the concept of dyadic therapy, as the core of the training program for all mental-health professionals, might have been progressive 20 years ago, but it seems much less vital and compelling today. It takes great courage for teachers to admit that their careers and training sequences may not represent ideal models for many careers in mental health today, but such might be the case. As Sabshin notes, "It seems wholly plausible . . . that more intensive studying of public health, sociology, anthropology, organizational structure, group process and community relationships . . . in community psychiatry may be an even superior developmental line and should be encouraged [p. 52]." In short, it would seem to us that the view that all training experiences, other than long-term dyadic psychotherapy, make only subsidiary contributions to the growth of clinical maturity must be open to question. The insights, skills, and self-knowledge that can be derived from family therapy, group therapy, and community work are unique, and transcend the experiences provided by dyadic office contact with patients.

We do recognize, however, that there are at least three related dangers associated with training in community mental-health centers. First, given the service pressures of mental-health centers, it can be argued that it is very difficult, even if supervisors hold the view that service needs should be considered secondary to training demands, to provide trainees with carefully graded and progressive responsibility for patient care. Clearly, it is important that no matter what treatment setting students are involved in, they should have time to read and think about their activities. But then how will the service obligations of the centers be met? In part, such service demands *are* being met by the utilization of specially trained indigenous workers to take over many of the treatment functions previously performed by members of traditional professional disciplines. In addition, the premise that long-term dyadic therapy is the treatment of choice for all patient problems is being replaced by the view that treatment modalities should be uniquely designed for specific patient groups (e.g., resocialization groups for chronic patients). This provision of treatment modalities especially tailored to patient needs should allow more efficient utilization of staff time and of other resources.

A second danger associated with training in community mental-health centers is the possibility that the trainee, even if not burdened with excessive patient-care demands, will be put into situations with which he is not yet equipped to deal. For example, an assignment to a walk-in clinic might confront the neophyte clinician with the responsibility for making rapid decisions about people in crisis. Such premature exposure to crises may needlessly make some trainees feel uncertain of their capacities. This might be especially true of clinical-psychology interns whose academic background and rigorous research training ill-prepare them for assuming patient responsibility and for the facts of life in clinical work. One possible response to this, given the availability of so many approaches to patient care, might be for such trainees to prematurely turn to community psychiatry "as a way of escaping the pain of involvement with individual patients [Kubie, 1968, p. 261]." Conversely, other trainees, who have assumed major responsibility for patient care, might develop a premature sense of competence, and thereby be rendered less available for learning and growth. Clearly, students' responsibilities should be carefully graded to their capacities, and there must be appropriate backup by senior people to ensure that the students' activities will serve as educational experiences rather than as a form of cheap labor.

The third danger assocated with training in mental-health centers involves the supervisory process. The organization of training programs in agency consultation, walk-in clinics, field-stations in the community, and rehabilitation and after-care clinics is meaningless unless adequate supervision is provided for the specific activities in which the students are engaged. Students are usually accurate in their assessment of what their teachers really want, and if long-term psychotherapy is the only area taught and supervised by the most stimulating teachers, the message will very quickly be communicated that the staff itself is quite ambivalent about students pursuing more diversified careers. It is imperative, then, that if new training programs are to be instituted, exciting supervisors and adequate curriculum time must be made available. Also, it is very important that supervisors understand in detail the nature of the treatment settings in which their supervisees are working, and take this into account in their supervisory work. Supervisory emphasis on intrapsychic life, genetic past, and psychodynamic causation is not only irrelevant, but can be disruptive to the work of a student in a crisis-intervention ward, which relies primarily upon a team approach and focuses on the patient's present adaptive functioning.

Another issue about supervision is especially relevant to centers where a single staff group is responsible for all the services provided to patients. While this type of organization has significant advantages for continuity of care, a serious problem for training can arise if a teacher is expected to supervise students in all treatment modalities and techniques. Such a task requires the supervisor to be expert in so many areas that his effectiveness as a teacher in any one area may be seriously hampered. Probably the teaching on these semiautonomous all-purpose units can be most effective if there are enough teaching personnel to allow for some degree of teaching specialization.

Developing a Professional Identity

Undoubtedly, a critical determinant in the professional role identification of many trainees is the model institutionalized in the training program in which they participate. For many years, psychotherapists have been trained in the philosophy of the dyadic therapy relationship, and the theory guiding professional work was undisputedly psychoanalysis. Consequently, the lone psychotherapist—anonymous, and detached from the sociopolitical life of his community—was the most prestigious role model available to our trainees, and the one to which most of our trainees aspired. Today, as a result of the dramatic theoretical, pragmatic, and moral changes in the mental-health field, there are not only more role models available for our trainees to identify with, but the status hierarchy appears to be shifting. Although an anticommunity mental health movement is apt to develop, it would appear that mental-health professionals who are trying to bring about major and basic changes in society through social and political action are ascending in prestige and influence.[7] Concomitantly, the prestige and glamor of the private practice of intensive psychotherapy may be decreasing.

The differences between community-oriented and psychodynamically oriented mental-health professionals transcend the concern of the latter with intrapsychic pathology and of the former with large-scale social issues. Representatives of these two points of view are likely to differ in their life-styles, values, talents, and ideologies. While there is a danger that trainees may get caught up in unproductive conflicts between these "competing" groups, we believe that advantages for training can also follow from an exposure to this conflict. Given an opportunity to work with both groups—an opportunity which, although available in most settings, is inherent to mental-health centers —the trainee is less likely to become a doctrinaire supporter of a single point of view—be it the status quo or the community-psychiatry bandwagon. He will be continuously challenged to examine the relative merits of both points of

[7]In this vein, it is noteworthy, as Sharaf, Schneider, and Kantor (1968) observed, that whereas 10 years ago the best predictor of whether a medical student would choose psychiatry as a specialization was "psychological mindedness," today, degree of "radicalism" is the best predictor.

view. While exposure to such diversity of opinion may result temporarily in considerable confusion and "identity crises," we feel that in the long run it will help trainees develop flexibility and eventually identify with and choose a professional role that best meets their needs and talents.

Despite both the antiindividual psychotherapy bias of many community-mental-health spokesman, and the growing recognition that the mental-health problems of this country cannot be solved by a simple increase in the number of well-trained individual therapists, we do not believe that the community-mental-health movement will result in the demise of dynamic personality theory and psychotherapy. Rather, it seems likely that dynamic psychotherapy, like "psychoanalysis" and "community psychiatry," will assume the position of a "subspecialty," and will no longer occupy the exalted position of primary theoretical underpinning for all mental-health activities. To some dynamic psychotherapists this trend is welcome, since future psychotherapists are more likely to pursue this field with a recognition of its specific role as a technique and theory, and their involvement will more likely be premised on interest than on the prestige associated with being an insight-oriented psychotherapist.

Training for Collaboration

The mental-health-center movement is markedly altering intraprofessional and interdisciplinary relationships. Concomitant with a greater democratization in the delivery of health services, there has been a definite move toward democratizing the relationships among staff members in mental-health centers. In part, this trend has arisen because of the recognition that we must aim beyond the territorial confines of traditional professional responsibilities if we are to meet the growing needs of society. This democratization is reflected in the growing use of multidisciplinary treatment teams, in the increased blurring of the boundaries among the mental-health professions, and in the growing reliance on indigenous nonprofessionals as mental-health workers. Let us briefly consider the impact of each of these changes on training.

The advantages for training that derive from participating on multidisciplinary teams include the opportunities to communicate with persons of diverse professional and lay backgrounds,[8] and to benefit from the different perspectives that each profession uniquely brings to the treatment process. For example, for the psychiatric resident or psychology intern, the opportunity to work in teams with psychiatric nurses could provide a model of nurturant profes-

[8]To a lesser extent, because of the mental-health centers' commitment to providing consultation to community agencies, trainees have an opportunity to work with schools, police, religious groups, and public-health officers.

sional patient care; for the psychiatric nurse such collaboration could provide models for the application of psychodynamic formulations in treatment programs. Collaboration with members of different disciplines during training can thus facilitate greater ease in conveying ideas and sharing responsibility for patient care. This is more than an exercise in goodwill, since in recent years mental-health workers have been spending less time in private practice and devoting more time to leadership and executive functions within organizations (Levinson & Klerman, 1966). In programs where the dyadic therapy model is the sole focus of training, students may be implicitly encouraged to bring this therapeutic model of interaction inappropriately into their relationships with colleagues. Teaching about the unique problems involved in collaborative work can provide an opportunity to learn alternative models of interaction—models that can facilitate effective assumption of administrative and leadership responsibility in later professional life.

The emphasis on multidisciplinary teams further derives from a concern with the critical manpower shortage in the mental-health professions. Therefore, within mental-health centers, the opposition of psychiatrists to the practice of psychotherapy by trained clinical psychologists, social workers, and psychiatric nurses is generally regarded as socially irresponsible. More and more in mental-health centers, primary clinical responsibility and leadership of the multidisciplinary teams is assumed by staff members from each of the different mental-health professions. In such a setting, nonmedical therapists are less likely than in the past to define themselves into a state of lessened therapeutic effectiveness through "subsidiary" status. Social workers may no longer need to humbly differentiate between "casework" and therapy; clinical psychologists may be able to more constructively use for clinical work the energy they now expend justifying the validity of their training; and psychiatric nurses may be able to define themselves in other ways than as "handmaidens" aiding the doctors in their "more important" work.

The diffusion of responsibility associated with this trend is creating a situation in which the different mental-health professions have no clearly defined goals or unique skills. This diffusion of role functions challenges deeply rooted power structures and vested interests and creates potential difficulties. As Redlich (1968) pointed out, "In spite of overlap there are great differences in the power, prestige and economic compensation the groups command resulting in overt and tacit power struggles, jealousies, and lack of cooperation." Perhaps present-day students, less invested in the role definitions of the past, will be able to work out the distribution of responsibilities and rewards in a more rational way than their predecessors. In any event, it seems likely that community-mental-health-center programs will eventually result in a realignment of the professions, perhaps in terms of functions (e.g., crisis-intervention, long-term psychotherapy, community consultation) instead of along traditional professional-discipline lines.

As was noted above, many mental-health centers have established programs for training and utilizing indigenous nonprofessional workers as mental-health aides. Such programs are designed to develop new mental-health manpower, improve the effectiveness of mental-health services in disadvantaged areas, and provide new jobs and careers for residents of low-income communities. The opportunity to work with such individuals poses important threats to the professional-in-training and also provides him with important benefits. On the positive side, indigenous workers can fill in the gaps in the student's knowledge about patients who come from lower socioeconomic classes. In addition, consistent interchange with less formally educated co-workers prevents the student from taking refuge in technical language; rather, he is forced to communicate clearly and simply. Working alongside nonprofessionals, moreover, can temper the sense of "noblesse oblige" that might accompany a middle-class clinician's efforts to "help" underprivileged patients.

This close contact with indigenous workers, however, is not without its painful aspects. Leadership does not come automatically because of professional title—working in teams involves visibility of one's clinical interactions to all the other members of the therapeutic team, and consequently a student's therapeutic limitations cannot be hidden or disguised. Moreover, professional trainees will find little comfort and security in blaming therapeutic failures on the alleged inferiority of their patients when they encounter individuals who, after a relatively brief training period, may have a greater impact on patients than they. While these experiences may be sobering, we feel it is essential for students to learn that professionals do not have a monopoly on therapeutic skill or effectiveness.

The Development of Professional Values

Training programs, in addition to their effect on clinical proficiency, strongly influence the development of a student's sense of professional ethics and values. Before concluding this essay, therefore, it is important to describe briefly the values communicated to students during their mental-health-center training experience.

Central to the philosophy of the mental-health-center movement is the effort to "guarantee and safeguard to a degree previously undreamed of, a basic right —the privilege of mental health [Bellak, 1964, p.00]." There seems to be little controversy about the worthiness of this goal. A great deal of concern and debate has been stimulated, however, about the impact that realization of this goal will have on both clinical practice and training. Advocates claim that mental-health centers will foster a sense of social responsibility and humanistic concern on the part of students, and an interest in markedly improving the quality of care provided to the disadvantaged. Critics feel that despite the idealistic origins of this goal, implementation will eventuate in an approach to patient care that is devoid of concern for the individual patient. This view is exemplified in the following statement by Shatan (1969, p. 319):

Under the guise of mounting a total crusade against illness, what does the Community Mental Health Movement really offer as a replacement for the clinical, humanistic emphases on the unique value of each individual? *The assembly-line techniques of industry*. . . . Assembly-line techniques which as presently applied, must lead to the industrialization and dehumanization of the mental health professions.

While there are no data at present to strongly support either view, our observations do not suggest that the development of mental-health centers has led to the dehumanization of patient care. We see no evidence that community-mental-health-center workers are less concerned than other mental-health professionals with the uniqueness or individuality of patients.

A more serious threat to the effectiveness of the mental-health-center movement, we believe, can arise from a policy that would uncritically follow the exuberant exhortations of some of the movement's strongest proponents. Lindemann (1969) exemplified this position when he urged the acceptance of a value orientation in which mental-health professionals "think not so much about excellent treatment of the individual case as about equal opportunities for all members of the community [p. xvi]." This strategy may represent a desirable compromise from a social-service standpoint, but from the point of view of the training of professionals, such a compromise of excellence seems hazardous. We thus share the concern voiced by Lustman (1966) and Wallerstein (1968) that community mental-health centers may produce a climate in which professional skills and rigor are denigrated in deference to benevolent ideology. For example, too great an emphasis on community-action programs and on the expanded use of subprofessionals and volunteers in responsible service capacities could result in the decline of training and practice standards. Mental-health-center staff, therefore, must explicitly support the view that good intentions are no substitute for competence, and that intensive and rigorous training is essential to the development of any type of therapeutic expertise. Unless mental-health centers produce a climate in which expertise and rigor are respected as much as benevolent ideology, the training of future clinicians will suffer and the movement will be unable to fulfill its promise.

Numerous problems are bound to occur as a result of attempts to integrate the new ideology and the traditional emphasis on excellence in work with individual patients. Nevertheless, such efforts are clearly justified if one accepts the implications of the following statement by Zwerling (1965):

We simply cannot afford to continue to do that which we know how to do because we do it so well, and to continue to train others to do it, and to pursue research on how to do it even better, in the face of all the indications that we may thus be isolating ourselves from the main body of the society we are sworn to serve.

REFERENCES

Arnhoff, F. N. The Boston mental health survey: A context for interpretation. In W. Ryan (Ed.), *Distress in the city.* Cleveland: Case—Western Reserve University Press, 1969.

Bellak, L. (Ed.) *Handbook of community psychiatry and community mental health.* New York: Grune & Stratton, 1964.

Caplan, G. *Principles of preventive psychiatry.* New York: Basic Books, 1964.

Caudill, W. *The psychiatric hospital as a small society.* Cambridge: Harvard University Press, 1958.

Conference on Graduate Psychiatric Education. *Training the psychiatrist to meet changing needs.* Washington, D.C.: American Psychiatric Association, 1964.

Cumming, J., & Cumming, E. *Ego and milieu.* New York: Atherton, 1962.

Dunham, H. W. Community psychiatry: The newest therapeutic bandwagon. *Archives of General Psychiatry,* 1965, **12**, 303–313.

Ewalt, J. R., & Ewalt, P. J. History of the community psychiatry movement. *American Journal of Psychiatry,* 1969, **126**, 43–52.

Fierman, L. B. Myths in the practice of psychotherapy. *Archives of General Psychology,* 1965, **12**, 408–414.

Freedman, A. M. Historical and political roots of the community mental health centers act. *American Journal of Orthopsychiatry,* 1967, **37**, 487–494.

Glasscote, R. M., Sanders, D. S., Forstenzer, H. M., & Foley, A. R. The community mental health center: An analysis of existing models. Washington, D.C.: Joint Information Service of the American Psychiatric Association and the National Association for Mental Health, 1964.

Goffman, E. *Asylums.* Garden City: Anchor Books, 1961.

Goldston, E. (Ed.) *Concepts of community psychiatry: A framework for training.* (U.S. Public Health Service Publication No. 1319) Bethesda, Md.: National Institute of Mental Health, 1965.

Greenblatt, M., York, R. H., & Brown, E. L. *From custodial to therapeutic patient care in mental hospitals.* New York: Russell Sage Foundation, 1955.

Gruenberg, E. M. Identifying cases of social breakdown syndrome. *Milbank Memorial Fund Quarterly,* 1966, **44**, Vol. 1, Pt. 2.

Hersch, C. The discontent explosion in mental health. *American Psychologist,* 1968, **23**, 497–506.

Hersch, C. From mental health to social action: Clinical psychology in historical perspective. *American Psychologist,* 1969, **24**, 909–916.

Joint Commission on Mental Illness and Health. *Action for mental health.* New York: Basic Books, 1961.

Jones, M. *The therapeutic community.* New York: Basic Books, 1953.

Kubie, L. S. Pitfalls of community psychiatry. *Archives of General Psychiatry,* 1968, **18**, 257–266.

Levinson, D., & Klerman, G. The psychiatrist in the organization: Problems in the synthesis of clinical and executive functions. Paper presented at the International Research Seminar on Evaluation of Community Mental Health Programs, Warrenton, Va., May 1966.

Lindemann, E. Introduction to *Distress in the city.* W. Ryan (Ed.). Cleveland, Ohio: Case—Western Reserve University Press, 1969.

Lustman, S. The meaning of the curriculum. Paper presented to the Plenary Session on the Psychoanalytic Curriculum at the meeting of the American Psychoanalytic Association, New York, December 1966.

Pasamanick, B. The development of physicians for public mental health. *American Journal of Orthopsychiatry.* 1967, **37**, 469–486.

Pasamanick, B., Scarpatti, F., & Dinitz, S. *Schizophrenics in the community.* New York: Appleton-Century-Crofts, 1967.

Redlich, F. *The university and community mental health.* New Haven: Yale University Press, 1968.

Rosenblum, G. The new role of the clinical psychologist in the community mental health center. *Community Mental Health Journal,* 1968, **4**, 403–410.

Sabshin, M. Theory and practice of community psychiatry training in the medical school setting. In S. Goldston (Ed.), *Concepts of community psychiatry: A framework for training.* (U.S. Public Health Service Publication No. 1319) Bethesda, Md.: National Institute of Mental Health, 1965.

Sharaf, M. R., Schneider, P., & Kantor, D. Psychiatric interest and its correlates among medical students. *Psychiatry,* 1968, **31**, 150–160.

Shatan, C. Community psychiatry—Stretcher bearer of the social order? *International Journal of Psychology,* 1969, **7**, 312–321.

Stanton, A. H., & Schwartz, M. S. *The mental hospital.* New York: Basic Books, 1954.

U.S., *Statutes at Large,* vol. 77. *Community mental health centers act of 1963,* Public law 88-164, 88th Cong., Oct. 31, 1963.

Wallerstein, R. S. The challenge of the community mental health movement to psychoanalysis. *American Journal of Psychiatry,* 1968, **124**, 1049–1056.

Whittington, H. G. The third psychiatric revolution—Really? *Community Mental Health Journal,* 1965, **1**, 73–80.

Zwerling, I. Some implications of social psychiatry for psychiatric treatment and patient care. Institute of Pennsylvania Hospital—*Strecker Monograph Series,* 1965, No. 11.

Contributions and Limitations for Professional Counselor Preparation: University Counseling Centers

Tim Gust

University of Hawaii

While competence in didactic courses is important, the experiential aspects of the counselor's training (his practicum, fieldwork, and/or internship) remain most crucial in determining his competence as a professional counselor. It is in the application of his learning that the counselor-in-training develops the basic skills that are necessary if he is to be technically competent and is to continue to grow in a meaningful, developmental manner. The site and type of practicum or internship, therefore, determines to a great extent the developmental growth pattern for the counselor. The purpose of this essay is to describe the contributions and limitations of the university counseling center as a training facility for professional counselors.

From the outset, this author's biases should be known; hopefully they will be substantiated within the essay. First, it is assumed that counseling psychology as a discipline forms the core or basis for professional counseling, whether it be in a school, a rehabilitation agency, or an employment-counseling setting (Roeber, 1965). In this regard, the major function of counselors is the enhancement of interpersonal relationships (Patterson, 1969). Second, the position is taken that the university counseling center offers one of the most ideal settings for practicum and internship training. Although other campus-based counseling facilities (e.g., university laboratory school) have the potential for offering programs of similar quality, it is believed that the university counseling center generally offers a broader-based and more comprehensive service, thereby making it the typical first choice for a professional training site. While it is recognized that expanding training needs require a variety of other community agencies for internship locations, the campus-based practicum provides one of the few controlled experiences wherein direct and sustained observation of counseling candidates can be made. The author's experiences in the counseling centers of the University of North Dakota and the University of Missouri—Columbia have a definite bearing on the descriptions to be developed. Specific staffing and program ideas are especially related to the University of Missouri—Columbia, Testing and Counseling Service.

CONTRIBUTIONS FROM UNIVERSITY COUNSELING CENTERS

Historical Background

Morrow (1946) reported the development and background of psychological internships from the earliest (ca. 1896) to about 1945. Bixler, Bordin, and Deabler (1946) focused more specifically on the training sequence and method in a college counseling center. Other publications (Embree, 1951; Super, 1956) focused upon the training program itself, or its application within a certain agency. All the early ideas, experiences, and recommendations contributed in some way to the evolving standards developed and published by the American Psychological Association (APA).[1]

Recognition of the role of the university counseling center in the training of counseling psychologists can be traced to the beginnings of the evolving discipline of counseling psychology. Substantial representation on various early committees of Division 17 of APA came from counseling psychologists employed by university counseling centers.[2] Furthermore, the standards recommended by Division 17 for the doctoral-level training of counseling psychologists indicate that "it is both historically and socially fitting that educational facilities remain the most important institutional home for psychological counseling functions"; and further that "the training program should qualify the counseling psychologist to work effectively in such . . . settings [APA, 1952b, p. 176]."

More specifically, the Division 17 reports on the practicum training of counseling psychologists (APA, 1952a) and the standards recommended for counseling-psychology internships (APA, 1960) make various recommendations with illustrations from university counseling centers. The latter report

[1]In addition to the original sources noted in the references, the APA reports referred to herein can be found as appendices in the following: A. S. Thompson, and D. E. Super (Eds.), *The Professional Preparation of Counseling Psychologists* (New York: Teachers College Press, 1964).
[2]Membership on early committees is indicated within each committee report (APA, 1952a; 1952b; 1956; 1960; 1961).

indicated that university and Veterans Administration facilities were the more commonly used settings for counseling internships. In a very recent review of internships in counseling psychology (Kirk & Chin, 1971), university and college counseling centers and Veterans Administration hospitals and regional centers continued to offer the most internship programs—51 and 52 respectively, as compared to 14 in rehabilitation centers and three in Jewish Vocational Services.

If one takes into account the unique historical position of the university counseling center in relation to both practice and training in counseling psychology, it is not surprising that this facility should offer the most unique opportunity for the training of psychological counselors.

Counselor Training Standards

Although the Division 17 reports related to practicum and internship training in general, it appeared that certain statements and conditions were especially pertinent to the university counseling center. The specific points that follow were abstracted from the original reports to illustrate this relationship. The complete reports, however, are recommended to the reader. The report on the practicum training of counseling psychologists (APA, 1952a) indicates among other issues that:

1. Ethical responsibility for trainee activities be held jointly by the training institution and the field agency.
2. The training center provide opportunities for laboratory (prepracticum) experiences to develop fundamental skills, fieldwork with clients under close supervision, and internship allowing responsibility for a variety of clients under supervision.
3. A variety of clients be available to allow for breadth and depth of experience.
4. The university training program and the training facility develop a written statement outlining the joint relationship, which would deal with trainee selection, planning of training experiences, and any other aspects that provide the trainee with a complete understanding of the relationship.

The report of the Division 17 Committee on Internship Standards (APA, 1960) defines internship as the terminal phase in the practicum training of the counseling psychologist, which follows a series of laboratory and clerkship or fieldwork experiences. The aspects of this report relating most specifically to the university counseling center indicate that:

1. It is imperative that the activities performed in the internship agency be integrated with the university program so as to be mutually facilitating. Careful collaborative planning between the internship agency and the university, together with the prospective intern, is required before a suitable plan can be arranged.
2. A deliberate attempt be made to provide the intern with opportunities to work with all types of client served by the agency, or to observe qualified counselors working with clients beyond the intern's qualifications, and to participate in case seminars.
3. It is highly desirable that the internship afford supervised experience in psychotherapeutic counseling—both short-term and more sustained counseling relationships.
4. Opportunities should be available for learning other aspects of the counseling psychologist's job, such as relating with colleagues and other professionals, parents, and referral agencies.
5. The intern should have an opportunity to learn how to supervise other graduate students and, if possible, some formal teaching responsibilities.
6. The intern should learn to appreciate the close relationship between his functioning as a counselor and his functioning as a research worker; he should be provided time and facilities to pursue personal or institutional research stemming from his daily work.
7. The direct supervisory function is primarily the responsibility of the agency; wherever possible interns should be exposed to more than one supervisor, preferably through a carefully planned rotation system.
8. Internship-agency strengths and weaknesses should be well known to the university's training personnel; the evaluation of the internship is a joint endeavor of the agency and the university.

If one considers the various agencies that might appropriately satisfy the above standards, it would seem that the university counseling center is the first choice. Not only physical proximity, but also the potential for interinvolvement between counselor-training program and counseling center enhances this choice. In addition, unique placement within the overall university setting makes possible research and training opportunities usually not available in noncampus counseling facilities.

Development of a professional training program requires some type of joint relationship between the counselor-training department and university counseling center. In the model developed below, this relationship is accounted for by joint appointments of staff to department and center. Joint appointment of staff is essential to the proper functioning of the overall training program.

A Model Counseling-Center Training Program

The roles and functions of senior faculty and staff in the counseling center will dictate the training opportunities for the counselor-trainee. To adequately describe the training function, it is necessary first to review these various roles and functions. While role and function definitions of counseling psychologists are far from solidified (Patterson, 1969; Warnath, 1968), it seems that the role of the university counseling center involves some combination of counseling, consultation, and training. Danskin (1965, p. 264) stated that the university counseling center should focus on the following ingredients:

1. A thorough understanding of the entering student.
2. A thorough understanding of factors that influence students in a college's environment.
3. [The development of] a majority of faculty and administrative persons who are both aware of the nature of their impact on students (or lack thereof) and concerned with seeing students change in desired ways.

The functions of counselors in this system would involve some balance of counseling, studying and writing, resource development, and training.

The university and college counseling-service guidelines (Kirk, Free, Johnson, Michel, Redfield, Roston, & Warman, 1971), officially adopted in November 1970 by the university and college counseling-center directors, are much more explicit and complete. Two complementary counseling-service functions, developmental and remedial, are seen as an integral part of the student's educational process. In addition, counseling-service professional staff are to be involved in academic and administrative planning and implementation in all aspects of student life. This document, which spells out such things as duties of staff, necessary physical facilities, and referral procedures, should be required reading for all college counseling-service personnel.

In the model developed below, the university counseling center satisfies its comprehensive service role through a carefully integrated program of counseling, consulting, research and training. While individual staff-members might not each have an even balance of activities in these areas, the center itself is careful to observe equilibrium. By using this paradigm of services, the counseling center satisfies its campus role and provides for the broadest and most unique training facility for counselors.

The *counseling* function involves the traditional activities of individual and group counseling of clients, with opportunities for selection and assignment of cases for both breadth and depth, as well as variety of experience for the counselor-in training. Counseling is both developmental and remedial.

The *consulting* function, probably the newest for some counseling centers, encompasses academic advising, curriculum development, teaching and learning functions, selection of students, and any other activities in which the consulting counselor can aid the academic division to better meet the needs of students. In addition, these functions extend to other student-personnel areas, including student affairs and activities, health center, housing, student finance, admissions and registration, campus security, physical plant, and so forth. Enhancing student opportunities for interpersonal development and functioning represents the focus of consulting efforts. To function adequately in these consulting relationships, a research component must be available.

Research functions include programmatic research arising from the need of the counseling center to analyze and evaluate itself, research stimulated through counseling experiences with clients, and research generated from consulting activities with various academic and nonacademic divisions. Unique opportunities for study of all aspects of student-body characteristics are available because of the central placement of the counseling service within the university framework.

The *training* function involves a carefully planned series of graduated, supervised experiences in each of the major areas of service as well as in training itself. In this manner counselors can be assured of receiving a broadbased initial and continuing-learning experience. The key to the success of the model is the interrelatedness and interdependency of all the functions.

Counselor-Trainee Experiences in Each Function

Within the counseling area, master's-level students can be involved in initial laboratory (prepracticum) experiences, and can begin to see clients under close supervision involving direct observations and audio and video recording. Doctoral candidates, involved as staff counselors on a half-time basis, can experience a variety of type, number, and level of clients as they move from a high degree of supervision to major responsibility for their clients. Group, family, and multiple counseling, as well as other varieties of counseling experiences, can be developed in terms of the competencies of senior staff.

Experiences in consulting activities will usually develop within the counseling intern's supervisory relationship with a particular senior staff-member. Moving from observation to actual involvement, the intern gains in his identity with the broad role of the practicing counselor. Consulting experiences permit the counselor-in-training to better understand the environmental pressures impinging upon his client.

Research experiences can be tailored to the intern's individual interests, his counseling or consulting experiences, or to ongoing programmatic efforts of the counseling center. In any event, relevancy of experiences in research should be evident to the intern. Various methods of disseminating research findings to campus departments should be reviewed and attempted, to add to the intern's breadth of experience.

Finally, the counseling intern can gain experience in training and supervision of counseling, supervision, consulting, and research. Because of the availability of at least three levels of practitioners (senior staff, doctoral interns, master's students), opportunities for supervision and training experiences are only limited by time and flexibility of programming.

"Do as I say but not as I do," *or* "Do as I do and do as I say"? A counselor-training program developed within a campus service facility like the university counseling center fulfills the latter admonishment. A university counseling center that furnishes the counselor-training program with a focal point for practicum and internship, allows for a "role-modeling" situation wherein counselors-in-training can work with professional counselors fulfilling the interdependent functions of counseling, consulting, research, and training.

Staffing

The staffing pattern becomes similar to the following:

1. Doctoral-level *senior* staff who are involved in counseling, consulting, teaching, supervision, and research.
2. Predoctoral-level *junior* staff (half-time salaried staff counselors) involved in individually tailored programs of individual and small-group counseling, plus assisting senior staff in consulting, research, teaching, and supervisory activities. These doctoral students would typically be taking didactic courses or completing their doctoral research in addition to this half-time internship.
3. Practicum students, usually pre–master's- level or immediately post–master's-level counselors, whose main role is that of students learning counseling and consulting skills and techniques. These students are unpaid, and while they are not staff, are included to acknowledge their presence in the overall supervisory structure. These students require the most supervisory time and are jointly supervised by the senior and junior staff.

LIMITATIONS OF THE COUNSELING CENTER

Some factors within the university-counseling-center setting may become limitations for counselors-in-training. If the counseling center has a limited clientele, such as college students only, or if its services are limited to only certain activities, such as individual therapy or vocational testing and counseling, the training program for counseling-interns will likely be too narrow. To broaden the training program, the counseling center can accept referrals from other community agencies, such as secondary and elementary schools, vocational rehabilitation, social services, employment services, and so forth. Besides accepting referrals from other community agencies, counselors-in-training, may be assigned to these other agencies, depending upon individual interests. Learning the basic skills of counseling, consulting, research, and training can be accomplished with university students and within the university environment. However, the counselor who expects to work in a different setting, such as an elementary school or with emotionally disturbed clients, should, during his training, spend time working in the different setting to become familiar with the unique aspects of the clients and the setting.

It is not unusual, in college counseling centers, to find counselors-in-training spending most of their time in individual- or group-counseling activities (Warnath, 1971). Counselors with such backgrounds have often been disillusioned when their first professional position turns out to involve activities other than therapeutic counseling. Although experience and supervision in the important basic skill of counseling can hardly be overdone, counselor-trainees must also become facile with the other functions mentioned, since the counselor's role in practice is rarely limited to one function. In fact, if counselor training is to be relevant for the future, the consulting, research, and supervisory functions may be *more* important than the counseling function. Many of the human-contact tasks can be appropriately performed by paraprofessional or support personnel (Carkhuff, 1966). This requires, however, a professional who can supervise the support personnel and also integrate and assimilate the activities they perform.

Furthermore, the preventative function, central in the counseling psychologists' role, implies that counselors spend more time in consultation, research, and "preproblem" solving than in so-called crisis-counseling. The counseling center must involve itself in facilitating the development of all individuals on the campus, not only those few whose problems have caused them to seek help. Enhancing the development of normal individuals without serious problems, through helping them learn alternative seeking and decision-making behaviors conducive to positive growth, has much greater payoff than does waiting for these same individuals to encounter difficulty in order to become eligible clients. The processes of positive planning, tentative decision making, and tolerance for ambiguity are some of the most important products of effective counseling that our clients can learn. The counseling center lacking this preventative focus limits its trainees' learning possibilities.

Another potential limitation hinges on the relationship with the academic counselor-training program. If real interstaff involvement is lacking, the training program for the student is inevitably less than ideal. There must be continuity in training from the beginning of the counselor-training program through to placement in the counselor's first position (Gust, 1970). This is best exemplified in a counseling center whose staff has regular joint appointments on the academic counselor-education staff.

EVALUATING THE TRAINING SITE

The evaluation of practicum and internship training sites has in the past received limited attention. Kirk's presentation (1970) probably exemplifies best why this is so. In discussing goals and issues in counseling-psychology internships, she raises the issue of extensity versus intensity of experience within counseling functions as well as within noncounseling functions such as consultation, supervision, research, and administration. In addition, the means by which the training goals can best be achieved are discussed. No clear standards emerge, and very little research exists to allow easy development of standards.

The criterion problem, central to counseling-effectiveness research, again looms as the critical factor. Does one evaluate the training site by assessing its physical facilities and training program; supervisor qualifications and methods of supervision; quality of counseling and/or consulting performed by the counseling intern and evaluated by the supervisor; or effectiveness of the intern as reported by the client or other consumer? As with counseling research in general, researchers will tackle different aspects of the problem according to their interests, capabilities, or the situation.

As an example of the present state of research on practicum supervision, Hansen and Warner (1971) reviewed articles in all APA- and APGA-affiliated journals for the 10-year period 1960–1969. The four journals reported 25 research articles (*Counselor Education and Supervision*—17, *Journal of Counseling Psychology*—six, *American Psychologist*—one, *Journal of Consulting Psychology*—one); topical divisions included "Role of the Supervisor," "Process of Supervision," and "Rating Systems in Practicum." Because most studies suffered from lack of adequate research design, the reviewers concluded that sufficient descriptive data had been collected, but admonished researchers to study counseling supervision through solid experimental investigations.

Recent developments that should stimulate further research are described below. Individuals desiring guidelines for counseling center operation, APA accreditation of training programs and internships, or issues in counseling-psychology internships should review the following reports (APA, 1971; Boneau & Simmons, 1970; Kirk, 1970; Kirk et al., 1971). In the area of evaluation of the overall counseling-psychology training program, Gerken (1969) presents an objective method of evaluation; a set of 150 attributes of counseling-psychology training programs, including their estimated importance and the judged level of accuracy with which they may be discerned. Based upon four years of work with APA Division 17 psychologists, these scales represent a comprehensive effort.

Evaluation of supervision offered in the training site appears to be another crucial issue. According to Arbuckle (1968), the function of training is to help counselor-trainees develop the humanness to be more effective in human relationships. In a study of group and individual counseling supervision, Lanning (1971) found that counselor-trainees expected to achieve relationships with their clients that were similar to the relationship they perceived with their counseling supervisors. According to Carkhuff (1969), the important variables to be considered in evaluating a training program center on the trainer's level of functioning on interpersonal dimensions related to constructive helpee change,[3] and the trainee's level of functioning on the same dimensions. Citing research findings, he stated that the level of the counselor-trainee's (supervisor) functioning would appear to be the most critical aspect of effective training.

The APA accreditation guides and Gerken's objective scales represent opportunities to enumerate and evaluate tangible attributes or *products* of training sites, whereas Carkhuff focuses attention upon the very *process* of training. Utilizing a composite of both process and products would appear to be the most rewarding to the individual seeking to carefully research the effectiveness of the training program. In theory, it may be possible to carefully separate out the various ingredients essential to the training site; but in practice the dynamic interactions of program, facilities, supervision, and counselor-in-training make the task most challenging to the skilled researcher.

In summary, the university-counseling-center training program, as outlined in this essay, allows meaningful levels of counselor training to be developed from prepracticum laboratory to internship-level experiences. These experiences, patterned after the roles and functions of senior staff in the counseling center, include counseling, consulting, research, and training. Counselors-in-training, therefore, can observe and participate in the applied functions of the senior staff, become involved in the supervision of peers and lower-level trainees, and receive supervision for their supervisory experiences. Only through a well-developed "layered" program of services and training can these concepts be applied. This type of program easily goes beyond the minimum recommendations and standards of APA.

[3]The dimensions include empathy, respect, concreteness, genuineness, self-disclosure, confrontation, and immediacy, as described, with rating levels from 1 to 5, with 3 being minimal, in R. R. Carkhuff & B. G., Berenson, *Beyond Counseling and Therapy* (New York: Holt, Rinehart and Winston, 1967).

References

American Psychological Association, Division of Counseling and Guidance, Committee on Counselor Training. The practicum training of counseling psychologists. *American Psychologist,* 1952, **7**, 182–188. (a)

American Psychological Association, Division of Counseling and Guidance, Committee on Counselor Training. Recommended standards for training counseling psychologists at the doctorate level. *American Psychologist,* 1952, **7**, 175–181.(b)

American Psychological Association, Division of Counseling Psychology, Committee on Definition. Counseling psychology as a specialty. *American Psychologist,* 1956, **11**, 282–285.

American Psychological Association, Division of Counseling Psychology, Committee on Internship Standards. Recommended standards for internships in counseling psychology. Multilith, 1960.

American Psychological Association, Division of Counseling Psychology, Report of a Special Committee. The current status of counseling psychology. Multilith, 1961.

American Psychological Association, Office of Educational Affairs. Accreditation: Procedures and criteria. Multilith, 1971.

Arbuckle, D. S. Counseling effectiveness and related issues. *Journal of Counseling Psychology,* 1968, **15**, 430–435.

Bixler, R. H., Bordin, E. S., & Deabler, H. L. Supervised training in a college counseling bureau. *Journal of Consulting Psychology,* 1946, **10**, 233–236.

Boneau, A., & Simmons, W. APA accreditation: A status report. *American Psychologist,* 1970, **25**, 581–584.

Carkhuff, R. R. Training in the counseling and therapeutic practices: Requiem or reveille. *Journal of Counseling Psychology,* 1966, **13**, 360–367.

Carkhuff, R. R. Critical variables in effective counselor training. *Journal of Counseling Psychology,* 1969, **16**, 238–245.

Danskin, D. G. My focus for a university counseling center. *Journal of College Student Personnel,* 1965, **6**, 263–267.

Embree, R. B., Jr. The use of practicum and internship in counselor training. *Educational and Psychological Measurement,* 1951, **11**, 752–760.

Gerken, C. An objective method for evaluating training programs in counseling psychology. *Journal of Counseling Psychology,* 1969, **16**, 227–237.

Gust, T. Extending counselor supervision. *Counselor Education and Supervision,* 1970, **9**, (3), 157–161.

Hansen, J. C., & Warner, R. W., Jr. Review of research on practicum supervision. *Counselor Education and Supervision,* 1971, **10**, 261–272.

Kirk, B. A. Internship in counseling psychology: Goals and issues. *Journal of Counseling Psychology,* 1970, **17**, 88–90.

Kirk, B. A., & Chin, A. H. Internship in counseling psychology. *Journal of Counseling Psychology,* 1971, **18**, 524–530.

Kirk, B. A., Free, J. E., Johnson, A. P., Michel, J., Redfield, J.E., Roston, R. A., & Warman, R. E. Guidelines for university and college counseling services. *American Psychologist,* 1971, **26**, 585–589.

Lanning, W. L. A study of the relation between group and individual counseling supervision and three relationship measures. *Journal of Counseling Psychology,* 1971, **18**, 401–406.

Morrow, W. R. The development of psychological internship training. *Journal of Consulting Psychology,* 1946, **10**, 165–183.

Patterson, C. H. What is counseling psychology? *Journal of Counseling Psychology,* 1969, **16**, 23–29.

Roeber, E. C. Roles and functions of professionally trained counselors. In J. F. McGowan (Ed.), *Counselor development in American society: Conference recommendations from invitational conference on government-university relations in the professional preparation and employment of counselors.* Columbia: University of Missouri Press, 1965.

Super, D. E. Internships in college counseling centers. *Counseling News and Views,* 1956, **9**, 16–18.

Warnath, C. F. Counseling psychology or adjunct psychology? *Counseling News and Views,* 1968, **20**, 2–6.

Warnath, C. F. *New myths and old realities.* San Francisco: Jossey-Bass, 1971.

Utilization of University Counseling Centers for Counselor Preparation

Barbara A. Kirk and Arnold H. Chin

University of California—Berkeley

Counseling centers, like most things in this world, come in varying "shapes and sizes." While sharing many common characteristics, they also differ in many respects. Differences may be a result of variations in local conditions, the philosophy and approach of counseling-center staffs, as well as other factors. In the following discussion of counseling centers as settings for counselor training, we have tried to focus on those aspects commonly shared by most centers, although, inevitably, some of what is said will likely be more reflective of our own point of view or the setting in which we work.

Counseling centers are helping agencies within institutions of higher education. As such, their objectives, functions, and clientele are largely defined by the institutions of which they are a part. Basically, through its various services, a counseling center aims to complement the efforts of other segments of the university community in realizing the broad educational and developmental objectives of the institution. Its major function and primary responsibility is the counseling of students to facilitate their development and to help them make the most of their university experience. Services are also frequently offered to faculty members, university departments, the administration, and other student-personnel workers as related to problems of student development, adjustment, and evaluation.

University and college students, the main clientele served by counseling centers, are rather homogeneous in some aspects, and quite heterogeneous in others. By and large, they represent the upper end of the population continuum with respect to intellectual ability and socioeconomic level. The bulk of undergraduate students are late adolescents with all the concerns and problems that are characteristic of this age group.

Traditionally, undergraduates have represented a goodly proportion of the student population in any school, if not the entire population, as in four-year colleges. In the past 15 years or so, however, with increasing emphasis on graduate education, schools with graduate programs have seen a rapid increase in the number of graduate students to the point where, in some institutions, they almost nearly equal the undergraduate population. These older students have definitely introduced considerable heterogeneity into the usual undergraduate mix. Not only are they older in years and usually further along in their development, but many are married and have started families. Consequently, the concerns they present are in many respects quite different from those of the undergraduates. The heterogeneity of college-student populations has also been enhanced in recent years by the greatly increased enrollment of minority and/or disadvantaged students, the increasing propensity of mature women to return to college to complete their education, and, more generally, the opening up of higher-education opportunities to anyone desirous and capable of making use of them. This diversity is particularly evident in large public institutions like the University of California—Berkeley, where one can find representatives of all types of student—students from every state, from almost 100 foreign countries, and from every social and economic category, covering a wide range in age.

Counseling services offered by most counseling centers usually include educational, vocational, and personal counseling. Increasingly, with greater numbers of older students in attendance at universities and colleges, marital counseling may also be offered. There is considerable variation among counseling centers with respect to the different types of counseling offered. Some centers emphasize personal counseling (a few offer this service exclusively), while others put the emphasis on vocational and educational counseling. Variations may be due to a number of factors, including differences in local conditions. For example, a counseling center on a campus with no psychiatric service may find itself, of necessity, doing a great deal of personal counseling or therapy. Regardless of the differences in emphasis, however, it is important to keep in mind that these different types of counseling are rarely that separable when dealing with a particular student. It is an exceptional case, indeed, wherein a student's concerns are so circumscribed that one particular approach is adequate in helping him to resolve them. More likely, difficulties in one area tend to generate difficulties in other areas, and if counseling is to be effective, the student and his relevant circumstances must be dealt with as a whole rather than piecemeal.

The kinds of assistance sought by students at counseling centers are as richly varied as the students themselves. A good number of concerns are determined by the fact that the majority of students on most campuses are late adolescents trying to cope with the developmental tasks of this period in a higher-educational setting. For these students, the college years coincide with a crucial developmental period in their lives, the transition from adolescence to adulthood.

During the short span of a few years, the average student faces the task of taking some major steps towards maturity. Generally, this involves establishing a clearer identification of himself and his relationship to the world around him. More specifically, he must develop his intellectual and interpersonal resources, and come to terms with whatever limitations are present in these areas, modify his relationships with adults and his parents in assuming increasing responsibility and independence, begin to evolve a coherent and workable value system, and develop realistic vocational goals, which will provide him with meaning and satisfaction in his adult years. Specifically, these students go to a counseling center to seek help in (1) learning about abilities, aptitudes, and interests; (2) choosing a field of study; (3) developing career goals; (4) exploring fields of work, career opportunities, and educational programs; (5) overcoming difficulties in learning and studying; (6) increasing personal and social effectiveness; and (7) learning to deal more effectively with personal problems that may be interfering with general functioning and development.

From the foregoing description, it is undoubtedly apparent that most students seen at counseling centers are relatively normal and functioning adequately. By and large, they are bright, alert, well-motivated persons with considerable inner resources. These factors often make it possible, in working with students, to accompish a great deal in a short period of time. Often, a brief, impactful counseling experience is sufficient to help a student resolve whatever concern may be confronting him at a particular time. Students with more serious behavioral disorders are also seen in counseling centers, but ordinarily it is not feasible for most centers to offer much in the way of intensive, long-term psychotherapy. The counseling goal with these students is to help them continue functioning rather than an attempt to effect major personality changes. Students who require more extensive help are usually referred to private or community resources whenever possible.

While counseling students is the predominant activity, most counseling centers are also engaged in other pursuits. The range of additional enterprises is quite wide, and may include (1) counseling services for alumni and the general public, (2) orientation programs for incoming students, (3) reading and study-skills programs, (4) research, (5) assistance to academic units and special programs in improving selection and admissions procedures, and (6) special testing services for students applying for admission to professional schools, graduate programs, and other universities.

More and more, counseling centers are also becoming aware of the importance of expanding their services beyond what has been offered traditionally. There is the realization that counseling centers must extend their activities beyond their own physical confines if they are to maximize their effectiveness. Any of the newer types of activity can be subsumed under what is commonly referred to as "outreach." Examples include (1) consultation with administration, faculty members, and other student-personnel workers regarding student adjustment, development, and evaluation; (2) training of nonprofessional personnel who work directly with students, such as residence-hall staff; and (3) the offering of counseling services outside the counseling center—e.g., in residence halls and academic units.

Essentially, what is involved in outreach is a transmission of the counseling approach to wherever it is welcomed and accepted throughout the academic community. The objective is to work with all interested members of the community in fostering an environment as conducive to development as possible.

Counseling centers, as can be seen from the foregoing description of their programs and goals, may offer special opportunities for the counselor-in-preparation, but there are also limitations. In the remainder of this essay, we attempt to make concrete and specific the learning experience (and experiences) for which the novice counselor can look to counseling centers. Many aspects of the approach to the learning experience detailed herein may not be unique to the counseling center, but are general to the philosophy of training and training practices. However, they are specified here to make the picture of training in the counseling center as real and as full as possible at this point in time.

"Guidelines for University and College Counseling Centers," (1969) a document at this time in process of development by a task force of university and college counseling-center directors, has this to say about training:

1. Training of graduate students is an appropriate and desirable responsibility of the Counseling Service. However, the primary service role of the agency must be maintained. Trainees and interns should be selected by the same criteria as staff members, and closely and continuously supervised by experienced, specialized personnel throughout. Training cases assigned to trainees should be selected in relation to their current level of competency in order to insure quality service to students.
2. A counseling program which is primarily dependent upon trainees for the provision of service shall *not* be considered adequate.

Since it is expected that these principles will be adopted as standards, spelling them out may be of especial relevance here.

The service versus training issue is basic to this matter. To whom does the counselor-educator or professor of counseling psychology have primary responsibility? To the student in his program. To whom does the counseling center have primary responsibility? The answer is not as clear. Is the learning experience of the trainee of such consequence that everything must be sacrificed to it? Does it matter anyway whether mistakes are made, errors in counseling? Don't experienced counselors make errors anyway, sometimes irreparable ones? How can people learn if they are not permitted, even encouraged, to plunge in and try things, find out how they work, and so learn from their own experience?

These points of view have merit, but only to a degree. It is human beings we are dealing with—their problems, their concerns, their lives—and safeguarding their interests is our prime responsibility. Some freedom and creativity can surely exist within the sober caution that must obtain in setting early limits. In attempting to satisfy the needs of both student and trainee, inevitably some compromise must take place—it is not a clear either/or dichotomy.

A counseling center is not a training laboratory in the usual sense. It is commonly established for the purpose of making a student's education most meaningful and rewarding to him, and for dissipating for the student any obstacles tending to prevent this goal. Often the counseling center is funded through student contributions in one form or another, rather than from instructional funds. Sometimes the funding is combined in a variety of proportions. Training is an established function of the majority of counseling centers, especially in large universities, where graduate training exists, and more especially counseling programs in education and/or psychology, and/or clinical programs in psychology. These counseling centers are usually related to such programs, and in a variety of ways.

Whereas at this time counseling centers agree that the primary service role of the agency must be maintained, training should be an important interrelated function—otherwise how will counseling centers maintain and expand their own personnel? With adequate care, and perhaps a more gentle pace, training needs may also be met, although the counselor-educator may at times chafe under restrictions placed on his trainees. One further value of the counseling center's emphasis on concern for the student: it transmits important learning to the trainee about the ethical considerations of his future profession.

The counselor-educator may not understand the complexity of the counseling function of the counseling center, and thus may not comprehend why his trainee cannot immediately be engaged in some central activity, perhaps in a segment of the counseling process, separated from the whole for this purpose. Students are complex human beings with complex problems not always readily discernible in advance. To deal with them as people, and with their manifold problems, requires considerable knowledge and skill. General knowledge will have been acquired in the classroom—personality theory, learning theory, theories of counseling, abnormal psychology, measurement, and so forth. The particular knowledge—the institutional structure and operations, the local labor market, the counseling process and procedures—must be acquired in the counseling center. More significant, the application of all knowledge to the individual, and the skills to work with him, must be acquired in the counseling center.

How can this be done? We should like to comment on various levels of preparation: practicum, fieldwork, internship, and then on the principles in the *Guidelines*, including selection of trainees, supervision of trainees, and selection of cases for them.

Practicum lends itself less well than more advanced levels to counseling-center involvement. There is the assumption that the trainee has previously had didactic preparation alone. A laboratory situation, controlled for training purposes, can initially permit more "action" on the part of the trainee than can an ongoing service organization—a "naturalistic" setting where the regular activities cannot be redesigned to fit training needs. Thus, initiation will be gradual, and frustration may be a factor.

At the University of California Counseling Center, where practicum students are only occasionally accepted, the "tools" of the trade are first established. The trainee is offered one or two hours of individual supervision a week, and between 6 and 10 hours of assignment to the Counseling Center. The practicum student first gets acquainted with his new milieu. He learns the history, purpose, and goals of the organization in which he is working. Depending upon where he took his undergraduate work, he is provided with formal and informal knowledge of operations on this campus, with the supervisor directing the method, content, and order of learning.

Very early demonstration of counseling interviewing is usually helpful to trainees. The purpose of the didactic learning becomes clearer and more real, and the trainee's opportunity to observe reduces his anxiety about being "thrown in" without knowing how to behave. Immediate observation at the beginning of practicum offers models.

Then comes the specific knowledge without which the practicum student may not be able to complete his first interview. Ordinarily practicum students are first assigned freshmen, for a variety of reasons, which will be discussed below. The tests most appropriate to the freshman level are next studied: taken, scored, norms selected, interpretation investigated by the trainee. When he is ready, he is given first-interview case data, and is asked to select appropriate tests, giving his reasons for using and/or preferring them. When this level is mastered, he is first asked for a formulation of test results in relation to case data, next to think and talk about how he would present them to the counselee, and what tentative goals might be. All the while, he is hearing about counseling in his interaction with other staff-members, may be reading cases, and is learning about cases selected for their variety.

Next comes acquaintanceship with occupational and educational information in a meaningful, applied way. He learns the local library—what is in it and how to use it; the local and national market for university graduates; and resources of all kinds, including the functions and responsibilities of other student-personnel services on the campus.

With some degree of mastery in these areas, he is ready to begin. This is typically done with role playing, usually after a demonstration interview or two. An experienced counselor, usually one with some talent in this, adopts a role known only to himself. The supervisor sits in on the interview, and compares his observations and perceptions with the trainee's. The role-player feeds back his reactions and feelings in relation to what the trainee did. A postsession thoroughly reviews the experience. As many role-playing sessions as necessary are conducted before the practicum student is considered reasonably ready to conduct his first interview.

When this occurs, the information available from application form and other records is discussed in detail with the trainee, for preparation, and for reduction of anxiety. He is usually *not* asked to record his first interview, and may not be asked to do so for the first several. He is, however, given planned access to his supervisor immediately following this interview in order that his questions and needs may be handled supportively.

Each interview from now on is reviewed before and after it takes place, whatever its position in the sequence. The number of interviews, therefore, is carefully controlled, in order that tapes may also receive intensive attention and/or interviews may be observed and considered in depth. The trainee is requested to listen to his own tapes one or several times before listening together with his supervisor. Where a number of trainees are in practicum together, group sessions may be very advantageous in developing interview techniques, and in learning how to establish goals and how to implement the counseling process.

For the fieldwork student, this all goes more rapidly. His prior learning must be carefully investigated and assessed, and is then built upon. It is expected that he, too, will likely spend something like one-quarter time with the counseling, possibly up to half-time, and will likely have two to three hours of individual supervision per week.

The intern, on the other hand, will spend no less than half-time for two years, or full time for one year, in the Counseling Center, be he predoctoral or postdoctoral. He will have prior practicum experience, and, hopefully, one or several field placements before coming to the Counseling Center. He usually will not require the elaborate filling-in of basics, but will commence, after appropriate orientation procedures, in much the same way as a new junior staff-member. His background must be fully understood, in order to determine the areas in which he most needs intensive and extensive training. He is afforded, at least initially, five hours a week of individual supervision, and is involved with the staff in all training and staff meetings, including case discussions with consultants, and discussions of philosophy, theory, issues, and research. He will have a substantial case-load, assigned with the purpose of broadening and deepening his experience, and will have other learning experiences designed for and with him in terms of his personal objectives, his competencies, and his interests (Kirk, 1970b).

Such experiences may include presentations to staff, research, outreach experiences, etc., but the predominant time and focus is upon the intensification and polishing of counseling skills.

Supervision should be by experienced, specialized personnel. Supervision, in our opinion, is the most difficult and demanding of the skills in the repertoire of the counseling psychologist. The approach is, perforce, a mix of both counseling and administration. The counseling aspect has to do with a relationship, creating the climate for learning; raising questions pertinent to the expanding awareness, sound judgment, and differentiated approach of the developing counselor; and, when and where necessary, involving his personal dynamics and reactions. The supervisor avoids being a therapist, but is duty-bound to work with the intrapsychic difficulties that affect the work of the trainee.

On the other hand, the supervisor is the administrator in the sense of governing the enterprise. If it is to be helpful, there must be continuous evaluation and feedback, the setting of limits, and the employment of the knowledge and experience of the supervisor for the wise and continuously alert guidance of the learning experience. It goes without saying that the supervisor must be a master craftsman, with enough experience to be able to meet the range of possibilities, as well as to know when he does not know, and to whom to turn.

Selection of cases for trainees poses another set of problems. Freshmen often seem most appropriate for several reasons. Other things being equal, they will be around longer and there is more opportunity to recoup for mistakes. They are younger, and there is a greater age-differential with the trainees, who should be less threatened by them. We know from our research that freshmen, especially girls, most need nurturance from counseling, and competence and skills are less crucial factors in working with them.

There are, of course, great individual differences in trainees. Initial assignments should take account of the trainee's own particular life and professional experiences to date, and the kinds of people he is most comfortable with in terms of age, sex, traits, and needs. Rarely, if ever, would a beginning trainee be assigned an inarticulate, resistive student, for example. It is no favor to a trainee at any level to be assigned cases with which he is not yet ready or prepared to deal. So there are dual purposes in assignment of cases: protection of the trainee, as well as quality of service to students.

As the trainee develops competency, the variety of cases assigned is gradually increased, at whatever pace is most profitable for the trainee. The range of cases and degree of competency are dependent upon the length of his experience, as well as upon his native aptitudes.

Other functions are also assigned at later stages in training: group counseling, outreach activities, and so on. These additional functions are related to the developing interests and competencies of the counselor. In a general sense, the internship experience can be seen as a guided tour in vocational evolution: as a process for the counselor, with the supervisor's help, to try experiences and evaluate them for himself toward establishing those most satisfying for his professional future, in one or several combinations. He will have some opportunity to determine whether, and to what degree, he wishes to engage in counseling per se, individual and/or group, student-personnel administration, liaison, consulting, teaching, and research.

Continued inservice training for staff has been dealt with elsewhere (Kirk, 1970a). Since it is never possible to know enough for counseling, and since counseling draws upon everything one knows, continued inservice training is a must. Besides, situations alter and conditions change, and the trainee must keep up with all such developments. At the intern level, at least, the trainee may well gain from being involved in and with the inservice training program for the whole staff in all its facets: encouragement to attend professional meetings when feasible, involvement in staff case discussions, research reports, reports on developments in testing and occupational information, review of issues in counseling and higher education, and discussion of policy and procedures in administration of the counseling center.

With the enormous territory encompassed by the field of counseling psychology, it is bewildering to try to establish definite sequential tasks for our trainees (Kirk, 1970b). At this point in the development of our field, we can, perhaps, only individualize making and evolving a training plan for our trainees, bringing each one along as far as possible in the allotted time. There is ample evidence of the need for at least a two-year internship, rather than the usual one-year internship; either a two-year predoctoral or a one and one arrangement, predoctoral and postdoctoral.

We have in this essay been attempting to describe the counselor-to-be's learning experience in college counseling centers. In doing so, we have discussed counseling centers—their goals, their programs, their relationships to their institutions of higher education, and the populations they serve. We have also discussed their roles, responsibilities, and opportunities for training; the issues they encounter in training; and something of the training process. What we have not until now communicated is the stimulating, exciting experience this setting offers to the counselor-in-training. It provides an able, functioning, youthful population with whom tangible results are ordinarily readily obtainable. It also provides the opportunity of seeing people grow and find direction, satisfying relationships, and self-fulfillment.

REFERENCES

University and College Counseling Center Directors Task Force III. Guidelines for university and college counseling services. 1969.

Kirk, B. A. In-service training and professional growth. In P. J. Gallagher and G. D. Demos (Eds.), *The counseling center in higher education.* Springfield, Ill.: Charles C Thomas, 1970. (a)

Kirk, B. A. The internship in counseling psychology: Goals and issues. *Journal of Counseling Psychology,* 1970, **17,** (1), 88–90.(b)

Issues

1. How might we evaluate a setting for practicum in terms of the criteria provided in this chapter? What are the practical steps by which the evaluation might be made, and by whom should it be done?
2. Should qualifications (versus guidelines) be established for practicum supervisors? If so, what should they be, and how would evaluations be made? What are the implications of such a move for programs preparing mental-health professionals?
3. Since most students do not know exactly the setting they would like to be in as professionals, it would seem that several practicum affiliations might be of value. Does this have different implications for master's and doctoral programs—e.g., in regard to level of expected functioning, orientation period, length of time required?
4. Is there a method, or are there methods, by which experiential learning, of the kind achieved in practicum, can be more meaningfully related to theoretical and research knowledge?

Annotated Readings

Adler, P. T. Internship training for a contemporary profession of psychology. *Professional Psychology*, 1970, **1,** 371–376.

> The special needs of impoverished urban communities have prompted a reorientation of traditional psychological services. As reflected in current intern-training programs, emphasis has been shifted to the performance of a variety of functions—including direct community involvement—away from the more limited office sessions. The first 10 weeks of internship is devoted to an intensive Basic Techniques Workshop, which, through seminars, evaluates subjects on the basis of case history, observation, interview, and diagnostic testing; and serves to acquaint interns with particular urban social settings while reviewing (and adapting) basic psychological techniques. The balance of the internship involves rotation through the various departments of the mental-health center. For six- to eight-week periods, the intern is alternately assigned to adult psychiatric inpatient service, emergency walk-in clinic, partial hospitalization unit, and child psychiatry. The program seeks to combine the ideal and real by forcing the intern to adapt traditional methods to nontraditional circumstances, thus expanding his range of competence and preparing him for the challenges of contemporary psychology.

Duncan, C. W. Counselors in private practice: A survey report. *Personnel and Guidance Journal,* 1968, **47,** 337–340.

> A questionnaire was mailed to every marriage counselor, child-guidance specialist, and psychologist listed in the yellow pages of Florida telephone directories. The replies were used to describe the profession of private-practice counseling. Sixty-seven percent of the sample replied. It was found that several professions offer counseling as a service, but there is not yet an established profession of private-practice counseling.

Pederson, A. M., & Weiner, I. B. Psychology training in emergency services. *American Psychologist,* 1970, **25,** 474–476.

> Based on data gathered from the Psychiatric Division of the Emergency Department at the University of Rochester, there has been an increased focus on psychological first aid in contrast to traditional, long-term treatment. This is especially in response to lower-class and nonwhite groups, which, for reasons of insufficient motivation or simple impatience, often fail to pursue referrals for care through other agencies. Complementing the available short-term treatments are follow-up sessions, which provide for return visits after the initial crises. Services also involve cooperation with other agencies (police, practitioners, etc.) where appropriate, and extension into the patient's home where necessary.
>
> As regards training, interns and fellows work with the emergency service for four months, during which time they assist in the interviewing and screening of patients, and sit in on later follow-up sessions. The program stresses direct participation in decision making, close work with professionals, exposure to the center's unique functions, and actual clinical responsibility for training assignments.

Quarrick, E. A., Jacobs, M., & Trick, O. L. A new role model for psychology students in a medical setting. *American Psychologist,* 1971, **26,** 317–319.

> At the psychiatric ward of the West Virginia University Medical Center, psychology graduate students replaced clerkship medical students for an experimental three-week stint. Although

494

the graduate students were not qualified to administer medication to their patients, they did participate wholly in group-therapy meetings, which are common fare in the ward. Assuming a disposition of toughness and confrontation, the graduates succeeded in winning confidence and respect. Patients showed no ill effects from the project and, in fact, subtle improvements were witnessed through the wealth of feedback.

The experiment afforded the graduate students an unusual opportunity for sustained interaction with psychiatric inpatients. It also demonstrated that many of the duties currently assigned to practitioners trained in medicine, might be adequately, if not advantageously, performed by psychologists and their trainees.

Suggestions for Further Reading

Hansen, J. C., & Moore, G. D. The off-campus practicum. *Counselor Education and Supervision,* 1966, **6**, 32–39.

Kelly, J. G. Antidotes for arrogance: Training for community psychology. *American Psychologist,* 1970, **25**, 524–531.

Kelly, J. G. Qualities for the community psychologist. *American Psychologist* 1971, **26**, 897–903.

Lehmann, S. Community and psychology and community psychology. *American Psychologist,* 1971, **26**, 554–560.

Levitt, H. The clinical psychology internship in the medical setting and the professional identity: The psychodiagnostic function. *Psychotherapy: Theory, Research and Practice,* 1967, **4**, 182–185.

Macht, L. B. Education and mental health: New directions for interaction. *Personnel and Guidance Journal,* 1969, **47**, 855–858.

McKay, W. R. Clients for the practicum. *Counselor Education and Supervision,* 1967, **7**, 75–76.

O'Brien, C., Bailey, R. E., & Fitzgerald, P. W. School counseling internship: An examination. *Counselor Education and Supervision,* 1966, **6**, 44–49.

Oseas, L. One kind of community psychology training program. *Professional Psychology,* 1970, **1**, 143–150.

Walker, C. E., Wolpin, M., & Fellows, L. The use of high school and college students as therapists and researchers in a state mental hospital. *Psychotherapy: Theory, Research and Practice,* 1967, **4**, 186–188.

Bibliography

CHAPTER 2

Abeles, N. Review of D. S. Arbuckle (Ed.), *Counseling and psychotherapy: An overview. Personnel and Guidance Journal,* 1968, **46**, 702–704.

Abroms, G. M. The new eclecticism. *Archives of General Psychiatry,* 1969, **20**, 514–523.

Albert, G. If counseling *is* psychotherapy—what then? *Personnel and Guidance Journal,* 1966, **45**, 125–129.

Amble, B., & Bradley, R. *Pupils as persons.* New York: Intext/Chandler, 1973, in press.

American Personnel and Guidance Association. The counselor: Professional preparation and role —A statement of policy. *Personnel and Guidance Journal,* 1964, **42**, 536–541.

American Personnel and Guidance Association, Association for Counselor Education and Supervision. Standards for the preparation of secondary school counselors—1967. *Personnel and Guidance Journal,* 1967, **46**, 96–106.

American Psychological Association, Division of Counseling Psychology, Committee on Definition. Counseling psychology as a speciality. *American Psychologist,* 1956, **11**, 282–285.

American Psychological Association, Division of Counseling Psychology. The scope and standards of preparation in psychology for school counselors. *American Psychologist,* 1962, **17**, 149–152.

Arbuckle, D. S. *Counseling: An introduction.* Boston: Allyn & Bacon, 1961.

Blocher, D. H. Issues in counseling: Elusive and illusional. *Personnel and Guidance Journal,* 1965, **43**, 796–800.

Brammer, L. M., & Shostrom, E. L. *Therapeutic psychology: Fundamentals of counseling and psychotherapy.* Englewood Cliffs: Prentice-Hall, 1960.

Brammer, L. M., & Shostrom, E. L. *Therapeutic psychology: Fundamentals of actualization counseling and psychotherapy.* (2nd ed.) Englewood Cliffs: Prentice-Hall, 1968.

Carkhuff, R. R. *Helping and human relations: A primer for lay and professional helpers.* New York: Holt, Rinehart and Winston, 1969. 2 vols.

Carkhuff, R. R., & Berenson, B. G. *Beyond counseling and therapy.* New York: Holt, Rinehart and Winston, 1967.

Duhl, F. J. A personal history of politics and programs in psychiatric training. In G. M. Abroms & N. S. Greenfield (Eds.), *The new hospital psychiatry.* New York: Academic Press, 1971.

Ellis, A. *Reason and emotion in psychotherapy.* New York: Lyle Stuart, 1962.

Goldman, L. Comment: Another log. *American Psychologist,* 1964, **19**, 418–419.

Hahn, M. E. Conceptual trends in counseling. *Personnel and Guidance Journal,* 1953, **31**, 231–235.

Hahn, M. E., & MacLean, M. S. *Counseling psychology.* (2nd ed.) New York: McGraw-Hill, 1955.

Lewis, E. C. *The psychology of counseling.* New York: Holt, Rinehart and Winston, 1970.

Mahrer, A. R. (Ed.) *The goals of psychotherapy.* New York: Appleton-Century-Crofts, 1967.

Patterson, C. H. *Counseling and psychotherapy: Theory and practice.* New York: Harper & Row, 1959.

Patterson, C. H. Comment: Counseling and/or psychotherapy? *American Psychologist,* 1963, **18**, 667–669.

Patterson, C. H. Counseling. *Annual Review of Psychology,* 1966, **17**, 79–110.

497

Patterson, C. H. *Theories of counseling and psychotherapy.* 2nd. ed. New York: Harper & Row, 1973. (b)

Patterson, C. H. Psychotherapy in the school. In D. S. Arbuckle (Ed.), *Counseling and psychotherapy: An overview.* New York: McGraw-Hill, 1967.

Patterson, C. H. Rehabilitation counseling: A profession or a trade? *Personnel and Guidance Journal,* 1968, **46**, 567–571.

Perry, W. G. On the relation of psychotherapy and counseling. *Annals of the New York Academy of Sciences,* 1955, **63**, 396–407.

Rogers, C. R. *Counseling and psychotherapy: Newer concepts in practice.* Boston: Houghton Mifflin, 1942.

Rogers, C. R. *Client-centered therapy: Its current practice, implications, and theory.* Boston: Houghton Mifflin, 1951.

Rogers, C. R. The necessary and sufficient conditions of therapeutic personality change. *Journal of Consulting Psychology,* 1957, **21**, 95–103.

Rogers, C. R. (Ed.) *The therapeutic relationship and its impact: A study of psychotherapy with schizophrenics.* Madison: University of Wisconsin Press, 1967.

Rothney, J. W. M. *Adaptive counseling in schools.* Englewood Cliffs: Prentice-Hall, 1972.

Rothney, J. W. M., & Sanborn, M. P. Wisconsin's research-through-service program for superior high school students. *Personnel and Guidance Journal,* 1966, **44**, 694–699.

Stefflre, B. S. Function and present status of counseling theory. In B. S. Stefflre (Ed.), *Theories of counseling.* New York: McGraw-Hill, 1965.

Stefflre, B. S., & Grant, W. H. (Eds.) *Theories of counseling.* (2nd ed.) New York: McGraw-Hill, 1972.

Super, D. E. Transition: From vocational guidance to counseling psychology. *Journal of Counseling Psychology,* 1955, **2**, 3–9.

Truax, C. B., & Carkhuff, R. R. *Toward effective counseling and psychotherapy: Training and practice.* Chicago: Aldine, 1967.

Tyler, L. E. Theoretical principles underlying the counseling process. *Journal of Counseling Psychology,* 1958, **5**, 3–8.

Tyler, L. E. *The work of the counselor.* (2nd ed.) New York: Appleton-Century-Crofts, 1961.

Tyler, L. E. *The work of the counselor.* (3rd ed.) New York: Appleton-Century-Crofts, 1969.

Wolberg, L. R. *The technique of psychotherapy.* (2nd ed.) New York: Grune & Stratton, 1967.

CHAPTER 3

Abroms, G. M. The new eclecticism. *Archives of General Psychiatry,* 1969, **20**, 514–523.

Altucher, N. Constructive use of the supervisory relationship. *Journal of Counseling Psychology,* 1967, **14**, 165–170.

American Psychological Association, Division of Counseling and Guidance, Committee on Counselor Training. Recommended standards for training counseling psychologists at the doctoral level. *American Psychologist,* 1952, **7**, 175–181.

American Psychological Association, Division of Counseling and Guidance, Committee on Counselor Training. The practicum training of counseling psychologists. *American Psychologist,* 1952, **7**, 182–188.

Arbuckle, D. S. Counselor, social worker, psychologist: Let's "ecumenicalize." *Personnel and Guidance Journal,* 1967, **45**, 532–538.

Arnold, D. L., & Hummel, D. L. Follow-up of graduates of the counselor training program at Kent State University. Unpublished manuscript, Kent State University, 1958.

Association for Counselor Education and Supervision. Committee on Professional Preparation and Standards. Standards for the preparation of secondary school counselors—1967. *Personnel and Guidance Journal,* **46**, 96–106.

Baker, R. L. Differences between guidance workers and teachers in knowledge of human behavior. *15th Yearbook, National Council on Measurements Used in Education,* 1959, 71–79.

Blane, S. M. Immediate effect of supervisory experiences on counselor candidates. *Counselor Education and Supervision,* 1968, **8**, 39–44.

Bordin, E. S. Curiosity, compassion, and doubt: the dilemma of the psychologist. *American Psychologist,* 1966, **21**, 116–121.

Bordin, E. S. (Ed.) *Training of psychological counselors.* Ann Arbor: University of Michigan, 1950.

Brammer, L. M. Eclecticism revisited. *Personnel and Guidance Journal,* 1969, **48**, 192–197.

Brayfield, A. H. Counseling psychology. *Annual Review of Psychology,* 1963, **14**, 319–350.

Bruce, P. Sources for personal validation. *Counselor Education and Supervision,* 1969, **8**, 327–330.

Carnes, E. F. A parting shot. *Counselor Education and Supervision,* 1966, **5**, 226.

Cash, W. L., Jr., & Munger, P. F. Counselors and their preparation. *Review of Educational Research,* 1966, **36**, 256–263.

Duhl, F. J. A personal history of politics and programs in psychiatric training. In G. M. Abroms & N. S. Greenfield (Eds.), *The new hospital psychiatry,* in press.

Expectations and commitments: A joint ACES/ASCA policy statement. Washington: American Personnel and Guidance Association, 1969.

Ekstein, R., & Wallerstein, R. S. *The teaching and learning of psychotherapy.* New York: Basic Books, 1958.

Gysbers, N. C., & Johnston, J. A. Expectations of a practicum supervisor's role. *Counselor Education and Supervision,* 1964, **4**, 68–74.

Hart, D. H., & Prince, D. J. Role conflict for school counselors: Training versus job demands. *Personnel and Guidance Journal,* 1970, **48**, 374–380.

Herr, E. L., & Cramer, S. H. Counselor role determinants as perceived by counselor educators and school counselors. *Counselor Education and Supervision,* 1965, **5**, 3–8.

Hill, G. E., & Green, D. A. The selection, preparation, and professionalization of guidance and personnel workers. *Review of Educational Research,* 1960, **30**, 115–130.

Johnston, J. A., & Gysbers, N. C. Practicum supervisory relationships: A majority report. *Counselor Education and Supervision,* 1966, **6**, 3–10.

Kehas, C. D. Guidance-in-education: An examination of the interplay between definition and structure. In V. F. Calia & B. D. Wall (Eds.), *Pupil personnel administration: New perspectives and foundations.* Springfield, Ill.: Charles C. Thomas, 1968.

Kehas, C. D. Toward a redefinition of education: A new framework for counseling in education. In S. C. Stone & B. Shertzer (Eds.), *Introduction to guidance: Selected readings.* Boston: Houghton Mifflin, 1970.

Kris, E. *Psychoanalytic explorations in art.* New York: International Universities Press, 1952.

Liddle, G. P., & Kroll, A. M. *Pupil services in Massachusetts schools.* Boston: Massachusetts Advisory Council on Education, 1969.

Malcolm, D. D. On becoming a counselor. *Personnel and Guidance Journal,* 1968, **46**, 673–676.

McCully, C. H. Professionalization: Symbol or substance. *Counselor Education and Supervision,* 1963, **2**, 106–111.

Miller, C. D., & Oetting, E. R. Students react to supervision. *Counselor Education and Supervision,* 1966, **6**, 73–74.

Munger, P. F., Brown, D. F., & Needham, J. T. NDEA institute participants two years later. *Personnel and Guidance Journal,* 1964, **42**, 987–990.

Ofman, W. The counselor who is: A critique and a modest proposal. *Personnel and Guidance Journal,* 1967, **45**, 932–937.

Parry, K. A. The effect of two training approaches on counselor effectiveness. Unpublished doctoral dissertation, University of Missouri, 1969.

Patterson, C. H. Counseling. *Annual Review of Psychology,* 1966, **17**, 79–110.

Peterson, D. R. *The clinical study of social behavior.* New York: Appleton-Century-Crofts, 1968.

Rioch, M. S., Elkes, C., Flint, A. A., Udansky, B. S., Newman, R. G., & Silber, E. National institute of mental health pilot study in training mental health counselors. *American Journal of Orthopsychiatry,* 1963, **33**, 678–689.

Silverman, M. S. Effects of differential practicum experiences on client and counselor perceptions of initial interviews. Unpublished doctoral dissertation, Northwestern University, 1969.

Sorenson, G., & Kagan, D. Conflicts between doctoral candidates and their sponsors: A contrast in expectations. *Journal of Higher Education,* 1967, **38**, 17–24.

Sorenson, G. Pterodactyls, passenger pigeons, and personnel workers. *Personnel and Guidance Journal,* 1965, **43**, 430–437.

Stoughton, R. W. The preparation of counselors and personnel workers. *Review of Educational Research,* 1957, **27**, 174–185.

Stripling, R. O., & Lister, J. L. Selection, preparation, and professionalization of specialists. *Review of Educational Research,* 1963, **33**, 171–178.

Sullivan, H. S. *The psychiatric interview.* New York: W. W. Norton, 1954.

Thompson, A. S., & Super, D. E. (Eds.) *The professional preparation of counseling psychologists: Report of the 1964 Greyston conference.* New York: Bureau of Publications, Teachers College, 1964.

Truax, C. B., & Carkhuff, R. R. *Toward effective counseling and psychotherapy: training and practice.* Chicago: Aldine, 1967.

Whiteley, J. M. Counselor education. *Review of Educational Research,* 1969, **39**, 173–188.

Wrenn, C. G. *The counselor in a changing world.* Washington: American Personnel and Guidance Association, 1962.

CHAPTER 4

American Personnel and Guidance Association, Association for Counselor Education and Supervision. Standards for the preparation of secondary school counselors—1967. *Personnel and Guidance Journal,* 1967, **46**, 96–106.

American Psychological Association, Committee on Counselor Training, Division of Counseling and Guidance. The practicum training of counseling psychologists. *American Psychologist,* 1952, 7, 182–188.

American Psychological Association, Committee on Counselor Training, Division of Counseling Psychology. *Counselor training, methods and procedures.* Columbia: University of Missouri, 1952.

Arbuckle, D. S. *Counseling: An introduction.* Boston: Allyn & Bacon, 1961.

Arnold, D. L. Counselor education as responsible self-development. *Counselor Education and Supervision,* 1962, **1**, 185–192.

Association of Counselor Education and Supervision, Committee on Counseling Effectiveness. Commitment to action in supervision: Report of a national survey of counselor supervision. Paper presented at the meeting of the American Personnel and Guidance Association, Las Vegas, March 1969.

Bandura, A. *Principles of behavior modification.* New York: Holt, Rinehart and Winston, 1969.

Bandura, A., Ross, D., & Ross, S. A. Imitation of film-mediated aggressive models. *Journal of Abnormal and Social Psychology,* 1963, **66**, 3–11.

Blane, S. M. Immediate effect of supervisory experiences on counselor candidates. *Counselor Education and Supervision,* 1968, **8**, 39–44.

Brammer, L. M., & Springer, H. C. A radical change in counselor education and certification. *Personnel and Guidance Journal,* 1971, **49**, 803–808.

Callis, R. A. Toward an integrated theory of counseling. *Journal of College Student Personnel,* 1960, **1**(4), 2–9.

Chenault, J. A. The diary report in counselor education. *Counselor Education and Supervision,* 1962, **1**, 193–198.

Combs, A. W., Avila, D. L., & Purkey, W. W. *Helping relationships: Basic concepts for the helping professions.* Boston: Allyn & Bacon, 1971.

Combs, A. W., & Snygg, D. *Individual behavior: A perceptual approach to behavior.* (Rev. ed.) New York: Harper, 1959.

Dagley, J. A taxonomy of counselor education objectives. Unpublished doctoral dissertation, University of Missouri—Columbia, 1972.

Davidson, T. N., & Emmer, E. T. Immediate effect of supportive and nonsupportive supervisor behavior on counselor candidates' focus of concern. *Counselor Education and Supervision,* 1966, **6**, 27–31.

Demos, G. D., & Zuwaylif, F. H. Counselor attitudes in relation to the theoretical positions of their supervisors. *Counselor Education and Supervision,* 1962, **2**, 8–13.

Embree, R. B., Jr. The use of practicums and internships in counselor training. *Educational and Psychological Measurement,* 1951, **11**, 752–760.

Gibson, J. J. Theories of perception. In W. Dennis (Ed.), *Current trends in psychological theory.* Pittsburgh: University of Pittsburgh Press, 1951.

Hatch, W. R. What standards do we raise? Report of meeting of Directors of National Defense Counseling and Guidance Training Institutes, U. S. Office of Education, Counseling and Guidance Institutes Branch, 1962.

Hill, G. E. The selection of school counselors. *Personnel and Guidance Journal,* 1961, **39**, 355–360.

Hunt, C. M. Developmental phases of counselor growth. *Counselor Education and Supervision,* 1962, **2**, 45–48.

Jones, A. Preparation of teachers and specialists for guidance service. *Review of Educational Research,* 1942, **12**, 124–133.

Joslin, L. C., Jr. *Knowledge and counseling competence: An investigation of two outcomes of a counselor education program.* (Doctoral dissertation, University of Michigan) Ann Arbor, Mich.: University Microfilms, 1962. No. 62–2748.

Kazienko, L. W., & Neidt, C. O. Self descriptions of good and poor counselor trainees. *Counselor Education and Supervision,* 1962, **1**, 106–123.

Loree, M. R. *Psychology of education.* (2nd ed.) New York: Ronald Press, 1970.

Mausner, B. Studies in social interaction: III. Effect of variation in one partner's prestige on the interaction of observer pairs. *Journal of Applied Psychology,* 1953, **37**, 391–393.

Miller, N. E., & Dollard, J. *Social learning and imitation.* New Haven: Yale University Press, 1941.

Mowrer, O. H. *Learning theory and behavior.* New York: John Wiley, 1960.

Mowrer, O. H. *Learning theory and the symbolic processes.* New York: John Wiley, 1960.

Patterson, C. H. Phenomenological psychology: An approach to human behavior. Paper presented at the meeting of the American Personnel and Guidance Association, Chicago, April 1962.

Pepinsky, H. B., & Pepinsky, P. N. *Counseling theory and practice.* New York: Ronald Press, 1954.

Reynolds, G. S. *A primer of operant conditioning.* Glenview, Ill.: Scott, Foresman, 1968.

Robinson, V. P. *Supervision in social case work: A problem in professional education.* Chapel Hill: University of North Carolina Press, 1936.

Roeber, E. C. Practicum and internship. Association for Counselor Education and Supervision, and American School Counselor Association. *Counselor education—A progress report on standards.* Washington: American Personnel and Guidance Association, 1962.

Rogers, C. R. *On becoming a person: A therapist's view of psychotherapy.* Boston: Houghton Mifflin, 1961.

Rosenbaum, M. E., & Tucker, I. F. The competence of the model and the learning of imitation and nonimitation. *Journal of Experimental Psychology,* 1962, **63**, 183–190.

Sanderson, H. *Basic concepts in vocational guidance.* New York: McGraw-Hill, 1954.

Springer, H. C., & Brammer, L. M. A tentative model to identify elements of the counseling process and parameters of counselor behavior. *Counselor Education and Supervision,* 1971, **11**, 8–16.

Super, D. E., & Bachrach, P. B. *Scientific careers and vocational development theory: A review, a critique and some recommendations.* New York: Bureau of Publications, Teachers College, 1957.

Thorndike, E. L. Measurement in education. *Teachers College Record,* 1921, **22**, 371–379.

Thorndike, R. L., & Hagen, E. *Ten thousand careers.* New York: John Wiley, 1959.

Thurstone, L. L. *Multiple-factor analysis: A development and expansion of the vectors of the mind.* Chicago: University of Chicago Press, 1947.

Tuma, A. H., & Gustad, J. W. The effects of client and counselor personality characteristics on client learning in counseling. *Journal of Counseling Psychology,* 1957, **4**, 136–141.

Tyler, L. E. *The work of the counselor.* (2nd ed.) New York: Appleton-Century-Crofts, 1961.

Walz, G. R., & Roeber, E. C. Supervisors' reactions to a counseling interview. *Counselor Education and Supervision,* 1962, **2**, 2–7.

Williamson, E. G. Supervision of counseling services. *Educational and Psychological Measurement,* 1948, **8**, 297–311.

CHAPTER 5

American Personnel and Guidance Association, Committee on Ethics. Code of ethics. *Personnel and Guidance Journal,* 1961, **40**, 206–209.

American Personnel and Guidance Association, Ethical Practices Committee. *Ethical standards casebook.* Washington: American Personnel and Guidance Association, 1965.

American Psychological Association. *Casebook on ethical standards of psychologists.* Washington: American Psychological Association, 1967.

American Psychological Association. Ethical standards of psychologists. *American Psychologist,* 1968, **23**, 357–361.

American Psychological Association. *Ethical principles in the conduct of research with human participants.* Washington: American Psychological Association, 1973.

Anderson, S. Group counseling in drug awareness. *School Counselor,* 1971, **19**, 123–126.

Arbuckle, D. S. (Ed.) *Counseling and psychotherapy: An overview.* New York: McGraw-Hill, 1967.

Arbuckle, D. S. Counselor, social worker, psychologist: Let's "Ecumenicalize." *Personnel and Guidance Journal,* 1967, **45**, 532–538.

Arbuckle, D. S. Current issues in counselor education. *Counselor Education and Supervision,* 1968, **7**, 244–251.

Arbuckle, D. S. Values, ethics and religion in counseling. Paper presented at the National Catholic Guidance Convention, Detroit, April 1968.

Arbuckle, D. S. *Counseling: Philosophy, theory and practice.* (2nd ed.) Boston: Allyn & Bacon, 1970.

Aubrey, R. F. School-community drug prevention programs. *Personnel and Guidance Journal,* 1971, **50**, 17–24.

Bailey, R. J. The preparation, certification and selection of personnel workers for the secondary schools of the United States. Unpublished doctoral dissertation, New York University, 1940.

Banks, W. M. The changing attitudes of black students. *Personnel and Guidance Journal,* 1970, **48**, 739–745.

Bare, C. E. Relationship of counselor personality and counselor-client personality similarity to selected counseling success criteria. *Journal of Counseling Psychology,* 1967, **14**, 419–425.

Berenson, B. G., & Carkhuff, R. R. (Eds.) *Sources of gain in counseling and psychotherapy.* New York: Holt, Rinehart and Winston, 1967.

Bergin, A. E., & Solomon, S. Personality and performance correlated of empathic understanding in psychotherapy. Paper presented at the meeting of the American Psychological Association, Philadelphia, September 1963.

Betz, R. L., Engle, K. B., & Mallinson, G. G. Perceptions of non-collegebound vocationally oriented high school graduates. *Personnel and Guidance Journal,* 1969, **47**, 988–994.

Beymer, L. Who killed George Washington? *Personnel and Guidance Journal,* 1971, **50**, 249–253.

Bijou, S. W. Implications of behavioral science for counseling and guidance. In J. D. Krumboltz (Ed.), *Revolution in counseling: Implications of behavioral science; major papers.* Boston: Houghton Mifflin, 1966.

Brammer, L. M., & Springer, H. C. A radical change in counselor education and certification. *Personnel and Guidance Journal,* 1971, **49**, 803–808.

Brazziel, W. F. Getting black kids into college. *Personnel and Guidance Journal,* 1970, **48**, 747–751.

Carkhuff, R. R. Training in the counseling and therapeutic practices: Requiem or reveille? *Journal of Counseling Psychology,* 1966, **13**, 360–367.

Carkhuff, R. R. *Helping and human relations: A primer for lay and professional helpers.* New York: Holt, Rinehart and Winston, 1969.

Counselor education: A progress report on standards. Washington: American Personnel and Guidance Association, 1962.

Dahl, S. Who is building the bridges? *Personnel and Guidance Journal,* 1971, **49**, 693–697.

Directory of counselor educators. Washington: U.S. Office of Education, December 1964.

Dreyfus, E. A. Humanness: A therapeutic variable. *Personnel and Guidance Journal,* 1967, **45**, 573–578.

Dworkin, E. P., & Dworkin, A. L. The activist counselor. *Personnel and Guidance Journal,* 1971, **49**, 748–753.

Eyde, L. D. Eliminating barriers to career development of women. *Personnel and Guidance Journal,* 1970, **49**, 24–28.

Eysenck, H. J. The effects of psychotherapy: An evaluation. *Journal of Consulting Psychology,* 1952, **16**, 319–324.

Gade, E. M. Implications of privileged communication laws for counselors. *School Counselor,* 1972, **19**, 150–152.

Gardner, J. Sexist counseling must stop. *Personnel and Guidance Journal,* 1971, **49**, 705–714.

Golann, S. E., & Magoon, T. M. A non-traditionally trained mental health counselor's work in a school counseling service. *School Counselor,* 1966, **14**, 81–85.

Gonyea, G. G. The "ideal therapeutic relationship" and counseling outcome. *Journal of Clinical Psychology,* 1963, **19**, 481–487.

Haettenschwiller, D. L. Counseling black college students in special programs. *Personnel and Guidance Journal,* 1971, **50**, 29–35.

Herbert, R. Ecology: A shared journey. *Personnel and Guidance Journal,* 1971, **49**, 737–739.

Hill, A. H., & Grieneeks, L. An evaluation of academic counseling of under- and over-achievers. *Journal of Counseling Psychology,* 1966, **13**, 325–328.

Hill, G. E. The profession and standards for counselor education. *Counselor Education and Supervision,* 1967, **6**, 130–136.

Hott, I. The school counselor and drugs. *School Counselor,* 1969, **17**, 14–17.

Hoyt, K. B. This I believe. In W. H. Van Hoose & J. J. Pietrofesa (Eds.), *Counseling and guidance in the twentieth century*. Boston: Houghton Mifflin, 1970.

Hurst, F. W. A university drug education project. *Personnel and Guidance Journal*, 1971, **50**, 11–16.

Kincaid, J., & Kincaid, M. Counseling for peace. *Personnel and Guidance Journal*, 1971, **49**, 727–735.

Levitt, E. E. The results of psychotherapy with children: An evaluation. *Journal of Consulting Psychology*, 1957, **21**, 189–196.

Manual for self-study by a counselor education staff. Washington: American Personnel and Guidance Association, March 1967.

Marsh, J. J., & Kinnick, B. C. Let's close the confidentiality gap. *Personnel and Guidance Journal*, 1970, **48**, 362–365.

May, R. (Ed.) *Existential psychology*. New York: Random House, 1961.

McDaniel, H. B. Counseling perspectives: Old and new. In J. D. Krumboltz (Ed.), *Revolution in counseling: Implications of behavioral science; major papers*. Boston: Houghton Mifflin, 1966.

Melloh, R. A. Accurate empathy and counselor effectiveness. Unpublished doctoral dissertation, University of Florida, 1964.

Moser, L. E. *Counseling: A modern emphasis in religion*. Englewood Cliffs: Prentice-Hall, 1962.

Pardue, J., Whichard, W., & Johnson, E. Limiting confidential information in counseling. *Personnel and Guidance Journal*, 1970, **49**, 14–20.

Paulson, B. B. Riposte. *Personnel and Guidance Journal*, 1967, **45**, 539–540.

Proctor, S. A. Reversing the spiral toward futility. *Personnel and Guidance Journal*, 1970, **48**, 707–712.

Ream, C. Youth culture: Humanity's last chance. *Personnel and Guidance Journal*, 1971, **49**, 699–704.

Rousseve, R. J. Toward an epitaph for the "non-judgmental" educator-counselor. *School Counselor*, 1971, **19**, 6–9.

Russell, R. D. Black perceptions of guidance. *Personnel and Guidance Journal*, 1970, **48**, 721–728.

Saalfeld, L. J. *Guidance and counseling for Catholic schools*. Chicago: Loyola University Press, 1958.

The scope and standards of preparation in psychology for school counselors. *American Psychologist*, 1962, **17**, 149–152.

Shertzer, B., & Stone, S. C. *Fundamentals of guidance*. (2nd ed.) Boston: Houghton Mifflin, 1971.

Shoben, E. J. Personal worth in education and counseling. In J. D. Krumboltz (Ed.), *Revolution in counseling: Implications of behavioral science; major papers*. Boston: Houghton Mifflin, 1966.

Smith, P. M., Jr. Men who think black. *Personnel and Guidance Journal*, 1970, **48**, 763–766.

Smith, P. M., Jr. Black activists for liberation, not guidance. *Personnel and Guidance Journal*, 1971, **49**, 721–726.

Spang, A. T., Sr. Understanding the Indian. *Personnel and Guidance Journal*, 1971, **50**, 97–102.

Standards for counselor education in the preparation of secondary school counselors; Report of committee on counselor education standards in preparation of secondary school counselors of Association for Counselor Education and Supervision. *Personnel and Guidance Journal*, 1964, **42**, 1061–1073.

Tillich, P. Report of a speech given at M.I.T. *Time*, 1961, **77**(17), 57.

Vance, B. The counselor—an agent of what change? *Personnel and Guidance Journal*, 1967, **45**, 1012–1016.

Van Kaam, A. *The art of existential counseling*. Wilkes-Barre: Dimension Books, 1966.

Van Kaam, A. An existential view of psychotherapy. In D. S. Arbuckle (Ed.), *Counseling and psychotherapy: An overview*. New York: McGraw-Hill, 1967.

Vontress, C. E. Cultural barriers in the counseling relationship. *Personnel and Guidance Journal*, 1969, **48**, 11–17.

Vontress, C. E. Counseling black. *Personnel and Guidance Journal,* 1970, **48**, 713–719.

Ward, E. J. A gift from the ghetto. *Personnel and Guidance Journal,* 1970, **48**, 753–756.

Washington, B. B. Perceptions and possibilities. *Personnel and Guidance Journal,* 1970, **48**, 757–761.

Watley, D. J. Counseling philosophy and counseling predictive skill. *Journal of Counseling Psychology,* 1967, **14**, 158–164.

Whiteley, J. M., Sprinthall, N. A., Mosher, R. L., & Donaghy, R. T. Selection and evaluation of counselor effectiveness. *Journal of Counseling Psychology,* 1967, **14**, 226–234.

Williamson, E. G. Youth's dilemma: To be or to become. *Personnel and Guidance Journal,* 1967, **46**, 173–177.

Wrenn, C. G. *The counselor in a changing world.* Washington: American Personnel and Guidance Association, 1962.

CHAPTER 6

Allport, G. W. *Pattern and growth in personality.* New York: Holt, Rinehart and Winston, 1963.

Barry, R. E., & Wolf, B. *Modern issues in guidance-personnel work.* New York: Bureau of Publications, Teachers College, 1957.

Bergin, A. E. The effects of psychotherapy: Negative results revisited. *Journal of Counseling Psychology,* 1963, **10**, 244–250.

Blocher, D. H. *Developmental counseling.* New York: Ronald Press, 1966.

Fromm, E. *Man for himself: An inquiry into the psychology of ethics.* New York: Rinehart, 1947.

Heath, S. R. *The reasonable adventurer.* Pittsburgh: University of Pittsburgh Press, 1964.

Hill, G. E. (Chm.) Standards for the preparation of secondary-school counselors, a report of the APGA committee on professional preparation and standards, sub-committee on standards for the preparation of secondary school counselors. *Personnel and Guidance Journal,* 1967, **46**, 96–106.

Koestler, A. *The act of creation.* New York: Macmillan, 1964.

Kohlberg, L. Development of moral character and moral ideology. In M. L. Hoffman & L. W. Hoffman (Eds.), *Review of child development research.* New York: Russell Sage Foundation, 1964.

Kubie, L. S. *Neurotic distortion of the creative process.* (2nd ed.) New York: Noonday Press, 1965.

Maslow, A. H. *Motivation and personality.* New York: Harper & Row, 1954.

Polanyi, M. *The study of man.* (2nd ed.) Chicago: Phoenix Books, 1963.

Polanyi, M. *The tacit dimension.* Garden City: Doubleday, 1966.

Rogers, C. R. The necessary and sufficient conditions of therapeutic personality change. *Journal of Consulting Psychology,* 1957, **21**, 95–103.

Rogers, C. R. Toward becoming a fully functioning person. In A. W. Combs (Ed.), *Perceiving, behaving, becoming.* Washington, D. C.: Yearbook Association for Supervision and Curriculum Development, 1962.

Schwab, J. J. *The teaching of science as enquiry.* Cambridge: Harvard University Press, 1962.

Shoben, C. J. Toward a concept of the normal personality. *American Psychologist,* 1957, **12**, 183–190.

Thompson, A. S., & Super, D. E. (Eds.) *The professional preparation of counseling psychologists: Report of the 1964 Greyston conference.* New York: Bureau of Publications, Teachers College, 1964.

Tiedeman, D. V. Predicament, problem, and psychology: The case for paradox in life and counseling psychology. *Journal of Counseling Psychology,* 1967, **14**, 1–8.

Tiedeman, D. V., & Field, F. L. Guidance: The science of purposeful action applied through education. In R. L. Mosher, R. F. Carle, & C. D. Kehas (Eds.), *Guidance: An examination.*

New York: Harcourt, Brace & World, 1965. (Originally published: *Harvard Educational Review,* 1962.)

Wise, W. M. Counseling individuals in liberal arts colleges. In E. J. McGrath (Ed.), *The liberal arts college's responsibility for the individual student.* New York: Teachers College Press, 1966.

CHAPTER 7

Bandura, A. *Principles of behavior modification.* New York: Holt, Rinehart and Winston, 1969.

Burck, H. D. The counseling revolution: Promises and problems. *Guidance Journal,* in press.

DeMott, B. Encounter in Mississippi. *Saturday Review,* January 20, 1968, 51–53+.

Gelatt, H. B., Jr. *The influence of outcome probability data on college choice.* (Doctoral dissertation, Stanford University) Ann Arbor, Mich.: University Microfilms, 1964. No. 64–9805.

Gendlin, E. T. *Experiencing and the Creation of Meaning,* New York, Free Press, McMillan, 1962 (reprinted 1970).

Gendlin, E. T. A theory of personality change. In P. Worchel & D. Byrne (Eds.), *Personality change.* New York: John Wiley, 1964.

Gendlin, E. T. Experiential Explication and the Problem of Truth. *Journal of Existentialism,* Vol. 6, No. 22, 1966.

Gendlin, E. T. The experiential response. In E. F. Hammer (Ed.), *Use of interpretation in treatment: Technique and art.* New York: Grune & Stratton, 1968. (a)

Gendlin, E. T. Focusing ability in psychotherapy, personality, and creativity. In J. M. Shlien (ed.), *Research in psychotherapy,* Vol. 3. Washington: American Psychological Association, 1968. (b)

Gendlin, E. T. Focusing. *Psychotherapy: Theory, Research and Practice,* 1969, **6,** 4–15.

Gendlin, E. T. Experiential Psychotherapy, chapter in *Current Psychotherapies,* Corsini, R. (ed.) Itasca, Illinois, Peacock Publishers, 1973.

Haberman, M. Guiding the educationally disadvantaged. In C. E. Beck (Ed.), *Guidelines for guidance: Readings in the philosophy of guidance.* Dubuque: W. C. Brown, 1966.

Hosford, R. E. Behavioral counseling—a contemporary overview. *Counseling Psychologist,* 1969, **1**(4), 1–33.

Hosford, R. E. Some reactions and comments. *Counseling Psychologist,* 1969, **1**(4), 89–95.

Ivey, A. E. The intentional individual: A process-outcome view of behavioral psychology. *Counseling Psychologist,* 1969, **1**(4), 56–60.

Krumboltz, J. D. (Ed.) *Revolution in counseling: Implications of behavioral science; major papers.* Boston: Houghton Mifflin, 1966.

Krumboltz, J. D. Changing the behavior of behavior changers. In A. C. Riccio & G. R. Walz (Eds.), *Forces for change in counselor education.* Washington: Association for Counselor Education and Supervision, 1967, 6(3SP), 222–229.

Krumboltz, J. D., & Schroeder, W. W. Promoting career planning through reinforcement. *Personnel and Guidance Journal,* 1965, **44,** 19–26.

Krumboltz, J. D., & Sheppard, L. E. Vocational problem-solving experiences. In J. D. Krumboltz & C. E. Thoresen (Eds.), *Behavioral counseling: Cases and techniques.* New York: Holt, Rinehart and Winston, 1969.

Krumboltz, J. D., & Thoresen, C. E. The effect of behavioral counseling in group and individual settings on information-seeking behavior. *Journal of Counseling Psychology,* 1964, **11,** 324–333.

Krumboltz, J. D., & Thoresen, C. E. (Eds.) *Behavioral counseling: Cases and techniques.* New York: Holt, Rinehart and Winston, 1969.

Krumboltz, J. D., Varenhorst, B. B., & Thoresen, C. E. Nonverbal factors in the effectiveness of models in counseling. *Journal of Counseling Psychology,* 1967, **14,** 412–418.

Magoon, T. M. Developing skills for educational and vocational problems. In J. D. Krumboltz

& C. E. Thoresen (Eds.), *Behavioral counseling: Cases and techniques.* New York: Holt, Rinehart and Winston, 1969.

Maltz, M. *Psycho-cybernetics: A new way to get more living out of life.* Englewood Cliffs: Prentice-Hall, 1960.

Postman, N., & Weingartner, C. *Teaching as a subversive activity.* New York: Delacorte Press, 1969.

Rosenthal, R., & Jacobson, L. *Pygmalion in the classroom: Teacher's expectation and pupils' intellectual development.* New York: Holt, Rinehart and Winston, 1969.

Ryan, T. A. *The effect of planned reinforcement counseling on client decision-making behavior.* (Doctoral dissertation, Stanford University) Ann Arbor, Mich.: University Microfilms, 1963. No. 64–1647.

Ryan, T. A. Effect of an integrated instructional counseling program to improve vocational decision-making of community college youth. U.S. Dept. of Health, Education and Welfare, Research Project No. HRD 413-655-0154, Grant No. 6–85–065, 1968.

Scott, J. F. So you're going to college. Public Affairs Pamphlet 394. (Obtainable from 381 Park Avenue South, New York, New York 10016.)

Thoresen, C. E., Hosford, R. E., & Krumboltz, J. D. Determining effective models for counseling clients of varying competencies. *Journal of Counseling Psychology,* 1970, **17**, 369–375.

Thoresen, C. E., & Krumboltz, J. D. Relationship of counselor reinforcement of selected responses to external behavior. *Journal of Counseling Psychology,* 1967, **14**, 140–144.

Thoresen, C. E., & Krumboltz, J. D. Similarity of social models and clients in behavioral counseling: Two experimental studies. *Journal of Counseling Psychology,* 1968, **15**, 393–401.

Ullmann, L. P. From therapy to reality. *Counseling Psychologist,* 1969, **1**(4), 68–72.

Varenhorst, B. B. Learning the consequences of life's decisions. In J. D. Krumboltz & C. E. Thoresen (Eds.), *Behavioral counseling: Cases and techniques.* New York: Holt, Rinehart and Winston, 1969.

Woody, R. H. Behavioral counseling: Role definition and professional training. *Counseling Psychologist,* 1969, **1**(4), 84–88.

Yabroff, W. Learning decision-making. In J. D. Krumboltz & C. E. Thoresen (Eds.), *Behavioral counseling: Cases and techniques.* New York: Holt, Rinehart and Winston, 1969.

CHAPTER 8

Adams, J. F. *Problems in counseling: A case study approach.* New York: Macmillan, 1962.

Adleman, R. H., & Walton, G. *The devil's brigade.* Philadelphia: Chilton, 1966.

Aldrich, C. K., & Nighswonger, C. *A pastoral counseling casebook.* Philadelphia: Westminster Press, 1968.

Aldridge, J. W. *In the country of the young.* New York: Harper's Magazine Press, 1970.

Alger, I. Video gives patients clearer view of themselves. *Journal of Rehabilitation,* 1967, May-June, 24–25 (Originally published: *Medical World News,* 1966, **1**, 1–2.)

Alger, I., & Hogan, P. The use of videotape recordings in conjoint marital therapy. *American Journal of Psychiatry,* 1967, **123**, 1425–1429.

Algren, N. *Man with the golden arm.* Garden City: Doubleday, 1949.

Altucher, N. Constructive use of the supervisory relationship. *Journal of Counseling Psychology,* 1967, **14**, 165–170.

American Personnel and Guidance Association. *Ethical standards casebook.* Washington: American Personnel and Guidance Association, 1965.

American Psychological Association. *Ethical standards of psychologists.* Washington: American Psychological Association, 1953.

Anonymous. Theology: literature in the divinity school. *Time,* Dec. 22, 1967, p. 51.

Arbuckle, D. S. *Counseling: Philosophy, theory and practice.* Boston: Allyn & Bacon, 1965.

Arbuckle, D. S. Counselor, social worker, psychologist: Let's "Ecumenicalize." *Personnel and Guidance Journal,* 1967, **45**, 532–538.

Association for Counselor Education and Supervision. Standards for the preparation of secondary school counselors—1967. *Personnel and Guidance Journal,* 1967, **46**, 96–106.

Axline, V. M. *Dibs: In search of self.* Boston: Houghton Mifflin, 1964.

Bach, G. R., & Widen, P. *The intimate enemy.* New York: William Morrow, 1969.

Back, K. W. The group can comfort but it can't cure. *Psychology Today,* 1972, **6**(7), 28–35.

Baldwin, J. *Giovanni's room.* London: M. Joseph, 1957.

Baldwin, J. *Another country.* New York: Dial Press, 1962.

Bandura, A. *Social learning and personality development.* New York: Holt, Rinehart and Winston, 1963.

Banfield, E. *The unheavenly city.* Boston, Little, Brown, 1970.

Baruch, D. W. *One little boy.* New York: Julian Press, 1952.

Baymur, F. B., & Patterson, C. H. A comparison of three methods of assisting underachieving high school students. *Journal of Counseling Psychology,* 1960, **7**, 83–89.

Bellow, S. *Herzog.* New York: Viking Press, 1964.

Benjamin, H. R. *The saber-toothed curriculum.* New York: McGraw-Hill, 1939.

Berenson, B. G., & Carkhuff, R. R. (Eds.) *Sources of gain in counseling and psychotherapy: Readings and commentary.* New York: Holt, Rinehart and Winston, 1967.

Berger, M. M. Integrating video into private psychiatric practice. *Voices: The Art and Science of Psychotherapy.* 1969–1970, **5**(4), 78–85.

Berger, M. M. (Ed.) *Videotape techniques in psychiatric training and treatment.* New York: Brunner/Mazel, 1970.

Bernard, H. W., & Fullmer, D. W. *Principles of guidance: A basic text.* New York and London: Intext Educational Publishers, 1969.

Berne, E. *The games people play.* New York: Grove Press, 1964.

Blocher, D. H. *Developmental counseling.* New York: Ronald Press, 1966.

Bloom, B. S. The thought process of students in discussion. In S. J. French (Ed.), *Accent on teaching: Experiment in general education.* New York: Harper & Brothers, 1954.

Brammer, L. M. Eclecticism revisited. *Personnel and Guidance Journal,* 1969, **48**, 192–197.

Brand, M. *Savage sleep.* New York: Crown, 1968.

Broedel, J., Ohlsen, M., Proff, F., & Southard, C. The effects of group counseling on gifted underachieving adolescents. *Journal of Counseling Psychology,* 1960, **7**, 163–170.

Brown, C. *Manchild in the promised land.* New York: Macmillan, 1965.

Brown, D. A. *Bury my heart at Wounded Knee.* New York: Holt, Rinehart and Winston, 1970.

Bruce, P. Sources for personal validation (or a soft-data man's struggle with his conscience). *Counselor Education and Supervision,* 1969, **8**, 327–330.

Bryan, A. I. The psychology of the reader. *Library Journal,* 1939, **64**, 7–12.

Bryson, S. Relationship between race of counselor and race of clients with level of understanding in an initial interview. Unpublished doctoral dissertation, Southern Illinois University, 1972.

Buchheimer, A., & Balogh, S. C. *The counseling relationship: A casebook.* Chicago: Science Research Associates, 1961.

Bugental, J. F. T. The person who is the psychotherapist. *Journal of Consulting Psychology,* 1964, **28**, 272–277.

Callis, R., Polmanteir, P. C., & Roeber, E. C. *A casebook of counseling.* New York: Appleton-Century-Crofts, 1955.

Camus, A. *The stranger.* (Trans. S. Gilbert) New York: Alfred A. Knopf, 1946.

Caplan, S. W. The effect of group counseling on junior high school boys' concepts of themselves in school. *Journal of Counseling Psychology,* 1957, **4**, 124–128.

Carkhuff, R. R., & Berenson, B. G. *Beyond counseling and therapy.* New York: Holt, Rinehart and Winston, 1967.

Carnes, E. F. A parting shot. *Counselor Education and Supervision,* 1966, **5**, 226.

Castaneda, C. *The teachings of Don Juan: A Yacqui way of knowledge.* Berkeley: University of California Press, 1968.

Castaneda, C. *A separate reality.* New York: Simon & Schuster, 1971.

Chodoff, P. Supervision of psychotherapy with videotape: Pros and cons. *American Journal of Psychiatry,* 1972, **128**, 819–823.

Clark, C. M. On the process of counseling supervision. *Counselor Education and Supervision,* 1965, **4**, 64–67.

Clavell, J. *Tai-Pan.* New York: Atheneum, 1966.

Clear, V. Paperback pedagogy. *Saturday Review,* Feb. 15, 1964, p. 73.

Clements, B. E. Transitional adolescents, anxiety, and group counseling. *Personnel and Guidance Journal,* 1966, **45**, 67–71.

Danet, B. N. Self-confrontation in psychotherapy reviewed: Videotape playback as a clinical and research tool. *American Journal of Psychotherapy,* 1968, **22**(2), 245–257.

Davis, S., Jr. *Yes I can.* New York: Farrar, Straus & Giroux, 1965.

Denig, R. K. *The Manoe-Denigs.* New York: T. A. Wright, 1924.

Dickenson, W. A., & Truax, C. B. Group counseling with college underachievers. *Personnel and Guidance Journal,* 1966, **45**, 243–247.

Dostoyevsky, F. *The house of the dead.* (Trans. C. Garnett) New York: Macmillan, 1915.

Dostoyevsky, F. *Crime and punishment.* (Trans. C. Garnett) New York: Modern Library, 1950.

Dostoyevsky, F. *The brothers Karamazov.* (Trans. Andrew R. MacAndrew) New York: Bantam Books, 1970.

Dreikurs, R. *Psychology in the classroom: A manual for teachers.* (2nd ed.) New York: Harper & Row, 1968.

Dunlop, R. S., & Hintergard, B. S. *The counselor's week: A simulation for counselor trainees.* New York and London: Intext Educational Publishers, 1968.

Eckman, P., & Friesen, W. V. Nonverbal behavior in psychotherapy research. In J. M. Shlien (Ed.), *Research in Psychotherapy.* Washington: American Psychological Association, 1968.

Ekstein, R. Supervision of psychotherapy: Is it teaching? Is it administration? Or is it therapy? *Psychotherapy: Theory, Research and Practice,* 1964, **1**, 137–138.

Ekstein, R., & Wallerstein, R. S. *The teaching and learning of psychotherapy.* New York: Basic Books, 1958.

Expectations and commitments: A joint ACES/ASCA policy statement. Washington: American Personnel and Guidance Association, 1969.

Fairbairn, A. *Five smooth stones.* New York: Crown, 1966.

Farrell, J. *Studs Lonigan.* New York: Modern Library, 1938.

Faulkner, W. *The sound and the fury.* New York: Modern Library, 1946.

Fellner, C. H. Paperback psychiatry. *Journal of Medical Education,* 1969, **44**, 585–588.

Fowles, J. *The magus.* Boston: Little, Brown, 1966.

Frankl, V. *Man's search for meaning: An introduction to logotherapy.* (Trans. I. Lasch) Boston: Beacon Press, 1963.

Freud, S. *Gesmammelte Werke,* Vol. 7. London: Imagos, 1946.

Friedan, B. *The feminine mystique.* New York: Norton, 1963.

Froehlich, K. E. Teaching psychotherapy to medical students through videotape simulation. In M. M. Berger (Ed.), *Videotape techniques in psychiatric training and treatment.* New York: Brunner/Mazel, 1970.

Fromm, E. *Escape from freedom.* New York: Farrar & Rinehart, 1941.

Fromm, E. *Man for himself.* New York: Rinehart, 1947.

Fromm, E. *The art of loving.* New York: Bantam Books, 1956.

Gannon, F. B. *The many faces of Kevin Michael Pullen: A guidance case study.* New York: College Entrance Examination Board, 1968.

Gazda, G. M. *Group counseling: A developmental approach.* Boston: Allyn & Bacon, 1971.

Gilbreath, S. H. Group counseling with male underachieving college volunteers. *Personnel and Guidance Journal,* 1967, **45**, 469–475.

Glanz, E. C. *Groups in guidance: The dynamics of groups and the application of groups in guidance.* Boston: Allyn & Bacon, 1962.

Gluech, B. C., Jr., & Stroebel, C. F. The computer and the clinical decision process: II. *American Journal of Psychiatry,* 1969, **125**, 2–7.

Golding, W. G. *Lord of the flies.* New York: Coward-McCann, 1962.

Goldman, L. Group guidance: Content and process. *Personnel and Guidance Journal,* 1962, **40**, 518–522.

Goodman, P. *Growing up absurd.* New York: Random House, 1960.

Green, H. *I never promised you a rose garden.* New York: Holt, Rinehart and Winston, 1964.

Greer, G. *The female eunuch.* London: MacGibbon & Kee, 1970.

Griffin, J. *Black like me.* Boston: Houghton Mifflin, 1961.

Gunther, B. *Sense relaxation below your mind.* New York: Collier Books, 1968.

Gysbers, N. C. Practicum supervision: I. Theory, learning theory. Paper presented at the annual convention of the American Personnel and Guidance Association, Boston, April 1963.

Hansberry, L. *A raisin in the sun.* London: Methuen, 1960.

Hansen, J. C. Trainees' expectations of supervision in the counseling practicum. *Counselor Education and Supervision,* 1965, **4**, 75–80.

Harrington, M. *The other America.* New York: Macmillan, 1962.

Harris, T. *I'm o.k.—you're o.k.* New York: Harper & Row, 1969.

Heath, R. *The reasonable adventurers.* Pittsburgh: University of Pittsburgh Press, 1964.

Heinlein, R. *Stranger in a strange land.* New York: Putnam, 1961.

Hesse, H. *Siddhartha.* (Trans. H. Rosner) New York: New Directions, 1957.

Hesse, H. *Peter Camenzind.* (Trans. W. J. Strachan) London: P. O. Wen, 1961.

Hesse, H. *Steppenwolf.* (Trans. B. Creighton) New York: Holt, Rinehart and Winston, 1963.

Hesse, H. *Demian.* (Trans.) New York: Harper & Row, 1965.

Hesse, H. *Beneath the wheel.* (Trans. M. Roloff) New York: Farrar, Straus & Giroux, 1968.

Hogan, R. A. Issues and approaches in supervision. *Psychotherapy: Theory, Research and Practice,* 1964, **1**, 139–141.

Hopke, W. E. A look in on guidance: A skit. *Counselor Education and Supervision,* 1963, **2**, 152–153.

Hoyt, D. P. An evaluation of group and individual programs in vocational guidance. *Journal of Applied Psychology,* 1955, **39**, 26–30.

Human Development Institute, Inc. Encounter tapes for personal growth groups. Atlanta: Bell & Howell Co., 1968.

Huxley, A. *Brave new world.* Garden City: Doubleday, Doran, 1932.

Ivey, A. E. Microcounseling: The counselor as trainer. *Personnel and Guidance Journal,* 1973, **51**(5), 312–316.

Jackson, E. P. Effects of reading upon attitudes toward the Negro race. *Library Quarterly,* 1944, **14**, 47–54.

Jourard, S. *Transparent self.* Princeton: Van Nostrand, 1964.

Kagan, N., & Krathwohl, D. R. *Studies in human interaction: Interpersonal process recall stimulated by videotape.* U.S. Department of Health, Education and Welfare, Office of Education, Bureau of Research, Final Report, Project No. 5–0800, Grant No. OE 7–32–0410–270, 1967.

Kell, B. L., & Burow, J. M. *Developmental counseling and therapy.* Boston: Houghton Mifflin, 1970.

Kell, B. L., & Mueller, W. J. *Impact and change: A study of counseling relationships.* New York: Appleton-Century-Crofts, 1966.

Kelman, S. *Push comes to shove.* Boston: Houghton Mifflin, 1970.

Kelz, J. W., & Trembly, E. L. *Supervised counseling experiences.* Boulder, Colo.: Pruett Press, 1965.

Kemp, C. G. Behaviors in group guidance (socio process) and group counseling (psyche process). *Journal of Counseling Psychology,* 1963, **10**, 373–377.

Kemp, C. G. *Foundations of group counseling.* New York: McGraw-Hill, 1970.

Kesey, K. *One flew over the cuckoo's nest.* New York: Viking Press, 1962.

Kesey, K. *Sometimes a great notion.* New York: Viking Press, 1964.

Knowles, J. *A separate peace.* London: Secker & Warburg, 1959.

Koestler, A. *Darkness at noon.* (Trans. D. Hardy) New York: Macmillan, 1941.

Koile, E. A. Counseling supervision: Models to choose from, models to move from. Paper presented at the annual convention of the American Personnel and Guidance Association, Dallas, March 1967.

Krumboltz, J. D., & Thoresen, C. E. The effect of behavioral counseling in group and individual settings on information-seeking behavior. *Journal of Counseling Psychology,* 1964, **11**, 324–333.

Laing, R. D. *Knots.* New York: Pantheon Books, 1970.

Lederer, W. J., & Burdick, E. *Sarkhan.* New York: McGraw-Hill, 1965.

Lewis, C. S. *The Screwtape letters.* New York: Macmillan, 1943.

Lewis, C. S. *Till we have faces.* New York: Harcourt, Brace, 1957.

Lewis, C. S. *The great divorce.* New York: Macmillan, 1963.

Lewis, O. *La vida.* New York: Random House, 1966.

Lewis, S. *Arrowsmith.* New York: Harcourt, Brace & World, 1945.

Lewis, S. *Main Street.* New York: Harcourt, Brace, 1948.

Lewis, S. *Babbitt.* New York: Harcourt, Brace, 1950.

Lewis, S. *Elmer Gantry.* New York: New American Library, 1967.

Lifton, W. M. *Working with groups: Group process and individual growth.* New York: John Wiley, 1961.

Lind, K. N. The social psychology of children's reading. *American Journal of Sociology,* 1936, **41**, 454–469.

Little, M., & Haley, A. *Autobiography of Malcolm X.* New York: Grove Press, 1965.

Lloyd-Jones, E., Barry, R., & Wolf, B. (Eds.) *Case studies in college student–staff relationships.* New York: Bureau of Publications, Teachers College, 1956.

Lloyd-Jones, E., Barry, R., & Wolf, B. (Eds.) *Case studies in human relationships in secondary school.* New York: Bureau of Publications, Teachers College, 1956.

Lloyd-Jones, E., Barry, R., & Wolf, B. (Eds.) *Guidance in elementary education: A casebook.* New York: Bureau of Publications, Teachers College, 1958.

Logue, P. E., Zenner, M., & Gohman, G. Video-tape role playing in the job interview. *Journal of Counseling Psychology,* 1968, **15**(5), 436–438.

Lorang, M. C. *The effect of reading on moral conduct and emotional experience.* Washington: Catholic University of America Press, 1946.

Loughary, J. W., Friesen, D., & Hurst, R. Autocoun: A computer-based automated counseling simulation system. *Personnel and Guidance Journal,* 1966, **45**, 6–15.

MacIver, J. *The frog pond.* New York: Braziller, 1961.

Malamud, B. *The assistant.* New York: Farrar, Straus & Cudahy, 1957.

Malamud, B. *The fixer.* New York: Farrar, Straus & Giroux, 1966.

Malcolm, D. D. On becoming a counselor. *Personnel and Guidance Journal,* 1968, **46**, 673–676.

Matthiessen, P. *Sal si puedes.* New York: Random House, 1969.

McCullers, C. *The heart is a lonely hunter.* Boston: Houghton Mifflin, 1940.

McCully, C. H. Professionalization: Symbol or substance. *Counselor Education and Supervision,* 1963, **2**, 106–111.

McGehearty, L. Case analysis: Consultation and counseling. *Elementary School Guidance and Counseling,* 1969, **3**(3), 217–222.

Mead, M. *Male and female.* New York: William Morrow, 1946.

Mezzano, J. A consideration for group counselors: Degree of counselee investment. *School Counselor,* 1967, **14**, 167–169.

Michener, J. A. *Hawaii.* New York: Random House, 1959.

Michener, J. A. *Caravans.* New York: Random House, 1965.

Miller, P. R., & Tupin, J. P. Multimedia teaching of introductory psychiatry. *American Journal of Psychiatry,* 1972, **128**, 1219–1223.

Morgan, R. *Sisterhood is powerful.* New York: Random House, 1970.

Munger, P. F., Brown, D. F., & Needham, J. T. NDEA institute participants two years later. *Personnel and Guidance Journal,* 1964, **42**, 987–990.

Nathanson, E. M. *The dirty dozen.* New York: Random House, 1965.

Neill, A. S. *Summerhill.* London: V. Gollancz, 1962.

Nylen, D., Mitchell, J. R., & Stout, A. *Handbook of staff development and human relations training: Materials developed for use in Africa.* National Training Laboratories for Applied Behavioral Science (NEA), 1967.

Ofman, W. The counselor who is: A critique and a modest proposal. *Personnel and Guidance Journal,* 1967, **45**, 932–937.

Ohlsen, M. M. *Group counseling.* New York: Holt, Rinehart and Winston, 1970.

O'Neill, E. *The ice man cometh.* New York: Random House, 1946.

O'Neill, E. *Long day's journey into night.* New Haven: Yale University Press, 1956.

Packard, Vance. *The hidden persuaders.* New York: David McKay, 1957.

Pancrazio, J. J., & Cody, J. J. A comparison of role-playing and lecture-discussion instructional methods in a beginning course in counseling theory. *Counselor Education and Supervision,* 1967, **7**, 60–65.

Paton, A. *Too late the phalarope.* New York: Scribner's, 1953.

Patterson, C. H. *Counseling and psychotherapy: Theory and practice.* New York: Harper & Row, 1959.

Patterson, C. H. *Counseling and guidance in schools: A first course.* New York: Harper & Row, 1962.

Perls, F. S. *In and out the garbage pail.* Lafayette, Calif.: Real People Press, 1964.

Pfeiffer, W. J., & Jones, J. E. *A handbook of structured experiences for human relations training.* Vol. 1. Iowa City: University Associates Press, 1969.

Plath, S. *The bell jar.* London: Faber, 1966.

Popham, W. J., & Husek, T. R. Implications of criterion-referenced measurement. *Journal of Educational Measurement,* 1969, **6**, 1–9.

Potok, C. *The chosen.* New York: Simon & Schuster, 1967.

Puzo, M. *The godfather.* New York: Putnam, 1969.

Radcliffe, H. *Well of loneliness.* London: Hammond, 1956.

Ramey, J. W. Teaching medical students by videotape simulation. *Journal of Medical Education,* 1968, **43**, 55–59.

Rand, A. *Atlas shrugged.* New York: Random House, 1957.

Reik, T. *Listening with the third ear.* New York: Farrar, Straus, 1952.

Reik, T. *The need to be loved.* New York: Farrar, Straus, 1963.

Riley, J. E., & Standley, F. L. Literature and counseling: The experience of encounter. *Counselor Education and Supervision,* 1968, **8**, 328–334.

Robinson, F. P. *Principles and procedures in student counseling,* New York: Harper, 1950.

Roeber, E. C. Practicum and internship. Association for Counselor Education and Supervision, and American School Counselor Association. *Counselor education—A progress report on standards.* Washington: American Personnel and Guidance Association, 1962.

Roeber, E. C. Practicum supervision: I. Theory, trait theory. Paper presented at the annual convention of the American Personnel and Guidance Association, Boston, April 1963.

Rogers, A. H. Videotape feedback in group psychotherapy. *Psychotherapy: Theory, Research and Practice,* 1968, **5**(1), 37–39.

Rogers, C. *On becoming a person.* Boston: Houghton Mifflin, 1961.

Rolland, R. *Michelangelo.* (Trans. F. Street) New York: Duffield, 1927.

Ross, A. O. *The exceptional child in the family: Helping parents of exceptional children.* New York: Grune & Stratton, 1964.

Rothney, J. S. M. *The high school student: A book of cases.* New York: Dryden Press, 1953.

Rothney, J. W. M. *Methods of studying the individual child: The psychological case study.* Waltham, Mass.: Blaisdell Publishing Co., 1968.

Saint-Exupéry, A. de. The little prince. (Trans.) New York: Harcourt, Brace & World, 1968.

Salinger, J. D. *Catcher in the rye.* Boston: Little, Brown, 1951.

Salinger, J. D. *Franny and Zooey.* Boston: Little, Brown, 1961.

Sanderson, H. *Basic concepts in vocational guidance.* New York: McGraw-Hill, 1954.

Satir, Virginia. *Conjoint family therapy.* Palo Alto, Calif.: Science & Behavior Books, 1964.

Semmel, M. I. *Toward the development of a computer-assisted teacher training system (CATTS).* (U.S. Office of Education Tech. Rep. No. 7.2) Bloomington: Indiana University, 1972.

Shaw, M. C., & Wursten, R. Research on group procedures in schools: A review of the literature. *Personnel and Guidance Journal,* 1965, **44**, 27–34.

Shostrom, E. *Man, the manipulator.* Nashville: Abingdon Press, 1967.

Shostrom, E. L. Witnessed group therapy on commercial television. *American Psychologist,* 1968, **23**, 207–209.

Skinner, B. F. *Walden II.* New York: Macmillan, 1962.

Smith, N. B. The personal and social values of reading. *Elementary English,* 1948, **25**, 490–500.

Snow, C. P. *Strangers and brothers.* New York: Scribner's, 1960.

Snyder, W. U. *Dependency in psychotherapy: A casebook.* New York: Macmillan, 1963.

Socio-Guidrama Series. Springield, N.J.: Methods and Materials Press.

Solzhenitsyn, A. *One day in the life of Ivan Denisovich.* (Trans. M. Hayward & R. Hingley) New York: Frederick Praeger, 1963.

Solzhenitsyn, A. *Cancer ward.* (Trans. R. Frank) New York: Dial Press, 1968.

Sorenson, G. Pterodactyls, passenger pigeons, and personnel workers. *Personnel and Guidance Journal,* 1965, **43**, 430–437.

Sound Seminar Series. New York: McGraw-Hill, 1968.

Speegle, P. T. The effectiveness of two techniques of counseling with students on academic probation. Unpublished doctoral dissertation, North Texas State University, 1962.

Spielberger, C. D., Weitz, H., & Denny, J. P. Group counseling and the academic performance of anxious college freshmen. *Journal of Counseling Psychology,* 1962, **9**, 195–204.

Spithill, A. C. The valuable allies. *Personnel and Guidance Journal,* 1968, **46**, 879–883.

Stalvey, L. M. *The education of a WASP.* New York: Bantam Books, 1971.

Steinbeck, J. *The grapes of wrath.* New York: Viking Press, 1936.

Steinbeck, J. *East of Eden.* New York: Viking Press, 1952.

Steinbeck, J. *Sweet Thursday.* New York: Viking Press, 1954.

Stoller, F. H. Group psychotherapy on television: An innovation with hospitalized patients. *American Psychologist,* 1967, **22**, 158–161.

Swenson, C. H., Jr. *An approach to case conceptualization.* Boston: Houghton Mifflin, 1968.

Thayer, L., Peterson, V., Carr, E., & Merz, D. Development of a critical incidents videotape. *Journal of Counseling Psychology,* 1972, **19**(2), 188–191.

Thoresen, C. E. The systems approach and counselor education: Basic features and implications. *Counselor Education and Supervision,* 1969, **9**, 3–18.

Toffler, A. *Future shock.* New York: Random House, 1970.

Tolkein, J. R. *Lord of the rings.* Boston: Houghton Mifflin, 1963. 3 vols.

Tollefson, N. F. *Counseling case management.* Boston: Houghton Mifflin, 1968.

Trethowan, W. H. Teaching psychiatry by closed-circuit television. *British Journal of Psychiatry,* 1968, **114**, 517–522.

Tucker, T. G. *Literature and life.* Melbourne: Whitcombe & Tombs, 1905.

Ullman, L. P., & Krasner, L. (Eds.) *Case studies in behavior modification.* New York: Holt, Rinehart and Winston, 1965.

Updike, J. *Rabbit redux.* New York: Alfred A. Knopf, 1971.

Updike, J. *Rabbit run.* New York: Alfred A. Knopf, 1960.

Voeks, V. *On becoming an educated person.* Philadelphia: W. B. Saunders, 1964.

Vriend, T. J. High-performing inner-city adolescents assist low-performing peers in counseling groups. *Personnel and Guidance Journal,* 1969, **47**, 897–904.

Wachtel, P. L. An approach to the study of body language in psychotherapy. *Psychotherapy: Theory, Research and Practice,* 1967, **4**(3), 97–100.

Walz, G. R. Practicum Supervision: I. Theory, self theory. Paper presented at the annual convention of the American Personnel and Guidance Association, Boston, April 1963.

Walz, G. R., Roeber, E. V., & Gysbers, N. C. Practicum supervision: II. Synthesis, integrated theory of supervision. Paper presented at the annual convention of the American Personnel and Guidance Association, Boston, April 1963.

Ward, V. W. Potential client's perceptions of self versus the ideal therapist. Unpublished master's thesis, University of Texas at Austin, 1971.

Warren, R. P. *All the king's men.* New York: Modern Library, 1953.

Watts, A. *The book: On the taboo against knowing who you are.* New York: Macmillan, 1967.

Weil, A. *The natural mind.* Boston: Houghton Mifflin, 1972.

Weinburg, C. The function of the creative writer in the training of teachers. *Journal of Teacher Education,* 1967, **18**, 216–221.

Weingarten, S. Boundaries of reading in satisfying needs. *Education,* 1964, **84**, 480–489.

Wildfang, P. Five groups' perceptions of self-ideal personality. Unpublished master's thesis, University of Texas at Austin, 1969.

Williams, T. *Cat on a hot tin roof.* New York: New Directions, 1955.

Williams, T. *Night of the iguana.* New York: New Directions, 1962.

Wilmer, H. A. Practical and theoretical aspects of videotape supervision in psychiatry. *Journal of Nervous and Mental Disease,* 1967, **145**(2), 123–130. (a)

Wilmer, H. A. Television: Technical and artistic aspects of videotape supervision of psychiatric teaching. *Journal of Nervous and Mental Disease,* 1967, **144**(3), 207–223. (b)

Wilmer, H. A. Innovative uses of videotape on a psychiatric ward. *Hospital and Community Psychiatry,* 1968, **19**, 129–133. (a)

Wilmer, H. A. Television as a participant recorder. *American Journal of Psychiatry,* 1968, **124**, 1157–1163. (b)

Wilmer, H. A. Use of the television monologue with adolescent psychiatric patients. *American Journal of Psychiatry,* 1970, **126**, 1760–1766.

Winborn, B., & Schmidt, L. G. The effectiveness of short-term group counseling upon the academic achievement of potentially superior but underachieving college freshmen. *Journal of Educational Research,* 1962, **55**, 169–173.

Wolberg, L. R. *The technique of psychotherapy.* New York: Grune & Stratton, 1954.

Wolfe, T. *You can't go home again.* New York: Harper & Brothers., 1940.

Wolfe, T. *The kandy-kolored tangerine-flake streamline baby.* New York: Farrar, Straus & Giroux, 1965.

Wolfe, T. *Electric kool-aid acid test.* New York: Farrar, Straus & Giroux, 1968.

Womer, F. B., & Frick, W. B. *Personalizing test use: A counselor's casebook.* Ann Arbor: School Testing Service, University of Michigan, 1965.

CHAPTER 9

American Psychological Association, Division of Counseling and Guidance Committee on Counselor Training. Recommended standards for training counseling psychologists at the doctorate level. *American Psychologist,* 1952, **7**, 175–181.

American Psychological Association, Division of Counseling and Guidance, Committee on Counselor Training. The practicum training of counseling psychologists. *American Psychologist,* 1952, **7**, 182–188.

American Psychological Association, Division of Counseling Psychology, Committee on Definition. Counseling psychology as a specialty. *American Psychologist,* 1956, **11**, 282–285.

American Psychological Association, Division of Counseling Psychology, Committee on Internship Standards. *Recommended standards for internships in counseling psychology.* Multilith, 1960.

American Psychological Association, Division of Counseling Psychology, Report of a Special Committee. *The current status of counseling psychology.* Multilith, 1961.

American Psychological Association, Office of Educational Affairs. *Accreditation: Procedures and criteria.* Multilith, 1971.

Arbuckle, D. S. *Counseling: Philosophy, theory, and practice.* Boston: Allyn & Bacon, 1965.

Arbuckle, D. S. Counseling effectiveness and related issues. *Journal of Counseling Psychology,* 1968, **15**, 430–435.

Arnhoff, F. N. The Boston mental health survey: A context for interpretation. In W. Ryan (Ed.), *Distress in the city: Essays on the design and administration of urban mental health services.* Cleveland: Case Western Reserve University Press, 1969.

Bellak, L. (Ed.) *Handbook of community psychiatry and community mental health.* New York: Grune & Stratton, 1964.

Berlin, I. N. The school counselor: His unique mental health function. *Personnel and Guidance Journal,* 1963, **41**, 409–414.

Bixler, R. H., Bordin, E. S., & Deabler, H. L. Supervised training in a college counseling bureau. *Journal of Consulting Psychology,* 1946, **10**, 233–236.

Boneau, A., & Simmons, W. APA accreditation: A status report. *American Psychologist,* 1970, **25**, 581–584.

Boy, A. V. Motivating students to seek counseling. *School Counselor,* 1959, **6**, 33–36.

Boy, A. V., & Pine, G. J. *Client-centered counseling in the secondary school.* Boston: Houghton Mifflin, 1963.

Boy, A. V., & Pine, G. J. *The counselor in the schools: A reconceptualization.* Boston: Houghton Mifflin, 1968.

Caplan, G. *Principles of preventive psychiatry.* New York: Basic Books, 1964.

Carkhuff, R. R. Training in the counseling and therapeutic practices: Requiem or reveille? *Journal of Counseling Psychology,* 1966, **13**, 360–367.

Carkhuff, R. R. Critical variables in effective counselor training. *Journal of Counseling Psychology,* 1969, **16**, 238–245.

Caudill, W. A. *The psychiatric hospital as a small society.* Cambridge: Harvard University Press, 1958.

Conference on Graduate Psychiatric Education. *Training the psychiatrist to meet changing needs.* Washington: American Psychiatric Association, 1964.

Cumming, J., & Cumming, E. *Ego and milieu: Theory and practice of environmental therapy.* New York: Atherton Press, 1962.

Danskin, D. G. My focus for a university counseling center. *Journal of College Student Personnel,* 1965, **6**, 263–267.

Dunham, H. W. Community psychiatry: The newest therapeutic bandwagon. *Archives of General Psychiatry,* 1965, **12**, 303–313.

Embree, R. B., Jr. The use of practicums and internships in counselor training. *Educational and Psychological Measurement,* 1951, **11**, 752–760.

Ewalt, J. R., & Ewalt, P. J. History of the community psychiatry movement. *American Journal of Psychiatry,* 1969, **126**, 43–52.

Fierman, L. B. Myths in the practice of psychotherapy. *Archives of General Psychiatry,* 1965, **12**, 408–414.

Frank, J. D. *Persuasion and healing.* New York: Schocken Books, 1963.

Freedman, A. M. Historical and political roots of the community mental health centers act. *American Journal of Orthopsychiatry,* 1967, **37**, 487–494.

Friedenberg, E. Z. *The vanishing adolescent.* Boston: Beacon Press, 1959.

Gerken, C. An objective method for evaluating training programs in counseling psychology. *Journal of Counseling Psychology,* 1969, **16**, 227–237.

Glasscote, R. M., Sanders, D. S., Forstenzer, H. M., & Foley, A. R. *The community mental health center: An analysis of existing models.* Washington: Joint Information Service of the American Psychiatric Association and the National Association for Mental Health, 1964.

Goffman, E. *Asylums: Essays on the social situation of mental patients and other inmates.* Garden City: Anchor Books, 1961.

Goldston, S. E. (Ed.) *Concepts of community psychiatry: A framework for training.* (U.S. Public Health Service Publication No. 1319) Bethesda, Md.: National Institute of Mental Health, 1965.

Greenblatt, M., York, R. H., & Brown, E. L. *From custodial to therapeutic patient care in mental hospitals: Explorations in social treatment.* New York: Russell Sage Foundation, 1955.

Gruenberg, E. M. Identifying cases of social breakdown syndrome. *Milbank Memorial Fund Quarterly,* 1966, **44**(1), Part 2.

Gust, T. Extending counselor supervision. *Counselor Education and Supervision,* 1970, **9**, 157–161.

Hansen, J. C., & Warner, R. W., Jr. Review of research on practicum supervision. *Counselor Education and Supervision,* 1971, **10**, 261–272.

Hersch, C. The discontent explosion in mental health. *American Psychologist,* 1968, **23**, 497–506.

Hersch, C. From mental health to social action: Clinical psychology in historical perspective. *American Psychologist,* 1969, **24**, 909–916.

Joint Commission on Mental Illness and Health. *Action for mental health.* New York: Basic Books, 1961.

Jones, M., et al. *The therapeutic community: A new treatment method in psychiatry.* New York: Basic Books, 1953.

Kirk, B. A. In-service training and professional growth. In P. J. Gallagher & G. D. Demos (Eds.), *The counseling center in higher education.* Springfield, Ill.: Charles C. Thomas, 1970.

Kirk, B. A. Internship in counseling psychology: Goals and issues. *Journal of Counseling Psychology,* 1970, **17**, 88–90.

Kirk, B. A. & Chin, A. H. Internship in counseling psychology. *Journal of Counseling Psychology,* 1971, **18**, 524–530.

Kirk, B. A., Free, J. E., Johnson, A. P., Michel, J., Redfield, J. E., Roston, R. A., & Warman, R. E. Guidelines for university and college counseling services. *American Psychologist,* 1971, **26**, 585–589.

Konopka, G. *The adolescent girl in conflict.* Englewood Cliffs: Prentice-Hall, 1966.

Kubie, L. S. Pitfalls of community psychiatry. *Archives of General Psychiatry,* 1968, **18**, 257–266.

Lanning, W. L. A study of the relation between group and individual counseling supervision and three relationship measures. *Journal of Counseling Psychology,* 1971, **18**, 401–406.

Levinson, D., & Klerman, G. The psychiatrist in the organization: Problems in the synthesis of clinical and executive functions. Paper presented at the International Research Seminar on Evaluation of Community Mental Health Programs, Warrenton, Va., May 1966.

Lindemann, E. Introduction to *Distress in the city,* W. Ryan (Ed.). Cleveland: Case—Western Reserve University Press, 1969.

Loughary, J. W., Stripling, R. O., & Fitzgerald, P. W. (Eds.) *Counseling, a growing profession: Report concerning the professionalization of counseling.* Washington: American Personnel and Guidance Association, 1965.

Lustman, S. The meaning of the curriculum. Paper presented to the Plenary Session on the Psychoanalytic Curriculum at the meeting of the American Psychoanalytic Association, New York, December 1966.

Meeks, A. R. Elementary school counseling. *School Counselor,* 1963, **10**, 108–111.

Morrow, W. R. The development of psychological internship training. *Journal of Consulting Psychology,* 1946, **10**, 165–183.

Munson, H. L. A rationale for elementary school guidance. Unpublished manuscript, College of Education, University of Rochester, 1966.

Pasamanick, B. The development of physicians for public mental health. *American Journal of Orthopsychiatry,* 1967, **37**, 469–486.

Pasamanick, B., Scarpatti, F. R., & Dinitz, S. *Schizophrenics in the community: An experimental study in the prevention of hospitalization.* New York: Appleton-Century-Crofts, 1967.

Patterson, C. H. What is counseling psychology? *Journal of Counseling Psychology,* 1969, **16**, 23–29.

Redlich, F. *The university and community mental health.* New Haven: Yale University Press, 1968.

Roeber, E. C. Roles and functions of professionally trained counselors. In J. F. McGowan (Ed.), *Counselor development in American society: Conference recommendations, invitational conference on government-university relations in the professional preparation and employment of counselors.* Columbia: University of Missouri, 1965.

Rosenblum, G. The new role of the clinical psychologist in the community mental health center. *Community Mental Health Journal,* 1968, **4**, 403–410.

Sabshin, M. Theory and practice of community psychiatry training in the medical school setting. In S. Goldston (Ed.), *Concepts of community psychiatry: A framework for training.* (U.S. Public Health Service Publication No. 1319) Bethesda, Md.: National Institute of Mental Health, 1965.

Sharaf, M. R., Schneider, P., & Kantor, D. Psychiatric interest and its correlates among medical students. *Psychiatry,* 1968, **31**, 150–160.

Shatan, C. Community psychiatry—Stretcher bearer of the social order? *International Journal of Psychology,* 1969, **7**, 312–321.

Stanton, A. H., & Schwartz, M. S. *The mental hospital: A study of institute participation in psychiatric illness and treatment.* New York: Basic Books, 1954.

Stiller, A. Social pressures and the guidance function. *School Counselor,* 1964, **11**, 233–237.

Super, D. E. *The psychology of careers: An introduction to vocational development.* New York: Harper & Row, 1957.

Super, D. E. et al. Internships in college counseling centers. *Counseling News and Views,* 1956, **9**, 16–18.

Swartz, H. Administrative aspects of the initiation of an elementary counselor program. *Report of the Fifth Annual Ohio Elementary School Guidance Conference,* Canton, Ohio, November 1965.

Teigland, J. J., Winkler, R. C., Munger, P. F., & Kranzler, G. D. Some concomitants of under-achievement at the elementary school level. *Personnel and Guidance Journal,* 1966, **44**, 950–955.

U.S., *Statutes at Large,* vol. 77. *Community Mental Health Centers Act of 1963,* Public law 88–164, U.S., 88th Congress, Oct. 31, 1963.

Wallerstein, R. S. The challenge of the community mental health movement to psychoanalysis. *American Journal of Psychiatry,* 1968, **124**, 1049–1056.

Warnath, C. F. Counseling psychology or adjunct psychology? *Counseling News and Views,* 1968, **20**, 2–6.

Warnath, C. F. *New myths and old realities.* San Francisco: Jossey-Bass, 1971.

Whittington, H. G. The third psychiatric revolution—really? *Community Mental Health Journal,* 1965, **1**, 73–80.

Zwerling, I. Some implications of social psychiatry for psychiatric treatment and patient care. Institute of Pennsylvania Hospital, *Strecker Monograph Series,* 1965, No. 11.

Author Index

Italic numbers indicate pages on which complete reference appears.

519

Subject Index